Constitutional Ratification without Reason

OXFORD CONSTITUTIONAL THEORY

Series editors:

MARTIN LOUGHLIN,
JOHN P MCCORMICK, AND
NEIL WALKER

Oxford Constitutional Theory has rapidly established itself as the primary point of reference for theoretical reflections on the growing interest in constitutions and constitutional law in domestic, regional, and global contexts. The majority of the works published in the series are monographs that advance new understandings of their subject. But the series aims to provide a forum for further innovation in the field by also including well-conceived edited collections that bring a variety of perspectives and disciplinary approaches to bear on specific themes in constitutional thought and by publishing English translations of leading monographs in constitutional theory that have originally been written in languages other than English.

ALSO AVAILABLE IN THE SERIES

Legitimation by Constitution
A Dialogue on Political Liberalism
Frank Michelman and Alessandro Ferrara

Authoritarian Liberalism and the Transformation of Modern Europe
Michael Wilkinson

Constitutionalism and the Paradox Principles and Rules
Between the Hydra and Hercules
Marcelo Neves

Constituent Power in the European Union
Markus Patberg

Religion, Law, and Democracy
Selected Writings
Ernst-Wolfgang Böckenförde
Edited by Mirjam Künkler and Tine Stein

Constituent Power and the Law
Joel Colón-Ríos

Law and Revolution
Legitimacy and Constitutionalism after the Arab Spring
Nimer Sultany

After Public Law
Cormac Mac Amhlaigh, Claudio Michelon, Neil Walker

Europe's Functional Constitution
A Theory of Constitutionalism Beyond the State
Turkuler Isiksel

Unconstitutional Constitutional Amendments
The Limits of Amendment Powers
Yaniv Roznai

Constitutionalism
Past, Present, and Future
Dieter Grimm

Euroconstitutionalism and its Discontents
Oliver Gerstenberg

Popular Sovereignty in Early Modern Constitutional Thought
Daniel Lee

Beyond the People
Social Imaginary and Constituent Imagination
Zoran Oklopcic

The Metaethics of Constitutional Adjudication
Bosko Tripkovic

Constitutional Ratification without Reason

JEFFREY A. LENOWITZ
Brandeis University

OXFORD
UNIVERSITY PRESS

OXFORD
UNIVERSITY PRESS

Great Clarendon Street, Oxford, OX2 6DP,
United Kingdom

Oxford University Press is a department of the University of Oxford. It furthers the University's objective of excellence in research, scholarship, and education by publishing worldwide. Oxford is a registered trade mark of Oxford University Press in the UK and in certain other countries

First Edition published in 2022

Impression: 2

Published in the United States of America by Oxford University Press
198 Madison Avenue, New York, NY 10016, United States of America

British Library Cataloguing in Publication Data

Data available

Library of Congress Control Number: 2021950728

ISBN 978–0–19–885234–6

DOI: 10.1093/oso/9780198852346.001.0001

Printed and bound by
CPI Group (UK) Ltd, Croydon, CR0 4YY

For my family

Acknowledgments

I have accrued many debts during the long time it took to write this book. So many that I will inevitably forget some of the people to whom I owe thanks. So, first, let me apologize to them for the oversight. This book began with my dissertation at Columbia University, and I must express my sincere gratitude to Melissa Schwartzberg and Jon Elster, my two wonderful advisors. Melissa Schwartzberg went above and far beyond. She molded me into a political scientist and led me through academia, writing a dissertation, the wilds of postgraduate life, and now the book publishing process itself. Simply put, this book would be non-existent or certainly of lesser quality without her encouragement, insightful advice, comments, occasional handholding, friendship, and constant inspiration. Jon Elster introduced me to the topic of constitution-making and taught me to think outside the bounds of traditional political theory and extend normative analysis where I thought it would not go. His supervision, comments, and guidance were crucial in the formative days of this project, and both his work and his sheer intellectual curiosity continue to serve as an ideal toward which I strive.

I owe thanks to many other faculty members who were then at Columbia. I benefitted greatly from being taught by Michael Doyle and Jeffrey Lax, both of whom I was lucky enough to have on my dissertation committee. Jean Cohen, David Johnston, Thomas Pogge, Joseph Raz, and Nadia Urbinati all greatly contributed to my training and the beginnings of this project. My experience at Columbia is inseparable from my friendship with Sandipto Dasgupta, whose support and presence in my life is as critical to me now as a professor as it was in the first days of graduate school. Much of this project, and my thinking more generally, was shaped during our late-night conversations and intellectual arguments. And I also need to single out for thanks David Szakonyi, an old and dear friend who joined me at Columbia and has provided crucial advice, commentary, and unrelenting encouragement on this project from its birth to the very end.

Many other friends, teachers, mentors, and colleagues both in and outside of Columbia also contributed to this project when I was in New York, with many continuing to be a source of help since I left. These include Carlo Invernizzi Accetti, Andrew Arato, Sam Brody, Sujit Choudhry, Axel Domeyer, Kevin Elliot, Felix Gerlsbeck, Guy Grossman, Jennifer Hudson, Turku Isiksel, Kimuli Kasara, Kate Krimmel, Bernard Manin, William McAllister, Laura Paler, Pasquale Pasquino, Ryan Pevnick, Ulrich Preuss, Kelly Radar, Andrew Rehfeld, Annie Stilz, Daniel Viehoff, and Ian Zuckerman. I also must express my utmost appreciation to my non-academic friends who made my life in New York, and still today, so much richer, and perhaps more importantly, routinely prevent me from taking myself too seriously. Among many, I want to thank Ali Naini, Kyle Reinford, Ted Sullivan, Conor Welch, and Dane Wisher.

After my doctoral studies I was lucky enough to receive a fellowship at Nuffield College, University of Oxford, where I immediately found myself immersed in a wonderful community of scholars and friends who supported me at every turn. I workshopped several chapters at Nuffield, all of which became better as a result. Special thanks go to Iain McLean, who ensured I got Condorcet and Early America right, and to David Miller, who pushed me to achieve greater precision in my moral argumentation. Others at Nuffield whose friendship and comments helped me push this project forward include Faisal Ahmed, Evrim Altintas, Chris Arnold, Emanuel Coman, Neli Demireva, Robin Hardin, Andy Harris, Anja Neudorf, Amy Nivette, Sergi Pardos, Lauge Poulsen, Olga Onuch, Sorana Toma, Jesse Tomalty, and Caleb Yong.

I left Oxford when I joined the Political Science Department at Brandeis University. I could not have landed at a more welcoming place. Since arriving, I have received nothing but encouragement and support from my colleagues. I thank each and every one of you. I especially want to acknowledge Bernard Yack, who gave pivotal feedback, guidance, and mentorship throughout the completion of this book, as well as Eva Bellin, Jill Greenlee, Dan Kryder, Gowri Vijayakumar, and Greg Childs, all of whom helped improve parts of this project with their advice, encouragement, or general support. I would also be remiss if I did not thank my department's academic administrators Rosanne Coloucoris and Martha Cronin, whose regular assistance, conversation, and Brandeis expertise helped me navigate campus and stay cheerful during long days writing alone in my office. Thanks also to my skilled research assistants, Dustin Fire and Zachary Kasdin, the latter of whom ended up teaching me a thing or two about constitution-making in his senior thesis, and several wonderful graduate students who kept me on my toes, especially Jeremy Cynamon, Yasser Kureshi, Holly Robbins, Adam Smith, and Paul Spalletta. Since I moved to the Boston area, Alex Gourevitch and Lucas Stanzyck not only supported me with their friendship, but also challenged me intellectually at every turn and helped improve upon my ideas in this book. I owe them both a great deal of thanks. Claire Edington and Dan Navon provided crucial encouragement and companionship as well, though I am still trying to forgive them for fleeing to sunny California.

I have presented parts of this book at numerous conferences, workshops, and seminars. Some of these include: the annual meetings of the American Political Science Association and the Association for Political Theory; the Meeting on Ethics and Political Philosophy in Braga; political theory workshops at the University of Chicago, CIDE, Ashoka University, Duke, the Universität Hamburg,

Nuffield College, and the University of Copenhagen; the University of Maryland Discussion Group on Constitutionalism; and an informal workshop held at the Safra Center. I thank everyone who participated, asked questions, gave comments, and chatted with me about the project both in and outside of these events. I especially want to recognize Elizabeth Beaumont, Corey Brettschneider, Chiara Cordelli, Kennan Ferguson, Katrina Forrester, Mark Graber, Michael Gillespie, Claudio Lòpez-Guerra, Alex Kirshner, Heinz Klug, Sanford Levinson, Elliot Mamet, Sankar Muthu, Andrew March, Gabriel Negretto, Julie Rose, Geneviève Rousselière, Richard Tuck, James Lindley Wilson, Emily Zackin, Michael Zuckert, and Christopher Zurn.

The following sources provided generous financial support for my research: the Edith C. Black Fellowship and the Mellon Interdisciplinary Graduate Fellowship at Columbia University, the Prize Postdoctoral Research Fellowship at Nuffield College, Oxford, and at Brandeis the Norman Award for Faculty Research, the Research Circle for Democracy and Cultural Pluralism Grant, and the Tomberg Research Fund. I would also like to thank John McCormick, for showing interest in my manuscript and eventually welcoming it into his, Martin Loughlin, and Neil Walker's excellent series, and to all of those who have helped me at Oxford University Press, including Jamie Berezin, Iona Jacob, Paulina Dos Santos Major, and the anonymous reviewers.

I wrote large portions of this book in Bursa, and must thank my Turkish family—Fatoş, Arif, Emel, Aliye, Ali, Nano, and everyone else—for their enthusiasm, love, and understanding, and for constantly thinking of creative places that I could work. The highlight will always be finishing a chapter in the fabric showroom at Kaçar Textile.

Last but not least is my family, to whom I dedicate this book. My parents, Janet and Jim Lenowitz, and my sister Robin, have encouraged and supported my intellectual pursuits since childhood. They provide a foundation of love and support cut with just the right amount of mockery and mirth that I rely upon daily. I am thrilled that we were recently joined by Steve, Lyra, and most recently Isaiah, who make a wonderful dynamic even better. Finally, I give my deepest thanks to my wife, Hande Inanc, and my son, Ozzie. Hande's encouragement and unfailing patience during the long process of drafting and revising kept me going, while watching her own success and research brilliance pulled me forward with inspiration. I do not know how I would have completed this book without her love and backing, and her willingness to constantly discuss, debate, and add to my arguments. Ozzie was born in the twilight of this project, and everything about my life has become better since. He is a fountain of joy and amusement that makes me happy no matter how frustrated I am with writing. In these final days, his cheerful yet insistent demands that I "go work Daddy" whenever I walked into a room helped get me to the finish line. I am assuming that he was excited to see me complete this project, not that he preferred to play with his mother.

Permission to reprint the following material is gratefully acknowledged.

- Modified parts of chapters 3 and 5 appeared as Jeffrey A. Lenowitz, "'A Trust that Cannot Be Delegated': The Invention of Ratification Referenda," American Political Science Review, 109:4, 803–16, © American Political Science Association, published by Cambridge University Press. See https://doi.org/10.1017/S0003055415000465
- A modified version of chapter 6 appeared as Jeffrey A. Lenowitz, "The People Cannot Choose a Constitution: Constituent Power's Inability to Justify Ratification Referendums," The Journal of Politics, 83:2, 617–23, © Southern Political Science Association, published by the University of Chicago Press. See https://doi.org/10.1086/709864

Contents

Abbreviations

CPJ	constituent power justification
CWA	Communications Workers of America
EU	European Union
IGO	intergovernmental organization
LJ	legitimacy justification
NGO	non-governmental organization
PML	procedural moral legitimation
PSL	procedural sociological legitimation
RJ	representation justification
SML	substantive moral legitimation
SSL	substantive sociological legitimation
TAL	Transitional Administrative Law (Iraq)
USJ	unique site justification
UN	United Nations
VCLT	Vienna Convention on the Law of Treaties

1
Questioning Ratification

Ratification is the procedure in which a draft constitution is submitted by its creators to the people or their representatives in an up or down vote determining implementation. It takes a variety of forms, sometimes being carried out via a national convention (Ethiopia 1994), sub-state conventions (U.S. 1789), sub-state legislative bodies (West German 1949), or, most commonly, a referendum (Kenya 2010).

Ratification is an old procedure. It has been an essential component of constitution-making since the beginning of written constitutions. The Massachusetts constituent legislature of 1778, the first body popularly elected to serve as a constituent authority, was also the first to use ratification. This practice slowly caught on, and today ratification procedures are ubiquitous. In the United States, a norm developed whereby all new state constitutions must be approved by a majority of the people through a referendum before enactment.[1] Worldwide, there has been an accelerating trend of popular ratification. Since 1970, more than half of all new constitutions came into effect only after a successful ratification.[2] Sixteen of the twenty-four constitutions created in the last decade were ratified.

While commonplace, ratification is always a choice; it is not a necessary component of constitution-making. None, for instance, of the landmark constitutions of India, South Africa, or Tunisia were ratified. Nonetheless, when ratification is used, it has power. It can influence the behavior of framers and subsequently alter the contents of what they write. It can lead to constitutional rejection, regardless of a draft constitution's political and social significance, the length and expense of its drafting process, or its perceived legitimacy or desirability. Ratification also imposes monetary costs. When it comes in the form of a referendum these

[1] Only 45 of the 146 constitutions adopted by the states became effective without ratification and all but three of these cases took place in the eighteenth century. This number is based on my own calculations and the following. Albert Lee Sturm, *Trends in State Constitution-Making, 1966–1972* (Council of State Governments 1973); "By Whom Shall a State Constitution Be Adopted," (1896) 9 Harvard Law Review 471–72; Albert Lee Sturm, "The Development of American State Constitutions," (1982) 12 Publius 57–98.

[2] Jennifer Widner, "Constitution Writing and Conflict Resolution Project" <http://www.princeton.edu/~pcwcr/>; Justin Blount, "Participation in Constitutional Design," in Tom Ginsburg and Rosalind Dixon (eds.), *Comparative Constitutional Law* (Edward Elgar 2011) 49; Justin Blount, Zachary Elkins, and Tom Ginsburg, "Does the Process of Constitution-Making Matter?" in Tom Ginsburg (ed.), *Comparative Constitutional Design* (Cambridge University Press 2012) 37; Jennifer Widner, "Constitution Writing in Post-Conflict Settings: An Overview," (2008) 49 William and Mary Law Review 1513–42, 1525. Number updated with my own calculations.

Constitutional Ratification without Reason. Jeffrey A. Lenowitz, Oxford University Press. © Jeffrey A. Lenowitz 2022.
DOI: 10.1093/oso/9780198852346.003.0001

can be quite extensive. Finally, ratification is endorsed by many. Constitutional consultants, non-governmental organizations (NGOs), international lawyers, and scholars frequently include ratification amongst their framing recommendations and constitution-making best practices manuals, citizens sometimes march on the streets demanding ratification, and some constitutions even require the process for future constitution-making endeavors.[3]

Ratification is thus a long-standing consequential constitution-making procedure that is optional yet common and recommended by experts. All of this raises the central question of this book: *why should constitutions be ratified*? Or, put differently, do the designers of constitution-making processes have good reasons to implement the procedure?

Strangely, this question is rarely asked, has never been the subject of academic study, and ratification in general has been overlooked. In fact, this is the first research project, let alone book, to study the procedure of ratification at all. No work of any form exists that explains the history of the procedure or systematically categorizes its type. The potential effects of the procedure are only mentioned in passing in a smattering of articles and books. Moreover, in the 240-year history of ratification, only two real attempts have been made to justify its implementation. The Berkshire Constitutionalists, a group of radicals in Western Massachusetts during the American revolution, were the first to try, and their arguments ultimately led to ratification's invention. The Marquis de Condorcet, in an essay written in 1789, is the only other person to write a serious contemplation of the reasons underlying the procedure.[4] His arguments were ignored and then forgotten. Most other mentions of ratification either assume the procedure's presence or simply hand wave toward normative concepts drawn from democratic theory without even minimal explanation.

This neglect is as troubling as it is surprising. In most cases, constitutions are created via a process that is designed. The resulting constitution-making process is the culmination of multiple decisions about what procedures to use in what order to generate a constitutional text. Ratification is one such procedural choice and is optional. What amounts to a veto on the results of one of the most critical decision-making processes a country undergoes should not be handed out, let alone recommended or treated as being part of the "best practices," without sufficient study. Ratification should be chosen for good reasons, but today such reasons are barely mentioned or never given. The main purpose of this book is to correct this oversight and provide some answers.

[3] For example, the Bolivian Constitution specifies that "The validity of the reform shall require approval by constitutional referendum." The Political Constitution of the State of Bolivia (2009), Art. 411, para. 411.

[4] These discussions of ratification are covered in detail in chapters 4 and 9, respectively.

This project was motivated by an earnest desire to uncover the reason or set of reasons that explain why ratification should be used. Ratification is a peculiar procedure somewhat unique to constitution-making. From one angle it looks superfluous or redundant. Why introduce an additional gatekeeper at the end of what is often a well-thought out participatory and representative decision-making process? Why make the fate of a bargain hinge upon the evaluation of those who played no role in the negotiations? From another angle, the answer seems obvious. After all, few procedures seem so democratic on their face. And few moments seem more appropriate for popular engagement and direct democratic action than the creation of the rules and structure of democratic government itself. Ratification, particularly a participatory version of it, seems like a natural component of constitution-making.

The surprise conclusion of this book contradicts my own and I imagine many others' intuitions. While the procedure is popular, looks pleasingly democratic, and seems supported by an array of arguments from normative democratic theory, I determine that there is no clear or obvious general justification for including ratification within the constitution-making process. I reach this conclusion by exploring the most plausible justifications, which I draw and reconstruct from the pre- and extra-constitutional functions of ratification, the origins of several ratification procedures, contemporary discussions of ratification and constitution-making more generally, and the application of central strains of democratic theory to the constitution-making context. These *core justifications for ratification* relate to constituent power, representation, and legitimacy.

Specifically, I ask whether the need for ratification stems from its function as a moment of constituent power, an instance where the people manifest and exercise their will to make a constitution their own. I consider whether ratification might be one of many or the sole site of constituent action and analyze how this affects the resulting justification. I then examine whether ratification plays a role in a representative process ongoing during constitution-making, and whether the importance of fostering representation justifies its use. Finally, I explore whether ratification helps generate a legitimate constitution. This entails articulating a three-part theory of legitimacy corresponding to the concept's legal, moral, and social manifestations, and analyzing the role of ratification within this scheme.

Ultimately, I find none of these arguments to be persuasive. This does not mean that ratification is always a mistake, but rather that a general argument in its favor appears lacking or incomplete, meaning that the procedure should not be a default one. In other words, consultants and constitution-makers should not approach ratification as if context-independent pro tanto reasons exist in favor of its use. Rather, until such an argument is made, decisions regarding whether to enact this optional procedure should be made with care, based on circumstances, and with the goals carefully spelled out and considered in addition to likely costs and effects.

The remainder of this chapter has five sections in which I elaborate on the above, further clarifying my subject matter and explaining why ratification needs justification. First, I set out basic background concepts and terms, explaining what I mean by a constitution and democratic constitution-making. Second, I define ratification, explain its various types, and describe various instances of the procedure. Third, I articulate what I mean by a justification for ratification, and what sorts of explanations and arguments I am not addressing. Fourth, I explain why ratification is a worthy object of study and why reasons are needed to explain its use. This involves a discussion of ratification's possible effects on the constitution-making process, its costs, and how the current literature on constitution-making leaves ratification unexamined. Fifth and finally I outline the upcoming chapters.

1. Basic Concepts

This book focuses on ratification procedures used in democratic constitution-making for sovereign states. To begin, an explanation of key terms is needed. In this section I define and explain constitution, constitution-making versus constitutional amendment, and the meaning of democratic constitution-making and its standard components.

1.1 Constitution

What is a constitution? There are likely as many different answers to this question as there are different constitutions, ranging from narrow to expansive. Aristotle, perhaps the earliest to write about constitutions, used numerous definitions in *Politics*, moving from describing constitutions as "an organization of offices in city-states" to claiming, "a constitution is a sort of life of city-state."[5] An expansive definition is certainly best if one hopes is to capture all that is needed to make constitutional government possible. An apt example for such a purpose would be Walter Murphy's definition, which describes a constitution as not only the constitutional text, but also "its dominant political theories, the traditions and aspirations that reflect those values, and the principal interpretations of this larger constitution."[6] Alternatively, one might want to split constitution into more than

[5] Aristotle, *Politics* (Hackett Publishing Company 1998) 75 [1278b9], 119 [1295a40].

[6] Walter Murphy, *Constitutional Democracy: Creating and Maintaining a Just Political Order* (John Hopkins University Press 2007) 43. See also Chris Thornhill, *A Sociology of Constitutions: Constitutions and State Legitimacy in Historical-Sociological Perspective* (Cambridge University Press 2011) 10. Thornhill detaches the definition of constitution from the existence of a specific written legal text, defining it as a legal order that constrains a political power in a specific way. This makes it possible for him to assert that both modern and pre-modern societies had constitutions.

one meaning, with the intent of grouping together all the various ways in which the term is used. For instance, Dieter Grimm claims that constitution has two different meanings: "Constitution in the first sense of the word refers to the nature of a country with reference to its political conditions. Constitution in the second sense refers to a law that concerns itself with the establishment and exercise of political rule."[7]

For the purposes of this book, however, I use "constitution" in a more constrained and singular sense. I define constitution as a written body of higher law that specifies the organization and structural features of a state (particularly those responsible for ordinary lawmaking), limits and regulates government organs and actors, and, usually, enumerates the basic rights of citizens, requires special procedures for alteration, and identifies itself as a constitution.[8] This definition takes inspiration from both Kelsen's description of a formal constitution and Paine's deflationary definition, which he wielded as a weapon in his fight against Burke and the immemorial constitution. Kelsen wrote that a "constitution in the formal sense," is "a certain solemn document, a set of legal norms that may be changed only under the observation of special prescriptions, the purpose of which it is to render the changes of these norms more difficult."[9] And Paine asserted that "a Constitution is not a thing in name only, but in fact. It has not an ideal, but a real existence ... a Constitution is a *Thing* antecedent to Government ... it is the Body of Element to which you can refer and quote article by article; which contains the principles upon which the Government shall be established, the manner in which is shall be organized, the powers it shall have ... "[10]

I use this somewhat narrow understanding of a constitution because my focus is on the discrete procedures used to draft the written text. I am interested in whether the framers of constitutions should present a draft of their handiwork to a ratifying agent for approval or disapproval. While traditions, legal interpretations, rule of law norms, and many other components come together to make constitutionalism possible, only the written document is the object of ratification.

Moreover, I am not focusing on any constitution that meets the above definition, for both international governmental organizations and states within a

[7] Dieter Grimm, *Constitutionalism: Past, Present, and Future* (Oxford University Press 2016).

[8] For a discussion of the difficulties in defining exactly what a constitution is using traditional designations such as a body of law that is harder to change, a document that addresses fundamental issues, or the legal code referred to as "the constitution," see Jon Elster, "Forces and Mechanisms in the Constitution-Making Process," (1995) 45 Duke Law Review 364–96, 364–367. See also Andrew Arato, *The Adventures of the Constituent Power* (Cambridge University Press 2017) 2–11; Zachary Elkins, James Melton, and Tom Ginsburg, *The Endurance of National Constitutions* (Cambridge University Press 2009) 38–40; Tom Ginsburg and Rosalind Dixon, "Introduction," in Tom Ginsburg and Rosalind Dixon (eds.), *Comparative Constitutional Law* (Edward Elgar 2011) 4–5; Dario Castiglione, "The Political Theory of the Constitution," (1996) XLIV Political Studies 417–35.

[9] Hans Kelsen, *General Theory of Law and State* (Transaction Publishers 2006) 124.

[10] Thomas Paine, *Rights of Man, Common Sense, and Other Political Writings* (Oxford University Press 1998) 122.

federal or colonial superstructure would then qualify. The European Union almost did have such a constitution. Hamburg, Texas, and Queensland and many other states or provinces within federal systems also have constitutions. My focus is the constitutions of sovereign states, those documents that lay out the highest body of law for an independent country. For it is the making of these constitutions that so often takes place outside of a pre-existing legal framework, and thus makes possible the design of a constitution-making process from scratch, and it is these cases that constitution-making guidelines, manuals, and consultants address. The arguments and theories I discuss may apply to sub- or super-state constitutions and their creation, but they also may not.

Given this definition of a constitution, the first is the June 29, 1776 Constitution of Virginia, established slightly over a month after the state declared independence in May of that year.[11] Some of the most recent, as of this writing, are the Constitution of Chad adopted by the country's parliament on April 30, 2018 and the Constitution of Cuba adopted via referendum on February 24, 2019.[12] In between drafters have created over 800 constitutions across the globe.[13]

1.2 Constitution-Making, Not Amendment

This book concentrates on a component of the constitution-making process, the set of procedures used to create a new constitution. New and old states with and without written constitutions embark on this process, and they do so for a variety of reasons. Constitution-making occurs to further efforts to transition away from conflict, to codify a recent regime change or to begin one, and to break away from a colonial past. New constitutions are also written to announce and create a new political entity, or more mundanely, to lock in gains by a particular party or to simply update a document that has become outdated over time.

Of course, creating a new constitution is not the only way to accomplish these objectives using the constitutional text. Countries that already possess a written constitution can instead choose to amend their existing body of higher law rather than replace it.[14] For those interested in constitution-making, a problem

[11] Hugh Blair Grigsby, *The Virginia Convention of 1776* (Da Capo Press 1969); John J. Dinan, *The Virginia State Constitution* (Oxford University Press 2011) 3–6.

[12] Reuters Staff, "Chad Parliament Approves New Constitution Expanding President's Powers" *Reuters* (May 4, 2018) <https://www.reuters.com/article/us-chad-politics/chad-parliament-approves-new-constitution-expanding-presidents-powers-idUSKBN1I11RC>; Ed Augustin, "Cuba Overwhelmingly Approves New Constitution Affirmin 'Irrevocable' Socialism" *The Guardian* (February 25, 2019) <https://www.theguardian.com/world/2019/feb/25/cuba-approves-new-socialist-constitution>.

[13] For a chart showing the acceleration of constitution-making activity, see Donald S. Lutz, *Principles of Constitutional Design* (Cambridge University Press 2006) 4.

[14] For a most comprehensive text on constitutional amendment, see Richard Albert, *Constitutional Amendments: Making, Breaking, and Changing Constitutions* (Oxford University Press 2019).

emerges: distinguishing the creation of a new constitution from significant amendment. Scholars have thus come up with a variety of strategies for making the distinction.

One route, used by Banks and Wilson, Widner, and Murphy, is to focus on the degree to which the government or the text changes as a result of the constitutional alteration.[15] Minor modifications that leave the fundamental structure of the state intact are considered amendments. Instances of true constitution-making involve either complete replacement, or alterations that change the basic nature of a political system. Examples of the latter might include Tanzania and Zambia, both of which altered their constitutions to shift from one party to multiparty rule in 1992 and 1991 respectively, and Morocco, which in 1996 added text to create a second parliamentary body. Another might be Turkey's 2017 transition to a super-presidential system via an amendment package that rewrote or repealed 40 percent of the constitutional text.[16] All four of these changes of existing constitutional texts radically shifted the political reality of their countries, and thus, in accordance with a context- and regime-based mode of identification, should be considered new constitutions.

However, this strategy runs into several problems. First is the impossibility of providing a uniform definition of what a fundamental change involves, given that political and historical context, the current distribution of power, as well as the details of the particular constitution in question all determine the significance of any particular constitutional alteration.

Second, focusing on the degree of change in the constitutional text or the resultant regime does not take seriously what those involved in the constitutional alteration see themselves as doing. Consider the 1990 Afghanistan Constitution, promulgated to replace the 1987 one, or any of the four constitutions Rafael Trujillo created to replace his first constitution for the Dominican Republic. Each of these new constitutions looked nearly identical to their predecessors and did little to change the nature of their government. But those involved took themselves as making a new constitution, rather than simply amending. Should these nonetheless be considered instances of amendment rather than constitution-making? Or, if citizens somewhere were out on the streets celebrating the creation of a new constitution, surely it would be strange to tell them that they did not change it enough, and that unbeknownst to them they were merely involved in amendment. Alternatively, if those changing a constitution understand themselves as merely amending an old document, this seems like it should also matter.

15 Widner, "Constitution Writing in Post-Conflict Settings: An Overview"; Arthur S. Banks and Kenneth A. Wilson, *Cross-National Time-Series Data Archive* (Databanks International 2019); Murphy, *Constitutional Democracy: Creating and Maintaining a Just Political Order*.

16 Albert, *Constitutional Amendments: Making, Breaking, and Changing Constitutions*, 7.

Another strategy for distinguishing constitution-making from amendment is to ignore the contents of the document and the effects it has on the regime and instead focus on the procedures used to alter the constitutional text. This procedural strategy is popular in more recent comparative constitutional studies, particularly those with a quantitative bent. For instance, Eisenstadt et al. apply "a narrow definition of change counting only constitutions resulting from explicit promulgations."[17] Though promulgation is some sort of procedure, usually the formal announcement of a new constitution, the authors unfortunately do not define exactly what they mean, and certain constitution-making events they include in their dataset are confusing.[18] For instance, they include an entry (signaling the creation of a new constitution) for Morocco 1992, which corresponds to textual alterations to the Moroccan Constitution that were widely reported to be amendments or reforms.[19] They also treat Tanzania 2011 as a constitution-making moment, though the only thing promulgated that year was a piece of legislation titled *The Constitutional Review Act*, which outlines a future constitution-making process that has yet to take place.[20]

Elkins, Ginsburg, and Melton, and later Wheatley and Mendez, take a different procedural path, choosing to treat changes made in accordance with procedures set out by the existing constitution as amendments, and changes made outside of the constitution as replacement.[21] This distinction accurately picks up on the fact that most constitutions have been made extra-legally, either because of a lack of a pre-existing constitution, a lack of sufficient replacement rules, or because their creators chose to ignore amendment procedures.[22] At the same time, some constitutions provide a legal path for creating a replacement document. For instance, Article 444 of the Ecuador Constitution details procedures through which a constituent assembly can be called to create a new constitution, and notes that, "the new Constitution, for its entry into force, shall require adoption by referendum with half plus one of all valid ballots cast."[23]

[17] Todd A. Eisenstadt, A. Carl LeVan, and Tofigh Maboudi, *Constituents before Assembly: Participation, Deliberation, and Representation in the Crafting of New Constitutions* (Cambridge University Press 2017) 27.

[18] Todd A. Eisenstadt, A. Carl LeVan, and Tofigh Maboudi, *Constitutionalism and Democracy Dataset, Version 1.0* (American University's Digital Research Archive 2017).

[19] Chicago Tribune Wire, "Moroccan Voters Pass Constitutional Reforms," *Chicago Tribune* (pre-1997 full text) <https://www.proquest.com/newspapers/moroccan-voters-pass-constitutional-reforms/docview/283393795/se-2?accountid=>.

[20] National Assembly of Tanzania, *The Constitutional Review Commission Act* (2011).

[21] Eisenstadt, LeVan, and Maboudi, *Constituents before Assembly: Participation, Deliberation, and Representation in the Crafting of New Constitutions*, 26–27; Elkins, Melton, and Ginsburg, *The Endurance of National Constitutions*, 55–59; Jonathan Wheatley and Fernando Mendez (eds.), *Patterns of Constitutional Design: The Role of Citizens and Elites in Constitution-Making* (Routledge 2016) 15.

[22] Gabriel L. Negretto, "Constitution-Making in Comparative Perspective," Oxford Research Encyclopedia of Politics, 4 <https://oxfordre.com/politics/view/10.1093/acrefore/9780190228637.001.0001/acrefore-9780190228637-e-66>.

[23] Constitution of the Republic of Ecuador (2008), Art. 444.

In contrast to these alternatives, I take what I refer to as a legal positivist position, one that is neither strictly substantive nor procedural. I consider an instance of constitutional change to involve constitution-making or replacement when those directly involved in the process, as well as core audiences such as local citizens and the international community, understand it as a moment of constitution-making rather than constitutional amendment.[24] Such moments usually involve major substantive changes to the governance and structure of a state, and usually depart from amending procedures specified in an existing constitution if present, but this is not always so. For purposes of quantitative analysis, this definition creates difficulties, as it requires close contextual study and case-by-case judgment calls on borderline cases.[25] This does not affect my own study, as I do not perform any such analysis, and most borderline cases I can identify do not involve ratification.

1.3 Democratic Constitution-Making: Meaning and Process

My focus is not simply the procedural recommendations for making any new constitution, but rather those that pertain to making democratic constitutions. I call this *democratic constitution-making*. This term refers to constitution-making processes meant to create a working constitutional democracy; it designates the intended outcome of a given constitution-making process rather than its substance. Democratic constitution-making is meant to exclude from consideration instances in which authoritarian or autocratic regimes create sham constitutions meant to entrench their rule or serve as mere democratic window-dressing.[26]

These are excluded because regimes interested in making sham constitutions usually refrain from seeking external advice and do not care about the actual normative implications of their design procedures. They want to create a constitution that pacifies their populace, sociologically legitimizes their rule, and increases their acceptability on the world stage. Thus, my arguments about the possible justifications of ratification procedures are neither addressed nor relevant to them. At the same time, I sometimes draw from cases of undemocratic constitution-making for examples and inspiration. This is because, though constitution-making occurs more often than most people think, it is still relatively rare, and this is even more true when it comes to democratic constitution-making.

[24] Negretto suggests something similar in "Replacing and Amending Constitutions: The Logic of Constitutional Change in Latin America," (2012) 46 Law & Society Review 749–79.

[25] This definition creates a different world of cases of constitution-making from, for instance, the *Comparative Constitutions Project*. According to them, between 1789 and 2006 there were 935 new constitutions. According to my calculations, there were only 816 new constitutions created in the time period. Note that both numbers include sham constitutions.

[26] David S. Law and Mila Versteeg, "Sham Constitutions," (2013) 101 California Law Review 863–952; Murphy, *Constitutional Democracy: Creating and Maintaining a Just Political Order*, 14.

What does modern democratic constitution-making look like? The exact contours of each constitution-making process are unique, but the general process breaks into five simplified stages, though the boundaries between them are porous: initiation, convoking, drafting, approval, and ratification.[27]

1.3.1 Initiation Stage

In the *initiation stage*, existing, transitional, or new power holders, often prompted by civil society forces, decide constitution-making is needed and begin the process.[28] Initiation is sometimes described as the *de-constituent* decision, in that it involves implicitly or explicitly deciding to abolish or attempt to abolish the former constitutional order (if still standing) and attempting to create a new one.[29] Thus, in Fiji, shortly after the 1992 elections, this stage involved both the Soqosoqo Vakavulewa ni Taukei, the party in power, and the opposition, meeting and deciding to review and ultimately replace the imposed and widely disliked 1990 constitution.[30] The initiation process for the 1991 Bolivian Constitution involved both a consultative referendum and an official referendum designed to assess support for beginning constitution-making.[31] In other recent cases of constitution-making, the initiation stage is led or supported by international actors, such as the United Nations (UN), and in post-conflict contexts frequently evolves from or is part of a prior peace-making process.[32]

Initiation can involve several bodies such as advisory committees and round tables and can produce a variety of quasi-legal/legal texts, from interim constitutions

[27] Different authors break up the constitution-making process in different ways: Elkins et al. break the process into writing, deliberation, and approval; Eisenstadt et al. use convening, debating, and ratification; Widner uses drafting, consultation, deliberation, adoption, and ratification; and Elster zooms in on the drafting body, breaking up the process into convoking the assembly, selecting delegates, determining the mandate, determining credentials, choosing decision-making procedures, and determining ratification. Elkins, Melton, and Ginsburg, *The Endurance of National Constitutions*; Eisenstadt, LeVan, and Maboudi, *Constituents before Assembly: Participation, Deliberation, and Representation in the Crafting of New Constitutions*, 28; Widner, "Constitution Writing and Conflict Resolution Project"; Jon Elster, "Arguing and Bargaining in Two Constituent Assemblies," (1999–2000) 354 University of Pennsylvania Journal of Constitutional Law 358.

[28] Another common initiating agent is a single foreign power engaged in decolonization, occupation, or custodianship. Thus, for instance, the initiating power for the constitution-making process that led to the 1979 Micronesian Constitution was the United States through its administration of the Trust Territories of the Pacific Islands. Brian Z. Tamanaha, "Battle between Law and Society in Micronesia," in Denis J. Galligan and Mila Versteeg (eds.), *Social and Political Foundations of Constitutions* (Cambridge University Press 2013) 585.

[29] Claude Klein and András Sajó, "Constitution-Making: Process and Substance," in Michel Rosenfeld and András Sajó (eds.), *The Oxford Handbook of Comparative Constitutional Law* (Oxford University Press 2012) 422–23.

[30] Brij V. Lal, "Constitutional Engineering in Post-Coup Fiji," in Andrew Reynolds (ed.), *The Architecture of Democracy: Constitutional Design, Conflict Management, and Democracy* (Oxford University Press 2002) 268–69.

[31] Gabriel L. Negretto, *Constitution-Building Processes in Latin America: International Idea Discussion Paper 3/2018* (2018) 11.

[32] Michele Brandt and others, *Constitution-Making and Reform: Options for the Process* (Interpeace 2011) 24.

to guiding principles. In Fiji, it involved a Joint Parliamentary Committee, a three-person review Commission, and terms of reference, which set out goals for the Commission and any draft they worked on.[33] According to some, the success or failure of the rest of the constitution-making process, especially in societies characterized by deep pluralism, often turns on the presence and quality of informal talks, inclusion efforts, and negotiations during initiation.[34] Note that it is usually in this stage that the remainder of the constitution-making process is designed, and it is thus here that designers likely choose whether to use ratification or not.

1.3.2 Convoking Stage

The initiation stage determines the nature of and ends with the *convoking stage*, in which the central constitution-making body—the entity formally entrusted with the work of writing and finalizing a draft of the constitution—comes together, either via self-declaration, appointment, election, or some combination of the latter two. In Mongolia, President Orchirbat ended the initiation phase of its 1991 constitution-making process by appointing a twenty-member Constitutional Drafting Commission, while the initiation phase of the constitution-making process that led to the 1996 Bolivian Constitution terminated upon the election and convening of the Bolivian constituent assembly.[35]

Central constitution-making bodies vary a great deal, and scholars of constitution-making disagree over how best to categorize them, let alone which type is most desirable.[36] Bodies are categorized in accordance with how they are populated (directly or indirectly elected, appointed by executives or parties), whether they are mandated to create a constitution, whether they possess legislative as well as constitution-making powers, and how large they are. Common central constitution-making bodies include constituent legislatures, constituent

[33] Lal, "Constitutional Engineering in Post-Coup Fiji", 268–70.

[34] Hannah Lerner, "Constituent Assemblies and Political Continuity in Divided Societies," in Jon Elster and others (eds.), *Constituent Assemblies* (Cambridge University Press 2018).

[35] Tom Ginsburg and Gombusuren Ganzorig, "Constitutional Reform and Human Rights," in Ole Brunn and Ole Odgaard (eds.), *Mongolia in Transition: Old Patterns, New Challenges* (Routledge 1996) 149; Lawrence S. Rothenberg and Mitchell S. Sanders, "Lame-Duck Politics: Impending Departure and the Votes on Impeachment," (2000) 3 Political Research Quarterly 523–36, 511; Phoebe King, "Neo-Bolivarian Constitutional Design," in Denis J. Galligan and Mila Versteeg (eds.), *Social and Political Foundations of Constitutions* (Cambridge University Press 2013).

[36] See, for example, Gabriel L. Negretto, "Democratic Constitution-Making Bodies: The Perils of a Partisan Convention," (2018) 16 International Journal of Constitutional Law 254–79; Fernando Mendez and Jonathan Wheatley, "Patterns of Constitution-Making over Time and Space," in Jonathan Wheatley and Fernando Mendez (eds.), *Patterns of Constitutional Design: The Role of Citizens and Elites in Constitution-Making* (Routledge 2016) 24–30; Jon Elster, "Legislatures as Constituent Assemblies," in Richard W. Bauman and Tsvi Kahana (eds.), *The Least Examined Branch: The Role of Legislatures in the Constitutional State* (Cambridge University Press 2006); Tom Ginsburg, Zachary Elkins, and Justin Blount, "Does the Process of Constitution-Making Matter?" (2009) 5 Annual Review of Law and Social Science 201–23, 204–9; Widner, "Constitution Writing in Post-Conflict Settings: An Overview", 1523–24; Brandt and others, *Constitution-Making and Reform: Options for the Process*, 232–73.

conventions, national conferences, round tables, and executive committees/commissions.

In democratic constitution-making, constituent assemblies—which includes constituent conventions and constituent legislatures—are the most frequent and recommended.[37] Constituent conventions (or as they are sometimes known, constitutional conventions) are assemblies convoked for the primary purpose of creating a new constitution, with the intention that they will dissolve upon the completion of this task and not undertake any ordinary legislative activity.[38] Delegates to conventions can be appointed or elected (directly or indirectly), with some conventions being populated by both methods. Constitutional conventions were present in the constitution-making processes that led to the U.S. Constitution, the German Federal Republic Constitution of 1949, the 1857 Constitution of Mexico, and the Australian Constitution of 1901, among many others.

Constituent legislatures are elected assemblies with the power both to pass ordinary legislation and create a constitution. They are not necessarily designed to dissolve immediately upon the approval of a new constitution. These are by far the most common constitution-making bodies. There are four types: mandated constituent legislatures, self-created constituent legislatures, self-created legislative assemblies, and constitutionally authorized constituent legislatures.[39] *Mandated constituted legislatures* are elected to enact a new constitution and pass ordinary legislation, usually occurring in situations where there is no existing legislative body or the existing one lacks sociological legitimacy. Examples include the legislatures that created the 1992 Slovakian Constitution and the 1978 Spanish Constitution.

Self-created constituent legislatures are normal legislative bodies that turn themselves into constituent assemblies without electoral approval, pre-existing constitutional authorization, or any other mandate. Such constituent legislatures were responsible for creating the majority of state constitutions in revolutionary America and the independence constitutions of Estonia and Croatia.[40] *Self-created legislative assemblies*, on the other hand, are constituent assemblies that, though elected as constitutional conventions, assume legislative powers. The Indian constituent assembly and the 1934 Brazilian constituent assembly are famous examples of this type. Finally, *constitutionally authorized constituent legislatures* are ordinary

[37] Negretto, "Democratic Constitution-Making Bodies: The Perils of a Partisan Convention," 255; Ginsburg, Elkins, and Blount, "Does the Process of Constitution-Making Matter?" 213.

[38] John Alexander Jameson, *The Constitutional Convention; Its History, Powers, and Modes of Proceeding* (Charles Scribner and Company 1867) 10; Negretto, "Democratic Constitution-Making Bodies: The Perils of a Partisan Convention," 256; Jon Elster, "The Optimal Design of a Constituent Assembly," in Helene Landemore and Jon Elster (eds.), *Collective Wisdom: Principles and Mechanisms* (Cambridge University Press 2012) 152.

[39] Elster, "The Optimal Design of a Constituent Assembly," 152–53; Elster, "Legislatures as Constituent Assemblies"; Negretto, "Constitution-Making in Comparative Perspective," 9–14.

[40] Negretto, "Constitution-Making in Comparative Perspective," 13; Roger Sherman Hoar, *Constitutional Conventions, Their Nature, Powers, and Limitations* (Little, Brown 1917) 141–48.

legislative bodies that legally transform themselves into constituent assemblies via procedures spelled out in an existing constitution or higher legal code.

1.3.3 Drafting and Approval

The *drafting* phase involves the writing of the constitution. Formally, this is the task of the central constitution-making body, whose members engage in arguing and bargaining as they hammer out a constitutional text. Popular imaginings of constitution-making likely consist of just these sorts of deliberations, with visions of learned assembly members debating constitutional provisions in the Indian constituent assembly, the Assemblée Nationale Constituante in France, and the South African constitutional assembly. At the same time, a variety of outside entities often play critical roles in the drafting process. International experts, intergovernmental organizations (IGOs), and constitution-makers from other countries are frequently consulted. Civil society groups and political parties are also often invited to contribute to the process, sometimes even submitting full or rival drafts of their ideal constitution. In Cambodia, the constituent assembly never even considered the draft constitution produced by its own twelve-member drafting committee, choosing instead to adopt the draft written independently by FUNCINPEC, the Royalist party, with edits by King Sihanouk.[41]

Sometimes an appointed commission or committee outside of and often existing before the central constitution-making body does most of the actual drafting. For instance, in 1922 a ten-person committee appointed by Michael Collins, the chairman of the Second Daíl (the provisional government in Ireland) met and created several drafts for Ireland's first constitution. One of these, after debate and modification by the Second Daíl and the British parliament, served as the primary text debated and enacted by the Third Daíl, a mandated constituent legislature, on October 25, 1922.[42] Other times, the central constitution-making body farms out the drafting to a committee composed of some of its own members, whose work is eventually sent back to the full body for debate, amendment, and an up or down vote. Thus, in India committees such as the Union Powers Committee and the Fundamental Rights Committee outlined the principles of the constitution, and then the Drafting Committee generated a draft.[43] In the process that led to Romania's 1991 Constitution, the mandated constituent legislature (a

[41] Stephen P. Marks, "The Process of Creating a New Constitution in Cambodia," in Laurel E. Miller (ed.), *Framing the State in Times of Transition: Case Studies in Constitution Making* (United States Institute of Peace Press 2010) 214–15.

[42] Paul Brady, "Social, Political and Philosophical Foundations of the Irish Constitutional Order," in Denis J. Galligan and Mila Versteeg (eds.), *Social and Political Foundations of Constitutions* (Cambridge University Press 2013) 272–73.

[43] Durga Das Basu, *Introduction to the Constitution of India* (20th edn, LexisNexis Butterworths Wadhwa Nagpur 2011) 17–19.

two-house parliament), delegated drafting to a twenty-six-member constitutional commission.[44]

However, sometimes the entire central constitution-making body does draft the text directly. Perhaps one of the most extreme examples of this took place during the constitution-making process that led to Brazil's 1988 Constitution, during which the entire 559-member mandated constituent legislature took part in drafting. To accomplish this, the Congress divided itself into eight committees, each of which were divided into three sub-committees. A central Committee on Systematization then harmonized the results.[45]

Contemporary constitution-making processes, in line with recommendations from constitutional consultants, international organizations, and constitutional scholars, are often designed to encourage and enable members of the public to participate and have input on the drafting process. There are a variety of ways for this to happen. To name a few, constitution-makers can meet with representatives of different interest or ethnic groups, hold public hearings, collect written submissions about what should be written into the constitution, solicit comments on a released draft constitution, convoke consultative deliberative bodies, or distribute questionnaires.

For example, each of the twenty-four sub-committees in the Brazilian process mentioned above devoted five to eight sessions hearing from groups representing different sectors of Brazilian society.[46] They also solicited citizen proposals and received over 64,000 in response.[47] The process used to create the 1995 Ugandan Constitution involved members of the Constitutional Commission touring the country, holding over 800 open seminars and consulting local leaders, and soliciting memoranda and reports from local councils, individuals, and citizen's groups.[48] The South African constitution-making process famously included a two-stage participatory and consultative process. The first took place from January to November 1995, as a lead-up to the creation of the draft constitution, and involved a national survey, the solicitation of constitutional ideas, public meetings, participatory workshops, and public hearings. In total, constituent assembly members directly interacted with over 115,000 people and received over two million submissions. The second phase of public participation concerned the draft constitution and took place from November 1995 to February 1996. The

[44] Bianca Selejan-Gutan, *The Constitution of Romania: A Contextual Analysis* (Constitutional Systems of the World, Hart Publishing 2013).

[45] Keith S. Rosenn, "Brazil's New Constitution: An Exercise in Transient Constitutionalism for a Transitional Society," (1990) 38 The American Journal of Comparative Law 773–802, 776–77.

[46] Ibid., 777.

[47] Jamal Benomar, "Constitution-Making after Conflict: Lessons for Iraq," (2004) 15 Journal of Democracy 81–95.

[48] Aili Mari Tripp, "The Politics of Constitution Making in Uganda," in Laurel E. Miller (ed.), *Framing the State in Times of Transition: Case Studies in Constitution Making* (United States Institute of Peace Press 2010) 163–64.

assembly distributed over 4.5 million copies of the draft and received over 250,000 comments.[49]

In the *approval stage* a final version of the constitution-making text is settled upon. In the absence of ratification, a positive result marks the end of the constitution-making process. The constitution is approved and then implemented. The primary actors in the approval stage are usually the central constitution-making body or one of its committees. Thus, the final draft of the Spanish Constitution of 1978 underwent approval by both chambers of the Cortes Generales, the mandated constituent legislature, before the ratification stage that involved a popular referendum.[50] Sometimes, existing governmental bodies that authorized the constitution-making body play a role in approval as well. For instance, two successive parliaments and the Finnish president approved the 2000 Constitution of Finland, drafted by an appointed Constitution 2000 Commission in conjunction with the government's Constitutional Law Committee, before it came into force on March 1.[51]

Note that in recent quantitative work seeking to measure the effects of constitution-making procedures, the approval stage is often confused with the ratification stage. Thus, for instance, Eisenstadt and Maboudi code a ratification process as participatory when it involves a free and fair referendum, and non-participatory or mixed if it involves approval by the elected constituent assembly, executive decree, or some other non-referendum means.[52] As I will explain below, this oddly groups together the inevitable and necessary final vote or decision of a drafting body (the approval stage) with ratification, a separate procedure and stage entirely.

2. Ratification

The *ratification stage* takes place after the approval stage and, when present, is the final stage of the constitution-making process instead of the latter. It consists in a ratification procedure, which I define as the following:

[49] Hassen Ebrahim and Laurel E. Miller, "Creating the Birth Certificate of a New South Africa: Constitution Making after Apartheid," in Laurel E. Miller (ed.), *Framing the State in Times of Transition: Case Studies in Constitution Making* (United States Institute of Peace 2010) 136–37; Siri Gloppen, *South Africa: The Battle over the Constitution* (Ashgate 1997) 256–58; Christina Murray, "Negotiating Beyond Deadlock: From the Constitutional Assembly to the Court," (2004) 32 International Journal of Legal Information 322–50, 106–12.

[50] Andrea Bonime-Blanc, "Constitution Making and Democratization: The Spanish Paradigm," in Laurel E. Miller (ed.), *Framing the State in Times of Transition: Case Studies in Constitution Making* (United States Institute of Peace 2010) 424–25.

[51] Seppo Tiitinen, "Constitutional Reform in Finland," *Constitutional & Parliamentary Information* (Association of Secretaries General of Parliaments 1999) 105–6.

[52] Todd A. Eisenstadt and Tofigh Maboudi, "Being There Is Half the Battle: Group Inclusion, Constitution-Writing, and Democracy," (2019) 52 Comparative Political Studies 2135–70.

Ratification: the submission of a constitution to an agent or group for their approval before final enactment, provided that:

(i) The independence condition: the agent is independent—not identical to, or controlled by, or controls—from the drafter.
(ii) The veto condition: the agent can only approve or reject the constitution.
(iii) The "acting for" condition: the agent plausibly claims to act for or in the name of the people.

These three conditions are not strictly necessary when identifying instances of ratification in previous constitution-making processes. There is room for discretion, and some case-by-case judgment is needed for borderline cases.

2.1 Conditions

The *independence and veto conditions* help distinguish ratification from the final vote in a complex drafting and approval process, and highlight that ratification involves the submission of a constitution to an agent that is distinct and independent from its drafters. Two examples further clarify these distinctions. The primary drafting body of the 1990 Namibian constitution was a seventy-two-member elected constituent assembly. During the drafting process, the assembly appointed an external committee of three lawyers to synthesize present and past proposals and competing constitutional drafts into a coherent whole. The expert group produced an explanatory memorandum and a complete draft of a constitution and submitted it to a standing committee of twelve specialists, who in turn created the final draft. The constituent assembly then discussed and eventually voted in favor of this constitution, which came into force in late March 1990.[53] The independence condition makes it clear that this final vote in the constituent assembly was not an instance of ratification, for the constituent assembly cannot be understood as independent from the expert and standing committees that it appointed, populated, and supervised. The Namibian constitution-making process thus lacked a ratification procedure, and the final vote of the constituent assembly was simply akin to the decisive vote in a legislature after a multi-stage drafting process.

Next, consider the drafting of the Estonian Constitution of 1992. This somewhat complicated process was initiated by the Estonian Supreme Soviet (the official legislative body) in August the year prior and involved the creation of a constitutional assembly consisting of sixty members, with thirty members coming from

[53] Marinus Wiechers, "Namibia's Long Walk to Freedom: The Role of Constitution-Making and the Right to Take Part in a Public Affair," in Laurel E. Miller (ed.), *Framing the State in Times of Transition: Case Studies in Constitution Making* (United States Institute of Peace Press 2010).

both the Supreme Soviet and the Estonian Congress (a rival grassroots legislative body formed in 1990). The constituent assembly produced a constitution in three months, asked for and received public comments, and approved a draft by supermajority on February 14, 1991. This draft was then sent back to the Supreme Council (the new name of the Supreme Soviet) for approval before submission to a referendum. The two bodies continued to negotiate, with the Supreme Council insisting on amendments, only some of which were ever made. The constitution was eventually authorized by the Supreme Council and submitted to the people in a ratification referendum. It was ratified on June 28, 1992, with 91.2 percent of those voting approving the document.[54]

Looking at the Estonian case, two ratifiers seem possible: the Supreme Council and the people in referendum. Both approved the draft constitution in an up or down vote, and both were not identical to the drafting body. However, the independence and veto conditions help us determine that the Supreme Council cannot be treated as a ratifier. In violation of the independence condition, the constituent assembly was not entirely independent of the Supreme Council, as the latter initiated the constitution-making procedure, planned the composition of the constituent assembly, and populated half of its members. Lest one thinks this is still a borderline case for ratification, the veto condition clarifies matters. The Supreme Council both asserted and exercised amendment power, and thus contributed to the drafting of the constitution. Ratifiers merely act as veto points, the Supreme Council did more than this, and therefore the Estonian constitution-making process had one ratification procedure: the referendum.

The "acting for" condition mainly serves to distinguish ratification procedures from instances in which autocrats or monarchs exercise a veto at the end of a constitution-making process. The 1923 Constitution of Romania, for instance, required the signature of King Ferdinand I to come into effect. The King had nothing to do with the drafting of the constitution, had little power over its authors, and merely approved rather than rejected the document. However, though meeting the first two conditions, the King—a monarch who inherited the position upon the death of his uncle—was not understood as a representative of the people and thus his acceptance does not count as ratification.[55]

[54] Rett R. Ludwikowski, "Constitution Making in the Countries of Former Soviet Dominance: Current Development," (1993) 33 Georgia Journal of International and Comparative Law 155–267.

[55] Cristina E. Parau, "Romania's Transnational Constitution: A Tradition of Elite Learning and Self-Empowerment," in Denis J. Galligan and Mila Versteeg (eds.), *Social and Political Foundations of Constitutions* (Cambridge University Press 2013) 513–14.

2.2 Types

Ratification divides into six types along two dimensions. The first dimension is the form of the agent involved in ratifying: a ratifying convention, an existing government body, or the people via a referendum. The second dimension is whether the ratifying agent is singular, representing the people as a whole, or many, representing the people of sub-state territories. Thus, the six types of ratification are: ratification by national convention, ratification by sub-state conventions, ratification by national government body, ratification by sub-state government bodies, ratification by national referendum, or ratification by sub-state referendum.

Ratifying conventions are independent bodies convoked for the sole purpose of approving or rejecting a constitution. They can be elected, appointed with the aim of being representative, or populated by a mixture of these two devices. *Ratification by national convention* occurs when the constitution is submitted to a single convention, acting for the entire state, for approval or rejection. The first known consideration of the procedure occurred in the Philadelphia Convention on July 23, 1787, when Governor Morris suggested that the federal constitution be submitted to "one general Convention, chosen & authorized by the people."[56] His suggestion was not even seconded. However, two years later the first instance of such a ratification procedure took place in the U.S. State of Georgia, when a constitution written and amended by two previous conventions was approved by a third elected especially for the purposes of ratification.[57]

More recently, both the 1994 Ethiopian and 2012 Somali constitution-making processes utilized national ratifying conventions. In Ethiopia, in accordance with the Article 10 of the 1991 "Transitional Period Charter," the appointed constituent legislature submitted its draft constitution to a newly elected national constituent assembly for the express purpose of ratification.[58] The ratifying convention in Somalia, known as the Somali National Constituent Assembly, consisted of 835 delegates chosen by 135 tribal leaders on the basis of descriptive representation principles. According to the "Protocol Establishing the Somali National

[56] Max Farrand (ed.), *The Records of the Federal Convention of 1787*, vol. 2 (Yale University Press 1911) 92.

[57] The second convention in the 1788–89 constitution-making process of the State of Georgia was supposed to be a ratifying convention. However, as many conventions decide to do, it exceeded its authority and amended the document. This, among other reasons, prompted the House of Assembly to call for the election of a second ratifying convention (and third convention overall) in February that same year. This, in a sense, supports the veto condition of my definition of ratification. Albert B. Saye, *A Constitutional History of Georgia: 1732–1945* (The University of Georgia Press 1948) 137–41. See chapter 3, section 4 for further discussion of Georgia's second constitution.

[58] Transitional Period Charter of Ethiopia (1991), part 4, Art.10. See Tsegaye Regassa, "The Making and Legitimacy of the Ethiopian Constitution: Towards Bridging the Gap between Constitutional Design and Constitutional Practice," (2010) 23 Afrika Focus 85–118; Kassahun Berhanu, "Ethiopia Elects a Constituent Assembly," (1995) 22 Review of African Political Economy 129–35. Note that, as Berhanu illustrates, the constituent assembly elections in Ethiopia were manipulated by the incumbent, the Ethiopian People's Democratic Front.

Constituent Assembly," this national convention was supposed to work in tandem with a ratification referendum, meaning that, as designed, the Somali process would have had two ratification procedures. However, security concerns related to Al-Shabob led to the cancellation of the referendum.[59]

Ratification by subnational conventions involves the submission of a draft constitution to multiple specially elected ratifying conventions convoked by subnational political units such as counties, provinces, or states. The only example of this ratification type occurred for the U.S. Constitution, which was submitted "to a Convention of Delegates, chosen in each State by the People thereof, under the Recommendation of its Legislature, for their Assent and Ratification."[60]

Ratification by government bodies involves the submission of a constitution to a government agent or branch that plays no other significant role in the drafting process. As with conventions, ratification by government bodies divides into two types depending upon the level of government in question. With *ratification by national government body*, the ratifier is a part of the national government. Such ratification procedures are rare, for if still standing, most governments at least partially control the constitution-making process and therefore violate the independence condition. Thus, when they do occur, ratification by national government body usually involves a provisional government, such as one set up during an internationally controlled peace process or secession effort. For example, the Transitional National Assembly created by the Arusha Peace Accords ratified the Rwandan Constitution, and an assembly consisting of the transitional government and the Bougainville People's Congress ratified the Constitution of Bougainville following the country's partial secession from Papua New Guinea in 2002.[61]

The ratifiers are part of subnational governments in *ratification by subnational government bodies*. Article XIII of the Articles of Confederation called for a version of this ratification type, demanding that any new governing document for the Confederation receive the explicit approval of all state legislatures. Famously, the Federal Convention in Philadelphia decided to ignore this article. In West Germany in 1949, the *Parlamentarischer Rat* went against the Allied request for

59 "Somalia: National Constituent Assembly Adopts New Constitution," Shabelle Media Network <http://allafrica.com/stories/201208020038.html>; Adnan Hussein, "Somalia Faces Tough Road in Its Transition to Federal Rule," Sabahi <http://sabahionline.com/en_GB/articles/hoa/articles/features/2012/05/21/feature-01>; Tesfatsion Medhanie, *Constitution-Making, Legitimacy and Regional Integration: An Approach to Eritrea's Predicament and Relations with Ethiopia* (DIIPER Research Series 2008).

60 Max Farrand (ed.), *The Records of the Federal Convention of 1787*, vol. 2 (Yale University Press 1914) 665.

61 Bougainville created a constitution for its own autonomous government but remains tied to Papua New Guinea in several ways. Edward P. Wolfers, "'Joint Creation': The Bougainville Peace Agreement and Beyond," (2010) 12 Accord 44–50; Priscilla Yachat Ankut, *The Role of Constitution-Building Processes in Democratization: Case Study—Rwanda*, 2005); Felip Reyntjens, "Constitution-Making in Situations of Extreme Crisis: The Case of Rwanda and Burundi," (1996) 40 Journal of African Law 234–42.

ratification by referendum, and instead submitted the *Grungesetz* to the West German *Landtage* (state parliaments) for ratification. They were likely motivated by the desire to make clear the provisional nature of any constitution created during occupation within their divided country, thinking that ratification by state legislator conferred less authority than the alternative.[62]

Ratification by referendum occurs when the constitution-making body or sitting government submits the constitution to the people directly for their explicit approval or rejection. The people, more precisely those with suffrage at the time, serve as the ratifying agent. The most common form of ratification, by a very large margin, is *ratification by national referendum*, where the votes of all of those with suffrage across a polity are aggregated together. National ratification referendums became increasingly popular in the late twentieth century. In fact, over half of all constitution-making processes since 1998 have made use of a referendum.[63] In just the last decade (2009–19) ratification referendums were held in sixteen countries including Cuba, Thailand, Egypt, Zimbabwe, and Madagascar. And, according to Elkins and Hudson, of the roughly 194 constitutions in force today, sixty-nine, or 35.6 percent, were ratified through a referendum.[64] In a real sense, a ratification referendum is the default ratification procedure today.

Ratification by sub-state referendums involves numerous referendums held in sub-state territories, with the constitution being approved if it is accepted in a majority or supermajority of them. For instance, the 1848 Constitution of Switzerland was submitted to voters in referendums held in each canton and declared ratified when a majority of these approved it. A similar procedure was used to approve the Australian Constitution thirty years later, with each colony holding a referendum.[65] Sometimes, complex ratification procedures seem to combine elements of sub-state and national referendums. For instance, the 2010 Kenyan constitutional referendum required both an overall majority of all those voting and at least 25 percent approval in five out of eight provinces. Even more

[62] H.W. Koch, *A Constitutional History of Germany in the Nineteenth and Twentieth Centuries* (Longman 1984) 339–55; Peter Merkl, *The Origins of the West German Republic* (Oxford University Press 1963) 114–16.

[63] Markkhu Suksi, *Bringing in the People: A Comparison of Constitutional Forms and Practices of the Referendum* (Martinus Nijhoff Publishers 1993). I supplemented Suksi's work with my own review for the years 1993–2018. For a graphical representation of the increase of referendums, see Ginsburg, Elkins, and Blount, "Does the Process of Constitution-Making Matter?".

[64] Zachary Elkins and Alexander Hudson, "The Constitutional Referendum in Historical Perspective," in David Landau and Hannah Lerner (eds.), *Comparative Constitution Making* (Edward Elgar 2019) 142.

[65] Paolo Dardanelli, "The Emergence and Evolution of Democracy in Switzerland," in Mary Malone (ed.), *Achieving Democracy: Democratization in Theory and Practice* (Continuum 2011) 149; Susan Crennan, "Federation," in Cheryl Saunders and Adrienne Stone (eds.), *The Oxford Handbook of the Australian Constitution* (Oxford University Press 2018) 94; Jonathan Wheatley and Micha Germann, "Outcomes of Constitution-Making: Democratization and Conflict Resolution," in Jonathan Wheatley and Fernando Mendez (eds.), *Patterns of Constitutional Design: The Role of Citizens and Elites in Constitution-Making* (Routledge 2016) 61.

complicated, the Iraqi ratification referendum required the approval of a simple majority of all those voting, as well as approval by more than one-third of all registered voters in sixteen out of eighteen governorates.[66]

In what follows, most of the examples I mention, or hypothetical constitution-making processes I reference, concern ratification procedures involving a referendum or convention. This means I somewhat de-emphasize ratification by governmental bodies on national and subnational levels. I do this for a simple reason. For a governmental body to serve as a ratifier it needs to be somewhat authoritative (so it can plausibly meet the "acting for" condition), still in power or standing, and not in control of the constitution-making process. This, as mentioned, is rare historically and also unlikely, mainly because a governmental body meeting the first two requirements has every reason to do all that it can to control the constitution-making process and the means to be successful. Thus, in most instances of constitution-making, standing authoritative governments usually at least partially control the constitution-making process, and therefore disqualify themselves from being ratifiers according to the definition I use. Nonetheless, the justifications I analyze are meant to apply to all ratification types, except where otherwise noted.

3. What Kind of Justification?

I claim that we need to know the reasons for using ratification. But what kind of reasons are these? I use the term "justification" to make clear that I am not after an explanation in the classically social scientific sense, and thus am not merely looking for explanatory reasons, i.e. reasons that contribute to the explanation of an occurrence.[67] Seeking explanations for ratification in particular instances is of course a perfectly valid exercise. Such an investigation would focus on the actors responsible for implementing the procedure and their motivations and expectations, and then attempt to describe the various causal pathways that led to the ratification moment. For example, one might inquire why, after a four-year closed drafting process, Emir Sheik Hamad bin Khalifa al-Thani decided to submit the final draft Constitution of Qatar to the people in a referendum when neither the 1972 provisional Constitution nor the people demanded it.[68]

Explanations are interesting, but I am in search of normative reasons, i.e. reasons that "count in favour of that for which they are reasons."[69] Reasons such

66 Brandt and others, *Constitution-Making and Reform: Options for the Process*, 299; *Iraq's Constitutional Process: Shaping a Vision for the Country's Future* (U.S. Institute of Peace 2005).

67 For the distinction between explanatory and normative reasons, see Joseph Raz, *From Normativity to Responsibility* (Oxford University Press 2011) 13–35.

68 Widner, "Constitution Writing and Conflict Resolution Project."

69 Raz, *From Normativity to Responsibility*, 18.

as these clarify why something is worth doing. I do not want to know why ratification is used when it is used, but rather why it should be used. However, even this is too broad. One might conduct a comparative study of several constitution-making processes and generalize about the various strategic reasons particular actors might have for pushing for ratification procedures of a certain type. For instance, a self-interested member of an ethnic group commanding a large majority of the population of a particular state might push for ratification via referendum with a simple majority threshold, while a member of a minority group in command of key provinces or states might seek ratification by sub-state conventions or legislatures.

These sorts of explanations for ratification, while interesting lines of inquiry that I will partially take up in the final chapter, are not the central focus of this book. Instead, I am seeking justifications consisting of normative reasons that are: context-independent, pro tanto, and operate ex ante. By *context-independent*, I mean that such a justification appeals to independent values unrelated to context and uses them to produce reasons for implementing ratification that apply, theoretically, to all cases of constitution-making and to all involved who are interested in its success. Such reasons are pro tanto in that they are defeasible, i.e. the justification gives a reason to use ratification, but circumstances can produce counter reasons that may override them. These reasons are ex ante in the sense that they apply at the beginning of the constitution-making process, rather than responding to occurrences that happen along the way. Thus, the reasons I am after are the sort that specify best practices in constitution-making design, ones that might find their way into policy recommendations or guidebooks distributed to those designing a new constitution-making process.

Elster's discussions of the optimal design of a constituent assembly is an example of the sort of justification I am looking for, though he did not use the term. This work is an extension of his larger project on the various ways in which self-interest and irrationality (passion, prejudice, and bias) can sometimes pollute collective decision-making, and how procedures can be designed to prevent this.[70] Elster emphasizes the importance of such a focus because of the frequent double-indeterminacy that plagues institutional evaluation from the standpoint of good outcomes. To evaluate an institution by its outcome we need, on the one hand, a normative theory that tells us what a good outcome is, and on the

[70] Jon Elster, "Constitution-Making in Eastern Europe: Rebuilding the Boat in the Open Sea," (1993) 71 Public Administration 169–217; Jon Elster, "Constitutional Bootstrapping in Philadelphia and Paris," in Michel Rosenfeld (ed.), *Constitutionalism, Identity, Difference, and Legitimacy: Theoretical Perspectives* (Duke University Press 1994); Elster, "Forces and Mechanisms in the Constitution-Making Process"; Jon Elster, "The Role of Institutional Interest in East European Constitution-Making," (1996) 5 East European Constitutional Review 169–217; Elster, "Arguing and Bargaining in Two Constituent Assemblies"; Elster, "Legislatures as Constituent Assemblies"; Jon Elster, "Clearing and Strengthening the Channels of Constitution Making," in Tom Ginsburg (ed.), *Comparative Constitutional Design* (Cambridge University Press 2012).

other hand, a causal theory that tells us if an institution is likely to lead to this desired outcome. A chief problem is that there are competing plausible normative and causal theories, and little agreed upon way to choose between them. In response, Elster suggests that we should shift our focus to the procedures likely to lead to good design, i.e. procedures that diminish partiality and irrationality from decision-making.[71]

Applied to constitutional design, this line of thinking emphasizes the importance of focusing on the constitution-making process, rather than simply dwelling on what an ideal constitution might look like. Given that there is no independent criterion that tells us exactly what a good constitution is for a particular polity, Elster suggests, the best we can do is design a constitution-making process that eliminates biases and other sources of irrationality and partiality. In pursuit of this goal, Elster outlines a series of procedures and conditions for constitution-making designed to amplify the collective wisdom of framers, defined as "impartial motivation conjoined with rational beliefs."[72] For example, he explains that ensuring that the assembly is not too small, instituting time limits, and separating the constitution-making body from the legislature reduces the effects of partial self- or group-interest.[73] Locating the constituent assembly away from major cities and cloaking the proceedings in full or partial secrecy tempers passions such as fear and vanity. In addition, designing selection mechanisms to an assembly in a way that encourages diversity and representativeness increases epistemic quality by facilitating optimal information gathering.

Each of the arguments Elster gives for his constitution-making suggestions are general and appeal to values—mainly the elimination of bias and other sources of irrationality—to produce reasons in support of his recommendations. These values are unrelated to a specific context and are relevant at the design stage. My goal in this project is to investigate whether similar justifications can be found in favor of implementing ratification. Such arguments could relate to the elimination of bias, or to other context-independent values.

4. Why Care about Ratification?

Why does ratification require or call for a justification of this type? My answer is simple: it is a mistake to recommend, accept the frequent use of, or implement an optional constitution-making procedure with significant effects without having

[71] Jon Elster, *Securities against Misrule: Juries, Assemblies, Elections* (Cambridge University Press 2013) 11–16.

[72] Elster, "The Optimal Design of a Constituent Assembly," 151.

[73] Of course, these recommendations have not gone unchallenged. Against Elster's preference for constituent conventions rather than constituent legislatures, see Negretto, "Democratic Constitution-Making Bodies: The Perils of a Partisan Convention."

reason to do so. Thus far, ratification has been ignored and no such reasons have been significantly developed or studied. This should be remedied. In this section, I will provide support for each component part of this claim.

4.1 Ratification Is Optional

As mentioned previously, ratification is an optional process. Now, in some sense, no constitution-making procedure is required given that, at least according to some theories, constitution-making necessarily abrogates the force of any existing legal regulation that might require a particular constitution-making procedure. But ratification is optional in a deeper and simpler sense: constitutions can be made without ever being submitted to any version of the procedure. This is not true for other procedures. For instance, a constitution cannot come into being unless those tasked with writing it are selected, the written text is generated through some process, and a final version of the text is settled on. However, constitutions have been born and implemented without ever being submitted to an up or down vote carried out by an agent or group independent from the drafters and acting for or in the name of the people.

Without ratification, a constitution comes into force during or shortly after the approval stage, when the drafting body and/or the authorities that convoked the drafting body approve it. For example, the Brazilian Constitution came into effect on October 5, 1988, after two subsequent majorities in the constituent assembly voted in its favor.[74] Similarly, the positive vote of 92 percent of the National Constituent Assembly of Tunisia effectively adopted the 2014 Tunisian Constitution.[75] Sometimes a triggering event is required for a new constitution to come into force after approval. Thus, for instance, though approved by the Estonian constituent assembly on June 15, 1920, the first Estonian Constitution only became active law in December 1920 following the election of a new legislature.[76] Regardless, these three and many other cases illustrate that constitutions can be created, enacted, and come into force without the use of any type of ratification procedure. Thus, using or not using the procedure is a choice that those constructing a constitution-making process must make.

[74] Rosenn, "Brazil's New Constitution: An Exercise in Transient Constitutionalism for a Transitional Society," 777.

[75] Duncan Pickard, "Prospects for Implementing Democracy in Tunisia," (2014) 19 Mediterranean Politics 259–64, 259.

[76] Henn-Jüri Uibopuu, "The Constitutional Development of the Estonian Republic," (1973) 4 Journal of Baltic Studies 11–35, 12.

4.2 Costs and Effects

Perhaps we would not need to inquire into ratification if the procedure had little or no effect or cost. Even though it is optional, if ratification simply rubber stamped the work of drafters—if it were a mere formality, a historical remnant, or a superficially symbolic process—then its lack of justification might be understandable or irrelevant. It simply would not matter if the procedure occurred or not. However, ratification is not perfectly neutral in this way, nor should one expect it to be. The procedure has several effects on constitution-making.

First, as a veto point, ratification can lead to the rejection of constitutions; sometimes the people or their delegate ratifiers say "No." In the United States, where 233 constitutional conventions have produced only 146 different constitutions, rejection by ratification is somewhat of a regular occurrence. In 1946, voters in France overwhelmingly rejected a constitution crafted by an assembly, perhaps because it gave too much power to the parliament.[77] In 1999, despite a vigorous government-led campaign to promote it, voters in Zimbabwe rejected a draft constitution by 54 percent.[78] Other examples of rejection include Switzerland in 1872, Estonia in 1932 and 1933, Albania in 1994, and Kenya in 2005. While such occurrences are relatively infrequent worldwide, ratification has and continues to lead to rejected constitutions.[79]

The rejection of a constitution in a ratification procedure has two subsidiary effects. On the one hand, in more cases than not, it puts an end to the constitution-making process, regardless of its length, importance, or the margin of defeat.[80] On the other hand, rejections can be quite costly. These costs might include the resources and time consumed by future constitution-making attempts, an increase in the difficulty of successfully creating a constitution in the future, the continued persistence of a state of anarchy or an outdated and harmful constitution and regime, and even an influx or resumption of violence in areas prone to conflict. Both Zimbabwe and Kenya saw a massive increase in violence seemingly related to the rejection of constitutions in referendums. In the former case, Mugabe encouraged

[77] Robert K. Gooch, "Recent Constitution-Making in France," (1947) 41 The American Political Science Review 429–32.

[78] Muna Ndulo, "Zimbabwe's Unfulfilled Struggle for a Legitimate Constitutional Order," in Laurel E. Miller (ed.), *Framing the State in Times of Transition: Case Studies in Constitution Making* (United States Institute of Peace Press 2010); John Hatchard, "Some Lessons on Constitution-Making from Zimbabwe," (2001) 54 Journal of African Law 210–16.

[79] According to Elkins and Hudson, "Failure accounts for only 11 of the 179 single-question referenda on new constitutions held since 1973." Elkins and Hudson, "The Constitutional Referendum in Historical Perspective," 158.

[80] One exception to this is the rejection, via referendum, of a proposed constitution for the Seychelles in November of 1992. The sitting government immediately initiated a new constitution-making process, and a new constitution, addressing many of the democracy deficits seen as the reason for the earlier rejection, was submitted to voters, and approved, in June 1993. John Hatchard, "Re-Establishing a Multi-Party State: Some Constitutional Lessons from the Seychelles," (1993) 31 Journal of Modern African Studies 601–12, 605–8.

supporters to invade white-owned farms and attack members of the Movement for Democratic Change (MDC), the rival party to the president's own party. In the latter, the rejection of the referendum in 2005 combined with a contested presidential election soon after led to a wave of violence in which 1,000 were killed and 500,000 displaced.[81]

Second, regardless of its outcome, a ratification procedure imposes both temporal and monetary costs. As an additional procedure in the constitution-making process, it lengthens the time it takes to create a new constitution. This is especially true for referendums in new democracies, which often require the establishment of functioning electoral management bodies, voter rolls, and ingredients necessary for a nationwide vote.[82] For a country in political turmoil, operating amidst a ceasefire, or in need of a new constitution for trade and economic purposes, such delays can be problematic. Perhaps the shortest ratification period was in Romania in 1991. The bicameral parliament, sitting together as a mandated constituent legislature, approved the document on November 21, 1991, and a referendum vote took place sixteen days later on December 8.[83] Longer processes, which are far more common, include the four months it took Swiss cantons to hold referendums on the proposed 1848 constitution, the six months it took between the election of the Ethiopian ratifying constituent assembly and its approval of the constitution, and the ten months needed to get nine states to sign on to the U.S. Federal Constitution.[84]

Monetary costs stem from the simple fact that an additional constitution-making process must be funded. This is especially true for ratification by referendum and constitutional conventions, as the other forms of ratification rely on already convoked political bodies. Thus, for instance, Australia's 1999 ratification referendum cost about A$43.5 million or US$66.8 million.[85] In 2018, Wafula Chebukati, the chairperson of Kenya's Independent Electoral and Boundaries Commission, estimated that a much-discussed future referendum on amendments

[81] Greg Linington, *Constitutional Law of Zimbabwe* (Legal Resources Foundation 2001); Bard Anders Andresassen and Arne Tostensen, "Of Oranges and Bananas: The 2005 Kenyan Referendum of the Constitution," (2006) 13 CHR–Michelsen Institution WP; Beth Elise Whitaker and Jason Giersch, "Voting on a Constitution: Implications for Democracy in Kenya," (2009) 27 Journal of Contemporary African Studies 1–20.

[82] See the Carter Center's worry about how a possible referendum in Tunisia would be carried out. *The Constitution-Making Process in Tunisia: Final Report* (The Carter Center 2014) 130.

[83] Stephen Holmes and Jon Elster, "New Constitutions Adopted in Bulgaria and Romania," (1992) 1 East European Constitutional Review 11–12, 11; Vlasta Maric and others, "Constitution Watch," (1992) 1 East European Constitutional Review 2–8, 5.

[84] Dardanelli, "The Emergence and Evolution of Democracy in Switzerland," 149; Berhanu, "Ethiopia Elects a Constituent Assembly," 129; Regassa, "The Making and Legitimacy of the Ethiopian Constitution: Towards Bridging the Gap between Constitutional Design and Constitutional Practice," 104.

[85] Australian Electoral Commission, *Costs of Elections and Referendums* (2019).

to the Kenyan Constitution would cost Sh12 billion or about US$98.7 million.[86] The costs of previous ratifying conventions are hard to come by, but we can approximate by looking at the costs of recent constitutional conventions used to create new constitutions or generate ideas for amending them. Thus, for instance, the recent Irish Citizen's Assembly of 2016–18 cost €2.36 million or US$2.6 million, though its members were appointed (bringing the costs down) and it only met for twelve days.[87]

Third, ratification has a variety of effects on the political and social environment of a country, for it inevitably turns what is often a process designed to promote consensus, ease conflict, emphasize compromise, and establish a new beginning into a political contest. Thus, for instance, civic education efforts, meant to promote constitutional knowledge and familiarity for the purposes of helping citizens contribute to constitution-making and be good future constitutional citizens, are regularly undone by the political campaigns produced by ratification. Such campaigns, as will be discussed in greater detail in chapter 6, section 5, have as their purpose persuasion, rather than education, and thus like ordinary political campaigns incentivize the spreading of half-truths, distortions, or misinformation for the purposes of ratification victory.[88] Things are worse when existing political parties take sides in the referendum battle, bringing in the fractious political contestation of the previous regime into the approval of the new government framework.

Further, absent unanimous acceptance, ratification guarantees and creates a set of losers for whom the constitution represents an outcome they or their ratification delegates explicitly voted against. In a referendum, every individual who voted no to a proposed constitution now faces a state framework which they formally rejected. As Simone Chambers notes, "putting deep constitutional issues to a referendum produces the disturbing results of a 'we the people who won' versus a 'we the people who lost.'"[89]

Fourth, as Arato suggests, "the process of drafting should be affected by knowing who will be the agent that will have to ratify the document."[90] Here, Arato is hinting at what Elster refers to as ratification's function as a downstream constraint on

86 Geoffrey Mosoku, "We Are Ready to Conduct the Referendum, Which Will Cost Sh12b: Iebc," *The Standard* (Nairobi October 8, 2018) <https://www.standardmedia.co.ke/politics/article/2001298246/we-are-ready-for-referendum-but-it-will-cost-you-billions-iebc>

87 Robert Hazel, "You Want a Constitutional Convention? This Is What You Need to Think through First," The Constitution Unit, UCL (October 8, 2014) <https://constitution-unit.com/2014/10/08/you-want-a-constitutional-convention-this-is-what-you-need-to-think-through-first/>; Leo Varadkar, *Written Answers: Tuesday, 26 March 2019* (2019).

88 Mark Tushnet, "Constitution-Making: An Introduction," (2012) 91 Texas Law Review 1983–2013, 1999–2000; Alicia L. Bannon, "Note: Designing a Constitution-Drafting Process: Lessons from Kenya," (2007) 116 Yale Law Journal 1830–72, 1840–41.

89 Simone Chambers, "Contract or Conversation? Theoretical Lessons from the Canadian Constitutional Crisis," (1998) 26 Politics and Society 143–72, 159.

90 Andrew Arato, *Constitution Making under Occupation: The Politics of Imposed Revolution in Iraq* (Columbia University Press 2009) 127.

constitution-makers.[91] The idea being that the known presence of ratification procedures, and the constant possibility of constitutional rejection if ratifiers are displeased, will lead framers to alter their behavior and at times write a different constitution than they otherwise would. Framers are conscious of this, they know they need to please their veto-equipped ratifiers and therefore seek clarity when its form is undecided. Thus George Grey forcefully objected to a proposal in the 1891 Australasian Federation Conference to approve a draft constitution before deciding upon the means of ratification, exclaiming "It is almost essential before we adopt the proposal [the constitution] ... that we should know the exact manner in which the people will have an opportunity of deciding this question. This is a step preliminary to the other, instead of one that ought to follow it."[92]

Ratification can work as a downstream constraint, altering the behavior of framers and the constitution they ultimately produce, through several pathways.[93] Most straightforwardly, the presence of ratification might lead framers to intentionally alter their goal constitution—the constitution each framer wants and tries to get the drafting process to produce—to one they believe will or can be made to survive the ratification process, which in turn will affect the overall content of the final document.[94]

Alternatively, ratification might also lead framers to avoid writing in provisions that they believe cannot be publicly justified or explained in accordance with existing societal norms. Or framers might believe that a ratifier's decision will partly consider—consciously or not—how constitution-makers behave during the drafting process and the arguments they give during the proceedings. In response, the framers will avoid taking certain actions or making certain arguments, which in turn would indirectly affect the contents of the constitution by determining what sorts of provisions framers write into the constitution and defend during deliberation over the eventual draft.[95] In other words, the sort of constitution framers write will be limited by the behavioral effects of any existing norms of appropriate reasoning or argument in the given context, and this effect will be heightened by the attention ratification shines on the constitution-making process.[96]

[91] Elster, "Forces and Mechanisms in the Constitution-Making Process," 374.

[92] *Official Report of the National Australasian Convention Debates: Sydney, 2 March to 9 April, 1891* (George Stephen Chapman, Acting Government Printer 1891) 903–4.

[93] In chapter 9, section 1.2, I analyze whether these constraints, which I call goal and justificatory constraints, make it more likely that a constitution is legitimate. Here I am simply claiming that the presence of ratification will make framers behave differently and write a different constitution, not that this constitution will be different in any predictable way.

[94] This is in addition to the constraint imposed by the expected preferences of other constitution-makers.

[95] This indirect effect is like one of the effects of signaling incentives described by Groseclose and McCarty. In the context of two-party negotiations in front of an outside audience, they found that the need to send signals to the third party influenced their decisions to accept or reject proposals. See Tim Groseclose and Nolan McCarty, "The Politics of Blame: Bargaining before an Audience," (2001) 45 American Journal of Political Science 100–119.

[96] Note that these effects occur regardless of a framer's motivation. A framer solely interested in creating a constitution that will forward her self-interest has to confine herself to provisions and behavior

Regardless of pathway, "the knowledge of that possibility [rejection] will keep framers within designated limits. Not wanting to be overruled, they will anticipate and feel constrained by the possible censure."[97] The resultant alterations to the constitution because of ratification might include granting constitutional status to matters that would otherwise be left to ordinary legislative procedures, specifying and entrenching assumed governing principles, or writing in provisions that reflect popular issues of the day. According to veto player theory, the addition of a ratifier (a new veto player) will result in less extreme changes from the status quo and, in the case of a ratification referendum, a slide toward the constitutional preferences of the "as-if" median voter.[98] Importantly, one cannot assume that ratification's effects through this pathway will be uniformly positive, i.e. will lead to a "better" constitution for the people as a whole, however one defines this. Ratification can just as easily lead framers to avoid beneficial compromises for "fear of being seen as selling out" during a ratification campaign, entrench racist or otherwise immoral provisions because of their popularity, or write in specific group benefits for no other reason than the electoral calculus needed to secure constitutional approval.[99]

Fifth, ratification can act as a *downstream enabler*, in some sense doing the opposite of a downstream constraint by freeing constitution-makers from the constraints imposed on them by upstream authorities. By this I mean that in instances in which the ratifying authorities are different from those involved in the convoking stage, framers might be more willing to discard the instructions given to them by their convokers because of their knowledge that a different agent will authorize their work during ratification. On one interpretation, this was an effect of ratification on the framers of the U.S. Constitution. As Rakove explains, "the principle of constitutional ratification thus carried the incidental benefit of licensing the delegates to consider whatever measure the public good demanded, regardless of the prevailing expectations and even their formal credentials."[100]

that she believes are acceptable to the ratifying authority, and the same is true of a framer motivated by her duty to pursue the public good and her desire to create the best constitution possible. One exception to this would be framers who want the constitution-making process to fail. Such constitution-making spoilers would still be affected by ratification, but in an opposite direction.

[97] Elster, "Constitutional Bootstrapping in Philadelphia and Paris," 80. Similarly, Voigt hypothesizes that "if the citizens are the ultimate deciders on accepting the constitution, members of the constitutional assembly have more incentives to take the preferences of the citizens explicitly into account." "The Consequences of Popular Participation in Constitutional Choice: Towards a Comparative Analysis," in Anne van Aaken, Christian List, and Christoph Luetge (eds.), *Deliberation and Decision: Economics, Constitutional Theory, and Deliberative Democracy* (Ashgate Publishing Ltd 2004) 200

[98] Simon Hug and George Tsebelis, "Veto Players and Referendums around the World," (2002) 14 Journal of Theoretical Politics, 466–67; George Tsebelis, *Veto Players: How Political Institutions Work* (Princeton University Press 2002); George Tsebelis, "Veto Players and Institutional Analysis," (2000) 13 Governance: An International Journal of Policy, Administration, and Institutions 441–74.

[99] Brandt and others, *Constitution-Making and Reform: Options for the Process*, 303.

[100] Jack N. Rakove, *Original Meanings: Politics and Ideas in the Making of the Constitution* (1st edn, A.A. Knopf 1996) 102.

4.3 The Absence of Justification

Attempts to create new constitutions are often pivotal moments in a country's history, and the procedures used to do so should be chosen with great care. Ratification is one such procedure, and as I have shown, practitioners, consultants, and scholars should be interested in the reasons for its use. Unfortunately, few such reasons have been forwarded or developed. This stems from the fact that, other than the above-mentioned eighteenth-century commentaries on ratification written by the Massachusetts' radicals and Condorcet, ratification has simply escaped study.

This used to be true for much of the constitution-making process. Over two decades ago, Jon Elster lamented that "Surprisingly, there is no body of literature that deals with the constitution-making process in a positive, explanatory perspective" and that there "is the absence of normative discussions of the constitution-making process" as well.[101] Elster and others' contributions on constitution-making brought attention to the topic and things have changed. Today, scholars increasingly recognize that process matters in the creation of constitutions. Choices concerning the institutions and methods used to make decisions when creating and implementing a constitution help determine its content and affect both the perception and reception of the process and the constitution itself. There is now a wealth of detailed process-oriented comparative case studies of constitution-making events, a field dedicated to applying formal economic methods to the study of constitutional change, and a growing body of empirical work on how procedural design choices affect the contents and durability of constitutions. In addition, various NGOs, academic centers, and transnational bodies regularly publish constitution-making reports, best practices manuals, and guidebooks meant to assist those engaged in constitution-making.

However, amidst both this new and older constitutional literature, ratification remains an overlooked subject of analysis. The procedure is often treated as epiphenomenal and ignored completely, seen as a vestige of previous constitutional or political authority, simply accepted without serious explanation, or reduced to a strategic advice. When it is recommended, it is done so based on uninterrogated and vague allusions to complex normative concepts.[102] The scholarly discussions of ratification that move beyond this, of which there are few, can be divided into the following categories. Most of them are not especially helpful for our endeavor, though I will end this section explaining two that are.

First are discussions of specific instances of ratification that appear within case studies or historical narratives of a constitution-making processes. These discussions simply detail what happened in a particular ratification process rather than concentrate on the reasons given for the procedure's use. One exception, as

[101] Elster, "Forces and Mechanisms in the Constitution-Making Process," 364.
[102] I cite examples of ratification being treated in this way throughout the remainder of the book.

I explain in chapter 3, concerns the ratification of the U.S. Constitution, for which several authors have tried to distill the reasons behind the use of state ratifying conventions.[103] But, even here, the reasons unearthed are contextual and never generalized to apply to constitution-making more broadly.

Second, and closest to what I am after, are Elster's own comments on ratification. As I have shown, Elster describes ratification as a downstream constraint on constitution-makers. He also describes the procedure as an act "intended to confer downstream legitimacy on the constitution," as something that holds framers to account, and as a mechanism that forces framers to compromise with one another.[104] These descriptions hint at possible reasons to use ratification, ones that I will develop in chapters 7 and 9, but are made in passing by Elster and left unexplored.

Third, there are a spate of articles that attempt to answer perennial questions about the U.S. founding by applying social scientific methods to the ratification of the U.S. Constitution. Thus, for instance, Riker and Fink argue that game theoretic methods shed light on how the federalists managed to "win" the ratification process, McGuire and Ohsfeldt use a principal-agent model and econometric tests to pin down the role economic interests played in ratification votes, and Anthony, Heckathorn, and Maser use cognitive mapping and transaction resource theory to explain violations of transitivity in inconsistent arguments made by both federalists and antifederalists in their ratification campaigns.[105] Again, nothing within these discussions hints at general reasons why ratification might be a desirable procedure.

The fourth group of discussions of ratification takes place within the recent wave of literature leveraging new large-n datasets to conduct quantitative analysis on constitution-making design. Studies in this genre seek to determine the effects that certain constitutional provisions and constitution-making procedures have on the contents of a constitution, the stability or longevity of governments, and the nature of the resulting regimes. Some of these works briefly look at ratification. For instance, Carey finds that ratification referendums "are not associated with any

[103] See Rakove, *Original Meanings: Politics and Ideas in the Making of the Constitution*, 102–8; Michael J. Klarman, *The Framers' Coup: The Making of the United States Constitution* (Oxford University Press 2016) 412–17; David E. Kyvig, *Explicit & Authentic Acts: Amending the U.S. Constitution, 1776–2015* (University Press of Kansas 2016) 42–65; Carlos E. Gonzalez, "Representational Structure through Which We the People Ratify Constitutions: The Troubling Original Understanding of the Constitution's Ratification Clauses," (2005) 38 UC Davis Law Review 1373–1504, 1392–1431 See also Richard S. Kay, "The Illegality of the Constitution," (1987) 4 Constitutional Commentary 57–80, 68–70.

[104] Elster, "Arguing and Bargaining in Two Constituent Assemblies," 369; Elster, "The Optimal Design of a Constituent Assembly," 169; Elster, *Securities against Misrule: Juries, Assemblies, Elections*, 210.

[105] Evelyn C. Fink and William H. Riker, "The Strategy of Ratification," in Bernard Grofman and Donald Wittman (eds.), *The Federalist Papers and the New Institutionalism* (Agathon Press 1989); Robert A. McGuire and Robert L. Ohsfeldt, "Self-Interest, Agency Theory, and Political Voting Behavior: The Ratification of the United States Constitution," (1989) 79 The American Economic Review 219–34; Denise L. Anthony, Douglas D. Heckathorn, and Steven Maser, "Rational Rhetoric in Politics: The Debate over Ratifying the U.S. Constitution," (1994) 6 Rationality and Society 489–518.

clear pattern of democracy, democratization, or executive restraint."[106] Eisenstadt, LeVan, and Maboudi show that the presence of a ratification referendum is not nearly as important as participation earlier in the constitution-making process when it comes to levels of democracy in the resultant regime.[107] Wheatley and Germann find that non-democracies are especially likely to use ratification referendums when creating new constitutions, and speculate that non-democratic actors, especially executives, use the procedure to consolidate their rule.[108] And Elkins, Ginsburg, and Blount conclude that constitutions approved by referendum contain a higher mean number of potentially elected government positions and are more likely to codify rights provisions, universal suffrage, a secret ballot, ordinary referendums, and opportunities for public participation in amendment.[109]

For the purposes of justifying ratification, this work is of little help. First, all of it reduces the procedure to the presence or absence of a referendum, missing out on informing us about other types of ratification. Second, much of the work suggests reasons to avoid ratification referendums, or at least not focus on them. Third, the positive findings are mere correlations. Ginsburg, Elkins, and Blount, who find the most normatively attractive associations with ratification, explicitly admit that it is wise to "reserve judgment about any causal inference with respect to these results."[110] The reason, as they explain, is simple: it is highly plausible that the same unobserved variable is responsible for both the decision to use a ratification referendum and the decision to include the positive provisions in the constitutional text. I discuss this literature and its relevance in greater depth in chapter 9.

Three additional works are worth discussing individually. The first is Steven Tierney's *Constitutional Referendums: The Theory and Practice of Republican Deliberation*.[111] At first glance, this excellent book looks likely to provide a justification for at least one type of ratification. Tierney's stated focus is on the constitutional referendum, which he defines as "any direct citizen vote on the specific issue of constitutional change or constitutional creation."[112] This includes referendums to amend constitutions, establish new forms of sub-state autonomy, transfer power from states to IGOs, and, most importantly for our purposes, create

[106] John M. Carey, "Does It Matter How a Constitution Is Created?," in Zoltan Barany and Robert G. Moser (eds.), *Is Democracy Exportable?* (Cambridge University Press 2009) 155–77.

[107] Eisenstadt, LeVan, and Maboudi, *Constituents before Assembly: Participation, Deliberation, and Representation in the Crafting of New Constitutions*, 51.

[108] Wheatley and Germann, "Outcomes of Constitution-Making: Democratization and Conflict Resolution," 56.

[109] Blount, Elkins, and Ginsburg, "Does the Process of Constitution-Making Matter?" 56–57; Zachary Elkins, Tom Ginsburg, and Justin Blount, 'The Citizen as Founder: Public Participation in Constitutional Approval," (2008) 81 Temple Law Review 361–82, 378.

[110] Blount, Elkins, and Ginsburg, "Does the Process of Constitution-Making Matter?" 55.

[111] Stephen Tierney, *Constitutional Referendums: The Theory and Practice of Republican Deliberation* (Oxford University Press 2012).

[112] Ibid., 11.

new constitutions. His motivating question is whether such referendums can be defended or even advocated for from the perspective of democratic theory, with an emphasis on a deliberative civic republican account. This means he is after a justification for referendums.

Unfortunately, little in the book pertains to ratification. Tierney barely mentions the procedure. Of the 132 constitutional referendums he mentions in the text, only eight were used to approve new constitutions. In fact, after defining them in the introduction, he only discusses ratification referendums directly at the end of the book to note that they might pose exceptions to his larger argument. Tierney's central conclusion is that "at least in undivided societies, the referendum can be a successful constitutional instrument provided adequate legal regulation serves to promote and protect a deliberative environment within which citizen participation can be fostered."[113] Put simply, Tierney justifies referendums by showing how their well-known defects and downsides can be avoided by redesigning the procedures and institutions of ordinary governance, with the aim of fully integrating the referendum into an ongoing deliberative democratic vision. This is unhelpful when it comes to justifying ratification referendums, in that constitution-making often takes place within divided societies, involves remaking rather than working within a stable legal framework, and Tierney's proposed solutions rely on ordinary features of the repeating game of democratic decision-making absent in the one-off constitutional context.

The next two works are partial exceptions to my claim that ratification has been overlooked. Section 3.5 of Interpeace's handbook for constitution-makers, *Constitution-making and Reform: Options for the Process*, discusses the use of referendums to approve constitutions. It does not use the term ratification referendum, but that is its subject. One short subsection, "Debating referendums," consists of four pages explicitly giving reasons for and against using the procedure. Unfortunately, this discussion is skeletal, its claims are left unexplained, and it falls prey to the tendency to think that referencing a normative concept in itself makes an argument. The authors list seven reasons for using a ratification referendum, though two of them are irrelevant for our purposes as they do not apply at the constitution-making design stage, and several of the others are repetitive. What is left is the following. Ratification should be used because: it instantiates "the right of the people to participate in the constitution-making process"; it serves as a mechanism of accountability and provides a "check on constitution-makers"; it helps legitimate a constitution; and it helps educate the populace.[114] The last reason can be dismissed because education efforts can occur and have occurred without a ratification referendum, and when they are linked to a referendum, as I discuss

[113] Ibid., 285.
[114] Brandt and others, *Constitution-Making and Reform: Options for the Process*, 299–301.

in chapter 6, section 5, they quickly become distorted and often overwhelmed by manipulative ratification campaigns. The first three reasons align precisely with the core justifications of constituent power, representation, and legitimacy discussed in the chapters ahead. In some sense, the rest of this book is an elaboration and examination of these brief claims, which are echoed in some form by most who mention ratification in a positive note.

Finally, there is Richard Tuck's *The Sleeping Sovereign: The Invention of Modern Democracy*.[115] This book traces the slow development of what Tuck refers to as the sovereign/government distinction in modern political thought.[116] The sovereign is the authority capable of making higher-order decisions about the organization and principles of the state and the government is that entity in charge of routine operations. Tuck claims that this distinction, properly understood, is what makes democracy possible in large modern states where direct citizen participation and real self-government is impossible on a day-to-day basis. Instead, self-legislation is confined to sovereign decision-making which, after the advent of constitutional government, means making and changing constitutional laws, while all other state operations are left to the people's agents. Hence, the sovereign is mostly asleep, content to doze while its deputies run its kingdom, but occasionally awakes to make changes to the constitutional framework.

Tuck presents his work as an exercise in intellectual and conceptual history. In the book he does not appear interested, nor does he discuss, the details of making or amending constitutions or any contemporary cases. Nonetheless, this work is a contemporary piece of scholarship relevant to our investigation, for it hints at the existence of a compelling justification for why constitutions need to be ratified. Starting from a unique interpretation of Rousseau, Tuck traces the evolution of an argument according to which sovereign power cannot be delegated, and instead must be exercised by the people directly. When it comes to creating constitutions, this means that a constitution can only be authorized, can only claim to be higher law, if it is approved by the people in a referendum. This argument, which Tuck not only finds through his investigation of eighteenth- and nineteenth-century political theory, but also ends up endorsing at the end of the book and in some of his Brexit writings, is a particular version of what I call a constituent power justification, the first core justification I tackle in this book. I enlarge and build upon it in chapter 5 and show its defects in chapter 6.

115 Richard Tuck, *The Sleeping Sovereign: The Invention of Modern Democracy* (Cambridge University Press 2016).

116 Tuck admits that this is nearly identical to the more famous constituted/constituent power distinction, though he traces its intellectual lineage slightly differently than traditional constituent power accounts. See chapter 4, section 4.

5. Structure

As mentioned, one likely reason ratification is recommended for and used in democratic constitution-making without sufficient argumentation is that, from a normative point of view, it seems so obvious. Numerous intuitions from democratic theory seem to justify the procedure. I focus on the most powerful of these to generate three core justifications for ratification: the *constituent power justification*, the *representation justification*, and the *legitimacy justification*. In the chapters that follow I construct the strongest forms of these justifications and analyze their strength.

The book proceeds as follows. The next two chapters are descriptive and historical in nature, providing both background information about the origins of ratification, and serving as a source of inspiration in our hunt for the procedure's justification. Readers should skip to chapter 4 if they are more interested in getting to the normative heart of the book. Chapter 2 focuses on the role and history of ratification in non-constitutional domains, specifically agency law, international law, and collective bargaining. In each of these domains, ratification is used to describe a procedure of a similar form. As I explain, this is no coincidence, for all types of ratification descend from a common procedure in the private law of Ancient Rome. This procedure entered early modern agency law, then treaty-making, then written constitution-making, and finally into collective bargaining practices. I detail the history and use of ratification in each of the non-constitutional areas and explain the procedure's evolving functions. In agency law, ratification serves the purpose of fixing a broken (illegitimate) decision-making process by transforming false agents into real ones. In early treaty-making, ratification serves as a means of pronouncing judgment on the behavior and credentials of ambassador agents. In later treaty-making, ratification serves as the site or a site of sovereign decision-making itself, or as a means of creating a bargaining advantage. And, in collective bargaining settings, ratification is thought to both add to the sociological and/or moral legitimacy of a contract and give the union a strategic advantage in negotiations.

Chapter 3 explores the early history of constitutional ratification and several of its types. Primarily, I focus on ratification's invention in Massachusetts by the Berkshire Constitutionalists, a group of political dissidents who shut down local courts in the Western part of the state from 1774 to 1780 in protest of attempts to create a new constitution without direct citizen approval. I also look at a similar but unsuccessful contemporaneous effort to implement ratification by members of the Mechanics Union in New York. Both these experiences concerned ratification via referendum, and thus in the remainder of the chapter I sketch out the origins of two other prominent ratification forms: regional ratification conventions and a polity-wide convention. These were developed, respectively, to approve the U.S. Constitution in 1787 and the second constitution for the state of Georgia in

1789. All three of these origin stories suggest versions of the core justifications to be examined in the chapters ahead.

The next three chapters focus on the first core justification of ratification: the constituent power justification (CPJ). As its name suggests, this justification relies on the theory of constituent power, made famous by Sieyès and Schmitt, according to which the people possess a unique primal power to create and unmake their constitutions. According to the CPJ, an authoritative constitution must be a popular creation and ratification serves as a moment that helps this become possible. In chapter 4, I explain the nature of constituent power, its theoretical presuppositions, and the central questions the concept raises. I next explain how specifying a CPJ is unusual, for constituent power theorizing usually operates on a level of abstraction, rather than muddying itself with the complexities of procedures. Finally, I develop and analyze several different types of CPJ, which vary depending on how they understand constituent power emerging throughout the constitution-making process and what role they see ratification playing. All these justifications, I argue, suffer from fundamental weaknesses. For instance, conceptualizing ratification as one of many moments of constituent power renders ratification either redundant or a means for the people to paradoxically disagree with themselves, while portraying the entire constitution-making process, ratification included, as an attempt to approximate the popular sovereign risks collapsing constituent power into nothing more than the claim that the people's preferences should be met.

Chapter 4 concludes by claiming that the remaining and most plausible CPJ is what I call the unique site justification (USJ), which understands ratification as the sole site in the constitution-making process where the people, the constituent power, materialize and authorize the constitution. This is the original argument made in favor of ratification by the Berkshire Constitutionalists, whose history I detailed in chapter 3. In chapter 5, I carefully reconstruct their argument from petitions, speeches, and voting logs. The Constitutionalists generated their demand for a popularly created constitution by combining a form of eighteenth-century contractualism with a new understanding of constitutions. Moreover, they confined constituent power to the post-drafting stage, making ratification necessary, and defined the right to ratify as unalienable, thereby disqualifying all forms of ratification other than a referendum. The result is a potent argument in favor of implementing a ratification referendum that leverages the full power of constituent power without any of the weaknesses detailed in chapter 4. Moreover, this USJ is not merely a historical argument. For instance, as mentioned above and as I end the chapter discussing, Richard Tuck recently revived it.

In chapter 6, I evaluate the USJ and conclude that it fails to persuade, thereby extinguishing the hope that constituent power might justify ratification. I make this argument by showing that for the procedure to serve as a way for the people to exercise popular sovereignty, it must be possible for them to make a *meaningful choice*, i.e. a choice made with a basic understanding of the contents of the constitution and any live alternative. The USJ's weakness, I argue, is that one should expect the average voter to be too uninformed to make such a choice. I consider three objections to this argument—that meaningful choice is so high that even drafters cannot meet it, that voting heuristics enable ratifiers to overcome their ignorance, and that targeted educational campaigns can sufficiently eliminate ignorance—and rebut them all. I conclude my treatment of constituent power dismissing it as a viable source of justification for ratification. I also make clear that rejecting the USJ is not anti-democratic, for ignorance is not similarly detrimental to many core arguments for democracy.

Leaving discussions of constituent power behind, chapter 7 turns to the second core justification of ratification: the representation justification (RJ). This argument, which relies on the general normative desirability of representation in democratic theory, claims that ratification should be implemented because it helps facilitate representation. The idea here is that drafters can be representatives of the people in the constitution-making process, that this is wanted, and that ratification helps make it possible. To explore this argument, I define political representation, explain its potential role in constitution-making, and argue that the only procedural role ratification might play in a representative process is as an accountability mechanism. The latter has two central purposes: to enable constituents to control their representatives and have presence in their actions. Ratification's ability to function as an accountability mechanism thus depends on its success in carrying out both. Unfortunately, I argue, the possible divergence between how a principal evaluates their representative framer and the draft constitution prevents ratification from reliably carrying out either, thereby undermining RJ. I end the chapter clarifying my argument by considering several objections.

The most common reason given in support of ratification is that it helps create a more legitimate constitution. Chapters 8 and 9 focus on this legitimacy justification, the final core justification of ratification covered in the book. Legitimacy is a tricky concept, often shrouded in vagueness and deployed inconsistently. Chapter 8 confronts this problem head-on, arguing that much of the confusion surrounding legitimacy comes from conflating its different types and ignoring exactly how procedures can have an impact on them. In its political application, legitimacy divides into three—moral, legal, and sociological legitimacy. However, while moral and sociological legitimacy apply to constitutions, legal legitimacy does not. Further, a procedure can affect the moral or sociological legitimacy of its outcome in two distinct ways: it can have a substantive effect, changing the contents of the outcome such that it meets some independently derived normative criterion, or a procedural effect, serving as the normative criterion itself that the outcome meets by virtue of resulting from the procedure. Combined, these two sets of distinctions produce four pathways through which a constitution-making procedure might legitimate a constitution. I call them substantive moral legitimation (SML), substantive sociological legitimation (SSL), procedural moral legitimation (PML), and procedural sociological legitimation (PSL). Chapter 8 ends by explaining these legitimation pathways and giving examples of each.

In Chapter 9, I evaluate the legitimacy justification by building up and evaluating what appear to be the most persuasive depictions of ratification legitimating a constitution through each of the four pathways. I treat SML and SSL together. Ratification might help ensure that the contents of a constitution fall within the substantive bounds of actual or perceived legitimacy in one of two ways. The procedure might act as a filter, an idea I draw from an extensive analysis of Condorcet's ratification essay, with ratifiers rejecting substantively illegitimate constitutions, or it might prompt framers to act differently, pushing them to avoid writing illegitimate constitutions in the first place. Both arguments, I explain, run into trouble. For instance, the latter mistakenly assumes without reason that ratifiers will make their decisions based on legitimacy and the former relies on the success of the filtration argument and overlooks the ability of framers to persuade ratifiers.

I then turn to the procedural pathways. PML is familiar, for a CPJ involves ratification serving just such a role. I also look at a more basic form of PML that adopts pure consent theory and conceives of ratification as a moment of necessary direct citizen consent. This, I show, is a persuasive argument for committed philosophical anarchists, but its implications are unpalatable to anyone else. Finally, I examine PSL, the idea that the mere occurrence of ratification induces people to believe that a constitution is legitimate. Ratification might have this effect because a significant majority of citizens believe that ratification is necessary, but this cannot be assumed. Alternatively, there might be a mechanism connecting the experience of ratification with the development of legitimacy beliefs, with the most likely being a connection between participation and legitimacy. The resultant participatory PSL argument is perhaps the most convincing justification considered in this book. However, as I conclude, it too suffers from critical problems: it relies on a series of controversial and unproven empirical assumptions, overlooks the limited addition of participation that ratification provides to modern constitution-making processes, and turns the implementation of ratification into an act of intentional and wrongful manipulation. The legitimacy justifications of ratification that I consider, as with those reliant on constituent power and representation, do not survive analysis.

Chapter 10 concludes the book and divides into three sections. The first section reviews the previous chapters and articulates my central finding: that the most likely or mentioned contenders to justify ratification are unpersuasive. The second section examines the implications of my findings, chief among them the conclusion that until better arguments are made, ratification should no longer be treated as a default procedure or one with context-independent merit. I also reflect upon other general lessons and observations that emerged during my investigation. These concern the applicability of democratic theory in unordinary contexts, a potential limitation of constituent power theory, the designation of constitution-makers as representatives, and the difficulties raised by appeals to legitimacy in the social sciences. Finally, I finish the chapter by sketching out four context-dependent arguments for using ratification. Note that while the justifications analyzed in previous chapters are from the perspective of one wanting to lay out optimum constitution-making guidelines, these argue from the perspective of an actor in a particular constitution-making process. These justifications frame ratification as a means of making up procedural legitimacy lost in a malfunctioning constitution-making process, of gaining a bargaining advantage within a constituent assembly, as appeasing a populace that simply expects or demands the procedure, and as breaking a deadlock in the drafting process.

2
Ratification beyond (and before) Constitutions

Though the focus of this book is the ratification procedures used at the end of constitution-making processes, ratification exists in other legal and political arenas. These include agency law, international law, and labor law. In each of these domains, the word ratification or its cognate is used to describe a procedure of a similar form. Namely, an instance in which *a principal (or its agent) has the opportunity to approve or reject a multiparty decision of which (another of) its agents took part, with approval making the decision binding on the principal.*[1] That ratification is used to describe similar procedures in a variety of domains is no coincidence, for ratification (the name and the procedure) first arose in the private law of Ancient Rome, and was later adopted into other domains with its basic structure intact. In fact, ratification's role in constitution-making came well after its role in private and international law, and the term was likely first applied to the final stage of constitution-making by people familiar with it from these contexts.

Of course, a comprehensive review of ratification in these domains would be a book unto itself, but this is not my intention here. Rather in this chapter I seek merely to sketch out the role and early evolution of ratification in these alternative settings. This has two benefits. First, it offers some insight into the pre-constitutional history and life of ratification, from its emergence in Roman law, to its incorporation in contract law in civil and common law systems, to its use in treaty-making practices and collective bargaining. Second, it gives us resources from which we can draw inspiration for our search for the justification of constitutional ratification. Observing how a similarly structured procedure operated in different contexts provides clues about the role and benefits for constitutional ratification. Moreover, while constitutional ratification is unexplored, the same is not true for ratification elsewhere.

Specifically, in the process of explaining ratification in agency, international, and labor law, I will show five distinct *functions* of ratification in these non-constitutional domains: a reparative function, an agent review function, a direct-action

[1] I am only reviewing examples of ratification in other legal and political domains when it refers to a special procedure. This, of course, is not the only way the term and its cognates have and are used. Most commonly, since at least the fourteenth century in English, ratification has been used as a synonym for approve in a legal sense.

Constitutional Ratification without Reason. Jeffrey A. Lenowitz, Oxford University Press. © Jeffrey A. Lenowitz 2022.
DOI: 10.1093/oso/9780198852346.003.0002

function, a bargaining advantage function, and a support function. Note that a function is neither a causal explanation for how a procedure came about, nor an argument in favor of the procedure's implementation. Rather, I use the term to mean a role that ratification plays within a given procedural context—what it enables or makes easier for agents to do, regardless of whether this was the initial reason for the procedure's creation or implementation.

1. Agency Law

Agency law consists of the legal procedures and consequences of consensual relationships in which one person (principal) agrees that another person (agent) shall, subject to the former's right of control, have the power through their actions to create and alter legal relationships on the principal's behalf, usually by interacting with third parties.[2] Ratification, in this context "the affirmance of a prior act done by another, whereby the act is given effect as if done by an agent acting with actual authority," is a standard component of agency law in both the civil and common law traditions.[3] It appears, for instance, in the civil codes of France, Germany, and Japan, and in the case law of countries such as the United States, New Zealand, and India.[4] This, as mentioned, is the result of ratification originating in the private law of the Roman Empire, from which both legal traditions draw influence.

1.1 Ratification in Roman Law

The earliest known discussion of what would become ratification are several passages alleged to be written by Ulpian, codified later in the Digest of Justinian, in which he discusses a procedure called *ratihabitio*. Three key lines are as follows:

> So ratification will make a business yours which initially was not yours, but was done with you in mind (*Ratihabitio constituet tumm negotium, quod ab initio tuum non erat, sed tua contemplation gestum*).
>
> For it is rightly said that in an offense ratification is comparable to mandate (*rectius enim dicitur in maleficio ratihabitionem mandato comparari*).

[2] *Restatement of the Law (Third) of Agency*, vol. I (American Law Institute 2006) 3.

[3] Ibid., 304. Joseph Story was correct in *Fleckner v. U.S. Bank* when he wrote that "and the civil law does not, it is believed, differ from the common law on this subject [ratification]." *Fleckner v. U.S. Bank*, 21 US 338 (1823).

[4] *Civil Code of France*, Arts. 1120, 1239, 1311, 1338, 1340; *German Civil Code*, sec. 184; *Civil Code of Japan*, Arts. 113a, 116; *Maharashtra State Mining Corportation V. Sunil*, 5 SCC 96 (2006); *Fleckner v. U.S. Bank*; *Kelner v. Baxter*, 2 CP 174 (1866).

> But even though payment be not to a genuine procurator but the principal ratifies the payment, there will be effective release since ratification is likened to mandate (*rati enim habitio mandato comparator).*[5]

To understand these passages and the function of ratification at the time, one must understand some of the basics of Roman contract law as it pertains to mandates. Between freemen, the Romans did not have a legal conception of agency; it was not possible for an authorized agent to contract with a third party on behalf of the principal such that the contract was between the principal and the third party, with both having a right to claim performance and an obligation to perform.[6] This stemmed from the Romans' adherence to the principle of privity, under which only those directly involved in a contract could be affected.[7] As Paulus notes in the Digest: "one promising for something to be given or done on behalf of another does not bind him, for each must promise for himself."[8]

Even without direct agency, Roman law still makes room for an agent to take action for a principal, albeit indirectly. One such pathway relies on a *mandatum*, a contract in which one person (promisor) agrees to do something for another (mandator) without payment.[9] Such indirect agency via mandate thus involves two contracts. First, a principal A enters into a mandate with another party B, in which B becomes a promisor by making a gratuitous promise to perform a requested service for A (with the understanding that A will indemnify B for any expenses and damages in carrying out the mandate).[10] B executes this promise by transacting with a third party C.[11] At no time is there a contract between A and C.[12]

So, for example, imagine that by a mandate Porcius asks Rufus to buy a pig for him for 100 *sesterces* or less and Rufus fulfills this mandate by completing a sale with Titus for that amount. This creates a contract of mandate, under which Rufus promises to do what he can to buy a pig for Porcius for the desired amount, and Porcius agrees to pay Rufus back for the pig plus any expenses. It would also create

[5] Alan Watson, Theodor Mommsen, and Paul Krueger (eds.), *The Digest of Justinian*, vol. I (rev. edn, University of Pennsylvania Press 1985) 100 (3.5.5.11); ibid., 583 (43.16.14), 704 (46.3.12.4).

[6] Reinhard Zimmermann, *The Law of Obligations: Roman Foundations of the Civilian Tradition* (Oxford University Press 1996) 46–47; Alan Watson, *The Spirit of Roman Law* (The University of Georgia Press 1995) 114–15.

[7] Paul du Plessis and Andrew Borkowski, *Borkowski's Textbook on Roman Law* (5th edn, Blackstone Press Limited 2015) 267.

[8] Watson, Mommsen, and Krueger (eds.), *The Digest of Justinian*, 176 (45.1.83).

[9] Henry John Roby, *Roman Private Law: In the Times of Cicero and of the Antonines* (reprint edn, Gaunt Inc. 1998) 116; Watson, *The Spirit of Roman Law*, 127–28; Watson, Mommsen, and Krueger (eds.), *The Digest of Justinian*, 86 (3.1). Note that I simply refer to the one who takes up the mandate as promisor, and not as procurator, which is the term used by Ulpian. This is mainly because of the shifting meaning of procurator throughout Roman law, and even within the Digest itself. See *Procurator* in ibid., Glossary.

[10] Gualtiero Procaccia, "On the History of Agency," (1976) 2 Tel Aviv University Studies in Law, 59.

[11] Plessis and Borkowski, *Borkowski's Textbook on Roman Law*, 286–87.

[12] Zimmermann, *The Law of Obligations: Roman Foundations of the Civilian Tradition*, 49. See also Peter Birks, *The Roman Law of Obligations* (Oxford University Press 2014) 128.

a contract of sale, where Rufus agrees to pay 100 *sesterces* to Titus and Titus agrees to deliver the pig to Porcius. However, Porcius and Titus are never in contract with one another.

Within this context, ratification applied to instances in which a promisor contracts with a third party on behalf of an agent, but is either not a real promisor (lacks *mandatum*) or is acting beyond the bounds of a mandate. So, for instance, imagine that Rufus contracts with Titus to buy a pig for Porcius at 100 *sesterces*, but lacks a mandate to conduct such a sale. This creates a problem for Rufus, as Porcius is being sent a pig but has not agreed to pay Rufus for the service. Rufus therefore has a debt. However, if Porcius ratifies Rufus' actions, if he formally agrees after the fact to treat the transaction as if Rufus was his agent, this retroactively makes Titus his authorized promisor. Porcius becomes a *mandator* and assumes Rufus' debt, agreeing to pay him or Titus directly for the pig sale, and the legal situation is as if Titus received a mandate in the first place and merely acted in accordance with it.

Thus, in the classical period of Roman law, ratification served the purpose of retroactively creating a mandated relationship where there was none before. In instances such as our pig sale, this did not change the contract of sale between the pseudo-promisor and the third party, but instead made it such that the person for whom the pseudo-promisor acted would behave as if he was a mandator from the beginning.[13] Porcius would provide the funds for the pig to Rufus, plus any expenses, as if he agreed to do so originally. To paraphrase Ulpian, it made the business Porcius' even though it was not originally his.

1.2 From Justinian to the *Codes Maximilianeus Bavaricus Civilis* and Edward Coke

Upon the rediscovery of the *Corpus Juris Civilis* in the eleventh century, ratification, like much of Roman law, became a part of canon law, the *ius commune*, and various European legal systems that followed.[14] Thus, Pope Boniface VIII's 1298 *Liber Sextus* includes ratification amongst the eighty-eight edicts that compose its *De Regulae Juris*. Regula X states that "there is no doubt that ratihabitio has a retroactive effect and is compared to mandatum (*ratihabitionem retrotrahi et*

[13] Ratification has no effect on third parties, for mandates have no such effects. Gualtiero Procaccia, "On the Theory and History of Ratification in the Law of Agency," (1978–79) 4 Tel Aviv University Studies in Law 9–32, 17 Earlier, Procaccia notes that ratification may have also played a different role in Roman law but fails to go into any detail.

[14] Procaccia, "On the History of Agency," 72. This and Procaccia's other article, cited above, meticulously trace this evolution. For general discussions of Roman law's influence on the development of early European legal systems, see Peter Stein, *Roman Law in European History* (Cambridge University Press 2004); John W. Cairns and Paul du Plessis (eds.), *The Creation of the Ius Commune* (Edinburgh University Press 2010); Walter Ullmann, *Law and Politics in the Middle Ages* (Cambridge University Press 1975); Franz Wieacker, *A History of Private Law in Europe* (Clarendon Press 1996).

mandato non est dubium comparari)." Johannes Andreae's 1340 *Glossa Ordinaria* to the same work alters the formulation slightly, stating, "indeed, ratihabitio has a retroactive effect and is equal to mandatum (*ratihabitio retrotrahitur et mandato aequiparatur*)."[15]

Ratification continued to be mentioned by legal scholars across continental Europe, particularly those writing within the canon law tradition who often simply replicated phrases from the Digest and the *Liber Sextus*. For instance, the Swiss ethicist and jurist Hubert van Giffen, also known as Obertus Giphanius, cites Ulpian and discusses ratification in his 1607 *Tractatus*, as does the Spanish jurist Diego de Covarrubias y Lieva in his earlier 1558 work.[16] Eventually, ratification became codified in early civil codes such as the Bavarian *Codex Maximilianeus bavaricus civilis* and Napoleon's *Code Civil des Français*, the latter of which is likely responsible for ratification's prevalence today in civil codes around the globe.[17]

Ratification entered the common law tradition by the thirteenth century. Bracton mentions it in *De Legibus Et Consuetudinibus Angliae*, written around 1250, and the procedure later takes centerstage in the 1302 case *Dean and Chapter of Exeter v. Serle de Lanlarazon*. In the latter, Serle is held responsible for an agreement to give back property, made by others in his name, that he assented to by failing to make a different agreement.[18] While recounting Justice Burnetoun's judgment, the Norman-French text switches to Latin, stating that: "*Ratio est quia ratihabitio retro trahitur et mandato comparator*" (The reason is that a confirmation relates back, and is equivalent to a command).[19]

Jumping forward, in a 1581 decision in *Anderson against Kinneir*, Ulpian was once again paraphrased, this time to explain the guilt of a woman who occupied a house unlawfully possessed by her sons, with the logic that her residence constituted a ratification of their action. As the Lords write: "she ratifiet and approvit all the deed as if it had been done at her command and assistance, et sic ratibabitio retro trahitur, et mandato equiparat."[20] In Henry Swinburne's popular *A Treatise of Spousals, or Matrimonial Contracts*, written some time before his death in 1624, he describes "*Ratihabitio retrotrahitur & mandato comparator*" as "a

[15] Procaccia, "On the Theory and History of Ratification in the Law of Agency," 19–20, translations are taken from the same text. For an excellent discussion about the transmission of juristic rules in Roman law to medieval and renaissance civil law, see Peter Stein, *Regulae Iuris: From Juristic Rules to Legal Maxims* (Edinburgh University Press 1966).

[16] Hubert Van Giffen, *Tractatus De Diversis Regulis Juris Antiqui Utilissimus* (1607) 117, 129–30; Diego de Covarrubias y Lieva, *Relectio Cap. Quamuis Pactum, De Pactis, Regul* (1558) 288.

[17] *Das Bayerische Landrecht (Codex Maximilianeus Bavaricus Civilis) Von Jahre 1756* (J. Schweizer 1894) 260 (4.9.3); *The Code Napoleon; or, the French Civil Code* (Charles Hunter 1824) 337(§1239), 1541(§998).

[18] Eugene Wambaugh, "A Problem as to Ratification," (1895) 9 Harvard Law Review 60–71, 60–61; Henry de Bracton, *On the Laws and Customs of England*, vol. 3 (Belknap Press 1977) 119; *Year Books of the Reign of King Edward the First: Year xxx–xxxi* (Longman, Green, Longman, Roberts, and Green 1863) 128.

[19] *Year Books of the Reign of King Edward the First: Year xxx–xxxi*, 128–29.

[20] *The Decisions of the Court of Session* (Bell & Bradfute 1802) 3607.

Notorious Rule, both of the Civil and Canon Law" when discussing whether a King ratifying his own marriage, negotiated by proxy, makes the marriage binding even though the marriage was to the wrong woman.[21]

It was however Coke's mention of the procedure in the fourth book of his *Institutes of the Laws of England*, initially published in 1634, which solidified ratification's place in the common law.[22] He writes:

> [F]or by the common law he that receiveth a trespass and agreeth to a trespass after it be done, is no trespasser, unless the trespass was done to his use, or for his benefit, and then his agreement subsequent amounteth to a commandment, for in that case, *Omni ratihabitio retrotrahitur et mandato aequiparatur*.[23]

Here, Coke makes clear that if *x* accepts *y*'s actions, done for *x*'s benefit, as *x*'s own, this is akin to *x* commanding *y* to take that action, for ratification is akin to mandate.[24]

Though the authors just mentioned and their contemporaries discussed the Roman legal practice of ratification, often using identical or paraphrased Latin phrases when discussing the topic, ratification meant something different for them than it did during Ulpian or Justinian's time. This was because direct legal agency came into existence in Europe and the Byzantine Empire, at least by the twelfth and thirteenth centuries. This can be seen, for example, in Maimonides' discussion of agents and partners in the Mishneh Torah, and a similar discussion in Pope Boniface VIII's *Regulae Juris*.[25] With agency now possible, a principal could appoint a legal agent to act on their behalf, with the effects being a legal action that directly changed the legal circumstance of the principal and the third party. This meant that ratification was no longer a tool to approximate direct agency retroactively, but a way to grant it retroactively. This brings us to a discussion about the modern form of ratification, for its core function and meaning have changed little since the introduction of agency.

[21] Henry Swinburne, *A Treatise of Spousals, or Matrimonial Contracts* (2nd edn, London 1711) 171.

[22] Wambaugh, "A Problem as to Ratification," 60.

[23] Edward Coke, *The Fourth Part of the Institute of the Laws of England* (W. Clarke and Sons 1809) 317.

[24] Attesting to the concepts ubiquity, a few decades later, near the end of his *Leviathan*, Hobbes mentions ratification as the means through which Moses rendered Phinehas' killing of Zimri and the Midianitish woman lawful ex post. He then explains that, "this presumption of a future ratification, is sometimes necessary for the safety of a commonwealth," for it allows anyone who can suppress a rebellion, even "without express law or commission," to do so with the knowledge that their actions can be made lawful by future ratification. Thomas Hobbes, *Leviathan* (Cambridge University Press 1996) 487.

[25] Maimonides, *Book 12: The Book of Acquisition* (The Code of Maimonides, Yale University Press 1951) 208; Israel Herbert Levinthal, "The Jewish Law of Agency," (1922) 13 The Jewish Quarterly Review 117–91; Procaccia, "On the History of Agency," 70; Procaccia, "On the Theory and History of Ratification in the Law of Agency," 21.

1.3 Ratification in Agency Law Today

Ratification today is a standard component of agency law in much of the world, where it overlaps and is relevant to a variety of legal subjects such as contract, commercial, and employment law.[26] In many jurisdictions, ratification comes in the form of Andraea's paraphrase of Ulpian's words, sometimes referred to as "the Second Maxim of Agency": *Omnis ratihabitio retrotrahitur et mandato priori acquiparatur*—every ratification relates back, and is equivalent to a prior authority.[27] To unpack this maxim, and ratification more generally, I mainly focus on its use in U.S. agency law, where it exists as a distinct doctrine in some jurisdictions, or simply as an oft-cited component of case law.[28] However, ratification, at least the part of the doctrine that I am interested in, is relatively uniform between the legal systems that incorporate it.

Ratification generally applies to situations in which an "agent" fails to form a contract between a principal and a third party by being deficient. Similar to the false promisor in Roman law, this agent may be deficient because (a) she is not an authorized agent of the principal at the time of the legal act, or (b) she acted outside the bounds of her authority. Regardless, such an agent cannot make a binding contract, for she lacks proper authority. This stems from the legal principle that neither a principal nor third party can be bound by a contract or other legal act concluded by an unauthorized agent.[29] German law provides an elegant explanation of the status of such a contract through the principle of *schwebende Unwirksamkeit* (pending invalidity), according to which a contract made by an unauthorized agent is neither void nor enforceable, but instead simply "floating" and awaiting either ratification or refusal.[30]

If it comes, ratification is "the affirmance of a prior act done by another."[31] In other words, as it is for Coke, ratification is the externally observable acquiescence

[26] For the most detailed English language discussions of ratification in modern law, see Edwin C. Goddard, "Ratification by an Undisclosed Principal," (1903) 2 Michigan Law Review 25–45; Floyd R. Mechem, *A Treatise on the Law of Agency* (Callaghan and Company 1914); Philip Mechem, "The Rationale of Ratification," (1952) 100 University of Pennsylvania Law Review; Ernest Wilson Huffcut, *The Law of Agency: Including the Law of Principal and Agent and the Law of Master and Servant* (2nd edn, Little, Brown, and Company 1901); Wambaugh, "A Problem as to Ratification"; Danny Busch and Laura Macgregor (eds.), *The Unauthorised Agent: Perspectives from European and Comparative Law* (Cambridge University Press 2009); *Restatement of the Law (Third) of Agency*.

[27] Goddard, "Ratification by an Undisclosed Principal," 25; Joseph Story, *Commentaries on the Law of Agency as a Branch of Commercial and Maritime Jurisprudence* (Little, Brown and Company 1863) 272; Mechem, "The Rationale of Ratification," 649.

[28] See for instance, *California Civil Code*, Art. 2310; *Louisiana Civil Code*, Art. 1843; *North Dakoa Century Code*, Art. 3.01.08.

[29] Danny Busch and Laura Macgregor, "Comparative Law Evaluation," in Danny Busch and Laura Macgregor (eds.), *The Unauthorised Agent: Perspectives from European and Comparative Law* (Cambridge University Press 2009) 387.

[30] Martin Schmidt-Kessel and Ana Baide, "Unauthorised Agency in German Law," in Danny Busch and Laura Macgregor (eds.), *The Unauthorised Agent: Perspectives from European and Comparative Law* (Cambridge University Press 2009) 120.

[31] *Restatement of the Law (Third) of Agency*, 304 (§4.01).

to be bound by a prior act taken by another. Assent can be express or implied, meaning that a principal can consent by taking express actions that make it clear that she consents to the actions of the false agent being able to change her legal situation, or by conduct justifiable only on the assumption that the principal intends to consent to the false agent's actions.[32] Regardless of how it is expressed, "ratification retroactively creates the effects of actual authority."[33] It fixes an incomplete transaction, changing the legal circumstance of a principal and a third party by putting both of them in the position they would have been in if the deficient agent had been a real agent. In short, it creates an agency relationship after the fact. In cases of (a), the ratification retroactively appoints the actor as an agent authorized to do the acts ratified, while for (b) the ratification operates as an extension of the agents authority to cover the acts ratified.[34]

Consider the following example:

> X, purporting to represent Y, enters into a contract with Z. X is not Y's agent in this instance. Later Y ratifies the transaction.

Before ratification, no duties and obligation actually exist for any party due to the initial contracting situation, other than any damages that might result from Z thinking she has made a binding contract and any debt owed by X if goods were delivered.[35] However, if Y ratifies the transaction, the effect is for X to become Y's agent at the time of the transaction. Thus, the transaction retroactively becomes real. Because of ratification, X and Z have a contract with one another, with the resulting duties and obligations that comes with it. In this way, ratification reaches back in time and grants X a power (of agency) that she did not actually have.

Of course, ratification is subject to certain conditions both at the time of the original action (T1) and during ratification itself (T2). These conditions are similar across different legal systems.[36] In T1, the false agent needs to have acted or purported to act as an agent on the principal's behalf.[37] A person cannot ratify the actions of just anyone and claim the legal consequences of them. In addition, the principal must have existed at the time of the original act. A corporation, for

[32] Huffcut, *The Law of Agency: Including the Law of Principal and Agent and the Law of Master and Servant*, 48; *Restatement of the Law (Third) of Agency*, 308 (§4.01) Of course, implied consent is a notorious tricky concept. See A. John Simmons, *Moral Principles and Political Obligations* (Princeton University Press 1979) 88–90.

[33] *Restatement of the Law (Third) of Agency*, 304 (§4.01), 316 (§4.02).

[34] Huffcut, *The Law of Agency: Including the Law of Principal and Agent and the Law of Master and Servant*, 42.

[35] Deborah A. DeMott, "Ratification: Useful but Uneven," (2009) 17 European Review of Private Law 987–1002.

[36] See Busch and Macgregor, "Comparative Law Evaluation," 404–21, which compares ratification in the legal systems of France, Belgium, Germany, the Netherlands, England, the United States, Scotland, and South Africa.

[37] *Restatement of the Law (Third) of Agency*, 321–24 (§4.02).

instance, cannot ratify the actions of a purported agent if they were not incorporated at T1.[38] Finally, the action taken by the false agent cannot be a nullity; one cannot retroactively authorize an agent to take an illegal act.[39]

In T2, the principal needs to have the legal capacity to ratify. This is coextensive with the legal capacity to have done the original act in T1 directly, rather than through an agent. Generally, this means that at the time of ratification the principal needs to be an adult of a sound mental state who is not under duress.[40] Moreover, part of having the legal capacity to ratify is that one is sufficiently informed of facts relevant to the original act or transaction, or aware of such lack of knowledge.[41] Finally, in most cases, partial or conditional ratification is impossible. One must ratify the entirety of an act or transaction taken by a false agent rather than pick and choose desirable components.[42] This is to ensure fairness with the third party.

1.4 Reparative Function

Though the details have changed, ratification has a similar role in the private law of Ancient Rome, the canon law of the Middle Ages, and the agency law of today. We can call it ratification's *reparative function*. Here, the procedure serves as a remedial measure, as a way to fix a contract or transaction gone wrong because of an agent's lack of authority. Ratification in the present eliminates missteps or deficiencies in a past principal-agent relationship, making it as if they never occurred and thereby retroactively authorizing an agreement, contract, or transaction. Note two things about this function. First, it assumes the possibility of a transaction going correctly, and is therefore parasitic on an account of what it takes for a contract, transaction, or other decision to be valid and authoritative in the first place. Second, the transformation wrought by ratification in agency law is to make an unauthoritative transaction authoritative in the eyes of those involved and the larger legal system of which the transaction is apart. Another way of putting this is to say that ratification serves as a means of legitimizing a faulty transaction.

[38] Ibid., 324–26 (§4.04)) There are exceptions. The legal systems of Belgium and the Netherlands, for instance, deviate from this requirement in certain circumstances, allowing corporations to ratify contracts made pre-incorporation. See Ilse Samoy, "Unauthorised Agency in Belgian Law," in Danny Busch and Laura Macgregor (eds.), *The Unauthorised Agent: Perspectives from European and Comparative Law* (Cambridge University Press 2009) 94–95; Danny Busch, "Unauthorised Agency in Dutch Law," in Danny Busch and Laura Macgregor (eds.), *The Unauthorised Agent: Perspectives from European and Comparative Law* (Cambridge University Press 2009) 176–77.

[39] The criteria for counting as a nullity, in the case of disabling ratification, varies across legal systems. See Busch and Macgregor, "Comparative Law Evaluation," 406–7.

[40] *Restatement of the Law (Third) of Agency*, 203–4 (§3.04), 324–25, 328 (§4.04).

[41] Ibid., 336 (§4.06).

[42] Ibid., 341 (§4.07).

2. Ratification in Treaty Law

Ratification has two roles in international law. The first arose in the early modern period and applies to what Grotius calls "Sponsions" or *sponsionum*.[43] These were agreements between nations by public agents not specifically authorized to make them, but often created through the exercise of a general implied power attached to their official stations. An example might be a prisoner exchange or a ceasefire negotiated by generals.[44] Such agreements were informal and could not bind a sovereign because the negotiators lacked delegated power. However, Grotius, followed by Pufendorf, Wolff, and Vattel, used the language and logic of ratification's agency law function to argue that such sponsions could become retroactively binding if a sovereign approved them after the fact.[45] Wolff goes so far to claim, "if indeed the sovereign power ratifies" a sponsion, "the sponsion is transformed into a treaty."[46] This is ratification serving in its *reparative function*, retroactively fixing an agreement that otherwise would not be valid. The sovereign's ratification reaches back in time, transforming the informal ceasefire or prisoner exchange into a properly authoritative agreement.

This agency law-inspired use of ratification in international law is minor and distinct from its second and more well-known role in treaty-making, where it often follows negotiations, signature, and accession.[47] Ratification in this more common sense, as Vattel explains, is the "deed by which the sovereign approves a treaty, and engages to observe it."[48] Or, as the Vienna Convention on the Law of Treaties (VCLT), the current central source of international law for treaty-making, defines the term, ratification is "the international act so named whereby a State establishes on the international plane its consent to be bound by a treaty."[49]

Today treaty ratification usually involves two standardized steps: (1) the execution, usually by signature, of an instrument of ratification by the executive, and (2) the exchange of this instrument with the other party for bilateral treaties or the submission of the instrument with a depository for multilateral treaties.[50] Ratification's mature role in international treaty ratification crystallized in the sixteenth century in Europe, corresponding with the beginnings of the slow shift from

[43] See Theodor Meron, "The Authority to Make Treaties in the Late Middle Ages," (1995) 89 The American Journal of International Law 1–20, 16n110.

[44] Henry Wheaton, *Elements of International Law* (2nd edn, Stevens & Sons 1880) 310.

[45] Samuel Pufendorf, *The Whole Duty of Man According to the Law of Nature* (Liberty Fund 2003) 247; Hugo Grotius, *The Rights of War and Peace*, vol. II (Liberty Fund 2005) 818–47; Christian Wolff, *Jus Gentium Methodo Scientifica Pertractatum*, vol. 2 (Clarendon Press 1934) 241–43 (465–68); Emer de Vattel, *The Law of Nations* (Liberty Fund 2008) 374–82, 481–2.

[46] Wolff, *Jus Gentium Methodo Scientifica Pertractatum*, 242 (468).

[47] Jeffrey S. Lantis, *The Life and Death of International Treaties: Doubled-Edged Diplomacy and the Politics of Ratification in Comparative Perspective* (Oxford University Press 2008) 2.

[48] Vattel, *The Law of Nations*, 373.

[49] *Vienna Convention on the Law of Treaties*, vol. 1155 (Treaty Series, United Nations 1969) I.2.b.

[50] Anthony Aust, *Modern Treaty Law and Practice* (3rd edn, Cambridge University Press 2013) 95.

treaties being mostly agreements between princes to being agreements between states.[51] From that time until the present, one can understand treaty ratification as having two different logics corresponding with two different forms.[52]

2.1 Ratification of Plenipotentiaries: Agent Review Function

Up until about the eighteenth century, treaty-making usually divided into three steps: the granting of Full Powers to negotiators (ambassador, ministers, etc.) by a sovereign, thereby making them plenipotentiaries; the deliberation and agreement on a final text by the negotiators; and the ratification of the text by the sovereign.[53] Such ratification initially took the form of oath-taking, which brought the treaty under canon law (in Europe), but eventually moved to a written form, which made the treaty binding upon rulers "under general principles of contract as they emerged from Roman law, feudal law and customary law systems."[54]

Under this form of treaty ratification, those negotiating treaties were usually understood to be agents of monarchs or princes invested with the competence to act as if they were the sovereigns themselves. These powers were granted in documents known as "Full Powers," and their presentation and discussion, including the precise authority that plenipotentiary negotiators held, usually occupied a significant portion of conference time during negotiations.[55] The object of ratification was not to go over the details of the treaty and then authorize it, for plenipotentiaries of the sovereign already possessed the power to make authoritative treaties. Rather, the object of ratification was the agent itself and its conduct. By ratifying, a sovereign declared that the agent negotiating and signing the treaty was rightfully its plenipotentiary and that he had acted within the proper scope of his Full Powers.[56] Thus the function of ratification was to publicly declare that the treaty negotiator

[51] An exemption might exist in the treaty practices in the classical period. For instance, in the Roman Republic before the second century BC, it appears that the people meeting in tribal assemblies under the presidency of the magistrate were, at least formally, charged with approving treaties. We might understand this as an example of treaty ratification. See Andrew Lintott, *Imperium Romanum: Politics and Administration* (Routledge 1993) 43; Polybius, *The Rise of the Roman Empire* (Penguin Classics 1980) 51 (1.11), 314 (6.14), 464 (15.1).

[52] J. Mervyn Jones, *Full Powers and Ratification: A Study in the Development of Treaty-Making Procedure* (University of Cambridge Press 1946) 66–107.

[53] Randall Lesaffer, "Peace Treaties from Lodi to Westphalia," in Randall Lesaffer (ed.), *Peace Treaties and International Law in European History* (Cambridge University Press 2004) 22.

[54] Ibid., 26–27.

[55] D.P. O'Connell, *International Law*, vol. 1 (Stevens & Son Limited 1965) 230–231; Jones, *Full Powers and Ratification: A Study in the Development of Treaty-Making Procedure*. Full Powers are still sometimes given, but they are often qualified by making explicit that signature is subject to ratification, and they are rarely discussed during multilateral conferences.

[56] Council of Europe, *Treaty Making: Expression of Consent by States to Be Bound by a Treaty* (Kluwer Law International 2001) 11; Hans Blix, "The Requirement of Ratification," (1953) 30 British Year Book of International Law 352–80, 354–55.

had exercised real authority granted by the sovereign, not overstepped its boundaries, and that the agreement was a real one. For, as Burlmaqui explains, "Treaties concluded by ministers, oblige the sovereign and the state only when the ministers have been duly authorized to make them, and have done nothing contrary to their orders and instructions."[57]

Ratification provided the "formal, necessary evidence of the authority under which an agent acted."[58] In the emerging system of international law, ratification became a critical step in which sovereigns, at least in Europe, assured each other that they recognized and had authorized those conducting their delicate negotiations. Thus, except in exceptional circumstances where ambassadors and diplomats involved in treaty negotiations exceeded their publicly given authority, sovereigns were considered obliged to ratify. The famous seventeenth-century diplomat, spy, and historian Abraham de Wicquefort spells this expectation out explicitly: "if the Embassador does not exceed the Bounds of his Powers ... the Prince is oblig'd to approve of him, and to ratify what has been negotiated in his Name, and by virtue of his Powers."[59] Later, citing Wicquefort's work (anonymous at the time), Pufendorf notes that even if one's plenipotentiary violates their secret commission, i.e. the agent reaches an agreement with an opposing country that violates private instructions as to what the sovereign finds agreeable, the sovereign is "still obligated to the third party for what the agent did," for "were this not true, there could be no safety in dealing with agents, since there would always be the fear that the secret instructions were different from the open, and no easier excuse could be found for invalidating everything done by agents ...."[60]

This early conception of treaty ratification is somewhat close to the private law version of ratification from which it descended. Like private law ratification, it involves a principal completing a contract by formally designating the actions of its agent as authorized. Moreover, the effects of ratification were usually seen as retroactive, in that treaty ratification made the treaty valid upon the (earlier) date of its initial signature by the agent.[61] However, similarities stop here. Unlike the private law context, early treaty ratification was a necessary step in all instances of treaty-making, and its purpose was to reaffirm that all parties in the treaty were real agents acting with authority, not to retroactively legitimate illegitimate agents. In fact, rather than being the very instance in which ratification might become relevant, in this context unauthorized agents or agents acting outside their instructions

[57] Jean-Jacques Burlamaqui, *The Principles of Natural and Politic Law* (Liberty Fund 2006) 524.

[58] Jones, *Full Powers and Ratification: A Study in the Development of Treaty-Making Procedure*, 158.

[59] Abraham de Wicquefort, *The Embassador and His Functions* (Bernard Lintott 1716) 406.

[60] Samuel Pufendorf, *De Jure Naturae Et Gentium Libri Octo*, vol. 2 (Clarendon Press 1934) 450 (3.9.2) For a discussion of seventeenth- and eighteenth-century debate on the class between public Full Powers and secret instructions, see Wheaton, *Elements of International Law*, 311–15.

[61] Wheaton, *Elements of International Law*, 314; Georg Friedrich Von Martens, *A Compendium of the Law of Nations* (Cobbett and Morgan 1802) 49.

were, at least according to Vattel, the only "strong and substantial reasons" that could allow a sovereign to "honorably refuse to ratify a compact."[62]

We can call ratification's role in early treaty-making its *agent review function*. The procedure provides a way to review an agent to ensure that she is duly authorized, and that she behaved in accordance with her given duties, instructions, and sphere of authority. The object of evaluation is the agent, not the specifics of the decision that she, along with others, reached.

2.2 Ratification of Treaties: Direct Action Function

The more recent form of treaty ratification that began in the late seventeenth and early eighteenth centuries and continues to this day is different. For one thing, the object of ratification is the content of the treaty itself, not the agent and its behavior. When countries ratify treaties today, they signal that they find the content of the treaty acceptable. "Today, it is the treaty, and not the signature, that is ratified."[63] This change was likely the result of the American and the French Revolutions and the advent of democratic constitutional government, which led to the introduction of popular domestic veto players in the process leading up to ratification.[64]

For instance, take the current Brazilian Constitution, under which, like many constitutions, the President has the power to appoint diplomats and conclude international conventions, treaties, and acts. However, the President's ratification power is "subject to the approval of the National Assembly."[65] Here, the old logic of treaty ratification being merely the verification that the negotiating agent was properly authorized and acting within its designated Full Powers makes little sense, for two related reasons. On the one hand, the President does not have absolute sovereign authority to conduct international negotiations to transfer to the diplomat, for all treaties need to be approved by a different branch of government before he or she can ratify it.[66] In this sense, under constitutions such as Brazil's, it is impossible for diplomats to be true plenipotentiaries, for they no longer hold the power to make full and binding agreements. This means that ratification must serve some purpose other than making sure a plenipotentiary acted within the scope of its full authority. On the other hand, when it occurs, ratification follows an intense deliberation over the appropriateness of the content of a treaty by agents other than the formal ratifier and the agent that appointed the diplomat, who then must approve the content before the executive can ratify. Ratification, therefore, ultimately depends on a review of the content of the treaty.

[62] Vattel, *The Law of Nations*, 340.

[63] Jones, *Full Powers and Ratification: A Study in the Development of Treaty-Making Procedure*, 159.

[64] Blix, "The Requirement of Ratification," 354; O'Connell, *International Law*, 231.

[65] The Constitution of the Federative Republic of Brazil (1988), Arts. 49, 84.7.

[66] William Edward Hall, *A Treatise on International Law* (4th edn, Clarendon Press 1895) 348.

Of course, many states do not have such provisions mandating legislative review of treaties before ratification, and do not limit executive power to such an extent when it comes to treaty-making.[67] Nonetheless, the emergence of countries that did was enough to slowly erode the practice of granting real Full Powers and to alter the norms and meaning of ratification.[68] According to O'Connell, this change became complete by 1878, when the protocol of the Congress of Berlin stated that it was ratification and not signature that gave treaties their definitive value.[69] Thus, unlike in the Middle Ages and early modern period, ratification today is no longer considered to be an obligation or a given following signature, and its refusal is no longer seen as an unfriendly act.[70]

It is easy to find recent examples of ratification refusal. India signed the UN Convention Against Torture in 1997 but has so far refused to ratify it. The number of treaties signed but not ratified by the United States is long. They include the 1966 International Covenant on Economic, Social and Cultural Rights, the 1989 Convention on the Rights of the Child, 1996 Comprehensive Test Ban Theory, and most recently the 2017 Paris Agreement. In fact, the United States signed but never ratified the VCLT itself. Clearly, it is no longer "a fraudulent and shameful abuse of the faith of treaties" to refuse to sign simply because one does not like the deal.[71]

Following from all of this, the ratification of a treaty no longer makes it retroactively binding from the time of signature, but serves as the site of primary legal and political action itself.[72] States become bound the moment that ratification instruments are exchanged or deposited.[73] As Judge John Bassett Moore once wrote, in his dissent to the Permanent Court of International Justice's ruling on *The Mavrommatic Palestine Concessions*, "the doctrine that governments are bound to ratify whatever their plenipotentiaries, acting within the limits of their instructions, may sign, and that treaties may therefore be regarded as legally operative and enforceable before they have been ratified, is obsolete, and lingers only as an echo from the past."[74] By ratifying a treaty, a head of state signals that they and other constituted bodies accept the content of a treaty and now bind their state by

[67] Some states, such as France, only introduce legislative review of treaties when they cover topics of particular importance such as large-scale trade. Malcolm N. Shaw, *International Law* (6th edn, Cambridge University Press 2008) 173.

[68] O'Connell, *International Law*, 242.

[69] Ibid., 243.

[70] Steiger Heinhard, "Peace Treaties from Paris to Versailles," in Randall Lesaffer (ed.), *Peace Treaties and International Law in European History* (Cambridge University Press 2004) 78–79.

[71] Vattel, *The Law of Nations*, 377.

[72] Lassa Oppenheim, *International Law: A Treatise*, vol. 1 (8th edn, David McKay Company Inc. 1955) 903.

[73] Blix, "The Requirement of Ratification," 355; Oppenheim, *International Law: A Treatise*, 903. Note that some scholars disputed this until at least the beginning of the twentieth century. See for instance Frederick Edwin Smith, *International Law* (6th edn, J.M. Dent & Sons 1927) 142.

[74] *The Mavrommatis Palestine Concessions (Greece v. U.K.)*, PCIJ (Permanent Court of International Justice) (1924).

international law (provided a sufficient number of other parties to the treaty also ratify).[75]

Ratification in this context plays a *direct action function.* Here, ratification serves as the site of authority itself. It is where an entity with ultimate authority for a specific agreement takes action, making a multi-stepped decision-making procedure authoritative and binding on itself and those it represents or acts for. This is not an instance in which a principal is correcting a lack of delegated authority to an agent or ensuring that an agent with delegated authority behaved appropriately, but rather one in which a principal acts directly. Thus, to go back to Brazil, the ratification of a treaty is the moment in which the President, now equipped with approval powers by the national assembly, formally binds Brazil to the treaty.

2.3 Bargaining Function

Robert Putnam's work on two-level games and foreign policy suggest a third function of ratification in the international arena. In "Diplomacy and Domestic Politics: The Logic of Two-Level Games," Putnam breaks international negotiations into two levels. On Level I, negotiators bargain until they reach a tentative agreement amongst themselves. On Level II, constituents decide whether to ratify the agreement, with ratification referring to "any decision-process at Level II that is required to endorse or implement a Level I agreement, whether formally or informally."[76] What this means is that a government negotiator, while seeking out a Level I compromise that all parties can accept, must also ensure that any resulting deal will be acceptable to enough of her legislators or constituents to secure ratification on Level II.

Putnam calls the set of all-possible Level I agreements that could be approved by a given Level II constituency a win-set.[77] Each country with some sort of ratification process has a win-set, and a successful Level 1 agreement therefore depends on finding and settling on an agreement that lies within the overlap of the win-sets of all parties involved. In other words, an international agreement is only possible if negotiators can agree upon a compromise that a significant number of their constituents can accept.

[75] The VCLT allows alternative means of concluding treaty-making, such as mere signature or exchange of instruments. For states that have a choice between procedures to conclude treaty-making, they are often thought to choose ratification when they are interested in the time delay that it provides, either to pass domestic legislation needed before the treaty goes into effect or to continue internal debates before making a final decision. Blix, "The Requirement of Ratification," 357; Shaw, *International Law*, 912; Aust, *Modern Treaty Law and Practice*, 95.

[76] Robert D. Putnam, "Diplomacy and Domestic Politics: The Logic of Two-Level Games," (1988) 42 International Organization 427–60, 436. Note that in this formulation, ratification is serving a direct-action function, in that the Level II ratification procedure is the site of authoritative sovereign decision-making.

[77] Ibid.

The size of a domestic win-set thus has several implications. On the one hand, having a smaller rather than larger win-set means that the scope of international agreement is smaller, and thus the chances of no agreement is greater. On the other hand, a smaller win-set can serve as a bargaining advantage for a Level 1 negotiator, for it might favorably restrict the range of compromises that the negotiator can plausibly make.[78] This links the nature of a ratification procedure directly to bargaining advantage, as the type of ratification used can affect the size and contours of the win-set. For instance, moving from a majority to a supermajority legislative voting threshold will shrink the win-set, for fewer agreements will be able to secure the support of the now greater number of ratifiers needed for passage.

Since Putnam's article, several scholars have shown how and when counties might choose to implement a ratification requirement, not implement one, or choose to make their existing ratification requirement stricter (or portray it as such) in an effort to secure greater bargaining advantage on specific issues.[79] According to Hodson and Maher, one rare instance of a country adopting harder ratification standards can be found in the United Kingdom's European Union Act of 2011, which gave parliament a greater say in the approving of European Union (EU) treaty revisions and increased the chances that such revisions would need to be authorized via referendum and/or subject to judicial review.[80] This Act certainly made it more difficult for EU treaty revisions to be ratified by the United Kingdom, for it eliminated a loophole exploited by several Prime Ministers to bypass parliament and the people. Whether the reduction in win-set size led to an increase in U.K. bargaining power remains unclear, especially because of the emergence of Brexit sentiments and the resulting 2016 referendum.

Putnam's work, and the literature it inspired, reveals the *bargaining function* of ratification.[81] Here, the procedure serves as a mean of shifting the bargaining landscape, changing the advantage of one group over another by restricting or expanding the scope of the set of agreements that the delegate of the former group can plausibly make. Note that this logic seems limited to situations in which two

[78] Ibid., 441.

[79] Dermot Hodson and Imelda Maher, "British Brinkmanship and Gaelic Games: EU Treaty Ratification in the UK and Ireland from a Two Level Game Perspective," (2014) 16 The British Journal of Politics and International Relations 645–61; Dieter Konold, "Farm Interests as Bargaining Chips: France in the Eu-Mercosur Free Trade Negotiations," (2010) 30 Journal of Public Policy 321–43; Jongryn Mo, "Domestic Institutions and International Bargaining: The Role of Agent Veto in Two-Level Games," (1995) 89 American Political Science Review 914–24; Andrew Moravcsik, "Integrating International and Domestic Theories of International Bargaining," in Peter B. Evans, Robert D. Putnam, and Harold K. Jacobson (eds.), *Double-Edged Diplomacy: International Bargaining and Domestic Politics* (University of California Press 1993).

[80] Hodson and Maher, "British Brinkmanship and Gaelic Games: EU Treaty Ratification in the UK and Ireland from a Two Level Game Perspective," 646.

[81] For an overview of the literature that sprung from Putnam's original article on two-level games, see Eugénia da Conceição-Heldt and Patrick A. Mello, "Two-Level Games in Foreign Policy Analysis," Oxford Research Encyclopedias–Politics <https://oxfordre.com/politics/view/10.1093/acrefore/9780190228637.001.0001/acrefore-9780190228637-e-496>.

or more players, representing different constituencies, are bargaining with one another, and a given ratification process will only apply to an individual player and its constituency.

3. Labor Law and Collective Bargaining

I now move from the realm of international law to collective bargaining, from the interaction of states cutting trade deals and negotiating ceasefires to workers and their employers hammering out wage increases and employment benefits. Ratification procedures are a frequent occurrence in collective bargaining practices, and common to the rules and laws that govern them throughout the world. In this context, ratification refers to the submission of a labor contract by negotiators and union elites to all union members (or those locals or chapters effected by the proposed contract) for their binding approval, usually through a referendum with a majority threshold. This vote can take place in person at a local meeting, by mail, or, increasingly, online.

3.1 Background

In 1988 Cappelli and Sterling wrote that "although the process of contract ratification is the final and perhaps most important step in the collective bargaining process, it has received remarkably little attention from the research community."[82] As with the ratification of constitutions, the ratification of labor contracts continues to be overlooked today. It remains, for instance, rarely studied when and where ratification procedures first became a component of collective bargaining, or the frequency of their occurrence throughout labor history.[83] Regardless, today the procedure is common in many countries, often being codified in union rules and constitutions.

Some unions, such as the Communications Workers of America (CWA), list ratification as an optional procedure to be used "if the delegates to an International Convention ... , or representatives at a Bargaining Council meeting, or the members themselves determine ratification to be desirable."[84] More frequently, the

[82] Peter Cappelli and W.P. Sterling, "Union Bargaining Decisions and Contract Ratifications: The 1982 and 1984 Auto Agreements," (1988) 41 Industrial & Labor Relations Review 195–209, 195.

[83] For some interesting works on the subject, see Herbert J. Lahne, "Union Contract Ratification Procedures," (1968) 91 Monthly Labor Review 7–10, 9; Alvin L. Goldman and Roberto L. Corrada, *Labour Law in the USA* (Kluwer Law International 2014); Paul Alan Levy, "Membership Rights in Union Referenda to Ratify Collective Bargaining Agreements," (1987) 4 Hofstra Labor and Employment Law Journal 225–67, 229; Oscar Molina, "Social Pacts, Collective Bargaining and Trade Union Articulation Strategies," (2008) 14 Transfer: European Review of Labour and Research 399–418, 399

[84] Communications Workers of America Constitution (2019), Art. 17, sec. 15.

procedure is required. The constitution of Unifor, the largest private sector union in Canada, states that "any contract entered into through collective bargaining or otherwise concerning terms of conditions of employment shall be ratified by a secret ballot vote of members at a meeting called to ratify the agreement, or by another established procedure."[85] In the United States, the Constitution of the National Association of Letter Carriers explains that "ratification shall be a mail referendum vote," and that "acceptance or rejection of proposed National Agreement shall be by majority of valid ballots returned by the voters."[86] The constitution of the New Zealand Nurses Organisation not only requires that all collective agreements be ratified by the affected membership, but also that these members be given the opportunity to participate in a simple majority vote to decide on the particular details of the ratification process to be used.[87]

In the United States, ratification is a procedure implemented voluntarily by unions. Nonetheless, when unions choose to use it, Title I of the Labor-management Reporting and Disclosure Act of 1959 (LMRDA) provides guidelines.[88] Under this regulation, union members participating in a ratification referendum must have the right to make a "meaningful vote," i.e. a vote in which procedures are followed, all members can participate, all viewpoints can be given and heard, and the outcome of the vote determines the conduct of union representatives.[89] As Levy notes, "the right to vote is 'meaningful' when the referendum process is allowed to work as it was intended: as a meaningful check on the exercise of leadership discretion."[90] Most countries follow the United States in leaving the decision to make use of ratification up to unions. New Zealand is an exception, for its Employment Relations Act of 2000 requires that all collective bargaining begins with an agreed upon ratification procedure that must be followed.[91]

Regardless of what leads to a ratification requirement, when present the procedure has teeth—union members have shown themselves willing to vote down even hard won negotiated contracts.[92] Between 1965 and 1967, during the heyday of ratification rejections in the United States, union members voted down about 15 percent of all contracts presented to them, which amounted to over 1500.[93]

[85] Unifor Constitution (2019), Art. 17b.

[86] Constitution of the National Association of Letter Carriers of the United States (2018), Art. 16.

[87] Constitution of the New Zealand Nurses Organisation (2018–19), Art.11.12.

[88] Labor-Management Reporting and Disclosure Act of 1959 29 U.S.C. § 411.

[89] For the relevant case law see Levy, "Membership Rights in Union Referenda to Ratify Collective Bargaining Agreements," 232–33.

[90] Ibid., 233.

[91] Parliament of New Zealand, Employment Relations Act (2000), sec. 51.

[92] Ratification rejection is especially common when positive company performance leads to high expectations that are not met by the contractual offerings. See Charles A. Odewahn and Joseph Krislov, "Contract Rejections: Testing the Explanatory Hypotheses," (1973) 12 Industrial Relations 289–96.

[93] William E. Simkin, "Refusals to Ratify Contracts," (1968) 21 Industrial and Labor Relations Review 518–40, 519. This rate of rejection, which appeared to have been an increase, led to a flurry of writing on the topic by concerned legal analysts and economists. However, contract rejection peaked at 15 percent, and worries faded away as, among other things, union membership decreased in the

Members of the International Association of Machinists even rejected a contract directly pushed by the U.S. President in 1966.[94] Rejections, though not as frequent, continue to this day. For instance in April 2019, workers at Harley Davidson's plants represented by the United Steelworkers Union voted to reject their employer's most recent contract.[95] In the same month, the New Zealand Education Institute Te Riu Roa, the largest education union in the country, rejected the Ministry of Education's collective bargaining offer, leading to a mega-strike of 50,000 teachers, the largest strike in New Zealand history, in May.[96] And in Winnipeg, Canada, in August 2019, the Amalgamated Transit Union Local 1505 rejected the city's fourth offer of employment terms.[97]

As with constitutions and treaties, once a labor contract is ratified, it is held to be binding and in force (provided that the representatives of the employers have also signed). However, there is a fundamental difference between ratification procedures in collective bargaining and ratification procedures in treaty- and constitution-making. Put simply, negotiations usually continue after a union membership rejects a proposed contract, and this is expected by both sides.[98] Negotiators from both sides often resume talks and work toward obtaining a new contract that can garner enough votes. For instance, in mid-July of 2016, a ratification vote among 40,000 AT&T wireless employees unionized through the CWA resulted in a rejection of a proposed benefits contract. Negotiations resumed, and the union approved a new contract at the end of the next month.[99]

Something similar does not occur when it comes to treaty and constitutional ratification. In these contexts, ratification nearly always occurs after the bargaining process has ceased. If a bilateral treaty is not ratified, the treaty does not go into

1980s. See Goldman and Corrada, *Labour Law in the USA*, 345; David I. Shair, "The Mythology of Labor Contract Rejections," (1970) 21 Labor Law Journal 88–94.

94 Clyde W. Summers, "Ratification of Agreements," in John T. Dunlop and Neil W. Chamberlain (eds.), *Frontiers of Collective Bargaining* (Harper & Row 1967) 77; David R. Jones, "Air Talks Reach 'Serious Impasse'" *New York Times* (July 15, 1966).

95 Patrick Leary, "Harley-Davidson Workers Reportedly Reject Contract Offer" *Milwaukee Business Journal* <https://www.bizjournals.com/milwaukee/news/2019/04/01/harley-davidson-workers-reportedly-reject-contract.html?iana=hpmvp_mil_news_headline>.

96 Katarina Williams, "School Mega-Strike Still under Consideration" *Manawatu Standard* (April 9, 2019), 7; Caroline Fleming, "'Biggest Strike NZ Has Ever Seen' on the Way as Teachers Turn Out" *Bay of Plenty Times* (May 28, 2019) A, A:2.

97 Danton Unger, "Transit Workers Reject Latest Offer; but Willing to Take Smaller Wage Hike in Exchange for Safer Working Conditions" *The Winnipeg Sun* (August 17, 2019) A.3, A.3.

98 To my knowledge, only one constituent assembly, the second New Hampshire constitutional convention, convoked with the understanding that it would continue sending draft constitutions to be ratified until one was approved. See my discussion of New Hampshire in chapter 3, section 3.1.

99 Aaron Pressman, "At&T Wireless Workers Approve New Benefits Contract" *Fortune Magazine* <http://fortune.com/2016/08/31/att-wireless-workers-approve-contract/>; Aaron Pressman, "At&T Sees It First Labor Problem in Years with Rejected Contract Proposal" *Fortune Magazine* <http://fortune.com/2016/07/18/att-labor-problems/>.

effect. If a multilateral treaty is not ratified by one of its members, that member is not a party to the treaty. And if a ratifier does not approve a constitution, the constitution-making process is usually over without a new constitution, and the status quo continues.

3.2 Functions

Four functions of ratification in a collective bargaining setting can be drawn from the scant literature on the topic, the first three of which are familiar. Most straightforwardly, ratification serves in its *direct action* function. Unions that require ratification, like sovereign states that utilize treaty ratification, only delegate the power to bargain to negotiators. The power to make an agreement authoritative and binding is left to union membership, and it is during the ratification vote that the union makes its real decision.[100] This argument can be given a democratic gloss, in that ratification procedures serve as an affirmation that the real power within workers unions lies with the workers themselves, who therefore must vote on the employment contract that will structure their working life. An unratified collective bargaining agreement in these instances is without force, as the source of authority, the workers, has yet to act.

Second, ratification might serve in its *bargaining function*, giving union negotiators a strategic advantage over their employer counterparts. Here, as with international treaties, the requirement of ratification serves as a credible commitment from negotiators that they can only accept a very favorable agreement.[101] That is, union negotiators can use the fact that any given contract must receive the approval of a majority or supermajority of their membership as a threat, an assertion of a smaller win-set, thereby taking certain potential contracts off the bargaining table in favor of a more desirable range of possibilities.[102]

A more extreme version of this strategy, made possible by the fact that negotiations continue post-ratification rejection, is for a union negotiator to agree to a contract and then encourage members to reject it during ratification, thereby demonstrating the credibility of her claim that certain demands must be satisfied

[100] Summers, "Ratification of Agreements," 79.

[101] Hans Haller and Steinar Holden, "Ratification Requirement and Bargaining Power," (1997) 38 International Economic Review 825–51; Charles S. Loughran, *Negotiating a Labor Contract: A Management Handbook* (The Bureau of National Affairs, Inc. 1984) 369.

[102] Note that, contra Haller and Holden, recent work by Cardona and Ponsatí suggests that choosing ratification over delegation (vesting full authority in a negotiator) is only beneficial when there are reasons to believe the negotiator is unreliable. Daniel Cardona and Clara Ponsatí, "Representing a Democratic Constituency in Negotiations: Delegation Versus Ratification," (2015) 45 Social Choice and Welfare 399–414.

before approval.[103] Of course, using ratification in this way to increase the chances of getting a more favorable agreement is risky, for it "involves a risk that no such favourable agreement is feasible and consequently no agreement is reached, even in situations where mutually beneficial agreements were possible."[104]

Third, ratification might also serve as a means of *agent review*. Here, ratification functions as a way of reviewing the performance of a labor negotiator to ensure that she is following the instructions and will of the membership. This has the effect of making negotiators especially attentive to the wants of their constituents, for they wish to produce an acceptable contract and avoid a strike.[105] At the same time, this agent review function can be deployed helpfully by the negotiators themselves, in that the lower cost of rejection (given that negotiations will continue) allows them to use contract ratification as a means of ensuring that their membership find the contract acceptable. By ensuring satisfaction, union leaders and negotiators can prevent membership from using more fatal agent review mechanisms, such as joining a different union or replacing the leadership.[106]

Fourth and finally is what I call the *support function*, according to which ratification serves as a means to increase the number of workers who find an adopted employment contract acceptable. The assumption here is that employment contracts should be supported by much of a union's membership, for this encourages stabilized labor relations and employee satisfaction.[107] Ratification might accomplish this in two ways. First, by requiring that any employment contract be approved by a majority or supermajority, the existence of an employment contract ratification referendum helps ensure that no contract comes into force that is actively opposed by a majority of the membership. Second, the mere occurrence of ratification might increase the support for a constitution, for a ratification vote incentivizes negotiators to sell the new contract to the electorate, and the sheer act of participation in the process might generate positive feelings toward the contract. Of course this latter point, that participation increases support, depends on the degree to which union members see their unions as democracies, which even the champion of this view, Clyde Summers, admits is not always the case.[108]

[103] Summers, "Ratification of Agreements," 78.

[104] Haller and Holden, "Ratification Requirement and Bargaining Power," 844.

[105] Summers, "Ratification of Agreements," 100.

[106] Ibid., 86; Michael L. Brookshire, "Centralized Bargaining Structures and Referendums," (1976) 2 Southern Business Review 12–27, 18–20; James E. Martin and Ruth D. Berthiaume, "Predicting the Outcome of a Contract Ratification Vote," (1995) 38 The Academy of Management Journal 916–28, 917. Simkin supports this function of ratification indirectly, by noting that an attempt to avoid ratification rejections by convincing unions to abandon the practice would not eliminate the bulk of the causes of rejection and instead "would simply channel those dissatisfactions toward more frequent changes of union leadership with implicit instructions to be tougher at the next negotiations." Simkin, "Refusals to Ratify Contracts," 537.

[107] Summers, "Ratification of Agreements," 83–84.

[108] Ibid., 85.

4. Conclusion

Our discussion of ratification before and beyond constitutions is not exhaustive in breadth (ratification procedures also appear in other arenas such as parliamentary procedure and juvenile guardianship law) or depth (not all aspects of ratification in agency, international, or labor law were explored), but it was not intended to be. Rather, it served the purpose of revealing ratification's pre-constitutional origins and central extra-constitutional uses, and making bare several functions of the procedure that will help us construct or identify justifications for constitutional ratification in the chapters ahead. To conclude, I will highlight and generalize these functions, briefly suggest how they might be relevant for justifying constitutional ratification, and point to places in the remainder of the book where these functions reappear.

Ratification has a *reparative function* when it serves the purpose of retroactively fixing a deficient agreement, decision, or contract in the past so that it becomes binding. This is the role ratification plays in private agency law and in the approval of sponsions made between overreaching state officials during international negotiations. Ultimately, this function is about legitimacy, normative or sociological, whereby ratification serves as a way of overcoming, and even making disappear, a legitimacy deficit in an earlier decision-making process. A justification based on constitutional ratification's reparative function would support the procedure on the basis of its importance on providing an opportunity to salvage the legitimacy of faulty constitution-making processes. For instance, in one sense the decision to submit the U.S. Constitution to constitutional conventions can be understood as a means of legitimizing what was an illegal attempt to replace, rather than revise, the Articles of Confederation. Though the delegates to the Philadelphia Convention never explicitly made this argument, as will be shown in chapter 3, section 3, traces of it can be seen in the various reasons they gave for using state conventions during their debates. I also directly address a reparative justification of ratification in chapter 4, section 3.4, discuss legitimacy more generally in chapters eight and nine, and return to the use of an ad hoc ratification procedure to repair an illegitimate constitution-making process in chapter 10, section 2.

The *bargaining function* casts ratification as a procedure that enables one negotiator in a bargaining context to increase their negotiating power by, among other things, plausibly shrinking their win-set by requiring the direct approval of those they represent. As discussed, ratification takes on this role in the context of treaty negotiations and collective bargaining. On its face, this looks like a difficult function with which to understand ratification during constitution-making. The reason why brings attention to a fundamental difference between the ratification of constitutions and the ratification of private contracts, treaties, and employment agreements.

In non-constitutional settings, a specific ratification procedure only applies to one of the parties involved in the transaction or negotiation. If X, falsely purporting to represent Y, contracts with Z, only Y (if she so chooses) will ratify the contract. The Treaty of Rarotonga, which established a nuclear weapon-free zone in the South Pacific, involved numerous ratification procedures, but each only involved and pertained to one of the treaty members. And when AT&T employees finally ratified their employment contract in 2016, this procedure did not involve members of the telecommunications company's board. The same is not true for the ratification of constitutions. Here, the ratification process involves everyone, directly or indirectly, who will be covered by the constitution. It is not a decision-making procedure applicable to only one member of a bargaining process, but rather one that involves all members and all they represent.

Thus, on its face, ratification cannot serve as a bargaining advantage for one of the actors involved in a constitution-making process, for it applies to all parties. However, as I discuss in chapter 10, section 3, such a dismissal might be too fast. While unable to serve as a general ex ante justification of constitutional ratification, ratification can still, in rare circumstances, be useful as a bargaining tool for those representing cohesive minority groups within a state or territory writing a new constitution. For instance, constituent assembly members acting on behalf of, and confident of the votes of, a large ethnic community can utilize a ratification referendum to push for favorable provisions on the basis of the need for securing the votes of their constituents. They will thus secure a bargaining advantage unavailable to less populous or cohesive groups. Therefore, though ratification would apply to all parties, it would instill a bargaining advantage to only some.

Ratification's *support function*, the idea that the procedure helps increase the degree that a decision is accepted by those it will affect, also concerns legitimacy, in particular sociological legitimacy. According to this function, ratification helps union negotiators ensure that the final employment agreement is supported by membership. A justification of constitutional ratification somewhat like the support function would argue that ratification helps to ensure a majority or super-majority of citizens view their constitution as legitimate, as something that they have good reasons for treating as authoritative, and that this is a desirable outcome. Chapter 9 is dedicated to discussing ratification's relationship with legitimacy.

Alternatively, according to the *agent review function*, ratification serves as a means of reviewing, controlling, and/or passing judgment on the behavior of one's agent or representative. Ratification functioned in this way in early modern treaty-making, in which sovereigns were expected to sign-off on international treaties unless they believed their representatives had bucked their instructions and delegated powers, and continues to do so today in instances of collective bargaining. A justification of constitutional ratification based on an agent review function would argue in favor of the procedure because of its ability to connect constituents and their agents in this way. As I will show in chapter 7, in the constitutional context this amounts to an argument in favor of ratification's role as an accountability mechanism in a representative process.

The most straightforward function of ratification is its *direct action function*. According to this function, ratification is simply the moment within a decision-making process where an agent with authority to bind itself and/or its constituents formally does so. In contemporary treaty-making, this is the moment when a head of state, often equipped with power stemming from legislative approval, formally makes a treaty binding on her state. One can also understand employment contract ratification in the same way. It is only during ratification, when all members vote, that the power to accept an employment contract is wielded. Justifying a ratification procedure as a moment within the constitution-making process where the people or their empowered agents take direct action dovetails nicely with constituent power, the idea that only the people have the power to create constitutional law. As I will show in chapters 4–6, an argument of this type was not only the first used to justify the procedure, but also continues to be attractive and popular to this day.

3
The Invention of Constitutional Ratification

While ratification's roles in private and international law date back to Ancient Rome and Medieval Europe respectively, its debut as a procedure of constitution-making had to wait until the eighteenth century when the practice of writing modern constitutions began. As mentioned, the Commonwealth of Virginia produced the first modern written constitution on June 29, 1776, simultaneously declaring their independence while outlining their future government.[1] This was followed by constitutions written for New Jersey, Delaware, Pennsylvania, Maryland, North Caroline, Georgia, New York, Vermont, and South Carolina over the next four years, all of which were implemented immediately following the approval stage. However, on March 20, 1780, the Constitution of Massachusetts went into effect after being accepted via town referendums, thereby becoming the first constitution ratified in history.

In this chapter I explain the origins of constitutional ratification, mainly by focusing on ratification's invention in Massachusetts in the 1770s and on a similar but unsuccessful effort to utilize the procedure in New York during the same period. I concentrate on this origin story not simply because a book on ratification warrants it, but also because, as will become clear in later chapters, those who first invented ratification articulated some of the strongest and most comprehensive arguments for the procedure.

The Massachusetts and New York experiences involved ratification via referendum. In the remainder of this chapter, I will sketch out the origins of two other prominent forms, which also took place in Early America. This includes the birth of regional ratification conventions during the drafting of the U.S. Constitution in 1787, and the creation of a polity-wide ratification convention in Georgia in 1789. More attention is paid to the Philadelphia experience because the ratification process of the U.S. Constitution is perhaps the most well-known ratification story in the world. While not as explicit, these origin stories also suggest possible justifications for ratification. Moreover, they reveal something that has been true about ratification since the beginning and helps explain one reason why it lacks a

[1] Both New Hampshire and South Carolina adopted constitutions earlier in 1776 than Virginia. However, both documents stated that they were temporary arrangements until conflict between the British and colonists ceased. Thus, I treat Virginia's constitution as the first.

Constitutional Ratification without Reason. Jeffrey A. Lenowitz, Oxford University Press. © Jeffrey A. Lenowitz 2022.
DOI: 10.1093/oso/9780198852346.003.0003

well-worked out justification: the procedure is often used for contextual reasons unrelated to its actual merits.

1. The Berkshire Constitutionalists

It was in 1778 Massachusetts that ratification first became part of the constitution-making process. The Berkshire Constitutionalists, a political faction that played an active role in the events leading up to the creation of the Massachusetts Constitution of 1780, invented the procedure. Using a method of dissent they initially pioneered to protest British rule, the Constitutionalists successfully prevented the local courts of law from sitting in Berkshire County and the surrounding towns from 1774 to 1780, effectively denying the civil authority of the newly independent government any jurisdiction in the area. They led this virtual rebellion to protest against what they saw as an illegitimate provisional government operating from Boston, to advocate for the principles of popular control of political authority, and most importantly to call for the creation of a new constitution that they would get to approve.

This period is well-traversed ground—as one historian notes, "for generations, historians . . . have been obsessed with the Massachusetts constitution of 1780"—and is covered in many treatments of Early American history and the development of American political thought.[2] Nonetheless, in this section I give a detailed history of constitution-making in Massachusetts, paying particular attention to the events that the Constitutionalists reacted to and played an active role within.

This focus is warranted because the history of the Berkshire Constitutionalists is the history of those who first came up with, argued for, and successfully implemented ratification. Their actions led to the procedure becoming the ubiquitous component of constitution-making that it is today and are thus of interest to anyone wanting to understand ratification generally. Moreover, the Constitutionalists provided normative justifications for their insistence that a new constitution be ratified. These are important, for today, nearly 250 years later, they remain the most sustained reflections on the need to ratify a constitution. However, the Constitutionalists' arguments did not come in the form of free-standing philosophical treatises and essays. Instead, their political theory and justification of ratification, described below and unpacked in chapter 5 and subsequent chapters, must be distilled from a variety of documents firmly embedded

[2] Marc W. Kruman, *Between Authority and Liberty: State Constitution Making in Revolutionary America* (University of North Carolina Press 1997) 15. Andrew McLaughlin illustrates Kruman's point at Andrew C. McLaughlin, "American History and American Democracy," (1915) 20 The American Historical Review 255–76, 264–65.

within the constitution-making events of the time, a task that requires the historical engagement here for its success.

In addition, focusing on this history has the benefit of revealing certain limitations of state constitution-making grand narratives.[3] Consider Gordon Wood's *Creation of the American Republic*, which despite its many attributes screens out state-specific political and theoretical variance by focusing on patterns of general state formation. For Massachusetts alone it filters out the early emphasis placed on ratification and overlooks the fact that higher law constitutional thinking arose in the mid-1770s, rather than a decade or two later. In addition, Wood's and similar accounts collapse the different reasons underlying the demand for ratification and constitutional conventions. Both serve to distinguish a constitution as higher law, but the call for ratification occurred earlier and, as I will show, was primarily based on a particular conception of constituent power rather than on the belief that a legislative body could not limit itself.[4]

1.1 Beginnings

For our purposes, the struggle to create a constitution for Massachusetts began on May 20, 1774, when the British parliament revised the colony's charter by passing the Massachusetts Government Act to punish colonists for their ongoing dispute with the Governor.[5] The Act's purpose was clear: as Lord North stated, it was meant "to take the executive power from the democratic part of Government."[6]

[3] See Gordon S. Wood, *The Creation of the American Republic, 1776–1787* (The University of North Carolina Press 1998) 312–42; Gordon S. Wood, "Foreword: State Constitution-Making in the American Revolution," (1992–93) 24 Rutgers Law Journal 911–26; Willi Paul Adams, *The First American Constitutions: Republican Ideology and the Making of the State Constitutions in the Revolutionary Era* (expanded edn, Rowman & Littlefield 2001) 25–95.

[4] Of course, studies focusing on early constitution-making in Massachusetts and the Berkshire Constitutionalists exist and are cited throughout this chapter and chapter 5. However, these tend to focus on the history rather than the ideas of the Constitutionalists or treat the latter in a distortive or purely descriptive manner. See Theodore M. Hammett, *The Revolutionary Ideology in Its Social Context: Berkshire County, Massachusetts 1725–1785* (Dissertation, Brandeis University 1976); Robert J. Taylor, *Western Massachusetts in the Revolution* (Brown University Press 1954); Ronald M. Peters, *The Massachusetts Constitution of 1780: A Social Compact* (The University of Massachusetts Press 1978) 29.

[5] "Massachusetts Government Act," in William MacDonald (ed.), *Select Charters and Other Documents Illustrative of American History: 1606–1775* (The MacMillan Company 1899) 122–30.

[6] Cited in Abner L. Braley, "Provisional Government of Massachusetts," in Albert Bushnell Hart (ed.), *Commonwealth History of Massachusetts*, vol. 3 (Russell & Russell 1966) 64. Before the Act, the Massachusetts government included a royally appointed Governor and Lieutenant Governor, a bicameral legislature (the General Court), and a judicial branch organized by the General Court and filled through royal appointment and local election. The lower house of the General Court was the popularly elected House of Representatives, and the upper house was the Council. Members of the Council were selected by the House and the outgoing Council. The Act eliminated terms limits for the Council and made them royal appointees, forbade town meetings without express gubernatorial consent, gave the Governor sole power to appoint and remove judges of the lower courts, and gave royally appointed sheriffs the power to choose jury members, rather than leave the decision up to town meetings. Samuel Eliot Morison, *A History of the Constitution of Massachusetts* (Wright & Potter Printing Co. 1917) 9–12.

Local dissent erupted immediately over this diminishment of popular power. In response, Governor Gage dissolved the General Court issued writs for a new assembly to be convened on October 5th.[7]

Gage's actions backfired; rather than punish dissent by depriving the colonists of governmental power, he effectively cut himself off from fully functioning local political units that continued business as usual.[8] Town governments remained in operation, committees of correspondences formed, conventions supplemented the court systems, and an increasing number of colonists began questioning the legitimacy of their now abrogated charter.[9]

The events of 1774 not only fanned the flames of dissent in the Northeastern counties and towns surrounding Boston, long the epicenter of resistance to British rule, but also awoke radicalism in the Western counties of Berkshire and Hampshire. Traditionally, due to geographic isolation, control by elite families loyal to the crown, and a general suspicion of Boston and its politics, the towns in these counties displayed relative indifference to the larger political and revolutionary questions of the day.[10] Nonetheless, some radical Whigs resided in the region, foremost of whom was the Reverend Thomas Allen, the pastor of the Congregational Church in Pittsfield and the future leader of the Berkshire Constitutionalists.[11] Allen used the opportunity to break free from the conservatism of the region's leaders and drum up support for the patriot cause. He soon headed the Pittsfield Committee of Correspondence and, along with his growing team of radical followers, traveled throughout the region advocating the revolutionary project.

Eventually, Allen and his followers engineered a form of protest that went beyond the organized condemnations of the Northeast: they physically shut down the royal courts of justice, the chief means of British administrative control at the local level.[12] In August, the town of Pittsfield petitioned the Inferior Court of

[7] Morison, *A History of the Constitution of Massachusetts*, 12.

[8] Oscar and Mary Handlin, "Introduction," in Oscar and Mary Handlin (eds.), *The Popular Sources of Political Authority* (Harvard University Press 1966) 4.

[9] Harry A. Cushing, "Political Activity of Massachusetts Towns During the Revolution," *Annual Report of the American Historical Association for the Year 1895* (Government Printing Office 1896) 105–10.

[10] Taylor, *Western Massachusetts in the Revolution*, 11–26, 77; John L. Brooke, "To the Quiet of the People: Revolutionary Settlements and Civil Unrest in Western Massachusetts, 1774–1789," (1989) 46 The William and Mary Quarterly 425–62, 435.

[11] Taylor, *Western Massachusetts in the Revolution*, 77. For biographical information on Allen, see *A Concise and Simple Narrative of the Controversy between Thomas Allen, A.M. Of Pittsfield and That Part of His Church and Congregation Which Have Lately Separated from His Pastoral Care* (Early American Imprints, Milo Smith & Co. 1809); Theodore M. Hammett, "Revolutionary Ideology in Massachusetts: Thomas Allen's "Vindication" of the Berkshire Constitutionalists, 1778," (1976) 33 The William and Mary Quarterly 514–27, 515; Frank A. DeSorbo, *Reverend Thomas Allen and Revolutionary Politics in Western Massachusetts* (Dissertation, New York University 1995); Richard D. Birdsall, "The Reverend Thomas Allen: Jeffersonian Calvinist," (1957) 30 The New England Quarterly 147–65.

[12] Allen pushed through Pittsfield and Berkshire's adoption of the non-importation agreement in June and July 1774. See DeSorbo, *Reverend Thomas Allen and Revolutionary Politics in Western*

Common Pleas not to transact any business during the term.[13] The language used in the petition betrays the political ideas and philosophy already in circulation at the time. For instance, it claims that "the people of this province fall in a State of Nature until our greavences are fully redressed by a final repeal of those injurious oppressive and unconstitutional acts. . . ."[14] Three days later, a crowd of 1500 people prevented the judges from sitting.[15] Soon after, on August 30th in the Hampshire County town of Springfield, an even larger crowd shut down the courts and forced court officials to swear not to enforce any part of the Massachusetts Government Act.[16] These were the first instances of counties overthrowing the royal courts, and patriots across the state approved and soon mimicked the Berkshiremen.[17] By September, all normal judicial procedures had ceased colony-wide.[18]

1.2 Early Resistance to the Charter-Based Government

Gage responded to "the many tumults and disorders" and the "unhappy state of the Province" by cancelling the planned convocation of the General Court and resorting to absolute military rule.[19] Representatives assembled regardless and in October formed the first of several Provincial Congresses that would govern the Commonwealth until July 1775. These bodies, lacking any constitutional or formal legal status, were meant to be temporary fixes—nothing more than a means

Massachusetts, 57–59; William Lincoln (ed.), *The Journals of Each Provincial Congress of Massachusetts in 1774 and 1775* (Dutton and Wentworth 1838) 653.

[13] Hammett, *The Revolutionary Ideology in Its Social Context: Berkshire County, Massachusetts 1725–1785*, 316. Four courts comprised the Massachusetts judicial system. Highest was the Superior Court of Judicature, which heard appeals cases and had original jurisdiction for major criminal and land-title cases. Next were the quarterly county courts. The General Sessions of the Peace, also known as the Court of Quarter Sessions, handled civil appeals and had original jurisdiction for cases concerning large sums and ordinary land titles. The Inferior Court of Common Please was one of the main governing bodies in each county, having jurisdiction over all but the most serious criminal cases and carrying out numerous administrative functions. Finally, the lowest courts were the Justices of the Peace, which handled minor violations of the peace. Taylor, *Western Massachusetts in the Revolution*, 27–30.

[14] Cited in J.E.A. Smith, *The History of Pittsfield (Berkshire Country), Massachusetts* (Lee and Shepard 1869) 198.

[15] Thomas Gage, "By the Governour—A Proclamation, September 18, 1774," in Peter Force (ed.), *American Archives: Fourth Series* (Northern Illinois University Libraries 1837) 809–10. See also Taylor, *Western Massachusetts in the Revolution*, 75–76.

[16] Steven E. Patterson, *Political Parties in Revolutionary Massachusetts* (University of Wisconsin Press 1973) 99.

[17] Braley, "Provisional Government of Massachusetts," 76; Smith, *The History of Pittsfield (Berkshire Country), Massachusetts*, 196, 325.

[18] Patterson, *Political Parties in Revolutionary Massachusetts*, 100.

[19] Gage, "By the Governour—A Proclamation, September 18, 1774," 809. See also Smith, *The History of Pittsfield (Berkshire Country), Massachusetts*, 326.

of loosely organizing the towns and linking them to the Continental Congress and to Gage while talks with the British continued.

However, the early battles at Concord and Lexington made reconciliation with the crown unlikely and the need for a more stable and comprehensive government became clear.[20] On May 5th the Second Provincial Congress declared that "no obedience ought, in future, to be paid" to Governor Gage. Eleven days later they applied to the Continental Congress for advice on how to set up a more permanent government.[21] In June, Congress responded, recommending that the colony "conform, as near as may be, to the spirit and substance of the charter," while treating the Governor and Lieutenant Governor "as absent and their offices vacant."[22] Though it essentially amounted to an admission that the unrevised charter remained valid, colonial leaders followed these recommendations precisely.[23] The Third Provincial Congress dissolved, new elections were held, and the first House of Representatives of the State of Massachusetts Bay convened on July 19, 1775. Shortly after, its members chose a new council to exercise gubernatorial powers in the absence of a governor.

Revamping the old charter displeased many, for it shackled the commonwealth to an ill-suited royal document that had been the chief instrument of its oppression. Moreover, the resultant government was inefficient and gave the power to appoint well-paid military and court officials to the General Court rather than local units, as was the custom under the Provincial Congresses.[24] Discontent only increased when, five months later, the Continental Congress recommended that South Carolina and New Hampshire create new governments from scratch.[25] To many in Massachusetts, it appeared that other states were being offered the opportunity to create their own government, while they were left with a recreated elite-driven political framework that drew its only authority from the very thing they were fighting against. Mild protests spread throughout the commonwealth, with dissension reaching its peak in Berkshire and Hampshire, where Allen and his followers transformed from simple patriots to the Berkshire Constitutionalists,

[20] Handlin, "Introduction," 9. See also "Letter to Continental Congress, May 16, 1775," in Lincoln (ed.), *The Journals of Each Provincial Congress of Massachusetts in 1774 and 1775*, 230.

[21] Lincoln (ed.), *The Journals of Each Provincial Congress of Massachusetts in 1774 and 1775*, 193; Handlin, "Introduction," 9.

[22] Worthington Chauncey Ford and others (eds.), *Journals of the Continental Congress, 1774–1789*, vol. 2 (U.S. Government Printing Office 1904–37) 83–84. See also John Adams, *The Works of John Adams*, vol. 3 (Little, Brown, and Co. 1851) 16–17; Edward M. Hartwell, "Referenda in Massachusetts and Boston," (1910) 12 Publications of the American Statistical Association 230–73, 245.

[23] The Continental Congress recommended returning to the 1691 charter, and therefore undid the changes of the Massachusetts Government Act. See Kruman, *Between Authority and Liberty: State Constitution Making in Revolutionary America*, 12.

[24] According to its critics, the General Court initially picked their friends or themselves for these lucrative posts. Morison, *A History of the Constitution of Massachusetts*, 10, 13; Braley, "Provisional Government of Massachusetts," 72–73.

[25] Smith, *The History of Pittsfield (Berkshire Country), Massachusetts*, 331. See also Taylor, *Western Massachusetts in the Revolution*, 79; Morison, *A History of the Constitution of Massachusetts*, 12–13.

a quasi-political party that quickly made its opposition to the new government known throughout the state.[26]

In December 1775, the Constitutionalists convinced a convention of the Berkshire Committee of Correspondences to formally refuse to support the provisional government.[27] Soon after, a town convention in Pittsfield successfully closed down the county courts. These actions echoed those taken in Berkshire a year earlier, but now Allen's group opposed the home-grown provisional government, rather than British authorities.[28] To explain their actions, the Pittsfield convention sent an explanation, written by Allen himself, to the General Court.[29]

This *Pittsfield Memorial* explains the Constitutionalists' "abhorrence of that Constitution now adopting in this province," attributes its defects primarily to the replacement of local control with the "nominating to office by those in power," and argues that there is no reason to create a government on top of the reviled charter, for the Continental Congress's advice was open to interpretation and invalidated by that given to South Carolina and New Hampshire. Allen goes on to make two demands: create an elected Governor and Lieutenant Governor and give local units sole power to appoint individuals to civil and military offices.[30]

These demands, and other criticisms articulated by the Constitutionalists in the document, derived from their straightforward application of revolutionary rhetoric and theory. The Berkshire Constitutionalists wanted independence immediately, so they called for the creation of an elected executive, thereby rejecting the pretense that the new government operated in the temporary absence of the royal Governor.[31] They were avid participants in a revolution buoyed by a commitment to popular sovereignty, so they rejected the General Court's decision to appoint judicial and military officials without local consultation. Moreover, they shared in

[26] Despite their internal protests, the Constitutionalists were strong patriots heavily invested in the war. See Hammett, *The Revolutionary Ideology in Its Social Context: Berkshire County, Massachusetts 1725–1785*, 73–81, 375; Richard D. Birdsall, "The Reverend Thomas Allen: Jeffersonian Calvinist," (1957) 30 The New England Quarterly 147–65, 149.

[27] "Resolves of the Stockbridge Convention, December 15, 1775," in Robert J. Taylor (ed.), *Massachusetts, Colony to Commonwealth: Documents on the Formation of Its Constitution, 1775–1780* (The University of North Carolina Press 1961). See also Taylor, *Western Massachusetts in the Revolution*, 80; Alexander J. Cella, "The People of Massachusetts, a New Republic, and the Constitution of 1780: The Evolution of Principles of Popular Control of Political Authority, 1774–1780," (1980) 14 Suffolk University Law Review 975–1006, 987; Patterson, *Political Parties in Revolutionary Massachusetts*, 136–37.

[28] According to Smith, the judiciary and civil magistracy were a strategic target of dissent, for "their obstruction would sufficiently arrest attention at Boston, while it would least embarrass the State in its operations against the enemy, and the people in their efforts to obtain a constitution." Smith, *The History of Pittsfield (Berkshire Country), Massachusetts*, 338.

[29] Hammett, *The Revolutionary Ideology in Its Social Context: Berkshire County, Massachusetts 1725–1785*, 323.

[30] Thomas Allen, "Pittsfield Memorial, December 26, 1775," in Oscar and Mary Handlin (eds.), *The Popular Sources of Political Authority* (Harvard University Press 1966) 61–64.

[31] Robert J. Taylor, "Introduction and Notes," in Robert J. Taylor (ed.), *Massachusetts, Colony to Commonwealth: Documents on the Formation of Its Constitution, 1775–1780* (University of North Carolina Press 1961) 14.

the general conspiratorial paranoia that served as an accelerant for the revolution across the colonies, as they tended to see, as Bailyn describes it, "overwhelming evidence . . . that they were faced with conspirators against liberty" on all sides.[32] Thus, they viewed the appointment of former colonial power holders and members of the sitting legislature to coveted high offices with suspicion.

1.3 The General Court Tries to Appease

The Berkshire Constitutionalists continued their dissent into 1776, growing in strength and influence. A February meeting of Berkshire committees, which Allen called and opened by reading aloud Paine's recently published *Common Sense*, resulted in the forced closing of the Court of Quarter Sessions, and the stripping of commissions from all recently appointed civil officers.[33] One month later, Allen similarly convinced twenty-eight towns in Hampshire County to forcefully close their Court of Quarter Sessions.[34]

This continued and increasing opposition to the provisional government, as well as the petitions sent to the General Court from Western anti-Constitutionalists seeking relief from these "unthinking, rash, and designing men," prompted the General Court to take further action. In May, they lowered judicial fee schedules and eliminated mention of the crown in its commissions.[35] By making the courts less expensive, and dropping the pretense of British authority, they hoped to reopen the courts by appeasing the Constitutionalists.[36]

[32] Bernard Bailyn, *The Ideological Origins of the American Revolution* (Harvard University Press 1992) 95. Thomas Allen's remarks in the *Pittsfield Memorial* map onto this revolutionary logic. For instance, he writes that "a secret poison has been spread thro' out all our Towns and great Multitudes have been secured for the corrupt Designs of an abandoned Administration." Allen, "Pittsfield Memorial, December 26, 1775," 62. See also Hammett, "Revolutionary Ideology in Massachusetts: Thomas Allen's 'Vindication' of the Berkshire Constitutionalists, 1778," 519. This article contains an introduction by Hammett and a previously unpublished 1778 essay by Thomas Allen titled, "A Vindication of the County of Birkshire in their Principles and Conduct, against the False and Maelovent Aspersions Cast on them by their Enemies, Respecting the present Mode of Government as it is Exercised in the State of Massachusetts Bay." Here and in later citations, I refer to Allen's text, not Hammett's introduction, when citing this source.

[33] Taylor, *Western Massachusetts in the Revolution*, 41; Smith, *The History of Pittsfield (Berkshire Country), Massachusetts*, 347. For a hostile report of Allen's speech to the townspeople of Richmond, see "Report of a Lecture by Thomas Allen on February 18, 1776," in Oscar and Mary Handlin (eds.), *The Popular Sources of Political Authority* (Harvard University Press 1966).

[34] Taylor, *Western Massachusetts in the Revolution*, 86. See also "A Letter from the Chesterfield Committee of Correspondence, March 4, 1776," in Robert J. Taylor (ed.), *Massachusetts, Colony to Commonwealth: Documents on the Formation of Its Constitution, 1775–1780* (The University of North Carolina Press 1961); "From the Proceedings of a Convention in Hampshire, March 11, 1776," in Robert J. Taylor (ed.), *Massachusetts, Colony to Commonwealth: Documents on the Formation of Its Constitution, 1775–1780* (The University of North Carolina Press 1961).

[35] For an account of local opponents, see Hammett, *The Revolutionary Ideology in Its Social Context: Berkshire County, Massachusetts 1725–1785*, 342–99.

[36] Taylor, *Western Massachusetts in the Revolution*, 86.

These efforts fell on deaf ears. The General Court acted too late, for by this time the Constitutionalists had abandoned their institutional focus for a broader demand: abandon the Royal Charter and establish a new constitution.[37] As Allen explains:

> [I]f Commissions should be recalled and the Kings Name struck out of them, if the Fee Table be reduced never so low, and multitudes of other things be done to still the people all is to us as Nothing whilst the foundation is unfixed the Corner stone of Government unlaid. We have heared much of Governments being founded in Compact. What Compact has been formed as the foundation of Government in this province?[38]

Until a new constitution, until this "cornerstone of government" be laid, no manner of appeasement would convince the Constitutionalists to cease their revolt.

These words appear in the *Pittsfield Petitions*, written by Allen and sent to the General Court on May 29, 1776 to further justify the Constitutionalists' dissent. Allen begins the document reaffirming that the townspeople "by no means object to the most speedy institution of Legal Government," being as "earnestly desirous as any others of this great Blessing." He then moves on to outlining their theory underlying the dissent.

Drawing from social contract theory,[39] Allen asserts that "the people are the fountain of power," that the "dissolution of the power of Great Britain over the Colonies" sent them into "a state of Nature," and that the only way to exit such a state and enjoy civil government capable of warding off "Tyranny and Despotism" is "the formation of a fundamental Constitution as the Basis and ground work for Legislation."[40] He then notes that "a Representative Body may form, but cannot impose said fundamental Constitution upon a people," for "the Approbation of the Majority of the people ... is absolutely necessary to give Life and being to it."

[37] Brooke, "To the Quiet of the People: Revolutionary Settlements and Civil Unrest in Western Massachusetts, 1774–1789," 439.

[38] "Pittsfield Petitions, May 29, 1776," in Oscar and Mary Handlin (eds.), *The Popular Sources of Political Authority* (Harvard University Press 1966) 92.

[39] I explain the details of this theory in chapter 5, section 2. Note that while I use "social contract theory" and "contractualism" throughout this text when referring to the Berkshire Constitutionalists and Early America, I do so because these are the terms used to describe the intellectual tradition today. This is anachronistic, for in the late eighteenth century the phrase "social compact" was much more common. Neither the Berkshire Constitutionalists nor their favorite author Locke used the phrase the "social contract." See Donald S. Lutz, "From Covenant to Constitution in American Political Thought," (1980) 10 Publius 101–33; Donald S. Lutz, *The Origins of American Constitutionalism* (Louisiana State University Press 1988) 18–34; J.S. Maloy, *The Colonial American Origins of Modern Democratic Thought* (Cambridge University Press 2008) 140–70.

[40] "Pittsfield Petitions, May 29, 1776," 90. This supports Kruman's claim, contra Wood and Adams, that "at the beginning of the Revolution, citizens distinguished readily between constitutional and statutory law and believed that the people themselves created and restricted government." Kruman, *Between Authority and Liberty: State Constitution Making in Revolutionary America*, 32.

He ends the petition making a single demand: "Your petitioners beg leave there to Request that this Honourable Body would form a fundamental Constitution for this province ... and that said Constitution be sent abroad for the Approbation of the Majority of the people in this Colony."[41] Here, Allen demands, for the first time in history, a ratification referendum. He conceptualizes it as the necessary means through which residents of Massachusetts can authorize a constitution and make it their own; a task that organized or constituted political entities cannot do by themselves.

The general demand for a new constitution spread throughout Massachusetts, gaining support from the Continental Congress' May 10th and 15th recommendation that the colonies establish governments in which all powers were to be "exerted under the authority of the people of the colonies," and from the Declaration of Independence promulgated two months later; both of which appeared to put the legitimacy of anything but a locally created constitution into question.[42] In response, on September 17, 1776 the General Court asked the towns for permission to transform itself into a constituent legislature and create a constitution, which would "be made public for the Inspection and Perusal of the inhabitants, before the Ratification thereof by the Assembly."[43]

Several things about this request followed local norms and traditions. The offering of inspection privileges had precedent, for since at least 1639 the various governments of Massachusetts Bay periodically submitted fundamental laws and important questions to the people for review and, on occasion, comment.[44] By assigning drafting and approval responsibilities for the constitution to itself, the General Court followed their neighboring colonies who had also used existing governmental bodies to create their new constitutions.[45] And, the use of "ratification" to mean formal acceptance, rather than to refer to a specific procedure, was

[41] "Pittsfield Petitions, May 29, 1776," 90–93.

[42] Worthington Chauncey Ford and others (eds.), *Journals of the Continental Congress, 1774–1789*, vol. 4 (U.S. Government Printing Office 1906) 342 and 357. See also Adams, *The First American Constitutions: Republican Ideology and the Making of the State Constitutions in the Revolutionary Era*, 61–62.

[43] "Resolution of the House of Representatives, September 17, 1776," in Oscar and Mary Handlin (eds.), *The Popular Sources of Political Authority* (Harvard University Press, 1966 1966) 99. See also Gaspar C. Bacon, "The State Constitution (1777–1780)," in Albert Bushnell Hart (ed.), *Commonwealth History of Massachusetts*, vol. 3 (Russell & Russell 1966) 183.

[44] For instance, in 1639 the General Court sent potential legislation to towns for review and comment by local elders, and more recently they had asked the towns for their opinion on the Declaration of Independence. See Charles Sumner Lobingier, *The People's Law or Popular Participation in Law-Making: From Ancient Folk-Moot to Modern Referendum* (The Macmillan Company 1909) 79; Hartwell, "Referenda in Massachusetts and Boston," 249.

[45] For example, as mentioned, earlier in 1776 provincial legislatures created and enacted new constitutions without popular review in South Carolina, New Hampshire, Virginia, and New Jersey. See Adams, *The First American Constitutions: Republican Ideology and the Making of the State Constitutions in the Revolutionary Era*, 66–72; Kruman, *Between Authority and Liberty: State Constitution Making in Revolutionary America*, 20–24.

common at the time.[46] However, two things are notable. First, the plan to combine the General Court and the Council into one body, a constituent legislature, was in fact unique, and suggests that even the General Court considered the normal bicameral legislature insufficient to create a constitution.[47] Second, and most critically for our purposes, by giving themselves final approval power, the General Court ignored one of the Berkshire Constitutionalists' central demands: that the people have final say over their constitution. That is, they rejected the inclusion of a ratification procedure.

At least 132 towns responded to the 1776 request.[48] Though ninety-two towns, a majority, approved it, the overall response displeased the General Court. Many towns did not respond, a significant number dissented, and a majority of the approving towns did so only under certain conditions. Most of the dissenting towns agreed on the need for a new constitution but objected to the proposal for several reasons. Six towns claimed that the members of the General Court did not have the power to create a constitution for they "were never elected by the people for that purpose."[49] Thirty-one towns took issue with the composition of the House, claiming that the representation was "very unequal and unsafe."[50] Eleven towns argued that it was a bad time to make a new constitution for many potential voters were off fighting the war and the General Court had more pressing matters to deal with.

Acton and Concord made the more sophisticated argument that an effective constitution cannot be created by the body it purports to limit, for constitutions are meant to secure certain rights and privileges from government encroachment,

[46] Donald S. Lutz (ed.), *Colonial Origins of the American Constitution: A Documentary History* (Liberty Fund 1998) 71, 164, 351, 386; Samuel Johnson, *A Dictionary of the English Language* (3rd edn, W.G. Jones 1768); *The Statutes at Large, from the 20th Year of the Reign of King George II to the 30th Year of the Reign of King George II*, vol. 7 (Mark Basket 1764).

[47] Kruman, *Between Authority and Liberty: State Constitution Making in Revolutionary America*, 30.

[48] Towns responded to requests from the General Court by sending records of their voting results. These records frequently included an explanation for the overall decision reached by each town and are known as "Returns." Below, all claims regarding the results of the 1776 request stem from my own analysis of the 126 surviving returns collected and printed by the Handlins, and six other returns that are either described or printed in other sources. See "Returns of the Towns on the Resolution of September 17, 1776," in Oscar and Mary Handlin (eds.), *The Popular Sources of Political Authority* (Harvard University Press 1966); Hammett, *The Revolutionary Ideology in Its Social Context: Berkshire County, Massachusetts 1725–1785*, 327; Harry A. Cushing, *History of the Transition from Provincial to Commonwealth Government in Massachusetts* (Columbia University 1896) 189; Smith, *The History of Pittsfield (Berkshire Country), Massachusetts*, 356.

[49] Return of Stoughton in "Returns of the Towns on the Resolution of September 17, 1776," 107. See also Lexington's Return at ibid., 150.

[50] Ibid., 165. A May 1776 law reformed the representative system and addressed the basis for many of these objections but had yet to circulate throughout the colony. See "An Act for More Equal Representation, May 4, 1776," in Oscar and Mary Handlin (eds.), *The Popular Sources of Political Authority* (Harvard University Press, 1966 1966) 201–4; J.R. Pole, *Political Representation in England and the Origins of the American Republic* (MacMillan 1966) 172–90; "Resolutions of an Essex County Convention, April 25, 1776" in Robert J. Taylor (ed.), *Massachusetts, Colony to Commonwealth: Documents on the Formation of Its Constitution, 1775–1780* (The University of North Carolina Press 1961).

and "the Same Body that forms a Constitution have of Consequence a power to alter it," and therefore "a constitution alterable by the Supreme Legislative is no Security at all."[51] Thirty-three towns joined them in embracing the logical corollary of this objection by requesting "a Convention be Chosen by the Inhabitants of the Several Towns and Districts in this State to form and Establish a Constitution for this State."[52] This request marked the first mention of a specially elected constitutional convention, which some consider to be "the most distinctive institutional contribution ... the American Revolutionaries made to Western politics."[53]

Seventy-four towns made a final objection, claiming that the General Court erred by not including popular ratification in their proposal. Despite the argument being of Constitutionalist origin, the most striking examples of this objection are found in the returns from Boston and Lexington. Boston claims that, "We apprehend that the People have some higher privileges, than a bare Inspection and Perusal of the Constitution under which they are to live."[54] Similarly, Lexington's return reads: "that ... it does not appear from thence, that there is any just Provision made for the Inhabitants, as Towns, or Societies, to express their approbation, or the Contrary, in Order to Such Ratification by the Assembly."[55]

The complaint over the lack of ratification was *the most popular objection* to the draft constitution. However, previous scholars overlooked this, likely because most of the towns voiced their dissent indirectly. In fact, only twenty-four of the towns that asserted the need for ratification actually dissented to the General Court's 1776 request. The remaining fifty-two towns approved the request, but only under the condition that ratification took place, frequently by repeating an altered version of the General Court's language. For example, the Hampshire towns of Greenfield and Colrain wrote: "that the same [draft constitution] be made public for the inspection perusal and *approbation* of the people before the ratification thereof."[56] Conway specified the need of obtaining the "Consent or Rejection" of each town, while Sheffield demanded that the constitution only be accepted if "agreed to by the People att Large."[57] Thus, a majority of the towns in Massachusetts deemed the

[51] "Return of Concord," in "Returns of the Towns on the Resolution of September 17, 1776," 152.

[52] Ibid., 157. Acton and Concord were the only two towns to make the request for a constitutional convention in their individual voting returns. However, a convention representing thirty-five Worcester County towns published a resolution on November 26, 1776, indicating their desire for a convention if possible. I counted these in my calculations, but only counted those towns whose original votes are either included in the published returns or summarized in the resolution.

[53] Wood, *The Creation of the American Republic, 1776–1787*, 342. Roger S. Hoar was perhaps the first to pinpoint Acton as being the source of the constitutional convention idea. He made this claim in opposition to Dodd, who falsely attributed the idea to a New Hampshire grants meeting in Hanover in 1777. Roger Sherman Hoar, *Constitutional Conventions, Their Nature, Powers, and Limitations* (Little, Brown 1917) 7; Walter F. Dodd, *Revision and Amendment of State Constitutions* (John Hopkins Press 1910) 6. See also Adams, *The First American Constitutions: Republican Ideology and the Making of the State Constitutions in the Revolutionary Era*, 86.

[54] "Boston Town Records," in "Returns of the Towns on the Resolution of September 17, 1776," 136.

[55] "Return of the Town of Lexington," in ibid., 150.

[56] Ibid., 103.

[57] Ibid., 103–5.

mere opportunity of perusal and inspection insufficient, and only a bare majority of sixty-eight towns approved the 1776 request. By 1776, the central tenet of the Berkshire Constitutionalists—*that only the direct consent of the majority can give life to a constitution*—had begun to gain widespread acceptance.

1.4 First Ratifications: Defeat and Success

On May 5, 1777, after months of inaction, the General Court tried again. They announced that the next session of the Court would create a new constitution, and asked each town to instruct and empower their future delegates to the House to meet "in one Body with the Council, to form such a Constitution of Government."[58] This request addressed prior complaints about delegates being unauthorized for constitution-making, and assuaged concerns about representation by making sure that the May 1776 reapportionment law had taken effect state-wide.[59] The General Court also responded to the Constitutionalists' demand by announcing plans for public ratification, with the public being defined as "at least two Thirds of those [men] who are free and twenty-one Years of Age, belonging to this State and present in the several meetings ...."[60] Specifically, each town was to hold a special meeting during which they would evaluate the draft constitution and draw up "a Return of their Approbation or Disapprobation." These returns were to included vote tallies, which the General Court would use to calculate whether an overall 2/3 majority had been reached. According to our typology, this procedure is ratification by national referendum, as it involves citizens voting directly on the constitution, and their votes being aggregated, even if this voting takes place within townhalls.

Most of the towns approved the proposal and sent delegates to Boston. The newly elected General Court resolved itself into a constituent legislature in June and submitted a constitution to the towns on February 28, 1778.[61] This was the first instance of ratification in history, and while marking a victory for the Constitutionalists, it was short lived. The first use of ratification also led to the first instance of constitutional rejection. The constitution failed by a spectacular margin of five to one,[62] with towns giving a wide range of reasons for their

[58] "Resolve of May 5, 1777," in Oscar and Mary Handlin (eds.), *The Popular Sources of Political Authority* (Harvard University Press 1966).

[59] Ibid.

[60] Bacon, "The State Constitution (1777–1780)," 184. See also "Resolve of May 5, 1777," 174–75. This marked an expansion of suffrage, for previously property qualifications regulated voter eligibility. See Adams, *The First American Constitutions: Republican Ideology and the Making of the State Constitutions in the Revolutionary Era*, 87. It is not uncommon for ratification provisions to specify expanded suffrage.

[61] "Journal of the Convention, June 17, 1777–March 6, 1778," in Oscar and Mary Handlin (eds.), *The Popular Sources of Political Authority* (Harvard University Press 1966); Taylor, "Introduction and Notes," 48–49; Morison, *A History of the Constitution of Massachusetts*, 15, 20.

[62] According to Morison, the count was 9,972 nays to 2,083 yeas. Morison, *A History of the Constitution of Massachusetts*, 16.

disapproval.[63] The most famous criticism is memorialized in Theophilus Parsons' *The Essex Result*, which provides an excellent summary of many political principles in circulation at the time. It focuses, for instance, on the lack of a Bill of Rights, insufficient separation of powers, and the unfairness of the proposed system of representation.[64] The Western towns criticized the proposed constitution from a more populist viewpoint, focusing on property requirements for the franchise, the appointment of officers by the governor and council, and the use of lifetime appointments for judges.[65]

The Berkshire Constitutionalists remained pertinacious, keeping the courts shut down in the Western counties, ignoring orders from the General Court to desist, and even going so far as to establish their own temporary judiciary.[66] In August 1778, the Constitutionalists sent the General Court another explanatory document. After defending the county against further charges of disloyalty and anarchy, and affirming that the courts would remain closed, this "*Berkshire County Remonstrance*" demanded that the General Court convoke a constitutional convention, "a special convention of Delegates from each Town in this State, for the purpose of forming a Bill of Rights and a Constitution or Form of Government," and even threatened secession in the absence of action.[67]

Note that this demand did not represent a new interest in the theoretical advantages of conventions—it completely lacks the principled justifications of other Constitutionalist writings—but instead seems indicative of the growing opinion that the General Court had no interest in creating a new constitution. Such thoughts were fueled by rumors circulating the commonwealth, such as the one expressed by a convention of Hampshire towns: "We Fear that there is Designing men in this State that Intends by Delaying the Forming a Bill of Rights and a free Constitution to Lull People to Sleep, or Fatigue them other ways so as to obtain a Constitution to their minds, Calculated to Answer their own Ends and wicked

63 "Returns of the Towns on the Constitution of 1778," in Oscar and Mary Handlin (eds.), *The Popular Sources of Political Authority* (Harvard University Press 1966); Morison, *A History of the Constitution of Massachusetts*, 16; Handlin, "Introduction," 22. Ackerman's assertion that the constitution failed because "the town meetings ... had insisted on state conventions to propose constitutions," lacks historical support. The returns of 1778, like those of 1776, reveal a plurality of reasons for rejection, only a few of which concern the lack of a constitutional convention. Bruce A. Ackerman, *We the People: Transformations* (Belknap Press of Harvard University Press 1998) 82.

64 Theophilus Parsons, "The Essex Result, 1778," in Oscar and Mary Handlin (eds.), *The Popular Sources of Political Authority* (Harvard University Press 1966); Taylor, *Western Massachusetts in the Revolution*, 88.

65 Taylor, *Western Massachusetts in the Revolution*, 88–90. DeSorbo claims that Allen saw *The Essex Result* as confirmation that eastern merchants were bent on preventing the erosion of their power. DeSorbo, "Reverend Thomas Allen and Revolutionary Politics in Western Massachusetts," 132. See also Smith, *The History of Pittsfield (Berkshire Country), Massachusetts*, 360.

66 Smith, *The History of Pittsfield (Berkshire Country), Massachusetts*, 359, 381. Hampshire County eventually allowed their courts to reopen in December 1777, due to the promise of a new constitution, but courts in Berkshire remained closed until 1780.

67 "Berkshire County Remonstrance, August 26, 1778," in Oscar and Mary Handlin (eds.), *The Popular Sources of Authority* (Harvard University Press 1966) 366–67.

Purposes."[68] Thus, in the Remonstrance, the Constitutionalists likely joined the growing number of people who thought the only means to a constitution, or at least to a people's constitution, would be the circumvention of the General Court.

Eventually, the General Court sent an investigating committee to Berkshire, which returned to Boston bearing the "*Statement of Berkshire County Representatives*," written again by Thomas Allen and dated November 17, 1778.[69] In it, Allen neither mentions a convention nor threatens secession, but instead repeats and enlarges his core contractual arguments—that the people are the fountain of power, that a constitution is the foundation of government and legislation, and that only the ratification of the people can give life to it. However, he makes one significant addition: a claim that the right to ratify a constitution is unalienable, and that attempting to give it away necessarily harms the people.[70] This unalienable right, as I discuss in chapters 5 and 7, is fundamentally linked to the suspicions expressed in the *Berkshire County Remonstrance*, in that political elites not only lack the power to create a constitution according to Allen, but allowing them to do so is to put everyone in danger. Ratification was needed, then, as a way of checking this potentially corrupt elite. This addition marks the culmination of Constitutionalist thought and the completion of their central theory of ratification.

On February 19, 1779, the House asked the towns of Massachusetts if they wanted to "have a new Constitution of Form of Government Made," and if so whether they wanted to "empower their Representatives ... to vote for the calling of a state Convention," the product of which would once again be distributed to the towns for ratification.[71] Though the strongest response came from their stronghold—every town in Hampshire and Berkshire County answered in the affirmative to both questions—the Constitutionalists did not reopen the courts.[72] Instead, hoping to avoid legitimating the General Court in the event of another constitutional rejection, the Constitutionalists kept the courts closed throughout the year.[73]

[68] "Opinions of Hampshire County Towns, March 30, 1779," in Oscar and Mary Handlin (eds.), *The Popular Sources of Political Authority* (Harvard University Press 1966) 386.

[69] Smith, *The History of Pittsfield (Berkshire Country), Massachusetts*, 381; J.E.A. Smith, "Chapter XIX: Town of Pittsfield (Continued)," in Thomas Cushing (ed.), *History of Berkshire County, Massachusetts, with Biographical Sketches of Its Prominent Men*, vol. 2 (J.B. Beers & Co. 1885) 304; DeSorbo, "Reverend Thomas Allen and Revolutionary Politics in Western Massachusetts," 138–39.

[70] "Statement of Berkshire County Representatives, November 17, 1778," in Oscar and Mary Handlin (eds.), *The Popular Sources of Authority* (Harvard University Press 1966) 375.

[71] "Resolve on the Question of a Constitution, February 20, 1779," in Oscar and Mary Handlin (eds.), *The Popular Sources of Political Authority* (Harvard University Press 1966) 383.

[72] Cella, "The People of Massachusetts, a New Republic, and the Constitution of 1780: The Evolution of Principles of Popular Control of Political Authority, 1774–1780," 996. For a table summarizing the Berkshire and Hampshire returns, see "Returns of the Towns on Resolves of February 20, 1779," in Oscar and Mary Handlin (eds.), *The Popular Sources of Political Authority* (Harvard University Press 1966) 388–90.

[73] Taylor, *Western Massachusetts in the Revolution*, 96. See also "A Berkshire Convention Addresses the Superior Court, May 3, 1779," in Robert J. Taylor (ed.), *Massachusetts, Colony to Commonwealth: Documents on the Formation of Its Constitution, 1775–1780* (The University of North Carolina Press 1961) 110.

Following a positive response to their request, the General Court called for the election of convention delegates in June 1779.[74] Approximately 300 delegates assembled in Boston on September 1, 1779, and the Massachusetts Constitutional Convention began. A small subcommittee consisting of Samuel Adams, James Bowdoin, and John Adams created the first draft of the constitution, with the latter doing most of the writing.[75] In the following two sessions of the convention, delegates debated and revised this draft in a process described by John Adams as "Locke, Sidney, and Rousseau and De Mably reduced to practice."[76]

In February and early March, the delegates discussed the procedural details of ratification.[77] Unknowingly beginning a tradition of constitution-making bodies diverging from the constraints set by their creators, the delegates did not even consider the procedures described by the General Court in its 1779 resolve, which gave itself responsibility for tallying the votes and enacting the constitution if approved.[78]

Rather, after much confused debate, the convention presented the following scheme: copies of the constitution would be sent to each town, discussed in town meetings, and all who qualified (freemen, twenty-one years or older) would vote on each clause. The towns would send these voting records, including any objections to each rejected clause, to the convention for tabulation. Delegates would either implement the constitution if all clauses obtained a two-thirds majority or alter the constitution to conform "to the Sentiments of two thirds of the Voters throughout the State" and then implement this revised version.[79] This clause by clause voting procedure appears to be a final contribution by the Berkshire Constitutionalists, for both Pittsfield and Williamstown ordered their convention delegates to push for something similar.[80]

[74] "Returns of the Towns on Resolves of February 20, 1779."

[75] Morison, *A History of the Constitution of Massachusetts*, 28–29; Cella, "The People of Massachusetts, a New Republic, and the Constitution of 1780: The Evolution of Principles of Popular Control of Political Authority, 1774–1780," 998. See also Samuel Eliot Morison, "The Struggle over the Adoption of the Constitution of Massachusetts, 1780," Massachusetts Historical Society Proceedings, vol. L (Massachusetts Historical Society 1917) 356.

[76] Cited in Handlin, "Introduction," 24. The bulk of the revisions took place in the third session of the convention, from late January to early March, when a harsh winter reduced the number of delegates to a maximum of eighty-two members.

[77] *Journal of the Convention for Framing a Constitution of Government for the State of Massachusetts Bay, from the Commencement of Their First Session, September 1, 1779, to the Close of Their Last Session, June 16, 1780.* (Dutton and Wentworth, Printers to the State 1832) 158–69.

[78] "The Call for a Convention, June 1779," in Oscar and Mary Handlin (eds.), *The Popular Sources of Political Authority* (Harvard University Press 1966). For a discussion of the tendency of constitution-makers to buck upstream directives, see Jon Elster, *Ulysses Unbound* (Cambridge University Press 2000) 107–10.

[79] *Journal of the Convention for Framing a Constitution of Government for the State of Massachusetts Bay, from the Commencement of Their First Session, September 1, 1779, to the Close of Their Last Session, June 16, 1780*, 168–69. Morison provides an excellent discussion of the debate regarding ratification procedures in Morison, "The Struggle over the Adoption of the Constitution of Massachusetts, 1780," 358–63.

[80] "Votes of Towns in Choosing Delegates, July–October 1779," in Oscar and Mary Handlin (eds.), *The Popular Sources of Political Authority* (Harvard University Press 1966) 412, 414.

Regardless of its source, this was an ill-founded ratification procedure. Its deficiencies are numerous. For instance, the plan for altering constitutional provisions approved by less than two-thirds of those voting neglects the possibility that an altered provision might no longer be acceptable to those who originally approved it. Moreover, it also fails to consider that individuals and towns might reject a proposal for conflicting reasons, making it impossible to create a provision congruent with supermajority will.

As it turned out, the convention never faced these sorts of complications because they had to deal with a more basic problem: many towns failed to follow directions. For instance, Hancock only reported voting results for three amended clauses and for a vote taken on the entire constitution as amended. Hadley reported the votes correctly for approved clauses, but gave the voting results on amended versions of defeated clauses, rather than on the original defeated clauses themselves.[81] Charlemont, Windsor, Rutland, and others only reported the results of a single vote on an amended version of the constitution.[82] Other towns, such as Groton, submitted complete voting returns but also voted that they would drop their objections and accept the original provisions if two-thirds of the state approved of them.[83]

When the committee appointed by the convention to tabulate the 181 voting returns began their work, they almost certainly came to a simple conclusion: it was impossible to determine whether each provision of the constitution obtained 2/3 approval. The committee, with eventual approval of the convention, solved this problem with "political jugglery," ignoring votes in favor of amended clauses or treated them as supporting the unaltered versions, and counting votes such as Groton's as being in favor of the original constitution.[84] This means, as Morison notes, "that in computing the vote for a given article the returns of practically all the towns that opposed it were either counted in favor of it or not counted at all."[85]

In this way, the committee "found" a two-thirds majority in favor of each article.[86] On June 15, 1780, the convention voted that "the People of the State of Massachusetts Bay have accepted of the Constitution" and on October 25th the

[81] "Returns of the Towns on the Constitution of 1780," in Oscar and Mary Handlin (eds.), *The Popular Sources of Political Authority* (Harvard University Press 1966) 478, 563.

[82] Ibid., 347–48, 505, and 866.

[83] Ibid., 650.

[84] Morison, "The Struggle over the Adoption of the Constitution of Massachusetts, 1780," 396–99; Morison, *A History of the Constitution of Massachusetts*, 21–22; Bacon, "The State Constitution (1777–1780)," 207–8; *Journal of the Convention for Framing a Constitution of Government for the State of Massachusetts Bay, from the Commencement of Their First Session, September 1, 1779, to the Close of Their Last Session, June 16, 1780*, 176–77.

[85] Morison, "The Struggle over the Adoption of the Constitution of Massachusetts, 1780," 398–99.

[86] Most of the constitution likely received supermajority support, for the juggling only seems to have affected two or three provisions. Taylor, "Introduction and Notes," 113. These controversial provisions were article III of the Declaration of Rights (religion); Chapter II, Section I, Article II (required Governor to be Christian); and Chapter VI, Article X (amendment procedures).

Constitution of the Commonwealth of Massachusetts went into effect, with John Hancock being elected Governor a day later. This constitution went to serve as the blueprint for other state constitutions as well as the federal constitution, and today it remains the world's oldest written constitution in active use.[87]

Though the final product was certainly more conservative than their ideal, the mere fact that a constitution ratified by the people came into existence marked the ultimate success of the Berkshire Constitutionalists. It also marked their end, or at least their transformation, for the establishment of a new framework of government on popular grounds meant the oppositional stance that kept the courts closed until 1780 had to become one of support. The Constitutionalists soon reopened the courts and integrated themselves into the new political life of Massachusetts. This led to the relocation of the capital of Berkshire County to the town of Lenox, a Constitutionalist stronghold. Moreover, many of the Constitutionalists' leaders became part of the very judiciary system they once impeded, with seven signers of the 1778 *Remonstrance* becoming justices of the peace within a year of ratification.[88]

In the end, however, their influence reaches further than the confines of the 1780 Massachusetts Constitution. For one thing, six years later, a different group of disgruntled Western Massachusettsans would borrow the Constitutionalists' tactics to fight against the state government, shutting down courts in Northampton and Worcester and beginning what would become known as Shay's rebellion.[89] In addition, the Constitutionalists birthed a new procedure, ratification, which soon began spreading across the American colonies, and eventually the world.

And, most relevant for our purposes, amidst their struggles the Constitutionalists were the first to theorize and create a sophisticated defense of ratification. Their theory, which I unpack and explain in chapter 5, justifies ratification by portraying it as an essential moment of *constituent power*, an instance in which the people directly wield their unique power to create authoritative higher law. Here, ratification takes on the direct action function described in the previous chapter, for it becomes the site where the agent with authority—the people themselves—take conclusive action.

At the same time, the Constitutionalists also frame the procedure as an essential tool through which the people can protect themselves against potentially corrupt drafters by reviewing their actions. This is like ratification's agent review function in early modern treaty-making. Chapter 7 concentrates on the implications of such a framing, which amounts to portraying and justifying the procedure as a type of accountability mechanism essential for maintaining a proper relationship of *representation* in the constitution-making process.

[87] Bacon, "The State Constitution (1777–1780)," 187–209.

[88] Brooke, "To the Quiet of the People: Revolutionary Settlements and Civil Unrest in Western Massachusetts, 1774–1789," 440–441.

[89] Leonard L. Richards, *Shay's Rebellion: The American Revolution's Final Battle* (University of Pennsylvania Press 2002) 9–11.

2. The Mechanics Union of New York City

While Thomas Allen and the Berkshire Constitutionalists were responsible for the first instance of ratification, and wrote the most in defense of the procedure, they were not the only radicals in the American colonies that both recoiled at the idea of a state constitution enacted without popular approval and put their dissatisfaction into print. In fact, on June 17, 1776, sixteen days after Allen sent out his *Pittsfield Petitions*, a letter appeared in *The New York Gazette*; and the *Weekly Mercury*, written in the name of the self-described "mechanicks in union, for the city and county of New York," making similar demands.[90]

Mechanics in eighteenth-century New York City were those whose occupations involved working with their hands.[91] Common mechanic professions ranged from blacksmith to shopkeeper to cooper to baker. Unlike in other great colonial towns, the mechanics in New York were especially politically active, likely due to the city having some of the lowest suffrage standards in the colonies. Paying a small fee, rather than owning land, was enough to give a white male the vote. Thus the mechanics formed the largest single group in the city's electorate, and they organized to flex their political muscle.[92]

Initially, politically engaged mechanics joined the more traditionally merchant-led Sons of Liberty, calling for resistance against the British and a move toward independence. However, by 1774 they had formed their own coalition, the Committee of Mechanics, an "organized, articulate, and militant" political force in its own right.[93] Some of their fellow patriots were unhappy with this development. In an infamous letter to John Penn, Governor Morris, taken by the mechanics' appearance at a meeting of the city's governing committee, wrote that: "The mob begins to think and reason. Poor reptiles! ... I see, and I see it with fear and trembling, that if the disputes with *Great Britain* continue, we shall be under the worst of all possible dominions; the domination of a riotous mob."[94]

Despite Morris' worries, the mechanics never transformed into a mob, but they did play a key role in New York City politics during the Revolution. They quickly became some of the strongest supporters of the Continental Congress in the city, furthering its efforts by blocking the movement of supplies and workman to the

[90] "The Respectful Address of the Mechanicks in Union, for the City and County of New-York, Represented by Their General Committee" *The New-York Gazette; and the Weekly Mercury* (New York June 17, 1776) 3.

[91] "After Carl Becker: The Mechanics and New York City Politics, 1774–1801," (1964) 5 Labor History 215–24.

[92] Roger J. Champagne, "Liberty Boys and Mechanics of New York City, 1764–1774," (1967) 8 Labor History 115–35, 124–28; Milton M. Klein, "Democracy and Politics in Colonial New York," (1959) 40 New York History 221–46, 232–34.

[93] Edward Countryman, *A People in Revolution: The American Revolution and Political Society in New York, 1760–1790* (John Hopkins University Press 1981) 162–63.

[94] Staughton Lynd, "The Mechanics in New York Politics, 1774–1788," (1964) 5 Labor History 225–46, 226.

British troops stationed in Boston.[95] In early 1775 the Committee of Mechanics joined with members of the radical merchant class to form a Committee of Inspection, with the task of enforcing Congress' non-intercourse policy. Eventually, this Committee's task expanded, and by spring 1776 they were effectively ruling the city in place of the British.[96]

Throughout this period, the mechanics regularly sent addresses to the New York Provincial Congress, many of which the city's newspapers published. For instance, on November 12, 1774, the mechanics emphasized their hopes that the Provincial Congress would cooperate with the more radical actions of the Continental Congress, ending their plea with a passive threat by declaring that "we shall ever by ready to aid and assist in carrying out the salutary Measure of the General Congress into Execution, to the utmost of our Power and Ability."[97] A year and half later, after outlining their grievances with British rule, the mechanics went so far as to urge the Provincial Congress to "instruct our most Honorable Delegates in Continental Congress, to use their utmost endeavors in that august assembly to cause these united colonies to become independent of Great-Britain."[98] Thus, the mechanics' June 17, 1776 letter concerning ratification was part of a pattern of requests to their local government.

The letter addressed what was already, for New York standards, a radical proposition urged forth by Morris in the colony's relatively conservative Provincial Congress. As mentioned, on May 15th, the Continental Congress directed the fledgling states to set up their own independent governments. In response, on May 24th, Morris moved that "a committee be appointed to draw up a recommendation to the people of this Colony, for the choosing of persons to frame a government for the said colony."[99] Worried that the current congress' deputies were not equipped with constitution-making power, Morris proposed that a new congress be elected as a mandated constituent legislature. He faced opposition—some of his fellow delegates thought that the existing congress already had the power to create a new constitution, while others thought that the entire endeavor was premature—but he was ultimately successful.[100]

95 Ibid., 228. The Committee of Mechanics in Boston sent a letter to the New York Mechanics asking for their help in this manner. See Mechanics of Boston, "To the Printer," *The New-York Journal; or, The General Advertiser* (New York September 29, 1774).

96 Carl Becker, *The History of Political Parties in the Province of New York, 1760–1776* (University of Wisconsin 1909) 161–63.

97 "Address from the Committee of Mechanicks," *The New-York Gazette; and the Weekly Mercury* (New York November 21, 1774) 3, 3.

98 "Address from the Committee of Mechanicks," *The Constitutional Gazette* (New York June 5, 1776) 2–3.

99 *Journals of the Provincial Congress, Provincial Convention, Committee of Safety and Council of Safety of the State of New York: 1775–1776–1777*, vol. 1 (Thurlow Weed 1842) 460.

100 Adams, *The First American Constitutions: Republican Ideology and the Making of the State Constitutions in the Revolutionary Era*, 84.

On May 26, 1776, the New York Provincial Congress followed Morris' recommendation, announcing that the abdication of their colonial governor and hostilities from the crown meant that the "old form of government is become, *ipso facto* dissolved," and that a new one was required. However, since "doubts have arisen, whether this Congress are invested with sufficient authority to frame and institute such new form of internal government and police," the Provincial Congress recommended that each county be given the opportunity to reauthorize their current representatives with "the express authority ... to institute a new internal form of government and police for this Colony," or "elect new members for that purpose."[101]

Though a significant step toward an outright declaration of independence from the British, the mechanics' response to this announcement was apoplectic. Written by the Chairman of the Mechanics Union, a pewter smith named Malcolm M'Euen, the letter voiced their dissent in thinly veiled sarcasm.[102]

> We could not, we never can believe you intended that the future delegates, or yourselves, should be vested with the power of framing a new constitution for this colony; and that its inhabitants at large should not exercise the right which God has given them, in common with all men, to judge whether it be consistent with their interest to accept or reject a constitution framed for that state of which they are a member.[103]

The mechanics' basic argument mirrors those made by Allen and his Constitutionalists 150 miles away. The power to create a new government was an unalienable God-given right held by all men in common. The British government and its colonial overseers had denied the people of New York this right thus far, and it was unthinkable to the mechanics that a home-based soon-to-be revolutionary congress was proposing to continue this denial. This would, among other things, continue to force the people of New York to be ruled by "oligarchic principles." As the Mechanics Union went on to explain, a legislature could never obtain the authority to create a constitution, for the people "cannot lawfully divest" such powers. Even if the majority of voters actually went along with congress' request, and authorized their representatives to make a constitution without ratification, this "would only proclaim our insanity, and for that reason, be void."

However, while the Berkshire Constitutionalists simply assumed that the people could have no hand in drafting the actual document, and thus necessarily

[101] *Journals of the Provincial Congress, Provincial Convention, Committee of Safety and Council of Safety of the State of New York: 1775–1776–1777*, 462–63.

[102] Richard L. Bowen, Jr., "New York Porter Mugs and Porterhouses," (1977) 7 The Pewter Collectors Club of America Bulletin 186–91, 187.

[103] "The Respectful Address of the Mechanicks in Union, for the City and County of New-York, Represented by Their General Committee."

needed ratification to exercise their unalienable right, the mechanics provided an argument for the same assertion. The mechanics explained that they understood their "own want of abilities," and admitted that the people were "not qualified for assisting in the framing of a constitution." In other words, the average citizen, for a variety of possible reasons, lacked competence to draft extraordinary law. Nonetheless, the mechanics argued, the cognitive demands of voting a constitution up or down were less, such that "the share of common sense the Almighty has bountifully distributed amongst mankind in general, is sufficient to . . . enable him to judge right what degree of safety, and what advantages he is likely to enjoy, or be deprived of, under any constitution proposed to him." Thus, by submitting a constitution to direct popular ratification, a constitution would become the people's "own joint work, as soon as the majority of them should have freely accepted it," and therefore become "truly binding on the people."[104] The mechanics thus justified ratification by relegating the moment of constituent power to the ratification process due to citizen ignorance. As I discuss in chapter 9, section 1, their emphasis on ignorance prefigured an argument Condorcet would make over a decade later to justify the use of a ratification referendum.

Unlike the Berkshire Constitutionalists, the mechanics' demands had no obvious effect. The Provincial Congress did not record any mention of the letter in their minutes and, unlike their responses to previous missives from the mechanics, did not bother to submit a formal reply to the local newspapers. In the mechanics' defense, the Berkshire Constitutionalists used direct action—they closed the courts—to ensure that their demands were heard. Such measures were unavailable to the mechanics, for mere months after their address the British began their attempt to retake the colonies by launching central attacks on Long Island and New York City.

Thus, the counties of New York acted in accordance with the May 26 directive, held meetings, and selected or reappointed new delegates, now equipped with authorization to create a new form of government. The new congress assembled on July 9, 1776, in White Plains, Westchester County, as New York City itself was no longer safe from the Royal Navy.[105] They quickly endorsed the Declaration of Independence and formally changed their name to "The Provincial Convention of the Representatives of the State of New York."[106] However, the convention tabled the matter of creating a new form of government for a year, as they were immediately consumed by war and because its conservative members wanted to minimize

[104] Ibid.
[105] Adams, *The First American Constitutions: Republican Ideology and the Making of the State Constitutions in the Revolutionary Era*, 85; *Journals of the Provincial Congress, Provincial Convention, Committee of Safety and Council of Safety of the State of New York: 1775–1776–1777*, 512. See Also Charles Z. Lincoln, *The Constitutional History of New York*, vol. 1 (The Lawyers Co-operative Publishing Company 1906) 483.
[106] Lincoln, *The Constitutional History of New York*, 487.

the chances of a radical document.[107] By November, the British had captured New York City, as well as five counties and parts of others.[108] Constitution-making, understandably so, was not a core issue at this time. As Gilbert Livingston and Christopher Tappen, congressional representatives appointed to the exploratory constitution-making committee wrote in their letter to Congress explaining their absence, "it would be well to secure a *State* to govern, before they discussed a form to govern it."[109]

Over the next year, the constitutional drafting committee appointed by the convention had trouble meeting, with its members scattered around the state helping the war efforts. The convention itself was forced to move locations repeatedly to avoid capture and attack.[110] Nonetheless, on March 12, 1777, James Duane presented John Jay's draft constitution to the convention.[111] The convention discussed the draft throughout the next month, ultimately enacting it without direct popular approval on April 20th.[112] The mechanics would have to wait nearly fifty years to have their demands met. In January 1822 New York's second constitution came into effect after being approved by a majority of all voters in a statewide referendum.

3. Ratification by Sub-State Conventions: Philadelphia

While the first ratification procedures authorized the constitutions of the newly emergent American states, perhaps the most famous instance of ratification took place when these same states came together to create the U.S. Constitution. The writings that emerged from the U.S. ratification process, the debates in the various conventions, the public participation that surrounded the whole episode, all have and will continue to be a source of interest to everyone from politicians to lawyers to academics to history enthusiasts.[113] However, less attention has been given to our concern, the debate over the ratification procedure itself.[114] These discussions

107 Peter J. Galie, *The New York State Constitution: A Reference Guide* (Greenwood Press 1991) 6–7.

108 Lincoln, *The Constitutional History of New York*, 45.

109 *Journals of the Provincial Congress, Provincial Convention, Committee of Safety and Council of Safety of the State of New York: 1775–1776–1777*, 590.

110 Lincoln, *The Constitutional History of New York*, 491–92.

111 *Journals of the Provincial Congress, Provincial Convention, Committee of Safety and Council of Safety of the State of New York: 1775–1776–1777*, 833.

112 Ibid., 838; Adams, *The First American Constitutions: Republican Ideology and the Making of the State Constitutions in the Revolutionary Era*, 86.

113 The entire ratification process in the United States is brilliantly explored and chronicled in Pauline Maier, *Ratification: The People Debate the Constitution, 1787–1788* (Simon & Schuster 2010). Unfortunately, Maier pays little attention to the actual discussion within the convention over the ratification procedure.

114 Four significant exceptions exist, though none directly discuss the reasons for or against ratification in general (I explain why below). See Jack N. Rakove, *Original Meanings: Politics and Ideas in the Making of the Constitution* (1st edn, A.A. Knopf 1996) 102–8; Michael J. Klarman, *The Framers'*

mainly transpired during the United States Constitutional Convention, which took place in Philadelphia from May 25 to September 17, 1787. In this section I review and dissect them, showing how the convention members ended up creating, explaining, and defending a new ratification variant, *ratification by sub-state conventions.*

3.1 Background to the Debates

When the Philadelphia Convention convened on May 14, 1787, the former American colonies were thirteen sovereign states loosely yet "perpetually" united in a "League of Friendship" under the treaty-like Articles of Confederation. The Congress of Confederation, consisting of delegates chosen by each state's legislature, managed any trans- or inter-state matters. This congress was weak, for despite the dreams of those such as Franklin and Dickinson, whose previous drafts of the Articles would have created a powerful central government, the states were free to do nearly whatever they wished under the adopted version.[115] States retained "sovereignty, freedom and independence, and every power, jurisdiction, and right" not explicitly delegated to Congress.[116] The most important of these delegated powers were the ability to declare war, make alliances, and make trade agreements, but all such actions required the approval, often absent, of at least nine state delegations.[117] Moreover, the states usurped these powers, and Congress had no ability to retaliate or enforce compliance.

Despite the desires of many, including members of the 1786 Annapolis Convention, the eventual directive given to the Philadelphia Convention did not call for a replacement of the Articles. Rather, it recommended something narrower.[118] According to Congress' February 21 resolution, the convention was to be held:

Coup: The Making of the United States Constitution (Oxford University Press 2016) 412–17; David E. Kyvig, *Explicit & Authentic Acts: Amending the U.S. Constitution, 1776–2015* (University Press of Kansas 2016) 42–65; Carlos E. Gonzalez, "Representational Structure through Which We the People Ratify Constitutions: The Troubling Original Understanding of the Constitution's Ratification Clauses," (2005) 38 UC Davis Law Review 1373–1504, 1392–1431. See also Richard S. Kay, "The Illegality of the Constitution," (1987) 4 Constitutional Commentary 57–80, 68–70.

115 Adams, *The First American Constitutions: Republican Ideology and the Making of the State Constitutions in the Revolutionary Era*, 278–82; Kyvig, *Explicit & Authentic Acts: Amending the U.S. Constitution, 1776–2015*, 34–35.

116 *Articles of Confederation* (1781), Art. II.

117 Rakove, *Original Meanings: Politics and Ideas in the Making of the Constitution*, 23–28.

118 "Proceedings and Report of the Commissioners at Annapolis, Maryland, 11–14 September 1786," in Merrill Jensen (ed.), *The Documentary History of the Ratification of the Constitution: Constitutional Documents and Records, 1776–1787*, vol. 1 (The State Historical Society of Wisconsin 1976) 184.

> for the sole and express purpose of revising the Articles of Confederation and reporting to Congress and the several legislatures such alterations and provisions therein as shall when agreed to in Congress and confirmed by the states render the federal constitution adequate to the exigencies of government and the preservation of the Union.[119]

This resolution makes two things clear. First, the convention was supposed to merely amend the Articles of Confederation. Second, such amendments were to go into effect only upon the approval of Congress and the state governments. In other words, Congress specified that the adoption of any changes to the Articles was to proceed in accordance with the troublesome amendment procedure already laid out in the thirteenth article of confederation; "nor shall any alteration at any time hereafter be made in any of them; unless such alteration be agreed to in a Congress of the United States, and be afterwards confirmed by the legislatures of every State."[120]

As is well known, the members of the Philadelphia Convention, or at least some of its most dominant members, quickly decided to go above and beyond Congress' resolution.[121] Instead of simply amending the treaty-like document, they proposed what amounted to an entirely new constitution meant to create a federal state.[122] Madison aptly summarizes the logic in favor of replacement rather than reform in Federalist 37, when he writes: "the existing Confederation is founded on principles which are fallacious; we must consequently change this first foundation, and with it the superstructure resting upon it."[123]

Nonetheless, the delegates still needed to figure out how to get their creation accepted and treated as higher law. The most obvious pathway was to simply follow Article 13, transforming the amendment procedure into a two-step ratification procedure involving approval by the Congress of the Confederation and then unanimous approval by the state legislatures. The debate over ratification, which was minimal despite taking place over ten days spread throughout the convention, was structured around this option. Specifically, the framers' debate can be broken down into four questions, the first three of which directly challenged the details of the Article 13 amendment process: (1) should the constitution be submitted to state legislatures or conventions? (2) How many legislatures or conventions needed

[119] "Confederation Congress Calls the Constitutional Convention, 21 February 1787," in Merrill Jensen (ed.), *The Documentary History of the Ratification of the Constitution: Constitutional Documents and Records, 1776–1787*, vol. 1 (The State Historical Society of Wisconsin 1976) 187.

[120] Merrill Jensen (ed.), *The Documentary History of the Ratification of the Constitution: Constitutional Documents and Records, 1776–1787* (The State Historical Society of Wisconsin 1976) 93.

[121] Ackerman, *We the People: Transformations*, 49–53; Kyvig, *Explicit & Authentic Acts: Amending the U.S. Constitution, 1776–2015*, 42–47.

[122] Rakove, *Original Meanings: Politics and Ideas in the Making of the Constitution*, 102.

[123] James Madison, Alexander Hamilton, and John Jay, *The Federalist Papers* (Penguin Books 1987) 243.

to approve the constitution before it would come into effect? (3) Does Congress get a vote? And, an unrelated question brought up near the end of the convention, (4) should the states be able to amend the constitution during ratification?

3.2 Legislatures or Conventions?

The convention spent the most energy on question (1), arguing the merits of using conventions or state legislatures to ratify the constitution on June 5, 9, and 20, July 23, and August 31. No other ratifying agent, such as a referendum or a national ratifying convention, was mentioned. The introduction of the Virginia Plan sparked early debate on this topic, for its fifteenth resolution vaguely stated that the draft constitution created by the Philadelphia Convention was to be, "submitted to an assembly or assemblies of Representatives, recommended by the several Legislatures, to be expressly chosen by the people, to consider & decide thereon."[124]

The arguments against this resolution, and in favor of submitting the constitution to state legislatures, were relatively straightforward and minimal. Sherman and Gerry noted that requiring legislative approval was most in tune with the Articles, while Gerry, Ellsworth, and Martin referenced the dangers of a more popular ratification instrument. Conventions, they argued, being such a direct manifestation of the people, might be uncontrollable, in tension with the state legislatures, or be so chaotic as to make agreement on anything impossible.[125] As Ellsworth noted, such conventions "were better fitted to pull down than to build up a Constitution."[126] Finally, Carrol claimed that if the federal constitution would effectively amend the state constitutions, then state constitutional amendment rules had to be followed. For Maryland at least, this meant seeking legislative approval.[127]

The delegates in favor of conventions, who were ultimately victorious, were far more detailed and varied in their reasons. First, they gave powerful pragmatic arguments, explaining that it would be easier to get the constitution passed in conventions as opposed to legislatures. For one thing, as King pointed out, "A Convention being a single house, the adoption may more easily be carried thro' it, than thro' the Legislatures where there are several branches."[128] That is, given the bicameral nature of many state legislatures, there would simply be fewer

[124] Max Farrand (ed.), *The Records of the Federal Convention of 1787*, vol. 1 (Yale University Press 1914) 22. Though this language left open the possibility of a national ratifying convention, rather than a state ratifying convention, this option was only mentioned once. On 31 August 1787 Morris suggested submitting the constitution to such a convention, but his suggestion was neither seconded nor discussed. Ibid., 475. See also Rakove, *Original Meanings: Politics and Ideas in the Making of the Constitution*, 385 n. 321.

[125] Farrand (ed.), *The Records of the Federal Convention of 1787*, vol. 1, 122–23; Max Farrand (ed.), *The Records of the Federal Convention of 1787*, vol. 2 (Yale University Press 1914) 89–91, 476.

[126] Farrand (ed.), *The Records of the Federal Convention of 1787*, vol. 1, 335.

[127] Farrand (ed.), *The Records of the Federal Convention of 1787*, vol. 2, 475.

[128] Farrand (ed.), *The Records of the Federal Convention of 1787*, vol. 1, 123.

votes to win if ratification took place via single conventions rather than multi-chamber state legislatures. In addition, as Madison, King, Ghorum, and Randolph emphasized repeatedly, the federal constitution would undoubtedly weaken the state legislatures, something their members would predictably be against.[129] Legislatures would thus, as Madison put it, "be more disinclined than conventions composed in part at least of other men" to vote in favor.[130]

Second, Madison and Mason stressed the necessity of making the federal constitution rest on a greater authority than the state legislatures, something that was impossible if the latter approved it. In this they assumed, or at least referred to, the popular belief at the time that conventions represented a unique and direct way of channeling popular will and authority.[131] Thus they linked ratification type with the *legitimacy* of a constitution. Making the federal constitution superior, Mason argued, was necessary in order to prevent future legislators from simply rejecting or ignoring it.[132] Madison repeatedly made a more complex argument, noting that by taking power away from the states, the federal constitution would effectively amend the state constitutions. Given that this was the case, the federal constitution could not be approved by the state legislatures, as they could never have the authority to amend the source of their own authority.[133] As Mason, joining in with Madison, also argued, the legislature "are the mere creatures of the State Constitutions, and can not be greater than their creators."[134] Thus, a constitution had to be the creation of something with greater authority, which meant a direct appeal to the popular sovereign itself acting through popular conventions. This point was perhaps most eloquently put by Madison in a letter to Washington written before the convention had even assembled, when he claimed that: "To give a new System its proper validity and energy, a ratification must be obtained from the people, and not merely from the ordinary authority of the Legislatures. This will be the more essential as inroads to the *existing Constitutions* of the States will be unavoidable."[135]

[129] Ghorum even added an extra argument, noting that ratifying conventions would produce better debate, given the inherent bias of the legislatures. See Farrand (ed.), *The Records of the Federal Convention of 1787*, vol. 2, 90.

[130] Farrand (ed.), *The Records of the Federal Convention of 1787*, vol. 1, 123. While Ellsworth argued in favor of ratification by legislatures in the convention, he ended up mimicking Madison's pragmatic argument in favor of conventions in his pro-ratification essays published under the pseudonym "A Landholder." See Colleen A. Sheehan and Gary L. McDowell (eds.), *Friends of the Constitution: Writings of the "Other" Federalists, 1787–1788* (Liberty Fund 1998) 286–7.

[131] Wood, *The Creation of the American Republic, 1776–1787*, chapter 8. Gonzalez argues that even the opponents of ratification via conventions acknowledged that the latter uniquely amounted to approval by the people themselves. See "Representational Structure through Which We the People Ratify Constitutions: The Troubling Original Understanding of the Constitution's Ratification Clauses," 1393–1407.

[132] Farrand (ed.), *The Records of the Federal Convention of 1787*, vol. 1, 122–23, 314–15; vol. 2, 88–89.

[133] In making this argument, Madison appealed to one of the bedrock ideas of what has become known as constituent power theory. See chapter 4, section 1.2 for a general discussion of this idea, and chapter five, section 3.2 for discussion of its use in colonial America.

[134] Farrand (ed.), *The Records of the Federal Convention of 1787*, vol. 2, 88.

[135] James Madison, *The Papers of James Madison*, vol. 9 (The University of Chicago Press 1975) 383.

Third, Madison asserted that ratification by state legislatures would transform what was to be the federal constitution into a mere treaty. He used this claim to make two points, both of which he had previously explored in his April 1787 "Vices of the Political System of the United States."[136] Implying that he saw clashes between state law and the federal constitution as inevitable, and the role of something like judicial review as important, he argued that submitting the constitution to popular conventions would make the constitution, from a legal perspective, superior to state laws.[137] Given that Madison was a federalist, and in favor of a strong central government, this was for him an unequivocally good thing. In addition, Madison, ever the Vatellian, claimed that, "in the case of treaties . . . a breach of any one article by any of the parties, frees the other parties from their engagements. In the case of a union of people under one Constitution, the nature of the pact has always been understood to exclude such an interpretation."[138] That is, Madison argued that to prevent every state from having the right to leave the union upon any breach of the constitution, the latter had to be ratified by conventions so that it would not be considered a treaty.[139]

In some sense, without downplaying the substantive merits of the arguments given, this entire debate can also be understood as a proxy for two larger and interrelated points of disagreement in the convention: between whether it was simply amending the Articles of Confederation or replacing them, and between whether what was needed from the constitution was the creation of a true national government or something that left state-centered authority intact. This is because no one seemed to disagree on two points: that ratification by convention violated the articles and signaled something beyond mere revision, and that ratification by state legislatures would doom the new constitution unless it departed from the Virginia Plan's vision of reducing the powers of state legislatures.[140]

3.3 Unanimity or Something Else?

The next ratification question addressed by the convention was how many states had to approve the constitution for it to go into effect. Discussions on the

[136] Ibid., 352. See also Klarman, *The Framers' Coup: The Making of the United States Constitution*, 415.

[137] Madison's argument about the right sort of ratification being paramount to making the federal constitution superior to state law echoed those he had made in letters to Jefferson and Pendleton earlier in the year. See Rakove, *Original Meanings: Politics and Ideas in the Making of the Constitution*, 99.

[138] Farrand (ed.), *The Records of the Federal Convention of 1787*, vol. 2, 93. Here, Madison seems to be referring to Vattel's hardline position that a violation of any part of a treaty gives the violated the right to dissolve the entire agreement. See Emer de Vattel, *The Law of Nations* (Liberty Fund 2008) II.12.202.

[139] As Madison makes clear in "Vices," he saw such treaty dissolution logic as applying to the articles. Madison, *The Papers of James Madison*, 352–53.

[140] See Gonzalez, "Representational Structure through Which We the People Ratify Constitutions: The Troubling Original Understanding of the Constitution's Ratification Clauses," 1399f1357; Kyvig, *Explicit & Authentic Acts: Amending the U.S. Constitution, 1776–2015*, 49.

topic took place on June 5, 16, and 19, July 23, August 30, and 31, and again on September 10. One option—in some sense the default—was to follow the Articles of Confederation's amendment provision and require unanimous consent of all the states. However, defenders for this option were few and the argument they made scarce. Gerry made no argument, but simply asserted that unanimity was necessary.[141] Patterson and Sherman urged unanimous consent because that is what the Articles required. In addition, Patterson, along with Carrol, argued that unanimity was necessary because the Confederation had been unanimously established, suggesting that the same decision-rule used to create something had to be used to abolish it, and that the adoption of a new constitution simultaneously meant the abolishment of the Confederation.[142]

The arguments against unanimity were forceful. On June 5th, the first day ratification came up in the Convention, Wilson clarified that a unanimity rule gives everyone a veto, meaning that it would allow "the inconsiderate or selfish opposition of a few States" to ruin any attempt to create a better federal government.[143] Ghorum refined the point further in mid-July, when he pointed out that requiring unanimous assent would mean that "all States are to suffer themselves to be ruined if Rho. Island should persist in her opposition to general measures."[144] Rhode Island refused to send members to the convention because of its legislature's opposition to a strong federal government, and its support for a new constitutional plan seemed highly doubtful. Unanimity, then, as convention members probably concluded, would almost certainly mean constitutional defeat.

Fourteen days later, on June 19th, Madison directly attacked Patterson and Carrol's assertion "that the Confederation having been formed by unanimous consent, could be dissolved by unanimous consent only." Madison, playing off of some of Patterson's claims, argued that such an idea imagines the Confederation to be a social compact or a treaty, both of which have unanimous beginnings. Social compacts either dissolve completely upon any member's "breach of the

[141] On September 10th, Gerry put some meat on his initial objections, warning that by choosing to use a threshold less than unanimity to dissolve the Confederation, the framers were making it easier to dissolve whatever they created on top of it. Farrand (ed.), *The Records of the Federal Convention of 1787*, vol. 2, 561.

[142] Farrand (ed.), *The Records of the Federal Convention of 1787*, vol. 1, 250; vol. 2, 475–79. Luther Martin of Maryland, who left the convention out of disgust, was particularly taken with Patterson and Carrol's arguments, repeating and enlarging upon them in his anti-Ratification "Genuine Information" essays, which he presented to the Maryland Legislature in November 1787 and published the following month. See Max Farrand (ed.), *The Records of the Federal Convention of 1787*, vol. 3 (Yale University Press 1914) 228.

[143] This view is echoed by Madison in Federalist 40, where he addresses the objection that the convention ignored the unanimity requirement of the Articles. Madison, Hamilton, and Jay, *The Federalist Papers*, 263. In both the Virginia and North Carolina ratifying conventions, Rhode Island's misbehavior was singled out specifically for why adhering to the unanimity requirement was an impossibility. See Klarman, *The Framers' Coup: The Making of the United States Constitution*, 413f.

[144] Farrand (ed.), *The Records of the Federal Convention of 1787*, vol. 2, 90. Rhode Island had refused to send delegates to the convention over fears that it would create too powerful a federal government; their dissent was likely viewed as highly probable.

fundamental principles of the compact" or authorize "the majority to bind the whole in all cases." In other words, Madison argues, if one conceptualizes the Articles of Confederation as a social compact, then not only is unanimity not needed to dissolve it, but rather one needs to accept that any individual state's actions can destroy the entire agreement or that a majority of states can dictate the contracts terms and shape for the rest. As Madison smugly notes, this is surely something "the Gentn. From N. Jersey [Patterson] would be amongst the last to admit." Treaties also, Madison notes, can be dissolved by the actions of single members, "unless it is expressly stipulated that a violation of particular articles shall not have this consequence." The Articles of Confederation contained no such stipulation, and thus unanimity was not required.[145]

On August 6th the Committee of Detail, appointed by the convention in late July to create a draft constitution reflecting all approved resolutions, released its report. Article XXI read as follows: "The ratification of the Conventions of ___ States shall be sufficient for organizing this Constitution."[146] As can be seen, by this point, the convention had rejected unanimity but had yet to decide on a specific number of states.[147] The debate to do so was scattershot and theoretically underdeveloped, consisting of quick appeals to the majoritarian principle or barely defended claims in favor of particular supermajority thresholds.[148] Wilson proposed seven because it was a bare majority. Madison supported his majoritarian impulses but suggested that the convention required the approval of seven or more states entitled to at least thirty-three members of the house of representatives, which would ensure that the constitution only came into effect with at least the support of both the majority of people and the majority of states. Sherman wanted ten because it was close to unanimity, Gouverneur Morris suggested a hybrid plan where different numbers were required depending upon whether the approving states were contiguous or not.

In the end, the convention chose a nine-state threshold as advocated by Mason, Pickney, and Randolph. Pickney gave no recorded explanation for his preference, while Mason and Randolph favored the number because it was a comfortable supermajority and familiar, with nine being the decision-making threshold for all congressional actions under the Articles of Confederation.[149]

[145] Farrand (ed.), *The Records of the Federal Convention of 1787*, vol. 1, 314–15.

[146] Farrand (ed.), *The Records of the Federal Convention of 1787*, vol. 2, 189.

[147] The delegates from Maryland had not moved on. They proposed on August 31 to fill in the blank with "13" but their motion was uniformly rejected by the other states. Farrand (ed.), *The Records of the Federal Convention of 1787*, vol. 1, 477.

[148] The arbitrariness of the arguments in favor of supermajority thresholds is no surprise, for as Melissa Schwartzberg demonstrates, while good general reasons sometimes exist for using a supermajority threshold, no such reasons exist for picking a specific majority rule. See Melissa Schwartzberg, "The Arbitrariness of Supermajority Rules," (2010) 49 Social Science Information 61–82.

[149] Farrand (ed.), *The Records of the Federal Convention of 1787*, vol 1, 123; vol. 2, 469, 477. The convention also agreed that though nine states were sufficient for the constitution to be ratified, only those who approved would be bound.

3.4 Congress and Amendment

The third and fourth questions pertaining to ratification took up must less time in the convention. The third concerned the remaining part of the Articles' amendment rule, that any change be first approved by the Confederation Congress. Article XXII of the Committee of Detail report initially included the requirement—"This Constitution shall be laid before the United States in Congress assembled, for their approbation ... "—, but at the behest of Pickney and Morris it was struck out in an 8 to 3 vote with no recorded discussion.[150]

However, on September 10th, the issue came up again. Gerry and Hamilton asked to revisit Article XXII, claiming that eliminating the formal requirement of abrogation mistreated Congress, with Gerry describing it as "improper and giving just umbrage to that body."[151] This objection was shut down quickly with two arguments. First, Fitzsimons explained that eliminating Congressional approval was necessary, for otherwise the convention would ask Congress to violate the Articles, the source of their own authority. In this sense, not requiring approval, but simply asking Congress to disseminate the constitution to the states, gave the legislature a role to play in the process without requiring illegality.[152] Second, Wilson pointed out that given Rhode Island, Maryland, and New York's hostility toward the constitutional project, there was no guarantee that Congress would accept the constitution. "After spending four or five months in the laborious and arduous task of forming a Government for our Country," Wilson explained, there was little reason to throw "insuperable obstacles in the way of its success."[153]

The final ratification related issue discussed at the convention concerned Randolph's proposal, which he raised repeatedly near the end of the convention, "that amendments to the plan might be offered by the State Conventions, which should be submitted to and finally decided on by another general Convention."[154] In other words, Randolph wanted to equip the state ratifying conventions with amendment proposing power, and create a second federal constitutional convention charged with reviewing the amendment suggestions, integrating them into a new text, and implementing the resulting constitution directly without further

[150] Farrand (ed.), *The Records of the Federal Convention of 1787*, vol. 2, 189, 478. There was precedent here, in that the Annapolis convention directly appealed to the states, not Congress, to call the constitutional convention. See Jensen (ed.), *The Documentary History of the Ratification of the Constitution: Constitutional Documents and Records, 1776–1787*, 184–85; Klarman, *The Framers' Coup: The Making of the United States Constitution*, 117.

[151] Farrand (ed.), *The Records of the Federal Convention of 1787*, vol. 2, 559.

[152] Madison later tried, unsuccessfully, to go beyond the convention's decision and have Congress explicitly approve of the constitution, rather than simply send it to the states. See Rakove, *Original Meanings: Politics and Ideas in the Making of the Constitution*, 109–10.

[153] Farrand (ed.), *The Records of the Federal Convention of 1787*, vol. 2, 562.

[154] Ibid., 631. See also his earlier proposals in the same vein at ibid., 479, 561.

ratification.[155] Mason seconded Randolph's proposal, and Gerry supported it, but both delegates seemed more interested in holding a second convention because of their dissatisfaction with the draft constitution, rather than having any particular opinions on the power of the ratifying conventions or the nature of the ratification process.[156] Pickney swatted the idea down, noting that "nothing but confusion and contrariety could spring form the experiment," and the proposal was unanimously rejected.[157]

The debates described above culminated in the now well-known ratification process used to approve the U.S. Constitution. It is formally outlined in two places. First, in the resolution sent by the Philadelphia Convention to the Confederation Congress on September 17, 1787: "Resolved, That the proceeding Constitution be laid before the United States in Congress assembled, and that it is the Opinion of this Convention, that it should afterwards be submitted to a Convention of Delegates, chosen in each State by the People thereof, under the Recommendation of its Legislature, for their Assent and Ratification . . . ."[158] Second, in Article VII of the U.S. Constitution, which reads "The ratification of the conventions of the nine states, shall be sufficient for the establishment of this Constitution between the states so ratifying the same." In other words, the draft U.S. Constitution was sent to the Confederation Congress, which distributed it to the state legislatures, instructing them to organize state ratifying conventions to approve or reject the constitution. When nine states ratified the document—Delaware, Pennsylvania, New Jersey, Georgia, Connecticut, Massachusetts, Maryland, South Carolina, and New Hampshire—it came into effect for all those states who ratified.

3.5 Why Ratify?

Given our focus on whether constitutions should be ratified or not, the known discussions that led to the decision to use sub-state conventions to ratify the U.S. Constitution, while interesting, are of little obvious help. None of the arguments given during the convention addressed general reasons to use ratification. From what we can tell, the framers did not seem to ponder the normative or deeper legal meanings of using ratification versus not using it, nor did they relate back to or discuss the conversations concerning the ratification of constitutions that had

[155] According to my definition, Randolph was proposing to complicate the drafting process and do away with ratification, as there would be no agent charged with solely approving or rejecting the constitution.

[156] Maier, *Ratification: The People Debate the Constitution, 1787–1788*, 44–45.

[157] Farrand (ed.), *The Records of the Federal Convention of 1787*, vol. 2, 632.

[158] Jensen (ed.), *The Documentary History of the Ratification of the Constitution: Constitutional Documents and Records, 1776–1787*, 517–18.

already transpired in Massachusetts, New York, and New Hampshire.[159] In fact, discussions during and surrounding the convention never seemed to consider the possibility of not having their creation ratified. Instead, the debates focused exclusively on what form the procedure should take.

Though disappointing for our purposes, this should not be unexpected. On the one hand, the conversations during the convention took place in the heat of constitution-making between those actively writing the constitution and wishing for its success (or demise). It should be no surprise then that so much of the debate over ratification concerned, either explicitly or implicitly, practicalities about how to get the constitution accepted and implemented, rather than general normative reasons in favor of a particular constitution-making procedure.

On the other hand, ratification, in a very real sense, was not optional for members of the Philadelphia Convention and likely unquestioned as a result. This was for two interrelated reasons, both having to do with the treaty-like structure of the Articles of Confederation and the initial goal of the Philadelphia Convention. First, the delegates at the convention did not have the authority to make any changes to the Articles of the Confederation directly. While they found a way to take liberties when it came to their original assignment, twisting their directive to amend the Articles to sanctioning the creation of an entire new governing document, they could not get around the fact that they were not practically or legally empowered to effect constitutional/Article/treaty change at any level. As Wilson famously put it during the convention, "he conceived himself authorized to conclude nothing, but to be at liberty to propose any thing."[160] Similarly, Patterson emphasized that the convention's object "is not such a Governmt, as may be best in itself, but such a one as our Constituent have authorized us to prepare, and as they will approve."[161]

In this sense, to relate back to our discussion in the previous chapter, the members of the constitutional convention were not traditional plenipotentiaries equipped with full powers, but rather more akin to modern treaty negotiators tasked with helping to shape a treaty the contents of which would be approved and made actionable by other state agents equipped with the relevant authority. The delegates never had the power to bind their sovereigns. This can be seen quite clearly in the various resolutions and acts issued by the twelve state legislatures to appoint their convention delegates.[162] In every state other than New Jersey, the delegates were given explicitly limited powers. Virginia's November 23, 1786 resolution, paraphrased or quoted by Pennsylvania, North Carolina, Delaware, and

[159] This is noticeable given that, as Bailyn notes, "the background experiences of constitution writing in the states … were constantly referred to in the Philadelphia convention … ." Bailyn, *The Ideological Origins of the American Revolution*, 325.

[160] Farrand (ed.), *The Records of the Federal Convention of 1787*, vol. 1, 253.

[161] Ibid., 150.

[162] Rhode Island refused to appoint or send delegates.

Georgia, and Congress's own February 21st directive cited above, is illustrative. The chosen representatives were

> hereby authorized as Deputies from this Commonwealth, to meet such Deputies as may be appointed and authorised by other States ...to join with them in devising and discussing all such alterations & further provisions, as may be necessary to render the Federal Constitution adequate to the exigencies of the Union, and in reporting such an Act for that purpose, to the United States in Congress, as, when agreed by them, and duly confirmed by the several states, will effectually provide for the same.[163]

In other words, the state legislatures empowered the convention delegates to merely deliberate and draft proposed changes to the Confederation, which would only go into effect upon the double approval of the Confederation Congress and the state legislatures.[164]

Second, and relatedly, though many of the convention delegates aspired to do more than amend a mere treaty, they were still trapped in the logic of one. Their attempt at transforming a loose confederation of sovereign states into a federal republic would go nowhere if at least some of the individual states did not endorse the constitution. It would be akin to states not signing on to a traditional treaty—the resultant document would govern nothing. This practical, rather than merely legal or moral problem, makes sense of Madison's repeated mention of avoiding making the constitution a mere "Treaty... of a particular sort."[165] He wanted to go beyond treaty-making, and thus sought to have the constitution ratified by a different manifestation of state authority than the state legislatures. The choice was never between ratification and no ratification, but rather between different institutional means for convoking the thirteen sovereigns of the American states to have them cede over part of their power. As Madison put it, he "found the difference between a system founded on the Legislature only, and one founded on the people, to be the true difference between a league or treaty, and a Constitution."[166]

Despite the lack of discussion about the virtues of ratification generally, it is still possible to tease out two skeletal justifications for the procedure from the arguments made at the convention. These arguments are somewhat familiar, as they portray the procedure as functioning in some of the ways detailed in the previous chapter, or else follow the arguments made by the Berkshire Constitutionalists and the New York Mechanics.

[163] Jensen (ed.), *The Documentary History of the Ratification of the Constitution: Constitutional Documents and Records, 1776–1787*, 197, 200, 203–4.
[164] These resolutions are collected in ibid., 195–225.
[165] Farrand (ed.), *The Records of the Federal Convention of 1787*, vol. 1, 122.
[166] Farrand (ed.), *The Records of the Federal Convention of 1787*, vol. 2, 93.

The first is the claim that ratification should be used because it plays an important role in enabling the people to create their constitution. As mentioned above and explained in the next two chapters, this justification relies on what would come to be known as the theory of constituent power, which applies the logic of popular sovereignty to constitution-making and concludes that only the people, rather than already constituted and established authorities, can rightfully create and authorize a constitution. The arguments within the convention regarding why state legislatures could not serve as ratifying authorities, especially the appeals to the legal supremacy of the constitution, suggest that many members of the Philadelphia Convention saw ratification as such a site of constituent power, i.e. as a procedure through which the people had to act directly.

The central argument went as follows: given that in a federal system a federal constitution would necessarily overrule or alter state legislation and state constitutions, state legislative bodies or any other branch of state government were automatically excluded from approving it, for "[i]t would be a novel & dangerous doctrine," as Madison explained, "that a legislature could change the constitution under which it held its existence."[167] Moreover, no constitution gave the legislature or any other body the power to unilaterally create or endorse a federal constitution. "Whither then must we resort?," Mason asks, "To the people with whom all power remains that has not been given up in the Constitutions derived from them."[168] Or as Madison later stated, "The people were in fact, the fountain of all power ... They could alter constitutions as they pleased."[169] Constituted bodies, according to the logic of constituent power and these arguments, lack the moral authority to approve a constitution. This power only lay with the people, which could be exercised through the popular device of a ratification convention. In summarizing the differences between the Virginia and New Jersey plans, Wilson made this distinction explicit, noting that in the former, which called for conventions, "ratification (is in this to be) by the people themselves," as opposed to the New Jersey plan, where ratification would merely be completed "by the legislative authorities according to the 13th art: of Confederation."[170]

However, note that the constituent power claim—that the people must create their own constitution—is not automatically supportive of any specific constitution-making procedure. While it claims that the people must play a role to some extent in the creation of the constitution, where and to what extent their participation needs to occur is an open question. Thus, more is required to explain why ratification is needed to accomplish this end. The New York Mechanics, for instance, provided an answer, claiming that the people only had the cognitive

[167] Ibid., 92–93.
[168] Ibid., 88.
[169] Ibid., 476.
[170] Farrand (ed.), *The Records of the Federal Convention of 1787*, vol. 1, 252.

abilities needed to evaluate a constitution, rather than assist in writing one. For the Philadelphia context, this means more is needed to explain why the people had to act during ratification, thus necessitating conventions over legislatures, rather than the people having emerged and acted at some other point in the constitution-making process.

One way of understanding the Philadelphia delegates' arguments is to see them as conceptualizing the procedure in an almost reparative function. Having state legislatures (and the Congress of the Confederacy) approve the constitution would ensure that these bodies completely controlled the constitution-making process—they already initiated it, authorized the convention, and selected its delegates—without ever having been transferred or delegated constituent power from the people. In this sense, up until ratification, all actors within the constitution-making process were acting without constituent authority. Thus, ratification by conventions was all-important as it would make up for these deficiencies and inject a temporary elected convention, thought to be a popular decision-making instrument separate and often antagonistic to constituted bodies, into the constitution-making process. I look specifically at this reparative use of ratification within a constituent power framework in chapter 4, section 3.2.

The second justification hinted at by the convention debates emphasizes the effects of ratification on beliefs, rather than its role in moral argumentation. This justification claims that ratification will increase the likelihood that citizens or elites or institutions to be governed by a constitution will see it as authoritative, and then argues or presumes that this is a positive development. This is a claim, as will be discussed in chapters 8 and 9, about ratification's positive effect on sociological legitimacy, i.e. on beliefs about moral legitimacy, and relates to the support function of ratification covered in the discussion of ratification in the collective bargaining setting. Just as the use of ratification in a union contract might increase the degree to which union members support the resultant agreement, here ratification might lead to greater beliefs in legitimacy amongst members of a polity.

Madison alludes to a version of this justification several times, again during his advocacy for using conventions to ratify rather than state legislatures, particularly when discussing the potential clash between the federal constitution and state laws. "A law violating a treaty ratified by a pre-existing law, might be respected by the judges as a law, though an unwise and perfidious one. A law violating a constitution established by the people themselves, would be considered by the Judges as null & void."[171] One way to understand this, is to read it as claiming that judges are more likely to see a constitution as legitimate, in the sense of being a supreme source of higher law that overrides all positive law, if it is ratified by the people (by which Madison means conventions) rather than state legislatures. Here the ratification

[171] Farrand (ed.), *The Records of the Federal Convention of 1787*, vol. 2, 93.

procedure itself is affecting legitimacy beliefs. Similarly, King asserted that "he preferred a reference to the authority of the people expressly delegated to Conventions, as the most certain means of obviating all disputes & doubts concerning the legitimacy of the new Constitution."[172] These and other statements suggest that at least some delegates advocated for ratification by convention because they believed the procedure would help ensure people would see the constitution, if approved, as legitimate and authoritative. While their arguments were meant to provide reasons in favor of a specific ratification process versus another, we can generalize them to apply to ratification overall.

4. Ratification by Convention: Georgia

The invention of a third type of ratification, ratification by a single national (or in this instance, state) convention, also occurred amidst the furious constitutional activity that defined the early history of the United States, but this time further south in Georgia during the creation of the state's 1789 constitution.

4.1 Background

Georgia's first constitution, created and enacted directly by a mandated constituent legislature in 1777, was widely disliked since its birth.[173] Complaints focused on the overly large unicameral legislature, the short rotation of the governorship, an unclear division of powers, excessive court costs, and other deficiencies related to the court system.[174] However, a tricky amendment rule, understood as applying to constitutional replacement as well, impeded organized attempts at alteration. Constitutional changes had to come from a constitutional convention, which the legislature would only call if it received "petitions from a majority of countries," with each "petition having to be signed by a majority of voters in each county within this state."[175]

While efforts to hold a convention to change the state constitution faced resistance and delays, the Georgia Assembly acted quickly to call a convention to consider the Constitution of the United States. The Congress of the Confederation formally sent out the constitution to the states on September 28, 1787, and Georgia's largest newspaper published it on October 13th. Within a week the state

[172] Ibid., 92

[173] Kenneth Coleman, *The American Revolution in Georgia: 1763–1789* (University of Georgia Press 1958) 81.

[174] John N. Shaeffer, "Georgia's 1789 Constitution: Was It Adopted in Defiance of the Constitutional Amending Process?," (1977) 61 The Georgia Historical Quarterly 329–41, 332–33.

[175] Ibid., 329; *Georgia Constitution* (1777), Art. LXIII.

assembly, already assembled in a special meeting to address growing conflict with the Muscogee, called for the election of the state ratifying convention. The convention assembled on December 28th, debated the federal constitution for one day, and unanimously ratified it on December 31st. The formal ratification ceremony took place two days later, and Georgia became the fourth state to ratify the U.S. Constitution.[176]

The approval of the federal constitution reenergized efforts to reform the state constitution, leading the state assembly to bypass the stringent amendment rule and simply convoke a constitutional convention on its own.[177] On January 31, 1788, the assembly appointed three people to represent each county, and delegated power to the Governor to call the constitutional convention as soon as nine states had ratified the federal constitution. In the process they approved a unique ratification process: the draft constitution would be circulated around the state, elections would be held for a second convention, and this convention would assemble in January to approve or reject the draft.[178]

Upon official word from the Congress of the Confederation that nine states had approved the U.S. Constitution, the Georgia Constitutional Convention assembled in Augusta on November 4, 1788. By the end of the month, they had created a constitution closely modeled on the federal constitution. Elections for the ratifying convention took place quickly, likely before anyone had time to study the proposed constitution, and it met on January 5th. Despite being "vested with full power ... for the sole purpose of adopting and ratifying, or rejecting" the proposed constitution, the ratifying convention decided to propose eleven amendments.[179] It adjourned, planning to publish the amendments, gauge public sentiment, and reassemble to adopt the constitution.

This was not meant to be. The newly elected state assembly, unhappy over the ratifying convention's decision to overreach and amend the draft constitution, ordered the election of another ratifying convention, this time empowered to accept the November constitution with or without any of the January amendments and an amendment proposed by the assembly itself.[180] In April 1789, Georgia voters

[176] Coleman, *The American Revolution in Georgia: 1763–1789*, 269–70; Shaeffer, "Georgia's 1789 Constitution: Was It Adopted in Defiance of the Constitutional Amending Process?," 335.

[177] Albert B. Saye, *A Constitutional History of Georgia: 1732–1945* (The University of Georgia Press 1948) 136; Coleman, *The American Revolution in Georgia: 1763–1789*, 27. This is the standard interpretation. However, Schaeffer disputes this conclusion, going to great lengths to show that if the 1777 amendment procedure is read broadly, and attention is paid to the surrounding debates over the 1789 constitution's creation, there was nothing illegal about it. Shaeffer, "Georgia's 1789 Constitution: Was It Adopted in Defiance of the Constitutional Amending Process?"

[178] Shaeffer, "Georgia's 1789 Constitution: Was It Adopted in Defiance of the Constitutional Amending Process?," 336; Coleman, *The American Revolution in Georgia: 1763–1789*, 271; Saye, *A Constitutional History of Georgia: 1732–1945*, 136.

[179] Coleman, *The American Revolution in Georgia: 1763–1789*, 272; Shaeffer, "Georgia's 1789 Constitution: Was It Adopted in Defiance of the Constitutional Amending Process?," 337–8.

[180] Shaeffer, "Georgia's 1789 Constitution: Was It Adopted in Defiance of the Constitutional Amending Process?," 339.

elected their third convention in a year a half. This second ratification convention assembled on May 4th and wasted no time. Debate lasted a single day, and on May 6th the convention ratified a version of the constitution that included most of the January amendments.[181]

4.2 Ratification Logic

Where did this ratification process come from? Prior to Georgia, only Massachusetts and New Hampshire ratified their constitutions, both by referendum. All the other American colonies/states had constitutions implemented directly after being written, and nothing in Georgia's previous constitution required a ratification procedure. How and why did the state assembly of Georgia create something new, a ratification procedure involving the submission of a draft constitution to a single convention consisting of delegates elected across the state? Can one discern general justifications for ratification from the reasons underlying this ratification variant's creation?

Answers are hard to find. The historical record of the debates at the state assembly are scant, consisting solely of motions and amendment proposals as well as vote counts. Public discussion on constitutional matters in newspapers at the time concerned what a new state constitution should look like, rather than how it should be created. Historical treatments of Georgia spend little time discussing the creation of the state's second constitution, focusing instead on its ratification of the federal constitution.

Nonetheless, two possibilities, not mutually exclusive, seem the most likely. On the one hand, perhaps the Georgia assembly simply wanted to mimic the procedure used by the Federal Convention, though they decided to use a single convention rather than sub-state conventions. This would be an example of what I call constitution-making borrowing, where designers of a constitution-making process mimic a successful high-profile constitution-making process. Borrowing is an explanation, and a common one at that, for why framers choose to construct a given constitution-making process in a particular way but does not serve as a justification for any specific procedural choice. It is no real justification for ratification to say we used the procedure simply because some other state or country did.

On the other hand, there is reason to surmise that the ratification procedure was the result of political compromise with more substantive weight. According to the Journal of the General Assembly of Georgia, on January 30, 1788, William Few, a member of the Continental Congress and a representative of Georgia at the Philadelphia Convention, moved that the assembly "name three fit and discreet

[181] Coleman, *The American Revolution in Georgia: 1763–1789*, 273.

persons from each county" to meet and create a new constitution. In other words, Few proposed the creation of a constituent assembly with members appointed by the legislature. An attempt was shortly made by Joseph Clay to amend the motion to require that, "a election be held in each county . . . for the purposes of choosing three fit and discreet persons." This proposal, which called for the election of a constitutional convention, failed by a vote of 38 to 25. However, in the records of the assembly Clay's proposal is immediately followed by Few making an addition to his original motion, in which he calls for copies of the draft constitution created by the new constituent assembly to be sent across the state for review, and for "every county . . . to choose three members each . . . for the sole purpose of adopting and ratifying; or rejecting the same."[182]

Perhaps then the use of a single ratifying convention resulted from bargaining about the site of constituent power. Some members of the Georgia legislature wanted the constitutional drafting body to be an appointed constituent assembly, with members handpicked by the legislators, while others wanted a proper constitutional convention, with the drafters being directly elected by the people themselves. The compromise was to use an appointed constituent assembly to draft the document in combination with a popularly elected ratification convention to approve or reject the results. While the appointed assembly excluded the people from the drafting process, a convention-based ratification procedure gave them an opportunity to participate in the constitution-making process rather than leave it entirely in the hands of constituted authorities. As with arguments advanced by the Berkshire Constitutionalists, the New York mechanics, and hinted at by the framers in Philadelphia, here a ratification procedure was needed as a moment of direct action for the people.

5. Conclusion

In this chapter I focused on the story of constitutional ratification's origins. Predominantly, this meant focusing on the events in revolutionary Massachusetts leading up to ratification's invention and first use, particularly the actions and arguments of the Berkshire Constitutionalists. These political dissidents shut down state courts amid the American Revolution for four years, reiterating their demand for and refining their justification of the opportunity to review and ratify any new constitution created for their state. I also introduced the New York Mechanics who, while not similarly successful in achieving direct ratification of their state

[182] General Assembly of Georgia, "Acts of the General Assembly of the State of Georgia Commencing the 1st of January, 1788," in *Early American Imprints: Series I Evans* (Readex 1984) microfilm 21107 (393–96). See also Shaeffer, "Georgia's 1789 Constitution: Was It Adopted in Defiance of the Constitutional Amending Process?," 336.

constitution, articulated contemporaneous arguments in favor of the procedure that mirrored and complemented those produced by the Constitutionalists.

While the Constitutionalists and the Mechanics invented constitutional ratification and gave the first and perhaps most substantive arguments in favor of the procedure, they concentrated on only one of its forms: ratification via referendum. Thus, in the remainder of the chapter, I explored the origins of two other ratification types: the use of subnational ratification conventions to approve the U.S. Constitution, and the use of a polity-wide convention to approve the State of Georgia's constitution. As a prelude to ratification's treatment today, where it is often unexamined and deployed uncritically, in both cases justifications for the use of ratification are not easy to find and did not seem to occupy the attention of those designing the constitution-making process. For the delegates at the Philadelphia Convention, this was likely because of the treaty-like nature of the Articles of Confederation and their absence of properly delegated power for constitution-making. This prevented them from creating a federal constitution without some explicit buy-in via ratification from the thirteen sovereign states. In the Georgia case, evidence of debate on the issue is simply lacking, with one likely explanation being that the designers of the constitution-making process simply decided to mimic the ratification procedure they had just used to approve the U.S. Constitution.

Nonetheless, in the process of outlining these origin stories, including the latter two, I unearthed several possible justifications for ratification that both relate to the pre- and extra-constitutional functions of ratification covered in the previous chapter and to some of the core justifications of ratification to be analyzed in the chapters ahead.

The first and most common, at least in these cases, portrays ratification as an instance of direct action. In modern treaty-making, this means ratification is the site in which those endowed with the actual power to authorize a treaty act. In the constitutional context, the idea is that the people must create and make a constitution their own at some point in the constitution-making process, and that ratification is justified because it provides a means for them to do so. This constituent power justification for ratification was critical to both the New York Mechanics' and the Berkshire Constitutionalists' advocacy for a ratification referendum, hinted at by the members of the Philadelphia Convention arguing for ratification by conventions rather than state legislatures, and perhaps served as the normative grounds for the bargain that apparently led to the use of a single ratification convention in Georgia.

The use of constituent power theorizing to justify ratification raises many questions. Why do the people need to make their constitution for it to be authoritative? What procedurally does it take for this happen? Why is ratification a necessary or particularly apt instance in the constitution-making process for the popular sovereign to emerge and act? These and other questions, and an examination of the strength of the constituent power justification more generally, will occupy us for the next three chapters.

A second justification proceeds by assigning ratification an agent review function and claiming that this is important or necessary. The procedure plays this role in early treaty-making and collective bargaining by providing an opportunity for principles to evaluate and temper the actions of their empowered agents or representatives. Kings and other sovereigns would use ratification to check up on the decisions of their empowered plenipotentiaries, while union members use it to weigh in on and retroactively influence the bargain struck by their negotiators. Applied to constitution-making, as the Berkshire Constitutionalists alluded to, this means that ratification is justified because it serves the essential role of providing a means for the people to discipline and review the work of their representative drafters. Why such a role is needed, and whether ratification can play it, will be the subject of chapter 7.

Finally, I showed elements of a justification for ratification that portrays the procedure in its support function, i.e. as a way of increasing the degree to which those subject to a decision support and accept it. This function first appeared in the context of collective bargaining, with some theorists suggesting that ratification procedures enable unions to increase the chances that their members will embrace a new employment agreement. Some of the framers of the U.S. Constitution hinted at just such a role for ratification by convention, when they claimed that the procedure was uniquely poised to convince elites that the new constitution took precedence over both ordinary and constitutional state laws. A general justification of this form claims that it is desirable for those to be governed by a new constitution to believe it is legitimate, and that ratification should be implemented because it is necessary for or makes more likely such legitimacy beliefs. Chapters 8 and 9 explore both this and other legitimacy-related arguments for using ratification.

4
Making the Constituent Power Speak

As discussed in chapter 2, around the beginning of the eighteenth century, ratification's role in treaty-making began to shift to what I call its *direct action function*. The delegation of full powers to plenipotentiaries began to disappear. No longer could ambassadors and foreign ministers make binding and authoritative agreements with their counterparts on their own, for they lacked the power to do so. Instead, the negotiation of treaties became separate from their authorization, which took place during treaty ratification. It was here, during ratification, that the sovereign power acted, putting its seal of approval on an agreement and making it binding provided its counterpart did the same.

The components of this role of treaty ratification—the inability of representatives to make agreements that bind the source of their own authority (the sovereign), the need for a final process during which the sovereign would take direct action and make an agreement its own—bear resemblance to and suggest the first core justification of constitutional ratification that I will investigate. These are arguments that seek to connect ratification with *constituent power*, the idea that the people alone have the power to make fundamental law.

Constituent power seems ready-made to provide an explanation for implementing constitutional ratification, for what, if anything, do ratification procedures involve if not the sovereign people exercising their will and making a constitution their own? According to such a *constituent power justification* (CPJ), any legitimate, authoritative, or rightful constitution must be the creation of the people, and ratification is the moment, or an essential moment, when this becomes possible. In other words, the reasons for implementing ratification stem from its intended function as a moment of higher lawmaking when the people are explicitly present.

This conceptualization of ratification as a moment of constituent power is both intuitive and expressed by a wide range of constitutional actors. It motivated both the Berkshire Constitutionalists and the New York Mechanics Union in their efforts to have their respective state constitutions approved by the people directly. At the Philadelphia Convention, shades of this argument appeared during the debate over whether to submit the U.S. Constitution to state ratifying conventions or the state legislatures. At the Pennsylvania Ratification Convention in 1787, James Wilson articulated the position clearly, claiming that "This . . . is not a government founded upon compact; it is founded upon the power of the people. They express in their name and their authority—"*We, the people, do ordain and establish, &c.*; from their

Constitutional Ratification without Reason. Jeffrey A. Lenowitz, Oxford University Press. © Jeffrey A. Lenowitz 2022.
DOI: 10.1093/oso/9780198852346.003.0004

ratification alone is it to take its constitutional authenticity, without that, it is no more than a *tabula rasa*."[1] Similarly, the Ukrainian Justice V.M. Kampo claimed that constituent referendums are based on "the exclusive right of the people to define and alter the constitutional order . . . that is, to realize constituent power."[2]

This and the following two chapters explore constituent power justifications of ratification. However, as I will show, these justifications gain some of their intuitive bite by blurring or avoiding the actual mechanics of constitution-making. Thus, our analysis is anything but straightforward, for constituent power theorizing usually operates on a level of abstraction above actual constitution-making procedures. This chapter breaks into four sections: I define the concept of constituent power and explain its relevance; explore some of the central questions that motivate its discussion; highlight the traditional immiscible relation between constituent power theory and the mechanics of creating a constitution; and then investigate several ways in which ratification might serve as an instance of constituent power and analyze the strength of the resulting justifications. Note that my focus is not on critically evaluating the coherence or strength of constituent power theorizing generally.[3] Rather, I seek to know whether, according to its own logic, it can produce plausible reasons for implementing ratification.

1. The Theory of Constituent Power

Constituent power, also known as the *pouvoir constituant* or the constitution-making power, is an old, central, and much written about concept in constitutional theory. It arose in conjunction with the creation of the first written constitutions, yet its roots date back to earlier theoretical discussions of the sovereignty/governance distinction, political resistance, authority, and the social contract.[4] Emmanuel

[1] James Wilson, *Collected Works of James Wilson* (Liberty Fund 2007) 254.

[2] V.M. Kampo, "Dissenting Opinion of Justice of the Constitutional Court of Ukraine V.M. Campo Pertaining to Decision No.6-Rp/2008 of April 16, 2008," (2009) 44 Statutes and Decisions 93–96, 94.

[3] For articles that do this, see David Dyzenhaus, "Constitutionalism in an Old Key: Legality and Constituent Power," (2012) 1 Global Constitutionalism 229–60; Carlos Bernal, "Constitution-Making (without Constituent) Power: On the Conceptual Limits of the Power to Replace and Revise the Constitution" in Richard Albert, Carlos Bernal, and Juliano Z. Benvindo (eds.), *Constitutional Change and Transformation in Latin America* (Hart Publishing 2019).

[4] The first English use of the term "constituent power" in a manner similar to how it is now understood is a subject of debate. Some claim that Thomas Young, a New York Radical, was the first to use the term. In 1776 he wrote "the people at large . . . are the supreme constituent power, and of Course their immediate Representatives are the supreme Delegate power; and as soon as the delegate power gets too far out of the hands of the constituent power, a tyranny is in some degree established." However, the British pamphleteer Junius used the term similarly six years earlier to refer to a type of power superior to the legislature. See Thomas Young, "Thomas Young to the People of the Grants," in Christopher Morgan (ed.), *The Documentary History of the State of New York* (Charles Van Benthuysen 1851) 563; Willi Paul Adams, *The First American Constitutions: Republican Ideology and the Making of the State Constitutions in the Revolutionary Era* (expanded edn, Rowman & Littlefield 2001) 63; Junius, "To the Printer of the Public Advertiser," *The Letters of Junius* (Leavitt, Trow & Co 1848) 29. For a discussion

Sieyès and Carl Schmitt are the most famous exponents of the fully developed concept, while Bodin, Hobbes, Machiavelli, Rousseau, Lawson, Locke, Paine, and others are frequently held to be important contributors.[5]

Put simply, constituent power is the unique power of the people (or the people themselves when exercising this power) to make and unmake their constitution, the set of fundamental laws that undergirds and creates their state. Specifically, when it comes to constitution-making, it is the power held by the body of individuals that inhabit the territory to be governed in accordance with the new constitution.[6] Constituent power is, as Schmitt summarizes, "the political will, whose power or authority is capable of making the concrete, comprehensive decision over the type and form of its own political existence."[7] A theory of constituent power thus claims that the constituent power must create the constitution for it to be authoritative, i.e. that the only valid constitution for a state is one made by its people.[8] This viewpoint is, for instance, instantiated in the preamble to the German Basic Law, which states that "the German people, in the exercise of their constituent power, have adopted this Basic Law."[9]

Contemporary work frequently uses "popular sovereignty" interchangeably with, or in the place of, "constituent power," likely because constituent power is an application of popular sovereignty onto the modern concept of a constitution.[10]

tracing the concept of constituent power to medieval and early modern law, see Daniel Lee, *Popular Sovereignty in Early Modern Constitutional Thought* (Oxford University Press 2016).

[5] See Murray G. Forsyth, "Thomas Hobbes and the Constituent Power of the People," (2006) XXIX Political Studies 191–203; Andrew Arato, *The Adventures of the Constituent Power* (Cambridge University Press 2017) 46; Murray G. Forsyth, "Hobbes's Contractarianism: A Comparative Analysis," in David Boucher and Paul Kelly (eds.), *The Social Contract from Hobbes to Rawls* (Routledge Press 1994) 42; Julian H. Franklin, *John Locke and the Theory of Sovereignty: Mixed Monarchy and the Rights of Resistance in the Political Thought of the English Revolution* (Cambridge University Press 1978); Bronislaw Baczko, "The Social Contract of the French: Sieyes and Rousseau," (1988) 60: Supplement The Journal of Modern History S98–S125, 100; Andreas Kalyvas, "Sovereignty, Democracy, and the Constituent Power," (2005) 12 Constellations 223–44, 227; Claude Klein, "A Propos Constituent Power: Some General Views in a Modern Context," in Antero Jyranki (ed.), *National Constitutions in the Era of Integration* (Kluwer Law International 1999) 31–32; Richard Tuck, *The Sleeping Sovereign: The Invention of Modern Democracy* (Cambridge University Press 2016); Martin Loughlin, "On Constituent Power," in Michael W. Dowdle and Michael A Wilkinson (eds.), *Constitutionalism Beyond Liberalism* (Cambridge University Press 2017); Lucia Rubinelli, *Constituent Power: A History* (Cambridge University Press 2020).

[6] Recent examples of this identification include: Philipp Dann and Zaid Al-ali, "The Internationalized *Pouvoir Constituant*—Constitution-Making under External Influence in Iraq, Sudan and East Timor," (2006) 10 Max Plank Yearbook of United Nations Law 423–63, 426; Markkhu Suksi, *Bringing in the People: A Comparison of Constitutional Forms and Practices of the Referendum* (Martinus Nijhoff Publishers 1993) 26.

[7] Carl Schmitt, *Constitutional Theory* (Duke University Press 2008) 125.

[8] Kalyvas, "Sovereignty, Democracy, and the Constituent Power," 237.

[9] *Grundgesetz Der Bundesrepublik Deutschland* (1949), preamble.

[10] Angelica Maria Bernal, *Beyond Origins: Rethinking Founding in a Time of Constitutional Democracy* (Oxford University Press 2017) 78–79; Ulrich K. Preuss, "Constitutional Powermaking for the New Polity: Some Deliberations on the Relations between Constituent Power and the Constitution," in Michel Rosenfeld (ed.), *Constitutionalism, Identity, Difference, and Legitimacy: Theoretical Perspectives*

By popular sovereignty, I mean the idea that no authority exists that can justify authoritative rule other than the will of the people to be ruled. This assertion rests on a dismissal of all prior sources of political authority. Divine appointment, beneficial consequences, superior force, age and tradition, none remain sufficient to ground coercive rule. By a modern conception of a constitution, I mean the idea of a constitution as a body of extraordinary law that is made and remade by real actors, rather than an informal ordering of state institutions and a bundle of normative principles. The latter evolves and gains authority because of its history and continued use, while the former requires an actor taking concrete steps to both create and authorize it.[11]

1.1 Extraordinary and Ordinary

To begin unpacking the theory and concept of constituent power I will start by exploring the ideal-typical distinction between ordinary and extraordinary law, two types of legal rules thought to be found in a constitutional system of government.[12] Ordinary law is familiar law, the body of positive law or legal rules that composes a working legal system; it contains anything from noise ordinances to tax codes to gun control regulations. Extraordinary law is constitutional law, the rules that determine how public power it to be exercised by organizing, defining, and limiting the institutions of government and setting out the formal procedures through which these institutions both govern and create ordinary law.[13]

Extraordinary law is "higher" than ordinary law in two central ways. First, since "the constitution is the highest level within national law," as Kelsen notes, it overrides ordinary law within a constitutional framework.[14] Thus, extraordinary law is controlling in cases of conflict with ordinary law, as evidenced by the judicial invalidation of ordinary acts of legislation when found to contradict constitutional laws within the same jurisdiction.[15]

(Duke University Press 1994) 468; Richard S. Kay, "Constituent Authority," (2011) 59 American Journal of Comparative Law 715–61, 27.

[11] Loughlin, "On Constituent Power," 151.

[12] For general discussions of the two types of legal rules, see H.L.A. Hart, *The Concept of Law* (2nd edn, Oxford University Press 1994) 89–96; Hans Kelsen, *General Theory of Law and State* (Transaction Publishers 2006) 115–19; Stephen Tierney, "Constitutional Referendums: A Theoretical Enquiry," (2009) 72 The Modern Law Review 360–83, 362.

[13] Larry Alexander, "What Are Constitutions, and What Should (and Can) They Do?" in Ellen Frankel Paul, Fred D. Miller, Jr., and Jeffrey Paul (eds.), *What Should Constitutions Do?* (Cambridge University Press 2011) 4.

[14] Kelsen, *General Theory of Law and State*, 124.

[15] Of course, hierarchical superiority also exists between ordinary laws. For instance, in federal systems such as the United States, valid federal legislation generally takes precedence over the statutes enacted by state legislatures. Extraordinary law is what lies at the very top of the legal hierarchy of a constitutional state. See Thomas C. Grey, "Constitutionalism: An Analytic Framework," in Roland

Some of the first written constitutions were described as "supremely normative" in this manner.[16] For instance, in *Federalist 78*, Hamilton insists that whenever an irreconcilable variance between two laws occurs, that which has the superior validity ought to be preferred, i.e. "the Constitution ought to be preferred to statute."[17] As explained in the previous chapter, several delegates to the Philadelphia Convention pushed for submitting the U.S. Constitution to ratifying conventions rather than state legislatures for just this reason; they thought it would help ensure that future courts treated the U.S. Constitution as extraordinary law when it came into conflict with subsequent state or federal legislation. Today, it is increasingly common to stipulate this sort of legal and normative superiority directly within a constitution. The beginning of Article 9 of the Ethiopian Constitution provides an example: "The Constitution is the supreme law of the land. Any law, customary practice or a decision of an organ of state or a public official which contravenes this Constitution shall be of no effect."[18]

Second, extraordinary law is higher because it authorizes and helps create ordinary law. As Althusius put it, "the greater is that which constituted the other."[19] This is why constitutional law occupies the top of Kelsen's legal hierarchy. As he explains, if "one legal norm determines the way in which another norm is created . . . the norm determining the creation of another norm is the superior, the norm created according to this regulation, the inferior norm."[20] Put differently, extraordinary law has higher status because it regulates the rules of the political game, part of which entails indirectly creating ordinary law by setting out the legally legitimate process of legislating.[21] Extraordinary law does this by constructing the institutions of government, outlining the rules they operate through, and assigning some of them the task of and the authority needed to legislate.

For theories of constituent power, the distinction between extraordinary and ordinary also applies to political actors and political power. This sets these theories apart from Kelsenian strains of legal positivism, where the validity of extraordinary law rests on an abstract and assumed norm, rather than the decision of a primal authority.[22] The legal and political institutions created and governed by the

J. Pennock and John W. Chapman (eds.), *Constitutionalism* (Nomos, New York University Press 1979) 195.

[16] Dann and Al-ali, "The Internationalized *Pouvoir Constituant*—Constitution-Making under External Influence in Iraq, Sudan and East Timor," 427.

[17] James Madison, Alexander Hamilton, and John Jay, *The Federalist Papers* (Penguin Books 1987) 439. Admittedly, it is unclear whether Hamilton had federal or only state law in mind.

[18] *Constitution of the Federal Democratic Republic of Ethiopia* (1994), Art. 9, sec. 1.

[19] Johannes Althusius, *Politica: An Abridged Translation of Politics Methodically Set Forth and Illustrated with Sacred and Profane Examples* (Liberty Fund 1995) 73.

[20] Kelsen, *General Theory of Law and State*, 124.

[21] Hannah Lerner, *Making Constitutions in Deeply Divided Societies* (Cambridge University Press 2011) 16.

[22] Schmitt explicitly attacks Kelsen on this point. See Schmitt, *Constitutional Theory*, 76. See also Joel Colón-Ríos, "The Legitimacy of the Juridical: Constituent Power, Democracy, and the Limits of Constitutional Reform," (2010) 48 Osgood Hall Law Journal 199–245, 208.

constitution are *constituted bodies*; the power they use is *constituted power*. This ordinary power manifests within existing legal institutions and procedures that form and limit its operation, determine its characters, and invest it with authority. All constituted bodies, from legislatures to judiciaries to the military, exercise constituted power in their day-to-day operation. Unlike constituted ordinary political power, extraordinary political power is exercised infrequently, and only to accomplish the very specific task of creating or remaking a constitutional order.[23] *Constituent power* is the name given to both the author of extraordinary law and the extraordinary power that it wields, though the former is also referred to as *constituent authority*.[24] Put simply, the constituent authority exercises constituent power when creating its constitution.

Admittedly, this definition of constituent power elides the distinction between *pouvoir constituent originaire* and *pouvoir constituent derive*, between the original or primary constituent power that creates a constitution and the derived or secondary constituent power that amends a constitution within an existing constitutional framework.[25] These twin concepts, developed by scholars such as Raymond Carre de Malberg and Roger Bonnard, are common within French constitutional theory. However, most scholars of constituent power follow Schmitt, arguing that the power to amend the constitution is not constituent power, and thus the distinction dissolves.[26] Derived or secondary constituent power describes a type of power that operates within the confines, to varying degrees, of constituted bodies and constitutional rules. While a constitutional amendment, even one produced by a popular referendum, can alter the constitution, its process is dictated by the constitution and thus it leaves the normative superiority and sovereignty of the constitution intact. Since, as I show below, constituent power is inherently unconstrained, derived constituent power appears not to be constituent power at all.[27]

[23] Kay, "Constituent Authority," 719; Bruce A. Ackerman, *We the People: Foundations* (Harvard University Press 1991) 6–10.

[24] Sometimes constituent authority is used in a different sense. For instance, Kay, somewhat mysteriously, uses it to refer to that "quality in a person or persons that enables them to produce an effective positive law constitution. Kay, "Constituent Authority," 720.

[25] For a thorough discussion of this distinction, see Asem Khalil, *The Enactment of Constituent Power in the Arab World: The Palestinian Case* (Dissertation, University of Fribourg 2006) 22–37. See also Stephen Tierney, *Constitutional Referendums: The Theory and Practice of Republican Deliberation* (Oxford University Press 2012) 11–13. For a discussion of why we should use primary and secondary constituent power, rather than original and derivative constituent power, see Yaniv Roznai, *Unconstitutional Constitutional Amendments* (Oxford University Press 2017) 120–123.

[26] Schmitt, *Constitutional Theory*, 150–158.

[27] For a subtle discussion of constituent power and its application to conceptualizing the limits of amending powers see Roznai, *Unconstitutional Constitutional Amendments*, especially chapter 6.

1.2 Characteristics

Three central characteristics of constituent power follow from the distinction between extraordinary and ordinary law and power. First, constituent power cannot be regulated by law or constituted authority.[28] Superficially, the emergence of constituent power and the mere occurrence of constitution-making signal a deep dissatisfaction with the current mode of government. This, at least practically, deprives its components of much of their sociological legitimacy, meaning that during the creation of a new constitution the constituted bodies, ordinary law, and constitution of the old regime would lack whatever power regulating the constituent authority entails.[29] Elster describes this reasoning in regards to a constituent assembly invested with constituent power: "Almost by definition, the old regime is part of the problem that a constituent assembly is convened to solve. There would be no need to have an assembly if the regime was not flawed. But if it is flawed, why should the assembly respect its instructions?"[30]

More fundamentally, the inability of constituent power to be regulated follows directly from the nature of the constitutional legal hierarchy; since constituent power is the source of constitutional law, and thus the source of all authority in a legal system, nothing within this system has the power to constrain it. To claim otherwise is to mistakenly insist, in the words of Price, that "there ought to be a power in the state superior to that which gives it being, and from which all jurisdiction in it is derived."[31] Thus, extraordinary law is unable to regulate constituent power because it is the creation of said power, and creations are always inferior to their makers.[32] This logic applies all the way down the hierarchy: constituted

[28] This includes international law as well, which is particularly at odds with the legal hierarchical logic of constituent power. Thus, attempts to impose international legal requirements on the nature of constitution-making procedures, for example the Mikmaq tribe's attempt to gain a specific type of representation in the Canadian Constitutional Conference by appealing to Art. 25 of the International Covenant on Civil and Political Rights (ICCPR), are incoherent and unpersuasive for constituent power theory, which holds that no norms, even international ones, are capable of binding or influencing the constituent power. Donald Marshall, Alexander Denny, and Simon Marshall, *Communication of the Sante' Mawi'omi Wjit Mikmaq under the Optional Protocol to the International Covenant on Civil and Political Rights* (1986). See also Angela M. Banks, "Expanding Participation in Constitution Making: Challenges and Opportunities," (2008) 49 William and Mary Law Review 1043–69, 1051–55; Thomas M. Franck and Arun K. Thiruvengadam, "Norms of International Law Relating to the Constitution-Making Process," in Laurel E. Miller (ed.), *Framing the State in Times of Transition: Case Studies in Constitution Making* (United States Institute of Peace Press 2010).

[29] Kalyvas, "Sovereignty, Democracy, and the Constituent Power," 227; Andrew Arato, "Carl Schmitt and the Revival of the Constituent Power in the United States," (1999–2000) 21 Cardozo Law Review 1739–47, 1741.

[30] Jon Elster, "Forces and Mechanisms in the Constitution-Making Process," (1995) 45 Duke Law Review 364–96, 370.

[31] Richard Price, "Two Tracts on Civil Liberty, the War with America, and the Debts and Finances of the Kingdom," in D.O. Thomas (ed.), *Richard Price: Political Writings* (Cambridge University Press 1991) 27.

[32] "No constitutional law can confer a constitution-making power and prescribe the form of its own initiation." Schmitt, *Constitutional Theory*, 132.

bodies and the ordinary law they create are unable to regulate constituent power because they cannot have a power or ability beyond that possessed by extraordinary law itself. As *Vindiciae Contra Tyrannos* explains, "For such is the force of the world: one who is constituted by another is held to be lesser; and one who receives his authority from another is inferior to his appointer."[33]

Of course, despite the fact that constituted bodies and law cannot regulate constituent power, they often try. In many instances, these attempts end in failure. Most famously, both the U.S. Federal Convention and the 1789 *Assemblée Nationale Constituante* violated the demands and restrictions imposed upon them by constituted bodies and pre-existing legal systems.[34] However, in other cases, the constituent power acts in accordance with existing procedures or institutional directives. For instance, the creation of the South African Constitution followed the procedures set out in the interim constitution enacted by the final apartheid parliament, and the 2010 Kenyan constitution-making process followed the procedures laid out in a 2008 amendment to the existing constitution regarding the proper legal methods for replacing the constitution.[35]

A proponent of constituent power theory has to interpret these events in one of two ways. She might claim that constituent power played no role in these processes, and that therefore either an illegitimate constitution was created or an old constitution was simply altered by constituted powers. Or, she might claim that in each case the constituent power did create the constitution, and that it chose rather than was forced to manifest and act in accordance with pre-existing procedures.[36] In this case, it is the fact that the constituent power chose to follow established provisions on constitution-making that gives the resulting constitution its authority, rather than the fact that the specified procedures were followed.

A second characteristic of constituent power is that it is extra-legal and self-authorizing.[37] It emerges *ex nihilo* and authorizes both itself and the resulting legal and political system by its sheer existence and action. Since "the power to constitute," Kalyvas states, "refers to the origins of higher constitutional norms, the very foundation of any valid legal system, it cannot be traced back to any juridical norm,

[33] Stephanus Junius Brutus, *Vindiciae, Contra Tyrannos* (Cambridge University Press 1994) 74. See Daniel Lee, "Private Law Models for Public Law Concepts: The Roman Law Theory of Dominium in the Monarchomach Doctrine of Popular Sovereignty," (2008) 70 The Review of Politics 370–99.

[34] Jon Elster, *Ulysses Unbound* (Cambridge University Press 2000) 108.

[35] Hassen Ebrahim, Kayode Fayemi, and Stephanie Loomis, *Promoting a Culture of Constitutionalism and Democracy in Commonwealth Africa: Recommendations to Commonwealth Heads of Government* (Commonwealth Human Rights Initiative 1999) 120; the Constitution of Kenya (Amendment) Bill (2008). See also Michele Brandt and others, *Constitution-Making and Reform: Options for the Process* (Interpeace 2011), 39. Also notable is the creation of the 1978 Sri Lankan Constitution, which was adopted pursuant to sec. 51 of the Constitution of Sri Lanka of 1972.

[36] In addition, as Kay explains, sometimes the masking of an exercise of constituent authority behind a façade of legality serves important political interests. See Richard S. Kay, "Constituent Authority," (2010) American Journal of Comparative Law, forthcoming, 733.

[37] Bernal, *Beyond Origins: Rethinking Founding in a Time of Constitutional Democracy*, chapter 3.

simply because a norm does not yet exist."[38] Thus, constituent power emerges from an "extra-legal zone" and is unsupported by any authoritative legal structure, yet serves as the source of all legal and political authority within a state. It therefore authorizes without being authorized, and founds without being founded.[39] This is why, for theories of constituent power, constitution-making is described as a break, an exception, or a rupture, a radically creative event that results in the formation of a genuinely new political order that traces its authority to nothing but the unauthorized constituent power and the facticity of its founding act.[40]

Third and finally, the constituent power is irreducible to the established legal and political order that it substantiates. In other words, the constituent power creates, rather than transforms into, constituted powers. It thus remains something distinct from the legal and political institutions of government it produces. Whether this means that constituent power disappears after the creation of a constitution is one of several central questions or ambiguities in the constituent power literature that I discuss below.

1.3 Questions

Of course, no settled or uniform version of a theory of constituent power actually exists. Instead, there are several key puzzles that divide different versions of the theory and drive debate. Three central questions, relating to identity, the longevity of constituent power, and the potential for action, structure contemporary discussions.

The first question—*the identity question*—pertains to identity and poses the well-known democratic boundary problem, the question of who exactly should be included when making democratic decisions, to the process of constitution-making itself.[41] It asks: what it meant by "the people" or "the nation?" Who is the subject of constituent power?[42] In the context of constitution-making, when polities are

[38] Kalyvas, "Sovereignty, Democracy, and the Constituent Power," 227. Kay writes something similar: "to inquire into the authority to make a new constitution is exactly to ask who may establish law without legal sanction." Kay, "Constituent Authority," 732.

[39] John Ferejohn, *Why the People: A Reflection on Democratic Constitutionalism* (Stanford University 2004) 3. See also Andreas Kalyvas, *Democracy and the Politics of the Extraordinary* (Cambridge University Press 2008) 93–94.

[40] Kalyvas, "Sovereignty, Democracy, and the Constituent Power," 228. Note that here one can see the social contract origins of constituent power theory, for the extra-legal and pre-juridical zone inhabited by constituent power is very much like the contractual concept of the state of nature or state of civil society. As Baczko explains: "the doctrine of the constituent power thus linked the principle of the social contract to political practice and aided their translation into action." Baczko, "The Social Contract of the French: Sieyes and Rousseau," 106.

[41] David Miller, "Democracy's Domain," (2009) 37 Philosophy & Public Affairs 201–28.

[42] Chambers notes that while "everyone agrees that popular sovereignty is a defining feature of modern constitutionalism, there appears to be an equally strong consensus that we can talk about a 'people' exercising constituent popular sovereignty only in a very loose way." Simone Chambers,

being remade or created, the identity of the people becomes even more important and real than in ordinary politics. Here it is a matter of deciding upon the people, rather than finding a way to glean their will. Two general answers to this identity question are common, each of which correlates to different conceptualizations of national identity and the relation between the people and their constitution.[43]

On the one hand, the people can be cast as an ethnos, a pre-political community constituted by some sort of commonness such as race, religion, history, culture, and the like.[44] This conception of the nation as "culture nation", to use Meinecke's terminology, was especially prominent in twentieth-century German and Eastern European constitutional theory.[45] It corresponds to a "nation-state constitution," understood as a reflection and protector of the aspirations, values, and culture of a pre-existing society.[46] According to Preuss, Schmitt had this conception in mind when discussing the sort of constituent power capable of creating a democratic state.[47] More recently, this conceptualization of the constituent power as ethnos appeared rather literally within the Estonian constitution-making process, when the franchise specified for the 1992 Constitutional Referendum was limited to those born in Estonia in 1940 and their descendants.[48]

On the other hand, the people as constituent power can be conceptualized as a demos or state nation, a political construction consisting of the totality of citizens in an existing state or one that emerges or begins during the constitution-making process.[49] Sieyès seems to understand the constituent power in just this way, describing the nation as the "body of associates living under a *common* law, *represented* by the same *legislature*, etc," and later as "the sum total of all the associates governed by, and obedient to, the law that is the work of their will."[50] This conception of the demos need not be static. For instance, both Espejo and Bernal

"Democracy, Popular Sovereignty and Constitutional Legitimacy," (2004) 11 Constellations 153–73, 154.

[43] Lerner, *Making Constitutions in Deeply Divided Societies*, 25.

[44] Preuss, "Constitutional Powermaking for the New Polity: Some Deliberations on the Relations between Constituent Power and the Constitution," 149–50.

[45] F. Meinecke, *Cosmopolitanism and the National State* (Princeton University Press 1970) 8.

[46] Lerner, *Making Constitutions in Deeply Divided Societies*, 25.

[47] Preuss, "Constitutional Powermaking for the New Polity: Some Deliberations on the Relations between Constituent Power and the Constitution," 151–52; Schmitt, *Constitutional Theory*, 257–59.

[48] This excluded 40% of the population, most of whom were ethnic Russians. Levent Gönenç, *Prospects for Constitutionalism in Post-Communist Countries*, vol. 50 (Law in Eastern Europe, Martinus Nijhoff Publishers 2002) 167–68.

[49] Kay, "Constituent Authority," 151; Preuss, "Constitutional Powermaking for the New Polity: Some Deliberations on the Relations between Constituent Power and the Constitution," 149–52.

[50] Emmanuel Joseph Sieyès, "What Is the Third Estate?" in Michael Sonenscher (ed.), *Political Writings: Including the Debate between Sieyès and Tom Paine in 1791* (Hackett Publishing Company 2003) 93; Emmanuel Joseph Sieyès, "Reasoned Exposition of the Rights of Man and Citizen," in Marc Allan Goldstein (ed.), *Social and Political Thought of the French Revolution, 1788–1797* (Peter Lang Publishers 1997) 142.

advance conceptions of the people as a demos that is always in the process of being made. As Espejo writes, "a people is always in the making and unmaking."[51]

The corresponding vision of a constitution to this demotic conception is a "liberal constitution." Such a constitution expresses a shared civic identity consisting in the ground rules of democracy and lawmaking as agreed upon by either a pre-existing citizenry or one formed during the constitution-making process itself. Recent constitution-making efforts in post-conflict settings, and the corresponding literature that arose alongside and in response to them, utilize and endorse this conception of the constituent power. Here, constitution-making is cast as a process through which competing social groups and communities unite as the constituent power and become a nation tied together through mutually agreed upon extraordinary law.[52]

The second question, *the outcome question*, asks: what happens to the constituted power after the constituting act? Underlying this question is the fundamental tension between the formless extra-constitutional constituent power and the formal constituted power, and the apparent impossibility of the two existing simultaneously. The constituent power becomes visible in moments of constitution-making as the pre-juridical supreme source of all future constitutional legitimacy, yet it is unclear what happens to the constituent power once it births the constituted form. If the constituent power disappears, does this mean that constitution-making involves a transfer of sovereignty to the constituted powers?[53] If the constituent power remains, how are constitutional laws more permanent and sacred than ordinary provisional legislation? As Loughlin and Walker point out, three general answers to this outcome question are dominant.[54] Some argue that constituent power is drained by and absorbed into the institutional and juridical sites of power that it constructs.[55] Others claim that constituent power remains as a latent revolutionary potential underlying and in tension with the constituted legal authorities.[56] And a final group claim that constituent power remains in the form of a general

[51] Paulina Ochoa Espejo, *The Time of Popular Sovereignty: Process and the Democratic State* (The Pennsylvania State University Press 2011) 3.

[52] See Laurel E. Miller, "Designing Constitution-Making Processes: Lessons from the Past, Questions for the Future," in Laurel E. Miller (ed.), *Framing the State in Times of Transition: Case Studies in Constitution Making* (United States Institute of Peace Press 2010) 627–8; Serdar Tekin, *Founding Acts: Constitutional Origins in a Democratic Age* (University of Pennsylvania Press 2016); Joanne Wallis, *Constitution Making During State Building* (Cambridge University Press 2014).

[53] See Forsyth, "Hobbes's Contractarianism: A Comparative Analysis," 42.

[54] Martin Loughlin and Neil Walker, "Introduction," in Martin Loughlin and Neil Walker (eds.), *The Paradox of Constitutionalism: Constituent Power and Constitutional Form* (Cambridge University Press 2007) 6.

[55] David Dyzenhaus, "The Politics of the Question of Constituent Power," in Martin Loughlin and Neil Walker (eds.), *The Paradox of Constitutionalism: Constituent Power and Constitutional Form* (Cambridge University Press 2007); Stephen Holmes, *Passions and Constraint: On the Theory of Liberal Democracy* (University of Chicago Press 1995).

[56] Antonio Negri, *Insurgencies: Constituent Power and the Modern State* (The University of Minnesota Press 2009); Bernal, *Beyond Origins: Rethinking Founding in a Time of Constitutional Democracy*.

commitment to popular sovereignty in constructive tension with the constituted powers.[57] As Habermas explains, "All the later generations have the task of actualizing the still-untapped normative substance of the system of rights laid down in the original document of the constitution."[58]

The third central question is *the action question*. It asks: how can the constituent power act?[59] This query stems from the observation that the people seem unable to act in ordinary politics without the presence of institutions and procedures designed to collect, form, and channel the popular will. As Madison asserted, "it is impossible for the people to spontaneously and universally to move in concert towards their object."[60] However, these institutions are unavailable to the constituent power. On the one hand, the occurrence of constitution-making means that any existing constituted bodies are relics from a previous regime that, as evidenced by the constitution-making activity itself, is no longer fully authoritative.[61] On the other hand, "no type of delegated power can modify the conditions of its own delegation," i.e. constituted bodies cannot be used as the means to modify the source of their own authority and the determinate of their own shape.

Moreover, the use of any formal institutions to enact the popular will qualifies as some sort of constraint, and the constituent power is that which cannot be constrained.[62] As Schmitt notes, "even the attempt to establish a definitive representative or interpreter of the people's will in some binding manner contradicts this theory," yet the "execution and formulation of a political decision reached by the people in unmediated form requires some organization, a procedure."[63] Thus, a paradox arises because the people seem unable to act without the constituted forms they have the sole authority to construct.[64] This action question reveals that when

[57] Akhil Reed Amar, "Popular Sovereignty and Constitutional Amendment," in Sanford Levinson (ed.), *Responding to Imperfection* (Princeton University Press 1995); Preuss, "Constitutional Powermaking for the New Polity: Some Deliberations on the Relations between Constituent Power and the Constitution"; Ackerman, *We the People: Foundations*; Joel Colón-Ríos, *Weak Constitutionalism: Democratic Legitimacy and the Question of Constituent Power* (Routledge 2012).

[58] Jürgen Habermas, "Constitutional Democracy: A Paradoxical Union of Contradictory Principles," (2001) 29 Political Theory, 774.

[59] Hans Lindahl, "Possibility, Actuality, Rupture: Constituent Power and the Ontology of Change," (2015) 22, 163–74.

[60] Madison, Hamilton, and Jay, *The Federalist Papers*, 264 #240.

[61] Kalyvas, *Democracy and the Politics of the Extraordinary*, 119; Kalyvas, "Sovereignty, Democracy, and the Constituent Power," 227; Schmitt, *Constitutional Theory*, 132; Elster, "Forces and Mechanisms in the Constitution-Making Process," 370.

[62] For recent attempts to reinvent constituent power to allow its exercise through constituted bodies, see Arato, *The Adventures of the Constituent Power*, 45–105; Andrew Arato, *Post Sovereign Constitution Making* (Oxford University Press 2016) 19–74; Oran Doyle, "Populist Constitutionalism and Constituent Power," (2018) 20 German Law Journal 161–80.

[63] Schmitt, *Constitutional Theory*, 128, 132.

[64] Somek writes: "The very act of founding a constitutional regime reveals a basic interdependency. While a multitude could not act as a community of citizens if it were not for legally constituted powers, these powers themselves depend for their realization on an activity which is not channeled by norms." Alexander Somek, "The Owl of Minerva: Constitutional Discourse before Its Conclusion," (2008) 71 The Modern Law Review 473–89, 476.

it comes to constitution-making, as Count Joseph de Maistre writes, the people sometimes appear to be "a sovereign that cannot exercise sovereignty."[65]

While all these questions are important and essential for understanding the concept of constituent power, it is the last one I want to pay attention to, for our concern is a subset of it. I am interested in the puzzling relationship between the constituent power and one of the mechanisms through which it constitutes. Specifically, does ratification serve as a vehicle through which the people exercise their constituent power?

2. Finding Constituent Power Justifications

The above discussion makes clear why constituent power theory is a likely candidate for justifying the implementation of ratification procedures. Constituent power theory claims that only the constituent power can create a valid constitution, and ratification, in its various forms, seems to be a perfect example of the people doing just that. However, testing this intuition requires bringing constituent power theory into contact with the actual procedures and institutions of constitution-making, something usually avoided by both constitution-makers and constitutional scholars.

2.1 Avoiding the Alchemist's Stone

Constitutions are made using fairly standardized institutions and procedures. Throughout the five phases of constitution-making discussed in chapter 1—initiation, convoking, drafting, approval, and ratification—a variety of discrete tasks take place. These can include choosing the various decision-making procedures to be used, educating the public, creating and populating constituent bodies, gathering expert recommendations, drafting the document itself, collecting public opinion, ensuring technical coherence, and ratifying and implementing the finalized constitution.[66] According to a theory of constituent power, somewhere

[65] Note that this question is also central to the debate between Kelsen and Schmitt regarding the genesis of a legal system. As mentioned, Kelsen solves the puzzle by turning the constituent power into a presupposed *Grundnorm* unifying and legitimizing the self-enclosed constituted system of legal norms, while Schmitt insists that the constituent power can act, and that therefore "a constitution is a conscious decision, which the political unity reaches *for itself* and provides *itself* through the bearer of the constitution-making power." Joseph Marie Maistre, "On the Sovereignty of the People," in Richard Lebrun (ed.), *Against Rousseau: "On the State of Nature" and "on the Sovereignty of the People"* (McGill-Queen's Press 1995) 45; Kelsen, *General Theory of Law and State*, 115; Schmitt, *Constitutional Theory*, 76.

[66] Interpeace's guidebook for constitution-making—*Constitution-making and Reform: Options for the Process*—lists twenty-four possible tasks or steps. Brandt and others, *Constitution-Making and Reform: Options for the Process*, 33.

amidst these tasks the constituent authority must emerge and act. The question is: where and when?

Discussions of constituent power usually avoid this question.[67] Instead, they stick to abstract theorizing and generalities. Claims that a particular constitution is authoritative because it is the product of the constituent power or popular sovereign are rarely followed by a detailed discussion of how the actual constitution-making process validates this claim.[68] When process is mentioned in these discussions one mostly finds vague statements such as "The Colombian people no doubt delegated their constituent power to the assembly" or unexplained equations of participatory creation with constituent power authorship.[69] For instance, a pamphlet discussing the Nepalese process claims that participatory constitution-making results in "a constitution that is owned by the people."[70] Similarly, a constitution-making manual written for Somali stakeholders emphasizes that participatory procedures create a constitution that is "the fundamental decision of the people to be governed."[71] What is missing from these sorts of statements is an explanation accompanying the claims. How did the Colombian people delegate their constituent power to the assembly? Why does increasing participation necessarily lead to constituent action? In which instances and how often does the constituent power act within the constitution-making process?

Such questions are not answered because, generally, authors tend to invoke the concept of constituent power, or to use popular sovereignty to mean the same thing, when making a general descriptive claim, stating a normative ideal, or gesturing toward some vague conception of legitimacy that a particular constitutional moment or constitution meets or falls short of. For legal scholars, as Claude Klein notes, the constituent power serves as "the alchemists' philosopher's stone," used to

[67] For a short but excellent exception to this tendency, see Jon Elster and others, "Introduction," in Jon Elster and others (eds.), *Constituent Assemblies* (Cambridge University Press 2018) 6–8. See also the recent eruption in literature discussing constitutional amendments and constituent power, which is both theoretically nuanced and attentive to procedure. For instance, Ludvig Beckman, "Democratic Legitimacy Does Not Require Referendum. On the 'Constitution' in Theories of Constituent Power," (2018) 14 European Constitutional Law Review 567–83; Roznai, *Unconstitutional Constitutional Amendments*; Colón-Ríos, *Weak Constitutionalism: Democratic Legitimacy and the Question of Constituent Power.*

[68] This is not to mention the numerous instances in which authors use the term "constituent power" simply to indicate parties that had any influence on the creation of a constitution. See Dann and Al-ali, "The Internationalized *Pouvoir Constituant*—Constitution-Making under External Influence in Iraq, Sudan and East Timor."

[69] William C. Banks and Edgar Alvarez, "The New Colombian Constitution: Democratic Victory or Popular Surrender," (1991) 23 Inter-American Law Review 39–92, 7. See also Felip Reyntjens, "Constitution-Making in Situations of Extreme Crisis: The Case of Rwanda and Burundi," (1996) 40 Journal of African Law 234–42, 238; Preuss, "Constitutional Powermaking for the New Polity: Some Deliberations on the Relations between Constituent Power and the Constitution," 158.

[70] *Participatory Constitution Making Process* (Participatory Constitution Building in Nepal Booklet Series, 2009) 1.

[71] Katharina Diehl and others, *Structures and Principles of a Constitution* (Max Planck Manuals on Constitution Building, 2009) 7.

somehow "account for the transition from the ante-judicial to an institutionalized legal system."[72]

In addition, for political theorists, philosophers, and others of the same ilk, constituent power and the image of popular founding serve as a means to reconcile the existence of fundamental rights and entrenched extraordinary law with a conception of self-government based on the will and consent of the governed.[73] The concept also takes centerstage when trying to explain, or legitimize, major shifts to constitutional systems that take place in violation of, or completely outside of, specified pathways of constitutional change.[74] When invoked for either of these purposes, constituent power is attributed to an entire constitution-making process without any attention being paid to what actually transpires, or without connecting what actually transpires with the normative concept.[75] Constituent power is thus normally a retrospective concept, one that is used to explain the appropriateness or the legitimating force of an instance of constitution-making that has already occurred.

For our prospective purposes, from the perspective of procedural design, these treatments of constituent power are unhelpful. In order to be of assistance in designing a constitution-making process, in selecting certain procedures and rejecting others rather than evaluating an entire process ex post, constituent power theory must move from the abstract to the particular; it must embrace and discuss the actual procedures and institutions used to create constitutions.

Of course, it might turn out that constituent power is simply not the sort of concept that can be of help when choosing decision-making procedures. This conclusion is not outlandish, for it seems to follow from constituent power's definition as something both extra-legal and extra-procedural. In a recent work, Richard Albert seems to suggest as much when he writes: "in the case of creating a new constitution, the range of valid exercises of constituent power is boundless. There are no rules of process to legitimate the outcome . . . ."[76]

Nonetheless, as compelling as this intuition is, I will set it aside. The fact remains that scholars, judges, and constitution-making participants, whether rightly or wrongly, do argue for the inclusion or exclusion of particular constitution-making

[72] Klein, "A Propos Constituent Power: Some General Views in a Modern Context," 31.

[73] Jed Rubenfeld, *Legitimacy and Interpretation* (Cambridge University Press 1998) 212.

[74] Bruce A. Ackerman, *We the People: Transformations* (Belknap Press of Harvard University Press 1998); Bruce A. Ackerman, *Revolutionary Constitutions: Charismatic Leadership and the Rule of Law* (Harvard University Press 2019).

[75] This is true for even sophisticated works of political theory, such as Tekin's *Founding Acts*, in which the author makes a persuasive argument about the importance of foundings and why constituent power must be exercised through a deliberative constitution-making process. However, nowhere does he go into detail about the procedures such a constitution-making process should involve, other than a brief discussion of the South Africa constitution-making process. Tekin, *Founding Acts: Constitutional Origins in a Democratic Age.*

[76] Richard Albert, *Constitutional Amendments: Making, Breaking, and Changing Constitutions* (Oxford University Press 2019) 73.

procedures using the language of constituent power. For instance, in the 2004 case, *Njoya and others v. Attorney-General and others*, concerning the Constitution of Kenya Review Act, applicants protested the Act because among other things it failed to involve an elected constituent assembly whose work would be directly submitted to the people in a referendum.[77] This, they argued, was the sole means of convoking the people to exercise their constituent power. Given this tendency of involving constituent power for procedural design purposes, I will take it seriously.

Thus, my chief concern with constituent power is its potential use in justifying the inclusion of a ratification procedure within a constitution-making process. Such a justification would claim that ratification should be used because it plays a central role in enabling the people to act. Again, one might find this justification suspicious from the outset. One might think that even if constituent power can explain some constitution-making procedures, it surely won't be ratification. The constituent power is about ensuring that the people create their constitution, and the literal creation of extraordinary law happens prior to ratification. However, this CPJ is still worth addressing, as a version of it was invoked repeatedly during ratification's constitutional beginning, and the contemporary literature on constitution-making regularly alludes to it. Interpeace's recent handbook, *Constitution-making and Reform: Options for the Process*, explains that: "Modern democratic theory and emerging international norms, such as self-determination, proclaim that the sovereignty of a nation is vested in the people. Since the constitution is the supreme law, a manifestation of national sovereignty, it is appropriate that the final word should rest with the people."[78] Similarly, in their opinion on the Kenyan case mentioned above, the High Court of Kenya concluded that, "Whether it be called a referendum or a plebiscite, that facility is a fundamental right of the people in the exercise of their constituent power."[79]

To state more formally, a CPJ claims that: only the constituent power can create a valid constitution; that ratification enables the constituent power to act; and that therefore ratification must be incorporated within the constitution-making process. Of course, thus far this justification is too general to justify ratification. What does it mean for ratification to enable the constituent power to act? How exactly does the procedure give "the final word" to the people? In addition, where does constituent action occur? Does the constituent power manifest solely in the ratification process or in other moments within the constitution-making process as well? As all of this makes clear, exactly when, where, and how the constituent power acts during constitution-making is essential for clarifying and explaining just how exactly constituent power justifies ratification. Below I explore several

[77] *Njoya & Others v. Attorney General & others*, KLR 4788 (High Court of Kenya) (2004).
[78] Brandt and others, *Constitution-Making and Reform: Options for the Process*, 299.
[79] *Njoya & others v. Attorney General & others*.

different types of constituent power justifications that emerge from addressing these questions.

2.2 Sieyès and the Problem of Assembling

The tendency for many discussions of constituent power and popular sovereignty to eschew the details of the constitution-making process likely results from a simple fact hinted at by the action question discussed above: the people cannot actually come together, draft a constitution, and enact it. At no point during the procedures and tasks commonly used to create a constitution is it clear that the people, whether ethnos or demos, are actually present and creating their constitution. For instance, the actual writing of a constitution is usually completed by a subcommittee of a constituent assembly and or an appointed constitutional commission, both of which frequently make recourse to drafts prepared through even less popular channels.[80] Participatory mechanisms such as public meetings and the collection of constitutional suggestions directly engage only a portion of the population and are often filtered by elected or appointed officials with incredible leeway.[81] Those dedicated to constituent power therefore have every reason to avoid discussing constitution-making procedures, for how constitutions are actually made, in some sense, seems in opposition to their master concept.

Sieyès ran directly into this conundrum in several of his works. For him, a constitution can only be established by the nation, a singular entity that must be distinguished "from an immense flock of people scattered over a surface of twenty-five thousand square leagues."[82] Constituted powers cannot decide upon matters that touch upon the present or future base of their authority, for to do so "would be a petition of principle or a vicious circle."[83] The constituent power resides in this unitary nation, its expression is the general will, and it cannot be alienated. Further, when exercising the constituent power, the nation "exercises the greatest and most

[80] For instance, the 1994 Ugandan Constituent Assembly worked from a draft constitution written by a Constitutional Commission whose members were appointed by the newly elected NRC government. Similarly, the bulk of the 1995 Estonian Constitution came directly from a draft written independently by the Estonian National Independence Party. James Wapakhabulo, "Managing the Constitution-Making Process in Uganda," in Goran Hyden and Denis Venter (eds.), *Constitution-Making and Democratisation in Africa* (Africa Institute of South Africa 2001) 116–23; "Constitution Watch," (1992) 1 East European Constitutional Review 2–8, 3.

[81] For example, the Zimbabwe Constitutional Commission held public meetings across the country, where they educated the public and solicited constitutional suggestions and commentary. Nine thematic committees were given the task of distilling the people's will from the thousands of submissions received, a feat that proved to be impossible. As one author wrote, "In such circumstances it was quite possible for a reasonably competent drafter to produce several very different constitutions and find justification in the submissions made to the commission for each one of them." John Hatchard, "Some Lessons on Constitution-Making from Zimbabwe," (2001) 54 Journal of African Law 210–216, 211.

[82] Sieyès, "Views of the Executive Means," 5. See also Sieyès, "What Is the Third Estate?," 133.

[83] Sieyès, "What Is the Third Estate?," 139.

important of its powers" and, because of its extra-legal nature, "must be free from every constraint, every procedural formality but that which it decides to adapt."[84]

In these and other passages, Sieyès puts forward a theory that tracks the conception of constituent power discussed above. He explains that constituent power is the sole source of all constituted power and constraints, that constitutions create and organize constituted powers, and that therefore only the constituent power can create a constitution. Since constituent power rests in the nation, its exercise being the general will, Sieyès claims that the nation must create its own constitution. And, because it is the source of all possible political constraints, the nation is inherently unconstrained when engaged in constitution-making.

Applying this theory of constituent power to the practical demands of constitution-making, specifically the writing of the French Constitution by the Estates Generale and the national assembly, led Sieyès to the logistical problem mentioned above. As he admits: "a great nation cannot in real terms assemble every time that extraordinary circumstances may require."[85] Put differently, it is simply impossible to assemble the nation and create a constitution. This is true for the obvious reason that an assembly of the entire nation, at least a modern one, cannot physically convene. Also, even if such an assembly were possible, it would be catastrophically stagnant due to its size and the deliberation necessitated by the constitution-making process.[86]

Sieyès was certainly not the first person to notice and struggle with the theoretical and practical difficulties plaguing attempts to use the will of the people to create a constitution. In the seventeenth century, both Royalists and Tories in England attempted to utilize this vulnerability in order to undercut arguments made by their opponents, who purported to speak for the people.[87] Also, about twenty years before Sieyès, Rousseau confronted the same problem, famously noting that:

> Laws are, properly speaking, nothing but the conditions of the civil association. The People subject to the laws ought to be their author ... but how will they regulate them? Will it be by common agreement, by a sudden inspiration? Has the body politic an organ to state its wills? Who will give it the foresight necessary to form its acts ... How will a blind multitude, which often does not know what it wills because it rarely knows what is good for it, carry out an undertaking as great, as difficult as a system of legislation?[88]

[84] Sieyès, "Reasoned Exposition of the Rights of Man and Citizen," 143.
[85] Sieyès, "What Is the Third Estate?" 139.
[86] Note that Sieyès is primarily concerned with the drafting of the constitutional text, suggesting that he sees this process as the key constituent moment.
[87] Edmund S. Morgan, *Inventing the People: The Rise of Popular Sovereignty in England and America* (W.W. Norton & Company, Inc. 1988) 94–119.
[88] Jean Jacques Rousseau, "Of the Social Contract," in Victor Gourevitch (ed.), *Rousseau: The Social Contract and Other Later Political Writings* (Cambridge University Press 1997) 68, 68 (II.6.10).

For Rousseau, this problem of enabling the constituent power to speak was especially daunting, given that mobilization issues aside, his theory also requires a fundamental moral transformation of the people to both comprehend and will the common good before they can set up self-governing. Rousseau solved this conundrum by giving up on popular and democratic constitution-making, at least when it comes to the founding of a new polity. In its place, he imported the ancient *deus ex machina*, the Lawgiver, to both educate the citizenry and construct a just system of legislation which the general will, via the assembly, will patrol and periodically alter.[89]

Sieyès however refused to let go of constituent power constitution-making despite its apparent impossibility. Rather than rely on a Lawgiver, he turned to a special type of representation. He writes, "it [the nation] has, on such occasions, to entrust the necessary powers to extraordinary representatives." Because the people cannot physically convene and create a constitution, Sieyès allows them to entrust constituent power to extraordinary representatives who can actually assemble.

On its face this solution is ambiguous, for what does "entrust" mean in this circumstance? If it indicates the delegation of constituent power to extraordinary representatives engaged in constitution-making, this subjects the nation to decisions reached by an external constituted body and amounts to locating constituent power somewhere other than the people themselves. This violates two central tenets of Sieyès' own conception of the constituent power. Sieyès' solution thus runs into an obstacle, stemming from the literal interpretation of popular sovereignty and extraordinary lawmaking that underlies constituent power theorizing. If the people alone exercise constituent power, but constitutions must be created by some sort of smaller body or bodies, how can a constitution ever be the product of constituent power?

Sieyès overcomes this obstacle by veering into the metaphysical. He radically equates the will of the extraordinary representatives to the will of the nation, arguing that the assembly "is a surrogate for an assembly of the nation," one that has "been put in place of the Nation itself as if it was it that was settling the constitution ... their common will has the same worth as that of the nation itself."[90] Extraordinary representatives assemble and create a constitution as if they *are* the nation itself, with a will of equal worth. In other words, Sieyès links will with representation, thereby transforming (not *transferring*) the will of the nation into the will of the extraordinary representatives, and the unrestrained

[89] Some interpreters of Rousseau portray the lawgiver as a constitutional consultant, one who drafts the constitution and presents it to the sovereign people for their acceptance, or at least as a figure that works in conjunction with the people. However, as appealing as these arguments are, I do not see how they are supported textually. Arato, *The Adventures of the Constituent Power*, 53; Joel Colón-Ríos, "Rousseau, Theorist of Constituent Power," (2016) 36 Oxford Journal of Legal Studies 885–908; Tekin, *Founding Acts: Constitutional Origins in a Democratic Age*, 57–68.

[90] Sieyès, "What Is the Third Estate?" 139.

constituent power of the people into the constituent power of the extraordinary representatives.[91]

For some, Sieyès' embrace of extraordinary representatives is revealing of his deep suspicions of direct democracy and the people more generally, or an instance of a pamphleteer not understanding the very theory he would go on to popularize. Tuck for instance claims that Sieyès is "the most important antagonist" to the constituent/constituted tradition that he made famous, while Colón-Riós writes that by embracing representation, Sieyès "extirpates much of its [his theory's] radical democratic force."[92] Such interpretations, however, only make sense if one wishes to confine constituent power to referendums, which Tuck, as we will see, is explicit about. Paradoxically, Colón-Riós, though his focus is on amendment, ends up advocating for a system of constitutional change involving a specially elected constituent assembly as a means of introducing constituent power back into constitutional democracy. He thus seems to embrace the very alternative that he faults Sieyès for advancing.

For the sake of argument, I will set these worries aside. Sieyès' vision of extraordinary representatives, assuming it is tenable and theoretically sound, enables him to avoid the problems plaguing an account in which constituent power is delegated and transferred to a constituted body. When it comes to extraordinary representatives, constituent power is not located in something external from the nation, because the will and actions of the assembly are the will and actions of the nation. Further, conceptualized in this manner, extraordinary representatives do not and cannot externally constrain the popular constituent authority, for their will and decisions are no longer external to those of the nation. Moreover, nothing external constrains the extraordinary representatives either, for their assembly "is not subject to any particular form" and can "assemble and deliberate as would the nation itself."[93]

2.3 Multiple Moments Justification

To restate, for Sieyès, extraordinary representatives wield constituent power when writing the constitution. Delegate Onslow Peters, during the Illinois Constitutional Convention of 1847, put this point more bluntly: "We are the sovereignty of the State. We are what the people of the State would be, if they were congregated here

91 Baczko, "The Social Contract of the French: Sieyes and Rousseau," 106–7.

92 Tuck, *The Sleeping Sovereign: The Invention of Modern Democracy*, 162; Colón-Ríos, *Weak Constitutionalism: Democratic Legitimacy and the Question of Constituent Power*, 85.

93 Sieyès, "What Is the Third Estate?" 140. For similar interpretations of Sieyès, see Andrew Arato, *Civil Society, Constitution, and Legitimacy* (Rowman & Littlefield Publishers 2000) 237; John Alexander Jameson, *The Constitutional Convention; Its History, Powers, and Modes of Proceeding* (Charles Scribner and Company 1867) 291.

in one mass meeting. We are what Louis XIV said he was, We are the State."[94] According to this model of constituent power constitution-making, one where the constituent power manifests somewhere earlier in the constitution-making process, what role can ratification play? What would it mean to require representatives embodying the will of the people to submit their creation to a ratification procedure?

Three interpretations seem possible. First, ratification is an attempt by some meta-authority above the constituent power to control constitution-making. According to a theory of constituent power, such an argument rests on a profound mistake—there is no authority higher than the constituent power—and therefore it produces no reasons in favor of ratification. Second, ratification might be a procedure left over or specified by the previous regime or constitution to constrain and check future constitution-making attempts. Again, this produces no reasons to implement ratification. Instead, it turns the procedure into a prototypical example of a constituted power trying to regulate the source of its own authority.

Third, ratification is simply another moment during constitution-making when the constituent authority emerges and acts. In the first instance, the constituent power takes the form of extraordinary representatives writing the constitution with the will of the people. In the second, constituent power manifests as the people review the constitution and decide if it is to their liking. This interpretation is an example of what I will call a *multiple moments* conceptualization of the relationship between constituent power and constitution-making procedures. Here, the people create their constitution by taking discrete actions during two or more moments of the constitution-making process. In each of these constituent power moments, the people act through a given procedure, institution, or mechanism.

Thus, for example, a multiple moments conceptualization of the constitution-making process that led to the 2002 Rwanda Constitution might claim that it contained three moments of constituent power: the Constitutional Commission exercised constituent power while drafting the constitution; the national assembly exercised constituent power when amending the constitution; and those voting in the ratification referendum exercised constituent power when they approved the constitution.[95] In each of these moments, albeit differently, the constituent power manifested and took action, and in combination these moments enabled the constituent power to create its governing document. Banks and Alvarez seem to conceptualize ratification in just this way when discussing the opportunities Colombian constitution-makers missed by choosing not to use popular

[94] Cited in Jameson, *The Constitutional Convention; Its History, Powers, and Modes of Proceeding*, 292.

[95] Priscilla Yachat Ankut, *The Role of Constitution-Building Processes in Democratization: Case Study—Rwanda* (International IDEA 2005) 16–19; Wellars Gasamagera, "The Constitution Making Process in Rwanda: Lessons to Be Learned" (7th Global Forum for Reinventing Government) 4–6.

ratification. They write, "Popular ratification . . . gives the people another chance to decide whether they want a new charter."[96]

Our first CPJ relies on this multiple moments conceptualization of constituent power and constitution-making.

> *Multiple Moments Justification*: Ratification should be implemented because it is one of several moments in the constitution-making process when the constituent power acts.

The general idea is that the constituent power must be the author of a constitution for it to be authoritative, that ratification assists in this by being one site among many in which the constituent power takes action, and that therefore the procedure should be implemented. Of course, as stated this justification is severely underdeveloped. For instance, some argument would be needed to explain why multiple moments of constituent action are necessary, or why ratification has to be or is an especially apt moment of constituent power's emergence. However, refining the argument further is unnecessary because of a more basic flaw within a multiple moments justification: any moment of constituent power after the first is either superfluous or contradictory.

Consider a constitution-making process with two moments of constituent power: (1) a Sieyèsian constituent assembly creates the constitution, followed by (2) regional ratifying assemblies voting on the draft, with approval requiring a supermajority. Here, since the will of the constituent assembly is necessarily the will of the people, the draft constitution is necessarily the creation of the constituent power. This is beyond contestation in a multiple moments justification. This means that in (2) the constituent power evaluates and decides whether to approve or reject its own creation. Two outcomes are possible. The constituent power accepts the constitution it created, or the constituent power rejects the constitution it created.

If the regional ratifying assemblies approve the constitution, then ratification is entirely redundant. Why spend the time and resources to implement a constitution-making procedure in which the constituent power is asked to evaluate its own handiwork? It is no justification at all to support a costly constitution-making procedure because it enables the people to vote in favor of what they just created. If the assemblies reject the constitution, this means that the constituent power rejected its own creation, which is incoherent. How is one to understand an author that presents its creation to itself only to refuse it? How can an author disagree with itself in such a manner? This suggests that there is little sense to a multiple moments justification. If one holds that constitution-making representatives or some other

[96] Banks and Alvarez, "The New Colombian Constitution: Democratic Victory or Popular Surrender," 88.

entity or procedure earlier in the constitution-making process embodies the will of the people and exercises constituent power, there seems to be no coherent justification for implementing ratification based on the need for further constituent action.

The nineteenth-century judge and scholar, John A. Jameson, reached this very conclusion. He concisely spells out the redundancy of ratification for a Sieyèsian theory of constitution-making and the constituent power in his entry on "Conventions, The Constitutional," in John Joseph Lalor's *Cyclopedia*. Describing the "French theory of convention," he writes

> that by reason of the impracticability of an actual assemblage of the sovereign body itself, the convention must be taken to be its plenipotentiary representative, and, as such, possessed of all the powers that the body would have were it "assembled on some vast plain," in a state of nature, without government, but purposing to ordain and establish one by its original authority; . . . A body which is virtually the people itself could not properly be required to refer its work to the people for approval. Hence, according to this theory, if a convention frame or amend a constitution, no submission of it to the people need be made.[97]

To repeat, this objection to justifying ratification by appealing to constituent power within a Sieyèsian framework applies to any attempt to justify ratification using a multiple moments justification. If previous moments in the constitution-making process involved the constituent authority determining the form and content of the constitution, i.e. creating the constitution, there is simply no reason to implement a redundant procedure in which the constituent power evaluates its own work. Doing so, at best, will lead to a contradiction between two different alleged manifestations of the constituent power, with no higher authority in existence to resolve the disagreement.

3. Constituent Power Dispersed

Objections to my quick treatment of the multiple moments justification are possible. For instance, one might claim that ratification is neither redundant nor contradictory, for if the people approve the constitution it means we can be confident that its creators were extraordinary, and if the people reject the constitution it means they were not. Ratification thus serves to ensure that the constituent power wrote the constitution. In this section I analyze three justifications of ratification that proceed along these lines. I motivate this discussion by considering an

[97] John Alexander Jameson, "Conventions, the Constitutional," in John Joseph Lalor (ed.), *Cyclopedia of Political Science, Political Economy, and of the Political History of the United States*, vol. 1 (Rand, McNally & Company 1882) 629.

objection to my reading of Sieyès, which claims that he explicitly endorses ratification in his later writings. This, one might argue, means that either Sieyès is internally contradictory or my analysis is inaccurate.

3.1 Sieyès and the Second Constituent Assembly

An objector to the above reading of Sieyès might point to the following passage in the "Reasoned Exposition of the Rights of Man and Citizen," where Sieyès seems to depict ratification as a moment of constituent power and recommend its implementation:

> They [the national assembly] will, consequently, act as a constituting power. And yet, since the existing Assembly does not precisely meet the requirements for the exercise of such a power, they declare that while the constitution that they are going to give the nation is provisionally obligatory, it will only become definitive after a new constituent power, convened specifically for this purpose, will provide it with the sanction necessitated by a rigorous application of principles.[98]

This passage can be interpreted in three ways. First, it might be an instance in which Sieyès portrays a ratification process involving a ratification assembly as a second moment of constituent power and thus endorses something like a multiple moments justification. This seems to be the interpretation of Lucien Jaume, who suggests that for Sieyès, alongside extraordinary representatives, "a procedure for ratification of the Constitution, once drafted, would have been required," because "the nation would have to be consulted in order to express the view of whether this Constitution was really theirs—that is to say, the expression of their constituent power."[99] Note that even if such an interpretation is correct, it does not provide us with a reason for submitting a constitution created by the people to the people, nor does it provide an additional constituent power-based justification for ratification, i.e. it does not salvage the multiple moments justification or help us construct a different type of constituent power justification. Instead, it simply portrays Sieyès as calling for a procedure that, as concluded above, looks unnecessary in the lights of his own theory.

Second, Sieyès might not be calling for ratification at all. In chapter 6 of "What is the Third Estate?" Sieyès explains two ways in which the Third Estate could "put itself in possession of the place in the political order that is its due" through the

[98] Sieyès, "Reasoned Exposition of the Rights of Man and Citizen," 136.

[99] Lucien Jaume, "Constituent Power in France: The Revolution and Its Consequences," in Martin Loughlin and Neil Walker (eds.), *The Paradox of Constitutionalism: Constituent Power and Constitutional Form* (Cambridge University Press 2007) 70.

national assembly.[100] The first path consists in the deputies of the Third Estate separating from the nobility and clergy, equating their will with the constituent will of the nation due to their majority status, and enacting a constitution. The second path is identical to the first, except the deputies do "not enact anything definitively," and instead create a provisional constitution. Afterwards, they must "demonstrate the need to give special powers to an extraordinary deputation" that would "settle, above all else, the great matter of the constitution."[101]

In the quoted passage, Sieyès might be articulating the second path for the Third Estate, recommending that the constituent assembly temporarily adopts a provisional constitution to govern France until a truly extraordinary constituent assembly convenes.[102] This second assembly would evaluate the provisional constitution and make any necessary changes.[103] According to this reading, only the second assembly would be a site of constituent power, there would be no multiple moments of constituent action, and ratification, defined as the up or down vote on a constitution by actors uninvolved in the drafting process, would never occur. Thus, this interpretation provides no alternative constituent power justification for ratification.

Third, Sieyès might be using ratification for reparative purposes and only recommending the procedure because of prior deficiencies in the national assembly. Though Sieyès notes that "the existing Assembly does not precisely meet the requirements for the exercise of such a [constituent] power," he does not spell out its shortcomings. Two seem likely. On the one hand, the membership of the national constituent assembly in July 22, 1789 (when the above was written) did not reflect Sieyès' initial vision. The assembly consisted of the same delegates elected by the three estates to serve in the Estates Generale in order to address the financial troubles plaguing France, not the sort of extraordinary representatives elected specifically for the purpose of creating a new constitution that Sieyès wished for and theorized in the first sections of "What is the Third Estate?"

On the other hand, the assembly engaged in constitution-making and ordinary governance, thus becoming both extraordinary and ordinary lawmakers. This is something Sieyès specifically warned against: "In politics, mixing up and conflating power is what constantly makes it impossible to establish social order."[104] The combination of these deficiencies might have led Sieyès to conclude that the national constituent assembly did not possess the constituent power of the people

[100] Sieyès, "What Is the Third Estate?" 151.
[101] Ibid., 152.
[102] Murray G. Forsyth, *Reason and Revolution: The Political Thought of the Abbè Sieyès* (Leicester University Press 1987) 102.
[103] This sort of process would be a nascent version of the interim constitutional arrangements deployed in the making of the 1997 South African Constitution.
[104] Sieyès, "What Is the Third Estate?" 143. See also Sieyès, "Views of the Executive Means," 34.

and did not necessarily articulate the general will. His endorsement of ratification can thus be read as an attempt to convoke the constituent power for the first time.

3.2 Ratification as Reparative

This third interpretation of the passage points to another potential CPJ, *the reparative function justification*, which casts ratification as a means of correcting prior missteps in the constitution-making process. Missteps cannot mean that the substance of the constitution does not match the will of the constituent power, for like Rousseau's general will, the will of the constituent power can only be known by its manifestation. That is, theoretically, there is no independent criteria one can use to evaluate the outcome of a supposed manifestation of the constituent power in order to tell whether it is authentic. Rather, by missteps, the reparative function justification refers to a given constitution-making procedure meant to manifest the constituent power not proceeding as planned. For instance, opposition parties to the ruling regimes in Egypt and Venezuela boycotted their respective constituent assemblies in 2012 and 2017.[105] This meant that sizeable parts of each country's population were not represented at the assembly. One can imagine an argument claiming that given this lack of representation or representativeness, it would be impossible to understand either assembly as one populated by extraordinary representatives enacting the will of the constituent power.

The justification in question can be stated as follows:

> *Reparative Function Justification:* Ratification should be implemented because it provides a moment of constituent power needed because of deficiencies that prevented an earlier moment or moments of constituent power from taking place.[106]

Several things are worth noting about this justification. For one thing, it is inspired by and reflects ratification's reparative role in agency law from Ancient Rome to the present. As discussed in chapter 2, in agency law ratification functions as a means to reach back and retroactively grant a representative or delegate the power

[105] Marina Ottaway and Nathan J. Brown, "Egypt's Transition in Crisis: Falling into the Wrong Turkish Model?" (Carnegie Endowment for the International Peace 2012) <https://carnegieendowment.org/2012/03/30/egypt-s-transition-in-crisis-falling-into-wrong-turkish-model-pub-47696>; Jennifer L. McCoy, "Venezuela's Controversial New Constituent Assembly, Explained" (*The Washington Post* August 1, 2017) <https://www.bbc.com/news/world-latin-america-41094889>.

[106] Once again, Banks and Alvarez seem to conceptualize ratification in just this way. They argue that the Colombian Constitution should have been submitted to popular ratification because doing so "effectively counters the positivist argument that the new Constitution was not authorized and is therefore illegal." In other words, they argued that ratification would have been a tool used to link the constitution with the constituent power despite previous insufficiencies in the constitution-making process. Banks and Alvarez, "The New Colombian Constitution: Democratic Victory or Popular Surrender," 81.

she was missing at the time of the transaction in question. Its effect is to make an unauthoritative transaction authoritative by repairing a deficiency. Similarly, the reparative function justification conceptualizes ratification as a means of repairing malfunctions earlier in the constitution-making process that prevented the constituent power from manifesting. As mentioned in the previous chapter, a similar argument was alluded to by some of the delegates at the Philadelphia Convention.

In addition, this reparative function justification implicitly endorses the dismissal of the multiple moments justification. By justifying ratification due to deficiencies in what were supposed to be prior constituent power moments, the reparative function justification implies that in the absence of these deficiencies, ratification would be unnecessary. Again, this mimics ratification's role in agency law, where its existence is parasitic on the possibility of an authoritative transaction that does not need ratification. In Roman law, there could be no conception of *ratihabitio* without *mandatum*, and in modern agency law there could be no ratification without the possibility of an ordinary contract binding from its inception.

All of this aside, does the reparative function justification justify the inclusion of ratification in constitution-making best practices? Is it a persuasive and successful CPJ? I argue that it is not because of two problems. First, it throws up all sorts of practical difficulties, some of which may be insurmountable. Who is the proper authority to judge whether the relevant deficiencies in the constitution-making process are present to warrant a reparative use of ratification? That is, who determines that, despite best laid plans, the constituent power failed to emerge and act? Additionally, how might ratification be added to a constitution-making process midstream, and who or what would have the authority to do so successfully? Things become all the more confusing because the obvious answer to these questions, the only answer, is the constituent power itself.

Second, and most importantly for our purposes, is that even if the previous worries could be resolved, the reparative function justification is not a proper CPJ. The central question motivating this book is whether general reasons exist for including ratification procedures within constitution-making processes before they begin, i.e. during the initiation phase when questions of procedural design are normally tackled. Our query is, should ratification be included in the general set of constitution-making best practices? This means that a CPJ, like any type of justification that would answer our question, must provide a normative reason for using ratification procedures from the beginning of the constitution-making process. The reparative function justification, which only justifies ratification if specific problems emerge during the process of creating a constitution, does not provide such a reason and is thus not an acceptable constituent power justification. It turns ratification into an ad hoc particular solution, rather than a justified component of constitution-making more generally.[107] I will thus set aside the reparative function justification, though I will return to it in chapter 10 when discussing contextual circumstances that might call for ratification.

3.3 Fallibility in Conjuring the Constituent Power

Up until now, in accordance with a multiple moments conceptualization of constituent power, I have embraced the Sieyèsian logic that the constituent power *can* and *does* act through a particular procedure or set of procedures. The actions of extraordinary representatives can be the real actions of the constituent power, the results of ratification can be the results of the constituent power making a judgment on the final draft, and the decisions of other properly calibrated constitution-making processes can in fact be the constituent power's decisions.

However, a critic of the multiple moments approach might argue that this has it all wrong, that by generalizing Sieyès' dubious claim that the will of extraordinary representatives simply is the will of the people, I ignore everything we know about how actual collective decision-making procedures operate. In attempting to extract a single decision from a diverse and large array of actors, problems can and often do arise. For instance, we know that procedures often produce unexpected or unwanted outcomes. Delegates to a constituent assembly might behave contrary to the wishes or needs of their constituents. A public comment period on a draft constitution meant to gather the thoughts of the nation might be overwhelmed by a disproportionate amount of responses from a minority group. Certain segments of a polity might boycott a referendum, refusing to lend their voice to what is supposed to be a moment of constituent power will-making. And elites structuring any given constitution-making procedure can use its rules to increase the likelihood of a desired outcome. Even if one wants to distinguish the constituent power from the mere accurate aggregation of popular preferences, which is the inclination of most constituent power theorists, such occurrences nonetheless appear worrisome.

In addition, if one sees the constituent power as a demos, such that it both acts within and is formed by the process used to write and enact a constitution, it will look different or be different from one constitution-making procedure to the next. It is unclear how a multiple moments conceptualization can integrate the idea of a changing constituent power without providing a story of which iteration of the constituent power should get our attention. Moreover, a multiple moments conceptualization fails to take seriously the unconstrained nature of constituent

[107] If one argues for the use of ratification as a means of double-checking previous attempts at manifesting the constituent power, this transforms the reparative function justification into a multiple moments justification, the problems of which were covered in the previous section.

power, its inability to be accurately channeled through institutions and procedures of any type. Finally, it overlooks the possibility that the constituent power, like the individuals of which it is composed, might change its mind. In other words, the constituent power might change its views on what an acceptable constitution looks like throughout the constitution-making process.

These sorts of problems disappear, our critic argues, if we adopt what can be called a multiple attempts conceptualization of constituent power. According to this conceptualization, no procedure is guaranteed to or can enable the constituent power to manifest and definitively take a stand on the constitution on its own. Thus, the constitution-making process contains multiple procedures and mechanisms designed, in combination, to ensure that the constituent power creates its constitution or, at the least, to increase the chances that this occurs.

Such a conception of constituent power constitution-making seems increasingly popular in contemporary constitutional theory. For instance, Serdar Tekin describes an optimal constitution-making process in which a variety of procedures allow "citizen consultation and participation during the drafting of the new constitution [to] come to the foreground," thereby making "the exercise of popular sovereignty ... not tied to a single act ... but to the deliberative process itself."[108] Similarly, in *Weak Constitutionalism*, Joel Colón-Ríos puts forward a constitutional theory according to which a constitutional regime's democratic legitimacy is contingent upon its providing a means for the constituent power to manifest periodically to revise or replace extraordinary law. To illustrate how this might work, he describes a process of constitutional change that involves a citizen-initiated referendum to convoke a constituent assembly, elections to the constituent assembly, followed by a ratification referendum to approve any changes. He notes that while "there is no single or correct set of arrangements that must be adopted in order to meet the demands of democratic legitimacy," "the fact that citizens are allowed to participate directly in the process makes it an exercise of constituent power ...."[109]

Two CPJs use such a conceptualization of constituent power in constitution-making. The first can be called the multiple attempts justification:

> *Multiple Attempts Justification:* Ratification should be implemented because it serves as one of several procedures that in combination help to ensure or make more likely that the constituent power creates its constitution.

This justification is like the reparative function justification, yet rather than being an ad hoc solution to particular deficiencies, ratification becomes a standard

[108] Tekin, *Founding Acts: Constitutional Origins in a Democratic Age*, 153.
[109] Colón-Ríos, *Weak Constitutionalism: Democratic Legitimacy and the Question of Constituent Power*, 168.

component of the constitution-making process because of the assumed imperfection or fallibility of any one procedural attempt to harness the constituent power when writing the constitution. The idea here is that by adding procedures that might convoke the constituent power, the designers of a constitution-making process increase the chances that the resulting constitution will end up being the product of the constituent will.

While the multiple attempts justification passes muster as a possible CPJ, it too is ultimately unpersuasive. It justifies ratification, and rejects a multiple moments conceptualization more broadly, by assuming that any constitution-making procedure meant to serve as a moment of constituent power's emergence and action might err. Without this assumption, the multiple attempts justification does not get off the ground. However, ratification is the final procedure in a constitution-making process, and in all of its various forms, it amounts to a simple veto point. Some popular authority, whether it is the people in a referendum or a special ratification convention, votes to approve or reject a constitution. Its decision will determine whether the constitution-making process ends in the enactment of a new constitution or the reversion to the status quo. Now, if a multiple attempts justification includes ratification in its assertion that no one procedure can reliably channel the constituent power, then the argument is unpersuasive. Why would an argument that hinges upon the necessary fallibility of all constitution-making procedures when it comes to serving as sites of constituent power advocate for the inclusion of a procedure which involves a definitive up or down vote that ends the process? If ratification might not involve the manifestation of the constituent power, why subject the fruits of the constitution-making process to it on the basis of the importance of constituent power?

Attempts to get around this concern run into problems. So, for instance, a defender of a multiple attempts justification could claim that ratification is special, in that it is guaranteed to accurately be a manifestation of the constituent power. If this is the case, it is unclear what role the constituent power does or needs to play in the earlier procedures of the constitution-making process. This transforms the multiple attempts justification into a different justification altogether, one that justifies ratification because it is the sole moment in the constitution-making process where the constituent power manifests. This *unique site justification* (USJ) is the subject of the following two chapters.

Alternatively, one might claim that while ratification is also fallible, adding the procedure simply increases the chances that the constituent power will manifest. This defense suffers from two problems. It is false unless accompanied by some sort of argument explaining why there is reason to believe that a given ratification procedure has a greater than 50 percent probability to serve as a site of constituent action. Again, it is unclear what such an argument even looks like. Further, it tells us nothing about ratification in particular, but instead simply produces a reason to add additional procedures of whatever form in the constitution-making process that might convoke the constituent power. Rather than being a defense of ratification specifically, this sort of argument is an invitation to infinite regress.[110]

Perhaps an advocate of the multiple attempts justification might admit that given the impossibility of guaranteeing that the constituent power emerges in the constitution-making process, a multiple attempts justification simply argues for the inclusion of ratification as one of several procedures that will best ensure that the final constitution is closest to the will of the constituent power, i.e. closest to what one has good reason to believe the people want out of their constitution. This, of course, is to miss the entire point of constituent power theorizing more generally. Producing a constitution that aligns with the actual or considered preferences of the people is not the goal, nor is such an outcome sufficient. What matters for the purposes of constituent power is that the people actually take action.

The second CPJ to assume one cannot be confident of any specific procedure convoking the constituent power argues for a broader approach. I call it the overall process justification:

> *Overall Process Justification:* ratification should be implemented because it is one procedure in a process that, taken as a whole, allows the constituent power to act.

According to this justification, one should understand a properly constructed constitution-making process as being the site of constituent action, rather than a particular procedure. In other words, it is not the case that extraordinary representatives become the constituent power and create a constitution, but rather that the entire process of constitution-making, with all its myriad procedures, has the effect of ensuring that the constituent power creates its constitution. What to make of this argument for ratification? It is perhaps the least persuasive of them all. This sort of conceptualization is a retreat to vagueness, a falling back to the tendency for scholars to treat constituent power as the philosopher's stone. It is to admit that constituent power is incapable of making procedural recommendations. This can be seen because such an argument produces no reasons for including any specific procedure, ratification or otherwise. Claiming that the constituent power acts through a process as a whole might explain why a constitution should be considered authoritative, but it is not a claim that can tell us what this process should look like.

[110] Condorcet makes a similar point in his discussion of ratification. When examining the possibility of appointing a second convention to ratify the work of the first he writes: "Either this new Convention must be given the power to change what the first has done, in which case a third would have to be elected to ratify these changes, and so on . . . ." Marquis de Condorcet, "On the Need for the Citizens to Ratify the Constitution," in Iain McLean and Fiona Hewitt (eds.), *Condorcet: Foundations of Social Choice and Political Theory* (Edward Elgar 1994) 274.

4. Conclusion

Constituent power theory appears to be the perfect candidate for justifying ratification. The people must create their constitution if it is to be authoritative, and ratification seems to provide just such an opportunity. However, as I have argued, figuring out the exact way ratification justifies constituent power proves more complicated than this intuition suggests.

In this chapter, I explored the theoretical background of constituent power and drew out its chief characteristics. Constituent power theory extends the distinction between ordinary and extraordinary to the realm of political power. It posits the existence of an ultimate source of authority that creates the constitution and legitimizes the state. This constituent power, identified solely with the people, legitimizes itself, cannot be constrained by external sources of authority, and remains independent from the constituted powers it produces.

A CPJ claims that constitutions must be created by the constituent power and identifies ratification as playing some sort of role in enabling the constituent power to manifest and take action. This makes identifying exactly when and where constituent power appears within the various procedures used to create a constitution an essential point of inquiry. As noted, constituent power theory is normally used retroactively to characterize constitution-making processes taken as a whole, and thus bringing the concept into contact with actual procedures is something that rarely occurs in the theoretical literature.

Starting from Sieyès' attempt to explain how the people could actually write a constitution when a mass assembly is impossible, I posited four possible constituent power justifications. The multiple moments justification claims that ratification serves as one of several essential moments of constituent power in the constitution-making process. The reparative function justification defends ratification by characterizing it as a moment of constituent power made necessary by prior deficiencies in the constitution-making process. The multiple attempts justification claims that the procedure was one of several imperfect attempts at creating, manifesting, and enabling the constituent power to act and make a constitution its own. And the overall process justification claims that ratification is a key part of a constitution-making process that taken as a whole counts as a site of constituent action. Each of these justifications fails for different reasons. The first makes ratification a redundant or incoherent process, the second makes the procedure into an ad hoc solution, the third is unpersuasive, contradicts itself, or misinterprets constituent power theory. And the fourth cannot produce a reasons in favor of ratification at all.

However, the flaws of these procedures push us toward a final constituent power justification that begs consideration. The multiple moments justification fails because any moment of constituent power manifestation makes all others unnecessary, such that the prior emergence of constituent power within a constituent assembly eliminates the need for ratification. However, what if no prior manifestation of the constituent power took place? What if the constituent assembly did not and was not supposed to be a moment of constituent action, meaning that ratification served as the sole site of constituent power?

A reparative function justification cannot be a constituent power justification, for it relies on observations made during constitution-making, thereby violating the ex ante perspective of the latter. However, as an ad hoc solution, the reparative function justification portrays ratification as a procedure through which the popular constituent power can act and create an authoritative constitution in the absence of other constituent moments, suggesting again that a ratification procedure involving the people might be sufficient for the purposes of constituent power theory.

One reason for the failure of the multiple attempts justification is that while the justification is motivated by the claim that any constitution-making procedure might err in channeling or enabling the constituent power to act, it must either exclude ratification from fallibility or else risk being unpersuasive. However, if one chooses the former and characterizes ratification as a moment in the constitution-making process when the constituent power inevitably acts, this eliminates the need for multiple attempts at constituent power. In other words, it suggests an image of constitution-making in which the constituent power acts only during ratification, i.e. where ratification is the sole site of constituent power.

The idea that ratification serves as the only site of constituent power, which the failure of these justifications suggests, points to a final type of constituent power justification. According to it, ratification should be implemented because the constituent power must create its constitution, and ratification is the only moment in the constitution-making process when the constituent power is able to act and make a constitution theirs. This USJ is immune to the deficiencies that plagued the justifications considered above and is the subject of the following two chapters. As I mentioned in the previous chapter, and as I will show in greater detail in the next, it also happens to be the argument used by the inventors of ratification, the Berkshire Constitutionalists, to explain their demand for the procedure. Further, this USJ is not only a thing of the past, as it has recently been resurrected and advocated by Tuck in his recent work on the sovereign/government distinction in modern political thought.

5
The Unalienable Right of the Berkshire Constitutionalists

> Indeed, it was as if all the imaginings of political philosophers for centuries were being lived out in a matter of years in the hills of New England.
>
> *Gordon Wood*[1]

Does conceptualizing ratification as a moment of constituent power justify its use? As argued in the previous chapter, it does not if one understands ratification to be one in a series of such moments. For instance, in Sieyès' theoretical landscape, ratification becomes an incoherent or redundant procedure, a second moment of constituent power that needlessly checks the work of framers already embodying the popular will. However, nothing about the nature of constituent power entails its manifestation in any particular stage or stages of the drafting process, and Sieyès' argument is simply one result, albeit a popular one, of applying constituent power theorizing to the procedures involved in creating a constitution. An alternative conceptualization of the emergence of constituent power, one different from Sieyès' and the other variations considered in chapter 4, might be able to explain ratification without resulting in similar problems.

In fact, such an account exists. It is embedded within the constitutional theory and writings of the Berkshire Constitutionalists, whose history I detailed in chapter 3. In the course of their battle with the state authorities, the Constitutionalists articulated the first argument for why a constitution should be ratified, and their writings remain some of the most extensive theoretical discussions of the topic to date. In short, the Berkshire Constitutionalists produced a theory of constituent power, located its exercise in the authorization of a constitution, and asserted that the right to create a constitution was unalienable due to its necessity in safeguarding the people from potentially corrupt elites. For the constitutionalists, this meant that no authoritative constitution was possible unless every eligible voter had the

[1] Gordon S. Wood, *The Creation of the American Republic, 1776–1787* (The University of North Carolina Press 1998) 285.

Constitutional Ratification without Reason. Jeffrey A. Lenowitz, Oxford University Press. © Jeffrey A. Lenowitz 2022.
DOI: 10.1093/oso/9780198852346.003.0005

opportunity to be a direct participant by approving or rejecting the constitution in a referendum.

In this chapter, I situate the Berkshire Constitutionalists' writings within the contractual tradition popular at the time and reconstruct their theory of constituent power from their speeches, voting returns, and legal petitions. I demonstrate how this theory drove them to activism centered on a demand for popular ratification, and how their arguments can be understood as providing a *unique site justification* (USJ), according to which ratification must be implemented because it is the sole and therefore necessary moment within the constitution-making process in which the constituent power acts and authorizes its constitution. This is not only a powerful justification for ratification, but also one that reconciles constituent power, constitution-making, and ratification yet remains immune to the problems that plague other constituent power justifications (CPJs). I end the chapter by demonstrating the continued allure of this conceptualization of constituent power and ratification referendums by showing how Richard Tuck endorses it in his 2017 book *The Sleeping Sovereign* and in his more recent writings on Brexit.

1. Historical Context, Theoretical Context

To reconstruct the Berkshire Constitutionalists' theory from their scattered writings, I need to draw not only from their history and historical context detailed in chapter 3, but also from the rich constellation of political ideas that informed them. This might seem like a daunting task, for like many during the Revolution, a variety of intellectual traditions surely influenced the Constitutionalists. Ideas mattered in Early America, but the exact nature and pedigree of these ideas has been the subject of an interpretive dispute for over half a century.[2]

However, matters are simpler than this makes them look. We are only interested in understanding the Berkshire Constitutionalists' approach to founding a new government after the demise of British authority, not the relative influence of theoretical traditions on the formation of early American political thought more generally. As I will show, this specific subject matter, as well as the language used by the Constitutionalists and the authors they cite, points solidly towards contractualism, a theoretical trope that cuts across schools of political thought in its usage. Thus, the writings of English Republicans such as Algernon Sidney, radical opposition Whigs such as the authors of *Cato's Letters*, and liberals such as Paine regularly

[2] The classic debate is between liberal and representative interpretations. For good summaries of this, see Joyce Appleby, *Liberalism and Republicanism in the Historical Imagination* (Harvard University Press 1992) 1–32; Lee Ward, *The Politics of Liberty in England and Revolutionary America* (Cambridge University Press 2004) 1–8; Dale S. Kuehne, *Massachusetts Congregationalist Political Thought, 1760–1790: The Design of Heaven* (University of Missouri Press 1996) 1–11.

appeal to contracts and compacts in which individuals cede personal liberties to create society and delegate limited powers to appointed rulers.[3]

Writings from the time, whether newspaper articles, legislative pronouncements, or religious speeches, make clear that Massachusetts was awash in social contract thinking, for they frequently use the language of contractualism. For instance, a 1772 article in the Massachusetts Spy notes that "a man when he enters into society is only *part* of a whole; from this result many benefits of which he could not experience in a state of nature." In their Proclamation of January 23, 1776, the General Court even invoked social contract theory to justify the Revolutionary War and call for public support, writing that "the Consent of the People is the only Foundation of [government] ... and therefore every Exercise of Sovereignty, against, or without, the Consent of the People, is Injustice, Usurpation, and Tyranny."[4]

In addition, social contractualism combined with, added to, and drew support from the century-old practice in New England of consensually creating new religious and political communities through covenants and compacts.[5] This practice, likely originating in the old Puritan belief that the history of humanity is the history of covenants, was particularly alive in Western Massachusetts during the Revolution, for most of its towns and churches were established, via compact, in the thirty years leading up to it.[6] Further, by the mid-eighteenth century contractualism was fully embedded in Congregationalism, the dominant form of Protestantism in the colony, and its clergy integrated contractual ideas drawn from Scottish Enlightenment and Whig political thought into their theological dogma.[7] Thomas Allen, the leader of the Berkshire Constitutionalists, was a trained Congregationalist pastor.

2. Constituent Power Rooted in Contractualism

Viewing the various claims made by the Berkshire Constitutionalists through the lens of contractualism yields a powerful six-part argument: (1) government is necessary; (2) its power comes from the people; (3) only the majority of civil

[3] Algernon Sidney, *Discourses Concerning Government* (Liberty Fund 1996) 88, 102; John Trenchard and Thomas Gordon, *Cato's Letters, or Essays on Liberty, Civil and Religious, and Other Important Subjects*, vol. 1 (W. Wilkins, T. Woodward, J. Walthoe, and J. Peele 1737) 247.

[4] "Proclamation of the General Court, January 23, 1776," in Oscar and Mary Handlin (eds.), *The Popular Sources of Political Authority* (Harvard University Press 1966) 65. See Donald S. Lutz, "The Theory of Consent in the Early State Constitutions," (1979) 9 Publius 11–42, 15–16.

[5] Donald S. Lutz, *The Origins of American Constitutionalism* (Louisiana State University Press 1988) 23–34.

[6] Robert J. Taylor, *Western Massachusetts in the Revolution* (Brown University Press 1954) 4; Kuehne, *Massachusetts Congregationalist Political Thought, 1760–1790: The Design of Heaven*, 35.

[7] Kuehne, *Massachusetts Congregationalist Political Thought, 1760–1790: The Design of Heaven*, 90–103; Abraham Williams, "An Election Sermon: Boston, 1762," in Charles S. Hyneman and Donald S. Lutz (eds.), *American Political Writing During the Founding Era: 1760–1805*, vol. 1 (Liberty Fund 1983).

society is capable of constructing and empowering an authoritative government; (4) this requires the creation of a constitution; (5) the people exercise their constituent power through authorization; and (6) the right to this power is unalienable. From these six claims, the Berkshire Constitutionalists concluded that (a) a constitution must be ratified and (b) that this must be done via referendum.

2.1 Social Contract Basics

For the Constitutionalists, the (1) "absolute necessity of legal government" stemmed from its ability to "prevent Anarchy and Confusion" and ward off "the destructive nature of Tyranny and lawless power." Government alone enabled man to secure civil and religious liberties by helping people "emerge from a state of Nature" and escape the constant dangers wrought by human deficiency and weakness.[8] The Constitutionalists' reading of political thought in conjunction with their religious heritage contributed to their embrace of this particularly dire state of nature narrative, for Puritanism emphasized government's divine role in warding off the selfish actions of fallen man, while Congregationalism stressed its earthly role in securing the conditions necessary to retain God-given liberties despite man's near-total depravity.[9]

Like the Levelers and the Whigs before them, the Constitutionalists also concluded that (2) "the people are the fountain of power," by denying any other source of political power.[10] Here, "power" refers to moral power, i.e. the right to use physical force in accordance with natural law or right.[11] In the political

[8] "Statement of Berkshire County Representatives, November 17, 1778," in Oscar and Mary Handlin (eds.), *The Popular Sources of Authority* (Harvard University Press 1966) 374; "Pittsfield Petitions, May 29, 1776," in Oscar and Mary Handlin (eds.), *The Popular Sources of Political Authority* (Harvard University Press 1966) 88, 93. Thomas Paine's *Common Sense*, which Allen read aloud to a 1776 Berkshire Convention, clearly articulates this position. After explaining how humans naturally form a society, he writes: "but as nothing but heaven is impregnable to vice, it will unavoidably happen, that in proportion as they surmount the first difficulties of emigration, which bound them together in a common cause, they will begin to relax in their duty and attachment to each other; and this remissness, will point out the necessity, of establishing some form of government to supply the defect of moral virtue." Thomas Paine, *Collected Writings* (The Library of America 1995) 7–8.

[9] See Williams, "An Election Sermon: Boston, 1762," 6. See also Kuehne, *Massachusetts Congregationalist Political Thought, 1760–1790: The Design of Heaven,* 41, 92–93; Theodore M. Hammett, *The Revolutionary Ideology in Its Social Context: Berkshire County, Massachusetts 1725–1785* (Dissertation, Brandeis University 1976) 220–221, 224. Note that this position is more Hobbesian or Pufendorfian than Lockean, in that government is seen as a universal necessity, rather than a convenience that men might choose to pursue if the state of nature becomes problematic. See John Locke, *Two Treatises of Government* (Cambridge University Press 2002) 21 [II.19]. See also A. John Simmons, *On the Edge of Anarchy: Locke, Consent, and the Limits of Society* (Princeton University Press 1993) 28.

[10] "Pittsfield Petitions, May 29, 1776," 90. Allen seems to have taken this phrase from James Burgh's popular *Political Disquisitions.* See James Burgh, *Political Disquisitions*, vol. 1 (Edward and Charles Dilly 1774) 4.

[11] See Morton White, *The Philosophy of the American Revolution* (Oxford University Press 1978) 187–95; Bernard Bailyn, *The Ideological Origins of the American Revolution* (Harvard University Press 1992) 55–93.

context, this power meant the right to make and enforce law, and to protect society more generally.[12] For the Constitutionalists, while the laws of nature and human behavior make government necessary, they do not assign authority to any particular person or group.[13] Individuals "by nature are free, and have no dominion one over another." Thus, the only source of moral power available is the rights or liberties individuals hold over themselves in a state of nature; "power originates in the people" and it does not and cannot arise from divine commissions, natural power relations, or any other non-popular source.[14] As one Congregationalist minister put it, "the *Voice of the People* ... is the *Voice of God*."[15]

If power comes from the people, how does a government come to hold or wield it? The Constitutionalists claimed (3) that individuals transfer or entrust some of their natural rights and liberties to a government through a series of consensual actions referred to as contracts or compacts. As Allen writes in the *Statement*, "Government is founded in Compact so it Origenates in the people."[16]

2.2 Two Types of Contractualism

The specifics of (3) require further discussion, for the details of transferring rights and liberties varied considerably between the different versions of social contract theory available to the Constitutionalists. Though somewhat artificially, one can divide these versions into two types: *classic contractualism* and *simple contractualism*.

Classic contractualism describes a three-stage process culminating in a mutual arrangement between two parties, the ruler and ruled, in which the ruled transfer power in the form of obedience and allegiance to a ruler in exchange for protection and order. Pufendorf provides a seminal description of this process: first, individuals create a "single and perpetual group" (civil society) of united "wills and strengths" through the *Compact of Civil Society*; second, the major part of civil society agrees "upon the form of government" in the *Decree of Form*; and third, rulers recognize the liberties of the people and "bind themselves to the care of the commons security and safety, and the rest to render them obedience" in the *Compact of Submission*.[17]

[12] Simmons, *On the Edge of Anarchy: Locke, Consent, and the Limits of Society*, 60.

[13] "Statement of Berkshire County Representatives, November 17, 1778," 375.

[14] "Instructions to Pittsfield Constitutional Convention Delegate, 1779," in Oscar and Mary Handlin (eds.), *The Popular Sources of Political Authority* (Harvard University Press 1966) 410.

[15] Williams, "An Election Sermon: Boston, 1762," 7.

[16] "Statement of Berkshire County Representatives, November 17, 1778," 375. See also Pittsfield's instructions to their delegates to the 1780 constitutional convention. "Albermarle County Instructions Concerning the Virginia Constitution, Sept–Oct, 1776," in Barbara B. Oberg and J. Jefferson Looney (eds.), *The Papers of Thomas Jefferson Digital Edition* (University of Virginia Press 2008) 410–411.

[17] Samuel Pufendorf, *De Jure Naturae Et Gentium Libri Octo*, vol. 2 (Clarendon Press 1934) 974–75. For a discussion of Pufendorf's influence on Whiggish thought during the Exclusion Crisis, see Ward, *The Politics of Liberty in England and Revolutionary America*, 109–13. Burlamaqui wrote another

This compact of submission resembles a legal contract, insofar as it involves two separate parties exchanging one thing for another and thereby binding themselves to specific performances. The compact of civil society is considered perpetual, and the decree of form treated as a separate event. Together, these shield institutions of government such as representative bodies in mixed constitutional regimes from the demise and recreation of compacts of submission, an effect heightened by situating the first two steps of the social contract in the distant and mythical past.

This classic contractual model was thus a boon to certain moderate British Whigs, for it allowed them to enlist yet tame popular sovereignty arguments developed by radicals during the English Civil War. Using it, they could justify resistance against a monarch on the basis of the people's power (by pointing to the violation of the compact of submission) while simultaneously maintaining and strengthening their defense of the Ancient Constitution and the other institutions of governance (which were buried in the past and thus immune to royal misbehavior). William Atwood, Algernon Sydney, and James Ferguson, for instance, articulated versions of this argument in their defense of the Glorious Revolution.[18]

In the colonies, classic contractual arguments of this sort were not only rampant, but eventually took on a form of their own. While traditionally the King's coronation oath and the people's acquiescence were taken to be the compact of submission, by the 1770s many colonists identified it with the charter or founding document of their colonies.[19] These "charters as compacts," and classic contractualism more generally, became critical to revolutionaries after their refusal to accept virtual representation came to its inevitable conclusion: since the British parliament had no authority over the colonies (the Decree of Form had deteriorated), the charters

influential version of this three-step model. See Jean-Jacques Burlamaqui, *The Principles of Natural and Politic Law* (Liberty Fund 2006) 293.

[18] See Edmund S. Morgan, *Inventing the People: The Rise of Popular Sovereignty in England and America* (W.W. Norton & Company, Inc. 1988) 94–121; Martyn P. Thompson, "Significant Silences in Locke's Two Treatises of Government: Constitutional History, Contract and Law," (1988) 31 The Historical Journal 275–94; Ward, *The Politics of Liberty in England and Revolutionary America*, 109–13, 265–68; J.G.A. Pocock, *The Machiavellian Moment: Florentine Political Thought and the Atlantic Republican Tradition* (Princeton University Press 1975) 45–46; Corinne C. Weston, "England: Ancient Constitution and Common Law," in J.H. Burns and Mark Goldie (eds.), *The Cambridge History of Political Thought, 1450–1700*, vol. III (Cambridge University Press 1991) 379–87; Melinda S. Zook, *Radical Whigs and Conspiratorial Politics in Late Stuart England* (The Pennsylvania State University Press 1999) 80–86, 154–64; Julian H. Franklin, *John Locke and the Theory of Sovereignty: Mixed Monarchy and the Rights of Resistance in the Political Thought of the English Revolution* (Cambridge University Press 1978) 105–10.

[19] For examples of charters see Benjamin Perley Poore (ed.), *Federal and State Constitutions, Colonial Charters, and Other Organic Laws of the United States*, vol. 1 (Government Printing Office 1877). For a discussion of the role charters played in the development of state constitutions, see Lutz, *The Origins of American Constitutionalism*, 35–49. See also Massachusetts House of Representatives, "A Letter to Dennis Deberdt, Esq; Agent for the House of Representatives" *The Boston Chronicle* (April 11, 1768), 145–48, available from *America's Historical Newspapers* (Readex 2022).

were the sole remaining legal connection to the metropole.[20] This explains the near exclusive focus on royal misbehavior in the *Declaration of Independence* and the surrounding debate, for justifying the revolution entailed showing that the King's repeated violations of the charter severed this final link.[21]

However, when it came to founding new governments, classic contractualism offered little help. The compact of submission, the reciprocal juristic agreement between rulers and ruled, broke down when representative institutions replaced independent magistrates as primary power holders.[22] Representatives not only represented but also were members of the people, and thus explaining obedience as the result of a contract between two separate parties was neither necessary nor conceptually coherent. In addition, Americans during the Revolution were intent on creating something new, which meant unsettling institutional arrangements rather than falling back on them. This rendered classic contractualism far less relevant, for it focused on protecting the rights and liberties of Englishmen by burying the compact of civil society and the decree of form in the distant past and emphasizing the history and unchangeable foundations of legitimate government.[23]

For these and other reasons, the Berkshire Constitutionalists, like many early Americans concerned with creating new governments, justified their constitutional project using simple contractualism, of which Locke is the central theorist.[24] Simple contractualism eliminates the compact of submission to present a two-stage story.[25] First, interested individuals create a civil society through mutual compact. Second, this society creates an empowered government.[26] At each stage, two rights or powers are transferred or entrusted to the newly created entity: the power "to do whatsoever he thinks fit for the preservation of himself and others within the permission of the *Law of Nature*," and "the *power to punish the Crimes* committed against the Law."[27] The former becomes a government's executive and

[20] See the *Declaration of Rights and Grievances*, promulgated on October 14, 1774, for a version of this argument. Worthington Chauncey Ford and others (eds.), *Journals of the Continental Congress, 1774–1789*, vol. 1 (U.S. Government Printing Office 1904) 68.

[21] Thad W. Tate, "The Social Contract in America, 1774–1787: Revolutionary Theory as a Conservative Instrument," (1965) 22 The William and Mary Quarterly 375–391, 377; Wood, *The Creation of the American Republic, 1776–1787*, 270–271, 282; Morgan, *Inventing the People: The Rise of Popular Sovereignty in England and America*, 243–45.

[22] Wood, *The Creation of the American Republic, 1776–1787*, 283. Pufendorf recognizes this difficulty and explains it at *De Jure Naturae Et Gentium Libri Octo*, 975.

[23] See Tate, "The Social Contract in America, 1774–1787: Revolutionary Theory as a Conservative Instrument," 386.

[24] Wood, *The Creation of the American Republic, 1776–1787*, 283.

[25] By simple contractualism I mean those versions of social contract theory which drew from or resembled Locke's theory in the manner I discuss below. Price, Priestly, and other British dissenters fall within this tradition, as do certain essayists at the Constitutionalists' time. I rely on Locke, for the Constitutionalists primarily cited or drew from his or his followers' works. See Richard Ashcraft, *Revolutionary Politics & Locke's Two Treatises of Government* (Princeton University Press 1986) 560–571; Franklin, *John Locke and the Theory of Sovereignty: Mixed Monarchy and the Rights of Resistance in the Political Thought of the English Revolution*, 87–126.

[26] Of course, these two steps sometimes become lost due to the varying ways in which Locke uses the term "government." See Ruth Grant, *John Locke's Liberalism* (Chicago University Press 1987) 101–4.

[27] Locke, *Two Treatises of Government*, 352 (II.128).

federative powers and the latter becomes its legislative power.[28] The combination of these two rights or moral powers, first transferred to the major part of civil society and then entrusted to a government, constitutes political power and rightful authority.[29]

The Constitutionalists' arguments not only track simple contractualism, but also reference several writers in the tradition. Allen cites the self-described Lockean Richard Price, an eighteenth-century Radical Whig pamphlet mostly comprised of restatements and excerpts of the *Two Treatises*, and Philip Furneaux's Lockean critique of Blackstone's classical contractualism.[30] Further still, William Whiting's "An Address to the Inhabitants of Berkshire County," a response to the Berkshire Constitutionalist by a discontented former member, criticizes Allen by claiming that he misinterprets and contradicts the contractualism of "the great Mr. Locke."[31] That Whiting, who knew Allen and eventually rejoined his group, thought an exegesis on the details of Lockean contractualism was an effective means of persuasion attests to the significance of these ideas for the Constitutionalists.

One additional feature of simple contractualism bears mentioning: different voting thresholds apply to each stage. The creation of civil society employs a unanimity threshold, for only individual consent can remove a person from the state of nature.[32] However, this consent to form and join civil society simultaneously entails agreeing to "submit to the determination of the majority" in (most) future political matters. The majority, then, is the sole means through which civil society can act prior to the creation of government.[33] From this, we can restate the third component of the Constitutionalists' argument: (3) only the majority of civil society is capable of creating an authoritative government.

28 Simmons, *On the Edge of Anarchy: Locke, Consent, and the Limits of Society*, 62–63.

29 Locke, *Two Treatises of Government*, 381–2 (II.171).

30 "Statement of Berkshire County Representatives, November 17, 1778," 376; Theodore M. Hammett, "Revolutionary Ideology in Massachusetts: Thomas Allen's 'Vindication' of the Berkshire Constitutionalists, 1778," (1976) 33 The William and Mary Quarterly 514–27, 522, 526. The above-mentioned packet is *The Judgment of Whole Kingdoms and Nations* (Printed for T. Harrison 1713). This was a renamed version of the 1709 pamphlet *Vox Populi, Vox Dei*, one of the best-selling British pamphlets in the eighteenth century. Allen attributes it to John Lord Somers, though other possible authors include Robert Ferguson, Gilbert Burnet, and Daniel Defoe, with the last being most likely. See Richard Ashcraft and M.M. Goldsmith, "Locke, Revolution Principles, and the Formation of Whig Ideology," (1983) 26 The Historical Journal 773–800; J.P. Kenyon, *Revolution Principles: The Politics of Party, 1689–1720* (Cambridge University Press 1977) 209–10.

31 William Whiting, "An Address to the Inhabitants of Berkshire County, Mass. (1778)," in Charles S. Hyneman and Donald S. Lutz (eds.), *American Political Writing During the Founding Era, 1760–1805*, vol. I (Liberty Press 1983) 462.

32 This is not a unanimity threshold in the normal sense, for dissenters become non-members rather than prevent the formation of civil society.

33 Locke, *Two Treatises of Government*, 331–33 (II.396–9).

2.3 The Necessity of a Constitution

The Constitutionalists' next claim, that (4) the first step in forming a government is to create a constitution, implies that authoritative non-constitutional government is impossible.[34] Allen and his followers reached this conclusion by combining social contractualism with the idea of a written constitution, and it is best understood by looking at an exchange between Allen and William Whiting, the ex-Constitutionalist sent to Pittsfield by the General Court to reopen the courts. Neither deviates far from simple contractualism, but their interpretations of how the theory applies to Massachusetts diverge significantly. This was possible because simple contractualism is vague about practical application and silent when it comes to the creation and function of a constitution.[35]

Whiting attempts to convince his fellow Berkshire County citizens of the weaknesses of the Constitutionalists' arguments by focusing on two of their frequent assertions: that "since the Dissolution of the power of Great Britain over these Colonies they have fallen into a state of nature," and "that the first step to be taken by a people in such a state for the Enjoyment or Restoration of Civil Government amongst them, is the formation of a fundamental constitution."[36] The Constitutionalists used these claims to justify their denial of the provisional government's authority. For them, the Declaration of Independence invalidated the sitting General Court's two possible sources of authority, the royal charter (already eroded by the King's despotism) and the Continental Congress' 1775 advice on how to create an interim government.[37] This meant that until the majority of the people formed one, no government in Massachusetts existed, the people were in a state of nature, and they were under no obligation to any constituted authority. Allen writes, "Hear then Goes Charter Covenants Compacts Laws and Constitution All is Redust to a parfect State of Nature."[38]

Whiting begins by attacking the first assertion. Citing Locke, he explains that individuals first leave the state of nature by consenting to form civil society and entrusting two of their alienable rights to the majority. Only then can the adoption

[34] By "government" I mean a form of political rule involving delegated power. This is consistent with how Locke most frequently uses the term. Ibid., 332, 402, 406–7, 410–11 (II.396, 205, 211, 219); Grant, John Locke's Liberalism, 104–18; Simmons, *On the Edge of Anarchy: Locke, Consent, and the Limits of Society*, 167–72.

[35] Tate, "The Social Contract in America, 1774–1787: Revolutionary Theory as a Conservative Instrument," 379; Forrest McDonald, *Novus Ordo Seclorum: The Intellectual Origins of the Constitution* (University of Kansas Press 1985) 145; Morgan, *Inventing the People: The Rise of Popular Sovereignty in England and America*, 256; Peter Laslett, "Introduction," in Peter Laslett (ed.), *Two Treatises of Government* (Cambridge University Press 2002) 78.

[36] "Pittsfield Petitions, May 29, 1776," 90.

[37] Hammett, "Revolutionary Ideology in Massachusetts: Thomas Allen's 'Vindication' of the Berkshire Constitutionalists, 1778," 526. The Continental Congress' advice was predicated on a future resolution between England and the colonies, and thus the declaration of independence negated it.

[38] Ibid., 521.

of a constitution or mode of government take place. Thus, constitutional government "is necessarily subsequent" to civil society. Next, Whiting claims that "no revolution in, or dissolution of, particular constitutions or forms of government, can absolve the members of the society from their allegiance to the major part of the community."[39] In other words, the destruction of its government does not automatically destroy civil society and eliminate the authority of the majority. When government dissolves, as Locke explains, "*it* [the Supreme Power] *reverts to the Society*."[40]

Whiting next claims, "that even admitting the declaration of Independence did actually annihilate the *Constitution* of the province of the Massachusetts Bay; yet it did not annihilate or materially affect the union or compact existing among the people."[41] Thus, Whiting enlists simple contractualism to show that the Constitutionalists made a mistake. The people were not in a state of nature; rather, "the inhabitants of the state of Massachusetts Bay, are now in a state of some measure familiar to that which every community must pass through, while they are emerging from a state of nature to that of a free and equal government. They are … in a state of civil society."[42]

If Whiting is correct, then the Constitutionalists misinterpreted simple contractualism or distorted it for rhetorical purposes. However, his critique relies on conceptualizing the Lockean state of nature as a social or historical condition that a person is either in or out of. Alternatively, one can see it as a moral relationship between one person and another. Specifically, two people are in a state of nature with one another if and only if they are not current voluntary members of the same legitimate civil society.[43] This not only squares with how Locke uses the state of nature—he claims that a person can be in a state of nature with fellow citizens under a tyrannical government and with visiting aliens, minors, and idiots under a consensual and rightful government—but also helps us understand the Berkshire Constitutionalists.[44]

Allen's and his followers' remarks on the state of nature make sense if they refer to the relationship between the people and any entity (other than the majority) that claims a right to rule in between the two contracts. Since only the majority has political power in civil society, and since, according to the Constitutionalists, the majority had yet to create a new government, the attempted use of force or

[39] Whiting, "An Address to the Inhabitants of Berkshire County, Mass. (1778)," 467.

[40] Locke, *Two Treatises of Government*, 427–8 (II.243). Lawson makes a similar point: "The continuance and dissolution of a legal power is also to be observed. As for real majesty it always continues, whilst the community remains a community." George Lawson, *Politica Sacra Er Civilis* (Cambridge University Press 1992) 226.

[41] Whiting, "An Address to the Inhabitants of Berkshire County, Mass. (1778)," 467.

[42] Ibid., 460.

[43] This conception of Locke's state of nature comes from Simmons, *On the Edge of Anarchy: Locke, Consent, and the Limits of Society*, 13–23 See also Grant, *John Locke's Liberalism*, 66.

[44] Locke, *Two Treatises of Government*, 277–78, 279–81, 307–8 (II.215, 218, 219, 260).

political power on the people by any entity other than the majority would constitute a wrongful coercive action. Specifically, it would be an example of usurpation, "the exercise of power which another has a right to . . . ," and indicate that the coercer refuses to recognize the majority as the rightful common judge and holder of governing power.[45] This sends the coercer into the state of nature in regards to civil society.[46] As Locke writes, "When any one, or more, shall take upon them to make Laws, whom the People have not appointed so to do, they make Laws without Authority" which means that "the People are not therefore bound to obey" and are able "to resist the force of those, who without Authority would impose any thing upon them."[47]

According to this logic, members of civil society in Massachusetts remained out of the state of nature with each other, but within it in regard to any entity other than the majority that claims or attempts to use political power, whether this be the refashioned General Court, the British government, or a particularly ambitious individual. Thus, without engaging in polemics or misunderstanding simple contractualism, the Constitutionalists could simultaneously speak of "the people" and call for a majoritarian ratification threshold and claim that they were in a state of nature. This is the most plausible defense of the Constitutionalists' state of nature claims, yet it relies on rejecting Whiting's next argument: that the provisional government rightfully ruled the Commonwealth.[48]

Whiting hoped to convince the residents of Berkshire County to reopen the courts by persuading them that they were in a state of civil society and therefore had to obey the majority, which now spoke through the General Court and its various subsidiary institutions. Thus, after attacking Allen's state of nature claims, he turns his attention to the Constitutionalists' second assertion, the claim that government requires a constitution. "The common cry in this county, that we have not foundation of government, is altogether groundless," Whiting argues, for even if Massachusetts has no constitution, it has not been shown "that there can be no foundation of government without it." In fact, "a compact or union among the people, by which they agree to submit themselves to be governed by the major

[45] Ibid., 398 [II.199].

[46] Richard Ashcraft, *Locke's Two Treatises of Government* (Allen & Unwin 1987) 202; Simmons, *On the Edge of Anarchy: Locke, Consent, and the Limits of Society*, 158–59. "Serving as a common judge" entails the exercise of executive, judicial, and legislative powers for Locke. See Grant, *John Locke's Liberalism*, 75.

[47] Locke, *Two Treatises of Government*, 408 (II.212). See Simmons, *On the Edge of Anarchy: Locke, Consent, and the Limits of Society*, 160–163, 171–72.

[48] The above departs from the interpretations of the Constitutionalist/Whiting debate given by Woods and Peters. Woods claims that Whiting mistakenly equates the constitution with the form of government while the Constitutionalists equated it with the social compact itself. Peters disagrees with Woods and claims that Whiting persuasively argues that there is no middle ground between the state of nature and civil society, something that the Constitutionalists refused to acknowledge. Ronald M. Peters, *The Massachusetts Constitution of 1780: A Social Compact* (The University of Massachusetts Press 1978) 101f131; Wood, *The Creation of the American Republic, 1776–1787*, 286.

part of the community, it itself, a sufficient and substantial foundation of government."[49] Here, Whiting, like many during the period, unquestionably equates the second compact to the adoption of a constitution and the creation of constitutional government. However, he also claims that non-constitutional government is possible, exists in civil society, and appropriately commands obedience.

To make this argument, Whiting exploits Locke's ambiguous remarks about the workings of civil society between the two contracts. Locke claims that after the first compact, rather than creating a government, the majority can abstain from the second contract and the creation of a separate form of government by choosing to rule society as a direct democracy, "making Laws for the Community from time to time, and Executing those Laws by Officers of their own appointing."[50] Whiting endorses this position but expands it far beyond the non-governmental form of direct democracy that Locke seems to have in mind. According to Whiting, to address the "peace and safety of the community," the majority in Massachusetts adopted "whatever modes and forms therefore, they had been accustomed to from the old charter, and still found would be useful and expedient for a free and independent society."[51] This reauthorized a charter-based government, making all members of civil society, such as the Berkshire Constitutionalists, obliged to obey the provisional authorities. For Whiting, then, a representative and multi-branched non-constitutional form of government was possible before the second contract.

At this point, two questions emerge: first, how can Whiting claim that the majority adopted or authorized the provisional government when even he admits that direct consent never occurred?[52] Whiting never gives a clear answer, but he seems to follow the logic of classic contractualism, stressing acquiescence and the lasting legitimacy of government institutions apart from the monarchy. He suggests that the use of the revised charter and the elections of General Court members counted as majority acceptance from which consent can be imputed, for these activities require the majority acting, giving consent, or at the least not

[49] Whiting, "An Address to the Inhabitants of Berkshire County, Mass. (1778)," 467.

[50] Locke, *Two Treatises of Government*, 354 (II.132). Locke and those influenced by him are notoriously vague when it comes to discussing civil society's ability to function in the absence of government. See McDonald, *Novus Ordo Seclorum: The Intellectual Origins of the Constitution*, 145; Tate, "The Social Contract in America, 1774–1787: Revolutionary Theory as a Conservative Instrument," 379; Morgan, *Inventing the People: The Rise of Popular Sovereignty in England and America*, 256. Lawson actually attempts an explanation twice, but they amount to brief suggestions with little explanation. Ibid., 88–89; George Lawson, *An Examination of the Political Part of Mr. Hobbs His Leviathan* (London 1657) 15; Lawson, *Politica Sacra Er Civilis*, 48. Locke is also silent on the creation and role of a constitution, and to the extent that he mentions one at all, it is in reference to the Ancient Constitution laying at the center of the debate raging between Filmer's royalist proponents and radical Whigs. Laslett, "Introduction," 78.

[51] Whiting, "An Address to the Inhabitants of Berkshire County, Mass. (1778)," 472.

[52] In fact, there was no "revised charter" to consent to. Rather, the provisional government operated in accordance with the original Province Charter, as it had been interpreted and reformulated over the near decade since its adoption, with powers delegated to royal authorities now exercised by the Council and the General Court.

resisting. The authority of the provisional government is further supplemented by the fact that it consisted in recycled institutions previously held to be authoritative.

Second, what is the point of a constitution if legitimate government is possible before the second compact? Whiting claims that a constitution clarifies unalienable rights and organizes the government and the armed forces. However, these cannot be what makes constitutional government unique for him, for the provisional government and its revised charter did the same. Instead, he hints at three ways in which constitutional government is unique: it is "*fixed* and *unalterable*," the majority approves its form directly, and its details are more rigidly clarified. Whiting values these things, he expresses his "wish that we had such a constitution of government and bill of rights firmly established," but holds that their absence does not make government impossible.[53]

Thus, for Whiting, government operated in the Commonwealth and every member of civil society owed it some level of obedience. The residents of Berkshire County had to obey the General Court and accept their membership into civil society or do neither and give up any opportunity to be a part of the provisional government and any future constitution-making process.[54]

The Berkshire Constitutionalists also combined constitutionalism with simple contractualism and agreed with Whiting on several points: they understood the second compact as involving the creation of a constitution, ascribed constituent power to civil society operating through the majority, and attributed similar functions to the constitution. Nonetheless, the Constitutionalists deviated from Whiting by insisting that no real government existed in Massachusetts because legitimate government requires a constitution.[55]

This divergence stemmed from two points of disagreement. First, the Constitutionalists denounced the possibility of consent via acquiescence being used to establish a new government. If the provisional government continued to usurp the majority's political power this would not somehow render it morally legitimate in their eyes, even if this went unnoticed by the bulk of the Commonwealth.[56] The provisional government did not receive authorization directly and could not be plausibly construed as an instrument of direct majoritarian rule. Second, the Constitutionalists ascribed two roles to a constitution that Whiting did not seem to share, both of which marked a further extension of Locke's theory: a constitution both provides "a sacred Barrier against Tyranny and Despotism," and "is the

[53] Whiting, "An Address to the Inhabitants of Berkshire County, Mass. (1778)," 470, 473, 474.

[54] Ibid., 467, 478.

[55] "Pittsfield Petitions, May 29, 1776," 92.

[56] The Constitutionalists suspected that the passage of time would make the provisional government and revised charter more sociologically legitimate. As Allen wrote: "We have feared, we now realize those fears, that upon our submission we shall sink down into a dead Calm and never transmit to posterity a single Right nor leave them the least Knowledge of so fair an Inheritance." "Statement of Berkshire County Representatives, November 17, 1778," 378. See chapters 8 and 9 for discussions of sociological legitimacy.

Basis and ground work of Legislation."[57] The "constitution as barrier" conception stemmed from the Constitutionalists' Calvinist conception of human beings and their belief in power's corrupting effect. As mentioned, they held the state of nature to be execrable because man, by his nature, is deficient and weak. While government is necessary because it alone shielded men from "Anarchy and Confusion," its protection is ultimately insufficient, for men may "use all manner of Deceit and Craft" and there is a "strong Byass of human Nature to Tyranny and Despotism."[58]

In other words, power could corrupt government officials and transform them into tyrants. This was no hypothetical possibility, for the Berkshire Constitutionalists and their ancestors had witnessed a variety of political actors undergo this transformation time and time again, leading them to conclude that "Tyranny Triumps thro' the world." Corruption actively hampered revolutionary efforts, for "men who has drank of this baneful poison could not be confided in to aid and assist their Country in the present Contest," and, in the Constitutionalists' minds, many of the men supporting and taking part in the provisional government had already succumbed to power's temptation.[59] In the face of such potential tyranny, the Constitutionalists sought relief in a constitution. "We have Nothing else in View," Allen writes, "but to provide for Posterity against the wanton Exercise of power which cannot otherwise be don than by the formation of a fundamental constitution," which secures "sacred Rights and Immunities against all Tyrants that my spring up."[60]

The Constitutionalists never directly explain how a constitution prevents tyranny or despotism, but their reasoning seems to be the following. Arguments such as Whiting's, in which political power is vested in representative governments without a constitution, rely on informal rules, habitual institutions, and the general good behavior of government actors to prevent despotism. For instance, to combat the Constitutionalists' claims that wicked men in the Commonwealth intended to enslave the people, Whiting argues that this is impossible, for councilors and representatives take oaths "to be true to the people of the state" and that elected politicians make good decisions because "they are sufficiently apprized that if they do not . . . they will not be elected themselves again."[61]

[57] Ibid., 375.

[58] "Pittsfield Petitions, May 29, 1776," 89; "Report of a Lecture by Thomas Allen on February 18, 1776," in Oscar and Mary Handlin (eds.), *The Popular Sources of Political Authority* (Harvard University Press 1966) 70.

[59] Thomas Allen, "Pittsfield Memorial, December 26, 1775,' in Oscar and Mary Handlin (ed.), *The Popular Sources of Political Authority* (Harvard University Press 1966) 62; "Statement of Berkshire County Representatives, November 17, 1778," 377. In a lecture in Richmond in February 1776, Allen warned of corrupt men and usurpers rising within the ranks of the colonists, and insinuated that the Provincial Congress and the General Court had been composed of designing men. "Report of a Lecture by Thomas Allen on February 18, 1776," 71.

[60] "Pittsfield Petitions, May 29, 1776," 91–92.

[61] Whiting, "An Address to the Inhabitants of Berkshire County, Mass. (1778)," 471.

For the Constitutionalists, these sorts of reassurances were insufficient. As the behavior of the British parliament and local councilors showed, corrupted leaders break informal rules and traditions, violate oaths, postpone or alter elections, and create new legislation to advance their interests.[62] Such behavior cannot effectively be stopped because civil society and non-constitutional government are in a relational state of nature with another; no common authority exists between them to patrol and punish misbehavior. A constitution solves this problem by being above the purview of government officials, organizing and constraining them in a visible manner by making public the conditions of their trust and the limits of their power, and clarifying the proper authority and means of resolution for the inevitable conflicts that power produces. Such a constitution makes it "peculiarly out of the Power of Designing men to Enroach on the Inherent and Unalienable rights of the People," serves as "Lines ... Drawn as rules of Government," and makes "the Servants of the People ... as much as may be in the Possession of the People."[63]

The majority thus endangers itself whenever it grants political power to a government without a constitution, for "whatever Building is reared without a foundation must fall into Ruins."[64] In an essay quoted by Allen, Richard Price expresses similar sentiments, noting that political power is "delegation for gaining particular ends," and that because "this trust may be misapplied and abused ... employed to defeat the very ends for which it was instituted, and to subvert the very rights it ought to protect ... all delegated power must be subordinate and limited." For the Constitutionalists, such subordination and limitation required a constitution.[65]

This brings us to the other role of a constitution that Whiting did not share. "The fundamental Constitution is the Basis and ground work of Legislation," Allen explains, and "Legislators stand on this foundation, and enact Laws agreeably to it." In other words, the entire legal and political system draws its authority from the constitution. At first glance, this simply expresses the distinction between higher and ordinary law that allows constitutions to serve as a barrier of tyranny. Allen makes this point by quoting from Furneaux's commentary on Blackstone's assertion that it "is the height of Political Absurdity" to envision a government without the power "to alter every part of its law."[66] Furneaux claims that Blackstone is

62 The General Court made organizational changes via legislation regularly. For instance, they recalculated representation in the Commonwealth in an Act dated May 4, 1774. "An Act for More Equal Representation, May 4, 1776," in Oscar and Mary Handlin (eds.), *The Popular Sources of Political Authority* (Harvard University Press, 1966) 78.

63 "Votes of Towns in Choosing Delegates, July–October 1779," in Oscar and Mary Handlin (eds.), *The Popular Sources of Political Authority* (Harvard University Press 1966) 418.

64 "Pittsfield Petitions, May 29, 1776," 91.

65 Richard Price, "Two Tracts on Civil Liberty, the War with America, and the Debts and Finances of the Kingdom," in D.O. Thomas (ed.), *Richard Price: Political Writings* (Cambridge University Press 1991) 28.

66 William Blackstone, *Commentaries of the Laws of England in Four Books*, vol. 1 (J.B. Lippincott Company 1893) 97n6; "Statement of Berkshire County Representatives, November 17, 1778," 376–77; Hammett, "Revolutionary Ideology in Massachusetts: Thomas Allen's 'Vindication' of the Berkshire Constitutionalists, 1778," 523–24.

mistaken, for "free states would be unfree" if there did not exist some "Liberties and previleges" that "Society has not given out of their own Hands to their Governors." These retained liberties and privileges, Furneaux explains, are enshrined in the constitution in order to limit and organize government, and set the terms for the entrustment of political power and the conditions under which it ends.[67]

However, the Constitutionalists are also making a deeper point. Legislators owe their very existence to the constitution, because without one there would be no reason to have government. Individuals form civil society and government to, among other things, create a means of living together and resolving conflict. A non-constitutional government lacks justification because it simply creates another source of conflict without resolution, this time between the people and government. The Constitutionalists' own fight with the General Court illustrates this scenario, for it was a protracted conflict over the proper source of government authority with no common judge to resolve the dispute. Adopting a constitution helps to avoid such situations by setting out bounds of authority and legislative procedures understood by the major part of civil society, and institutionalizing mechanisms of dispute resolution. In this sense, all governmental authority comes from the constitution.[68] As Allen's citation of *The Judgment of Whole Kingdoms* explains: "Every subjects allegiance is first oweing to the Constitution and to the Ruler only in the source and virtue of what Every member of the Political society is Bound unto by the Terms of the Original pact or settlement."[69]

Thus, for the Constitutionalists a legitimate government did not exist in Massachusetts from 1774 until 1780 because there was no constitution. By refusing to reopen the courts they did not rebel, but simply ignored the orders of a usurping authority. An authoritative government used political power entrusted to it by the major part of civil society, with the terms of this trust codified in a constitution. Thus, as the Berkshire Constitutionalists explained, (4) "the first step to be taken by a people in such a state for the Enjoyment or Restoration of Civil Government amongst them, is the formation of a fundamental constitution," and until then the people "are but beating the Air and doing what will and must be undone afterwards."[70]

[67] "Statement of Berkshire County Representatives, November 17, 1778," 376–77; Hammett, "Revolutionary Ideology in Massachusetts: Thomas Allen's 'Vindication' of the Berkshire Constitutionalists, 1778," 523–24; Philip Furneaux, *Letters to the Honourable Mr. Justice Blackstone* (T. Cadell 1770).

[68] Note that by legislative authority the Constitutionalists seem to have in mind all political power concerning the making, enforcement, and interpretation of laws.

[69] Hammett, "Revolutionary Ideology in Massachusetts: Thomas Allen's 'Vindication' of the Berkshire Constitutionalists, 1778," 522.

[70] "Pittsfield Petitions, May 29, 1776," 90–91.

3. Constitutional Creation and Constituent Power

By combining simple contractualism and the concept of a written constitution, and holding that government was impossible with the latter, the Berkshire Constitutionalists argued that creating a government essentially meant creating a constitution, and that the ability to do so belonged solely to the majority of civil society. In this way, they espoused an early theory of constituent power.

3.1 Authorization and the Legislature

However, as discussed in the previous chapter, constituent power theories run into a basic conundrum: creating a constitution requires, at a minimum, writing one, and it is unclear what role the majority can play in this process. The most intuitive solution, having every member of civil society directly take part in the drafting process, is impossible for all but the smallest communities. Thus, alternative ways to combine popularly held constituent power with the process of constitution-making must be found. Several exist.

One is to have an individual or group write and enact the constitution, and somehow associate or identify its actions with the will of the majority. For instance, construing constituent power as something that can be entrusted or delegated enables principal-agent dynamics. The people temporarily entrust their constituent power to a group of elected delegates who write the constitution at the people's behest. Alternatively, Sieyès conceptualized constituent power as non-communicable, and bypassed the problem of direct authorship though a conception of extraordinary representation, in which special representatives embody and become identical to, rather than represent, the will of the people when creating the constitution.[71] Another solution involves a Rousseauian or Platonic Lawgiver who, through certain extraordinary attributes, is able to create a constitution that so perfectly aligns with the nascent will of the majority that its creation can be attributed to them. These options place emphasis on the identity of the framers and the nature of the drafting process, with the idea that only the right sort of framers in the right sort of conditions can embody the majority will. By doing so, these and similar solutions depict constitution-making as a single unbroken procedure undertaken by the constituent power.

Beginning in the Pittsfield Petitions, the Berkshire Constitutionalists introduced a different approach: they divided the process into drafting and authorization stages, with authorization involving the approval or rejection of the draft

[71] Emmanuel Joseph Sieyès, "What Is the Third Estate?" in Michael Sonenscher (ed.), *Political Writings: Including the Debate between Sieyès and Tom Paine in 1791* (Hackett Publishing Company 2003) 139.

constitution and being the unique site of constituent power. "The Approbation of the Majority of the people of this fundamental Constitution," Allen notes, "is absolute necessary to give Life and being to it."[72]

In other words, (5) the people exercise their constituent power and create their constitution when they ratify it. When it comes to constituent power, what matters is who gets to approve the constitution, not who writes the document or how they do it. In combination with the previous four claims, this completes the Constitutionalists' general argument for ratification. Only the people can create legitimate government, creating a constitution is equivalent to creating a government, and constituent power is only exercised during the authorization process. Thus, the people must have the opportunity to approve or reject the constitution before implementation.

3.2 Who Ratifies?

Demanding that the people ratify does not specify a particular ratification procedure. The people might, for instance, delegate their constituent power to existing legislatures or a special ratifying convention. The Constitutionalists' next claim eliminates such possibilities by denying the permissibility of any form of ratification other than a direct popular vote, i.e. a referendum.[73] Allen explains:

> Legislators stand on this foundation, and enact Laws agreeably to it. They cannot give Life to the Constitution: it is the approbation of the Majority of the people at large that gives Life and being to it.... A Representative body may form but cannot impose said Constitution upon a free people. The giving Existence to the fundamental Constitution of a free state is a Trust that cannot be delegated. For any rational person to give his vote for another person to aid and assist in forming said Constitution with a view of imposing it on the people without reserving to himself a Right of Inspection Approbation Rejection or Amendment, imports, if not impiety, yet real popery in politicks.... In this the very essence of true Liberty consists, viz. in every free state the Constitution is adopted by the majority.[74]

This and similar passages contain two entangled arguments.

[72] "Pittsfield Petitions, May 29, 1776," 90.

[73] Condorcet would express this position less than twenty years later. Marquis de Condorcet, "The Principle of, the Justifications for, the New Constitution," in Marc Allan Goldstein (ed.), *Social and Political Thought of the French Revolution, 1788–1797: An Anthology of Original Texts* (Peter Lang 1997) 417.

[74] "Statement of Berkshire County Representatives, November 17, 1778," 375. "Popery in politicks" referred to the idea that there is an entity in the state with supremacy. For an example of such usage, see Granville Sharp, *A Declaration of the People's Natural Right to a Share in the Legislature* (Applewood Books 2009) xxxiv.

The first attacks the possibility of existing legislative bodies authorizing a constitution. According to the Constitutionalists, such a plan circulated as early as mid-1776, when "several of the Justices newly created without the Voice of the People" suggested that "the Representatives of the People may form just what fundamental constitution they please and impose it upon the people."[75] To Allen and his followers, such a plan was "the rankest kind of Toryism, the self same Monster we are now fighting against."[76] Later that same year, the General Court's first request, to create and enact a constitution without any real town consultation, confirmed these suspicions.

The Constitutionalists' argument is a slight reformulation of the familiar claim that a constituted body cannot constitute itself; one that we saw reemerge in the Philadelphia Convention when it was deployed to justify disallowing state legislatures from serving as ratifying authorities. On the one hand, like any organ of government, legislative bodies receive their power and authority from the people. However, as discussed above, political power can only rightfully be given to governmental organs organized and limited by formal rules. These rules come from the constitution, and since constitution-making events take place in the absence of an operable constitution, any existing legislative branch or body of government lacks ordinary authority, let alone the extraordinary power to create a constitution. "A Legal Representative is a Creature of the Constitution of a state, or Kingdom," several Hampshire County towns explained, in reference to General Court members, and "we Desire to know how such a Creature can Exist in a Legal Sense prior to that Constitution on which his being and Existance Depends."[77]

On the other hand, the act of creating a constitution involves creating the source of authority for any governmental organ or branch. Therefore, a government entity cannot create the constitution because this would involve creating its own creator, authorizing the very source of its own authority. As Allen notes, "the whole Legislature of any state is insufficient to give Life to the fundamental Constitution of such state, it being the foundation on which they themselves stand and from which alone the Legislature derives its Authority."[78]

3.3 An Unalienable Right

The second argument for confining constituent power to popular ratification is wider reaching. The Constitutionalists claim that *any* type of representative or delegated entity, not just a legislative body or other branch of government, is

[75] "Pittsfield Petitions, May 29, 1776," 91.
[76] Ibid., 90–91.
[77] "Opinions of Hampshire County Towns, March 30, 1779," in Oscar and Mary Handlin (eds.), *The Popular Sources of Political Authority* (Harvard University Press 1966) 385.
[78] "Statement of Berkshire County Representatives, November 17, 1778," 377.

unable to create and authorize a legitimate constitution. This is because constituent power cannot be delegated or entrusted, for (6) the right to create a constitution by authorization, i.e. the right to ratify, is unalienable.

The Berkshire Constitutionalists first discuss unalienability in the following passage:

> The people at large are endowed with certain alienable and unalienable Rights. Those which are unalienable, are those which belong to Conscience respecting the worship of God and the practice of the Christian Religion, and that of being determined or governed by the Majority in the Institution or formation of Government. The alienable are those which may be delegated for the Common good, or those which are for the common good to be parted with. It is of the unalienable Rights, particularly that of being determined or governed by the Majority in the Institution or formation of Government of which something further is necessary to be considered at this Time.[79]

Here, Allen mentions three unalienable rights: the right of religious belief (inner worship); the right of religious practice (external worship); and the right to be determined by the majority in the institution or formation of government, which can be restated as the right to ratify.

To clarify, in the context of seventeenth- and eighteenth-century philosophy, a "right" referred to a moral power, the ability to effect or do something using physical strength in a manner approved by or not in violation of reason and the natural law that it tracks. Many of the popular natural rights theorists at the time elucidated rights in this way. For instance Burlamaqui, following a tradition stemming back to Gerson through Suarez to Pufendorf, defined the term as "a power that man hath to make use of his liberty and natural strength in a particular manner ... so far as this exercise ... is approved by reason."[80]

A right is unalienable if it cannot voluntarily be given away or exchanged by its owner.[81] This is distinct from forfeiture, prescription, defeasibleness, and the like; it is a property that describes how consensual acts can lead to the intentional transfer of a right and has nothing to do with whether a right can be lost because of wrongdoing, taken away by force, or outweighed by competing considerations. Further, unalienable rights overlap but are not equivalent to those rights not ceded

[79] Ibid., 374–75.

[80] Burlamaqui, *The Principles of Natural and Politic Law*, 69; Samuel Pufendorf, *Two Books of the Elements of Universal Jurisprudence* (The Works of Samuel Pufendorf, Liberty Fund 2009) 91, 221; Quentin Skinner, *The Foundations of Modern Political Thought: The Age of Reformation*, vol. 2 (Cambridge University Press 1978) 121, 176; White, *The Philosophy of the American Revolution*, 186–92; Richard Tuck, *Natural Rights Theories: Their Origin and Development* (Cambridge University Press 1979) 25.

[81] Terrance McConnell, "The Nature and Basis of Inalienable Rights," (1984) 3 Law and Philosophy 25–59, 31.

to civil society or government.[82] The rights remaining with individuals after each of the two contracts include unalienable rights, but also include all natural rights, such as Locke's "liberty … of innocent delights," that do not need to be ceded in order to fulfill the purpose of civil society or government.[83] Finally, an unalienable right is not necessarily a natural right, i.e. a right that exists before any contracting takes place. It is only a right that cannot be voluntarily transferred, and its genesis remains an open question.

Thus, the Berkshire Constitutionalists' assertion that the right to ratify is unalienable amounts to the claim that civil society cannot transfer its morally sanctioned ability to approve or reject a constitution to any entity other than itself. Why did the Berkshire Constitutionalists think that this, or the other rights Allen picked out, were unalienable? The answer to this question is not straightforward, for using different conceptions of unalienability, each with a different explanation for why some rights cannot be alienated, is commonplace in the philosophical and religious works of the time.[84] However, Francis Hutcheson, who first introduced the terminology of alienable/unalienable rights and greatly influenced early American political thought, helps us differentiate them into types. According to Hutcheson, to determine if rights are alienable or not, one must consider: "1st. If the Alienation be within our natural Power, so that it be possible for us in Fact to transfer our Right; and if it be so, then, 2nd. It must appear that to transfer such Rights may serve some valuable Purpose."[85] Using this distinction, one can divide unalienable rights into two types: naturally unalienable and morally unalienable.

A right is *naturally unalienable* if it concerns an ability or power that a person cannot physically transfer to another. Hutcheson gives the example of the right to private judgment, which he claims occurs automatically in the mind in response to external evidence and stimuli. This right is naturally unalienable, because even if they want to, individuals cannot give another person the ability to make judgments for them, let alone transfer the right to do this.[86] Locke invokes

[82] Thus, Peters is incorrect when describing unalienable rights as "criteria … by which the legitimate extent of political authority could be determined." Peters, *The Massachusetts Constitution of 1780: A Social Compact*, 75. See also Simmons, *On the Edge of Anarchy: Locke, Consent, and the Limits of Society*, 62.

[83] Locke, *Two Treatises of Government*, 352 (II.128). See also Theophilus Parsons, "The Essex Result, 1778," in Oscar and Mary Handlin (eds.), *The Popular Sources of Political Authority* (Harvard University Press 1966) 330; Simmons, *On the Edge of Anarchy: Locke, Consent, and the Limits of Society*, 62; "Instructions to Stoughton Constitutional Convention Delegate, 1779," in Oscar and Mary Handlin (eds.), *The Popular Sources of Authority: Documents on the Massachusetts Constitution of 1780* (Harvard University Press 1966) 424.

[84] See, for example, Richard Price's gloss on the unalienability of the rights to internal worship, external worship, self-legislation, and property; Price, "Two Tracts on Civil Liberty, the War with America, and the Debts and Finances of the Kingdom," 33.

[85] Francis Hutcheson, *An Inquiry into the Original of Our Ideas of Beauty and Virtue in Two Treatises*, ed. Wolfgang Leidhold, The Collected Works and Correspondence of Francis Hutcheson (Indianapolis: Liberty Fund, 2004), 185. See White, *The Philosophy of the American Revolution*: 196–202.

[86] Even if one does not accept Hutcheson's particular conception of cognition, the point stands, for attempting to give someone the power to make judgments for us would necessarily involve making the constant judgment that their judgments are the correct ones.

something like natural unalienability in his toleration writings; he argues that one reason magistrates can never acquire the right to coerce in religious matters is because "no man can, if he would, conform his faith to the dictates of another," for "to believe this or that to be true does not depend upon on our will."[87] The discourse on religion in late eighteenth-century Massachusetts also contained similar arguments. For instance, the Congregationalist Pastor Abraham Williams notes in his election sermon that "Human Law can't control the Mind.—The Rights of Conscience are unalienable; inseparable from our Nature; —they ought not—they cannot possible be given up to Society."[88] In this way, natural unalienability explains the Constitutionalists' treatment of the right belonging to inner worship as unalienable, for a person cannot give another the ability to dictate their genuine faith and religious belief. However, it does not explain the right to ratification or external worship, for there is nothing physically impossible about alienating either.[89]

A right is *morally unalienable* if it is possible for a person to control and alienate the activity or object in question, but not without violating moral law. This definition of moral unalienability could yield an endless number of variations, each correlated with a different conception of morality. However, in the context of early America, these variations narrowed down to two: *non-ownership moral unalienability* and *no-reason moral unalienability.*

A right that someone does not possess is non-ownership morally unalienable. For instance, a person might be able to take some action *x* but be unable to transfer the right to do *x* because she does not possess it. Locke uses non-ownership moral unalienability to explain the impossibility of voluntary enslavement or submission to absolute rule.[90] Both, he argues, involve alienating the right to destroy our lives. This is impossible, because individuals do not possess the right; God only entrusted them with the right to control their life, not the right to end it.[91] "Nobody

[87] John Locke, "A Letter Concerning Toleration," *The Works of John Locke*, vol. 5 (12th edn., Rivington 1824) 11, 40. This argument relies on Locke's claim that coercion works on the will.

[88] Williams, "An Election Sermon: Boston, 1762," 8.

[89] Though popular at the time, there is something contradictory about natural alienability, for it is hard to see how a person has a right to abilities and actions that he cannot control and objects that he does not possess. This is particularly problematic for Pufendorf, Hutcheson, Jefferson, and the like, who linked rights to the will and intentions. See White, *The Philosophy of the American Revolution*, 199–200.

[90] Locke's argument might also fit into another conception of moral unalienability popular in the late eighteenth century: the idea that a right is unalienable if it stems from a duty. This conception, discussed by Burlamaqui, Jefferson, and others, holds that alienating a right to do *x* derived from a duty to do *x* is impossible, for this would involve taking on a duty not to do *x* and thus contradict the original duty. I ignore this alternative type of moral unalienability because of its similarity to non-ownership moral unalienability, and its absence from most discussions of unalienability in the Massachusetts discourse at the time. See Burlamaqui, *The Principles of Natural and Politic Law*, 74; White, *The Philosophy of the American Revolution*, 209–10.

[91] See also *The Judgment of Whole Kingdoms and Nations*, 18. This only pertains to an individual's ability to alienate a right. Thus, a right to life might be unalienable, but subject to forfeiture under certain conditions. According to Tuck, Grotius first stated such a position. See Tuck, *Natural Rights Theories: Their Origin and Development*, 70.

can give more power than he has himself, and he that cannot take away his own life cannot give another power over it."[92]

Non-ownership moral unalienability does not explain the right to practice religion as one chooses, but what about the right to ratification? Consider two possible explanations: civil society cannot alienate the right to ratify the constitution because individuals possess it; and the majority cannot alienate the right to ratify the constitution because civil society possesses it. The first explanation fails because civil society possesses the right to ratification, which stems from the rights of self-preservation and punishment ceded by individuals upon entering civil society. The second explanation also fails, for it mistakenly treats the majority as a distinct agent separate from civil society, rather than the means through which the will and decision of civil society is determined in accordance with the agreement made in the first contract.

This leaves *no-reason morally unalienability*, which applies when alienation is always irrational, i.e. when the reasons against alienating a right necessarily win out over those in favor. This conception is a descendant of the Grotian idea of interpretive charity seized upon by English Radicals in the seventeenth century, who argued that while it is logically possible for free men to renounce all of their natural rights, charity dictates that we assume that our predecessors were rational, and therefore could not have intended to leave themselves and future generations without any critical rights.[93] Moving from classic to simple contractualism eliminates the focus on the original contract and the ancient constitution, turning the principle of interpretive charity into a general form of unalienability that, I argue, best explains the right of ratification. Here, the irrationality of alienating certain rights is treated like a defeating condition, i.e. a condition like fraud, duress, or insanity, the presence of which automatically voids a contract, or in this case voids any attempt at alienation.[94]

How do certain rights always lack sufficient reasons for alienation? Allen claims "alienable [rights] may be delegated for the Common good, or those which are for the common good to be parted with." This can be read in two ways. On the one hand, Allen simply explains that those rights delegated for the common good are alienable rights. On the other hand, Allen describes alienable rights as those rights the alienation of which can benefit the common good. This latter interpretation suggests that unalienable rights are those rights that harm the common good when alienated. From this, and taking into consideration that Allen is referring explicitly

[92] Locke, *Two Treatises of Government*, 284 (II.223). See Simmons, *On the Edge of Anarchy: Locke, Consent, and the Limits of Society*, 115–16; White, *The Philosophy of the American Revolution*, 210; Peters, *The Massachusetts Constitution of 1780: A Social Compact*, 80; McConnell, "The Nature and Basis of Inalienable Rights," 45. My interpretation diverges from these authors, in that they collapse what I call non-ownership moral unalienability into natural alienability.

[93] Tuck, *Natural Rights Theories: Their Origin and Development*, 143–52.

[94] See Simmons, *On the Edge of Anarchy: Locke, Consent, and the Limits of Society*, 137.

to those rights held by civil society, the good of which is the "common good," I can define alienation against reason as alienating a right when doing so harms the good of the rights holder.

This produces the following definition of no-reason moral unalienability: *a right is unalienable if alienating it is always contrary to the good of its holder.* Undergirding this conception is the idea that the alienation of a right, considered in isolation, has a negative effect on a rights holder. Thus, rational rights holders only alienate rights if doing so, in some way, has a greater positive impact on their well-being, whatever this might entail. And unalienable rights are those rights that always leave the rights holder in a worse position following alienation, regardless of context.

Seen in this light, no-reason moral unalienability is familiar. Hobbes expresses a similar logic when he writes: "Whensoever a man transfers his right or renounces it, it is either in consideration of some right reciprocally transferred to himself or for some other good he hope thereby . . . and therefore there be some rights which no man can be understood by any words or other signs to have abandoned or transferred."[95] And Parsons claim that certain rights are "are unalienable and inherent, and of that importance, that no equivalent can be received in exchange."[96]

No-reason moral unalienability explains the right to practice religion and the right to ratify the constitution. In regards to the former, the Constitutionalists' explanation likely follows Hutcheson's, who explains that, "it can never serve any valuable purpose, to make Men worship him in a way which seems to them displeasing to him."[97] Since the point of practicing religion is to take actions one believes God desires and to be judged accordingly, allowing another person to dictate one's religious practice eliminates its value, adds nothing, hurts the individual rights holder, and is therefore without reason.[98] Since such alienation is irrational, the right to practice one's religion as one pleases is unalienable. This reasoning is echoed by a 1780 voting return by the Berkshire town of New Salem, which argues that "Religion must at all times be a matter between GOD and individuals, then we see not the least propriety or fitness, in the Peoples Investing their Legislature with any spiritual Jurisdiction Over the Subject."[99]

95 Thomas Hobbes, *Leviathan* (Cambridge University Press 1996) 66.

96 Parsons, "The Essex Result, 1778," 330; Simmons, *On the Edge of Anarchy: Locke, Consent, and the Limits of Society*, 137–38; Peters, *The Massachusetts Constitution of 1780: A Social Compact*, 80.

97 Francis Hutcheson, *An Inquiry into the Original of Our Ideas of Beauty and Virtue in Two Treatises* (Liberty Fund 2004) 185.

98 As with internal worship, this stance on external worship bears the influence of the Constitutionalists' theological commitments. Congregationalists, such as the Constitutionalists, likely subscribed to Calvin's adoption of Luther's two kingdoms conception, which held that secular government was profoundly distinct from religious government. See, for instance, the town of Granville's discussion in their 1780 Returns, "Returns of the Towns on the Constitution of 1780," in Oscar and Mary Handlin (eds.), *The Popular Sources of Political Authority* (Harvard University Press 1966) 557.

99 Ibid., 482–83. See also Parson's discussion of worship in Parsons, "The Essex Result, 1778," 330.

In these terms, the right to ratification is unalienable because any alienation endangers or harms civil society (the rights holder) and is therefore without reason. Why would this be the case? The Constitutionalists explain:

> [T]o suppose the Representative Body capable of forming and imposing this Compact or constitution without the Inspection and Approbation Rejection or Amendment of the people at large would involve in it the greatest Absurdity.... This imports uncontroulable Dominion over their Constituents for what should hinder them from making such a constitution as invests them and their successors in office with unlimited Authority, if it be admitted that the Representatives are the people as to forming and imposing the fundamental Constitution of the state upon them without their Approbation and perhaps in opposition to their united sense—In this the very essence of true Liberty consists, viz in every free state the Constitution is adopted by the Majority.[100]

This argument tracks and expands the Berkshire Constitutionalists' earlier argument against non-constitutional government. An entity entrusted with constituent power, i.e. entrusted with the right to authorize the constitution before its final enactment, might approve a constitution and form of government directly harmful to the people, and be completely within its power when doing so. Moreover, there is no way to prevent this occurrence, for the Constitutionalists believed that individuals in civil society cannot reliably control or check governing bodies in the absence of a constitution. In this sense, the dominion of those endowed with constituent power is indeed, as Allen suggests, uncontrollable.

For example, a constitutional convention might be created for the restricted purpose of creating a particular kind of constitution, with explicit instructions that it would dissolve upon the completion of its task. Nonetheless, if entrusted with the power to create a constitution without consulting the majority, this convention could write and draft any constitution it wanted, including one that turned the convention into a perpetual government with near absolute powers, and then authorize and implement it. In the absence of a higher law document and a pre-existing means of regulating its behavior, it would either be difficult or impossible for individuals in civil society to prevent it from doing so.

Moreover, the Constitutionalists must have recognized that the authorization of a constitution by a body endowed with constituent power might make the constitution appear morally legitimate, even if the authorizers violated the terms of their trust. This effect would be heightened by the tradition of covenanting and the general popularity of contractual and constitutional thought in Massachusetts at the time, which likely made anything resembling a social contract appear somewhat

100 "Statement of Berkshire County Representatives, November 17, 1778," 377.

acceptable. Thus, alienating the right to ratify a constitution, which amounts to alienating constituent power, involves giving an external body the moral power to take actions the effects of which are either long-lasting or permanently harmful to civil society, in a context in which institutional safeguards and regulatory mechanisms are absent. To the Constitutionalists, no potential benefit could offset such risk, and therefore the right to ratify is unalienable. Constitutions not only must be ratified, but this must be done directly by the people in some form of referendum.

4. *The Sleeping Sovereign* and the Unique Site Justification

The USJ is the argument produced by those who first invented ratification. However, it is not of mere historical interest. On the one hand, it remains the most coherent and worked out version of an argument that seeks to justify ratification by appealing to popular sovereignty and constituent power. Thus, the regular stream of constitutional consultants and constitutional lawyers that seek to connect the two are best interpreted as making a USJ argument.

On the other hand, in the realm of contemporary political theory, it is having something of a renaissance. For instance, as mentioned in chapter 1, Richard Tuck recently resurrected the argument in his book, *The Sleeping Sovereign: The Invention of Modern Democracy*.[101] The book, a contribution to the history of political thought, explicitly focuses on following the development of what Tuck refers to as the sovereign/government distinction—the sovereign being the authority able to make the higher-order decisions about the organization and values of a state. Upon the advent of constitutional government, this means the sovereign is the authority capable of creating and changing constitutional law. The government is that which is tasked with running the state's day-to-day operations, in other words all those institutions and agents that execute the functions of a state not having to do with writing and amending the constitution. This distinction, as Tuck himself admits, is nearly identical to the constituent/constituted distinction within constituent power theory—the sovereign is constituent power and the government is constituted power—, though Tuck traces its origins to Bodin, Hobbes, and Rousseau, and views Sieyès as its antagonist rather than its most famous proponent.

For Tuck, the sovereign/government distinction played and continues to play an important role: it is what makes democracy possible in large-scale modern states. In this sense, his historical reconstruction of the distinction is also a reconstruction of the invention of modern democracy; as Tuck notes "it allowed for

[101] Richard Tuck, *The Sleeping Sovereign: The Invention of Modern Democracy* (Cambridge University Press 2016).

the appearance of a new kind of democracy, appropriate for the modern world, in which citizens could all be true legislators in fundamental matters but leave less fundamental ones to their agents."[102] Further still, as some readers of Tuck make even more explicit, his project simultaneously involves the elucidation of "the original theory of modern constitutionalism."[103] Tuck attributes these roles to the sovereign/government distinction because he sees it as the key to unlocking the perennial problem of democracy once it moved outside the realm of small-city states. How can a concept of self-government, one that seems to require an active and circumscribed citizenry, apply in large commercial and eventually modern states? How can democracy, real democracy, thrive in such contexts without reducing the role of citizens to that of choosing elites to rule over them. The answer, according to Tuck, which Rousseau hit upon while building on the ideas of Bodin and Hobbes, is to separate sovereignty from government, and enable the people to play a role in self-legislation by limiting it to the occasional making and unmaking of their constitutional law.[104] In between these rare moments of constituent power the people sleep, i.e. step back from politics, and let the government/constituted power handle things.

Now, there is much to question in Tuck's narrative on a variety of levels. It would be helpful, for instance, if he explained more precisely how his account differs from standard discussions of the history and evolution of the constituent/constituted power distinction, or at least took any account of some of the existing literature on the topic. In addition, it remains unclear what one gains by writing Sieyès out of the distinction by interpreting sovereignty/constituent power as requiring the use of direct public consultation. Further, Tuck never explains why a deep appreciation of the theoretical necessity of the public's engagement during the creation of fundamental law necessitates emphasizing, and seemingly celebrating, their absence during the long periods of ordinary politics. Such a conclusion, perversely, brings Tuck closer to Schumpeter and more contemporary minimalists than he is likely comfortable with.

More directly, it is tempting to push against Tuck's interpretation of Rousseau, upon which much of the book's argument rests.[105] For instance, Tuck describes the sovereign assemblies of Rousseau's theory as so "limited and foundational" that they can be compared to Jefferson's scheme of holding constitutional conventions every nineteen years.[106] This seems problematic for conceptual and textual reasons.

[102] Ibid., 141.

[103] David Singh Grewal and Jedediah Purdy, "The Original Theory of Constitutionalism," (2018) 127 The Yale Law Journal 2–42, 6.

[104] Tuck, *The Sleeping Sovereign: The Invention of Modern Democracy*, 249.

[105] See Jeffrey Lenowitz and Melissa Schwartzberg, "Insomnia and Other Constitutional Pathologies," (2019) 16 Modern Intellectual History 295–308, 302–5.

[106] Tuck, *The Sleeping Sovereign: The Invention of Modern Democracy*, 136 n. 127; Jean Jacques Rousseau, "Of the Social Contract," in Victor Gourevitch (ed.), *Rousseau: The Social Contract and Other Later Political Writings* (Cambridge University Press 1997) 119–20 (III.18).

Conceptually, moments of sovereign assembly lawmaking that only take place once or twice a generation seems directly at odds with Rousseau's central project, which seeks to secure personal freedom by linking it to ongoing self-legislation via the general will. Textually, Rousseau describes the assembly and citizenry as far more engaged than Tuck's interpretation allows. For instance, Rousseau notes that "As soon as public service ceases to be the Citizen's principal business . . . the state is close to ruin," and "in a well conducted assembly everyone flies to the assemblies."[107]

However, for our purposes these questions and potential criticism are immaterial. Rather, what is relevant is how Tuck's historical account and implicit normative theory tracks USJ. The people are not only the sole site of sovereignty, but this sovereignty cannot be alienated in the sense of being exercised by representative bodies. In other words, the people cannot exercise their unique ability to create fundamental law by selecting representatives to create a constitution. Doing so amounts to a betrayal of the idea of sovereignty and is the basis for Tuck's original recasting of Sieyès as an enemy of modern democracy.[108] Rousseau's great pronouncement, for Tuck, was the rejection of the idea "that a sovereign people could be represented *in its sovereignty* through deputies," and his further insistence that "no sovereign agent is entitled to transfer its sovereignty."[109]

What this means is that the people exercise their sovereignty only when voting on constitutions, and perhaps amendments to them, directly. Referendums on constitutions are therefore not only justified but also necessary. In this sense, while the theoretical origins of the sovereignty/government distinction lie in canonical titans of political thought, Tuck locates the origins of the distinction's operationalization in the Girondins and in eighteenth-century Revolutionary America, specifically in who I call the Berkshire Constitutionalists.[110] It was these thinkers, for Tuck, who figured out how to "give an institutional structure to the idea of a legislative sovereign underlying but separate from the normal governmental structure."[111] They alone "realized that they could give an appropriate institutional expression to the idea of democracy at the level of sovereignty but not government by the institution of a referendum on the articles of a written constitution."[112]

Moreover, Tuck is not satisfied in merely tracing a historical line of political thought, i.e. uncovering the sovereign/government distinction and showing how it became operationalized with the invention of constitutional plebiscites. Rather, he seems to support the theory he uncovers and thus advocate for USJ.[113] That he

[107] Rousseau, "Of the Social Contract," 113 (III.15).
[108] Tuck, *The Sleeping Sovereign: The Invention of Modern Democracy*, 162–80.
[109] Ibid., 138–39.
[110] Ibid., 145–61, 189–96.
[111] Ibid., 143.
[112] Ibid., 254.
[113] Philp claims something similar at Mark Philp, "Review of Richard Tuck's 'The Sleeping Sovereign: The Invention of Modern Democracy'," (2019) CXXXIV The English Historical Review 469–72, 471.

does so can be seen in two instances. On the one hand, Tuck ends *The Sleeping Sovereign* positioning his sovereign/government account against what he sees as the dominant approach of constitutional theory today. This approach, which Tuck describes as liberal anti-Jacobin constitutionalism, involves following Sieyès in countering the populist specter of mob-like direct democracy by rejecting the idea that sovereignty is "a power located in a specific site" and instead conceptualizing it as consisting of "multiple sites of representation" and thus being merely "an expression of the fact that there are no political constraints on what an independent community can do."[114]

Tuck spends the majority of *The Sleeping Sovereign*'s conclusion arguing against this approach, mainly by picking apart what he sees as the "three major reasons for the modern disinclination to accept the radical seventeenth- or eighteenth-view that a sovereign people can act like a monarchical sovereign through the process of majority voting . . . ."[115] He follows this discussion by not only embracing the sovereign/government distinction, and thereby implicitly USJ, but also accepting what he sees as its controversial but necessarily implication: that the basis for a properly enacted legitimate constitution's authority is the constant decision of its populace to not rise up and change it. As he explains, "it is quite reasonable to say that the fact that Constitution has not been amended or repealed by the *present* sovereign means that the present sovereign, with all its other beliefs and commitments, wishes the law to stand."[116]

On the other hand, many of Tuck's interventions in the Brexit debate make positive recourse to the idea he explores in *The Sleeping Sovereign.* As he noted in his July 17, 2017 speech on Brexit to the Policy Exchange, while he "didn't discuss the EU directly in the lectures" that became *The Sleeping Sovereign*, "it was already at the back of my mind."[117] In this speech, Tuck argues that one of the central problems of the European Union (EU) for the United Kingdom, from a democratic perspective, is that entering it involved accepting a sort of higher law beyond the reach of the sovereign.

EU policy was accepted by parliament and ratified via referendum, but the U.K. sovereign has no way to change it; "only a process of intergovernmental negotiation, issuing in chances which no one country can impose on itself, can alter the essential character of the EU's constitutional structure."[118] Thus the constituent power of the United Kingdom effectively became cut-off from the higher law that constrains and organizes its government. The only way out, for Tuck and his fellow Lexiteers, was to "repudiate the *whole* structure."[119] As Tuck and his co-author

[114] Tuck, *The Sleeping Sovereign: The Invention of Modern Democracy*, 256.
[115] Ibid., 257.
[116] Ibid., 282.
[117] Richard Tuck, "Brexit: A Prize in Reach for the Left" Policy Exchange https://policyexchange.org.uk/pxevents/brexit-a-prize-in-reach-for-the-left/.
[118] Ibid.
[119] Ibid.

Chris Bickerton plainly argue, "Brexit is therefore all about sovereignty ... The message of the Brexit vote was the people no longer want to play this secondary role as a 'delegated power.' They want once again to be sovereign and to put government back in its place."[120]

5. Conclusion

In this chapter I argued that the Berkshire Constitutionalists developed a theory of constitutionalism and constitution-making that justifies ratification via constituent power without running into the problems plaguing alternative CPJs. To this end I reconstructed their theory, filling in the gaps and interpreting some of their vague statements by reference to the political and intellectual context in which they were enmeshed. The Constitutionalists, I argue, held that the basics of Lockean contractualism were true: the protection of liberty requires government, all political power comes from the people, and government must obtain its authority through a process consisting of two voluntary contracts. To this they added the idea of a written constitution, a document that formally structures and empowers the institutions of government and protects civil society from the effects of power combined with man's innate corruptibility. The adoption of this constitution became the second Lockean contract, and thus the Constitutionalists claimed that constituent power—the ability to create a legitimate constitution—belongs solely to the people in civil society.

Creating a constitution involved two steps, writing and authorizing, and according to the Constitutionalists constituent power resided solely in the second. In other words, the people only exercise their unique ability to create a constitution when reviewing and approving or rejecting an already written constitution, i.e. when ratifying. This means that the identity of the drafters and the details of the drafting process are irrelevant in terms of constituent power, and helps explains why, at least initially, the Constitutionalists had no problem with previously constituted authorities such as the General Court writing the constitution, just so long as they eventually submitted their creation to the people.

This division of the constitution-making process into two steps, and the confinement of constituent power to the second, is why the Constitutionalists' theory escapes the problems that afflict all other CPJs. The drafters of the constitution are neither identified with nor taken to embody the people in civil society, and their actions do not constitute the exercise of constituent power. At no point in the constitution-making process does constituent action occur prior to ratification. Thus, there is no possibility of redundancy or contradiction, and ratification

120 Christopher Bickerton and Richard Tuck, "Popular Sovereignty and 'Taking Back Control': What It Means and Why It Matters," The Full Brexit <https://www.thefullbrexit.com/popular–sovereignty>.

is neither reduced to a reparative function nor cast as one of several attempts or a part of a multi-stage attempt at ascertaining the constituent will.

Perhaps, one might want to conclude that even if authorization is the proper site of constituent power, it can be carried out by extraordinary representatives, delegates, or some other entity distinct from the people acting in a referendum. The Constitutionalists' conception of the people's right to authorize their constitution as unalienable rebuts this objection. Alienating constituent power, which non-popular ratification entails, necessarily harms civil society; this is why the right to exercise constituent power is unalienable. Not only must a constitution be ratified to go into effect, but the ratifying authority, according to the Constitutionalists, must always be the people directly.

Framing constituent power as unalienable was the final theoretical move that allowed the Constitutionalists to place the full weight of contractualism behind their specific demand for popular ratification. As has already been mentioned, views on the state of nature, popular sovereignty, contracting, and the like abounded in the press, sermons, speeches, and pamphlets at the time, and Allen and his Constitutionalists successfully articulated a theory that integrated all of them into an argument supporting one simple demand: submit the constitution to the people before formal enactment. While their larger political theory allows for the delegation of rights and powers between individuals and civil society and government, and while their support of representative government makes their belief in representation and fiduciary relationships clear, the authorization of a constitution was something that the majority of civil society had to do for itself. As Allen starkly put it: "Representatives are the people as to Legislation; but as to the formation and Imposition of the Constitution upon the people they cannot be."

Thus, at the beginning of popular constitution-making in America, and in the world at large, ratification procedures played a critical role. While the identity of framers and the way they drafted constitutions were important, insofar as the right kind of framers would prevent vested interests from distorting the foundations of the government and lead to well-structured fundamental law, the people only fully exercised their constituent power when voting up or down the proposed constitution. Under this formulation, ratification (but only via referendum) receives justification from its function, i.e. as the sole means through which constituent power is exercised.[121] In the next chapter we will test USJ's persuasiveness.

[121] Schmitt's position on ratification constantly changes in *Constitutional Theory*. However, at one point he says something very similar to what I am describing here: "The people's constitution-making will always expresses itself only in a fundamental yes or no and thereby reaches the political decision that constitutes the content of the constitution." Carl Schmitt, *Constitutional Theory* (Duke University Press 2008) 132.

6
Ignorance and the Constituent Power

The Berkshire Constitutionalists articulated a robust justification for ratification based on constituent power. Starting from two premises, that authoritative constitutions must be created through the exercise of the people's constituent power and that this power is inalienable, this *unique site justification* (USJ) holds that ratification is necessary because it is the sole opportunity in the constitution-making process for the constituent power to emerge. By isolating constituent power in the ratification process, and conceptualizing ratification as the moment in which the people can act, this theory avoids the redundancy, incoherence, and theoretical inconsistencies that bedevil other attempts to justify ratification by appealing to constituent power.

USJ, of course, cannot justify all types of ratification. It confines constituent power within the ratification process by conceptualizing the procedure as being uniquely able to allow the direct exercise of inalienable popular sovereignty. Ratification, therefore, must involve a way for the people to act directly on the constitution without the use of intermediary agents. The only ratification procedures that do so are those that make use of some sort of constitutional referendum. This might involve an aggregation of provincial referendums as in 1780 Massachusetts, or a single national referendum. This reduced scope does not undermine USJ, but simply means that representative forms of ratification cannot be justified by claiming that ratification is the unique site at which constituent power is exercised.

In this chapter I argue USJ faces its own limitations, joining the other constituent power justifications (CPJs) in being unable to justify ratification. Specifically, I claim that USJ requires conceptualizing a ratification referendum as involving the people making an informed decision. However, the nature and context of the procedure makes it impossible to be confident that it does anything more than reveal the decision of a likely ill-informed and manipulated electorate faced with a coercive choice.

I make this argument in five steps. First, I argue that for a ratification referendum to serve as a means through which the people exercise their constituent power, it must be possible for them to make a *meaningful choice*, i.e. a choice made with a basic understanding of the constitution and any live alternative. This requirement stems directly from the logic of constituent power, and not from any assumptions about what democracy more generally requires. Second, I claim that USJ fails because one can expect the average voter to be too uninformed to make such a choice. In the third, fourth, and fifth sections I further specify my argument

Constitutional Ratification without Reason. Jeffrey A. Lenowitz, Oxford University Press. © Jeffrey A. Lenowitz 2022.
DOI: 10.1093/oso/9780198852346.003.0006

by addressing three objections to my dismissal of USJ: that even constitutional framers will fall short of the meaningful choice threshold; that information shortcuts eliminate the problem of constitutional ignorance; and that education programs can eliminate information deficits. I conclude by summarizing my argument and taking stock of constituent power's ability to justify ratification and provide procedural recommendations more generally.

1. What Kind of Choice?

USJ justifies a ratification referendum by conceptualizing it as the sole and necessary moment in the constitution-making process when the constituent power makes its decision. Thus, the choice a voter makes when presented with a draft constitution is an essential one. What must this choice look like? What kind of choice must the relevant portion of the population be capable of when they vote on the constitution?

1.1 Choice Not Outcome

At the least, a voter must be free to make a choice. A referendum with a single option ballot, or one in which armed soldiers or skilled mesmerists force citizens to vote a certain way cannot reasonably be construed as the expression of the sovereign will. For instance, one cannot look at the ratification process for the 1973 Philippines Constitution, in which ratification took place by voice vote in village assemblies under the stern gaze of soldiers and policemen, and understand its outcome as the result of constituent action.[1] Voters must be able to choose whether or not they wish to accept the proposed constitution if their decisions are to be understood as the exercise of constituent power. To say otherwise would be to vacate constituent power theory of any meaning at all.

Beyond being free, what other requirements must the vote meet to satisfy the logic of constituent power? Consider the following hypothetical situations:

A. Citizens vote on a constitution that was never publicly discussed or distributed.
B. Constitution-makers discuss, distribute, and advertise Constitution Blue. On the day of the referendum, Constitution Blue is secretly replaced with Constitution Green. Most voters are unaware of the switch.

[1] Aurel Croissant, "Ways of Constitution-Making in Southeast Asia: Actors, Interests, Dynamics," in Marco Bünte and Björn Dressel (eds.), *Politics and Constitutions in Southeast Asia* (Routledge 2017) 32.

C. Citizens vote on a constitution written in a language that they cannot understand.

Could the results of these referendums be understood as the expression of constituent power? Our intuition, rightly, suggests no. The people do not exercise their popular sovereignty if they have no idea what they are voting on. Thus, it seems, voters must be able to access and understand the contents of the document they are tasked with evaluating.

Note that our conclusion does not change if voters would have voted in an identical fashion had they been able to review and understand the constitution. If every citizen in A would have cast the same vote if they had seen and heard about the constitution beforehand, there is still a problem. They did not have access nor understand what they were voting on when they voted. Nor does it change if it turns out that voters approved a constitution that is objectively better than the status quo and likely reversion point of rejection. It does not matter if the citizens in C have a better life under Constitution Green then they did before the vote. That voters inadvertently made a choice that happened to align with their considered preferences or happened to be best for them is immaterial for USJ, for such outcomes do not change the fact that the people did not really *choose* their constitution.

Constituent power theorizing emphasizes that only the people have the power and authority needed to create the extraordinary law that will govern them in the future, and USJ claims that ratification referendums are necessary because they provide the only means of enabling the constituent power to exercise this authority—to act and create—during the constitution-making process. The above hypotheticals cannot be construed as moments of constituent action, for the decisions made by the voters within them are not acts of creation. If voters are supposed to create via their ratification referendum vote, at a minimum they must be able to evaluate the proposed constitution and act upon their evaluation.

1.2 Meaningful Choice

Given that, for USJ, the primary function of a ratification referendum vote is to provide the means for the constituent power to act, create, and authorize a constitution, thus making it a product of their action and will, the subjective viewpoint of voters toward the constitution becomes paramount. Voters must be aware of and understand what they are creating and authorizing; the constitution cannot be both an accident and an intentional product of popular will. Thus, as much as possible, the choice voters make in a referendum should reflect how they evaluate the constitution and compare it to the likely outcome of constitutional rejection. In order to do this, voters need to apply their own values, beliefs, and interests when making their choice. Put differently, the logic of constituent power requires that actions taken by the constituent power be not merely an exercise of will, but an exercise of will augmented by reason. I call this *meaningful choice*.[2]

A voter makes a meaningful choice while voting on a ratification referendum: if she understands that she is voting on a constitution and that her vote will help determine whether not the proposed constitution goes into effect; if she comprehends what the constitution says and what kind of government it will likely create; if she can reasonably imagine the likely results of constitutional rejection, whether this be a continuation of the status quo, the resumption of civil war, or the beginning of another constitution-making process; and if she can compare the constitution with the possible results of rejection and, in accordance with her interests and beliefs, freely choose the alternative that she prefers.

In other words, a ratification referendum is only an instance in which "the collective acts in the strong sense of exercising its constituent power in view of enacting a legal order *ex novo*" if individual voters are capable of making an agent-relative sensible choice about their constitution, i.e. a decision that stems from reasons relating to their evaluation of the contents of that constitution.[3] When this is possible, one can say that a constitutional ratification referendum satisfies meaningful choice, or that individuals have met the meaningful choice threshold.

1.3 Other Choice Thresholds

The nature of meaningful choice becomes clearer upon comparison with other choice situations and requirements. Consider the demands placed on voters by minimalist conceptions of democracy, according to which democracy is merely the "institutional arrangement for arriving at political decisions in which individuals acquire the power to decide by means of a competitive struggle for the popular vote." In other words, for minimalists, democracy is the institutional arrangement under which elites make decisions, the people select the elites, and the people compete to become one of these elites.[4]

Minimalists relegate political questions and issues to elites, believing that, as Schumpeter puts it, the "psychic economy of the typical citizen" is unfit to

[2] Calling this "meaningful choice" takes inspiration from judicial interpretations of sec. 101(a)(1–2) of the Labor Management Reporting Disclosure Act (LMRDA). This provision is taken to require that all union members have equal rights to vote, deliberate, and discuss union business. It also guarantees that union members' right to vote is "meaningful," where "meaningful" is understood as requiring fair procedures, educational opportunities, and all the conditions necessary for ensuring that a ratification referendum on a labor contract serves as a real check on union leadership. See Paul Alan Levy, "Membership Rights in Union Referenda to Ratify Collective Bargaining Agreements," (1987) 4 Hofstra Labor and Employment Law Journal 225–67, 232–33.

[3] Hans Lindahl, "The Paradox of Constituent Power: The Ambiguous Self-Constitution of the European Union," (2007) 20 Ratio Juris 485–505, 495.

[4] Joseph A Schumpeter, *Capitalism, Socialism, and Democracy* (3rd edn, Harper & Row 1950) 242, 269, 262.

handle such complexities.[5] Thus, the sole requirement of citizens is to vote during elections, "to cast his vote to the party he believes will provide more benefits than any other."[6] Whether voters know anything about the issues their representatives will have to address and how they are likely to address them is unimportant. Instead, voters simply need to vote, on the basis of something that makes sense to them.[7]

The threshold of meaningful choice is higher than that required by minimalist conceptions of democracy. For USJ, voters need to be able to understand the constitution, the nature of the choice, and the likely repercussions of their actions. Ratifiers must be able to decide whether or not they want to live in a state structured by the proposed constitution. For democratic minimalists, no such requirements are in place. A voter needs to be able to make a free choice in an election, but it matters not whether this choice is based on an understanding of the ideology of the candidates or a split-second evaluation of their haircuts.

The doctrine of informed consent in health care law and bioethics is as robust as the previous were minimal, requiring that physicians receive informed, voluntary, and decisionally-capacitated consent before treatment.[8] A patient is informed only if they understand the medical situation and prognosis, the recommended care, any potential alternatives, and the risks and benefits, and conclusively demonstrate their comprehension. Further, this knowledge cannot be merely abstract and technical, for patients must also apply it to their own situation.[9] A patient's consent is voluntary if it is free from coercion, which includes explicit and implicit threats as well as any potential curtailment of options that arise from the patient's belief that she will be harmed or deprived of benefits, even when such fears are unfounded.[10] The consent must also take place in the absence of undue inducement, where the possibility of a potential reward for agreeing to treatment might cloud individual judgment.[11] Finally, decisional capacity means that patients must have the capacity to understand and communicate, the ability to reason and deliberate, be in

[5] Ibid., 285.

[6] Anthony Downs, *An Economic Theory of Democracy* (Harper & Row 1957) 36.

[7] See also Adam Przeworski, "Minimalist Conception of Democracy: A Defense," in Ian Shapiro and Casiano Hacker-Cordsn (eds.), *Democracy's Value* (Cambridge University Press 1999).

[8] See generally Martin Gunderson, "Justifying a Principle of Informed Consent: A Case Study in Autonomy-Based Ethics," (1990) 4 Public Affairs Quarterly 249–65; Neil C. Manson and Onora O'Neil, *Rethinking Informed Consent in Bioethics* (Cambridge University Press 2007).

[9] As Lo explains, "[I]t is not enough to understand ... that angioplasty or bypass surgery will probably relive chest pain but there is considerable perioperative mortality. In addition, the patient ... must realize that her chest pain and shortness of breath might be improved by angioplasty or surgery but that she might die because of surgery." Bernard Lo, "Assessing Decision-Making Capacity," (1990) 18 Law, Medicine, & Health Care 193–201, 195.

[10] Quarraisha Abdool Karim and others, "Informed Consent for HIV Testing in a South Africa Hospital: Is It Truly Informed and Truly Voluntary," (1998) 88 American Journal of Public Health 637–40.

[11] "General requirements for informed consent," 45 CFR 46.116.

possession of a set of values and goals that can be applied directly to the medical choice at hand, and genuinely acknowledge that they have a choice.[12]

The threshold of informed consent is considerably higher than that required for it to be meaningful. Meaningful choice does not require individual voters to demonstrate their sustained contemplation of the issue in question or their personalization of what is otherwise abstract and technical information. It is sufficient for a voter to understand what a constitution means and be able to decide whether she prefers the likely result of its rejection or the system of government she imagines it will create. This decision might be based on uninterrogated values, a few mistakes, weak preferences, biases or prejudices, or beliefs created in the absence of considering all known alternatives, and will likely take place amidst some coercion. But, as long as it stems from someone with the ability and opportunity to consider the contents of the constitution, the voter's choice is acceptably meaningful.[13]

2. Condorcet's Prediction

In his essay on ratification, Condorcet writes:

> Given the current state of education, there is no doubt that most citizens are not sufficiently enlightened to judge a constitutional plan. In order to do so, they would need to know the reasons behind each clause and be able to work out their consequences. Most citizens lack the ideas needed to do this. Direct ratification would therefore not be true ratification, and the nation would seem to have exercised a right when it had not actually done so.[14]

[12] Mark R. Wicclair, "Patient Decision-Making Capacity and Risk," (1991) 5 Bioethics 91–101; David Archard, "Informed Consent: Autonomy and Self-Ownership," (2008) 25 Journal of Applied Philosophy 19–34.

[13] The threshold of meaningful choice is quite like the "deliberative" requirements supported by Stephen Tierney in his book, discussed in chapter 1, on constitutional referendums. Adhering to a civic republican deliberative conception of democracy, he claims that "the very idea that a constitutional referendum can be an act of constitutional authorship by a public acting together hinges on the idea that millions of people can and will deliberate on the question." However, because "the kind of discursive deliberation that can take place within a small group is not possible ... at the macro level," he goes on to adopt a less demanding conception of deliberation tailored for macro rather than micro political contexts. Specifically, he embraces Goodin's idea of "internal-reflective deliberation," which means voters learning about the issues in question, reflecting upon them, and reaching an informed decision. Stephen Tierney, *Constitutional Referendums: The Theory and Practice of Republican Deliberation* (Oxford University Press 2012) 210–225; Robert E. Goodin, *Innovating Democracy: Democratic Theory and Practice after the Deliberative Turn* (Oxford University Press 2008); Robert E. Goodin and Simon J. Niemeyer, "When Does Deliberation Begin? Internal Reflection Versus Public Discussion in Deliberative Democracy," (2003) 51 Political Studies 627–49.

[14] Marquis de Condorcet, "On the Need for the Citizens to Ratify the Constitution," in Iain McLean and Fiona Hewitt (eds.), *Condorcet: Foundations of Social Choice and Political Theory* (Edward Elgar 1994) 273.

The gist of Condorcet's claim is as true today as it was in 1789. USJ is unpersuasive because the average voter taking part in a ratification referendum will likely be too ignorant on constitutional matters to satisfy even a minimal conception of meaningful choice. In this section I explain why this expectation of ignorance is warranted, and explore relevant empirical work supporting this claim.

From the start, two clarifications are in order. First, in claiming that the average person lacks sufficient knowledge to make a meaningful choice, I am not joining recent skeptics of democracy in arguing that individuals are too ill-informed or irrational for modern forms of self-government.[15] While I follow these authors in identifying voter ignorance as a problem, my argument diverges from their own in two key respects. On the one hand, I am only claiming that the information needed for the specific task of evaluating a constitutional design is neither common knowledge nor something one should expect even an ideally participatory, civic-minded citizenry to possess. I make no claim as to the sort of information voters would need to carry out their ordinary political functions in an informed manner and whether one can expect them to possess it. On the other hand, the criterion of meaningful choice, and the level of comprehension and knowledge it demands, applies only to ratification referendums conceptualized as moments of constituent power. Nothing I argue suggests that it is problematic if voters fail to meet the demands of meaningful choice in ordinary elections or referendums.

Second, when talking about the level of knowledge and information needed to make a meaningful choice, I am not suggesting that an informed voter is one who has *the right* constitutional preferences or makes *the best* constitutional decisions. Rather, I simply mean a person who possesses sufficient information to understand and form preferences on the proposed constitution.

2.1 Expect Constitutional Ignorance

Why are voters likely to be too ignorant to make a meaningful choice? To answer this, we must clarify what exactly a voter needs to know in order to vote meaningfully in a ratification referendum. As mentioned, the task of a ratifier is to determine whether she prefers a proposed constitution to the status quo or whatever else is likely to result from constitutional rejection. Contra the New York Mechanics, "the

[15] Christopher H. Achen and Larry M. Bartels, *Democracy for Realists: Why Elections Do Not Produce Responsive Government* (Princeton University Press 2016); Jason Brennan, *Against Democracy* (Princeton University Press 2016); Ilya Somin, *Democracy and Political Ignorance: Why Smaller Government Is Smarter* (Stanford Law Books 2013); Bryan Caplan, *The Myth of the Rational Voter: Why Democracies Choose Bad Policies* (Princeton University Press 2007).

share of commonsense the Almighty has bountifully distributed amongst mankind" is not sufficient for this task.[16] Rather, a ratifier must "have sufficient knowledge and judgment to reject a proposed constitution that is inferior and accept one that is not."[17] This, as McWhinney puts it, is "an inherently technical domain, demanding some degree of constitutional expertise."[18]

Specifically, a ratifier needs to know enough to: comprehend the purpose and function of constitutions; understand the basic implications of most provisions; anticipate (to a degree) how the various provisions will come together to create a government with a set of interlocking institutions; approximate the fit between the constitution and the current political/social context; and understand how the text compares to other possible alternatives. Voters can only decide whether a proposed constitution or the likely outcome of rejection best matches their existing values and preferences by possessing such knowledge. Without it, it is hard to see how the people's approval or rejection of a constitution is a meaningful decision reached by the constituent power, for it would represent a judgment on a matter not understood.[19]

The complexity of merely evaluating a constitution, which is only part of the task facing the ratifier (the other is anticipating and evaluating the likely result of rejection), can be demonstrated by considering the Venezuelan Constitution approved in 1999. On its face, it seems like a modern progressive constitution. It declares that Venezuela is a state of law *and* justice, incorporates an extensive list of civil and social human rights, and prioritizes women's equality. It creates an innovative system of five governmental powers by creating two new branches of government: the "electoral power" and the "public power." The electoral power consists of a national electoral council in charge of regulating and safeguarding proper electoral procedures in state elections and, when invited or ordered by the Supreme Court, civil society, and union elections. The citizen power assures that each of the other four powers adhere to their constitutionally determined functions, and consists of the attorney general, the defender of the people, and the comptroller general.[20]

[16] "The Respectful Address of the Mechanicks in Union, for the City and County of New-York, Represented by Their General Committee" *The New-York Gazette; and the Weekly Mercury* (June 17, 1776) 3, 3.

[17] Dennis C. Mueller, *Constitutional Democracy* (Oxford University Press 1996) 322.

[18] Edward McWhinney, *Constitution-Making: Principles, Process, Practice* (University of Toronto Press 1981) 26.

[19] Interestingly, court cases exist in which the judiciary has struck down referendum-based laws on the grounds that the people did not understand the implications of the proposition on which they voted. For example, in *Bates v. Jones*, 127 F.3d 839 (9th Cir. 1997), Judge Reinhardt invalidated a terms limit measure created through referendum because "a state initiative measure cannot impose such a limitation when the issue of whether to impose such a limitation of those rights is put to the voters in a measure that is ambiguous on its face and that fails to mention in its text, the proponents' ballot arguments, or the state's official descriptions, the severe limitation to be imposed."

[20] The Constitution of the Bolivarian Republic of Venezuela (1999).

However, lurking beneath these cheery provisions lay several dangerous constitutional features. The constitution grants the legislative branch the power to appoint and remove the justices of the highest court as well as most members of the two new branches, frequently by simple majority vote and without having to provide proof of misconduct or other objective grounds for removal.[21] This effectively eliminates the independent balancing power of these non-elected branches. The legislative branch can delegate lawmaking power to the President without limit, and the President obtains the power to dissolve the national assembly in the event of three votes of censure against the executive appointed Vice-President.[22] Moreover, the constitution exempts the military, for the first time in Venezuelan constitutional history, from any civilian control other than the executive itself.[23] In sum, amidst the 360 articles and over 100 pages that compose the Venezuelan Constitution, lie a series of provisions that stealthily helped equip Chavez with authoritarian powers.[24] This conclusion would remain hidden, however, to all those without a relatively high level of knowledge and expertise about constitutional design and comparative institutions.[25]

A ratification referendum voter can therefore only make a decision on the merits if she knows the basics of constitutional theory, institutional design, jurisprudence, the current distribution of power and interest, and the foundations of the existing political order if present. Unfortunately for USJ, there is no reason to believe that the average citizens anywhere will possess such esoteric knowledge.[26] This information is specialized, takes significant time and effort to learn, and the average person—whether in a stable democracy, post-conflict territory, or deteriorating autocracy—has little incentive or reason to acquire it.[27] One should no more expect the average person to know how to rebuild a car engine or perform

[21] Allan R. Brewer-Carias, "The 1999 Venezuelan Constitution-Making Process as an Instrument for Framing the Development of an Authoritarian Political Regime," in Laurel E. Miller (ed.), *Framing the State in Times of Transition: Case Studies in Constitution Making* (United States Institute of Peace Press 2010) 519.

[22] The Constitution of the Bolivarian Republic of Venezuela, Arts. 203, 236 (§208, 221).

[23] Brewer-Carias, "The 1999 Venezuelan Constitution-Making Process as an Instrument for Framing the Development of an Authoritarian Political Regime," 519–20.

[24] The Constitutional Assembly also shut down and packed competing institutions in order to eliminate any possible sources of opposition to Chavez and his party David Landau, "Constitution-Making Gone Wrong," (2013) 64 Alabama Law Review 923–80, 939–49.

[25] Cases like Venezuela cast doubt on Landemore's claim that "epistemically speaking, referendums probably ensure that really bad constitutions are avoided," in that she assumes the features that make a constitution bad will be obvious rather than buried in technicalities. Hélène Landemore, "Inclusive Constitution-Making: The Icelandic Experiment," (2015) 23 The Journal of Political Philosophy, 175.

[26] Albert Lee Sturm, *Thirty Years of State Constitution-Making, 1938–1968; with an Epilogue: Developments During 1969* (National Municipal League 1970) 79.

[27] Downs, *An Economic Theory of Democracy*; Somin, *Democracy and Political Ignorance: Why Smaller Government Is Smarter*, 107–19. If Downs is correct about the irrationality of being informed about ordinary politics, this is even more true when it comes to knowing information of use only during constitution-making.

a pneumonectomy, than to understand, for instance, the intricacies of creating an effectively balanced multi-branch government. This makes a ratification referendum unable to serve as a key moment of constituent action within constitution-making, for one cannot rely on voters to know enough to be able to evaluate the draft presented to them. This expectation of voter ignorance is supported, albeit mostly indirectly, by several empirical studies.

2.2 Ignorance in Fact

The ignorance of voters when it comes to general political issues is a well-established object of study. Political scientists began focusing on the political ignorance of the average U.S. citizen in the mid-twentieth century, and soon found that "voters fell short" of the democratic ideal of an electorate able to choose candidates on the basis of a comprehensive understanding of platforms and issues.[28] Contemporary work supports and expands upon these initial observations, repeatedly finding that large numbers of American voters are ignorant when it comes to basic political facts, the fundamentals of government (functions, offices, and personnel), and current political issues. As Neuman reports, "[E]ven the most vivid concepts of political life . . . are recognized by only a little over half the electorate."[29] Of course, though the most documented, political ignorance is not the unique domain of American voters. Similar studies demonstrate comparable levels of ignorance in other countries such as Australia and Great Britain.[30]

Two things are worth emphasizing here. First, the type of information these studies test for concerns, at least partly, details about institutional structure and the basic workings of government. While some argue this is irrelevant for voters in ordinary elections, it is precisely the sort of information a voter needs to compare a draft constitution with the status quo. Second, the United States, Australia,

[28] Bernard R. Berelson, Paul F. Lazarsfeld, and William N. McPhee, *Voting: A Study of Opinion Formation in a Presidential Campaign* (University of Chicago 1954) 308.

[29] Paul M. Sniderman, Richard A. Brody, and Philip E. Tetlock, *Reasoning and Choice: Explorations in Political Psychology* (Cambridge University Press 1991) 15; Angus Campbell and others, *The American Voter* (The University of Chicago Press 1960); Michael X. Delli Carpini and Scott Keeter, *What Americans Know About Politics and Why It Matters* (Yale University Press 1996) 65; W. Russell Neuman, *The Paradox of Mass Politics: Knowledge and Opinion in the American Electorate* (Harvard University Press 1986) 16; Arthur Lupia and Matthew McCubbins, *The Democratic Dilemma: Can Citizens Learn What They Need to Know* (Cambridge University Press 1998) 1. See also Michael R. Alvarez and John Brehm, *Hard Choices, Easy Answers: Values, Information, and American Public Opinion* (Princeton University Press 2002); Richard G. Niemi and Herbert F. Weisberg, *Controversies in Voting Behavior* (4th edn, CQ Press 2001); Cambell and others, *The American Voter*, 170.

[30] Ian McAllister, "Civic Education and Political Knowledge in Australia," (1998) 33 Australian Journal of Political Science 7–23, 11–12; D.T. Denver and Gordon Hands, *Modern Constituency Electioneering: Local Campaigning in the 1992 General Election* (Frank Cass 1997).

and Great Britain are all long-standing and stable functioning democracies characterized by high levels of transparency, national civic education programs, high levels of general education, a well-developed civil society, and an independent media, all of which make it easier for the average citizen to acquire basic political knowledge. Citizens of countries or territories emerging from autocracy, civil war, frequent regime changes, or sustained political instability, without a tradition of democracy or constitutionalism, i.e. citizens in territories most prone to constitution-making today, are even less likely to acquire political knowledge of this kind.

Now, the studies mentioned above mainly focus on normal elections. When it comes to referendums, ignorance appears to be as or even more widespread.[31] In 1998, 79 percent of polled Californians agreed that ballot measures were often too complicated and confusing for voters to understand what happens if the initiative passes.[32] A large majority of voters in Colorado, Oregon, Washington, and California agreed that "the initiative and referendum measures on the ballot are usually so complicated that one can't understand what is going on," while 90 percent of voters on a New Zealand referendum on electoral reform were unable to give reasons for their decision to vote for or against the introduction of proportional representation.[33] Three-quarters of the electorate of California Proposition 10 on rent control accidently voted against the side they supported.[34] Similar findings exist even for Switzerland, where referendums are frequent political occurrences. For instance, on the basis of their analysis of forty-one ballot measures, Gruner and Hertig concluded that less than 20 percent of the voters were well-informed of the issues at hand. Another study looking at ballot measures from 1981 to 1999 found that 30 percent of all voters could not give reasons for their votes, while 50 percent were unable to give more than one.[35]

The general ignorance of voters in referendums is so well-attested that it forms the basis of most recent discussions of referendum voting. As Luskin notes, "[W]ith the fact of widespread public ignorance now firmly established, there has been a

[31] I distinguish between three types of referendums: "ordinary referendums" take place on non-constitutional matters; "constitutional referendums" pertain to constitutional matters; and "ratification referendums" are those that concern the approval or rejection of a new constitution. For a discussion of the different forms of referendums and initiative see Markkhu Suksi, *Bringing in the People: A Comparison of Constitutional Forms and Practices of the Referendum* (Martinus Nijhoff Publishers 1993); Joseph F. Zimmerman, *The Referendum: The People Decide Public Policy* (Praeger Publishing 2001); Ian Budge, *The New Challenge of Direct Democracy* (Polity Press 1996); Thomas E. Cronin, *Direct Democracy: The Politics of Referendum, Initiative, and Recall* (Harvard University Press 1989).

[32] J. Fred Silva, *The California Initiative Process: Background and Perspective* (Resource Material for the Speaker's Commission on the California Initiative Process 2000) 31.

[33] Cronin, *Direct Democracy: The Politics of Referendum, Initiative, and Recall*, 74; Mads Qvorthup, *A Comparative Study of Referendums: Government by the People* (Manchester University Press 2002) 37.

[34] David Magleby, *Direct Legislation: Voting on Ballot Propositions in the United States* (The John Hopkins University Press 2001).

[35] Thomas Christin, Simon Hug, and Pascal Sciarini, "Interests and Information in Referendum Voting: An Analysis of Swiss Voters," (2002) 41 European Journal of Political Research 759–76.

shift from 'denial' to 'extenuation.'"[36] Scholars interested in defending the practical and normative advantages of direct democracy no longer argue that voters fully or even partially comprehend the relevant issues. Instead, they concentrate their efforts on explaining how "relatively uninformed voters ... cast the same votes they would have cast if better informed" and how voters uninformed about the details, specific subject matter, and consequences of most referendums nonetheless figure out what outcomes match their preferences.[37]

Moreover, ignorance when it comes to referendums should come as no surprise, for as Bowler and Donovan note, "If ... voters lack factual information, a constraining ideology and an ability to deal with issues in highly publicized candidate races, how can they be expected to sort through the complex policy choices they face in the low information setting of direct democracy?"[38] Referendums often address unfamiliar topics and pertain to particular policies and issues that require a great degree of technical information to comprehend.[39] And, as scholars from Weber to Schumpeter to Dahl have noted, citizens do not and should not be expected to obtain the levels of expertise needed to decide on the complex issues that make up even that average policy question tackled by politicians day to day.[40] Complicating matters further, referendums usually fall outside the normal schedule and machinery surrounding elections and their corresponding campaigns.

Thus, when compared to election votes, referendums demand a more complex decision, concern less familiar issues, require uncommon political knowledge, and take place in an environment where information channels are unfamiliar, less available, or both. All of this is even truer for constitutional referendums, those pertaining to constitutional matters, for such issues are often further away from the daily lives of voters and the ordinary course of politics, and tend to be the exclusive domain of political elites.[41] It is no surprise, for instance, that a poll taken shortly

[36] Robert C. Luskin and others, *Deliberation and Referendum Voting* (The Center for Deliberative Democracy, 2005) 1.

[37] Arthur Lupia, "Shortcuts Versus Encyclopedia: Information and Voting Behavior in California Insurance Reform Elections," (1994) 88 The American Political Science Review 63–76, 63. I address the shortcuts and heuristics literature below.

[38] Shaun Bowler and Todd Donovan, *Demanding Choices: Opinion, Voting, and Direct Democracy* (University of Michigan Press 1998).

[39] Christin, Hug, and Sciarini, "Interests and Information in Referendum Voting: An Analysis of Swiss Voters," 759.

[40] Simon Hug, "Some Thoughts About Referendums, Representative Democracy, and Separation of Powers," (2009) 20 Constitutional Political Economy 251–66, 256.

[41] For example, common issues in ordinary referendums include: conscription (New Zealand 1949); family planning (Portugal 1998, Ireland 1992); nuclear power (Taiwan 1994, Sweden 1980); international treaties (Spain 1986, Austria 1994); electoral reform (New Zealand 1992, Switzerland 1991), the structure of parliament (Bangladesh 1991, Lithuania 1996); full faith and credit bonds (Maine 1998, New York 1997); tax policies (Oregon 1985, Iowa 1999); gay rights (Maine 1998, Washington 2012); and affirmative action (Washington 1998, California 1996). Zimmerman, *The Referendum: The People Decide Public Policy*; Lawrence LeDuc, *The Politics of Direct Democracy: Referendums in a Global Perspective* (Broadview Press 2003) 21–33.

before the 2016 Italian Constitutional Referendum found that 79 percent of voters either did not understand the referendum or only understood it superficially.[42]

Comparing a proposed constitution to the status quo or likely result of constitutional rejection is undeniably more complex than evaluating the likely consequences of most ordinary or constitutional referendum. Constitutions can contain hundreds of provisions on almost every aspect of political life, and evaluating them requires imagining what sort of government they would create in combination, while referendums usually pertain to a few specific issues and pose narrow alteration to existing law and policy.[43] Moreover, constitutions can contain obscure provisions covering topics that are even further from ordinary life than the sorts of issues likely to populate single-issue constitutional referendums. This is only heightened by the trend in constitution-making for constitutions to become more detailed and larger in scope.[44] One should thus expect at least as much and likely more ignorance when it comes to ratification referendums.[45]

The limited empirical work on ratification referendums and high impact constitutional referendums supports this expectation. For instance, Eurobarometer 214 indicates that one-third of European voters had not heard of the Constitution for Europe after its signing in 2004, and over half got basic questions wrong regarding its content.[46] Hobolt demonstrates that a third of Dutch voters and a quarter of Spanish voters attributed their negative vote on the referendum to lack of information and subsequent confusion.[47] Similar findings exist on the country level. A large portion of voters on the Australian Constitutional Referendum of 1999 not only had "dim knowledge about how the existing constitutional system works and little or no insight into what the proposed changes would involve," but a later study on a representative sample showed a significant number of these voters switching their vote after being properly informed.[48] Similarly, 81 percent of a representative

[42] "Sondaggio Ipr & Tecne 24 Ottobre 2016—Referendum" (2016) <http://scenaripolitici.com/2016/10/sondaggio-ipr-tecne-24-ottobre-2016-referendum.html>.

[43] George Tridimas and Takis Tridimas, "Electorates v. Politicians: The 2005 French and Dutch Referendums on the Eu Constitutional Treaty," in Anneli Albi and Jacques Ziller (eds.), *The European Constitution and National Constitutions: Ratification and Beyond* (Kluwer Law International 2006) 278.

[44] The advantages and disadvantages of a longer more detailed constitution versus a shorter one is a matter of some debate. See Zachary Elkins, James Melton, and Tom Ginsburg, *The Endurance of National Constitutions* (Cambridge University Press 2009) chs. 4–5; George Tsebelis and Dominic J. Nardi, "A Long Constitution Is a (Positively) Bad Constitution: Evidence from OECD Countries," (2016) 46 British Journal of Political Science 457–78.

[45] Elkins and Hudson support this intuition when they emphasize how evaluating constitutions, versus amendments, is cognitively more challenging due to the former's multidimensionality and increased length. This, they suspect, is part of the reason why ratification referendums are approved at a much higher rate that amendment referendums. Citizens do not understand what they are voting on in ratification referendums, and thus slide into yea-saying. Zachary Elkins and Alexander Hudson, "The Constitutional Referendum in Historical Perspective," in David Landau and Hannah Lerner (eds.), *Comparative Constitution Making* (Edward Elgar) 161.

[46] European Commission, *The Future Constitutional Treaty* (2005).

[47] Sara Binzer Hobolt, "Taking Cues on Europe? Voter Competence and Party Endorsements in Referendums on European Integration," (2007) 46 European Journal of Political Research 151–82, 154.

[48] John Higley and Ian McAllister, "Elite Division and Voter Confusion: Australia's Republic Referendum in 1999," (2002) 41 European Journal of Political Research 845–61. Luskin et al. show the

sample of voters on the Charlottetown Accord of 1996, which was effectively a vote on a new Canadian constitution or at the least a major restructuring of the original document, agreed that "most people didn't understand what the referendum was all about."[49] And finally, research on the Brexit referendum suggests that the average voter was deeply confused about some of the most relevant issues in a manner that was favorable to the Leave campaign, and that this confusion remained even two years after the vote.[50]

Because of the likelihood of such voter ignorance, USJ is unpersuasive as a general and context-independent argument in favor of ratification. The justification requires that the procedure be capable of serving as a central moment of constituent power in the constitution-making process, but the likely presence of uninformed citizen ratifiers incapable of making a meaningful choice on the proposed constitution undermines its capability to do so. Ratification referendums cannot be relied upon to give voice to the constituent power, and therefore arguments from constituent power cannot justify their widespread implementation.

However, before accepting this conclusion, which means giving up on the capacity of constituent power to justify ratification altogether, several defenses of USJ must be addressed. These claim that: (1) the meaningful choice threshold demands too much, because even constitutional framers will fall below it; (2) information shortcuts allow citizens to vote competently even without the required level of information; and (3) education campaigns can and are used to sufficiently educate voters. I address these objections in the sections that follow.

3. Ignorant Framers

The first defense of USJ claims that the level of knowledge demanded by meaningful choice is so unreasonably high that the actual framers of the constitution will not meet it. Most constitution-makers are not constitutional scholars and experts in institutional design, and we should not expect future framers to be any different. Thus, the standard of meaningful choice is an indefensible basis for criticizing USJ, since it faults citizens for not being more informed than the authors of the constitution. Here, framers or authors refer to all those involved in the drafting

effects of voter ignorance in the referendum by demonstrating how a sample of voters, after engaging in deliberative and educative processes, expressed a desire to change their votes. See Luskin and others, *Deliberation and Referendum Voting*.

[49] Harold D. Clarke and Allan Kornberg, "The Politics and Economics of Constitutional Choice: Voting in Canada's 1992 National Referendum," (1994) 56 The Journal of Politics 940–62.

[50] Ipsos MORI and UK in a Changing Europe, "The Perils of Perception and the EU" <https://www.ipsos.com/ipsos-mori/en-uk/perils-perception-and-eu>; Ipsos MORI and the Policy Institute at King's College London, "Brexit Misperceptions" <https://www.kcl.ac.uk/policy-institute/assets/brexit-misperceptions.pdf>.

stage who have a hand in writing, debating, amending, and voting on the constitution before it reaches its final form. This includes members of roundtables, constitutional conventions, constitutional commissions, and national assemblies.

Now, one response to this objection is to dismiss it as irrelevant. The threshold of meaningful choice stems from conceptualizing ratification as providing a unique moment for the constituent power to act. It is not meant to apply to framers, and whether they meet it reveals nothing. However, I will forego this response. The intuitive bite of the defense comes from the fact that constitution-makers need to be far more informed than a citizen ratifier to do their job. Meaningful choice requires that one possess sufficient information to roughly evaluate a constitution and compare this to a similar evaluation of the present political system or whatever else is likely to emerge from constitutional rejection. Framers need to (or at least should) know much more than this; in a sense their task is to compare the status quo to all possible constitutional alternatives rather than just one. If they do not know enough to make a meaningful choice on an already written constitution, how do they know enough to write one? Meaningful choice, this suggests, is far too demanding.

This defense is initially persuasive because it is partially true. Most members of a democratically elected or representatively appointed constitution-making body will be too ignorant to make a meaningful choice. Consider the composition of some actual democratic constitution-making bodies. The members of the 1991 Constituent Assembly in Colombia ranged from traditional party delegates, ex guerillas, indigenous leaders, businessmen, social and labor leaders, peasants, journalists, academics, lawyers, and clerics.[51] Similarly, the authors of the 1995 Ugandan Constitution included a constituent assembly composed of politicians and party members, women's rights advocates, army personnel, trade union advocates, and youth leaders.[52] Members of the twenty-five-person Stjornlagarad, Iceland's 2011 Constitutional Council, included an Economics professor, ethicist, farmer, pastor, theater director, physician, and a consumer spokesperson.[53]

Discounting the relatively small group of delegates with significant legal and political knowledge, most of the participants in these constitution-making processes knew very little about the purpose and role of constitutions, the basics of institutional design, and the exact working of their existing government, and they are not

[51] Kirsti Samuels, *Constitution Building Processes and Democratization: A Discussion of Twelve Case Studies* (International IDEA 2006) 11; Donald T. Fox, Gustavo Gallon-Giraldo, and Anne Stetson, "Lessons of the Colombian Constitutional Reform of 1991: Toward the Securing of Peace and Reconciliation?" in Laurel E. Miller (ed.), *Framing the State in Times of Transition: Case Studies in Constitution Making* (United States Institute of Peace Press 2010) 472.

[52] John Waliggo, "The Main-Actors in the Constitution-Making Process in Uganda," in Goran Hyden and Denis Venter (eds.), *Constitution-Making and Democratisation in Africa* (Africa Institute of South Africa 2001) 57–58; Devra C. Moehler, *Distrusting Democrats: Outcomes of Participatory Constitution Making* (University of Michigan Press 2008) 61–63.

[53] "Iceland Election Results Announced," Iceland Review Online <https://www.icelandreview.com/news/iceland-election-results-announced/>.

exceptional in this regard. Many past and future constitution-making bodies are or will be full of framers ignorant on constitutional matters. However, this is only true when they are first selected.

The drafting process is designed to encourage constitution-making competence. I will divide this up into two rough stages. In the first, the training stage, constitution-makers study materials related to framing before the drafting begins. This includes the records of constitution-making in other countries and states, issue papers prepared by volunteers and hired constitutional consultants, academic research on constitution-making and constitutional design, and constitution-making handbooks produced by non-governmental organizations (NGOs), international governmental organizations (IGOs), and academic institutions.[54] For instance, members of the Nepali Constituent Assembly received a book entitled *Creating the New Constitution: A guide for Nepali Citizens*, prepared by International IDEA, which explains Nepali constitutional history and "provides an analysis of different options that emerge when making a new constitution."[55] In addition, framers receive demographic data, local constitutional and political histories, and reports on the strengths and weaknesses of present and past institutions. The members of the 1867 New York Constitutional Convention, for example, received two large convention manuals detailing all contemporary American state constitutions and comprehensive statistics on every aspect of New York State.[56] Moreover, contemporary constitution-makers often make recourse to rich online resources. This includes constitutionnet.org, a site run by International IDEA offering constitutional histories, online instruction manuals, and updates on constitution-making projects around the world, as well as the Comparative Constitutions Project's website constituteproject.org, an online depository of up-to-date multilingual versions of all constitutions that can be searched and compared.

Much of this training and exposure to constitutional information takes place within structured educational programs. For instance, during the Namibia

[54] Examples of such manuals include: Michele Brandt and others, *Constitution-Making and Reform: Options for the Process* (Interpeace 2011); Nanako Tamaru and Nano O'Reilly, *A Women's Guide to Constitution Making* (Inclusive Security 2018); Markus Bockenforde, Nora Hedlin, and Winluck Wahiu, *A Practical Guide to Constitution Building* (International Institute for Democracy and Electoral Assistance 2011); Jamal Benomar, *Constitution-Making and Peace Building: Lessons Learned from the Constitution-Making Processes of Post-Conflict Countries*, August 2003); Philipp Dann and Zaid Al-ali, "The Internationalized *Pouvoir Constituant*—Constitution-Making under External Influence in Iraq, Sudan and East Timor," (2006) 10 Max Plank Yearbook of United Nations Law 423–63. Djordjevic, a former constitution-maker in Yugoslavia, claims that French, Belgian, German, and Spanish constitutions were consulted frequently by framers. Jovan Djordjevic, "The Creation of the 1974 Constitution of the Socialist Federal Republic of Yugoslavia," in Robert A. Goldwin and Art Kaufman (eds.), *Constitution-Makers on Constitution Making: The Experience of Eight Nations* (American Enterprise Institute 1988) 190 See also the numerous resources available at http://www.constitutionnet.org.

[55] Yash Ghai and Jill Cottrell (eds.), *Creating the New Constitution: A Guide for Nepali Citizens* (International IDEA 2008) 1.

[56] Franklin B. Hough, *New York Convention Manual* (Weed, Parsons & Company 1867).

constitution-making process "lectures, seminars, discussions, and workshops were held on a wide range of topics pertaining to constitutions, systems of government, the role of political parties in a multiparty democracy, and the international protection of human rights."[57] Framers in Rwanda underwent similar training in constitution building seminars.[58] These programs, according to International IDEA's instructions for them, serve as a means of educating framers on the nature and purposes of constitutions generally, how constitutions are used, legal language, the importance of structure, the main elements of constitutions, relevant portions of international law, and how existing or previous constitutions functioned.[59]

In addition, constitution-making bodies frequently tour other countries for advice and invite international and local constitutional experts to give guidance. International advisory boards visited Eritrea, the Nicaraguan Constitutional Assembly consulted local constitutional scholars, and the secretariat to the Constitutional Loya Jirga in Afghanistan prepared background papers with assistance from NATO and the UN. Ugandan constitutional commissioners visited the United States and several European countries to discuss constitutional options, members of the Nepalis Constituent Assembly observed direct democratic processes in Switzerland, and delegates from the Indonesian People's Consultative Assemblies observed the working of constitutional courts in Thailand and South Korea.[60]

Finally, as mentioned in chapter 1, through a variety of inclusive procedures including travelling commissions, nationwide surveys, comment solicitation, town-hall meetings, and the submissions of drafts for public review, constitution-makers seek out and obtain public opinion data related to constitutional desires and previous experience with political institutions. For instance, the Ugandan Constitutional Commission received memoranda summarizing the viewpoints expressed in over 800 local government council meetings attended by the public, toured the country holding town-hall meetings, solicited essays on the constitution by primary, secondary, and university students, and collected relevant newspaper op-eds and general comments by interested individuals. In all, over 25,000 submissions were received and processed by the commission.[61] Framers not only

[57] Jamal Benomar, "Constitution-Making after Conflict: Lessons for Iraq," (2004) 15 Journal of Democracy 81–95, 90.

[58] Dann and Al-ali, "The Internationalized *Pouvoir Constituant*—Constitution-Making under External Influence in Iraq, Sudan and East Timor," 9.

[59] Brandt and others, *Constitution-Making and Reform: Options for the Process*, 56.

[60] Hassen Ebrahim, Kayode Fayemi, and Stephanie Loomis, *Promoting a Culture of Constitutionalism and Democracy in Commonwealth Africa: Recommendations to Commonwealth Heads of Government* (1999); Benomar, "Constitution-Making after Conflict: Lessons for Iraq," 91; Brandt and others, *Constitution-Making and Reform: Options for the Process*, 58–60. Note that Interpeace suggests that constitutional trips by framers are frequently used as excuses for shopping trips and escape.

[61] Moehler, *Distrusting Democrats: Outcomes of Participatory Constitution Making*, 56–57. Commissioners also toured throughout Zimbabwe and Rwanda. See John Hatchard, "Some Lessons on Constitution-Making from Zimbabwe," (2001) 54 Journal of African Law 210–16, 212; Katharina Diehl

receive such vast amounts of relevant constitution-making information, but they are given the time and resources to process it. Framers usually create the constitution on a full-time basis and are paid for doing so; this allows them to devote themselves to becoming competent. They are also often supplied with legal assistants and researchers to assist them.

In the second stage, the bargaining and drafting stage, framers experience a new set of learning mechanisms. Drafting a constitution requires that participants interact, for a group with diverse preferences cannot draft a complex document in isolation from one other. Framers, particularly in modern constitution-making processes that encourage diversity and representativeness, are likely to start the process disagreeing with one another when it comes to substantive issues, priorities, and wording. Since the delegates' task is to create and agree upon a single constitution meant to be long-lasting and stable, and such multi-layered disagreement exists, the convention becomes the site of a cooperative mixed motive conflict, i.e. a situation in which the delegates have conflicting motives to cooperate (they need to produce a constitution) and to compete (they each want the final constitution to be as close to their ideal constitution as possible).[62]

Thus, constitution-making bodies often involve arguing, bargaining, learning, and voting, and stop only when the required number of delegates agree to one of potentially many equilibria, i.e. to a particular draft of the constitution that contains numerous provisions which were once the subject of dispute.[63] This process, made necessary by the need to create an agreed upon constitution, promotes further learning. Constitution-makers are forced to listen to differing values, opinions, interests, and beliefs. This grants them new perspectives on issues and enables them to better see complexity. After the training stage, "most constitution-makers understand some of the constitutional issues as stake, but likely only those issues that affect them and their own communities."[64] Through deliberation, these information imbalances can be remedied. As decades of deliberative democracy research tells us, the need to persuade and compromise can force participants to refine and become more familiar with their own intuitions, knowledge, and preference set, as well as become acquainted with those of their interlocutors.

Citizen ratifiers do not undergo the educational experience of drafting a constitution. They do not necessarily argue and bargain and compromise with each other, for they are not involved in creating a constitution. Instead, they simply must vote yes or no on a referendum. Ratifiers might be exposed to some of the

and others, *Structures and Principles of a Constitution* (Max Planck Manuals on Constitution Building, 2009) 9.

[62] Thomas Schelling, *The Strategy of Conflict* (Harvard University Press 1980) 60.
[63] Jon Elster, *Explaining Social Behavior: More Nuts and Bolts for the Social Sciences* (Cambridge University Press 2007) 401–26.
[64] Brandt and others, *Constitution-Making and Reform: Options for the Process*, 57.

educational material given to framers during training, but they likely have insufficient time to read, reflect, and process the received information. More importantly, designers of constitution-making processes have some degree of control over the education of constitutional framers. As I discuss section 5 below, the same is not true for citizen ratifiers. No one can guarantee that ratifiers will read the education material given to them, attend constitution-making seminars, and differentiate between relatively objective educational resources and referendum propaganda. In the end, most constitution-makers in previous instances of constitution-making have emerged from the process far more competent than a citizen ratifier must be to make a meaningful choice, and future constitution-making processes are likely to be designed to have a similar effect. This defense of USJ thus fails, for most framers likely easily surpass the threshold of meaningful choice by the time they endorse a text.[65]

4. Information Shortcuts

The second defense of USJ claims that ignorant voters can meet the requirements of meaningful choice by relying on information shortcuts to vote as if they are informed. This argument makes use of voting studies that arose in response to the findings of political ignorance mentioned above. The central point of these studies, the authors of which I call "the heuristics school," is that even with limited factual knowledge, voters make competent political decisions by using rules of thumb "to figure what they are for and against in ways that make sense in terms of their underlying values and interests."[66] These rules or heuristics include such things as partisan cues, candidate ideology, elite or interest group endorsement, polls, and past election results.[67]

[65] My argument is that framers can reliably be sufficiently educated, not that they always are or that they always will be in the future. One notable failure of adequately familiarizing constituent assembly members with all the details needed for constitution-making occurred in the Micronesian process, which resulted in some of its members requesting an extension due to their confusion. As the delegate making the request wrote: "I am very much cornered that the language we are using in this Convention is a second language to all of us and is not well understood by most of us, if not at all." Brian Z. Tamanaha, "Battle between Law and Society in Micronesia," in Denis J. Galligan and Mila Versteeg (eds.), *Social and Political Foundations of Constitutions* (Cambridge University Press 2013) 589.

[66] Bowler and Donovan, *Demanding Choices: Opinion, Voting, and Direct Democracy*, 168.

[67] See Henry E. Brady and Paul M. Sniderman, "Attitude Attribution: A Group Basis for Political Reasoning," (1985) 79 American Political Science Review 1061–78; Richard D. McKelvey and Peter C. Ordeshook, "Information, Electoral Equilibria, and the Democratic Ideal," (1985) 48 Journal of Politics 909–37; Richard R. Lau and David P. Redlawsk, "Voting Correctly," (1997) 91 American Political Science Review 585–98; Lupia and McCubbins, *The Democratic Dilemma: Can Citizens Learn What They Need to Know*; Jeffrey J. Mondak, "Public Opinion and Heuristic Processing of Source Cues," (1993) 15 Political Behavior 167–92; Richard R. Lau and David P. Redlawsk, "An Experimental Study of Information Search, Memory, and Decision Making During a Political Campaign," in James Kuklinski (ed.), *Citizens and Politics, Perspectives from Political Psychology* (Cambridge University Press 2001); Samuel Popkin, *The Reasoning Voter: Communication and Persuasion in Presidential Campaigns*

4.1 Heuristic School

The heuristics school begins from the premise, taken from behavioral decision theory and cognitive psychology, that individuals are "limited information processors" who necessarily use shortcuts to make reasonable decisions while preserving cognitive resources.[68] These shortcuts, or heuristics, allow people to decide most of their choices, from the undemanding and trivial to the complex and important, on the basis of very simple types of information.[69] Though imprecise, using shortcuts is necessary because it is impossible for individuals to know detailed information about or conduct research on the consequences of the thousands of choices that confront them daily.[70] When used appropriately, these heuristics enable individuals to successfully accomplish the tasks confronting them without having to worry about every little factual detail.

The heuristics school applies this insight to political decisions, finding that "limited information need not prevent people from making competent vote choices since voters rely on cues and heuristics to overcome their information shortfalls."[71] Here, a competent vote choice is one that a voter would make with full information.[72] Central to this argument is the distinction between knowledge and information: "knowledge is the ability to predict accurately the consequences of choices," while "information is the data from which knowledge may be derived."[73] The heuristic school argues that while knowing the sort of detailed political facts tested in political information surveys might make a voter knowledgeable to the extent that she can vote in alignment with her preferences, the same is true for

(University of Chicago Press 1991); Benjamin I. Page and Robert Y. Shapiro, *The Rational Public: Fifty Years of Trends in Americans' Policy Preferences* (University of Chicago Press 1992).

[68] Susan T. Fiske and Shelly E. Taylor, *Social Cognition* (2nd edn, McGraw-Hill 1992).

[69] The foundations of this school can be traced to Amos Tversky and Daniel Kahneman, "Judgment under Uncertainty: Heuristics and Biases," (September 1974) 185 Science 1124–31.

[70] Arthur Lupia and John G. Matsusaka, "Direct Democracy: New Approaches to Old Questions," (2004) 7 Annual Review of Political Science 463–82, 468.

[71] Hobolt, "Taking Cues on Europe? Voter Competence and Party Endorsements in Referendums on European Integration," 154.

[72] Lau and Redlawsk, "Voting Correctly," 586. Though I cannot discuss it in detail here, there are several problems with this definition of competency and the ways in which it is measured. For instance, many attempts at surmising how a person would behave if they were properly informed slide into paternalism, assume an unrealistic separation of values and factual information, and falsely equate full information with the capability of making reasonable inferences. Similarly, many of these studies measure competent voting behavior by looking at the actions of those voters who are the most informed. This leads to at least two deficiencies. On the one hand, it equates better informed with actually informed. That is, it overlooks the possibility that the most informed group of voters in a population may nonetheless be extremely confused and ignorant. On the other hand, it assumes away differences between informed and uninformed voters that might resist statistical measure, i.e. cultural backgrounds, moral standards, cognitive styles, etc.

[73] Lupia and McCubbins, *The Democratic Dilemma: Can Citizens Learn What They Need to Know*, 20; Arthur Lupia, "How Elitism Undermines the Study of Voter Competence," (2006) 18 Critical Review 217–32, 226.

knowing a different sort of information, i.e. the type of data processed in accordance with heuristic principles. For example, in the right conditions, a voter who does not know what the New York City Comptroller does, let alone anything about the candidates running for the office, might vote along partisan lines or follow the recommendations of a trusted news source and reach the same decision she would reach after weeks of research on the matter. A voter might not know or comprehend the details of a referendum requiring firearm manufactures to install a new safety feature on their weapons, but by simply following or doing the opposite of what the National Rifle Association recommends, they can arrive at a vote that reflects their existing values and interests on the issue.

The heuristics-based defense of USJ claims that voters can rely on partisan cues, elite endorsements, and other shortcuts to vote as if they were fully aware of the provisions of the proposed constitution and capable of comparing a proposed system of government to their present political situation. This argument appears to be supported by studies on Quebec's sovereignty referendums of 1992, the 1994 Norwegian referendum on EU membership, and the referendums on the 2005 Constitution for Europe.[74] Though not ratification referendums on a national constitution, each were high stakes referendums concerning constitutional issues that would have significantly readjusted their respective constitutional order. And in all of these instances, rather than engage in "abstract exercises in constitutional design using copious information about the payoffs of alternative outcomes," voters appeared to have relied on heuristics.[75]

4.2 Three Problems with a Shortcuts Defense

Appealing to information shortcuts cannot save USJ for three main reasons. First, the heuristics school might be wrong. Those generally critical of the heuristics school, particularly its use of information shortcuts to downplay the implications of factual political ignorance, claim that voters might not rely on information shortcuts regularly, that there is no evidence that voters actually vote competently when using them, and that if used, heuristics are only helpful to informed voters.[76]

[74] Harold D. Clarke, Allan Kornberg, and Marianne C. Stewart, "Referendum Voting as Political Choice: The Case of Quebec," (2004) 24 British Journal of Political Science 345–55; Andreas R.T. Schuck and Claes H. De Vreese, "Public Support for Referendums: The Role of the Media," (2011) 34 West European Politics 181–207; Hobolt, "Taking Cues on Europe? Voter Competence and Party Endorsements in Referendums on European Integration"; Andrew Glencross and Alexander Trechsel, "First or Second Order Referendum? Understanding the Votes on the EU Constitutional Treaty in Four EU Member States," (2011) 34 West European Politics 755–72.

[75] Clarke, Kornberg, and Stewart, "Referendum Voting as Political Choice: The Case of Quebec," 354–55.

[76] Sniderman, Brody, and Tetlock, *Reasoning and Choice: Explorations in Political Psychology*; Larry M. Bartels, "Uninformed Votes: Information Effects in Presidential Elections," (1996) 40 American Journal of Political Science 194–230; James H. Kuklinski and Paul J. Quirk, "Conceptual Foundations of Citizen Competence," (2001) 23 Political Behavior 285–311; Mary N. Franklin, Cees van der Eijk,

Bartels, for instance, notes that "it is easier to assume than to demonstrate that cues and shortcuts do, in fact, allow relatively uninformed voters to behave *as if* they were fully informed." Further, on the basis of six presidential elections in the United States, he concludes that "the behavior both of individual voters and of the electorate as a whole deviates in significant and politically consequential ways from the projected behavior of a 'fully' informed electorate."[77]

Supporting these critics are studies purporting to show that referendum outcomes "become tied to the popularity of the government in power, even if the ostensible subject of the referendum has little to do with the reasons for government popularity (or lack of popularity)."[78] Thus, Clarke et al. demonstrate that the outcome of the 1992 constitutional referendum in Canada indicated the citizens' desire to sanction the ruling political party more than their preferences on the subject matter of the proposed amendments.[79] Other research indicates that referendums frequently devolve into "second-order elections," where voters "make extensive use of irrelevant cues such as long term party loyalties or momentary rough evaluations of the party in government" and thus arrive at decisions divergent from fully informed citizens voting on the issues.[80] In other words, it is entirely possible that citizens use information shortcuts to make complex voting decisions, but that the results of doing so is in no way correlated with what their informed decision would be.[81] If such criticisms of heuristics are right, information shortcuts become a weak defense of USJ.

Second, even if one accepts that information shortcuts can enable ignorant voters to vote competently, appealing to them to save USJ is unpersuasive because the context of ratification referendums makes shortcuts unreliable. Even proponents of heuristics admit that information shortcuts sometimes fail to

and Michael Marsh, "Referendum Outcomes and Trust in Government: Public Support for Europe in the Wake of Maastricht," (1995) 18 West European Politics; Delli Carpini and Keeter, *What Americans Know About Politics and Why It Matters*.

77 Bartels, "Uninformed Votes: Information Effects in Presidential Elections," 195, 198. See also Achen and Bartels' discussion in Achen and Bartels, *Democracy for Realists: Why Elections Do Not Produce Responsive Government*, 37–41.

78 Franklin, Eijk, and Marsh, "Referendum Outcomes and Trust in Government: Public Support for Europe in the Wake of Maastricht," 1.

79 Clarke and Kornberg, "The Politics and Economics of Constitutional Choice: Voting in Canada's 1992 National Referendum." Another example of this phenomenon is the 1962 French referendum on changing the constitution, which was more a plebiscite for de Gaulle than anything else. See David B. Goldey, "The French Referendum and Election of 1962," (1963) 11 Political Studies 287–307. I thank Jon Elster for pointing me to this example.

80 Henrik Oscarsson, "The Ideological Response: Saying No to the Euro," in Claes H. de Vreese (ed.), *The Dynamics of Referendum Campaigns: An International Perspective* (Palgrave Macmillan 2007) 206 See also Qvorthup, "A Comparative Study of Referendums: Government by the People," 205.

81 In fact, such a worry seems supported by the original psychological research on heuristics, which emphasized the inevitable introduction of bias and miscalculation into individual decision-making reliant on shortcuts. Daniel Kahneman, Jack L. Knetsch, and Richard H. Thaler, "Anomalies: The Endowment Effect, Loss Aversion, and Status Quo Bias," (1991) 5 The Journal of Economic Perspectives 193–206; Tversky and Kahneman, "Judgment under Uncertainty: Heuristics and Biases."

guarantee competent decision-making. This occurs when shortcuts *misfire* (lead to non-preferred outcomes), are *used incorrectly* (are applied to an incompatible setting), or are *inaccessible* (the information normally processed with the heuristic is unavailable or indecipherable).[82] For example, imagine that whenever I make home improvement decisions I follow the advice of my neighbor, who is a contractor. If my neighbor gives me bad advice, the heuristic misfires. If I consult her on automotive repair or consult the wrong neighbor, I misapply the heuristic. And, if she goes into a coma, the heuristic becomes inaccessible.

Certain conditions make political shortcuts more likely to fail in these ways. Heuristics are likely to misfire when cue-givers are ignorant about the subject matter in question. Voters tend to misapply heuristics when lacking the contextual and historical information needed to know which elites, interest groups parties, or media source supports outcomes conducive to their own values. As Delli Carpini and Keeter note, "the heuristics model is based on *low* information rationality, not *no* information rationality."[83] Finally, heuristics are likely to be unavailable when regular cue-givers are either absent, fail to send signals on the subject matter at hand, or contradict each other.

Most generally, shortcuts operate when politics resembles a repeated game. Here, uninformed players can make competent political decisions because experience has taught them that relying on specific decision-making proxies leads to desirable outcomes. However, constitution-making often occurs in moments of disruption—when the game is breaking or already broken. Thus, it is no surprise that the context of ratification referendums precisely meets the conditions for heuristic failure.

The subject matter of a ratification referendum is complex and deals with issues unfamiliar to both average citizens and elites. A local newspaper, community leader, or other cue-giver might understand elections or an ordinary referendum and give more or less consistent voting advice, but become confused and hence unreliable when it comes to constitutional evaluation, a subject matter outside of its normal purview. Similarly, citizens might lack the background knowledge needed to know which competing information leader to trust. Thus, the complexity and unfamiliarity of a ratification referendum can easily lead to misfires and misapplication.

[82] These distinctions are my own, but for similar criticisms of heuristics, see Bartels, "Uninformed Votes: Information Effects in Presidential Elections"; James H. Kuklinski and Paul J. Quirk, "Reconsidering the Rational Public: Cognition, Heuristics, and Mass Opinion," in Arthur Lupia, Matthew McCubbins, and Samuel Popkin (eds.), *Elements of Reason: Cognition, Choice, and the Bounds of Rationality* (Cambridge University Press 2000).

[83] Delli Carpini and Keeter, *What Americans Know About Politics and Why It Matters*, 52. See also Lau and Redlawsk, "An Experimental Study of Information Search, Memory, and Decision Making During a Political Campaign"; Kuklinski and Quirk, "Conceptual Foundations of Citizen Competence." Emphasis added.

In addition, ratification referendums concern the rules of a new political system, and thus do not necessarily align with existing cleavages formed within the old. Parties and interest groups frequently split over proposed constitutions, making their cues inaccessible. Moreover, coalitions that favor or oppose a draft constitution are likely to be new, unfamiliar, and unpredictable, for constitutions unsettle vested interests, benefiting and harming groups with little in common previously. For instance, the coalition that opposed the 1970 proposed Arkansas Constitution consisted of local judges and prosecutors, minor county officials, and the liquor industry, making any signals sent by them hard to interpret.[84] More generally, constitution-making is normally an infrequent one-shot game, thus there is a lack of accumulated experience and reliable expectations with which individuals can form heuristics or appeal to existing ones. This makes the chance of misapplication rather high. Finally, constitution-making frequently occurs in political contexts of great instability, meaning that previous systems of information shortcuts are likely disrupted and new ones yet to form. "The ordinary influences that operate and secure a full vote on matters of moment," as Sir Samuel Griffith noted in his objection to popular ratification in the 1891 Australasian Federal Conference, "would be to a great extent wanting."[85]

Direct evidence of such heuristic failure in ratification referendums does not exist for lack of study, but evidence from high stakes constitutional referendums provides some support. The Australian Republican Referendum in 1999 concerned two questions: the first asked voters if they wanted Australia to become a republic with a President, appointed by their parliament, replacing the Queen and Governor General; the second asked whether a preamble should be placed at the beginning of the constitution.[86] 55 percent of those voting in the referendum rejected it, though opinion polls showed voters favoring the creation of a republic two to one throughout the 1990s. According to deliberative polling conducted afterwards, voters "got the referendum quite wrong," in that, if fully informed, they would not have favored rejection.[87] This suggests that if used, heuristics did not lead voters to a competent decision. Higley and McAllister partially attribute these results to what amounts to shortcut failures: citizens did not understand the issues and their normal heuristics were indecipherable. Specifically, party and leader cues were contradictory, for the Labor party divided on the method of election for the

[84] Elmer E. Cornwell, Jay S. Goodman, and Wayne R. Swanson, *State Constitutional Conventions: The Politics of the Revision Process in Seven States* (Praeger 1975) 170–173; Kay Collett Goss, *The Arkansas State Constitution: A Reference Guide* (Greenwood Press 1993) 10–12.

[85] *Offical Report of the National Australasian Convention Debates. Sydney, 2 March to 9 April, 1891* (George Stephen Chapman, Acting Government Printer 1891) 901.

[86] Though this constitutional referendum did not amount to a ratification referendum, the changes were substantial and many of the same conditions that would weaken heuristics for ratification referendums were present.

[87] Luskin and others, *Deliberation and Referendum Voting*, 10.

head of state, the Liberals divided on the republic issues, and the Prime Minister campaigned against the referendum that his government had proposed.[88]

The 2000 Danish national referendum on the euro provides further evidence of cue-giver confusion and subsequent heuristic inaccessibility and misfiring. Political parties at the extreme left and right joined forces in a No campaign, leaving the centrist parties weakly united for a Yes. Campaign messages were confused and vague, and voters received no clear heuristical data to act upon.[89] Like the Australian case, this confusion resulted from the subject of the referendums, which fell outside the normal political landscape.

The third and strongest reason to resist the voting shortcuts defense is also the simplest: how citizens vote is irrelevant for USJ. Even if most voters in future constitutional ratification referendums will always rely on information shortcuts, and these shortcuts will always lead them to a competent vote, this still does not rescue the argument. That is because USJ requires that referendums meet the threshold of meaningful choice, which concerns how a voter makes her choice—by her ability to vote on a constitution for reasons relating to her evaluation of its contents in comparison with the likely result of rejection—and not on the outcome of a referendum.

The claim that heuristics enable ignorant voters to make the same decisions as informed voters is comforting in the face of worries about the health of democracies filled with ignorant citizens, for it explains how even if politically ignorant, voters are still able to arrive at political outcomes that match their preferences, and thus democracy still provides a way of ensuring that government rules in accordance with the will of its citizenry. However, this outcome-based focus is anathema to USJ, where primary importance is ascribed to the direct intentional exercise of the people's sovereign power for non-consequentialist reasons. This is why a happy outcome to a referendum in which voters never looked upon the constitution cannot satisfy USJ, for voters cannot author a constitution they never see. Thus, even if heuristics enable ignorant voters to make agent-relative sensible decisions in a ratification referendum, the vote is still not an instance of the people deciding upon their constitution, for they remain unable to comprehend and own their decision. In other words, heuristics cannot enable an unaware voter to make a meaningful choice.

[88] Higley and McAllister, "Elite Division and Voter Confusion: Australia's Republic Referendum in 1999," 859.

[89] Claes H. de Vreese, "Context, Elites, Media and Public Opinion in Referendums: When Campaigns Really Matter," in Claes H. de Vreese (ed.), *The Dynamics of Referendum Campaigns: An International Perspective* (Palgrave Macmillan 2007) 10; Hanspeter Kriesi, "The Participation in Swiss Direct-Democratic Votes," in Claes H. de Vreese (ed.), *The Dynamics of Referendum Campaigns: An International Perspective* (Palgrave Macmillan 2007).

5. Educating the People

The third defense of USJ is simple: voter ignorance can be countered by education efforts. If the people are too ignorant to evaluate the constitution, we should simply educate them beforehand. Of course, using education campaigns to target political ignorance is not a new idea; it is why most ordinary referendums and initiatives include education efforts, why civic education is an essential component of public education, and why international donors and civil society groups increasingly promote voter information campaigns for ordinary elections. When it comes to constitution-making, framing bodies, along with the assistance of sitting governments, NGOs, IGOs, civil society organizations, the media, and constitutional consultants, frequently design and implement massive voter outreach and education programs.[90] In fact, over half of the last 194 instances of constitution-making involved such programs.[91]

Such education programs employ an array of tactics over the course of the constitution-making process with the purported aim of teaching citizens about constitutionalism, institutional design, and the constitution-making process, so that they can participate and evaluate their constitution. Framers in Brazil broadcasted the proceedings of the constituent assembly on public television, and a state media center ensured that news outlets explained the day-to-day developments; this resulted in 716 television programs, 700 radio programs, 3000 hours of video, and 4871 interviews with members of the assembly.[92] In South Africa, framers distributed posters, brochures, leaflets, a biweekly newsletter, and even comic books. They also produced television and radio programs, set up a multi-lingual "Constitutional Talk Line," held 486 workshops targeted at disadvantaged communities, hosted numerous constitutional public meetings, set up an official website, and distributed 4.5 million copies of the draft constitution.[93]

Eritrean framers launched an extensive educational program specifically tailored to address the country's 80 percent illiteracy rate. Using songs, traveling plays, concerts, poetry, and illustrated books, the program directly engaged with an

[90] For instructions on how to organize such a process, see Brandt and others, *Constitution-Making and Reform*, 91–107.

[91] Vivien Hart, "Constitution Making and the Right to Take Part in a Public Affair," in Laurel E. Miller (ed.), *Framing the State in Times of Transition: Case Studies in Constitution Making* (United States Institute of Peace Press 2010) 37.

[92] Keith S. Rosenn, "Conflict Resolution and Constitutionalism: The Making of the Brazilian Constitution of 1988," in Laurel E. Miller (ed.), *Framing the State in Times of Transition: Case Studies in Constitution Making* (United States Institute of Peace Press 2010) 445.

[93] Ebrahim, Fayemi, and Loomis, *Promoting a Culture of Constitutionalism and Democracy in Commonwealth Africa: Recommendations to Commonwealth Heads of Government*; Laurel E. Miller, "Designing Constitution-Making Processes: Lessons from the Past, Questions for the Future," in Laurel E. Miller (ed.), *Framing the State in Times of Transition: Case Studies in Constitution Making* (United States Institute of Peace Press 2010) 630; Brandt and others, *Constitution-Making and Reform: Options for the Process*, 93–94; Synnove Skjelton, *A People's Constitution: Public Participation in the South-African Constitution-Making Process* (Institute for Global Dialogue 2006).

estimated 500,000 members of the population.[94] In Uganda, the education process lasted four years and included seminars for 10,000 community leaders, the dissemination of previous constitutions and specially prepared information packets, 800 educational seminars led by constitution commissioners, over forty multi-lingual radio programs, twenty television programs, and countless information seminars held by trained leaders or local council officials.[95]

Education programs could work. The average citizen, given the right time, setting, and motivation, could learn enough to make a meaningful choice. And it is impossible to say that such programs have never worked for a ratification referendum. Sufficient studies to ground this claim do not exist. Nonetheless, two reasons push one to doubt the ability of education campaigns to sufficiently and reliably lower voter ignorance for ratification referendums.

First, little evidence exists showing that previous educations programs overcame voter ignorance. This is true whether one looks at elections or referendums. A recent meta-analysis of coordinated trials found no evidence overall that non-partisan voter information campaigns shape voter behavior.[96] Further, nearly all of the findings on voter ignorance mentioned in the previous section were based on surveys and experiments run in contexts where educational programs preceded the vote. For example, expensive multi-media education programs preceded the referendums on the EU constitution, yet a third of respondents in a Eurobarometer survey reported never having heard of the constitutional treaty, and over half said they knew little about its substance. Similarly, 54 percent of survey respondents in Uganda agreed that the constitution was too complicated for them to understand, and 33 percent could not answer a question about its purpose, despite the lauded and comprehensive campaign. In both South Africa and Eritrea, where comprehensive education programs sought to prepare citizens for participation, most public suggestions sent to framers were unrelated to constitutional issues or "not susceptible to being translated into the language of a modern constitution."[97]

Second, combatting constitutional ignorance through neutral education programs is made exceedingly difficult by the *ratification campaigns* that begin upon promulgation of the draft constitution. These campaigns have a goal that is both easier to meet and in direct tension with that of education programs. Whereas education programs aim at giving voters the knowledge they need to understand and evaluate their constitution, ratification campaigns, like ordinary political

[94] Miller, "Designing Constitution-Making Processes: Lessons from the Past, Questions for the Future," 631; Bereket Habte Selassie, "Constitution Making in Eritrea: A Process-Driven Approach," in Laurel E. Miller (ed.), *Framing the State in Times of Transition: Case Studies in Constitution Making* (United States Institute of Peace Press 2010).

[95] Moehler, *Distrusting Democrats: Outcomes of Participatory Constitution Making*, 55–57.

[96] Thad Dunning and others, "Voter Information Campaigns and Political Accountability: Cumulative Findings from a Preregistered Meta-Analysis of Coordinated Trials," (2019) 5 Science Advances 1–10.

[97] Miller, "Designing Constitution-Making Processes: Lessons from the Past, Questions for the Future," 631.

campaigns, merely want to persuade the public to vote a certain way, often by any means necessary. Educating is no more important to a ratification campaign than misleading; both are appropriate means of bringing voters to the desired decision.

Moreover, studies show that campaigns are likely to be influential when the decision to be made is complex, concerns a topic that is new or rare and lacks a history of public debate, and involves issues on which voters lack long-standing opinions. Disagreement between or ignorance of traditional cue-givers, the absence of other reliable heuristics, and the presence of contradicting messages further heightens campaign effectiveness.[98]

It is just these conditions that characterize the context of ratification referendums. The subject and issues of constitution-making are unfamiliar. Voters are uninformed or newly informed, making their opinions more malleable. Constitution-making is normally rare and there is usually little history of public debate. Ratification campaigns thus take place in contexts where voters, despite any proceeding educational programs, are extremely likely to be influenced by calculated campaigns.[99]

Of course, being influenced by a ratification campaign is not necessarily detrimental to making a meaningful choice. That is, a meaningful choice threshold does not require the unrealistic absence of persuasion or non-objective discussions of the constitution. The problem is that ratification campaigns address voters most prone to manipulation and influence, are designed to convince these voters to make a particular choice, and take place when normal obstacles to manipulation—regulatory institutions, laws, and norm—are relatively absent. The result is that "efforts at self-education are thwarted by manipulative campaigns designed to oversimplify the issue and appeal to the electorate's worst instincts."[100]

Voters are often subjected to "sharply contested, but ill-defined and unsubstantiated, visions of alternative political futures," and "bombarded by conflicting claims about the costs and benefits of accepting or rejecting a referendum proposal."[101] Specifically, campaigns for referendums manipulate voters in one of several ways: they foreground particular true facts, changing their meaning by eliminating context or means of comparison; provide misinformation or strategically

[98] David M. Farrell and Rüdiger Schmitt-Beck, *Do Political Campaigns Matter? Campaign Effects in Elections and Referendums* (Routledge 2002); Lawrence LeDuc, "Referendums and Elections: How Do Campaigns Differ?" in David M. Farrell and Rüdiger Schmitt-Beck (eds.), *Do Political Campaigns Matter? Campaign Effects in Elections and Referendums* (Routledge 2002). See also Tamir Sheafer, "Detecting Campaign Effects in Imbalanced Campaigns: The Likud's Interparty Referendum over Sharon's Disengagement Plan," (2005) 10 The Harvard International Journal of Press/Politics 85–93.

[99] de Vreese, "Context, Elites, Media and Public Opinion in Referendums: When Campaigns Really Matter"; Lawrence LeDuc, "Opinion Formation and Change in Referendum Campaigns," in Claes H. de Vreese (ed.), *The Dynamics of Referendum Campaigns: An International Perspective* (Palgrave Macmillan 2007).

[100] Julian N. Eule, "Judicial Review of Direct Democracy," (1990) 99 Yale Law Journal, 1555–56.

[101] Luskin and others, *Deliberation and Referendum Voting*; Clarke, Kornberg, and Stewart, "Referendum Voting as Political Choice: The Case of Quebec."

incomplete information; prime one aspect of a vote and make it determinate; or prime an issue or factor that is unrelated to the vote entirely.

In both the Danish and Swiss referendums on the euro, held in 2000 and 2003 respectively, the No campaigns relied on unrelated issue priming, portraying the vote as one about patriotism, fears of a central bank, and commitments to social welfare, rather than focusing on the actual substance of the referendum.[102] In the campaigns preceding the Albanian Constitutional referendum in 1997, both sides "spent a relatively limited amount of time on substantive issues."[103] The Democratic Party, leading the charge of the "No" campaign, resorted to misinformation. For instance, they attacked Article 18, a ban on arbitrary discrimination, by claiming that it violated the European Convention on Human Rights (ECHR) and was meant to restrict individual liberties. In response, the "Yes" campaign resorted to a purely defensive position, failing to emphasize what the constitution would actually do, meaning that voters, 90 percent of whom approved the constitution, likely did so on the basis of limited and distorted information.[104]

In Poland in 1997, the state electoral commission launched an extensive information campaign meant to educate the public about the new constitution and lay out arguments for and against it. However, "this effort largely descended into an electoral campaign in the nature of propaganda rather than education." In turn, opponents of the constitution provided incomplete information on several articles, framing provisions about future collaboration with international organizations, child maturity and freedom of consciousness, and a consultative Monetary Policy Council, as attempts to deprive Poland of its sovereignty, take children away from their parents, and give state finances to a powerful unaccountable agency.[105]

Similarly, the proposed constitutions of the 1970 Arkansas State Constitutional Convention and the 1968 Rhode Island Convention both immediately became the site of numerous and conflicting public relations campaigns that resorted to rumor-mongering, exaggerated interpretations of constitutional provisions, and simultaneous celebrations and condemnations of the drafting process.[106] Those opposed to the Arkansas draft, for example, successfully convinced a large portion of the electorate that the constitution would benefit elites and increase taxes, though neither of these claims followed logically from the text.[107] Finally, the yes campaign

[102] LeDuc, "Opinion Formation and Change in Referendum Campaigns," 33.

[103] Scott N. Carlson, "The Drafting Process for the 1998 Albanian Constitution," in Laurel E. Miller (ed.), *Framing the State in Times of Transition: Case Studies in Constitution Making* (United States Institute of Peace Press 2010) 321.

[104] Ibid., 330, 354.

[105] Lech Garlicki and Zofia A. Garlicka, "Constitution Making, Peace Building, and National Reconciliation: The Experience of Poland," in Laurel E. Miller (ed.), *Framing the State in Times of Transition: Case Studies in Constitution Making* (United States Institute of Peace Press 2010) 401.

[106] Patrick T. Conley, *The Rhode Island State Constitution: A Reference Guide* (Praeger 2007) 32–34; Cornwell, Goodman, and Swanson, *State Constitutional Conventions: The Politics of the Revision Process in Seven States*, 170–173; Goss, *The Arkansas State Constitution: A Reference Guide*, 10–12

[107] Cornwell, Goodman, and Swanson, *State Constitutional Conventions: The Politics of the Revision Process in Seven States*, 173.

for Australia's 1967 Aboriginal referendum successfully sold what amounted to an increase in federal government power over population determination as a vote on a broad increase in Aboriginal rights.[108]

Such manipulation wrought by ratification campaigns usually goes unchecked by educational programs, and this should be expected. The driving forces behind education programs—constitution-makers, civil society organizations, and sitting governments—usually come to take sides on the draft constitution upon its release, as their incentives to neutrally educate citizens become overridden by competing ones for a particular outcome. Education programs thus frequently cease or transform into ratification campaigns. While some external NGOs or IGOs may wish to continue neutral education programs, the effects of these are limited by the likely absence of local support.

The 2005 referendum on the Kenya Constitution is a perfect example. The government, NGOs, and local civil society organizations immediately ceased education efforts upon promulgation of the draft document, choosing instead to support either the pro-constitution Bananas or anti-constitution Orange campaigns, neither of which made significant efforts to discuss the contents of the constitution. Both campaigns were led by political elites using the opportunity to position themselves in advance of the 2007 elections, and both did their best to turn the vote into one on ethnicity, rather than on constitutional design.[109] The Orange campaign falsely claimed that the constitution disadvantaged younger citizens, enlarged presidential power, legalized abortion, and gave the President a life-long term, and simultaneously reframed support of the constitution as explicit support for the unpopular Kibaki government.[110] The Banana campaign responded weakly, choosing instead to engaged in indirect vote-buying than disseminating information about what the constitution entailed.[111]

The attempted defense of CPJ by appealing to education campaign thus fails for two reasons. First, educational programs already take place for elections, ordinary referendums, and ratification referendums, yet electorates remain uninformed. The immense size of the chasm between voter knowledge and what it takes for voters to make a meaningful choice on a ratification referendum makes it hard to imagine future education programs having regular success where so many others have failed. Second, education programs are likely to be overwhelmed by powerful ratification campaigns that operate in a context in which campaign effects are known to be high, normal safeguards are absent, and the electorate is especially

[108] Paul Kildea and Rodney Smith, "The Challenge of Informed Voting at Constitutional Referendums," (2016) 39 UNSW Law Journal 368–400, 390.

[109] Beth Elise Whitaker and Jason Giersch, "Voting on a Constitution: Implications for Democracy in Kenya," (2009) 27 Journal of Contemporary African Studies 1–20, 9.

[110] Alicia L. Bannon, "Note: Designing a Constitution-Drafting Process: Lessons from Kenya," (2007) 116 Yale Law Journal 1830–72, 1839–40.

[111] Bard Anders Andresassen and Arne Tostensen, "Of Oranges and Bananas: The 2005 Kenyan Referendum of the Constitution," (2006) 13 CHR-Michelsen Institution WP, 7, 18.

prone to manipulation. As Condorcet notes, when the electorate are given the right to ratify a constitution, "the men who really exercised this right would be those whose eloquence, reputation, and standing earned them temporary sway."[112]

Of course, given the right conditions, educational programs might be able to successfully bring voters up to a level of constitutional competence sufficient for making a meaningful choice and resisting campaign manipulation. However, USJ demands more than just this possibility. It seeks to broadly recommend a ratification referendum as a standard component of a constitution-making process by depicting the procedure as a moment in which the constituent power acts. Thus one must be confident that voters will be able to make a meaningful choice. As of now, the reception of voters to education efforts and the nature and effects of spontaneous ratification campaigns remain too unpredictable.[113] The possibility of meaningful choice cannot reasonably be guaranteed, and therefore USJ is an insufficient context-independent justification for ratification.

6. Conclusion

As explained in chapter 4, a constituent power justification defends the necessity of ratification by appealing to the long-standing tradition of constituent power and its conceptual associates popular sovereignty, ordinary and extraordinary law, and fear of government oppression and domination. Specifically, a constituent power justification claims that ratification is a necessary component of the constitution-making process because constitutions must be created by the constituent power, and ratification plays some sort of essential role in making this happen. However, bringing constituent power theorizing into contact with the mechanics of the constitution-making process and clarifying the kind of role ratification might play reveals weaknesses in this type of justification.

If ratification is one of many instances of constituent action in the constitution-making process it becomes redundant or incoherent. If the procedure plays a reparative role, making up for prior failures to convoke or manifest the constituent power, it becomes a mere ad hoc solution. If ratification becomes one of several attempts meant to enable the constitution power to act, the concept of constituent power itself becomes lost from the justification or the reasons for using ratification simply disappear. Finally, if ratification is just part of process through which the

[112] Condorcet, "On the Need for the Citizens to Ratify the Constitution," 273.

[113] LeDuc explains: "[T]he most volatile referendum campaigns are likely to be those in which there is little partisan, issue, or ideological basis on which voters might tend to form an opinion easily. Lacking such information, they take more time to come to a decision, and that decision becomes highly unpredictable and subject to change over the course of the campaign, as new information is gained or new events unfold . . . . The potential volatility in such circumstances is very high, because there little in the way of core beliefs or attitudes to anchor the opinions formed." LeDuc, "Opinion Formation and Change in Referendum Campaigns," 41.

constituent power acts, no procedural recommendations become possible from the concept. Thus, as I argued, the multiple moment justification, the reparative function justification, the multiple attempts justification, and the overall process justification failed to justify the use of ratification procedures.

The failings of these types of constituent power justifications suggested a final possibility. Rather than envisioning ratification as one of many possible moments of constituent action or constituent action approximations, ratification can be understood as the sole moment during the constitution-making process when the constituent power acts. This USJ escapes the deficiencies plaguing other forms of CPJ by limiting constituent action to ratification. And, as seen in chapter 5, it is the type of argument made by the Berkshire Constitutionalists, the inventors of ratification, and their discussion remains the most comprehensive explanation for ratification to date. USJ is also still present, having recently been rearticulated by Richard Tuck throughout the course of his exegesis on the history of the distinction between sovereignty and government and his arguments in favor of Brexit via referendum. Moreover, the argument lurks behind many of the brief asides in the constitutional literature that link-up ratification with popular sovereignty and constituent power.

However, as argued in this chapter, USJ ultimately fails to explain the need for ratification. The justification claims that ratification is necessary because it is the sole moment in the constitution-making process where the constituent power acts and creates its constitution. It makes this argument by characterizing constituent power as inalienable, which means that USJ only justifies ratification procedures that make use of referendums. However, for a referendum vote to serve as a site of constituent action, individual voters must make a meaningful choice on the constitution. That is, they must choose whether to accept a proposed constitution based on their understanding of the document and the likely result of its rejection. This does not import a thick conception of what it means for the people to express its will, but instead relies on the simple idea that something cannot be taken to be the intentional creation of an agent if she did not understand what she was willing and creating.

This standard of meaningful choice is unlikely to be met because voters will be too ill-informed, for the information required to evaluate a constitution in accordance with meaningful choice is technical, hard to obtain, and of little value in normal circumstances. Since one should expect voters to be unable to make a meaningful choice, ratification referendums cannot be understood as the moment when the popular sovereign takes its decision. The USJ fails to persuade, and constituent power, despite its intuitive appeal, fails to even map onto, let alone explain and justify, the procedure of constitutional ratification. Contemporary defenders of ratification referendum like Tuck cannot then appeal to popular sovereignty, the popular will, or other variants of constituent power thinking to advocate for the submission of a constitution to the people. To continue to do so in the face of evidence that voters are likely to be confused and/ or misled about their decisions requires both vacating constituent power of any meaning and treating citizens with disrespect. It is to collapse a celebration of democracy and self-rule into a symbolic gesture.

It is again important to emphasize that this argument is not anti-democratic. The inability of voters to make a meaningful choice on a proposed constitution says nothing about their ability to competently vote in an election or ordinary referendums, even one that pertains to constitutional issues. This is so because the standard of meaningful choice only applies to ratification referendums that purport to be the site of constituent action. When voters go to the ballot box to vote for a President or legislator, to decide upon a tax referendum, or even to decide upon a particular constitutional amendment, their actions are not meant to be those of the constituent power. Theories of democracy, at least most prominent ones, do not and should not demand such a high level of knowledge.

This chapter and the two preceding it might also imply something about the usefulness, or lack thereof, of the pure concept of constituent power for the purposes of procedural design. The concept might have its uses. It is an enlightening way to explain and understand how constitutions made outside of prescribed legal pathways of constitutional change can nonetheless still be authoritative. It provides a normative explanation for why constitutions are rightfully seen as resting on top of the traditional legal hierarchy and gives theoretical resources for resisting attempts to locate the raw power of the people in parliaments, courts, or populist parties. Nonetheless, our discussion here pushes against the idea that constituent power theorizing can help us choose particular procedures. It can tell us to open up a constitution-making process, to make it popular and participatory to some extent, but any attempts at deploying the concept more specifically runs into the sorts of problems canvassed here.[114] Constituent power underdetermines a constitution-making process, despite the best intentions of those who wish to use the concept to select procedures.

[114] See Arato's criticism of Colon-Rios along these lines in Andrew Arato, *Post Sovereign Constitution Making* (Oxford University Press 2016) 291.

7
Representation through Accountability

If ratification does not serve as a moment of constituent power, as a means of injecting direct popular action into the constitution-making process, perhaps it plays a less direct role and instead enables representation. Further, maybe it is this role that justifies the procedure. In other words, maybe ratification should be implemented because it helps to foster a desirable representative relationship between the people and the framers of their constitution.

Admittedly, this line of thought might seem counterintuitive. An instance in the constitution-making process in which citizens or their delegates directly vote the constitution up or down seems to be a primary site of action itself, one in which ratifiers serve as central actors, and not merely a mechanism or element in a larger representative process.[1] When delegates are involved in ratification, such as when constitutions are submitted to national or regional conventions, ratification seems to contain its own representative process. And, when ratification comes in the form of a referendum, it looks as likely to play a role in constitution-making representation as citizen referendums play in the normal workings of contemporary representative democracies.[2]

But, this dismissal is too fast. Ratification has connections to representation and principal-agent dynamics more generally that need to be taken seriously. Constitution-making certainly looks like a decision-making process involving representation, as it involves a small group of individuals, oftentimes elected, creating law for or at the behest of a larger body of citizens. And ratification, which involves the evaluation of the work of these agents, looks like it could be part of the institutions and procedures that facilitate this representation. Specifically, as I will argue, it resembles an accountability mechanism.

As seen in chapter 2, many of ratification's non-constitutional variants seem to be a part of something that looks like a representative process. In agency law—from Ancient Rome to the present—ratification serves a *reparative function*, providing a means of retroactively authorizing a would-be agent or (pseudo-agent) so her actions can count for her principal. In early treaty-making and collective bargaining the procedure has an *agent review function.* In the former it allowed sovereigns to review the authorization and behavior of their agents during negotiations to ensure

[1] I thank Bernard Manin for pointing this out.

[2] Maija Setälä, "On the Problems of Responsibility and Accountability in Referendums," (2006) 45 European Journal of Political Research 699–721.

Constitutional Ratification without Reason. Jeffrey A. Lenowitz, Oxford University Press. © Jeffrey A. Lenowitz 2022.
DOI: 10.1093/oso/9780198852346.003.0007

that their actions remained within the bounds of their delegated powers. In the latter, ratification functions as a means to ensure that union representatives always bargain with the best interests of their union in mind, for any agreement they come up with will be reviewed by membership. Ratification's *agent review function* in particular, as I will show, closely resembles the role of accountability mechanisms in representative government.

Discussions of constitutional ratification itself also link the procedure to representation. The Berkshire Constitutionalists, as noted in chapter 5, held ratification to be essential because of, among other things, their worry that in its absence, unscrupulous representatives might hijack the constitution-making process with nothing to stop them. It was this concern that lead Allen to repeatedly claim that the right of ratification was an unalienable right. Widner, in her analysis of constitution-making amidst conflict, treats ratification via referendum as a factor in measuring the level of representation and participation.[3] That is, the presence of a referendum is seen as an increase in representation. Additionally, Vivien Hart explicitly presents a ratification referendum as "a means of holding representatives to account and creating legitimacy for the constitution."[4]

This chapter follows these and other associations, investigating whether constitutional ratification might be justified based on its role in facilitating representation. I call this second core justification a representation justification of ratification, or RJ. In what follows, I articulate the strongest version of RJ, explain its appeal, and yet conclude that it comes up short. The importance of representation cannot serve as a means to justify the procedure. I make this argument in four steps. First, I sketch out RJ, the concept of political representation, and how it might apply to constitution-making. Second, I argue that ratification's only compelling role in fostering representation is to serve as an accountability mechanism. This follows from its temporal placement within the constitution-making process and is suggested by its non-constitutional functions. I explain what an accountability mechanism is and what roles it plays in representation, and restate RJ taking accountability into account. Third, I argue that ratification cannot reliably serve as a source of accountability because of what I call "the problem of double duty," which occurs whenever there is a plausible divergence between how a principal evaluates his representative framer and draft constitution. Fourth, I bolster and flesh out my rejection of RJ by considering three objections to it.

[3] Jennifer Widner, *Constitution Writing and Conflict Resolution*, 2005) 7–8.

[4] Vivien Hart, "Constitution Making and the Right to Take Part in a Public Affair," in Laurel E. Miller (ed.), *Framing the State in Times of Transition: Case Studies in Constitution Making* (United States Institute of Peace Press 2010) 36.

1. Representation Justification

An RJ seeks to harness our intuitive preference for and familiarity with representative government, and representation more generally, to justify the use of ratification procedures. Specifically, it claims that one should implement a ratification procedure in a constitution-making process because it plays an important role in creating or maintaining a representative relationship between constituents and their constitutional framers. Put differently, RJ states: (P1) framers can be representatives; (P2) there are good reasons for framers to be representatives; (P3) ratification procedures contribute to the constitution-making representative process; therefore (P4) one has good reason to implement ratification.

1.1 Scope Restriction

From the outset, it is clear that P1 restricts the scope of RJ to those constitution-making processes capable of involving representation, or at the least that the justificatory force of RJ is going to vary between different constitution-making processes depending upon the nature of their drafting bodies. For instance, it is unpersuasive to claim that representation is involved in a constitution-making process in which a dictator writes a new constitution for himself.

Less fantastically, consider the drafting of the 2001 Constitution of Senegal and the 2002 Constitution of Timor-Leste. In Senegal, a "Technical Commission of Experts," consisting of six elites selected by the President, drafted a constitution, distributed it to party and legislative leaders for a quick fifteen days of review and comment, and then made minor revisions to the document.[5] In Timor-Leste, an eighty-eight-person elected constituent convention drafted, reviewed, and revised the draft constitution.[6]

The Timor-Leste constitution-making process appears to involve representation. Each member of the convention was chosen like a representative and acted for their constituency. Thirteen of the members were chosen in first-past-the-post district elections, and their constituency was their respective district. The rest of the convention members were elected nationally in proportional representation elections; their constituencies were the voting population as a whole. Things are more difficult when it comes to the Senegalese constitution-making process, for it is unclear who, if anyone, counted as a representative. The

[5] Souleymane Bachir Diagne, "The Constitution of a 'Laïc' African and Muslim Country: Senegal," in Asli Ü. Bâli and Hannah Lerner (eds.), *Constitution Writing, Religion and Democracy* (Cambridge University Press 2017) 137–38.

[6] Annemarie Devereux, *Timor-Leste's Bill of Rights: A Preliminary History* (Australian National University Press 2015) 18–22; Joanne Wallis, *Constitution Making During State Building* (Cambridge University Press 2014) 82–84.

technical commission consisted of the Minister of Justice, two constitutional law professors, an agent of the President of the republic, an agent of the government, an agent of the constitutional council, and one jurist acting for civil society, yet all were appointed by and served the President. Who were the relevant constituencies? The office of the President? The constitutional council? Civil society more generally? Looking to the review process as the site of representation does not make things much easier.

My interest throughout this book is to interrogate the strongest form of the various possible justifications for ratification. As such, in this chapter I will confine my attention to constitution-making processes that seem to maximize the chances of RJ being persuasive. When it comes to drafting a constitution, this means focusing on processes such as those used in Timor-Leste, i.e. those that most closely resemble traditional sites of representation by involving elected drafting bodies such as a constituent legislature or constituent convention. It is of course possible for representation to exist between a constituent and an agent they did not choose, but these are not the easiest cases. If RJ is successful here, I can then ask whether it applies to a more diverse array of drafting processes.

1.2 Focusing the Argument

Someone who is interested in interrogating RJ might focus on any of the first three propositions. For instance, one might question P1 more generally, asking whether framers, even those that are elected, can be representatives at all. Is it right to group members of a constituent convention with ordinary representative legislators? Do convention members, who are elected to perform one central task and then return home without a chance at reelection, have much in common with legislators who are in a long-term, often renewable, relationship with constituents that involves regular back and forth communication over a diverse array of decisions? Do constitution-makers represent the people when they are involved in a task that, in some sense, will remake the people?

In P1's favor is the fact that many consider and treat constitution-makers as representatives. For example, the United Nations Development Programme (UNDP) held a workshop for members of the Nepal Constituent Assembly titled "Effective Representation" and distributed training manuals that referred to them as "representatives chosen by the people to manage the transition process."[7] Numerous constitutions and constitution-makers refer to constitutional drafters as representatives explicitly. The preambles of the constitutions of Argentina and Brazil

[7] See *Participatory Constitution Making Process* (Participatory Constitution Building in Nepal Booklet Series) 1; *Support to Constitution Building: Introductory Workshops/Interaction Programmes* (United Nations Development Programme, Nepal).

both contain the phrase, "We, the representatives of the people . . . ."[8] James Wilson referred to himself and his fellow framers of the U.S. Constitution as "merely the proxies of our constituents."[9]

Further, the scholarly literature on constitution-making is full of articles and books referring to members of constituent assemblies as representatives. Friedman and Stokes, in one of the few empirical studies about the behavior of framers, assume that they are representatives without discussion.[10] Elkins, Ginsburg, and Blount seem to treat representation as automatic in constitution-making processes involving elected framers.[11] And Wandan persuasively claims that constitution-makers are best understood as ordinary representatives, for this is the only way to accurately understand how constitution-making agency is exercised and created.[12]

Alternatively, one might question P2, the source of the normative weight of RJ. Is there a good reason to encourage or facilitate representation at the constitution-making level, or conceptualize framers as representatives? Doesn't doing so worryingly place emphasis on fulfilling the present need of parties and groups and allowing for the expression of current political disagreement, rather than focusing on establishing long-term rules of the game? This seems especially likely when constitution-making serves as a component of the conflict resolution process, for in these instances representative framers are most likely to "entrench disagreement without providing avenues for change," and "incorporate too many interests of an already constituted future politics in the politics of constitution-making."[13]

On the other hand, several arguments in favor of conceptualizing framers as representatives seem plausible. Perhaps representative framers are desirable because they provide a way of preserving the principle of popular sovereignty in the absence of direct democracy, or because they increase the likelihood of constituent buy-in to the constitution and the government it will structure, or because the best ways to encourage the norms of representative democracy in a future state is to inject them into the constitution-making process itself.[14] Alternatively, perhaps representation

8 *Constitución Argentina* (1853 (rev. 1994)) preamble; *Constituição Da República Federativa Do Brasil* (1988 (rev. 2017)) preamble.

9 James Wilson, *Collected Works of James Wilson* (Liberty Fund 2007) 255.

10 Emmanuel Joseph Sieyès, "What Is the Third Estate?" in Michael Sonenscher (ed.), *Political Writings: Including the Debate between Sieyès and Tom Paine in 1791* (Hackett Publishing Company 2003) 140; Robert S. Friedman and Susan Stokes, "The Role of Constitution-Maker as Representative," (1965) 9 Midwest Journal of Political Science 148–66, 149.

11 Zachary Elkins, Tom Ginsburg, and Justin Blount, "The Citizen as Founder: Public Participation in Constitutional Approval," (2008) 81 Temple Law Review 361–82, 364.

12 Solongo Wandan, "Nothing out of the Ordinary: Constitution Making as Representative Politics," (2015) 22 Constellations 44–58.

13 Jamal Benomar, *Constitution-Making and Peace Building: Lessons Learned from the Constitution-Making Processes of Post-Conflict Countries* (United Nations Development Programme 2003) 4; Andrew Arato, *Civil Society, Constitution, and Legitimacy* (Rowman & Littlefield Publishers) 148.

14 Laurel E. Miller, "Designing Constitution-Making Processes: Lessons from the Past, Questions for the Future," in Laurel E. Miller (ed.), *Framing the State in Times of Transition: Case Studies in Constitution Making* (United States Institute of Peace Press 2010) 627; Vivien Hart, *Democratic Constitution Making*, July 2003) 3–4; Devra C. Moehler, *Distrusting Democrats: Outcomes of Participatory Constitution Making* (University of Michigan Press 2008) 32–33; Arato, *Civil Society, Constitution, and Legitimacy*,

is the best way to ensure that diverse viewpoints and experiences are brought into the drafting process. One could even take this argument in an epistemic direction, claiming that having citizens elect a group of representatives that are especially competent, diverse, and more able to deliberate will produce a better constitution than alternatives.[15] Or, in accordance with the recent constructivist turn in representative theory, perhaps a representative constitution-making process is actually the most democratic way a diverse citizen body can make a constitution.[16]

However, instead of focusing on either P1 or P2, I will focus on P3. Does a ratification process, when present, help facilitate or encourage representation at the constitution-making level? Does the procedure somehow help maintain the relationship of representation between the people and those arguing and bargaining over the constitutional text? If P3 holds up, if ratification plausibly serves as a component of a representative relationship within constitution-making, I can then go back to the other components of RJ. However, if P3 proves to be implausible, which is what I will argue, RJ fails without further discussion.

1.3 Political Representation

Even confining attention to P3, I still need to explain what representation means. This however is complicated. The concept is mired in theoretical and interpretive controversy and disagreement.[17] Brennan and Hamlin summarize the state of the literature succinctly when they write: "Ideas of representation in political theory are notoriously diffuse and recalcitrant."[18] Today, political representation stands for something more than a pragmatic solution to large states or the inevitable application of the division of labor to government, but exactly what this might be remains open to debate.[19] Hannah Pitkin's claim that political representation is a particular form of acting for others is generally accepted, but this description, as even she admitted, is broad and can mean any number of things.[20]

230; Levent Gönenç, *Prospects for Constitutionalism in Post-Communist Countries* (Martinus Nijhoff Publishers 2002) 112; Jon Elster, "Constitution-Making in Eastern Europe: Rebuilding the Boat in the Open Sea," (1993) 71 Public Administration 169–217, 178–79.

[15] Robert E. Goodin and Kai Spiekermann, *An Epistemic Theory of Democracy* (Oxford University Press 2018) 245–54.

[16] Mónica Brito Viera, "Introduction," in Mónica Brito Viera (ed.), *Reclaiming Representation: Contemporary Advances in the Theory of Political Representation* (Routledge 2017); Nadia Urbinati, *Representative Democracy: Principles and Genealogy* (University of Chicago Press 2008).

[17] See Andrew Rehfeld, "What Is Representation? On Being and Becoming a Representative," in Mónica Brito Viera (ed.), *Reclaiming Representation: Contemporary Advances in the Theory of Political Representation* (Routledge 2017) 50–51 for an excellent summary of the difficulties in answering this question.

[18] Geoffrey Brennan and Alex Hamlin, "On Political Representation," (1999) 29 British Journal of Political Science 109–27, 109.

[19] Nadia Urbinati, "Representation as Advocacy," (2000) 28 Political Theory 758–86, 758.

[20] Hannah F. Pitkin, *The Concept of Representation* (University of California Press 1967).

For example, scholars today continue to disagree over the nature of appropriate representative behavior, the importance of fostering inclusion or exclusion, the compatibility of representation with democracy, and how existing theories can accommodate new political forms beyond the nation-state.[21] More recently, a new wave of scholarship has sought to untether representation from strict adherence to formal institutions altogether.[22]

Moreover, this great debate over the meaning and point of political representation is made all the more confusing because scholars have the tendency to "speak about representation in two different ways: substantively and conceptually," without noting the difference. Substantive discussions properly concern the meaning and functioning of representative government, while conceptual discussions concern the shared concepts that "represent" and its derivatives refer to.[23]

Here, I seek to bypass the substantive debates by focusing on the concept of representation and putting forward one general enough to apply to a variety of different theories of political representation. In doing so, I am inspired by Andrew Rehfeld's numerous efforts to clarify and demystify the concept.[24] I hold that representation is an institutionalized relationship in which representatives mediate between constituents and political decision-making.[25] Specifically, it involves:

> An agent *a*, who stands-in for a constituency *b*, for an audience *c*, for the purpose of some activity *d*, during which the agent x's (acts for or on behalf of *b*).

A is the representative, the agent who is acting in place and for another. *B* is the represented, the individual or group that *a* is acting for. This group can be pre-existing or called into being by the institutions of representation themselves.[26] *C* is the entity appealed to for validation, the thing whose acceptance that *a* stands-in for *b* makes it possible for *a* to stand-in for *b*. All three of these can be an individual or a group. *D* is the activity for which and during which the representing is

[21] For an overview of representation literature in contemporary democratic theory, see Nadia Urbinati and Mark Warren, "The Concept of Representation in Contemporary Democratic Theory," (2008) 11 Annual Review of Political Science 387–412; Viera, "Introduction."

[22] Michael Saward, "Authorisation and Authenticity: Representation and the Unelected," (2009) 17 The Journal of Political Philosophy 1–22; Lisa Disch, "Toward a Mobilization Conception of Democratic Representation," (2011) 105 American Political Science Review 100–14.

[23] Rehfeld, "What Is Representation? On Being and Becoming a Representative," 51.

[24] Andrew Rehfeld, "Towards a General Theory of Political Representation," (2006) 68 The Journal of Politics; Andrew Rehfeld, "Representation Rethought: On Trustees, Delegates, and Gyroscopes in the Study of Political Representation and Democracy," (2009) 103 American Political Science Review 214–30; Rehfeld, "What Is Representation? On Being and Becoming a Representative"; Andrew Rehfeld, "The Concepts of Representation," (2011) 103 American Political Science Review 631–41.

[25] This excludes any non-relational uses of representation. See Malcolm E. Jewell, "Legislator-Constituency Relations and the Representative Process," (1983) 8 Legislative Studies Quarterly 303–37, 306.

[26] Iris Marion Young, *Inclusion and Democracy* (Oxford University Press 2000) 130; Melissa S. Williams, *Voice, Trust, and Memory: Marginalized Groups and the Failings of Liberal Representation* (Princeton University Press 1998) 203–5.

supposed to take place. A representative does not represent her constituency for all time in all domains, but rather has a demarcated activity and time to represent, both of which are set by *d*. Finally, *x* is how *a* is supposed to go about standing-in for *b* during *d*; this is set by the substantive theory of representation one endorses.

To illustrate this definition, consider the elected representative of Oregon's fifth congressional district. The winner of the congressional election is *a*, who since 2009 and as of 2021 is Kurt Schrader. *B* is the around 700,000 people who live in the 5,362 square miles that compose the district. *C* are Schrader's fellow members of the U.S. Congress who treat him as one of their own due to the fact that he won a properly run election for the seat. The tasks associated with acting as a congressperson in the U.S. House of Representatives compose *d*, and *x* varies from one substantive theory of representation to the next. *X*-ing might entail doing precisely what Schrader's constituency wants as it relates to his duties as a congressman; doing what a properly informed constituency would have good reason to do; doing what Schrader promised to do or what Schrader believes will lead to his reelection; paying particular attention to the wants and perspectives of those members of Oregon's fifth who have been historically marginalized; or any number of a combination of these things.[27]

In addition to this conceptual definition of representation, I will make two further distinctions. First, I am only concerned with representation within the political realm, for this is our subject matter. What representation means in a courtroom, or an Olympic playing field, or in an artwork, is not my concern. Second, I am interested in what can be called justified representation, the type of representation that we generally think there is reason to advocate for within democratic theory. Manuel Estrada Cabrera and Jorge Ubico, in some sense, both represented the Guatemalan people, in that they claimed to act in their name, were treated as such by international private actors such as United Fruit Company, and profited by trading the nation's resources. Nonetheless, this is not the sort of representation that would justify the implementation of ratification, i.e. it is not a normatively desirable form of representation. What I am concerned with instead is the sort of representation aligned with the basic norm that those affected by collective decisions should have an opportunity to influence them.[28] This means that while there are still numerous acceptable versions of *x*, all must somehow involve making the viewpoints, voices, or preferences, real or hypothetical, of an absent public present in decision-making contexts.

[27] Pitkin, *The Concept of Representation*; Williams, *Voice, Trust, and Memory: Marginalized Groups and the Failings of Liberal Representation*; Suzanne Dovi, *The Good Representative* (Blackwell Publishing 2007); Jane Mansbridge, "Rethinking Representation," (2003) 97 American Political Science Review 515–28.

[28] See Robert Alan Dahl, *On Democracy* (Yale University Press 2000) 37–38; Jürgen Habermas, *Between Facts and Norms: Contributions to a Discourse Theory of Law and Democracy* (The MIT Press 1996) 107; Urbinati and Warren, "The Concept of Representation in Contemporary Democratic Theory," 395.

This conceptual definition of representation applies straightforwardly to constitution-making processes. The framer is *a* and the soon to be governed populace is *b*. The act of drafting a constitution is *d*, *c* consists of other framers and perhaps the international community, and again *x* will vary across reasonable theories of political representation.

2. Ratification's Potential Role

Now that I have a general definition of the concept of representation and understand how it applies to constitution-making, I turn to the central issue of this chapter: does ratification play a role in a constitution-making representative process, and if so, what is this role? Given that ratification is a formal procedure, the role it might play will be a procedural one. That is, ratification's role in a constitution-making representative process would be to serve as one of the formal procedures that structure and help to maintain the relationship of representation. Luckily, "what has been in contention since the establishment of representative government concerns primarily the nature of the nature of the activity of representing, not the procedures . . . that induce political representation."[29] These procedures, which are historically stable and relatively uncontroversial, usually include a selection device, a means of communication, and an accountability mechanism.[30]

Selection devices—such as an election, lottery, or appointment based on expertise or mirror representation—allow principals to choose agents, empower them to serve as representatives, and at times specify their roles.[31] Means of communication refer to the formal and informal avenues through which constituents and their representatives exchange information. They range from petitions, protests, and town halls, to meetings, speeches, debates, interviews, and, increasingly, interaction on social media. Accountability mechanisms are the procedures through which representatives are held to account through sanction or reward. Elections and recall votes are the most common accountability mechanisms in standard instances of representation in electoral democracies, with less common mechanisms including civic review boards, implementation studies, and official hearings.[32]

[29] Bernard Manin, Adam Przeworski, and Susan Stokes, "Introduction," in Adam Przeworski, Bernard Manin, and Susan C. Stokes (eds.), *Democracy, Accountability, and Representation* (Cambridge University Press 1999) 3.

[30] Pitkin, *The Concept of Representation*, chapters 2, 3.

[31] See Terry Macdonald, *Global Stakeholder Democracy: Power and Representation Beyond Liberal States* (Oxford University Press 2008) 165–68. For more on mirror representation see Mansbridge, "Rethinking Representation"; Rehfeld, "Representation Rethought: On Trustees, Delegates, and Gyroscopes in the Study of Political Representation and Democracy"; Anne Phillips, *The Politics of Presence* (Oxford University Press 1995).

[32] Young, *Inclusion and Democracy*, 132.

As mentioned, if representation takes place during the constitution-making process, then the central task of representative framers (d) is to create a constitution. Ratification, of course, takes place after this undertaking is finished. And, among the central and other more ancillary representative procedures, an accountability mechanism is the only one that takes place after the central task of representation is complete. Thus, if ratification plays a procedural role in inducing representation, it is as an accountability mechanism.[33]

Unsurprising, this is the process that ratification seems most suited for, as approving or disapproving their handiwork seems like an apt way for constituents to reward or punish framers for doing a good or bad job. If the framers are members of a constituent convention or constituent legislature, which usually dissolve upon the adoption of a constitution, it might be the sole formal accountability mechanism available.

Likewise, ratification's *agent review function* in early treaty-making and collective bargaining looks like a type of accountability mechanism. In the former, a sovereign reviews its plenipotentiary's actions, ensures that she acted appropriate and with authority, that she *x*-ed, and signals this by signing or rejecting the treaty. In the latter, union members review the work of their union representatives by accepting or rejecting a new contract.

Moreover, constitutional ratification is conceptualized as an accountability mechanism in some of the few existing discussions of the procedure. For instance, Elster notes that "it is certainly desirable that self-created constituent legislatures should be held accountable in some way, either by reelection or by downstream ratification of the constitution."[34] Similarly, as noted above, Hart includes "electoral review" of the constitution as one procedure in the constitution-making process that can ensure that "the principle of the accountability of decision-makers" is met.[35] Thus, P3 can be restated as following: ratification procedures assist in the constitution-making representative process by serving as accountability mechanisms.

2.1 Basics of Accountability Mechanisms

Examining this reformulated P3 requires that I first explain the nature and purpose of an accountability mechanism. As mentioned, an accountability mechanism is a procedure or set of procedures that gives principals or third parties the ex post

[33] This is not to say that accountability mechanisms solely operate after *d*, but rather that they are the only procedures that can. For instance, the ability of constituent to hold recall elections serves as an accountability mechanism that can operate during rather than after the representative activity.

[34] Jon Elster, *Securities Against Misrule: Juries, Assemblies, Elections* (Cambridge University Press 2013) 345.

[35] Hart, "Constitution Making and the Right to Take Part in a Public Affair," 33.

ability to sanction and reward agents on the basis of their performance, how they *x*-ed, which in turn gives these agents incentives to justify and explain their actions.[36] Of course, not every ex post action that evaluates representative behavior counts as an accountability mechanism. For example, the shouts and threats of violence from the streets of Paris and the galleries of the Estates Generale in 1789 were public evaluative responses, but the ad hoc, uncontrollable, and violent nature of such practices makes them too unpredictable to institute or plan for.[37] Thus, when I refer to accountability mechanisms, particularly from an institutional design perspective, I mean those that are integrated into the representative process, and ad hoc responses to unfavorable actions taken by representatives cannot be so integrated.

Accountability in this context has three interrelated dimensions: an *explanatory dimension* in which a representative explains her actions to her constituents, an *evaluative dimension* in which constituents form a judgment, and a *sanctioning dimension* in which constituents sanction (or reward) their representative in accordance with this judgment.[38] All three of these dimensions are important, and distorted conceptions of accountability arise from overemphasizing or ignoring one of them. For instance, some strains of deliberative democratic theory have ignored sanctioning and overemphasized the explanatory dimension of accountability, focusing on the importance of representatives giving reasons for their decisions and the institutions that foster this occurrence.[39] The resulting conception of accountability is insufficient, for an unelected autocrat immune from sanctioning might explain every detail of her decision-making process yet remain accountable to no one but herself. Or, as Rehfeld illustrates the point, a representative who steals money from constituents unable to sanction is not accountable simply because she explains she needed the money to buy a new car.[40] A proper

[36] The increasing tendency to use "accountability" to stand for a myriad of concepts unrelated to holding an agent to account has diluted the meaning and force of the concept. See Richard Mulgan, "'Accountability': An Ever-Expanding Concept," (2000) 78 Public Administration 555–73. One example of this in the constitution-making literature can be seen in the Commonwealth Human Rights Initiative's constitution-making recommendations, which reduce accountability to a combination of transparency and public education. See Hassen Ebrahim, Kayode Fayemi, and Stephanie Loomis, *Promoting a Culture of Constitutionalism and Democracy in Commonwealth Africa: Recommendations to Commonwealth Heads of Government* (1999) 16.

[37] See Bernard Manin, *The Principles of Representative Democracy* (Cambridge University Press 1997) 168; Susan Maslan, "Resisting Representation: Theater and Democracy in Revolutionary France," (1995) Representations 27–51.

[38] Rehfeld and Maloy describe similar dimensions of accountability but neglect constituent evaluation and representation explanation respectively. See Andrew Rehfeld, *The Concept of Constituency: Political Representation, Democratic Legitimacy, and Institutional Design* (Cambridge University Press 2005) 189; J.S. Maloy, *The Colonial American Origins of Modern Democratic Thought* (Cambridge University Press 2008) 25; Rehfeld, *The Concept of Constituency: Political Representation, Democratic Legitimacy, and Institutional Design*, 189.

[39] Amy Gutmann and Dennis F. Thompson, *Democracy and Disagreement* (Harvard University Press 1996) As Maloy claims, they "depict the face of democratic accountability with a tongue but no teeth." Maloy, *The Colonial American Origins of Modern Democratic Thought*, 182.

[40] Rehfeld, *The Concept of Constituency: Political Representation, Democratic Legitimacy, and Institutional Design*, 189.

accountability mechanism equips the represented (or their agent) with power and the capacity to exercise it, and solely concentrating on the explanatory dimension deprives them of this.

Two additional features of accountability mechanisms need mentioning. First, as Grant and Keohane explain, accountability "implies that some actors have the right to hold other actors to a set of standards, to judge whether they have fulfilled their responsibilities in light of these standards, and to impose sanctions if they determine that these responsibilities haves not been met."[41] In other words, accountability mechanisms, and holding someone accountable more generally, require the existence of some *standard of conduct*. Usually this standard of evaluation is *x*, which might include such variables as the proper aims of *a*, the means through which *a* defines these aims, and the source of judgment *a* is to use when trying to reach them.[42] For instance, in a theory claiming that representatives should use their own personal judgment to maximize the public good as their constituents define it, constituents should base their evaluations of the actions and explanations of their representatives in accordance with how far they believe the representatives adhered or deviated from this standard.[43] As ample research has demonstrated, and as recent theories of representation have emphasized, these standards are not necessarily independent of representatives.[44] Representatives might rely on issue framing to change some of the preferences or beliefs that compose the standard, or representatives' actions might crystallize and make more specific what before were mere vague and nascent interests or preferences in an electorate.[45] For all but the most ardent methodological individualist, this should be unproblematic. A standard of conduct can still constrain an agent even if the agent is able to partially influence the standard.

Note that the nature of this standard, and who is charged with enforcing it, varies between two types of accountability mechanisms. Most of the time, as with

[41] Ruth W. Grant and Robert O. Keohane, "Accountability and Abuses of Power in World Politics," (2005) 99 American Political Science Review 29–43, 29.

[42] This is a modified version of the three distinctions Rehfeld finds in the trustee/delegate debate. Rehfeld, "Representation Rethought: On Trustees, Delegates, and Gyroscopes in the Study of Political Representation and Democracy," 215.

[43] James D. Fearon, "Electoral Accountability and the Control of Politicians: Selecting Good Types Versus Sanctioning Poor Performance," in Adam Przeworski, Bernard Manin, and Susan C. Stokes (eds.), *Democracy, Accountability, and Representation* (Cambridge University Press 1999) 55.

[44] Clarissa Rile Hayward, "Making Interest: On Representation and Democratic Legitimacy," in Ian Shapiro and others (eds.), *Political Representation* (Cambridge University Press 2009); Disch, "Toward a Mobilization Conception of Democratic Representation."

[45] See, for example, some of the literature on framing effects: William A. Gamnson and Andre Modigliani, "Media Discourse and Public Opinion on Nuclear Power: A Constructionist Approach," (1989) 95 American Journal of Sociology 1–37; Paul M. Sniderman and Sean M. Theriault, "The Structure of Political Argument and the Logic of Issue Framing," in Willem E. Saris and Paul M. Sniderman (eds.), *Studies in Public Opinion: Gauging Attitudes, Nonattitudes, Measurement Error and Change* (Princeton University Press 2004); Dennis Chong and James N. Druckman, "A Theory of Framing and Opinion Formation in Competitive Elite Environments," (2007) 57 Journal of Communication 99–118.

elections, those being represented determine the standards of conduct (sometimes with the help or influence of the representatives themselves) and enforce them through the accountability mechanism.[46] I call this, following Ferejohn and Rosenbluth, a *political accountability mechanism*. This is opposed to a *legal accountability mechanism*, characterized by formal standards enforced by a third party outside of the representative relationship and not directly controlled by those being represented.[47] Examples of legal accountability mechanisms include criminal sanctions and most cases of impeachment, all of which involve representatives being sanctioned on the basis of found violations of codified law by third parties such as courts or other representatives.

Second, accountability mechanisms must have *specificity*, they must target particular representatives or particular groups of representatives.[48] Constituents or third-party enforcers use accountability mechanisms to evaluate the actions and behaviors of those acting for them. Such particularity is important, for the presence of multiple representatives in democratic settings is predicated on the existence or constant possibility of pluralism, meaning that the actions needed to represent one constituency might be different than those needed to represent another.[49] Representatives therefore must be evaluated and held accountable separately or in groups. Accountability mechanisms would be unable to hold anyone to account if their subject was the general behavior of all representatives, rather than particular representatives, insofar as this would sever the bond between any particular constituency and their representative or group of representatives, and treat all representatives equally even when their behavior differed.

In summary, accountability mechanisms allow principals or third parties to reward or sanction particular representatives or groups of representatives on the basis of their adherence to formal and informal standards of conduct. This description, however, still leaves unexplored the function of accountability mechanisms. What larger purpose are they supposed to serve? Two central functions exist: accountability mechanisms are a means of controlling representatives and an avenue through which constituents can assert their presence or lack thereof in their agent's actions.

[46] These standards are often the same as the terms upon which a representative was authorized by her constituents. See Mark E. Warren, "Deliberative Democracy and Authority," (1996) 90 The American Political Science Review 46–60, 46.

[47] John Ferejohn and Frances Rosenbluth, "Electoral Representation and the Aristocratic Thesis," in Ian Shapiro and others (eds.), *Political Representation* (Cambridge University Press 2009) 279–80.

[48] This does not exclude accountability mechanisms from applying to more than one person, as they do in systems of party-list proportional representation. In these instances, the particularity of accountability remains, for, except in extreme instances, a party only populates a proportion of the total number of all representatives. Among such systems, open-list proportional representation maximizes accountability. Lukas Rudolph and Thomas Däubler, "Holding Individual Representatives Accountable: The Role of Electoral Systems," (2016) 78 Journal of Politics 746–62.

[49] See Jürgen Habermas, *The Inclusion of the Other: Studies in Political Theory* (The MIT Press 1996) 108.

2.2 Means of Control

Most intuitively, accountability mechanisms are meant to give constituents the ability to influence their representatives to behave in a desired way.[50] The threat of sanctions, or the desire of reward, is thought to deter the powerful from abusing their positions and deviating from representing their constituents in the desired manner. In this way, "though they always operate *ex post*, accountability mechanisms exert effects *ex ante*."[51]

The background assumption of this explanation of accountability mechanisms is that, if left to their own devices, representatives might sometimes shirk their responsibility and fail to *x* (represent their constituents).[52] Thus, constituents dole out sanctions and rewards based on the degree to which their representatives meet the relevant standards of conduct, with the intention of incentivizing their representatives to act in the desired manner.[53]

Accountability mechanisms function as a means of control, but they face real limitations in this task. For example, imagine a simplistic theory of representation in which *x* involves enacting the majority preferences of *b*, one's constituents. A representative might nonetheless fail to represent for several reasons. The preferences of her constituents might change over time without her notice, be partially formed or non-existent on many issues, be contradictory, or simply be expressed ineffectively.[54] Some of her constituents might communicate their preferences more loudly than others, making it harder for her to assess the majority opinion at any given time. Constituents might express contradictory preferences, or preferences for paths of action and outcomes that do not match.[55] And, voter myopia or ignorance might cause a divergence between what actions constituents believe *x*-ing demands and what the representative knows *x*-ing actually entails.[56] These and

[50] Brian F. Crisp and others, "Elections as Instruments for Punishing Bad Representatives and Selecting Good Ones," (2014) 32 Electoral Studies 658–69. Some scholars even claim that accountability mechanisms are only about control. See Maloy, *The Colonial American Origins of Modern Democratic Thought*, 7; Terry Macdonald and Kate Macdonald, "Non-Electoral Accountability in Global Politics: Strengthening Democratic Control within the Global Garment Industry," (2006) 17 The European Journal of International Law 89–119.

[51] Grant and Keohane, "Accountability and Abuses of Power in World Politics," 30.

[52] For discussions of shirking, see James B. Kau and Paul H. Rubin, "Ideology, Voting, and Shirking," (1993) 76 Public Choice 151–72; Joseph P. Kalt and Mark A. Zupan, "The Apparent Ideological Behavior of Legislators: Testing for Principal-Agent Slack in Political Institutions," (1990) 33 Journal of Law and Economics 103–32.

[53] See Manin, *The Principles of Representative Democracy*, 178–79; Bernard Manin, Adam Przeworski, and Susan Stokes, "Elections and Representation," in Bernard Manin, Adam Przeworski, and Susan C. Stokes (eds.), *Democracy, Accountability, and Representation* (Cambridge University Press 1999) 40–43.

[54] Larry M. Bartels and Christopher H. Achen, *Democracy for Realists: Why Elections Do Not Produce Responsive Government* (Princeton University Press 2016).

[55] Susan C. Stokes, "What Do Policy Switches Tell Us About Democracy," in Bernard Manin, Adam Przeworski, and Susan C. Stokes (eds.), *Democracy, Accountability, and Representation* (Cambridge University Press 1999) 126.

[56] Sometimes voter myopia drives politicians to influence rather than respond to public opinion. Jose Maria Maravall, "Accountability and Manipulation," in Bernard Manin, Adam Przeworski, and Susan C. Stokes (eds.), *Democracy, Accountability, and Representation* (Cambridge University Press 1999) 156.

similar problems can lead a representative to fail to *x*, and no amount of extra ex post motivation brought by potential sanctions and rewards can solve the problem.

My senator, for instance, might be driven by an intense desire to please her constituents and get reelected, but if misinformed about what we want, her actions will not be appropriately responsive. Problems such as these plague almost any possible configuration of *x* that depends on beliefs, values, or preferences of constituents that need to be communicated to the representative across conditions of informational asymmetry. They also apply to both political and legal accountability mechanisms. A representative worried about being impeached or fined will find it no easier to assess what her constituents want from her then one driven by a desire for reelection.

In addition, accountability mechanisms are not the sole means of control. Ex ante efforts leading to the selection of the right kind of representative can have similar effects. If voters are able to select a representative who resembles them in a meaningful way—because of a shared background, values, experiences, etc.—then the chosen representative is more likely to *x*, regardless of the presence or absence of an accountability mechanism. Such a representative would "look within . . . to a contextually derived understanding of interests, interpretive schemes ('common sense'), conscience, and principles," and take a course of action likely to meet voter approval.[57] For instance, a person who believes that political decisions should be made on the basis of their religion would choose a political representative that feels the same way, and by choosing such a person end up with a representative likely to behave in a manner they approve.

Thus, while control is certainly a role played by accountability mechanisms, it is an imperfect one. The procedure, as it turns out, is neither necessary nor sufficient for getting representatives to behave a certain way.

2.3 Presence and Reflexivity

A second explanation and function of accountability mechanisms is more central and more complicated: accountability mechanisms serve as the procedural means through which the paradox of representation is transcended by principals gaining non-physical presence in the actions of their partially independent representatives.[58] By the "paradox of representation," I refer to Hannah Pitkin's claim that the

[57] Mansbridge, "Rethinking Representation," 520–21. See also Fearon, "Electoral Accountability and the Control of Politicians: Selecting Good Types Versus Sanctioning Poor Performance," 59; Dovi, *The Good Representative*, 158; Jane Mansbridge, "A 'Selection Model' of Political Representation," (2009) 17 The Journal of Political Philosophy 369–98; Philip Pettit, "Varieties of Public Representation," in Ian Shapiro and others (eds.), *Political Representation* (Cambridge University Press 2009).

[58] David Runciman, "The Paradox of Political Representation," (2007) 15 The Journal of Political Philosophy 93–114, 93–99.

modern conception of representation demands "the making present *in some* sense of something which is nevertheless *not* present literally or in fact."[59]

The basic idea behind this paradox is the following: representation involves one agent acting for another agent (*x*-ing) who is physically absent from the action in question, i.e. the represented is not literally present. However, this description applies to many relationships that are not representative in character. A person I hire to water my plant is not my representative, nor is a friend who picks up my prescriptions when I am sick. Representation is unique because, among other things, the actions taken by my representative implicate me; in some way they are meant to be actions taken by me that I am responsible for. The actions of the plant caretaker and my friend do not have this effect. It is in this way, by implicating the represented and giving her a stake in the action, by granting a kind of artificial yet felt presence, that representation makes the non-present present. As Vieira and Runciman note, "It is my *presence* in the action of someone else—the fact that another person is not merely trying to help me but is acting *for* me—that allows me to call that person my representative."[60]

Examining the mandate/independence debate clarifies the meaning of non-physical presence and how a properly conceptualized understanding of representation makes it possible.[61] The two extremes of this somewhat staged debate are familiar. Mandate theorists claim that representation involves mandated delegates following the explicit instructions of their constituents, while independence theorists claim that it involves independent trustees making decisions using only their own judgment. As Pitkin suggests, both positions derive from misinterpreting the paradox of representation in opposite yet equally flawed ways.

Practical problems aside, the system of representation favored by mandate theorists hardly looks like representation at all. Constituents using imperative mandates deprive their agents of autonomy and thus rule directly themselves. They are the ones taking political action and making decisions, with their delegates merely serving as passive executors of their will.[62] In this set-up, nothing is absent.

[59] Pitkin, *The Concept of Representation*, 9; Hannah F. Pitkin, "Commentary: The Paradox of Representation," in Roland J. Pennock and John W. Chapman (eds.), *Representation* (Atherton 1968) 41 Pitkin shortened her articulation of the paradox in her later article on representation, where she simply states: representation "implies a paradox (being present and yet not present)." Hannah F. Pitkin, "Representation and Democracy: Uneasy Alliance," (2004) 27 Scandinavian Political Studies 335–42, 335.

[60] David Runciman and Monica Brito Vieira, *Representation* (Polity Press 2008) 68.

[61] For a brief discussion of the history of this debate, see Rehfeld, *The Concept of Constituency: Political Representation, Democratic Legitimacy, and Institutional Design*, 217.

[62] For Kelsen and Rousseau, this is exactly what representation must entail. In addition, during the French Revolution, Francois Robert applied this conception of representation to constitution-making, arguing "that the deputies to the national assembly [France, 1790] must have imperative mandates." See Hans Kelsen, *General Theory of Law and State* (Transaction Publishers 2006) 289–92; Francois Robert, "Republicanism Adapted to France," in Marc Allan Goldstein (ed.), *Social and Political Thought of the French Revolution, 1788–1797: An Anthology of Original Texts* (Peter Lang 1997) 214; Jean Jacques Rousseau, *The Government of Poland* (Hackett Publishing Company, Inc. 1985) 36–37.

There is nothing to *represent*, and thus no representation takes place.[63] Thus, a theory of mandated delegates overemphasizes presence to such an extent that representation ceases to be a possibility, for delegates unable to make independent decisions cannot take actions for and be in a relationship with the constituents that control them completely.[64]

Representation as independent trusteeship is deficient for the opposite reason: a lack of constituent presence and an emphasis on absence. Constituents empower trustees to take actions on their behalf using their own judgment, but while this grants a needed flexibility absent from mandated delegates, it also means that representatives can repeatedly deviate from *x* without formal consequence. As Pitkin notes, "[I]f the situation is such that we can no longer see the constituents as present there is no representation, and if the man habitually votes the opposite of their wishes we can no longer see them as present in his voting."[65] In other words, independent trustees can repeatedly take actions contrary to what their constituency wants, which makes it both impossible to conceive of the constituency as present in their actions and intuitively farfetched to describe them as representatives. This problem is exacerbated by the fact that theories of trusteeship are silent when it comes to proper representative behavior, i.e. they contain nothing about what it means to *x* or how it can be evaluated. They lack standards of conduct. This suggests "that there is no such thing as not representing a person as one should" and that representatives always *x* as a result.[66] Besides depriving presence of any real meaning, this further weakens trusteeship as a mode of representation because, as mentioned, whatever the appropriate conception of representation may be, "It implies standards for, or limits on, the conduct of the representative."[67]

As Pitkin notes, "[I]nsofar as the mandate-independence controversy contains a conceptual dispute based on the meaning of representation, both sides are right.... The representative must really act, be independent; yet the represented must be in some sense acting through him."[68] What is needed, to use Manin's term, is "partially independent" representatives, i.e. representatives occupying the middle ground between fully instructed automatons directly following the explicit orders of their constituents, and completely free actors making decisions and taking actions completely unconstrained from the will of those they represent.[69] Only such partially independent representatives are capable of giving non-physical presence to literally absent constituents.

[63] This explains why Weber classifies imperative mandates as characteristic of direct democracy. See Max Weber, *Economy and Society: An Outline of Interpretive Sociology*, vol. 1 (University of California Press 1978) 289; Manin, *The Principles of Representative Democracy*, 163–66.
[64] Pitkin, *The Concept of Representation*, 151.
[65] Ibid., 153.
[66] Ibid., 55.
[67] Ibid., 33.
[68] Ibid., 154.
[69] See Manin, *The Principles of Representative Democracy*, 163–67.

Accountability mechanisms come to the rescue here, serving as at least one means through which partially independent representatives become possible. They allow constituents to transcend the paradox of representation by being both absent and present. Pitkin hints at how this occurs when she writes: "the substance of the activity of representing seems to consist in promoting the interests of the represented, in a context where the latter is conceived as capable of action and judgment, but in such a way that he does not object to what is done in his name."[70]

Put simply, accountability mechanisms give constituents (*b*) the opportunity to publicly declare whether or not they were present in the actions of their representatives (*a*), and to do so through the distribution of rewards or sanctions (sanctioning dimension). This in turn motivates principals to evaluate their agents (evaluative dimension), which compels agents to align with and explain their actions in terms of *x* (explanatory dimension), and both of these effects combine to help foster and ensure a continual relationship between the representative and the represented that avoids explicit instructions yet resists the equation of representative action to constituent will. As Manin claims, "In representative government, the electorate judges *ex post facto* the initiatives taken in a relative autonomous manner by those it has placed in power. Through their retrospective judgment, the people enjoy genuinely sovereign power."[71]

One knows that the represented have presence, that they have a stake in and a partial responsibility for the actions of their representatives, when they reward or refrain from sanctioning their representatives during the moment of accountability. On the other hand, one knows that political representation, in the relational sense, was fractured—for the represented were not present in the actions and behavior of their purported representatives—when constituents voice their objections through sanction.[72] This near absence of representation, the deterioration of presence, is always a possibility, for as mentioned above no institutional set-up or accountability mechanism can guarantee that delegates will behave appropriately.

3. Ratification as Accountability Mechanism

As noted in section 1.1, my strategy is to test RJ by considering the most favorable constitution-making process for the justification. For the drafting process, this

[70] Pitkin, *The Concept of Representation*, 155.

[71] Manin, *The Principles of Representative Democracy*, 183.

[72] Of course, this may be put too strongly, in that even if individuals always reelect their representatives when they see themselves as having presence in their actions, all instances of reelection do not necessarily signal presence; i.e. other factors might lead to reelection. This is probably one of the reasons that Runciman concentrates on the "non-objection criterion," the negative account of what constitutes the activity of representation, such that "representation takes place when there is no objection to what someone does on behalf of someone else." Runciman, "The Paradox of Political Representation," 95.

means looking at those that involve an elected constitution-making body. For the ratification process, this means focusing on a ratification referendum, for this is the ratification type most likely to serve as an accountability mechanism. Like an election or recall vote, it gives constituents a direct formal means to punish or reward their representative. It is certainly possible to hold a representative to account through the actions of a delegate or even another representative. For instance, one can understand the mechanism of impeachment when used for elected presidents as a means for voters to sanction their executive representative through the actions of their legislative representatives. Nonetheless, a direct accountability mechanism is more common and less complex to analyze.

3.1 Looks Like One

Can a ratification referendum serve as an accountability mechanism? It certainly resembles one. As already noted, the procedure is an ex post institutionalized evaluation of the product of the framers' work. It occurs at the correct temporal moment of the constitution-making process, avoids the unpredictability and imprecision of informal mechanisms, and is carried out directly by the people who are to live under the constitution, i.e. the very people that representative framers would purportedly represent.

The education programs and ratification campaigns, detailed in chapter 6, section 5, that precede ratification referendums serve as the explanatory dimension, with framers seeking to explain the choices they made to their constituents. Constituents deciding how to vote in a referendum is the evaluative dimension, and the rejection or acceptance of the constitution is the sanctioning dimension.

Note however that the sanctioning dimension of ratification as an accountability mechanism is a bit unusual, for whether approving or rejecting a constitution counts as a sanction or a reward depends upon the representative framer's stance on the constitution. This is usually easy to surmise, for in most constitution-making processes that involve elected framers, these framers directly vote on the constitution before submission to a ratification procedure. Assuming that these votes are transparent, constituents can use them to learn how to hold their representative framers to account. Thus, if one's representative voted in favor of the constitution, then rewarding her and signaling one's presence involves voting in favor of ratification, while sanctioning and denying presence involves voting against the constitution. However, if she voted against the constitution, then voting against ratification counts as a reward, and voting in favor of ratification counts as a sanction.

Constitution-making, which normally occurs outside of law, is more likely to make use of a political accountability mechanism, in that there are normally no enforceable codified standards nor designated agents of enforcement with which to police their behavior. A partial exception might be instances of constitution-making policed by a transitional constitution, for this document would contain certain legal standards regulating the content of the constitution that framers will eventually produce and how they must go about producing it.[73]

Moreover, on its face, ratification referendums seem poised to serve both central functions of an accountability mechanism. First, ratification referendums seem to give constituents some degree of control over their framers by serving as a downstream constraint to the constitution-making process, for the framers' knowledge that their work must be approved by a final authority and their behavior scrutinized by their constituents should influence the decisions that they make within the drafting process.[74] Can ratification help create the conditions necessary for constituents to have and express their presence in the actions of their representatives? Again, a ratification referendum seems like an apt procedure. A person would signal their presence by voting like their representative did on the constitution and signal their absence by voting the opposite of their representative.

A ratification referendum therefore appears to be a moment of accountability that encourages framers to x without explicit instruction, fosters two-way communication, and ultimately establishes presence and allows for the transcendence of Pitkin's paradox of representation. Note that using ratification for this purpose links accountability to a discrete task of the representative. This would be problematic in most instances of ordinary representation, for representatives are frequently responsible for a variety of decisions and actions, and thus institutionally hitching their accountability to a particular task would mistakenly formalize an evaluative distortion. However, this distortion does not occur for representative framers, for their sole task (as a representative) is to write a new constitution.

3.2 Problem of Double Duty

Despite the above-mentioned strengths, there is a central problem that makes ratification unable to reliably serve as an accountability mechanism. Consider the following two situations. In both, a constitutional convention of elected delegates approved a draft constitution by supermajority vote, which is now being presented for ratification in a national referendum:

[73] The 1993 Interim Constitution for South Africa, for instance, specified numerous constitutional principles that any new constitution had to comply with. Constitution of the Republic of South Africa (1996).

[74] Representative control is one reason given in support of the use of decision-controlling referendums (referendums in which the agenda setter and the initiator of the referendum are different political actors). See Setälä, "On the Problems of Responsibility and Accountability in Referendums," 716; Pier Uleri, "Introduction," in Michael Gallagher and Pier Uleri (eds.), *The Referendum Experience in Europe* (Macmillan Press 1996).

Bad Framer: My delegate successfully pursued an agenda antagonistic to my values and beliefs in the convention. She did not *x*. For instance, she tried and succeeded in creating a constitutional provision that prohibits people of my ethnic background from holding certain political offices. My delegate supports and votes in favor of the draft constitution. I dislike the constitution but prefer it to what I expect to be the result of a ratification rejection.[75]

Good Framer: My delegate pursued an agenda in line with my values and beliefs. Many of her proposals failed, as other delegates outvoted her. However, when voting on the final draft constitution, she voted in favor of it. She knew that it was an imperfect document but calculated that it was the best possible. I believe that she *x*-ed. I do not like the resultant constitution and prefer what I anticipate being the result of a failed ratification. I do not begrudge my delegate for her vote, I understand and approve of her motivations, I just arrived at a different conclusion.

In both of these examples, there is a critical asymmetry in my evaluation of the "representative" and the constitution. In Bad Framer, I want to vote in favor of the constitution because I prefer it to the status quo or predicted reversion point.[76] However, if ratification is serving as an accountability mechanism, I want to reject the constitution, for I do not see myself present in the actions of my representative. The opposite problem emerges in Good Framer. I evaluate the constitution negatively. It is not a document I want structuring the future of my polity and I want to vote against it. At the same time, for accountability purposes, I want to approve the constitution. My representative *x*-ed, she followed my standards of conduct and represented me, giving me real presence in a decision-making context in which I was literally absent.

These examples show a deficiency in using ratification as an accountability mechanism. Doing so makes the procedure responsible for two separate evaluations and decisions (*double duty*), and these can diverge from one another (*evaluative divergence*). A ratifier deciding how to vote in a ratification referendum accountability mechanism is actually answering two questions with only one opportunity to respond: were you present in/ do you support the actions of your representative? And do you want the draft constitution to go into effect? When a ratifier's answers to these two questions differ, when her evaluations diverge, she cannot answer one "correctly" without answering the other "incorrectly." She cannot accurately assert

[75] Something similar sometimes occurs during union contract votes, when members accept a constitution that falls short of their wishes in order to avoid the costs of being laid off or being called to strike. Ross Stagner and Hjalmar Rosen, *Psychology of Union-Management Relations* (Wadsworth Publishers, Inc. 1965).

[76] By predicted reversion point I mean the anticipated results of constitutional rejection, which may differ from the current status quo. See Kenneth A. Shepsle, "The Positive Theory of Legislative Institutions: An Enrichment of Social Choice and Spatial Models," (1986) 50 Public Choice 135–78, 163n122.

her presence or lack thereof without voting against her wants when it comes to the draft constitution. That is, if evaluative divergence occurs, the sanctioning dimension of accountability drops out for a voter who wishes to make a choice on the constitution that aligns with their evaluation of the document. This problem of double duty is possible because there is no necessary correlation between a voter's evaluation of a draft constitution and her evaluation of her constitutional representative yet treating ratification as an accountability mechanism makes it responsible for both.

Voters in a ratification process meant to serve as both an accountability mechanism and a means to approve or reject a constitution have three basic strategies they can use to deal with double duty. First, a voter might give primacy to the constitutional choice, meaning they base their vote solely on whether they prefer the proposed constitution to the expected results of rejection. However, this means that if their evaluation of the constitution and their representative diverges, they cannot sanction or reward their representative and thus the accountability mechanism does not function. Second, a voter might do the reverse and give primacy to representative accountability, therefore perversely making a decision about the future organization of her polity for reasons unrelated to constitutional content. In this instance, evaluative divergence would cause the voter to reject a constitution she likes or accept a constitution she dislikes.

Third, a voter might somehow make her decision on the basis of both the behavior of her representative and the proposed constitution, perhaps taking preference or evaluative intensity into account. Nonetheless, the voter would eventually make a decision and, if her evaluations diverged, she would either fail to hold her representative accountable or inaccurately express her opinion on the proposed constitution, regardless of how she weighted the two. None of these outcomes are acceptable; ratification cannot function as a reliable accountability mechanism, for doing so collapses two different critical decisions into one that becomes inadequate whenever they conflict.

Evaluative divergence does not stem from there being other tasks that need to be taken into consideration when evaluating a framer, for there are none, but rather from several sources. The examples above illustrate the two most likely. First, Bad Framer shows how a very undesirable status quo or reversion point can lead to evaluative divergence by making the actions of a representative nearly irrelevant for the purposes of evaluating the constitution. It is akin to asking a starving person to evaluate whether someone selected a good meal for them by choosing to accept or reject the offered food. In the case of Bad Framer my delegate did not *x*, and the constitution she helped create is not one that I like. Nonetheless, I view the result of a rejected constitution so negatively that I am compelled to endorse practically any document presented to me. Thus, a divergence arises due to the double duty of the ratification referendum as accountability mechanism. One can imagine situations like these arising when a ratification referendum ends a constitution-making process of a polity trying to transition out of a civil war or away from dictatorial or autocratic rule.

Second, Good Framer shows evaluative divergence arising from the simple fact that constitution-making is usually a collective decision-making process, and therefore the end result is not consistently determined by the behavior of any single or group of participants. Since the actions of all participants can affect a collective decision-making outcome, my delegate's efforts and goals might not fully determine the constitutional text. The intervention of other framers, in other words, can cause a deviation between how my representative behaves and the contents of the proposed constitution.

To restate, the central problem of double duty is that, when evaluative divergence occurs, voters cannot accurately assert or deny their presence in their representative's actions without voting against their wants when it comes to the draft constitution. Holding one's representative up to standards, judging her, and sanctioning or rewarding her accordingly, is made difficult or impossible by the need to take into account a separate question. Thus, ratification cannot serve as a mechanism for maintaining the partially independent nature of representatives that makes it possible for them to transcend the paradox of representation and give real presence to absent constituents. Further, double duty also likely decreases the already limited ability of the accountability mechanism to give constituents power and control over their representatives, for representatives will know that they will be judged not simply on their ability to *x*, but also based on the desirability of a group output as it compares to the anticipated reversion point. This means that P3 is false, and RJ cannot justify ratification.

4. Objections

To further clarify the problem of double duty to RJ, I now focus on three potential objections to its relevance. The first claims that voters in representative government frequently consider outcomes when voting in elections, and that therefore the problem of double duty is either overblown or requires also claiming that classic instances of accountability are equally deficient. The second objection claims that certain constitution-making processes avoid the problem of double duty, and that therefore RJ is successful in at least some instances. The third objection looks to ratification's role as an accountability mechanism in non-constitutional contexts, and simply asks how the procedure brings accountability in instances of early modern treaty-making and collective bargaining, but not in the creation of new constitutions.

4.1 Outcomes Are Often Used

An objector might make the following argument: in representative governments, voters frequently rely on their evaluations of the outcomes of the legislative process—bills and policies—when holding their individual representative accountable.[77] Sometimes voters use outcomes as one of many inputs, other times they serve as the sole evaluative criteria. Outcomes might be used in this manner when more detailed information about the specific behavior of individual representatives is unavailable, when voters are unwilling or unable to accept the costs associated with a closer evaluation, or when voters make evaluative mistakes out of ignorance, passion, manipulation, and the like. Regardless of the cause, voters frequently use collective decision-making outcomes to evaluate individual representatives, and according to the above argument this means that ordinary accountability mechanisms are deficient, and that representation is not present or not possible in most representative governments. If we want to resist this conclusion, then the above argument against ratification's function as an accountability mechanism must be rejected.

This objection mistakenly assumes that the crux of my argument is the assertion that using one's evaluation of a draft constitution is an imprecise or distortive means of judging the behavior of a representative. Perhaps it might be, but this is beside the point. Rather, my central claim is that ratification cannot serve as an accountability mechanism because this makes one action (voting yes or no to a proposed constitution) responsible for two tasks (holding framers accountable and accepting or rejecting a constitution) that might demand different responses because of evaluative divergence. In these instances, when representative behavior and the draft constitution demand opposite responses, it becomes impossible for a constituent to meet both through the one action available to her. If she holds her representatives accountable, she destroys ratification's function as a means to accept or reject a constitution; if she votes on the constitution itself, then ratification ceases to be an accountability mechanism.

In normal electoral accountability mechanisms, constituents might use outcomes to help them decide whether to keep their representative in office (reward) or replace her with someone else (sanction), and one might reasonably argue that this leads to poor or inaccurate evaluations of a representative's *x*-ing for some of the same reasons that double duty is a problem, i.e. because a representative's overall

[77] For instance, the foundational texts in the empirical literature on retrospective voting claim that voters use the state of the economy, an outcome, to evaluate political incumbents. See Anthony Downs, *An Economic Theory of Democracy* (Harper and Row 1957); Morris P. Fiorina, *Retrospective Voting in American National Elections* (Yale University Press 1980); V.O. Key, *The Responsible Electorate* (Vintage 1966). Admittedly, recent studies question the generalizability of this model by showing its inapplicability to local rather than state and national elections. See Christopher R. Berry and William G. Howell, "Accountability and Local Elections: Rethinking Retrospective Voting," (2007) 69 The Journal Of Politics 844–58.

performance as a representative may differ from the outcomes of the collective decision-making processes that they take part in. Nonetheless, using outcomes to evaluate does not make the election vote responsible for choosing legislation in addition to evaluating representatives. If a representative acts perfectly yet the legislative outcomes are undesirable, this does not make it impossible for voters to fulfill their responsibilities when voting. They are not expected to make a decision about the outcomes of previous legislative processes when they choose a person to be their representative. In other words, regardless of the degree to which outcomes inform a voter's decision, they do not vote on the outcomes directly and their vote will not directly affect the fate of previous legislative decisions.[78] Thus the problem of double duty does not apply to ordinary accountability mechanisms.

4.2 Make It Secret

A second objection claims that one can design a constitution-making process to ensure that the problem of double duty does not emerge. Such a process would be one in which the only means of evaluating the behavior of a representative is the draft constitution subject to ratification. For instance, imagine a constitution-making process involving a constitutional convention that operated in complete secrecy, did not publicize intra-convention voting, and kept its members sequestered until after a ratification referendum in order to prevent them from expressing their opinions on the draft.

Those asked to ratify a constitution stemming from this secret process would never face the problem of double duty or confront evaluative divergence, for the draft constitution would be the sole basis for their determination of whether they were present in the actions of their representative. They would be unable to differentiate between the desirability of the constitution and the degree to which they felt their representative *x*-ed and therefore they would never wish to approve a constitution and sanction a representative, or vice versa. Thus, such an objection argues, P3 is unproblematic, and assuming P1 and P2 are also true, RJ is persuasive in some cases. Ratification is therefore justified by its role in representation provided that the constitution-making process is of the right type.

This is a clever objection, but a faulty one. First, note that it is of extremely limited reach. It only salvages RJ by relegating it to constitution-making processes that have never existed, may be impossible to orchestrate, and are likely objectionable for many reasons unrelated to ratification.

Second, the secret constitution-making process does not fully eliminate the possibility of evaluative divergence. The objector believes that it does because of the

[78] Similarly, retrospective voters solely interested in their economic welfare do not vote directly on the economy, but simply use it to make their decision.

assumption that a voter cannot dislike a constitution yet also want to approve it. This, as seen in Bad Framer, is a false assumption. A predicted reversion point of a rejected constitution might be so bad that an otherwise unwanted constitution becomes preferable. Thus, a voter in a referendum following a secret constitution-making process might wish to sanction their representative because they think the constitution is awful, but nonetheless also wish to approve the constitution because they view it as better than the predicted alternative. The problem of double duty emerges even here because such a voter cannot do both with the one decision available to her in ratification.

Third, this objection fails because it eliminates the *specificity* of the ratification referendum, thereby preventing it from serving as an accountability mechanism. A citizen cannot hold her representative to account because she does not know and cannot know how her representative behaved. Therefore, the accountability mechanism would sanction or reward all representatives similarly, regardless of their behavior. As mentioned in section 2.1, this is to sever the link between a representative and her principals, making accountability impossible. Thus, in seeking to avoid the problem of double duty, the second objection proposes a secret constitution-making process that makes a ratification referendum unable to hold anyone to account. Since in this instance ratification cannot serve as an accountability mechanism, P3 is negated, and RJ remains incomplete and unpersuasive.

4.3 Double Duty in Other Domains

As mentioned, ratification functions as an accountability mechanism of sorts in early modern treaty-making and in collective bargaining practices. A third objection claims that either ratification cannot do so in these constitutional domains, or that the problem of double duty is not so severe after all. If the possibility of evaluative divergence makes ratification unreliable as an accountability mechanism in constitution-making, it should do the same when it comes to approving a treaty drafted by a plenipotentiary or a contract negotiated by a union representative.

There are two weaknesses to this objection. First, the problem of double duty looks like less of an issue for these other versions of ratification-as-accountability mechanism because of features both have that are absent from the constitution-making context. This is especially true for early modern treaty-making for, as discussed in chapter 2, section 2.1, the practiced coexisted with a norm, discussed by Wicquefort and Pufendorf, that sovereigns would ratify treaties unless their representatives violated their publicly given authority and instructions. To use this chapter's terminology, the norm dictated that the only acceptable reason for ratification refusal was the presence of an unauthorized agent or an agent that failed to *x*. Wicquefort illustrates this norm through a series of examples of sovereigns following through on agreed upon details of treaties before they were ratified by their counterparts because of their confidence in the authority and behavior of the treaty negotiators and the automatic nature of ratification. For instance, he discusses the making of 1678 treaty between the King of France and Navarre and the United Provinces of the Netherlands, during which the King decided to honor the treaty and cease hostilities before ratification by the United Provinces.[79]

This norm essentially neutralizes the problem of double duty by forbidding the use of ratification to evaluate the treaty as a whole. Evaluative divergence becomes a non-issue, because the sovereign ratifier was not supposed to evaluate anything other than the behavior of his plenipotentiary. As should be clear, no such norm currently exists in the constitution-making context. The average participant in a ratification procedure, especially a ratification referendum, is unlikely to see themselves as duty bound to sign off on a draft constitution unless their representatives misbehaved.

When it comes to ratification in collective bargaining, there are also reasons to believe that evaluative divergence is less frequent. For instance, the collective bargaining process does not usually stop when membership rejects a labor contract. In most instances, rejection means that negotiators for both sides go back to the bargaining table and try again. This has the effect of making it less likely that situations like Bad Framer arise, where an extremely unwanted status quo or reversion point drives evaluative divergence. In addition, collective bargaining involves two parties in opposition, employers and employees. The individuals representing each side work together as a team united against their common opponent. This lessens though does not eliminate the possibility of a situation like Good Framer, where voters feel differently about the constitution and their representative's behavior.

Second, even if I accept the substance of the objection, it does not challenge my critique of ratification as an accountability mechanism. Double duty is a problem for our purposes because RJ seeks to justify ratification on the basis of it serving as a unique means of bringing accountability to constitution-makers. The fact that it cannot perform as an accountability mechanism consistently or predictably, because of evaluative divergence and the problem of double duty, is therefore quite damaging to RJ. In contrast, no one is trying to justify the use of ratification in early modern treaty-making or collective bargaining based on its role in providing accountability to these procedures. The assertion made in chapter 2 is simply that it (sometimes) might have functioned or been understood as a way of reviewing agents in these domains. If it turned out that the problem of double duty haunted ratification in collective bargaining, and someone was trying to justify the implementation of the procedure in this context by its role in providing accountability, then this justification would face similar obstacles.

[79] Abraham de Wicquefort, *The Embassador and His Functions* (Bernard Lintott 1716) 405.

5. Conclusion

Whether taken to be an institutional innovation designed to guarantee popular sovereignty, an instrumental substitute for stronger forms of democracy inconsonant with modern times, a means of securing a human right to participation demanded by international law, or something else entirely, representation occupies a central and celebrated place within democratic theory and is nearly unanimously treated as something worth institutionalizing in contemporary states.[80] A possible connection between representation and ratification, which is suggested by the frequent conceptualization of framer as representatives and the long-standing association of ratification with representation, seems to then be an attractive source of justification for the latter. In this chapter I followed this intuition by building out and interrogating RJ, a justification for ratification based upon its relationship with political representation. RJ claims that ratification is justified because framers (P1) can and (P2) should be representatives and (P3) ratification plays a crucial role in enabling this to happen.

Ratification is an ex post procedure that occurs after the writing of the constitution, the would-be task of representative framers. This means that ratification's role in a constitutional representative process must be similarly ex post. Out of the numerous mechanisms and procedures that might contribute to institutionalizing political representation, an accountability mechanism is the only one that meets this criterion. This transforms P3 into: ratification plays an essential role in constitution-making by serving as an accountability mechanism.

Upon analysis, ratification is not up for this role. Despite its initial appearance as a viable means to secure representative control and make presence a possibility, the two primary roles of an accountability mechanism, ratification cannot reliably accomplish either. If ratification serves as an accountability mechanism, a voter has one vote to signal her acceptance or rejection of a proposed constitution, and reward or sanction her representative framer. However, these two tasks might demand different actions, particularly because constitutions usually stem from collective decision-making processes, such that the behavior of a single representative may not correlate with the final constitution. A voter might want to accept the constitution yet sanction her representative or reject a constitution yet reward her

[80] For examples of the first two arguments, see Urbinati, *Representative Democracy: Principles and Genealogy*; Benjamin Barber, *Strong Democracy: Participatory Politics for New Age* (University of California Press 1984). Brennan and Hamlin usefully categorize arguments such as Urbinati and Barber's as first-best arguments and second-best arguments respectively; first-best arguments see representation as a politically superior alternative to the imperfections of direct democracy, and second-best arguments see representation as a practicable means of achieving an approximation of the unobtainable ideal of direct democracy. "On Political Representation," 111. For how representation might be demanded by international law, see Thomas M. Franck and Arun K. Thiruvengadam, "Norms of International Law Relating to the Constitution-Making Process," in Laurel E. Miller (ed.), *Framing the State in Times of Transition: Case Studies in Constitution Making* (United States Institute of Peace Press) 6–7.

representative. Such a divergence is always possible, and when it occurs ratification must fail at one of its given tasks. Thus, *RJ fails*, for one cannot justify ratification on the basis of it playing a role in the representative process that it is ill-suited to perform.

I will end this chapter with one final reflection, suggested by my conclusions, though its implications are beyond the scope of this book. The likeliest candidate for a constitution-making accountability mechanism, ratification, is wanting. If one believes that representation requires, or at least significantly benefits from an accountability mechanism, this presents a problem. What can or does provide accountability for constitution-making representatives? At least in standard constitution-making processes, there is no other plausible formal candidate, i.e. no ex post procedure exists through which those represented by framers can hold them to account. The fact that "there is no chance for the public to punish representatives who fail to fulfill their mandate" does not expose a "weakness of accountability" as one scholar suggests, but rather points to its complete absence.[81] Part of this, of course, stems from the one-off nature of the constitution-making process. Whether it ends in a new constitution, or results in a reversion to the status quo, the constitution-making process ends shortly after the representative activity concludes.[82] It is therefore not surprising that the constitution-making process itself does not contain further procedures of accountability. What are the implications of this? Without accountability, are constitution-makers representatives at all? How can the paradox of representation be surmounted without a moment in which those represented can assert their presence or absence?

These questions suggest three lines of inquiry for future work. The first is to investigate whether informal mechanisms provide accountability in constitution-making. For instance, many framers run for office or reelection following the constitution-making process. These future elections might serve as a type of accountability mechanism for their role as framers. Alternatively, perhaps general reputational effects from taking part in an often-public high stakes decision-making process provide a form of accountability as well. One worry about this solution, however, is that both of these are more likely to assist with the control side of accountability rather than the assertion of presence.

Second, perhaps a new constitution-making procedure is needed to create accountability for framers. Like all accountability mechanisms, it would take place ex post to the representative action and provide principals with some means of sanctioning and rewarding their delegates. After the drafting of a constitution by elected framers, each constituency might hold a referendum with the specific purpose of punishing or rewarding their framer. Or, an independent commission

[81] Hart, "Constitution Making and the Right to Take Part in a Public Affair," 34.

[82] The exception to this would be a self-created constituent legislature that stays in power after a failed constitution-making process.

might convene to review the behavior and actions of each framer and levy the appropriate rewards or punishments. This latter possibility would be similar to the Athenian *euthynai*, which the Greeks used to hold retiring magistrates to account.[83] In both of these mechanisms, the awards and punishments could be anything from monetary rewards or fines to the commission or denial of political positions.

Such fanciful accountability mechanisms are theoretically possible, though the constitution-making context is bound to create complications not found in ordinary settings. For instance, it is unclear what evaluative criteria would be appropriate for judging the actions of framers, and the infrequency of constitution-making would prevent principals or members of a special commission from answering this question from experience. In addition, the legal authority of an accountability mechanism for framers is ambiguous, for on the one hand the implementation of a new constitution overrides previous institutional prescriptions, and on the other hand is it unlikely that framers would include a mechanism that might be used to punish them into the constitution that they write.

Third, as discussed in the first section, perhaps one should avoid seeing the absence of an accountability mechanism as problematic, and instead question P2, the idea that those who draft constitutions should be political representatives. This is a common assumption, but what are the reasons for holding it? That is, why should one conceptualize framers, or want them to be, political representatives? The intuitive response is to make recourse to the vast array of arguments in favor of representative government and the institution of representation more generally, or to ignore the issue and simply assume representation occurs when framers are elected, because elections and representation go hand in hand in contemporary representative democracies.[84] However, either response is theoretically sloppy, for it involves equating the writing of a constitution with other instances of political decision-making that might benefit from representation, when constitution-making is clearly a unique enterprise of its own.

Better arguments do exist. For example, perhaps the constitutional process should mirror the desired political system to be created, as a way of jumpstarting the necessary norms needed for political stability. As Arato explains, "most democratic theories do not and cannot recognize any source of legitimacy other than direct or electoral participation by full members of the political community. If it

[83] Jon Elster, "Accountability in Athenian Politics," in Adam Przeworski, Bernard Manin, and Susan C. Stokes (eds.), *Democracy, Accountability, and Representation* (Cambridge University Press) 268; Mogens Herman Hansen, *The Athenian Democracy in the Age of Demosthenes: Structure, Principle, and Ideology* (Oxford University Press) 222; Deirdre Dionysia Von Dornum, "The Straight and the Crooked: Legal Accountability in Ancient Greece," (1997) 97 Columbia Law Review 1483–1518.

[84] Elkins, Ginsburg, and Blount give an example of the latter tendency, when they reason as follows amidst a discussion of public participation in constitutional design: "... in either case the main deliberative body is selected by the public. We can thus presume some level of representation in the decisions that the deliberative body undertakes." Zachary Elkins, Tom Ginsburg, and Justin Blount, "The Citizen as Founder: Public Participation in Constitutional Approval," (2008) 81 Temple Law Review 361–82, 364 See also Yash Ghai, *The Role of Constituent Assemblies in Constitution Making*) 23.

is important that the rules of the game provide for democratic participation, it is equally or even more important that the rules of the game emerge in a democratic manner."[85] In other words, if one desires to create a democratic system of government, the corresponding democratic conception of moral legitimacy needs to be fostered as early as possible, and insofar as representation is seen as an essential means of legitimating democratic political decisions in the absence of direct citizen participation, it has to be present in constitution-making as well. Therefore, as Gönenç notes, since "the indispensable tenet of contemporary democratic politics has been the participation of the people in making collective choices through their representatives," "constitutional choices are no exceptions. They are generally made by the representatives of the people in modern democratic political systems."[86]

One can think of reasons to avoid understanding framers as representatives as well. For instance, doing so might have negative effects, for it can deemphasize the long-term role of constitutions in establishing the rules of the game for the political process in a country—by creating the basic institutions and procedures for political action, enumerating the fundamental rights of citizens, and setting out the procedures for its own revisions—and instead place focus on the importance of giving current societal interests their say, fulfilling the already present needs of parties and groups, and allowing for the expression of political disagreement. This is especially prevalent, and dangerous, when constitution-making occurs during or after conflict resolution processes, for in these instances representative framers are most likely to "entrench disagreement without providing avenues for change," and "incorporate too many interests of an already constituted future politics in the politics of constitution-making."[87]

[85] Arato, *Civil Society, Constitution, and Legitimacy*, 230. Similarly, Hart writes that: "A democratic constitution is no longer simply one that establishes democratic governance. It is also a constitution that is made in a democratic process." Hart, *Democratic Constitution Making*, 3–4.

[86] Gönenç, *Prospects for Constitutionalism in Post-Communist Countries*, 112. See also Jon Elster's brief discussion of process legitimacy in Elster, "Constitution-Making in Eastern Europe: Rebuilding the Boat in the Open Sea," 178–79.

[87] Benomar, *Constitution-Making and Peace Building: Lessons Learned from the Constitution-Making Processes of Post-Conflict Countries*, 4; Arato, *Civil Society, Constitution, and Legitimacy*, 148.

8
Legitimacy Types and Procedures

Perhaps the most likely source of justification for ratification is the concept of legitimacy. The idea here is a simple one. The desired outcome of a constitution-making process is not merely a written document, but rather one that is legitimate. Ratification, such an argument goes, makes this outcome more likely. As Elster remarks, ratification "is intended to confer downstream legitimacy on the constitution."[1]

The intuition that legitimacy is a promising source of justification is supported by several reasons. First is the simple observation that, though few seem to think or write about the reasons underlying ratification, those that do usually point to the procedure's association with legitimacy. This comes in two forms. Some authors link ratification to legitimacy directly. Miller, for instance, claims that "[ratification] referendums can be valuable in constitution making, conferring a degree of legitimacy on the process and its outcome." Muna Ndulo, a consultant to constitution-making processes in Kenya, Zimbabwe, Somalia, and Sudan, suggests that in order to give a constitution "maximum legitimacy," a ratification referendum should be "entrenched in African constitutional practice as a mechanism for obtaining the mandate of the people on constitutional matters." Somewhat similarly, Selassie explains that the use of a special constituent assembly to ratify the Eritrean Constitution was necessary because of "the issue of legitimacy," the central assumption of which is "that the government is established by and on behalf of the people."[2] Tushnet asserts that "a ratification is desirable, if not required, in part to ensure that the new constitution has domestic legitimacy."[3] Mendez and Wheatley,

[1] Jon Elster, *Ulysses Unbound* (Cambridge University Press 2000) 113.

[2] Laurel E. Miller, "Designing Constitution-Making Processes: Lessons from the Past, Questions for the Future," in Laurel E. Miller (ed.), *Framing the State in Times of Transition: Case Studies in Constitution Making* (United States Institute of Peace Press 2010) 623; Muna Ndulo, "Zimbabwe's Unfulfilled Struggle for a Legitimate Constitutional Order," in Laurel E. Miller (ed.), *Framing the State in Times of Transition: Case Studies in Constitution Making* (United States Institute of Peace Press 2010) 193; Muna Ndulo, "Constitution-Making in Africa: Assessing Both the Process and Content," (2001) 21 Public Administration and Development 101–17; Bereket Habte Selassie, "Constitution Making in Eritrea: A Process-Driven Approach," in Laurel E. Miller (ed.), *Framing the State in Times of Transition: Case Studies in Constitution Making* (United States Institute of Peace Press 2010) 74

[3] Mark Tushnet, "Constitution-Making: An Introduction," (2012) 91 Texas Law Review 1983–2013, 1999.

Constitutional Ratification without Reason. Jeffrey A. Lenowitz, Oxford University Press. © Jeffrey A. Lenowitz 2022.
DOI: 10.1093/oso/9780198852346.003.0008

in their 2013 empirical study of constitution-making, refer to the ratification procedure simply as "the mode of legitimation."[4]

On the other hand, some authors indirectly connect ratification to legitimacy by grouping ratification with other participatory procedures such as constituent assembly elections and public consultations and promoting all of them because "broad public participation contributes to the constitution's legitimacy."[5] Examples of this participation equals legitimacy logic abound.[6] A UN Guidance Note from the Secretary-General advises constitution-makers to focus on "the impact of inclusivity and meaningful participation on the legitimacy of new constitutions." In its 2011 briefing paper for the Constituent Assembly of Tunisia (later issued again in 2012 for Egypt), Democracy Reporting International recommends a participatory constitution-making process because it forms "the basis for the normative legitimacy of the constitution."[7] A Max Planck manual on constitution-building prepared for Somali stakeholders emphasizes that "the legitimacy of a constitutional process rests on the extent to which the process was participatory, open, democratic, inclusive, transparent, accommodating different interests and respecting the will of the majority as well as minorities."[8] Vivien Hart, in an essay on democratic constitution-making, concludes that "the legitimacy of constitutional agreements at the end of the twentieth century depends upon openness in two senses: a process both open-ended and open to participation."[9] And, finally, Medhanie explains that participatory constitution-making secures the consent of elites, stakeholders, and society as a whole, and that this "consent is actually the source of the constitution's legitimacy."[10]

Medhanie's musings point to a second reason to see legitimacy as a source for ratification's justification: the long tradition of consent-based accounts of

[4] Jonathan Wheatley and Fernando Mendez, "The Constitution-Making Process: An Analytical Framework," in Jonathan Wheatley and Fernando Mendez (eds.), *Patterns of Constitutional Design: The Role of Citizens and Elites in Constitution-Making* (Routledge 2016) 17.

[5] Jamal Benomar, *Constitution-Making and Peace Building: Lessons Learned from the Constitution-Making Processes of Post-Conflict Countries*, 2003) 11. For two quantitative studies that include the presence of a ratification referendum as an indicator of participation and inclusiveness, see John M. Carey, "Does It Matter How a Constitution Is Created?" (Exporting Democracy: What Democracies Can and Cannot Do); Zachary Elkins, Tom Ginsburg, and Justin Blount, "The Citizen as Founder: Public Participation in Constitutional Approval," (2008) 81 Temple Law Review 361–82.

[6] For a discussion of some of the potential shortcomings to participatory constitution-making, see Michael Lusztig, "Constitutional Paralysis: Why Canadian Initiatives Are Doomed to Fail," (1994) 27 Canadian Journal of Political Science 747–71, 5.

[7] UNSG, *Guidance Note of the Secretary-General: United Nations Assistance to Constitution-Making Processes*, 2009) 4; Philipp Dann and others, *Lessons Learned from Constitution-Making: Processes with Broad Based Public Participation* (Democracy Reporting International 2011) 4.

[8] Katharina Diehl and others, *Structures and Principles of a Constitution* (Max Planck Manuals on Constitution Building, 2009) 7.

[9] Vivien Hart, *Democratic Constitution Making*, Special Report 107 (United States Institute of Peace 2003) 1. See also Susanna D. Wing, *Constructing Democracy in Transitioning Societies of Africa: Constitutionalism and Deliberation in Mali* (Palgrave Macmillan 2008).

[10] Tesfatsion Medhanie, *Constitution-Making, Legitimacy and Regional Integration: An Approach to Eritrea's Predicament and Relations with Ethiopia* (DIIPER Research Series, 2008) 7.

political authority, which, as we already saw, informed the originators of ratification. Starting in at least the late sixteenth and early seventeenth centuries, thinkers such as Buchanan, Hooker, Althusius, and Hobbes, soon to be followed by Pufendorf, Lock, and later Rousseau, developed conceptions of legitimate government predicated on an original or ongoing act of individual or collective consent. These accounts continue to influence political thinking to this day, and though they differ in regards to their details and implications for political obligation, state form, revolution, and the like, all seem to provide some sort of explanation for why constitutions must be ratified. Simply put, a constitution, and the government and state it structures, must be consented to by its citizens in order to obtain coercive authority over its populace. What better procedure for consenting to a constitution than to ratify it?

Third, a growing body of empirical work claims to demonstrate the legitimating effects of direct participation in creating systems of rules. For instance, in several studies about the importance of legitimacy on observed legal compliance, where legitimacy is defined as a citizen's belief that she ought to obey the law, Tyler finds that individual experience with political and legal authorities plays a central role. In particular, he claims that "procedural justice is the key normative judgment influencing the impact of experience on legitimacy," and that "one important element in feeling that procedures are fair is a belief on the part of those involved that they had an opportunity to take part in the decision-making process."[11] Similarly, on the basis of several lab experiments, Frohlich and Oppenheimer found that subjects who had a hand in choosing distributional principles "are more confident in their choices and more satisfied, and their confidence grows in contrast with their counterparts who have a [identical] principle imposed on them."[12] Numerous other studies provide further support for the idea "that personal influence in the procedure generates legitimacy," and that "direct voting in referendums is one such way to exercise influence in the process."[13] These sorts of findings suggest that

[11] Tom. R Tyler, *Why People Obey the Law* (Yale University Press 1990) 163. See also Tom R. Tyler, "Enhancing Police Legitimacy," (2004) 593 The Annals of the American Academy of Political and Social Sciences 84–99; Tom R. Tyler and Jonathan Jackson, "Popular Legitimacy and the Exercise of Legal Authority: Motivating Compliance, Cooperation and Engagement," (2014) 20 Psychology, Public Policy, and the Law 78–95; Tom R. Tyler, "Procedural Justice, Legitimacy, and the Effective Rule of Law," (2003) 30 Crime and Justice 283–357. I argue that a mismatch between Tyler's conceptualization of legitimacy and his means of measuring the concept undercuts his claims in Jeffrey A. Lenowitz, "On the Empirical Measurement of Legitimacy," in Melissa Schwartzberg and Jack Knight (eds.), *Political Legitimacy: NOMOS LXI* (New York University Press 2019).

[12] Norman Frohlich and Joe A. Oppenheimer, *Choosing Justice: An Experimental Approach to Ethical Theory* (University of California Press 1993) 121.

[13] Mikael Persson, Peter Esaiasson, and Mikael Gilljam, "The Effects of Direct Voting and Deliberation on Legitimacy Beliefs: An Experimental Study of Small Group Decision-Making," (2006) European Political Science Review 1–19; Shaun Bowler, Todd Donovan, and J.A. Karp, "Enraged or Engaged? Preferences for Direct Citizen Participation in Affluent Democracies," (2007) 60 Political Research Quarterly 351–62; James D. Fearon, "Deliberation as Discussion," in Jon Elster (ed.),

ratification procedures, particularly referendums which seem like rich instances of participation, might play a major role in creating a legitimate constitution.

Fourth, we know that several of ratification's functions in its non-constitutional domains point to legitimacy. In its first incarnation, in Roman law, and later in agency law more generally, ratification served in its reparative function as a means of correcting a legitimacy deficit earlier in the process. The procedure served as a means to fix mistakes from a prior transaction in order to render it binding. Similarly, ratification's support function, found in its use as a component of collective bargaining, is to maximize the number of union members who viewed a labor contract as acceptable and, in some sense authoritative.

In this and the following chapter, I pursue these leads and examine whether ratification had legitimating effects and whether they provide sufficient reasons for its implementation. To start, in this chapter, I investigate what legitimacy means and how procedures can lead to it. For, though the conception is often used confidently in both academic and everyday settings, what legitimacy actually refers to is frequently unclear. Consider some of the claims about ratification, participation, and legitimacy mentioned above. They are not only ambiguous but resist evaluation. Though they make recourse to legitimacy, it is unclear what legitimacy means, how the concept applies to constitutions, and how constitution-making procedures such as ratification can confer it.

Here, I address these deficits in four steps. First, I argue that in its political application, legitimacy divides into three types: moral, legal, and sociological. Second, I show that moral and sociological legitimacy apply directly to constitutions but that legal legitimacy collapses into sociological legitimacy when higher law is its object. Third, I explain that constitution-making procedures can affect the actual or perceived normative status of their outcome in two ways. They can have a substantive effect; meaning that they affect the contents of the outcome such that it meets some independently derived normative criteria. Or, they can have a procedural effect, meaning that the procedure itself serves as the normative criterion, which the outcome meets by virtue of being produced by the procedure in question. Fourth, by combining the previous distinctions I produce four pathways through which constitution-making procedures might legitimate constitutions: substantive moral legitimation, procedural moral legitimation, substantive sociological legitimation, and procedural sociological legitimation. I explain each of these pathways and give examples of how they might apply to certain constitution-making procedures. This paves the way for the following chapter where I analyze potential justifications of ratification using these distinctions.

Deliberative Democracy (Cambridge University Press 1998); J. Brockner and others, "The Moderating Effect of Self-Esteem in Reaction to Voice: Converging Evidence from Five Studies," (1998) 75 Journal of Personality and Social Psychology 394–407.

1. What Is Legitimacy?

Confusion and disagreement surround the concept of legitimacy. The term is used differently depending upon author, context, and purpose. While legitimacy is often used to indicate that something is valid or right, what this actually means is frequently left unexplained or underdeveloped. Much of this confusion stems from failing to differentiate between types of legitimacy, each equipped with its own evaluative criteria. Specifically, when it comes to the political context, legitimacy splits into three interrelated types: moral, sociological, and legal legitimacy.[14] Roughly put, something is *morally legitimate* if there is an acceptable moral justification for its claim to authority; *sociologically legitimate* if a significant portion of the relevant population believes it to be justified or morally legitimate; and *legally legitimate* if it is lawful according to the legal order of which it is a part.

Of course, as we will see, there is significant overlap and frequent causal connections between these types of legitimacy. Government officials might be morally legitimate authorities because they were lawfully elected and thus legally legitimate; a judicial interpretation might be unlawful because it violates the bounds of morality; a rule might become lawful simply because people believe it to be right; and all instances of sociological legitimacy rely on basic beliefs in moral legitimacy. Despite this, it is nonetheless worth distinguishing between each of three types of legitimacy, for doing so brings increased clarity to discussions of constitutional legitimacy and will assist us in evaluating how a constitution-making procedure such as ratification might help create a legitimate constitution.

Before proceeding, it begs mention that a significant portion of the argument below, most obviously the strict distinction between moral and legal legitimacy, assumes that the basic tenants of legal positivism are true. At the least, it requires accepting Austin's foundational claim that one can describe and apply law without resorting to moral argumentation.[15] This is not the place to defend the merits of

[14] I take this conceptual taxonomy from Richard Fallon's article on constitutional legitimacy, though I alter, add to, and depart from his substantive understanding of each legitimacy type Richard H. Fallon, Jr., "Legitimacy and the Constitution," (2005) 118 Harvard Law Review 1787–1853. For a similar distinction between types, though less explicit, see Andrew Arato, *Post Sovereign Constitution Making* (Oxford University Press 2016) 130–31. Colón-Ríos mentions all three kinds of legitimacy, but defines each differently and then redefines the concept as solely having to do with pedigree. Joel Colón-Ríos, *Weak Constitutionalism: Democratic Legitimacy and the Question of Constituent Power* (Routledge 2012) 105–6. For other less developed or detailed conceptions, see Andrew Arato and Zoltan Miklosi, "Constitution Making and Transitional Politics in Hungary," in Laurel E. Miller (ed.), *Framing the State in Times of Transition: Case Studies in Constitution Making* (United States Institute of Peace Press 2010) 386 n. 384; Bruce Gilley, *The Right to Rule: How States Win and Lose Legitimacy* (Columbia University Press 2009) 7; David Beetham, *The Legitimation of Power* (MacMillan 1991); Leslie Green, "Law, Legitimacy, and Consent," (1998) Southern California Law Review 795–825, 797; Wilfried Hinsch, "Justice, Legitimacy, and Constitutional Rights," (2010) 13 Critical Review of International Social and Political Philosophy 39–51.

[15] John Austin, *The Province of Jurisprudence Determined* (Cambridge University Press 1995) 159 See also Joseph Raz, *The Authority of Law* (2nd edn, Oxford University Press 2009) 40.

legal positivism against competing jurisprudential considerations; instead I simply assume its truth and admit that my arguments will have less resonance to natural law theorists and other non-positivists.[16]

1.1 Moral Legitimacy

Moral legitimacy is the conceptual center around which both legal and sociological legitimacy revolve; neither makes much sense without it. Moral legitimacy relates to "moral justifiability or respect-worthiness," the latter usually interpreted as necessitating some sort of duty of compliance toward that which is morally legitimate.[17] More precisely: *x is morally legitimate if and only if x's claim to authority is morally justified.* This definition makes use of the concept of practical authority, which a person or group possesses if its demands in a particular arena provide reasons for action meant to preempt or override those directly related to the action in question.[18]

Consider a state, the most common political subject of moral legitimacy. A state claims to be authoritative when it asserts a right to rule—a right to issue commands and directives relating to keeping the public order, maintaining itself, and exercising coercive force—and demands some sort of deserved and dutiful non-selfish compliance from its citizenry as a result. A state claiming authority expects citizens to comply with its edicts simply because it makes them. Citizens should pay their taxes because the state demands payment, not because tax payments contribute to national security or because failing to do so results in punishment. In claiming authority a state is asserting that there are sufficient moral reasons to treat its edicts as preemptive in this fashion.

States claiming to be authoritative are morally legitimate when their claim to have a right to rule is justified and as a result they are owed a duty of obedience.[19]

[16] See H.L.A. Hart, *The Concept of Law* (2nd edn, Oxford University Press 1994); Hans Kelsen, *General Theory of Law and State* (Transaction Publishers 2006); Green, "Law, Legitimacy, and Consent"; Raz, *The Authority of Law*; Jules L. Coleman, *The Practice of Principle* (Clarendon Press 2001).

[17] Fallon, "Legitimacy and the Constitution," 1786. Note that in response to philosophical anarchists, several authors have claimed that moral legitimacy does not necessary entail political obedience. See M.B.E. Smith, "Is There a Prima Facie Obligation to Obey the Law?," (1973) 82 Yale Law Journal 950–76; Rolf Sartorius, "Political Authority and Political Obligation," (1981) 67 Virginia Law Review 3–17; Allan Buchanan, "Political Legitimacy and Democracy," (2002) 112 Ethics 689–719; Kent Greenawalt, *Conflicts of Law and Morality* (Clarendon Press 1987) 47–59.

[18] Joseph Raz, *The Morality of Freedom* (Oxford University Press 1986) 23–99; Joseph Raz, *Between Authority and Interpretation: On the Theory of Law and Practical Reason* (Oxford University Press 2009) 126–66; Raz, *The Authority of Law*, 3–33, 233–91. I add "override" to Raz's description of authoritative reasons as preemptive in order to accommodate competing conceptions of practical authority that characterize the reasons as extremely weighty, rather than fully preemptive. Scott Shapiro, "Authority," in Jules L. Coleman and Scott Shapiro (eds.), *The Oxford Handbook of Jurisprudence and Philosophy of Law* (Oxford University Press 2002).

[19] Raz, *The Morality of Freedom*, 26; Raz, *The Authority of Law*, 6.

Here, the existence of moral reasons for a state's claim to authority generates the relevant duties of obedience. The nature of the obedience, the type of duty produced by morally justified authority, and the recipient of the duty remain controversial topics. Obedience might amount to not actively undermining the state, not interfering with the state, obeying some or all of the state's commands, or even assisting and supporting the state. The generated duty might be content-dependent or independent, absolute, prima facie, or preemptive. Citizens might owe obedience to the state itself, its government, or the people in whose name it acts.[20] We however can remain neutral on these questions; moral legitimacy simply consists in a morally justified claim to authority and an owed duty of obedience of some sort.

Note that morally legitimate authority is distinct from *de facto authority*. A state is de facto authoritative when its claim to authority is successful rather than morally justified. Such a state claims a right to rule, acts as if it has a right to rule, and succeeds in establishing and maintaining its rule.[21] Whether a state is morally legitimate is irrelevant for the purposes of determining de facto authority.[22] Thus, a state can claim to be authoritative without being a de facto or a legitimate authority, can be a de facto authority without being a legitimate authority, and can be a legitimate authority without being a de facto authority.

1.2 Sociological Legitimacy

Sociological legitimacy piggybacks on moral legitimacy. It is the people's belief that their regime's claim to authority is morally justified—meaning that they see content-independent reasons for following its orders—and their resultant acquiescence or obedience as a result. This concept descends from Max Weber, who defined it as "the probability that to a relevant degree the appropriate attitudes will exist, and the corresponding practical conduct will ensue" and held it to be "the

[20] For examples of these debates see A. John Simmons, *Justification and Legitimacy: Essays on Rights and Obligations* (Cambridge University Press 2001) 122–57; Ronald Dworkin, *Law's Empire* (Harvard University Press 1986) 191; Raz, *The Morality of Freedom*, 38–69; Shapiro, "Authority."

[21] Raz, *The Morality of Freedom*, 26; Christopher McMahon, *Collective Rationality and Collective Reasoning* (Cambridge University Press 2001) 50.

[22] While it is conceptually possible to imagine a non de facto morally legitimate authority, certain views on what actually makes an authority morally legitimate might make this impossible. For instance, if one of the primary moral justifications for having a political authority is to secure stable social coordination, and this is only possible (without violating other significant moral principles) if the authority is de facto, then all legitimate political authority is necessarily effective and de facto. However, as Raz notes: "[T]his is the result of substantive political principles ... It is not entailed by a conceptual analysis of the notion of authority, not even by that of the concept of political authority." Raz, *The Authority of Law*, 9. One example of a non de facto yet morally legitimate authority might be the Polish government in exile in London in 1940. Nonetheless, while it did not successfully rule Poland, the government in exile was recognized as authoritative by the bulk of the Polish population. Raz, *Between Authority and Interpretation: On the Theory of Law and Practical Reason*, 128.

basis of every authority."[23] Sociological legitimacy is thus a common explanation for the de facto authority of a state, in that it is thought to be extremely difficult for a government to effectively govern a modern polity unless a significant portion of the population believes it has a right to rule.

In the terms of our disaggregated conception of legitimacy, a regime is sociologically legitimate to the degree that its citizens believe it to be morally legitimate. Obedience, according to Weber, tends to follow such beliefs. Here, obedience is what criminologists and socio-legal scholars term "legitimate normative obedience," i.e. obedience due to a belief in the rightful authority of officials, rather than due to instrumental reasons or general moral beliefs about proper behavior.[24] We can thus formally define sociological legitimacy in the following manner: *x is sociologically legitimate if a significant portion of the population that x claims authority over believes x to be morally legitimate and complies with its directives as a result.*[25]

Note that sociological legitimacy is, as Friedrich notes, "a question of fact."[26] It is fundamentally a descriptive concept, for it describes whether or not a certain percentage or number of citizens have certain attitudes or beliefs toward a political object, and whether they act a certain way because of them.[27] Sociological legitimacy is thus distinct from moral and legal legitimacy, both of which are evaluative concepts, in that its measurement is completely dependent on attitudinal and behavioral characteristics of a given set of individuals, rather than reliant on objective or semi-objective external criteria.[28] However it remains a normative concept, in that it concerns beliefs in moral legitimacy and the obedience that such beliefs entail.[29] Thus, attempts to

[23] Max Weber, *Economy and Society: An Outline of Interpretive Sociology*, vol. 1 (University of California Press 1978) 214. See also Robert Grafstein, "The Failure of Weber's Conception of Legitimacy: Its Causes and Implications," (1981) 43 The Journal of Politics 45–472.

[24] Tyler, *Why People Obey the Law*; Anthony Bottoms and Justice Tankebe, "Beyond Procedural Justice: A Dialogic Approach to Legitimacy in Criminal Justice," (2012) 102 The Journal of Criminal Law & Criminology 119–17, 120; Carl Friedrich, *Man and His Government* (McGraw-Hill 1963) 234.

[25] Sociological legitimacy might be maintained and supported by a simultaneous belief among citizens that their fellow citizens consider an authority morally legitimate, and perhaps will impose sanctions in response to deviance. Nonetheless, these sorts of beliefs are distinct from those beliefs that constitute sociological legitimacy. Horne ignores this distinction in her social norm approach to legitimacy. Christine Horne, "A Social Norms Approach to Legitimacy," (2009) 53 American Behavioral Scientist 400–15.

[26] Friedrich, *Man and His Government*, 234.

[27] Sociological legitimacy is thus variable between time periods, groups, and governmental organs.

[28] As Clark notes, "the test for legitimacy is not the truth of the philosopher, but the belief of the people." Ian Clark, "Legitimacy in a Global Order," (2003) 29 Review of International Studies 75–95, 80.

[29] Fallon notes a weak sense of sociological legitimacy that means observed popular acquiescence, regardless of reason, and Venter explicitly defines legitimacy for constitutions as depending on whether "those who are governed by it, including the organs of the state, acquiesce to its terms." Legitimacy is certainly employed by some political scientists in this way, most likely due to its relative ease of empirical measurement, but such usage overly distorts the concept. For instance, according to this weaker sense of sociological legitimacy, the governments of Mugabe, Pinochet, and Than Schwe were sociologically legitimate. Fallon, "Legitimacy and the Constitution," 1795–96; Francois Venter, "Constitution

completely reduce the concept to rationally calculated obedience misuse the term.[30]

1.3 Legal Legitimacy

The final type of legitimacy is legal legitimacy: *x is legally legitimate if x is lawful according to the legal system of which x is a part*. In this sense, legal legitimacy is equivalent to the positivist conception of legal validity, according to which something is legally valid if and only if it belongs to a legal system in force in a certain country or enforceable within it.[31] Thus, to say that an Environmental Protection Agency order is legally legitimate is to say that it is legally enforceable and valid within the legal structure of the United States. This is distinct from saying that it is sociologically legitimate (meaning that U.S. citizens see it as issuing properly from a morally legitimate authority) or morally legitimate (meaning that actual moral reasons supporting the EPA's claim to authority exist in this domain).

Two additional features of legal legitimacy are worth clarifying. First, ascribing legal legitimacy to an object involves making a legal statement, i.e. a statement in which "the fact that certain laws belong to certain legal systems" is a "necessary condition of the truth."[32] The truth conditions of legal legitimacy, unlike moral and sociological legitimacy, consist in specific legal facts rather than moral properties or actually existing beliefs. Second, legal legitimacy as a concept nonetheless relies upon normative and sometimes even moral presuppositions. Assertions of legal legitimacy establish that something has the legal effects that it claims because it is a valid component of the relevant legal system. This is why legal legitimacy is identical to legal validity, which means "the specific existence of norms."[33] Legal systems presume their own normativity, and thus claiming that a specific law or political action properly belongs to an accepted legal system is to suggest that the law or political action deserves compliance as a result. Thus, it is not uncommon

Making and the Legitimacy of the Constitution," in Antero Jyranki (ed.), *National Constitutions in the Era of Integration* (Kluwer Law International 1999) 21.

[30] Ronald Rogowski, *Rational Legitimacy: A Theory of Political Support* (Princeton University Press 1974).

[31] Raz, *The Authority of Law*, 153.

[32] Joseph Raz, "On Lawful Governments," (1970) 80 Ethics 296–305, 300. In a sense, Raz's discussion in this article about the three different contexts in which the concept of a legal system is deployed anticipates Fallon's tripartite legitimacy distinction. Ibid., 302–4. I follow Leslie Green in interpreting Raz's discussion of lawful government as an explanation of legal legitimacy: Green, "Law, Legitimacy, and Consent," 797. Finally, for a discussion of legal statements, see H.L.A. Hart, *Essays in Jurisprudence and Philosophy* (Clarendon Press 1983) 21–48.

[33] Kelsen, *General Theory of Law and State*, 30.

for assertions of legal legitimacy to assume the moral legitimacy of a legal system as a whole.[34]

2. Legitimate Constitutions

We now need to apply these legitimacy types to a constitution. What does it mean for a constitution to be morally, sociologically, or legally legitimate?

2.1 Morally and Sociologically Legitimate Constitutions

A morally legitimate constitution is a constitution with morally justified authority; it is a constitution that justifiably structures a given state, creates the legal system, sets limitations on government power, and is owed some form of respect and compliance as a result. Such a constitution demands that a specific right be protected from government infringement, or that one organ of government has a check on another organ, or that the edict of one of its constituted bodies be complied with, not because of the individual merit of the right or the check, not because citizens agree with these provisions, and not because the edict is reasonable, but because the constitution demands it and moral reasons exist for respecting this demand. To use Michelman's term, a morally legitimate constitution is "respect-worthy," in that it creates a legal and political system the inhabitants of which have good reasons to respect even when they disagree with specific laws or policies and fail to change them.[35]

This concept of moral legitimacy is intentionally incomplete. It says nothing about what counts as a moral reason in support of a claim to authority, for this comes solely from the comprehensive moral theory one endorses. Thus, how one determines whether a constitution's claim to authority is morally justified will vary from one moral theory to the next. For instance, according to Rawls' liberal principle of legitimacy, a morally legitimate constitution is one "the essentials of which all citizens as free and equal may reasonably be expected to endorse in the light of principles and ideals acceptable to their common human reason."[36] Raz would hold that a legitimate constitution is one that meets the normal justification thesis

[34] Raz explains that "if the constitution and the other rules that establish legal authorities are morally justified, so are the authorities that the establish, and the laws made by those authorizes are morally binding." Joseph Raz, *On the Authority and Interpretation of Constitutions: Some Preliminaries* (Cambridge University Press 1998) 189.

[35] Frank I. Michelman, "Ida's Way: Constructing the Respect-Worthy Governmental System," (2004) 72 Fordham Law Review 345–65, 346–47.

[36] John Rawls, *A Theory of Justice* (revised edn, Harvard University Press 1999) 137.

and the independence condition, while for Simmons and perhaps Locke a legitimate constitution would simply be one directly consented to by its citizens.[37]

A sociologically legitimate constitution, on the other hand, is a constitution that a relevant portion of the population believes is morally legitimate and treats as authoritative as a result.[38] This means that citizens consider the constitution to be *the* constitution, that the government functions in accordance with the constitution's provisions, that legal reasoning stops at the constitution, and that most people believe that all of this occurs for good moral reasons. The provisions of a sociologically legitimate constitution, as well as the institutions that it structures, are thus taken to be appropriate, deserving of respect, and generally justified. Moreover, the citizenry actually complies because of such beliefs.[39] An extreme example of a sociologically legitimate constitution appears in Paine's utopic depiction of the early United States, where the constitution "was a political bible of the state," and "[s]carcely a family was without it."

Sociological legitimacy is the legitimacy type most frequently relied upon in the constitution-making literature. Ndulo, for example, refers to a legitimate constitution as one the people feel that they own, and therefore respect, defend, and obey, and Banks and Alvarez claim "that constitutional legitimacy is determined by the people's acceptance of the Constitution, the fit between the new set of rules and society."[40] Most explicitly, Arato and Miklosi explain that they "are ultimately concerned with the sociological sense of the term *legitimacy* as established by Max

[37] Joseph Raz, "The Problem of Authority: Revisiting the Service Conception," (2006) 90 Minnesota Law Review 1003–44; Raz, *The Morality of Freedom*; Simmons, *Justification and Legitimacy: Essays on Rights and Obligations*, 123–56.

[38] Measuring sociological legitimacy, regardless of context or object, is inherently difficult. When it comes to constitutions a variety of approaches, all of which are reductive and imperfect, have been used. Widner uses the level of violence five years after constitution-making in post-conflict countries. Moehler uses constitutional support, measured through four survey questions designed to assess whether respondents felt that the constitution included their views, represents the national political community as a whole, is worthy of compliance, and should be preserved. De Raadt takes a more elite-based focus, relying on incidents of constitutional conflicts in the area of executive-legislative relations as well as disputes about the competencies of constitutional courts, while Elkins et al. rely on constitutional durability. Zachary Elkins, Tom Ginsburg, and James Melton, "The Lifespan of Written Constitutions" (World Justice Forum); Devra C. Moehler, *Distrusting Democrats: Outcomes of Participatory Constitution Making* (University of Michigan Press 2008); Jennifer Widner, "Constitution Writing in Post-Conflict Settings: An Overview," (2008) 49 William and Mary Law Review 1513–42; Jennifer Widner, *Constitution Writing and Conflict Resolution*, 2005); Jasper de Raadt, "Contested Constitutions: Legitimacy of Constitution-Making and Constitutional Conflict in Central Europe," (2009) 23 East European Politics and Societies 315–38.

[39] Two things are worth noting. First, citizens might believe that one provision of the constitution needs to be changed, while still maintaining that the document as a whole is justified. Second, the sociological legitimacy of a constitution is different from the sociological legitimacy of the government. Thus, a sociologically illegitimate government might operate in a state structured by a sociologically legitimate constitution. This is especially likely if said government is seen as departing from the provisions of the constitution.

[40] William C. Banks and Edgar Alvarez, "The New Colombian Constitution: Democratic Victory or Popular Surrender," (1991) 23 Inter-American Law Review 39–92, 43.

Weber, having to do with a significant part of a population ... considering a political order as a whole or the government based on it ... justified or valid."[41]

2.2 The Irrelevance of Legal Legitimacy

Unlike moral and sociological legitimacy, a conceptual problem emerges when one applies legal legitimacy to a constitution. A legally legitimate constitution would be a constitution that is legal according to the legal system of which it is a part. However, in constitutional governments the constitution creates the legal system; it lies at the end of any chain of legal reasoning regarding the lawfulness of an object or action and undergirds all legal rules and regulations. Thus, claiming that a constitution is legally legitimate seems confused, for the criterion of legal legitimacy, lawfulness, is set by the object whose legitimacy is being asserted.

Two possible solutions to this conundrum exist. The first is that constitutions can contain reflexive standards of legal legitimacy. Many constitutions contain sections that seems to serve this purpose. For instance, the final provision of the 1948 Constitution of the Italian Republic states:

> This Constitution shall be promulgated by the provisional Head of State within five days of its approval by the Constituent Assembly and shall come into force on 1 January 1948. The text of the Constitution shall be deposited in the Town Hall of every Municipality of the Republic and there made public, for the whole of 1948, so as to allow every citizen to know of it.[42]

This provision, one might argue, makes the Italian Constitution self-legitimizing, for it contains steps that, if followed, produce a lawful constitution.

Despite the ubiquity of such provisions, this purported solution falls short. On the one hand, the implication of a constitution that violates its own enactment provisions is unclear. When something is legally illegitimate it is not legal and lacks legal force. If a constitution provides its own criterion of legal legitimacy yet fails to satisfy it, then the constitution is legally invalid, which implies that it cannot serve as a source of legal legitimacy for anything, itself included. If the Italian Constitution was promulgated ten days after its approval it should be illegal and legally illegitimate. However, by being illegitimate, it cannot determine lawfulness, meaning that it would not be legally illegitimate for there is no acceptable source of constitutional legality. This circularity plagues any attempt to locate the source of legal legitimacy for a constitution in the same constitution, for legitimacy

[41] Arato and Miklosi, "Constitution Making and Transitional Politics in Hungary," 385 n. 384.
[42] Italian Constitution. Final and Transitional Provisions, XVIII.

presupposes the possibility of illegitimacy, which requires that the relevant criterion is separate from the object being evaluated.

On the other hand, constitutional self-legitimation simply falls short of what people mean when they assert legal legitimacy. Consider a hypothetical put forward by Frederick Schauer. He presents and signs a new constitution for the United States that includes a provision announcing its establishment upon his signature. This constitution is legally legitimate in its own terms, for it satisfies its own internal condition of validity. The same is true for the actual U.S. Constitution, but the fact that it is the legally legitimate constitution of the United States, while Schauer's is not, points to the insufficiency of a purely internal criterion of legal legitimacy. We can make this distinction, "not because of anything internal to one document or the other, because internally they are equally valid. Rather, we know that one is the Constitution and the other is not because of what we know empirically and factually about the world."[43]

The second solution claims that the legal or political system being replaced can provide the relevant criteria of lawfulness by dictating how future constitutions are to be made or what they must include. Here, legal legitimacy is meant to come from legal continuity. Examples of this logic abound in constitution-making history: Louis XIV demanded that he receive a veto over and within the constitution; the Allied powers demanded the creation of a highly decentralized government in West Germany and the popular ratification of the constitution; and the South African Interim Constitution specified the process of constitution-making and constrained the final document's content by imposing thirty-four binding constitutional principles.[44] In 1992, the Hungarian Constitutional Court retroactively endorsed this vision of legality when it claimed: "[T]he exchange of systems took place on the basis of legality ... in a formally unimpeachable manner through adhering to the lawmaking rules of the previous lawmaking order."[45]

According to this argument, legal legitimacy depends upon the degree to which constitutions and their creators follow the mandates of the previous legal authority. This solution fails for several reasons. For one thing, it arbitrarily makes

[43] Frederick Schauer, "Amending the Presuppositions of a Constitution," in Sanford Levinson (ed.), *Responding to Imperfection: The Theory of Practice of Constitutional Amendment* (Princeton University Press 1995) 153.

[44] Jon Elster, "Forces and Mechanisms in the Constitution-Making Process," (1995) 45 Duke Law Review 364–96, 373–75; Hassen Ebrahim, Kayode Fayemi, and Stephanie Loomis, *Promoting a Culture of Constitutionalism and Democracy in Commonwealth Africa: Recommendations to Commonwealth Heads of Government* (1999) 121; Aili Mari Tripp, "The Politics of Constitution Making in Uganda," in Laurel E. Miller (ed.), *Framing the State in Times of Transition: Case Studies in Constitution Making* (United States Institute of Peace Press 2010) 162–66. Such constraints on the constitution-making process have mixed success; the French Assembly ignored both of the King's requests and the German framers resisted much of the desired decentralization, while framers in Uganda and South Africa closely followed the instructions given to them.

[45] Cited in Andrew Arato, *Civil Society, Constitution, and Legitimacy* (Rowman & Littlefield Publishers 2000) 103. For further discussion of the decision, see Alajos Dornbach, "Special Reports: Retroactivity Law Overturned in Hungary," (1992) 7 East European Constitutional Review 7–8.

legal legitimacy impossible for those constitutions created in a context where constitution-making directives are absent. The constitutions of completely new states, or states in which the previous regime had nothing to say about the creation of its replacement's constitution, could never be legally legitimate. In addition, this solution perversely gives existing regimes the power to set the terms of legal legitimacy for the constitutions that are meant to replace them.

Most importantly, however, allowing existing regimes to determine the legal legitimacy for new constitutions confuses the actual legal role of a constitution and constitution-making. Constitutions are the ultimate legal foundation for a juridical system and their creation negates the legal authority of any previous foundation.[46] It therefore makes little sense for the legal legitimacy or lawfulness of a constitution to depend on its observance with a command from its precursor, for to do so suggests that this prior legal source, rather than the new constitution, is juridically superior.[47] Thus, since something is legally legitimate if it is lawful according to the legal system of which it is a part, and constitutions create and define legal systems instead of operating within them, legal legitimacy in the normal sense does not apply to constitutions.

2.3 Collapse into Sociological Legitimacy

Despite this conclusion, it remains possible to differentiate a lawful constitution from one that is not. We know that the constitution adopted in 1787 in Philadelphia is valid higher law for the United States while the Articles of Confederation are not.[48] We know that the Constitution of the Federal Republic of Brazil is not a lawful constitution for Suriname and Guyana. Such judgments are possible because social facts determine the legality of constitutions. The same is true for ordinary law in a stable legal system, except that the relevant social facts are of a particular type: legal facts. A given law is a law if it is an actual component of a legal system, meaning that its origins followed the proper legal procedures and its contents do not violate higher legal norms, i.e. if it is legally legitimate. When it comes to constitutions, legal facts are indeterminate, for a constitution is their ultimate source. Thus, the relevant social facts are therefore not legal, but instead relate to specific attitudes and behavior of the relevant population and legal officials.

[46] Unless a new constitution refers to the old constitution, or judicial interpretation consults prior legal systems when appropriate precedent is absent.

[47] Banks and Alvarez, "The New Colombian Constitution: Democratic Victory or Popular Surrender," 62.

[48] This is despite the fact that Art. VII of the U.S. Constitution violated the Articles of Confederation by allowing for secession, removing amendment power from the Continental Congress and state legislatures, and specifying a new means for constitutional revision. Bruce A. Ackerman, *We the People: Transformations* (Belknap Press of Harvard University Press 1998) 34–35.

We can identify the constitution of a given polity by looking for the document that is treated like higher law; i.e. the document that lies at the end of judicial reasoning, determines and limits the interaction of governmental organs, prescribes how laws are actually created, and safeguards fundamental rights. The people and government of Suriname and Guyana do not follow the Brazilian Constitution or treat it as authoritative, and it is therefore not the legal constitution for these countries. In contrast, the document ratified in Philadelphia in 1789 is valid law in the United States because it is treated as such.[49]

This logic maps onto Hart's discussion of the primary rule of recognition: the rule that identifies the ultimate source of legal validity in a legal system.[50] This rule of recognition consists in the practice of legal and political officials; i.e. a rule pointing to *x* as the source of legal validity consists in the fact that legal and political officials treat *x* as the ultimate source of legal validity.[51] In a constitutional setting, the rule of recognition points to the constitution as the ultimate source of legal validity. Therefore, the legal legitimacy of a constitution hinges on the practice of officials recognizing the constitution as the actual and proper constitution of the polity in question.[52]

For newly constitutionalized polities, especially constitutional democracies, we might imagine that something more is needed than a rule of recognition applicable only to officials. One can imagine Schauer's constitution also including provisions appointing his friends and family to all governmental positions, all of whom are inclined to treat his constitution as the ultimate source of legality, yet this would not make his constitution the lawful one. For a new constitution to be legally legitimate, a significant portion of the population also needs to treat it as the highest law in the land. In other words, for new constitutions, legal legitimacy depends on the practice and behavior of government officials, which constitution-making procedures will unlikely affect, and the sociological legitimacy of the constitution.[53] Therefore, when examining the effects of ratification on creating a legitimate constitution, only moral and sociological legitimacy are relevant.[54]

[49] Fallon, "Legitimacy and the Constitution," 1805.

[50] Hart, *The Concept of Law*, 92–120.

[51] Ibid.

[52] A constitution is the ultimate source of legal validity pointed to by a rule of recognition and not the rule of recognition itself. Constitutions are codified higher law that can be amended, repealed, and intentionally replaced by enactment, while rules of recognition are social practices that cannot change until the social practices that they are change. This mistake is regularly made in the constitution-making literature. See for instance Ginsburg, Elkins, and Blount's claim that "Because the constitution . . . provides the ultimate rule of recognition for lawmaking processes, it requires the greatest possible level of legitimation in democratic theory." This claim is confused, for a social practice is not something that is or is not legitimate, in any sense of the concept. Tom Ginsburg, Zachary Elkins, and Justin Blount, "Does the Process of Constitution-Making Matter?" (2009) 5 Annual Review of Law and Social Science 201–23, 206; Raz, *On the Authority and Interpretation of Constitutions: Some Preliminaries*, 160–161.

[53] See Fallon, "Legitimacy and the Constitution," 1804.

[54] The irrelevance of legal legitimacy to constitution-making is important in its own right, in that it means constitution-makers can bypass tedious legal arguments about whether particular constitution-makers should follow existing statute when trying to create new legitimate constitutions. Instead,

3. Creating Legitimacy

In order to assess constitution-making procedural recommendations based on legitimacy, we need something more than a clear understanding of what it means for a constitution to be legitimate. For instance, referring to sociological legitimacy, which he describes as "the facts about whether or to what degree people actually believes themselves to be obliged to submit to authority," Tushnet asserts that, "ratification [referendum] is desirable, even if not required, in part to ensure that the new constitution has domestic legitimacy."[55] This claim is incomplete because it lacks an explanation connecting a ratification referendum to sociological legitimacy. Does participating in a referendum change an individual's belief? Does a referendum screen out all sociologically illegitimate constitutions? Or, are individuals simply more likely to believe in the authority of a document approved in a referendum? We thus need to look at how procedures can impact legitimacy.

A procedure can positively affect the actual or perceived normative status of its outcome in two general ways: it can alter the substance of the outcome, such that it meets or comes closer to meeting some independent normative criterion, or it can serve as the normative criterion itself and validate its own outcome. I call the former a substantive effect and the latter a procedural effect.[56] For example, under ideal conditions a procedure in which a person dividing a cake receives the last piece has a substantive effect on its outcome, for it makes it more likely that the size and distribution of cakes pieces (the outcome) meets an independently known criterion of fairness (equal size pieces).[57] Alternatively, a game of roulette with informed players has a procedural effect on its outcome, for the distribution of winnings is normatively acceptable or believed to be normatively acceptable because it results from the rules and procedures of the game itself.

Applying this distinction to constitutions and legitimacy, we can say the following. A constitution-making procedure, alone or in combination with others, can legitimate a constitution by influencing its contents such that it becomes more likely to meet an independent criterion of legitimacy; this is *substantive legitimacy*. The procedure affects the contents of a constitution, and it is this content that makes the document legitimate or illegitimate by meeting some standard. Alternatively, a constitution-making procedure, alone or in combination with others, can involve *procedural legitimation*, i.e. generate a constitution that is legitimate simply because

decisions to ignore, follow, pretend to follow, or retroactively meet pre-existing legal rules for constitutional replacement or change should be based on what is actually relevant, i.e. whether the chosen procedures are likely to lead citizens and elites into accepting the constitution as authoritative.

55 Tushnet, "Constitution-Making: An Introduction," 1988–99.

56 For a similar distinction, see Peter Esaiasson, Mikael Gilljam, and Mikael Persson, "Which Decision-Making Arrangements Generate the Strongest Legitimacy Beliefs? Evidence from a Randomised Field Experiment," (2012) 51 European Journal of Political Research 785–808, 787.

57 Rawls, *A Theory of Justice*, 74–76.

it resulted from the procedure or procedures in question. Here the procedure can serve as a necessary or sufficient condition. That is, something might be legitimate because a certain procedure produced it or might be illegitimate if a certain procedure did not. In both of these instances, the procedure directly affects the legitimacy of the constitution rather than the provisions the document contains.

4. Pathways to Constitutional Legitimacy

Combining the two types of legitimacy applicable to constitutions with the procedural and substantive distinction produces four pathways through which a constitution-making procedure might legitimate a constitution: *substantive moral legitimation* (SML), *substantive sociological legitimation* (SSL), *procedural moral legitimation* (PML), and *procedural sociological legitimation* (PSL). If a constitution-making procedure helps to legitimize a constitution it will do so through at least one of these pathways. When constitutional consultants claim that a given procedure should be included within a specific constitution-making process because of its legitimizing effect, they should specify and explain which of the four pathways make sense of their claim. In this final section I describe each of these legitimation pathways and give examples of how they can apply to constitution-making procedures and be used to justify them.

4.1 Substantive

The substantive legitimation pathways involve a procedure affecting the content of a constitution, and it is this content that makes the constitution legitimate. SML occurs when *p* affects the contents of a constitution such that it is more likely to fall within the boundaries of morality as it applies to legitimacy. I use the term "boundaries" to indicate that morality underdetermines the contents of a constitution.[58] By this I mean that according to any plausible conception of morality choosing specific constitutional provisions likely requires decisions based on non-moral reasons, such that moral justification will exist for many different constitutions in each context. This follows from two observations.

On the one hand, certain moral values are incommensurable, meaning that their value is incomparable.[59] Framers might have to choose between prioritizing one

[58] Raz, *On the Authority and Interpretation of Constitutions: Some Preliminaries*, 171–74, 193 n. 120.

[59] Raz, *The Morality of Freedom*, 321–66; James Griffin, "Incommensurability: What's the Problem?" in Ruth Chang (ed.), *Incommensurability, Incomparability, and Practical Reason* (Harvard University Press 1997) 35–51; David Wiggins, "Incommensurability: Four Proposals," in Ruth Chang (ed.), *Incommensurability, Incomparability, and Practical Reason* (Harvard University Press 1997) 52–66; Donald Regan, "Value, Comparability, and Choice," in Ruth Chang (ed.), *Incommensurability, Incomparability, and Practical Reason* (Harvard University Press 1997) 129–50.

such value over another and will be unable to rely on moral reasons when doing so. For instance, we can imagine two different constitutions, one that maximizes individual rights protection at the cost of weakening popular sovereignty, and the other which does the opposite. If the protection of basic rights and empowering the people are incommensurable moral values, both constitutions—though very different—could be morally legitimate. A framer choosing between them might be able to rely on good reasons, perhaps those related to context, to make a decision, but these will not be the sort of moral reasons that determine the legitimacy of a constitution.

On the other hand, it is highly unlikely that only one form of a provision or constitutional arrangement can satisfy a given moral principle. Moral reasons are not so specific, i.e. even single moral values without incommensurable competition can underdetermine institutional choice. Thus, we can imagine a democratic republican theory that includes the following moral principle: a legitimate constitution must provide formal mechanisms that allow the governed to equally influence political officials, so that each can help determine the contents of the laws and policies these officials enact. Even if this principle had no competitors, any number of constitutional arrangements might reasonably meet it. For instance, a representative government limiting campaign contributions and making use of proportional representation would be as legitimate as one employing single-member constituencies with plurality voting, the right of recall, and publicly funded elections.[60] Thus, due to both incommensurability and the non-specific nature of moral values, it is appropriate to speak of the boundaries of a morally legitimate constitution rather than attempt to spell out its exact contents.

SSL takes place when *p* affects the content of a constitution such that it is more likely to appear morally legitimate to the citizens it purports to govern. The idea here is that certain attributes of a constitution are more conducive to making it authoritative in the eyes of its citizenry, and that *p* makes such attributes more likely to appear within the text. For instance, imagine that constitutions containing bills of rights are more likely to be seen as legitimate than those without them. If *p* increases the likelihood that a bill of rights appears in a constitutional text, then *p* would involve substantive sociological legitimation.

For an example of SML and SSL, consider a situation in which designers of a constitution-making process are choosing between transforming the existing legislature into a self-created constituent legislature or convening an independent constitutional convention. Assume that a convention is more likely to draft a constitution that is impartial when it comes to factions, special interests, and generations. That is, constitutions created by conventions are more likely to be designed to benefit and treat all present and future members of a polity in an equal manner.

60 This is just an example, and perhaps there are good causal and moral reasons for choosing one of these alternatives over the other.

There might be many reasons for this. A convention separates the constitution-making process from the ongoing activities of the sitting government, thereby diminishing the chance that partial governmental interests will be written into the constitution.[61] Further, a convention more easily allows for the creation of new electoral rules to determine the drafting body, which can be set up to ensure a balanced representation of group interests in the convention, with the assumption that this too will amplify the impartiality of the text. Finally, the use of a constitutional convention makes it possible that some of the drafters will be non-legislators, and therefore not used to working for the short-term interests of their constituents with reelection in mind. Under certain conditions, this might also increase the chances that the constitution will aim at the long-term equal health of the state and people, rather than that of the current dominant constituency.[62]

If a morally legitimate constitution is one that, among other things, is impartial, then using a convention is a means of SML, because the procedure makes it more likely that the substance of a constitution falls within the bounds of morality. If, on average, citizens are more likely to believe an impartial constitution is morally legitimate, i.e. that good moral reasons exist for its claim to ultimate legal authority, then using a convention is a means of SSL. The procedure helps to alter the constitution's contents in such a way that it becomes more likely to trigger legitimacy beliefs in the relevant populace. An SML argument in favor of using conventions would point to the decision-making body's effect on moral legitimacy, while an SSL argument would point to the decision-making body's effect on legitimacy beliefs. Both arguments would seek to justify a constitutional convention by assuming the desirability of a legitimate constitution.

4.2 Procedural

The procedural legitimation pathways trace the legitimating effects to the procedure, rather than the procedure's effects on the constitution. PML occurs when a constitution is morally legitimate just because it stemmed from a constitution-making process involving *p*. Something about the nature of *p*, by itself or in combination with other procedures, produces a constitution that is morally legitimate because of its genesis rather than its content.

[61] Elster, "Forces and Mechanisms in the Constitution-Making Process." For a recent argument against those that support constitutional conventions over constituent legislatures, see Gabriel L. Negretto, "Democratic Constitution-Making Bodies: The Perils of a Partisan Convention," (1995) 16 International Journal of Constitutional Law 254–79.

[62] At the same time, we should be wary of falling into the fallacy of composition and simply concluding that decreasing the number of biased members in a constitution-making body will automatically yield a less biased constitution. See Adrian Vermeule, *The System of the Constitution* (Oxford University Press 2011) chapter 1.

Whether PML is even possible depends upon whether one holds a compatible moral theory. For instance, as mentioned above, according to a Rawlsian framework a constitution's moral legitimacy will depend upon whether free and equal citizens can be expected to endorse its basic features in the light of principles and ideals acceptable to their common human reason. Under this conception a PML pathway does not exist, for moral legitimacy is completely determined by the contents of the constitution. For a Rawlsian, the only moral legitimation pathway is SML.

PSL on the other hand takes place when a constitution is more likely to be considered morally legitimate by its subjects because it came from a constitution-making process involving *p*. Advocates of participatory constitution-making make this sort of argument when they recommend inclusive and participatory constitution-making procedures because "a high level of popular participation" is "necessary for a constitution to be regarded as legitimate and relevant by the citizenry." Such recommendations remain neutral on the effect of participatory procedures on the substance of the constitution and instead ascribe a legitimizing effect to the act of participation itself.[63] In PML, then, a procedure works on the constitution itself, affecting its moral status, while in PSL it works on individuals, influencing and changing their behavior and perceptions toward the constitution.

Again, some of the decisions related to the creation of the constitution drafting body can help illustrate these pathways. Consider a debate about how to populate it. Some might argue in favor of electing rather than selecting members to the drafting body, pointing to PSL effects of elections. The idea here would be that a populace is more likely to see constitution-makers that they choose as legitimate, and more likely to view a constitution as legitimate if it is created by legitimate drafters. For support, one might appeal to research showing that people tend to see authorities as more legitimate, when they have a hand in choosing them.[64] This might be because elections, via peer effects, inform voters that their leaders (or framers) are worthy, or because people simply see themselves as obliged to follow the results of a process that they participated in.[65] Regardless, the results of such an argument, at least from a legitimacy perspective, would be that constitutional commissions, roundtables, and other appointed drafting bodies should be dismissed, and constituent legislatures, constitutional conventions, and national conferences be considered, and that basis of the argument would be the effect of procedures themselves on the mental-states of the populace, not the content of the constitution.

[63] Elkins, Ginsburg, and Blount, "The Citizen as Founder: Public Participation in Constitutional Approval," 362.

[64] Guy Grossman and Delia Baldassarri, "The Impact of Elections on Cooperation: Evidence from a Lab-in-the-Field Experiment in Uganda," (2012) 56 American Journal of Political Science 964–85.

[65] Morris Zelditch, "Processes of Legitimation: Recent Developments and New Directions," (2001) 64 Social Psychology Quarterly 4–17.

Even among elected constitution-making bodies, there are choices. Imagine again a debate about whether a given elected legislative body should transform itself into a self-created constituent legislature, and create a new constitution, or whether a new election should be held for a mandated constituent legislature or a constitutional convention. A PML argument could claim that only the people possess the power to create a legitimate constitution for themselves, but that they can choose to entrust or delegate this power by electing constitution-makers. Thus, only mandated constituent legislatures or constitutional conventions can create legitimate constitutions, for their members were chosen explicitly to write a constitution. An ordinary legislature, even one that transforms itself publicly into a constituent legislature, lacks such a capability, for its members were only elected to serve as ordinary legislators.

Deciding to use a constitutional convention or mandated constituent assembly leads to a further question regarding the specific electoral rules used to select delegates. Imagine that one knows that a constitution is unlikely to be sociologically legitimate unless citizens are able to identify with at least one of its member, i.e. see the document as resulting from a process involving someone like them. This means that the constitution-making body needs to meet what Elster calls the criterion of representativeness, i.e. it would need to "reflect, in miniature, the diversity of the nation." Thus, one could make a PSL argument for the implementation of proportional representation with little to no threshold and a single district, to be supplemented by a quota system for especially small and marginalized groups, because such a voting system would maximize representativeness and, as a result, maximize the chances of the constitution being considered rightfully authoritative by the populace.

5. Conclusion

Framing ratification as a means of creating a legitimate constitution is both an intuitive and relatively popular means of justifying the procedure. A legitimate constitution is thought to be the goal of any democratic constitution-making process, and thus if ratification can assist in obtaining one, that would be a very strong reason for implementing the process. This chapter set the stage for analyzing such a justification by putting forth a conceptual framework for the concept of legitimacy, how it applies to constitutions, and how procedures can lead to it. Such a framework is necessary because references to legitimacy in general, and in the constitution-making literature in particular, are either vague or inconsistent. To this end I articulated two types of legitimacy relevant to constitutions, moral legitimacy and sociological legitimacy, and two ways that procedure can legitimate a constitution, by having a procedural or a substantive effect. Combined, these distinctions produce four pathways through which a constitution-making procedure might legitimate a constitution: procedural moral legitimation, procedural sociological legitimation, substantive moral legitimation, and substantive legal legitimation. In the next chapter I test the legitimacy justification of ratification by seeing whether the procedure might plausibly operate through one of these four pathways.

9
Legitimation Device

This chapter continues our exploration of the third core justification of ratification, the legitimation justification, which asserts that ratification should be implemented in a constitution-making process because it helps to create a legitimate constitution. As the previous chapter demonstrated, if ratification has such an effect, it does so through one of four legitimation pathways: substantive sociological legitimation (SSL), substantive moral legitimation (SML), procedural sociological legitimation (PSL), and procedural moral legitimation (PML). In what follows, I build and examine what appear to be the strongest depictions of ratification playing a role through each of these pathways. I conclude that it remains highly dubitable whether ratification leads to legitimacy through any of the four pathways, and that the legitimation justification of ratification is thus far weaker than it initially appears.

In this chapter, I do not claim to be comprehensive. There are countless ways ratification might assist in the procedural or substantive legitimation of a constitution and I cannot canvass them all. I also do not purport to have the final say on many of the explanations I do cover. Most of my arguments do not amount to total refutations. Rather, my goal is to demonstrate that the most plausible explanations of how ratification might legitimate a constitution, even when treated as charitably as possible, still face numerous hurdles, rely on controversial and unproven empirical assumptions, and often overlook the differences between constitution-making and ordinary democratic decision-making. This makes them, at best, unstable and therefore unreliable ground from which to justify the use of an optional and costly procedure.

1. Substantive Legitimation

Maybe ratification plays a substantive role in constitutional legitimation. That is, perhaps the fact that a constitution is ratified makes it more likely that its contents fall within the bounds of morality (SML) or appear to do so for a significant portion of the relevant populace (SSL). But how might this occur? Ratification is a process through which an already drafted constitution is approved or rejected as a whole, so its effects on the substance of the text seem limited.[1] Ratifiers cannot

[1] I am excluding those rare instances in which ratifiers are asked to vote separately on certain provisions separated from the main text. To my knowledge this practice is isolated to state constitution-making in the United States.

Constitutional Ratification without Reason. Jeffrey A. Lenowitz, Oxford University Press. © Jeffrey A. Lenowitz 2022.
DOI: 10.1093/oso/9780198852346.003.0009

directly insert desired provisions or vote out those they find problematic. They are merely given a finished product and asked to vote it up or down.

Instead, ratification might affect the contents of a constitution and substantively legitimate it in one of two ways: by directly stopping, through rejection, illegitimate constitutions created by drafters from coming into effect; or by affecting drafters in such a way that they avoid writing illegitimate constitutions in the first place. This applies for both moral and sociological legitimacy, though one has to assume that a significant number of citizens ascribe legitimacy or illegitimacy to a constitution at least partially based on its contents for SSL to be possible. This might be doubtful for some of the reasons canvassed in chapter 6, i.e. many citizens do not have worked out preferences on the contents of a constitution. Nonetheless, for now, for the purposes of analyzing these legitimacy pathways, I will set this problem aside.

Note that some of the empirical evidence mentioned in chapter 1 suggests an association between ratification and certain constitutional provisions that can be construed as supporting the idea that ratification plays a role in substantive legitimation. For instance, Ginsburg, Elkins, and Blount found that constitutions approved by ratification referendum "appear more likely to provide for universal suffrage, a secret ballot, a referendum process in ordinary governance, and a public role in approving constitutional amendments."[2] It is easy to portray such findings as providing evidence for a ratification referendum's role in SSL or SML. One simply has to argue, not implausibly, that these constitutional features, more likely to occur in constitutions approved by referendum than those never submitted to one, are either features of a morally legitimate constitution or features thought necessary for a constitution to be legitimate.

However, such an inference is too quick. As noted in chapter 1, these empirical findings are mere correlations. As the authors candidly write, "[I]t seems prudent to reserve judgment about any causal inference with respect to these results," for since the "processes are themselves selected at some upstream point in constitution making, it is likely that the association between public involvement on the one hand and rights and democracy on the other reflects the common impact of an unobserved variable."[3] In other words, it is entirely likely that the same factor or factors that lead those in the initiation stage of constitution-making to choose to use a ratification referendum also lead drafters to write a constitution that spells out universal suffrage, a secret ballot, etc. This would make the association between ratification referendums and these features spurious due to the presence of a confounding variable. Ratification would not be helping to cause the purportedly

[2] Justin Blount, Zachary Elkins, and Tom Ginsburg, "Does the Process of Constitution-Making Matter?" in Tom Ginsburg (ed.), *Comparative Constitutional Design* (Cambridge University Press 2012) 55.

[3] Ibid., 57.

legitimizing features of a constitution, and thus the found correlation could not form the basis for an argument justifying the procedure. To conclude more about this found correlation, one either need to look at more rigorous empirical work that allows causal inferences—which has yet to be produced and may not be possible due to case scarcity and complexity—or examine various ways in which ratification might lead to textual change. The latter is the subject of this section.

1.1 Ratification as a Filter

Perhaps ratification serves as a legitimacy filter, ensuring that only legitimate constitutions come into force. The idea here is that ratifiers will reject actually or perceived morally illegitimate constitutions during the ratification process. This depiction of *ratification as a filter* is an example of either an SML or SSL claim. It describes a substantive effect because it assumes the existence of a content-based criterion of legitimacy and depicts ratification as having the ability to ensure that only constitutions that meet it are adopted. It pertains to both moral and sociological legitimacy, depending on whether ratifiers are meant to identify and reject constitutions that actually fall outside the bounds of morality, or merely those that they or their constituents believe do so.

Justifying ratification via its role as a legitimacy filter is also one of the few arguments for ratification fleshed out in the history of political thought, as Condorcet argued in favor of the procedure by depicting it as a filter in his little discussed 1789 essay on ratification, and later in his introduction to the theory underlying the ill-fated Girondin Constitution.[4] In order to fully understand his argument, and to evaluate ratification's ability to serve as a legitimacy filter more generally, it is helpful to first canvass some of Condorcet's other claims in his essay, many of which focus on rejecting various versions of ratification.

1.1.1 Condorcet on Ratification

At the beginning of the French Revolution, Condorcet was not a member of the Estates Generale, national assembly, or the national constituent assembly. He did not formally enter the politics of Revolutionary France until September 1789, when he was elected to the government of Paris and began chairing its committee for writing a municipal constitution.[5] Nonetheless, as a scholar and public intellectual

[4] Marquis de Condorcet, "On the Need for the Citizens to Ratify the Constitution," in Iain McLean and Fiona Hewitt (eds.), *Condorcet: Foundations of Social Choice and Political Theory* (Edward Elgar 1994); Condorcet, "A Survey of the Principles Underlying the Draft Constitution," in Iain McLean and Fiona Hewitt (eds.), *Condorcet: Foundations of Social Choice and Political Theory* (Edward Elgar 1994).

[5] Henry E. Bourne, "Municipal Politics in Paris in 1789," (1906) 11 The American Historical Review 263–86, 285n2; Keith Michael Baker, *Condorcet, from Natural Philosophy to Social Mathematics* (University of Chicago Press 1975) 268; Iain McLean and Fiona Hewitt (eds.), *Condorcet: Foundations of Social Choice and Political Theory* (Edward Elgar 1994).

long fascinated with institutional design, he paid much attention to the day-to-day debates. Thus, in August, while the national constituent assembly reflected on how to construct a new constitution for France in the wake of the demise of the Ancien Régime, Condorcet wrote a series of essays relating to the constitutional project. One of these is "On the Need for the Citizens to Ratify the Constitution."[6]

The subject of the essay is clarified in its first sentence: "Can the citizens give an assembly the power to establish a constitution or to accept one on their behalf without retaining the right to ratify it themselves, or should they retain this power?"[7] Condorcet thus assumes the existence of a right to ratify and asks if any of three potential means of ending a constitution-making process is acceptable: no ratification, ratification by convention, or ratification by referendum. He spends the majority of the essay giving a series of arguments, some of which were referenced in previous chapters, against these latter two types of ratification.

He first focuses on ratification by referendum. Like many of his contemporaries and the Berkshire Constitutionalists, Condorcet did not understand direct popular ratification as something possible through a national plebiscite.[8] Rather, he imagined that individuals would vote yes or no to a draft constitution within local assemblies. The results of these votes would be transmitted by the assemblies to the constitutional convention for tabulation. The convention would then announce the adoption of a new constitution if a majority of citizens in a majority of all assemblies approved it, or else make the specific changes needed to secure majority approval.[9]

Condorcet presents two objections to ratification of this sort. First, as discussed in chapter 6, he claims that citizens are "not sufficiently enlightened to judge a constitutional plan."[10] Because citizens are too ignorant to take a coherent stance on a constitution, their votes would either be irrational or the result of manipulation, neither of which is desirable.

His second objection applies specifically to this ratification referendum via assembly process. "How," as he puts it, "could 40,000 or so French assemblies possibly express a will on a plan that would necessarily be quite complicated." If a large enough percentage of voting assemblies rejected the constitution, it would be impossible to tell from their votes what needed to change in order to create an acceptable document. If voting assemblies voted on each clause separately, "the clauses approved by a plurality would form an incomplete constitution,"

[6] Albert Soboul, *The French Revolution 1787–1799: From the Storming of the Bastille to Napoleon* (NLB 1974) 147–51.

[7] Condorcet, "On the Need for the Citizens to Ratify the Constitution," 271.

[8] See Richard Tuck, *The Sleeping Sovereign: The Invention of Modern Democracy* (Cambridge University Press 2016) 149–51.

[9] This is different than the methods used to approve the Massachusetts and New Hampshire constitutions, in that the Americans required approval by a majority of individual votes, rather than a majority of town halls.

[10] Condorcet, "On the Need for the Citizens to Ratify the Constitution," 273.

and attempting to correct the rejected provisions would lead to a disjointed document.[11]

This second objection should seem familiar, in that Condorcet is simply generalizing the problems that befell the 1780 Massachusetts Constitutional Convention when it attempted to tabulate town voting returns.[12] This might be a coincidence. Alternatively, and intriguingly, it might suggest that Condorcet heard about the Massachusetts experience, especially the vote juggling needed to get the constitution approved, from someone familiar with the event. There is no evidence of this, but it is possible. While for obvious reasons the problems faced by the Massachusetts Convention were not publicly reported, either in the American colonies or in France, Condorcet spent time with Thomas Jefferson, Benjamin Franklin, Filippo Mazzei, John Adams, and François-Jean de Chastellux, all of whom likely knew what had transpired in Boston. John Adams, for instance, was actually one of the people responsible for counting the votes at the Massachusetts Convention, and Chastellux had met and discussed the convention with Samuel Adams, another participant, during his visit to the American states.[13]

"Having agreed that the citizens should not retain the direct right to accept or reject the constitution," Condorcet next examines whether, "having requested one assembly to form a constitution, they must then give another assembly the right to ratify the constitution proposed by the first." Condorcet rejects such ratification by convention by arguing that it leads to infinite regress, for a body elected to ratify a constitution would need the power to make changes if it rejected the constitution, "in which case a third would have to be elected to ratify these changes, and so on" until acceptance by a convention.[14] In the best case, Condorcet notes, this would unhealthily extend the time needed to approve a constitution. This argument, of course, is only persuasive if one assumes that a constitution-making process that ends in the rejection of a draft constitution is unacceptable. For Condorcet, such an assumption would have been unquestionable; from within the heat of the French Revolution the alternative to a new form of government likely looked to be pure violence and chaos.[15]

Condorcet goes on to point out that ratification by a ratifying convention also seems redundant. It involves entrusting representatives with the right to ratify, and thus, "approval by such a Convention would contribute nothing more to rights

[11] Ibid., 273–74.

[12] See chapter 3, section 2.

[13] Chastellux recounts this discussion in his *Travels in North America*. See Marquis de Chastellux, *Travels in North America in the Years 1780, 1781, 1782* (New York 1828) 128.

[14] Condorcet, "On the Need for the Citizens to Ratify the Constitution," 274.

[15] Condorcet also touches upon the possibility of the local assemblies that appointed members to the Estates Generale being used to ratify the constitution. He cautions against this, arguing that not only will these assemblies likely be without authority, but, in an echo of arguments made at the Philadelphia Convention, that they will also be biased toward self-interest rather than the good of the nation. See ibid., 275–76.

than approval by a National Assembly which was authorized to establish a constitution."[16] Here, Condorcet is simply noting that if the people can transfer their right to ratify to a ratification convention, it is unclear why they should not transfer the right to the constitution-making body itself rather than going to the trouble of introducing another procedure. Thus, in a sense, he is questioning the payoff of multiplying sites of participation when it comes in the form of additional instances of representative decision-making. As I will show in the next section, this suggests an argument against, or at least a weakness of, certain attempts to justify ratification because of its role in procedurally legitimating the constitution.

At this point in his argument, only the first of the three options for concluding a constitution-making process remains: citizens give up the right to ratify and no ratification takes place. Condorcet suggests that this is an acceptable outcome, for while it is true that "whatever form is used to establish the constitution, it is probable that I will not accept a great many of its proposals," it is nonetheless better to have a constitution written and approved by elected framers than to preserve an individual right to ratify and, in the process, risk increasing the time a polity goes without a constitution. "Would slight imperfections in the constitution cause more harm," he asks, "than would result from a delay of perhaps several years, during which time France would be without a constitution, or would have only an uncertain one?"

Up until this point, Condorcet's essay makes a consistent and powerful argument: there is little reason to submit a constitution for ratification via referendum or convention/assembly. However, rather than end his essay here, Condorcet quickly reverses course. He introduces a defense of ratification via referendum by making an SML argument depicting ratification as a legitimacy filter. Claiming that his prior analysis concerning the dangers of submitting a constitution to the people is only persuasive when it comes to constitutions that offend mere opinion, Condorcet writes that, "[i]f my rights and those of my fellow citizens are violated, then I must of course make a forceful protest. I need not worry about delaying the establishment of an unjust constitution; on the contrary, my aim must be to prevent such a constitution from ever being established."[17] In other words, Condorcet claims that avoiding a constitution that violates basic rights is of the utmost priority, such that worries about time delays or other procedural complications are irrelevant in comparison.

He goes on to suggest a two-step direct ratification procedure narrowly tailored to prevent rights violations. First, the assembly should write a declaration of rights.[18] This should be submitted to citizen assemblies, after which all citizens

[16] Ibid., 276.

[17] Ibid., 277.

[18] Condorcet had published, albeit anonymously, his own version of a declaration of rights in London earlier in 1789. See Marquis de Condorcet, "Declaration of Rights," in Iain McLean and Fiona Hewitt (eds.), *Condorcet: Foundations of Social Choice and Political Theory* (Edward Elgar 1994). Characteristic

will be "required to pronounce, not whether it has been well or badly drafted, but whether it omits any of the true rights of man or contains any principles which violate one of these rights." Next, the assembly should submit the constitution to the assemblies. Once again, citizens should not "judge whether it is well or badly organized, but . . . confirm that it contains no violation of the declaration of rights, or else to point out any particular clause which does constitute a violation."[19] In both of these steps, the failure to obtain a majority approval of the declaration of rights or the constitution would result in the drafters amending their handiwork in response to objections and submitting it back to the voters, continuing to do so until sufficient approval is reached.

Condorcet was so taken with this ratification proposal that, four year later, he integrated it into his "A Survey of the Principles underlying the Draft Constitution," which he presented to the national constituent assembly in February 1793 as a means of explaining the theory behind the Girondin Constitution. He explains that "approval [of the constitution] is a clear indication that . . . no part of it violates their rights; but rather that it seems to offer a complete guarantee of these rights." Rejection, on the other hand, "means that the citizens do not consider that the constitution provides a complete guarantee of their rights, or . . . violates their rights instead of protecting them."[20] Thus, for Condorcet, ratification of this particular type is justified because, if things go according to plan, ratification filters out any constitution that violates basic rights. This is an SML if one assumes that, for Condorcet, avoiding basic rights violations is a necessary feature of a morally legitimate constitution. From what he writes in this essay and elsewhere, this assumption seems warranted.

1.1.2 Assessing the Filter

I will overlook the two-stage specifics of Condorcet's proposal and instead concentrate on two assumptions made by his and any similar attempts to construe a ratification procedure as a filter for illegitimate constitutions: (i) that ratifiers will make their decision on the basis of legitimacy; and (ii) that ratifiers are able to detect

of Condorcet, it is oddly complex for a bill of rights, and makes frequent mention of the importance of voting thresholds.

[19] Condorcet, "On the Need for the Citizens to Ratify the Constitution," 277. Splitting the constitution-making process into two is not as outlandish as Condorcet's proposal might initially seem. In a sense, the practice of laying down guiding principles before the drafting process, made popular by the thirty-four guiding principles set by the multiparty negotiating process in South Africa, reflects a similar approach.

[20] Condorcet, "A Survey of the Principles Underlying the Draft Constitution," 194–95. For an alternative translation, see Marquis de Condorcet, "The Principle of, the Justifications for, the New Constitution," in Marc Allan Goldstein (ed.), *Social and Political Thought of the French Revolution, 1788–1797: An Anthology of Original Texts* (Peter Lang 1997) 416. For an excellent discussion on Condorcet's jury theorem and its implications, see McLean and Hewitt (eds.), *Condorcet: Foundations of Social Choice and Political Theory*, 34–40.

whether or not a constitution is morally legitimate. Both of these assumptions can be challenged. For the sake of simplicity, I focus on the SML variant of the ratification as filter argument when talking about (i), though the problem I raise applies to SSL equally.

The first assumption is that the criterion of choice for all or most ratifiers is whether or not a constitution is morally legitimate. That is, that ratifiers will reject a constitution if it is morally illegitimate and accept a constitution that is neutral or legitimate because of their concern for legitimacy. For Condorcet, this means that ratifiers will look for significant rights violations in the text and reject the constitution if they find one.

Condorcet attempts to build this presumption into his proposal by urging the assembly to remind voters that they are to vote against the constitution *only* if it violates their fundamental rights. Confining voters' attention to rights violations was essential for him, as he long worried that most citizens in France, and likely anywhere, lacked the competence for complex and particular political decisions. In the language of his jury theorem, he worried that the average voter would be worse than random at making such decisions, such that a decision reached by a large number of citizens would almost certainly be the incorrect one.[21] This worry was the basis for the rejection of direct democracy in his famous 1785 "Essay on the Application of Mathematics to the Theory of Decision-Making," where he explains that "a pure democracy, indeed, would only be appropriate to a people much more enlightened, must freer from prejudices than any of those known to history."[22]

Evaluating an entire constitution is undoubtedly a complex political decision, and thus submitting one to local assemblies for citizens to directly vote on would result in an incorrect and unwanted outcome. This is why Condorcet noted earlier in his ratification essay that voters were "not sufficiently enlightened to judge a constitutional plan." However, for him, recognizing basic rights was not a complicated task. For, as he explained in his 1789 *Ideas on Despotism*, "the natural rights of man are known in general to all those with a sound mind and a noble soul."[23] In other words, Condorcet is conceptualizing ratification as a moral application of his jury theorem, and assuming that unlike with constitutional evaluation as a whole, voters have a better than random competence at identifying rights violations. Indeed, he concludes the ratification essay making this very point: "By limiting

[21] Though Condorcet does not mention average decision-making competence, the theory still holds when using it. See Philip J. Boland, "Majority Systems and the Condorcet Jury Theorem," (1989) 38 Journal of the Royal Statistical Society Series D (The Statistician) 181–89, 184.

[22] Marquis de Condorcet, "Essay on the Application of Mathematics to the Theory of Decision-Making," in Keith Michael Baker (ed.), *Condorcet: Selected Writings* (Bobbs-Merrill 1976) 49. Condorcet instead advocated for a single assembly of enlightened men that would be large enough that a decision by a bare majority would guarantee a true judgment.

[23] Marquis de Condorcet, "Ideas on Despotism: For the Benefit of Those Who Pronounce this Word without Understanding It," in Guillaume Ansart (ed.), *Condorcet: Writings on the United States* (The Pennsylvania State University Press 2012).

the individual right of the citizens to pronouncing only on what is or is not contrary to their rights, we are enabling them to retain control over the establishment and maintenance of the social order precisely to the extent that their enlightenment permits."[24] Thus, by confining voters to making the simple decision on the presence or absence of rights violations, Condorcet tries to amplify v, the probability that a voter chooses the correct outcome, and thus override the disastrous consequences of large scale decision-making by the unenlightened.

Unfortunately, for Condorcet's plan and for any argument that seeks to position ratification as a legitimacy filter, there is no way to ensure that ratifiers adopt legitimacy as their decisive reason for deciding whether to reject or accept a constitution. Ratifiers, regardless of how you direct them, might accept or reject constitutions for all sorts of reasons that may or may not correlate with a decision made on the basis of legitimacy.

Ratifiers might reject a constitution because they hate the sitting government and believe that voting down the constitution is an effective form of punishment, or because they view it as a political bargain rather than as a document meant to maximize the public good. In 1967, voters in New York likely voted down a proposed constitution for the latter reason, with many disgusted at what they perceived as bargaining inappropriate for constitution-making, specifically the decision by Democrats to allow religious primary school funding in the hopes of capturing the Catholic vote.[25]

Alternatively, voters might approve a constitution simply because it represents a change from an undesirable status quo, even if they nonetheless see its contents fall outside the bounds of what they view as a morally legitimate constitution.[26] This is likely what happened in the 2005 referendum for the Constitution of the Democratic Republic of Congo, where voters seemed to care less about its content and more about their beliefs that it could be a road out of conflict.[27] This effect might be heightened by ratifiers being especially risk-averse in the constitution-making setting, due to their familiarity with a failed status quo and the genuine unknown of a draft constitution.[28]

Some voters might see themselves as constitutional scholars, accepting or rejecting the constitution based on whether it meets their beliefs, however well

[24] Condorcet, "On the Need for the Citizens to Ratify the Constitution," 278.

[25] See *New York Times*, November 5, 1967, 10E; and Henrik N. Dullea, *Charter Revision in the Empire State: The Politics of New York's 1967 Constitutional Convention* (Rockefeller Institute Press 1997).

[26] Yash Ghai and Jill Cottrell (eds.), *Creating the New Constitution: A Guide for Nepali Citizens* (International IDEA 2008).

[27] James Thuo Gathii, "Popular Authorship and Constitution Making: Comparing and Contrasting the DRC and Kenya," (2008) 49 William and Mary Law Review 1109–38.

[28] Elkins and Hudson explain this, in accordance with prospect theory, as voters seeing themselves in a domain of losses, facing two bad choices, and thus willing to gamble on a new constitutional regime regardless of their specific reservations. Zachary Elkins and Alexander Hudson, "The Constitutional Referendum in Historical Perspective," in David Landau and Hannah Lerner (eds.), *Comparative Constitution Making* (Edward Elgar 2019) 162.

developed or informed, about what a good constitution must look like. And others might simply listen to a friend or local official or newspaper. If a significant number of ratifiers use such non-legitimacy-related criteria when deciding whether to approve or reject a constitution during ratification, then ratification will not be a predictable or effective filter for legitimacy, and the acceptance of a constitution would only signal that ratifiers have reasons, or what they think are reasons, for not rejecting the constitution. This problem emerges regardless of ratification type. An elected member of a ratifying convention, a citizen voting in a referendum, or a sub-state governmental actor all might very well make their ratifying decision for reasons unrelated to legitimacy.

Thus, ratifiers might accept or reject legitimate or illegitimate constitutions and there is therefore no reason to be confident that the ratification legitimacy filter ever does much filtering at all. While the caricature of Condorcet as a naïve idealist, formed based on too much attention being given to the *Sketch for a Historical Picture of the Progress of the Human Mind*, is surely wrong, his belief that one could ensure that voters make decisions on the basis of specific reasons, at least in this instance, was hopelessly optimistic. To put the problem more precisely: justifying ratification by portraying the procedure as a means of filtering out illegitimate constitutions only works if, at the least, ratifiers will see illegitimacy as a decisive reason for rejecting a constitution. Since there is no way to ensure, and no reason to presume, that ratifiers will adopt this choice criterion, this justification for ratification fails.

Additionally, the second assumption, that ratifiers can detect a morally illegitimate constitution, is also problematic, but in a way that mainly applies to the attempt to justify ratification referendums via SML. In this limited case, voters are supposed to be able to assess whether a constitution is morally illegitimate. The problem, once again, is voter ignorance. If voters are too uninformed to evaluate a constitution, then they might very well be too uninformed to assess its moral legitimacy. This problem is compounded by the likelihood that constitutions, if illegitimate, are likely to be so for subtle reasons. If framers accidentally created a constitution that falls outside the bounds of morality, then its moral flaws will likely be less than obvious. If they intended to create a constitution that is illegitimate, and they know that ratifiers will reject an illegitimate constitution, then they will do all they can to hide their morally problematic provisions.

Condorcet's own metric of moral legitimacy is a perfect example of this problem. Though Condorcet repeatedly suggests that recognizing rights violations in a constitution is relatively straightforward, his own discussion of the simplicity of this task seems to give the game up. After explaining the ease with which citizens would identify problematic constitutional provisions, how "only a few clauses of the constitution could threaten rights, and these are necessarily the simplest," he writes the following:

> We must ensure that equality is scrupulously respected in the way in which people are given citizenship rights and allowed to enjoy these rights. We must also ensure that there is equality in the National Assembly; that the various provinces are proportionally represented according to the principle which conforms with national equality; that judicial power is independent of any particular authority, but subject to the laws; that the government, also bound by the laws, can make neither laws nor exemptions, nor-exercise arbitrary power. In this way, we shall protect rights, and while the constitutional laws may be good or bad, they could no longer be unjust.[29]

This directive is not simple. Identifying whether a modern constitution instantiates such principles is not the easy task that Condorcet wants to suggest. The fact that Condorcet's own declaration of rights runs to fifteen pages and covers much technical discussion further undermines his assumption.[30]

To make the point differently, let us assume that one moral boundary for a legitimate constitution is that it establishes an independent judiciary with the power to check the other branches of government. Imagine a constitution that sets up a complicated scheme of judicial administration which relegates ultimate power to a political appointee of a legislative body or executive with dismissal power.[31] In such an instance, one might conclude that the constitution would be illegitimate according to the above-mentioned criteria, but in order to reach this judgment a voter would have to read the constitution, understand it, know enough about institutional design, and resist the inevitable bombardment of misinformation that would accompany the ratification campaign. The idea of ratification as a filter assumes that ratifiers are able to use their votes to exercise quality control on the constitution. If they are uninformed, however, this becomes at the least unreliable.

Now, one might argue that the above misinterprets the filter argument. We should instead see it as a simpler epistemic claim about ratification. How and why voters reach their decision on the constitution is irrelevant. The latter was a concern for evaluating the Unique Site Justification (USJ) because it mattered that voters were aware of and responsible for their decisions in a deep and meaningful way. For an epistemic argument such as ratification-as-filter, only outcomes are important, not the reasons for them. What matters is that on average ratifiers will be better than random at voting correctly, which in this instance means rejecting illegitimate constitutions and accepting neutral or legitimate ones. If this is true, and if we ensure our ratification procedure involves at least a large assembly, we

[29] Condorcet, "On the Need for the Citizens to Ratify the Constitution," 278.

[30] Condorcet, "Declaration of Rights."

[31] Here I am imagining a more extreme version of the President of the National Judicial Office specified in Art. 13 of the current Hungarian Constitution. For a critique of this office, see European Commission for Democracy Through Law, *Opinion on the Fourth Amendment to the Fundamental Law of Hungary* (Council of Europe 2013).

can all but guarantee a correct outcome. That we cannot control how ratifiers make their decision, and that some ratifiers won't be able to distinguish a legitimate constitution from an illegitimate one, is beside the point.

This objection cannot save the ratification-as-filter argument. It persuades by hiding its unexplained premise: that ratifiers will be better than random at voting correctly. What is needed is a reason for holding this assumption. The most intuitive explanation is that ratifiers possess the capacity to identify illegitimate constitutions, and will reject them on this basis, which is what I considered above. The weaknesses of this explanation are problematic not because the explanation carries some independent normative weight, but rather because it means there is no obvious reason to maintain that ratifiers will likely reject illegitimate constitutions. Absent an alternative explanation, this particular substantive legitimacy justification for ratification remains unconvincing.

Before moving on, I want to make two further observations. First, conceptualizing ratification referendums as a moral legitimacy filter is also in tension with the possibility that voters, or a majority of them, want to implement a morally illegitimate constitution.[32] When this is the case, ratification will not function as a filter. For instance, voters in Alabama overwhelmingly approved the state's 1901 constitution, which included provisions for racial segregation and poll taxes and was written, "to establish white Supremacy in this State."[33] Similarly, if the Croatian Constitution of 1990 was submitted to the people in a referendum, it is entirely possible that the majority Croatian population would have endorsed the draft, despite the fact that the constitution specifically excluded Croat Serbians from being considered one of the constituent nations of the republic.

Second, it is worth noting that historically, even without adopting a very specific conception of what the boundaries of a morally legitimate constitution are, it seems that ratification's performance as a filter for illegitimate constitutions is inconsistent. Referendums led to the approval of Chavez' authoritarian constitution in 1999 and the rejection of Mugabe's oddly decent constitution in 2000. Voters in Kenya rejected a proposed constitution in 2005 yet ratified an extremely similar document in 2010. In Rwanda in 2003, voters overwhelmingly approved a constitution that violated numerous political and social rights. In some sense, the fact that ratification by referendum is the favored way for autocrats to end their constitution-making processes attests to the device's inability to filter much of anything.[34]

[32] See Gabriel L. Negretto, "Constitution-Making and Liberal Democracy: The Role of Citizens and Representative Elites," (2020) 18 International Journal of Constitutional Law 206–32, 213.

[33] Cited in Wayne Flynt, "Alabama's Shame: The Historical Origins of the 1901 Constitution," (2002) 53 Alabama Law Review 67–76, 70.

[34] Jonathan Wheatley and Micha Germann, "Outcomes of Constitution-Making: Democratization and Conflict Resolution," in Jonathan Wheatley and Fernando Mendez (eds.), *Patterns of Constitutional Design: The Role of Citizens and Elites in Constitution-Making* (Routledge) 56, 162.

1.2 Ratification as Content Control

Perhaps ratification leads to a substantively legitimate constitution by affecting events earlier in the constitution-making process. Specifically, maybe the presence of ratification makes it unlikely that framers will write a morally or sociologically illegitimate constitution in the first place. This depicts ratification as a *means of content control*, as a way of affecting the contents of a constitution by changing the behavior of its drafters. The procedure creates legitimate constitutions not because ratifiers reject all the illegitimate ones, but because the anticipation of a future ratification and the threat of rejection leads framers to make different drafting decisions than they otherwise would. As mentioned in chapter 1, Elster describes this function of ratification as a "downstream constraint." This constraint, I argue, breaks into two. Ratification can be a means of content control by acting as what I call a goal constraint or as a justificatory constraint.[35]

Ratification serves as a *goal constraint* when constitution-makers restrict their goal constitution, the constitution that they wish to produce, to a range they believe is acceptable to future ratifiers. That is, framers working to create a constitution that aligns with their own preferences or goals, regardless of whether these stem from reason or passions or interests, will do so under the constraints imposed by what they expect is necessary to satisfy the minimum number of ratifiers needed for ratificatory approval.[36] They will, for instance, avoid institutional choices that they predict will be too controversial and include those they believe to be necessary for ratifiers. As Elster notes, the minutes of the U.S. federal convention "are very revealing in this respect, with their constant references to what might or might not be approved by the ratifying conventions."[37]

Ratification as a *justificatory constraint* is a bit more complex. Here, framers do not change their goal constitution to meet substantive preferences that they believe ratifiers have on the contents of the constitution, but rather avoid writing in provisions that they believe are unjustifiable in accordance with existing norms. To understand this, consider how societal norms might affect the contents of a constitution indirectly by constraining drafters. The underlying idea is that norms might exist making certain types of explanation or arguments off-limits, and thus any provision that can only be justified using off-limits argumentation will not appear in the constitutional text.

Elster's various discussions of the civilizing force of hypocrisy and the masking of self-interest during political debate provide an example. Consider a delegate to a public constituent assembly operating in the context of a norm of impartiality.

[35] Jon Elster, "Forces and Mechanisms in the Constitution-Making Process," (1995) 45 Duke Law Review 364–96, 374.

[36] Ibid.

[37] Jon Elster, "The Optimal Design of a Constituent Assembly," in Helene Landemore and Jon Elster (eds.), *Collective Wisdom: Principles and Mechanisms* (Cambridge University Press 2012) 148–72, 169.

Such a delegate will find it in his interest to cast his arguments in the language of impartiality in order "to avoid the opprobrium associated with the overt appeal to private interest in public debates," "to present his position in a way that precludes compromising or bargaining," or "to persuade others if he believes they are susceptible of being swayed by impartial argument."[38] Elster explains that, among other things, this has the effect of limiting the sorts of positions a delegate can pursue and write into a constitution, for some will too obviously stem from self- or party-interest and not admit to impartial justification. Thus, the existence of some norm of impartiality, or other similar functioning norm, can result in a constitution with different contents when compared to what would exist in its absence.

Ratification might play a role in this mechanism, and thus affect the content of a constitution by acting as a justificatory constraint, in two ways. On the one hand, the existence of a ratification procedure, especially one that involves the public in some capacity, might heighten the attention placed on the drafting of a constitution. That is, the public might pay more attention to the debates surrounding the drafting of a constitution if they know they are to play some role in its approval. Framers will know this, and thus the constraining effects of the relevant norms, such as the norm of impartiality described above, might be heightened as well. On the other hand, framers might anticipate themselves or others having to defend their drafting choices during the lead up to a ratification vote and therefore avoid drafting decisions that cannot be justified in accordance with the operating norms. Thus, for instance, in the context of a norm of impartiality, if a certain constitution-making provision too plainly appeared to be the result of sheer self-interest or partiality, and resists any plausible alternative public justification, a constitution-making body might have to alter it or eliminate it altogether.

For ratification's role as a goal constraint to serve as the basis of an SSL or SML content control justification of the procedure, drafters must believe that ratifiers will reject a constitution if it falls outside the bounds of morality, in reality or as the ratifiers perceive it, and shift their goal constitution in response. Note that this does not mean that they have to conceptualize the constraint as having to do with legitimacy, but rather that the effect of the constraint is to screen out illegitimate constitutions. Similarly, an SSL or SML justification of ratification that relies on the idea of ratification as a justificatory constraint must assume that norms exist that would prevent framers from using the sorts of arguments that would be required to justify an actual or perceived morally illegitimate constitution. To continue with our previous example, if one of the boundaries of a morally legitimate constitution

[38] Jon Elster, "Deliberation and Constitution Making," in Jon Elster (ed.), *Deliberative Democracy* (Cambridge University Press 1998) 101–2. See also Jon Elster, *Explaining Social Behavior: More Nuts and Bolts for the Social Sciences* (Cambridge University Press 2007) 406–7; Jon Elster, *Alchemies of the Mind: Rationality and the Emotions* (Cambridge University Press 1998) 371–78; Jon Elster, "Constitution-Making in Eastern Europe: Rebuilding the Boat in the Open Sea," (1993) 71 Public Administration 169–217, 183.

is that it is not biased toward certain segments of the population, then a norm of impartial justification heightened by the increased attention brought by ratification might have the effect of ensuring or increasing the chances of such an impartial constitution.

Both of these constraint mechanisms initially seem plausible, and therefore likely to provide firm foundations for a legitimacy-based justification of ratification. However, there are reasons to question the efficacy of both and the strength of the justification more generally. First, note that the effects of both constraints are additive, in the sense that forms of these constraints operate even without ratification. Framers involved in democratic constitution-making already care about what citizens will think about the constitution, for a disliked document will be poorly received. No set of framers involved in creating a democratic constitution would completely ignore the preferences and beliefs of the citizens to be governed by their creation when formulating their goal constitution. This is all the more true when the constitution-making body is populated by delegates from civil society or ethnic groups, who, at least in their official capacity, are meant to translate the preferences of those they represent into constitutional text.

Further, as already described, if justificatory norms regarding the permissible bounds of argumentation exist, they will also operate to an extent without ratification, especially in today's ever more transparent drafting processes. A desire to avoid informal ostracism, hits to one's reputation, and bad press will already give drafters reasons to advance arguments and provisions that fall within the normative bounds of permissibility. This is not to say that ratification won't heighten either effect, but rather to remind us that the correct comparison is not to the behavior of drafters who disregard popular opinion and care nothing for norms of argument. This means that if ratification functions as a goal or justificatory constraint, its effects will be more subtle than initially imagined.

Second, ratification's function as a goal constraint and justificatory constraint requires that constitution-makers believe that ratifiers will reject constitutions that cannot be justified in accordance with a specific norm or are illegitimate more generally. That is, for ratification to function as a means of content control during drafting, framers have to believe that ratification can, in a sense, *function as a legitimacy filter*. As discussed above, there might be little reason for this belief and constitution-makers, then, might not hold it.

For example, a constitution-maker creating a constitution for Burundi might plausibly believe that ratifiers will not reject a constitution if it is slightly illegitimate, or completely illegitimate, or if some of its provisions can only be justified by violating some societal norms of argumentation, because she knows that ratifiers will approve anything in the hopes of changing their status quo. Such a framer might feel no or very little concern with writing in provisions to benefit a particular group or minimizing certain rights, or even having to make arguments to this effect in the public domain. Similarly, and especially for ratification referendums, a constitution-maker might believe that ratifiers are so uninformed about constitutional design that there is little likelihood for them to identify a morally dubious provision or argument.[39] Both ignorance and competing decision-making factors can decrease the chances that ratification can serve as a filter, and if ratifiers know this, ratification's goal and justificatory constraint functions will often be ineffective.

The third problem relates to incompleteness in the above argument. It is not exactly correct to say that ratification's function as a goal and justificatory constraint depends on framers' beliefs that ratifiers will reject a legitimacy norm-violating or illegitimate constitution. Rather, it depends on their belief that ratifiers cannot be convinced to approve a constitution despite its actual or perceived moral deficiencies or misled into thinking an illegitimate constitution is legitimate. As mentioned in chapter 6, ratification campaigns almost always accompany ratification referendums. The same is true for other ratification types, though these campaigns might be more or less public depending upon the publicity of a ratification procedure. These campaigns are incredibly effective due to the technical nature of constitution-making evaluation, the high-stakes nature of the decision, the frequently unstable nature of the status quo, and the disruption of normal cue-givers.[40]

The potential belief by framers that they can persuade or mislead voters to accept constitutions that they might otherwise reject due to legitimacy related appraisals further weakens the goal and justificatory constraint functions of ratification, especially via referendum. This does not mean that ratification would have no effect—certain provisions might be so obviously morally problematic that they would resist any attempted persuasion or manipulation—but it weakens the procedure's ability to predictably legitimate through this pathway substantially.[41]

Fourth, conceptualizing ratification as a goal constraint is similar to the control function of an accountability mechanism in traditional forms of representation, in that it assumes that the threat of ratification failure and the desire for ratification passage will cause framers to respond positively to the preferences and needs of prospective ratifiers.[42] Even if one accepts that ratifiers have preferences related to legitimacy, are willing to make a decision based upon them, and are not caught

[39] See the discussion chapter 6, sections 2.1 and 2.2 for why such ignorance should be expected.

[40] Framers can also encourage ignorance by limiting the time between promulgation and ratification. Such a strategy appears to be common. Pinochet submitted Chile's 1980 constitution without any public discussion under incredibly tight time constraints; while, as mentioned in chapter 1, the Constitutional Commission in Romania only allowed sixteen days for the electorate to review the draft. Jennifer Widner, "Constitution Writing and Conflict Resolution Project" <http://www.princeton.edu/~pcwcr/>.

[41] Recent work by Elkins and Hudson demonstrates that from 1789–2016, 94% of all constitutions put to referendum were approved. Does this mean that nearly all constitutions submitted to a referendum were deemed legitimate, or that citizens are unlikely to reject a constitution regardless of its content? Elkins and Hudson, "The Constitutional Referendum in Historical Perspective."

[42] See chapter 7, section 2.2.

up in the manipulative net of ratification campaigns, the procedure's effectiveness at causing framers to write a more legitimate constitution will be hampered by similar problems. As discussed in chapter 7, section 2.2, there are many: ratifiers might have contradictory conceptions of what it means for a constitution to be legitimate, framers might have difficulty assessing what these legitimacy beliefs consist in due to communication issues, and ratifiers' legitimacy beliefs might shift through the course of constitution-making. Each of these issues will substantively reduce the effectiveness of ratification as a goal constraint.

In the end, one can be no more confident in the reliability of ratification to cause framers to write more legitimate constitutions than one can be in the procedure's ability to filter out illegitimate ones. As noted, ratification might occasionally do both. It might sometimes lead to the rejection of a constitution over its illegitimate contents and framers might sometimes omit or add in language to meet substantive legitimacy requirements they suspect ratifiers will impose. However, neither legitimating pathway should be seen as routine, and thus both are weak sources of justification for the procedure.

2. Procedural Moral Legitimation

Unlike substantive legitimation, I will examine the two procedural legitimation pathways separately. As mentioned, procedural legitimation occurs when a constitution is legitimate because of how it was made, rather than its content. The fact that ratifiers approved a constitution either contributes to the moral reasons in favor of its claim to authority (PML) or appears to do so from the perspective of those it governs (PSL). In this section I consider two families of arguments associated with the former: those that appeal to constituent power and those that appeal to consent.

2.1 Return to CPJ

Portraying ratification as a means of PML is to claim that the occurrence of ratification, alone or in combination with other procedures, is a sufficient means of creating a morally legitimate constitution, regardless of the procedure's effect on outcomes. Something about the process of submitting a constitution to a ratifier produces moral reasons in support of its claim to authority. Assuming that one goal of constitution-making is to produce a legitimate constitution, this gives a strong reason to implement some sort of ratification procedure.

The logic of such a PML-based justification of ratification should be familiar, for constituent power justifications (CPJs) are examples. Put in the language of moral legitimacy, a theory of constituent power claims that a constitution's claim to authority is only morally justified if it is the product of a process that involves the constituent power in a primary role. Contemporary scholars of constituent power often say this explicitly. For instance, Colón-Riós claims: "the question of democratic legitimacy is not about the procedure that the constitution establishes for law-making . . . , but about the procedures through which the constitution was adopted," with a specific focus on the "actual role that citizens played during the moment of constitution-making."[43] Thus, according to a CPJ, the people must exercise their constituent power and create the constitution for it to be morally legitimate, and ratification is what makes or helps to make this possible. For the reasons covered in chapters 4 and 6, this PML-based justification fails to persuade.

2.2 Consent Theory

Of course, the Berkshire Constitutionalists, and aspects of the constituent power tradition more generally, descended from a particular interpretation of Locke's theory of the original contract. This hints at a more general argument that links ratification with PML by claiming that the procedure morally legitimizes a constitution by allowing individual citizens to directly consent to it. This argument derives from consent theory—by which I mean any theory, Lockean or otherwise, that grounds moral legitimacy solely in individual consent. For such a theory, authority is exclusively concerned with the right to impose new duties by binding directives and to have these directives obeyed. Since individuals are free and autonomous beings, such a right can only arise upon consent, the performance of an informed non-coerced voluntary act signaling a deliberate undertaking of corollary obligations and the resultant acceptance of a restriction on future choices.[44]

A consent theorist might argue that ratification (via referendum only) is a *necessary* component of the constitution-making process because it uniquely allows individuals to directly consent to their governing document and undertake obligations. This gives the constitution, and the state that results, a morally justified right to rule over all those consenting.[45] According to our framework, this is an example of a PML pathway, because it concerns moral reasons for authority and claims that a referendum legitimates a constitution because of the occurrence of the procedure itself, rather than any specific effect it has on the contents of the produced document.

[43] Joel Colón-Ríos, *Weak Constitutionalism: Democratic Legitimacy and the Question of Constituent Power* (Routledge 2012) 115.

[44] A. John Simmons, *Moral Principles and Political Obligations* (Princeton University Press 1979) 57–71; A. John Simmons, *Justification and Legitimacy: Essays on Rights and Obligations* (Cambridge University Press 2001) 122–57 See also Leslie Green, "Law, Legitimacy, and Consent," (1989) 62 Southern California Law Review 795–825.

[45] Note that traditionally consent theorists talk about the state or government more generally, and do not depict the constitution as the object of consent.

A justification of ratification on these grounds can of course be dismissed by rejecting consent theory directly. However, even without doing so, several challenges emerge. First, consent might be a basis of political legitimacy more generally but just not apply to constitutions. Michelman, for example, argues that well-written constitutions are necessarily vague, open to interpretation, and flexible when it comes to the moral concerns that factor into an account of legitimacy based on informed consent. Consent to a constitution is therefore impossible because the kind of things people need to know to consent and take on obligations are the very things that are only decided upon once the constitution goes into effect. To a similar end, Hardin argues that adopting a constitution does not entail future commitments and obligations, for as a coordination device a constitution simply raises the cost of trying to do things some other way. The logic of consent arguments, which rely on the notion of a contract and the exchange of obligations, duties, and power, is therefore inapplicable.[46]

However, even if one ignores these concerns and accepts the applicability of consent theory to constitution-making, a more major problem arises. Put simply, a consent-based PML argument for ratification requires one to endorse a view according to which most or even all past, present, and future constitutions are illegitimate for a majority or supermajority of those they govern. This follows from three observations.

First, because unanimity would make the adoption of a constitution nearly impossible, ratification referendums normally utilize majority or supermajority thresholds.[47] This means that a constitution is illegitimate for everyone who voted against it, for they formally did not consent. The same is true for all qualified voters who forgot to vote, were physically unable to vote, or voted under conditions of coercion, for none of them consented.

Second, consent theory demands that individuals intend to consent when they do, for obligations do not adhere if a person accidently agrees to undertake them or undertakes them without knowing their substance.[48] If I am stretching at a

[46] Frank I. Michelman, "Ida's Way: Constructing the Respect-Worthy Governmental System," (2004) 72 Fordham Law Review 345–65, 362–63; Frank I. Michelman, "Is the Constitution a Contract for Legitimacy?," (2003) 8 Review of Constitutional Studies 101–28, 120–121; Russel Hardin, *Liberalism, Constitutionalism, and Democracy* (Oxford University Press 1999) 113.

[47] Despite suggestions by Rousseau, Tullock, and Buchanan, and others, to my knowledge no constitution has come into force under a voting rule requiring unanimity. Jean Jacques Rousseau, "Of the Social Contract," in Victor Gourevitch (ed.), *Rousseau: The Social Contract and Other Later Political Writings* (Cambridge University Press 1997) 49 (I.5.3); James M. Buchanan and Gordon Tullock, *The Calculus of Consent: Logical Foundations of Constitutional Democracy*, vol. 3 (The Collected Works of James M Buchanan, Liberty Fund 1999) chapter 7. Some ratification referendums use a specified minority threshold. For instance, the referendum on the 1953 Constitution of Denmark required 45% approval by all those voting. The constitution went into force after it was approved by 46%. See "New Constitution Approved by Referendum—Minimum Age for Franchise to Be Reduced to 23 Years," (1953) IX Keesing's Contemporary Archives 12950.

[48] For further discussions about what it takes to consent, see Joseph Raz, *The Morality of Freedom* (Oxford University Press 1986) 80–85; Simmons, *Moral Principles and Political Obligations*, 75–83.

meeting when someone asks for volunteers to raise their hands, I am not obliged to volunteer for it was not my intent. Similarly, if I agree to see a movie with a friend who lives in my neighborhood, and I later find out that the movie is only playing in a theater eight hours away, I am not obliged to attend the movie because I did not understand what was involved and did not intend to commit to such a long journey.[49] Applied to ratification, such a standard means that voters who do not and cannot understand the implications of a proposed constitution cannot consent to its terms and undertake the appropriate obligations. As shown in chapter 6's discussion of meaningful choice, a standard that is *less strict* than that demanded for an act of consent to be binding, we have reasons to expect that many if not most voters will be too uninformed during ratification to intentionally consent in the relevant way.

Third is the well-worn problem of consent and future generations. If a constitution is only morally legitimate for individuals that intentionally and freely consented to it in a ratification referendum, it will be morally illegitimate for all those born or coming to age after the vote. In his essay on ratification, Condorcet worried about this very problem, noting that the successful ratification of a constitution "becomes meaningless as soon as these individuals cease to form a plurality of the nation."[50] Moreover, the constitution could not become morally legitimate through some other way, for instance by producing desired public goods, just distributions, or needed coordination effects, for the very reasons that make consent necessary in the beginning preclude alternative sources of moral legitimacy from being relevant later.[51]

Several responses to this are possible. One temptation might be to repackage traditional tacit consent arguments to apply to constitutions, such that citizens consent to their constitution by residence, paying taxes, political participation, etc.[52] Tuck even makes such a defense when he claims that "it is quite reasonable to say that the fact that the Constitution has not been amended or repealed by the *present* sovereign means the present sovereign, with all its beliefs and commitments, wishes the law to stand." Unfortunately, this is not reasonable. Changing even an easy to amend constitution is quite onerous and depends on navigating complex institutional, informational, and political realities. As Hume said long ago in his own battle against tacit consent, "[W]e may as well assert, that a man, remaining

[49] I assume in this example that my ignorance is blameless and therefore excusable.

[50] Condorcet, "On the Need for the Citizens to Ratify the Constitution," 272.

[51] In other words, other explanations of how a decision-making process procedurally, morally legitimates its outcome might only apply to the first generation, but allow different sources of moral legitimacy to come into play later on. Pure consent theory cannot allow this, for its arguments are motivated by the claim that personal consent is the only way a someone can gain justified control over an aspect of a person's life.

[52] Henry Beran, *The Consent Theory of Political Obligation* (Croom Helm 1987); Michael Walzer, *Obligations: Essays on Disobedience, War, and Citizenship* (Harvard University Press 1970) 111–14; John Locke, *Two Treatises of Government* (Cambridge University Press 2002) chapter 8, §§119–22, 347–49.

in a vessel, freely consents to the dominion of the master; though he was carried aboard while asleep, and must leap into the ocean, and perish, the moment he leaves her."[53] Moreover, numerous arguments over the years have shown the inadequacies of tacit consent, and how its only persuasive forms require jettisoning the very moral foundations of consent theory.[54]

Another response might be the following: one can avoid the moral illegitimacy of constitutions for future generations by creating mechanisms that enable them to consent. Condorcet seems to endorse such a strategy when, at the beginning of his ratification essay, he recommends that, "we simply fix the duration of the new constitution at the term beyond which it would cease to be legitimate; that is, at 18 or 20 years," with these numbers representing "the time it takes for half of the citizens alive when the law was passed to be replaced by new ones."[55] Similarly, and inspired by Condorcet, Jefferson claimed that we should "provide in our constitution for its revision at state periods," and that "every constitution then, and every law, naturally expired at the end of thirty-four years. If it be enforced longer, it is an act of force and not of right."[56]

Condorcet and Jefferson's discussions hint at a mechanism for renewing consent, but neither is specific about the details. I can imagine two possibilities. One is to make use of an all-encompassing constitutional sunset provision—similar to those used in South Africa's 1993 Interim Constitution and Poland's Small Constitution of 1992—that sets an expiration date for a constitution, upon which a new constitution-making process will automatically begin.[57] The other is a constitutional provision that requires a periodic referendum question that asks voters whether they consent to their constitution or wish for something different.

[53] David Hume, *Essays: Moral, Political, and Literary* (Liberty Fund 1985) 475.

[54] George Klosko, *Political Obligation* (Oxford University Press 2005) 122–40; Simmons, *Moral Principles and Political Obligations*, 75–100.

[55] Condorcet, "On the Need for the Citizens to Ratify the Constitution," 272. Condorcet based his calculations on contemporary mortuary data and a voting age of either twenty-five or twenty-one years. Admittedly, he departs from a strictly individualistic conception of consent and reciprocal obligation and instead endorses societal level consent of a particular type. He writes: "[A]ny law accepted by the plurality of inhabitants of a nation can be taken as having unanimous support: given the need either to accept or to reject the law and to follow the plurality opinion, anyone who rejects a proposed law will already have decided to abide by it if it is supported by the plurality." Here Condorcet combines an argument similar to a two-contract interpretation of Locke, according to which a majority decision indicates unanimous consent because of a prior unanimous agreement to abide by whatever the majority decides, with his own jury theorem. The prior agreement to abide by what the majority decides follows rationally from the fact that, given a large body of voters with a probability of greater than half of voting correctly, the decision reached by the majority will almost certainly be the correct one. I thank Iain McLean for providing clarification on this matter. Ibid., 272, 276.

[56] "Letter to Samuel Kercheval, July 12, 1816," in Thomas Jefferson, *Thomas Jefferson: Writings* (Library of America 1984) 1401–02 "Letter to James Madison, September 6, 1789," in *The Papers of Thomas Jefferson Digital Edition* (University of Virginia Press, Rotunda 2008), vol. 15, 392–97 For further information about Jefferson's interaction with Condorcet, see Iain McLean and Arnold B. Urken, "Did Jefferson or Madison Understand Condorcet's Theory of Social Choice?" (1992) 73 Public Choice 445–57.

[57] See Ozan O. Verol, "Temporary Constitutions," (2014) 102 California Law Review 409–64.

Sieyès seems to hint at just such a thing in Article 36 of his *Reasoned Exposition of the Rights of Man and Citizen*, when he writes that "it is worthwhile to establish fixed dates," for a people to exercise "their right to review and reform its constitution."[58] Moreover, such a provision actually exists. Fourteen U.S. states have automated convention referendum. Citizens in these states are asked, usually every ten years, to vote on whether or not to hold another constitutional convention.[59] For instance, the secretary of state in Rhode Island must submit the question "Shall there be a convention to amend or revise the constitution?" to the qualified electorate every ten years from the most recent convention.[60] Further, the constitutions of the Republic of Palau and the Federated States of Micronesia also call for an identical question to be placed in front of voters at least every fifteen and ten years respectively.[61] For these cases, one can conceptualize voting against a convention as signaling consent to the existing constitution, while voting for a new convention indicates dissent.

Three things are worth noting about either of these solutions to the generational problem. First, it means that consent-based PML justifications of ratification not only apply solely to ratification referendum, but also only to constitutions that include all-encompassing sunset provisions or something like a mandated convention referendum. This decreases the scope of the justification considerably and makes it problematic ex ante when one does not know a constitution's contents. Historically, none but the above-mentioned constitutions have included such provisions. Second, there might be good reasons for avoiding either of those two options. Madison outlines such reasons in his letters to Jefferson and Turberville, where he warns that regular replacement might, among other things, prevent constitutions from serving as a source of institutional stability, engender factions, "give greater agitation to the public mind," and open up the possibility for constitutional gaps and anarchy.[62] In addition, routinized convention referendums are susceptible to manipulation by sitting legislatures and other power holders

58 Emmanuel Joseph Sieyès, "Reasoned Exposition of the Rights of Man and Citizen," in Marc Allan Goldstein (ed.), *Social and Political Thought of the French Revolution, 1788–1797* (Peter Lang Publishers 1997) 150.

59 These states are Alaska, Connecticut, Hawaii, Illinois, Iowa, Maryland, Massachusetts, Missouri, Montana, New Hampshire, New York, Ohio, Oklahoma, and Rhode Island. See *The Book of the States: 2011* (The Council of State Governments 2011) 17. For a discussion about the genesis of these automatic convention referendums, see John J. Dinan, "'The Earth Belongs Always to the Living Generation': The Development of State Constitutional Amendment and Revision Procedures," (2000) 62 Review of Politics 645–74

60 The Constitution of the State of Rhode Island (1986), Art. 14 sec. 12.

61 Constitution of the Federated States of Micronesia (1978), Art. 14 sec. 12; Constitution of the Republic of Palau (1979), Art. 14 sec. 11. The Polish Constitution of 1791 contained a similar provision. The Governance Act (Poland) (1791), Art. 6.

62 "Letter to Thomas Jefferson, February 4, 1790," in *The Papers of James Madison Digital Edition* (University of Virginia Press 2010); "Copy in Substance of a Letter to G. L. Turberville, Esq., Nov, 2, 1788," in James Madison, *The Writings of James Madison: 1787–1790*, vol. 4 (G.P. Putnam's Sons 1903) 299.

adverse to the possibility of a decrease in their power. For example, in U.S. states these incumbents use the convention question to show that institutional change is a regular possibility, while simultaneously taking steps, such as timing the vote to ensure minimal participation and leaving the referendums unsponsored and unadvertised, to ensure that a convention never occurs.[63]

Third, and perhaps most critically, referendums on whether to hold a new convention, and referendums on replacement constitutions, run into the same problems catalogued before—those who forget to vote, are physically unable to vote, are too ignorant to vote, or vote against the constitution (or unsuccessfully in favor of a new convention) do not give their consent. For them, according to consent theory, the constitution is illegitimate.[64]

To summarize, a consent theorist could justify ratification by a consent-based PML argument, claiming that ratification is a unique moment in the constitution-making process where individuals can consent to their constitution and make it legitimate. The implication of such an argument is that all constitutions created thus far, except for fourteen U.S. state constitutions and the constitutions of two small island nations, have been and are morally illegitimate for all generations following the founding generation. Moreover, all constitutions created thus far, and all future constitutions, are or will be illegitimate for the uninformed, the coerced, formal dissenters, and non-voters. This means that for most people in all possible states shortly after founding there is or will be no good content-independent moral reason to support a constitution's claim to authority, and therefore no corresponding independent reason to respect and uphold its provisions. For those already loyal to consent theory, whose theoretical commitments push them toward an acceptance of philosophical anarchism, the view that no existing or plausible government is likely to be legitimate, such a conclusion is acceptable, and ratification is strongly justified as the only means of making the constitution legitimate to anyone. For everyone else, these outcomes are a good reason to question the straightforward application of consent theory's applicability to constitutions, or at the least to look elsewhere for a general justification of a ratification procedure.

63 See Gerald Benjamin, "The Mandatory Constitutional Convention Question Referendum: The New York Experience in National Context," (2002) 65 Albany Law Review 1017–50.

64 In an address to the French national assembly in 1791, Barnave gives another, albeit bizarre, argument against scheduled moments of constituent action, claiming that doing so inappropriately restricts the constituent power by telling it when it should or should not arise. Antoine Barnave, "On National Conventions and Constituent Power," in Marc Allan Goldstein (ed.), *Social and Political Thought of the French Revolution, 1788–1797: An Anthology of Original Texts* (Peter Lang 1997) 273.

3. Procedural Sociological Legitimation

In his notes for a speech in favor of revising the Virginia Constitution of 1776, Madison writes that it would be "advisable to have it ratified by them [the people]," in order to make it "more stable and secured agst. The doubts & imputations under which it now labors."[65] We can now understand this recommendation, and other remarks by Madison and his allies at the Philadelphia Convention, as linking ratification with PSL, for they suggest that the populace will be more likely to consider a constitution legitimate if it was approved through a ratification procedure.[66] Dennis Mueller suggests something similar, claiming that "a conscious and literal acceptance of the provisions of the constitutional contract should induce greater compliance with its provisions than if it is felt to have been chosen by someone else."[67] Advocates of participatory constitution-making attribute such an effect to ratification when they claim that procedures can legitimate a constitution by increasing participation, "that public involvement in the constitution making process is essential for constitutional legitimacy," and that ratification, as "the modal form of participation in constitutional design," is justified on these grounds.[68] Again, such arguments emphasize the effects that procedures have on belief rather than on the constitution itself. These types of arguments are attractive; it is easy to believe that a morally-laden political concept such as participation leads to legitimacy in the real world, and in operating democracies this may frequently be the case.[69] Nonetheless, an explanation is need for this purported effect, something that many constitution-making experts seem to forget. How might ratification contribute to content-independent sociological legitimacy?

[65] James Madison, *The Papers of James Madison*, vol. 8 (The University of Chicago Press 1973) 79.

[66] More specifically, ratification might contribute to legitimacy, be necessary for legitimacy, or be sufficient for legitimacy.

[67] Dennis C. Mueller, *Constitutional Democracy* (Oxford University Press 1996) 180. He goes on to argue that following this logic a very high supermajority threshold should be used for a ratification referendum, as this will maximize the number of citizens who see the constitution as more legitimate, while not resulting in an increase in the chances of constitutional rejection because "the costs of true anarchy" are too high.

[68] Tom Ginsburg, Zachary Elkins, and Justin Blount, "Does the Process of Constitution-Making Matter?" (2009) 5 Annual Review of Law and Social Science 201–23, 206; Katy Le Roy, *Public Participation in Constitution-Making: The Pacific Islands*, 2011) 45. See also Preuss Ulrich K. Preuss, "Perspectives on Post-Conflict Constitutionalism: Reflections on Regime Change through External Constitutionalization," (2006) 51 New York Law School Law Review 467–94, 494.

[69] For good overviews of the arguments for and against participation in constitution-making see Devra C. Moehler, "Public Participation and Support for the Constitution in Uganda," (2006) 44 The Journal of Modern African Studies 275–308, 277–80; Zachary Elkins, Tom Ginsburg, and Justin Blount, "The Citizen as Founder: Public Participation in Constitutional Approval," (2008) 81 Temple Law Review 361–82.

3.1 Present Belief

The simplest explanation is that people believe ratification is necessary for legitimacy, such that its occurrence helps legitimize a constitution and its absence does the opposite. This relies upon a pre-existing social norm or belief being present in the people, one that links the moral authority of a new constitution to whether it was ratified. One can certainly imagine specific contexts in which such a social norm or belief might develop, most of which reflect path dependency. A polity with a long-standing tradition of amending constitutions or approving new constitutions via referendums might have one.[70] For example, if the Swiss government implemented its Federal Constitution of 1999 without submitting it to a referendum, the people would likely have rejected its moral authority. The same is true if a U.S. state attempted to implement a new constitution without submitting it to the electorate.[71] In both contexts, the people associate and expect constitutional change to conclude with the people voting directly via a referendum. Departing from this would arouse suspicion and arm opponents of the constitution with an easy way to cast it in a negative light.[72]

A norm or belief linking legitimacy to ratification might also exist in a polity governed by a constitution that remains sociologically legitimate and includes a provision requiring ratification. Such instances are going to be rare however, because few national constitutions have such provisions and constitution-making often occurs upon the literal or normative deterioration of present-day authorities.[73] Nonetheless, state constitution-making in the United States provides an example. Today, twenty-seven state constitutions include such provisions. For instance, section 3(c) of Article XII of the Missouri Constitution reads: "Any

[70] Similarly, Bowler and Donovan found that those who expected democracies to provide avenues of participation other than elections were more likely to support the use of ordinary referendums. Shaun Bowler, Todd Donovan, and J.A. Karp, "Enraged or Engaged? Preferences for Direct Citizen Participation in Affluent Democracies," (2007) 60 Political Research Quarterly 351–62.

[71] Since 1780, U.S. states have adopted 146 different constitutions. Ninety-seven of these were popularly ratified and many more were submitted to referendums and rejected. All but three constitutions promulgated without ratification preceded the civil war. These were the 1913 and 1921 Louisiana constitutions and the Virginia Constitution of 1902, though subsequent constitutions for both states include provisions requiring referendums for all new constitutions. Today, twenty-seven state constitutions include automatic ratification provisions. In general, then, there is an informal norm and likely strong expectation for constitutions to be approved by the electorate before going into effect. See LA Constitution, Art. XVIII, sec. 2; VA Constitution, Art. XII, sec. 2; Albert Lee Sturm, *Trends in State Constitution-Making, 1966–1972* (Council of State Governments 1973) 11; *The Book of the States: 2011*, 16; Albert Lee Sturm, "The Development of American State Constitutions," (1982) 12 Publius 57–98, 1; G. Alan Tarr, *Understanding State Constitutions* (Princeton University Press 1998) 24.

[72] This argument also works if conditions are such that people can be convinced that a constitution not ratified is illegitimate. For instance, most U.S. residents likely have no idea that state constitutions are nearly always ratified. However, if a state constitution-making process decided to forego ratification, opponents of the process could easily weaken the legitimacy of the constitution that emerged by pointing out that its framers departed from tradition or law by failing to make use of a cherished direct democracy device.

[73] Elster, "Forces and Mechanisms in the Constitution-Making Process," 370.

proposed constitution or constitutional amendment adopted by the convention shall be submitted to a vote of the electors of the state at such time." U.S. states create new constitutions in times of stability—constitution-making occurs in order to solve institutional inefficiencies or reflect recent demographical changes rather than to create a political authority where one is absent—and therefore old constitutions maintain their legitimacy until they are replaced. Thus, violating constitutionally specified procedures such as ratification would negatively impact the perceived legitimacy of the new constitution.

Similarly, a norm or belief might arise in polities where a recent constitution-making attempt failed due to rejection during ratification, even if such a norm was absent pre-rejection. Albanian constitution-making in the 1990s provides an example of just such a context. In 1994, President Berisha submitted a draft constitution to the people for ratification in a referendum. There was no precedent for this action, no one else called for a referendum, and the recognized transitional constitution at the time required supermajority approval in parliament and no popular approval. Berisha, whose party lacked the votes to push through their desired draft, made recourse to a referendum in the hopes of implementing the constitution in the face of opposition. The plan backfired when 59 percent of those voting in a November referendum rejected the constitution.[74] When a new government took office in 1997, constitution-making began anew. In such circumstances it is hard to imagine a new constitution coming into effect without popular approval. Any attempt to do so would have easily fit into a narrative of elite control and popular manipulation. Thus, it is not surprising that the new government made use of referendum ratification. In November of 1998, 50 percent of all eligible voters went to the polls, 90 percent of them approved the constitution.[75]

While worth noting, these contextual and path dependent explanations of procedural sociological legitimacy are insufficient for our purposes of justifying ratification. While in certain instances implementing ratification might lead to sociological legitimacy because of predictable social norms or beliefs based on past history and institutional experience, for most constitution-making events, in

[74] Opposition parties opposed the draft constitution because, among other reasons, it enlarged the powers of the President and reduced those of the judiciary. Berisha originally proposed that the draft be submitted to a separate constituent assembly for approval, but after all parties other than the DP condemned this plan, he decided to use the referendum. This entailed pushing through a law in parliament amending the transitional constitution to allow the President to propose referendums without parliamentary approval. In the weeks leading up to the November referendum, the opposition parties banded together to highlight Berisha's constitutional violation and to encourage voters to vote against Berisha by rejecting the constitution. Turnout for the vote was about 80%. "Constitution Watch: Country-by-Country Updates on Constitutional Politics in Eastern Europe," (1995) 4 East European Constitutional Review 2–35, 2–4.

[75] An OSCE report notes: "[S]ince the failed 1994 referendum, all parties agreed that new constitutions need to be approved by referendum." Organization for Security and Co-operation in Europe, *The Republic of Albania: Referendum on the Constitution*, 22 November 1998, 1999) 5; "Constitution Watch: Country-by-Country Updates on Constitutional Politics in Eastern Europe and the Ex-USSR," (1998) 7 East European Constitutional Review 2–44, 2, 3.

both the present and future, conditions will be different, or such a judgment will be impossible to make. In other words, there is no reason to assume that the presence of a specific norm linking legitimacy beliefs to the presence of ratification is more likely than not.[76]

3.2 Participation Leads to Legitimacy

What is needed for a persuasive PSL argument is a more generally applicable reason to believe that ratification leads to sociological legitimacy for content-independent reasons. The likeliest is based on a purported causal link, championed by participatory constitution-making advocates, between participation and legitimacy beliefs.[77] Such an argument claims that ratification is a sufficient or necessary form of participation. The procedure, by enabling citizens to participate, helps foster belief that the produced constitution is legitimate. This explanation "focuses on the additional value of taking part in the constitution-making process itself; it works to the extent that arrangements generate stronger legitimacy beliefs when chosen endogenously than when exogenously imposed."[78] Ndulo makes this type

[76] At the same time, if ratification continues to be included among the best practices of constitution-making, if these best practices continue their slow transformation into international norms or laws, and if constitutions continue to be submitted to ratification procedures as a result, we might get to a point where active citizens everywhere internalize a ratification norm, such that a constitution implemented without ratification would be condemned as sociologically illegitimate. In other words, the continued use and recommendation of ratification might create this PSL pathway and make possible a PSL-based justification in the future. However, I do not believe we are there yet.

[77] Examples include Michele Brandt and others, *Constitution-Making and Reform: Options for the Process* (Interpeace 2011) 9; Angela M. Banks, "Expanding Participation in Constitution Making: Challenges and Opportunities," (2008) 49 William and Mary Law Review 1043–69; Vivien Hart, "Constitution Making and the Right to Take Part in a Public Affair," in Laurel E. Miller (ed.), *Framing the State in Times of Transition: Case Studies in Constitution Making* (United States Institute of Peace Press 2010); Laurel E. Miller, "Designing Constitution-Making Processes: Lessons from the Past, Questions for the Future," in Laurel E. Miller (ed.), *Framing the State in Times of Transition: Case Studies in Constitution Making* (United States Institute of Peace Press 2010); Jennifer Widner, "Constitution Writing in Post-Conflict Settings: An Overview," (2008) 49 William and Mary Law Review 1513–42, 1516; Silvia Suteu and Stephen Tierney, "Squaring the Circle? Bringing Deliberation and Participation Together in Processes of Constitution-Making," in Ron Levy and others (eds.), *The Cambridge Handbook of Deliberative Constitutionalism* (Cambridge University Press 2018). Note that there is now pushback on the idea that constitution-making processes should highly emphasize participation, with several critics pointing out that this prevents the elite compromises and bargains necessary for a coherent durable constitution and a stable political order. See Michael Lusztig, "Constitutional Paralysis: Why Canadian Initiatives Are Doomed to Fail," (1994) 27 Canadian Journal of Political Science 747–71; Gabriel L. Negretto and Mariano Sánchez Talanquer, Constitutional Origins and Liberal Democracy in Comparative Perspective (ICON*S Conference: Public Law in Times of Change?); Donald L. Horowitz, "Constitution-Making: A Process Filled with Constraint," (2006) 12 Review of Constitutional Studies 1–17; Donald L. Horowitz, "Conciliatory Institutions and Constitutional Processes in Post-Conflict States," (2008) 49 William and Mary Law Review 1213–48; Abrak Saati, *The Participation Myth: Outcomes of Participatory Constitution Building Processes on Democracy* (Umeå University, Department of Politics 2015).

[78] Peter Esaiasson, Mikael Gilljam, and Mikael Persson, "Which Decision-Making Arrangements Generate the Strongest Legitimacy Beliefs? Evidence from a Randomised Field Experiment," (2012) 51 European Journal of Political Research 785–808, 787.

of argument when he touts ratification because of its ability to prevent a constitution from being "perceived as being imposed."[79] Ghai and Galli similarly explain that: "If people have participated, they are more likely to have a commitment to it, even if they have not fully understood the process or the constitution, or indeed even if their participation was largely ceremonial."[80] Moreover, as discussed in chapter 2, section 3.2, a similar logic is behind the *support function* of the ratification of labor agreements during collective bargaining. The idea here being that labor agreements should be ratified by membership because doing so increases the chances that individual workers will view the resulting contract positively.

3.2.1 The Core Argument

I begin analyzing this PSL pathway by making explicit three of its often-unmentioned implicit component claims. First, is the claim (a) that individuals are more likely to consider rules and policies legitimate if they participate in their creation, i.e. that participation leads to sociological legitimacy. This is a popular idea, one that often goes hand in hand with similar claims about participation and moral legitimacy made prominent by deliberative and participatory democratic theorists.[81] Many explanations for (a) exist. People might be less critical of something they think they helped create or more confident in what they see as their own creation. Participation might lead to greater familiarity with outcomes, with familiarity being conducive to legitimacy. That is, people might see something as more rightfully authoritative when they understand it better. Individuals might be more likely to exaggerate the positive and downplay the negatives in outcomes for which they feel responsible. Or participation might simply increase the opportunity for generating consensus beliefs. All of these might lead people to view an outcome as more legitimate because of participation.[82]

[79] Muna Ndulo, "Zimbabwe's Unfulfilled Struggle for a Legitimate Constitutional Order," in Laurel E. Miller (ed.), *Framing the State in Times of Transition: Case Studies in Constitution Making* (United States Institute of Peace Press 2010) 193.

[80] Yash Ghai and Guido Galli, *Constitution Building Processes and Democratization*, 2006) 14. According to Alexander Hudson, several members of the South African constitution-making process held similar views. See Alexander Hudson, "Political Parties and Public Participation in Constitution Making: Legitimation, Distraction, or Real Impact," (Forthcoming) Comparative Politics 1–21.

[81] See for instance Josh Cohen, "Deliberation and Democratic Legitimacy," in Alan Hamlin and Philip Pettit (eds.), *The Good Polity: Normative Analysis of the State* (Blackwell 1989); Archon Fung, "Democratic Theory and Political Science: A Pragmatic Model of Constructive Engagement," (2007) 101 American Political Science Review 443–58; Archon Fung, "Putting the Public Back into Governance: The Challenges of Citizen Participation and Its Future," (2015) 75 Public Administrative Review 513–22.

[82] See James D. Fearon, "Deliberation as Discussion," in Jon Elster (ed.), *Deliberative Democracy* (Cambridge University Press 1998); Archon Fung, "Varieties of Participation in Complex Governance," (2006) 66 Public Administration Review 66–75; Carol Pateman, *Participation and Democratic Theory* (Cambridge University Press 1970); Benjamin Barber, *Strong Democracy: Participatory Politics for New Age* (University of California Press 1984); Philipp Dann and others, *Lessons Learned from Constitution-Making: Processes with Broad Based Public Participation* (Democracy Reporting International 2011) 4; John M. Carey, "Parchment, Equilibria, and Institutions," (2000) 33 Comparative Political Studies 735–61.

An array of empirical findings seems to provide support for such a general causal link between participation and legitimacy. For instance, using survey data, Johnson finds that participation is "persistently associated with attitudes expressive of democratic legitimacy," even when accompanied by negative evaluation of outcomes.[83] As mentioned in the previous chapter, Oppenheimer and Frohlich found that subjects who choose their own distributional principles were "more confident in their choices and more satisfied" than those who had an identical principle imposed on them. Sutter et al. discovered a significant positive effect of endogenous institutional choice on the level of cooperation in comparison to the same exogenously implemented institutions in groups participating in public goods games. Similarly, Esaiasson et al. observed that voting and deliberation led to higher levels of legitimacy beliefs in school children; Grossman found that Ugandan coffee farmers were more likely to contribute to public goods when their leaders were elected; and Olken demonstrated that Indonesian villagers were far more satisfied, willing to contribute, and perceived greater benefits from development projects chosen through plebiscites rather than local assemblies.[84]

In addition, Tom Tyler, whose theory of how legitimacy is manufactured is one of the most influential in the social sciences, claims to find a strong indirect relationship between participation and legitimacy via the concept of procedural justice. He demonstrates this relationship in a wide variety of studies pertaining to cooperation with the police, employee rule compliance, tax avoidance, and court interactions.[85] Tyler argues that procedural justice, which occurs when authorities are perceived to "wield their power in fair, just, and neutral ways," is "a mechanism for creating and maintaining legitimacy."[86] Procedurally just treatment strengthens

[83] Carolina Johnson, "Local Civic Participation and Democratic Legitimacy: Evidence from England and Wales," (2014) 63 Political Studies 765–92, 765.

[84] Norman Frohlich and Joe A. Oppenheimer, *Choosing Justice: An Experimental Approach to Ethical Theory* (University of California Press 1993) 121; Benjamin A. Olken, "Direct Democracy and Local Public Goods: Evidence from a Field Experiment in Indonesia," (2010) 104 American Political Science Review 243–67; Mikael Persson, Peter Esaiasson, and Mikael Gilljam, "The Effects of Direct Voting and Deliberation on Legitimacy Beliefs: An Experimental Study of Small Group Decision-Making," (2006) European Political Science Review 1–19; Matthias Sutter, Stefan Haigner, and Martin G. Kocher, "Choosing the Carrot or the Stick? Endogenous Institutional Choice in Social Dilemma Situations," (2010) 77 Review of Economic Studies 1540–66; Guy Grossman and Delia Baldassarri, "The Impact of Elections on Cooperation: Evidence from a Lab-in-the-Field Experiment in Uganda," (2012) 56 American Journal of Political Science 964–85.

[85] Tom. R Tyler, *Why People Obey the Law* (Yale University Press 1990); Tom R. Tyler and Yuen J. Huo, *Trust in the Law: Encouraging Public Cooperation with the Police and Courts* (Russell-Sage Foundation 2002); Tom R. Tyler, "Procedural Justice, Legitimacy, and the Effective Rule of Law," (2003) 30 Crime and Justice 283–357; Tom R. Tyler, Patrick E. Callahan, and Jeffrey Frost, "Armed, and Dangerous(?): Motivating Group Adherence among Agents of Social Control," (2007) 41 Law & Society Review 457–92; Tom R. Tyler and Steven Blader, "Can Businesses Effectively Regulate Employee Conduct? The Antecedents of Rule Following in Work Settings," (2005) 48 The Academy of Management Journal 1143–58; Tom R. Tyler, Jonathan D. Casper, and Bonnie Fisher, "Maintaining Allegiance Towards Political Authorities," (1989) 33 American Journal of Political Science 629–52.

[86] Tom R. Tyler and Jonathan Jackson, "Popular Legitimacy and the Exercise of Legal Authority: Motivating Compliance, Cooperation and Engagement," 81; Tom R. Tyler, "Evaluating Consensual Models of Governance: Legitimacy-Based Law," in Jack Knight and Melissa Schwartzberg (eds.), *Political Legitimacy: NOMOS LXI* (New York University Press 2019) 281.

the social bonds between individuals and institutions, causing the former to identify with the latter and eventually internalize the belief that they should obey and cooperate.[87]

Participation comes into play because it increases the chances that a procedure or process appears just by affecting the three main antecedents of procedural justice evaluations. The first, "quality of decision-making," relates to the perceived fairness of the procedures used to reach the decision. The second, "quality of treatment," concerns whether individuals are treated with dignity and respect throughout the decision-making process, and the third is focused on the degree to which an individual understands the actions of a decision-maker and their reasons for taking them.[88] Participating in a procedure, Tyler and his co-authors assert, positively affects all three antecedent evaluations, leading to perceived procedural justice and thus sociological legitimacy.

The second central claim is (b) that this positive causal relationship between participation and legitimacy, as has been found in the contexts of ordinary governance, policing, the workplace, etc., also exists within the constitution-making process. In other words, according to (b), participation also leads to legitimacy when it comes to constitution-making. This assumes that when it comes to what matters for sociological legitimacy, constitution-making is not so different from more familiar and ordinary decision-making settings. People are still people, and when they see themselves as playing a role in creating something, they are more likely to see the result as authoritative.

Again, empirical work exists supporting (b). For instance, Samuels concludes that participatory constitution-making empowers the people and creates public support, highlighting the success of the highly participatory Rwanda and South Africa constitution-making experience, and the failure of the elite-driven processes in Nigeria and Bahrain.[89] Elkins, Melton, and Ginsburg claim that more inclusive drafting processes enhance the likelihood of constitutional endurance and citizens' respect for the constitution, both of which might be associated with sociological legitimacy.[90] And Eisenstadt, LeVan, and Maboudi claim to show, through their

[87] Tom R. Tyler and Jonathan Jackson, "Future Challenges in the Study of Legitimacy and Criminal Justice," in Justice Tankebe and Alison Liebling (eds.), *Legitimacy and Criminal Justice: An International Exploration* (Oxford University Press 2013) 88.

[88] Tyler, "Procedural Justice, Legitimacy, and the Effective Rule of Law," 298–300; Anthony Bottoms and Justice Tankebe, "Beyond Procedural Justice: A Dialogic Approach to Legitimacy in Criminal Justice," (2012) 102 The Journal of Criminal Law & Criminology 119–17, 144–46.

[89] Kirsti Samuels and Vanessa Hawkins Wyeth, *State-Building and Constitutional Design after Conflict* (International Peace Academy 2006) Banks argues that the Rwanda constitution-making experience was characterized by participation without power, such that participatory opportunities gave those without power little additional influence on the outcome. However, Banks does not address whether those without power knew that they had little additional influence in the proceedings. If they were ignorant of internal exclusion it might make little difference in regards to sociological legitimacy whether or not they actually obtained additional power through participation. Banks, "Expanding Participation in Constitution Making: Challenges and Opportunities."

[90] Zachary Elkins, James Melton, and Tom Ginsburg, *The Endurance of National Constitutions* (Cambridge University Press 2009) 81 and elsewhere; Blount, Elkins, and Ginsburg, "Does the Process

analysis of a dataset including all successful constitution-making events between 1974 and 2014, that participatory constitution-making has a lasting and systematic effect on democratization, which in turn suggests that "it legitimizes citizen authorization."[91]

The third and final claim is the simple observation that (c) ratification involves participation of the relevant sort. Of course, the strength of (c), and ultimately the degree to which ratification will assist in sociologically legitimating a constitution, is going to vary according to ratification type. For instance, with ratification by referendum, voters will participate by physically voting on a constitution and taking part in any education or persuasion campaigns surrounding the referendum.[92] Ratification by existing government bodies and conventions can involve participation of two types. On the one hand, if the conventions or government bodies are elected, people will participate by taking part in the electoral process. On the other hand, regardless of the mode of delegate selection, channels can be created that enable people to participate by communicating with their ratifying delegates.

Admittedly, whether or not ratification ultimately makes the sociological legitimacy of a constitution more likely is an empirical claim for which there is little direct evidence for or against. No studies exist that test whether the average person or a population as a whole is more inclined to see a constitution as authoritative if and because they take part in a participatory ratification procedure. Nonetheless, this participation-based PSL pathway for ratification is convincing; (a), (b), and (c) seem plausible. Ratification does appear to amplify the opportunities for individuals to participate in the constitution-making process, and if participation leads to legitimacy, ratification certainly looks like a pathway through which the creation of a sociologically legitimate constitution becomes more probable. Assuming that one wants to create a sociologically legitimate constitution, it looks like we have finally found a firm foundation from which ratification can be justified.

of Constitution-Making Matter?" 54–57. Much, however, is obscured by the authors measure of inclusiveness, which is a complex proxy which takes into account elements of the ratification process, drafting process, and the number of direct democracy mechanisms within the created constitutional text itself. For a discussion of this, see Jonathan Wheatley and Fernando Mendez, "The Constitution-Making Process: An Analytical Framework," in Jonathan Wheatley and Fernando Mendez (eds.), *Patterns of Constitutional Design: The Role of Citizens and Elites in Constitution-Making* (Routledge 2016) 10.

[91] Todd A. Eisenstadt, A. Carl LeVan, and Tofigh Maboudi, *Constituents before Assembly: Participation, Deliberation, and Representation in the Crafting of New Constitutions* (Cambridge University Press 2017) 3.

[92] For a discussion of participation in constitution-making via referendums and electing constituent bodies, and how such procedures can lead to problems in constitutional orders without codified regulations for constitutional replacement, see Gabriel L. Negretto, "Constitution Making in Democratic Constitutional Orders: The Challenge of Citizen Participation," in Saskia Ruth, Yanina Welp, and Laurence Whitehead (eds.), *Let the People Rule? Direct Democracy in the Twenty-First Century* (ECPR Press 2017).

3.2.2 Weaknesses

Though ratification as a means of procedural sociological legitimation via participation is perhaps the most convincing grounds for justifying ratification that I analyze in this book, it is still a weak and uncertain justification. Specifically, in this section I argue that there are good reasons to be skeptical of (a), (b), and (c). Further, in the following section, I suggest that justifying a procedure solely by appealing to procedural sociological legitimacy might be morally problematic in itself.

First, while a variety of theories provide arguments in support of (a), there are reasons to doubt much of the empirical work that is supposed to test, show, and vindicate it. Put simply, it is unclear if any of this work actually concerns legitimacy at all. Most generally, this is because legitimacy is a concept especially resistant to targeted study, in ways that most authors ignore. As Gordon and Huber make clear, it is extremely difficult to select cases or design experiments that isolate legitimacy from other sources of the behavioral change used to measure its presence.[93] For instance, one might be tempted to look to diffuse support of a regime as evidence of legitimacy, but this overlooks the fact that "individuals may value an authority or institution over feasible alternatives for a variety of reasons," only some of which might have to do with legitimacy. This problem is exacerbated because the very choices, institutions, or actions by an authority that would predictably affect legitimacy beliefs will also likely change the other non-legitimacy sources of support, meaning that "empirical research will not be able to isolate the causal effect of legitimacy absent strong assumptions."[94] Further difficulties arise because in certain contexts individuals influence each other, such that a change in one person's legitimacy beliefs and their corresponding actions are likely to indirectly affect both for other people. This makes "isolating which actors' perceptions of legitimacy affect their (versus others') behavior difficult."[95] What all of this means is that research claiming to show an effect of participation on legitimacy might actually show an effect of participation on something else entirely or no effect at all.

Relatedly, operationalizing sociological legitimacy is anything but straightforward. In many if not most cases, the meaning of the concept is lost amidst attempts to measure it. Consider how Tyler and his various co-authors, who have spent three decades thinking about how to measure legitimacy, operationalize the concept. Their recent work breaks legitimacy into three measurable dimensions: a perceived obligation to obey; trust/support for authorities; and moral alignment/solidarity.[96]

[93] See Sanford C. Gordon and Gregory A. Huber, "The Empirical Study of Legitimate Authority: Normative Guidance for Positive Analysis," in Jack Knight and Melissa Schwartzberg (eds.), *Political Legitimacy: NOMOS LXI* (New York University Press 2019).

[94] Ibid., 353–54.

[95] Ibid., 343–44.

[96] Tyler and Jackson, "Popular Legitimacy and the Exercise of Legal Authority: Motivating Compliance, Cooperation and Engagement"; Tyler and Jackson, "Future Challenges in the Study of Legitimacy and Criminal Justice"; Tom R. Tyler, "Procedural Justice and Policing," in E. Allan Lind (ed.), *Social Psychology and Justice* (Routledge 2019).

Difficulties emerge because these dimensions, measured individually and used to construct a legitimacy score, are inadequate components or proxies for legitimacy.

For instance, measuring legitimacy via Tyler's three dimensions can produce false positives: a person can feel obligated to obey a legal authority, trust a legal authority, or believe they share a common normative outlook with a legal authority, all while simultaneously believing the legal authority is illegitimate. I might plausibly believe that I should listen to my boss or that my boss generally makes decisions that comport with my moral outlook, but nonetheless believe that his authority is illegitimate because he only got the position out of nepotism. The three dimensions can also produce false negatives: a person can distrust their authority or believe the normative outlook of an authority is wrong yet nonetheless see that authority as legitimate. Many democratic citizens might distrust their elected officials, see their moral compasses as fundamentally broken, but nonetheless believe that their claim to rule is legitimate because of the procedures through which they were chosen. Further, the dimension of moral alignment, which is present when a person sees her legal authorities as having compatible moral values as herself, introduces a confounding variable into the measure of legitimacy itself. Moral values can be independent reasons for a person thinking they should obey an authority, apart from legitimacy beliefs. All of this is to show that in some of the most cited social scientific research on participation and legitimacy, the measure of legitimacy used is unreliable and possibly corrupted.[97] Participation might impact something, but this something might not be legitimacy.

Moving on to (b), there are in fact reasons to doubt that general findings linking participation to legitimacy in ordinary politics and workplaces apply to the extraordinary context of constitution-making. Even if people are more likely to believe that a law or policy or project choice is legitimate if they help create it, the same may not be true when it comes to the creation of the rules that determine how such laws or policies or project choices are to be made and what they may or may not contain. Creating a constitution is different than choosing a distributive policy, deciding upon a range of development projects, taking part in judicial proceedings, electing a legislative representative, or completing a corporate project, in ways that seem likely to matter.

For instance, the decisions taken regarding the look and feel of a new constitution take place outside the bounds of an operating system of norms and rules. As mentioned earlier, constitution-making is not a repeated game in the same way as decision-making in ordinary political, legal, and workplace contexts, and thus the importance of participation in it might not grow and be internalized in the same manner. In addition, the procedures used to create new constitutions are often

[97] For more on this topic, see Jeffrey A. Lenowitz, "On the Empirical Measurement of Legitimacy," in Melissa Schwartzberg and Jack Knight (eds.), *Political Legitimacy: NOMOS LXI* (New York University Press 2019).

novel and unfamiliar, and the uniqueness of the constitution-making event might make normative evaluations of them, such as those relating to procedural justice, difficult or at least less than automatic. One cannot assume that legitimating beliefs arise in the same way and for the same reasons when we move to a completely different and rare decision-making context; (b) cannot be taken for granted.

Suspicion of (b) is also supported by empirical research. Moehler's study of the creation of the 1995 Ugandan Constitution, a constitution-making process frequently praised for its inclusive and participatory nature, is one of the most comprehensive studies on this topic. Drawing upon both qualitative and quantitative analysis, Moehler concludes that, "contrary to the optimistic predictions of most academics and activists, my evidence indicates that participation did not have a direct effect on constitutional legitimacy" and "participants were no more or less supportive of the constitution than were the citizens who did not get involved."[98] Instead, Moehler found that local elites, rather than public participation, influenced whether citizens viewed the constitution as legitimate. One reason this occurred, a reason relevant to the importation of Tyler's process-based model of legitimacy to constitutions, is because "in transitioning states, most citizens lack the information and skills to assess the fairness of the constitution-making process on their own, and so they turn to local leaders for guidance."[99] Thus, supporters of the constitution used the inclusion of participatory processes to convince some citizens that the constitution-making process was fair, but this did not prevent opposition leaders from convincing their followers otherwise.

Likewise, in a study of post-Soviet constitution-making in Central and Eastern Europe, de Raadt concludes that "open constitution-making procedures do not necessarily produce legitimate constitutions and that closed constitution-making is no certain cause for contestation."[100] While Jackson, through an analysis of constitution-making in Germany and Japan in the 1940s, Eastern Europe and South Africa after 1989, and the 2005 Iraqi Constitution, concludes that participatory processes, like non-participatory processes, sometimes create legitimate constitutions and sometimes do not.[101] Further, an experiment meant to stimulate

[98] Moehler, "Public Participation and Support for the Constitution in Uganda," 276, 301 See also Devra C. Moehler, *Distrusting Democrats: Outcomes of Participatory Constitution Making* (University of Michigan Press 2008).

[99] Moehler, "Public Participation and Support for the Constitution in Uganda," 276.

[100] He focuses on constitution-making in Bulgaria, the Czech Republic, Estonia, Hungary, Poland, Romania, and Slovakia. Jasper de Raadt, "Contested Constitutions: Legitimacy of Constitution-Making and Constitutional Conflict in Central Europe," (2009) 23 East European Politics and Societies 315–38, 317.

[101] Vicki C. Jackson, "What's in a Name? Reflections on Timing, Naming, and Constitution-Making," (2008) 49 William and Mary Law Review 1249–1305. In addition, the fate of the 1996 Eritrean Constitution and the 1997 Thailand Constitution attest to the fact that incredibly participatory processes can produce constitutions that neither citizens nor elites deem legitimate. The Eritrean Constitution has yet to be implemented nearly two decades after being ratified in a two-step process by both the national assembly and a special ratificatory constituent assembly, while the Thai Constitution almost immediately lost the support of the coalition that created it, was soon violated extensively by Prime Minister Thaksin who nonetheless maintained popular support, and eventually died in a 2006 coup. Bereket

participatory constitution-making in high school classrooms found "no support for the idea that participation in constitution making in and of itself generates stronger legitimacy beliefs."[102]

It is also unclear if the large N quantitative works mentioned above, by Elkins, Melton, and Ginsburg, and Eisenstadt, LeVan, and Maboudi, are actually supportive of (b).[103] They might have nothing to do with sociological legitimacy.[104] For one thing, neither work can invalidate the worry that a confounding variable is responsible for both the use of participatory processes in constitution-making and the outcomes the authors are measuring. In addition, despite sometimes hinting that legitimacy is their topic, neither sets of authors directly claim to show or measure anything about it. Elkins et al. demonstrate that inclusive constitution-making is associated with greater constitutional endurance and higher levels of citizen respect, but a whole host of factors affected by participation yet distinct from sociological legitimacy might be the cause. Similarly, while an increase in sociological legitimacy is one possible reason for Eisenstadt et al.'s finding that participatory constitution-making leads to greater levels of democratization, it is just one of many variables that might have this effect, none of which the authors study or sufficiently control for. Further, more recent work by Eisenstadt and Maboudi show that group inclusion, the involvement of a diverse array of interest group advocates, rather than popular participation, is actually the variable associated with higher levels of democratization.[105] Similarly, Negretto's recent work demonstrates, at least for existing electoral democracies, that elite cooperation at the constitution-making stage improves liberal democracy, while citizen participation generally has little effect.[106]

At this point, we cannot confidently embrace (b). There is reason to question and doubt the assumption that participation in constitution-making has the same effect on citizens as it has in other arenas. The empirical work on the matter, while growing, remains scant and conflicting, with the most in-depth study on the issue suggesting that participation isn't as tightly connected to legitimacy as many assume. Perhaps increasing participation leads to temporary excitement about the

Habte Selassie, "Constitution Making in Eritrea: A Process-Driven Approach," in Laurel E. Miller (ed.), *Framing the State in Times of Transition: Case Studies in Constitution Making* (United States Institute of Peace Press 2010); Bjorn Dressel, "Thailand's Elusive Quest for a Workable Constitution, 1997–2007," (2009) 31 Contemporary Southeast Asia 296–325.

102 Esaiasson, Gilljam, and Persson, "Which Decision-Making Arrangements Generate the Strongest Legitimacy Beliefs? Evidence from a Randomised Field Experiment."

103 See nn. 90 and 91.

104 Further, as Negretto shows, what participation means is ambiguous in both the theory and coding of Constituents Before Assembly. See Gabriel L. Negretto, "Replacing and Amending Constitutions: The Logic of Constitutional Change in Latin America," (2012) 46 Law & Society Review 749–79, 157–58.

105 Todd A. Eisenstadt and Tofigh Maboudi, "Being There Is Half the Battle: Group Inclusion, Constitution-Writing, and Democracy," (2019) 52 Comparative Political Studies 2135–70.

106 Negretto, "Constitution-Making and Liberal Democracy: The Role of Citizens and Representative Elites," 224.

constitution-making process, but as Klein and Sajo make clear, even when "participation has created constitutional enthusiasm this may not result in lasting or widespread acceptance of the constitution, especially where high expectations of empowerment do not materialize."[107]

Finally, the claim (c) that ratification involves participation of the relevant sort is incomplete. To understand this, consider Condorcet's discussion of the virtues of submitting a constitution to a ratifying convention. He notes that "approval by such a Convention would contribute nothing more to rights than approval by a National Assembly which was authorized to establish a constitution."[108] This calls attention to the fact that ratification does not occur in a vacuum. If used, it occurs at the end of the constitution-making process after a host of other procedures. Many of these can involve citizen participation that, if one assumes (a) and (b) and overlooks the above-mentioned problems, purportedly lead to sociological legitimacy. Thus, the question is not only whether the sort of participation provided through ratification leads to sociological legitimacy, but whether it adds anything that other participatory procedures in the constitution-making process do not already provide.

As discussed in chapter 1, there are five basic stages in the constitution-making process: initiation, convoking, drafting, approving, and ratifying. Participation is increasingly prominent and recommended by contemporary best practices in the first three stages of a constitution-making process. In the initiation stage, citizens can use formal and informal channels to suggest guiding principles, weigh in on the future procedures to be used to create the constitution, and give real suggestions on constitutional content. Examples of this can be seen in the long and tumultuous convoking phase of the ongoing Chilean constitution-making process. In the 2016 "Encounter" phase citizens participated by submitting their suggestions for a future draft via an online form and attending over 8000 local small group meetings and eighty-six large regional and provincial meetings.[109] In late October 2019, street protests in Santiago that began over a subway fare spread across the country, transforming into a nationwide demand for a new constitution. And, on October 25, 2020, voters decided via referendum not only to create a new constitution, but also to do so through a fully elected constituent convention as opposed to a hybrid body where half the members would be sitting legislators.[110]

[107] Claude Klein and András Sajó, "Constitution-Making: Process and Substance," in Michel Rosenfeld and András Sajó (eds.), *The Oxford Handbook of Comparative Constitutional Law* (Oxford University Press 2012) 424.

[108] Condorcet, "On the Need for the Citizens to Ratify the Constitution," 276.

[109] Carlos Bernal, "How Constitutional Crowdsourcing Can Enhance Legitimacy in Constitution Making," in David Landau and Hannah Lerner (eds.), *Comparative Constitution Making* (Edward Elgar 2019) 236 See also Claudia Heiss Bendersky, Ernesto Riffo Eigueta, Jorge Contesse, and Cristián Sanhueza, *An Assessment of the Chilean Constituent Process* (Observatory of the Chilean Constituent Process 2018).

[110] Pascale Bonnefoy, "Chile's President Says He Will Support a New Constitution," *New York Times* (November 12, 2019), A12; Pascale Bonnefoy, "'An End to the Chapter of Dictatorship': Chileans Vote to Draft a New Constitution," *New York Times* (October 26, 2020), A11.

During the convoking stage, if the central constitution-making body is to be a constituent legislature or constituent convention, citizens can participate by electing delegates to the constitution-making body and taking part in the campaigns surrounding these elections. In addition, during the drafting phase the public can suggest specific provisions, institutional mechanisms, or rights to be included in the text. They can also be consulted to settle divisive issues that come up during drafting and asked to comment on draft versions of the text. Designers of constitution-making processes can use a variety of mechanisms to consult the people on these issues, including: non-binding issue-specific referendums; requests for written submissions; town hall meetings; questionnaire-based surveys; deliberative seminars, town hall meetings, soliciting comments through the internet, phone lines, texting, and various social media outlets.

Examples of such participatory procedures abound. The Ugandan Constitutional Commission developed its agenda of constitutional reform through a variety of participatory processes. These included holding and attending 140 district seminars, with an estimated attendance of 70,000 people, and soliciting constitutional ideas through newspapers and a nationwide student essay context.[111] In Zimbabwe, the Constitutional Commission established by Mugabe toured all eleven provinces of the country, holding 4,321 open meetings during which individuals could express their views on the contents of the constitution. Over 500,000 people attended these general meetings, and 150,000 more attended specialized meetings meant to target overlooked minority groups.[112]

Constitution-makers in Kosovo set up an interactive website in which citizens could read drafts as they were being produced, make comments, and exchange their views.[113] In Eritrea, public meetings on constitutional proposals were held in 157 locations involving more than 110,000 participants, with an additional 11,000 Eritreans participating in similar meetings in locations outside the country.[114] In South Africa, constitution-makers organized workshops with civil society organizations, established a well-used telephone talk line, held general meetings, and solicited comments during all three stages leading to the final draft.[115] In 2011, members of the Icelandic Constitutional Council posted twelve draft constitutions

[111] Allegedly, on the basis of these mechanisms, the commission successfully lobbied for constitution-making authority to be placed in an elected constituent assembly rather than the legislature. Brandt and others, *Constitution-Making and Reform: Options for the Process*, 348–49; Moehler, *Distrusting Democrats: Outcomes of Participatory Constitution Making*, 281.

[112] John Hatchard, "Some Lessons on Constitution-Making from Zimbabwe," (2001) 54 Journal of African Law 210–16, 211.

[113] Brandt and others, *Constitution-Making and Reform: Options for the Process*, 127.

[114] Miller, "Designing Constitution-Making Processes: Lessons from the Past, Questions for the Future," 633.

[115] Ibid., 631; Nico Steytler, "South Africa," in John Kincaid and G. Alan Tarr (eds.), *Constitutional Origins, Structure, and Change in Federal Countries* (McGill-Queen's University Press 2005); Synnove Skjelton, *A People's Constitution: Public Participation in the South-African Constitution-Making Process* (Institute for Global Dialogue 2006).

on their webpage and on Facebook, receiving more than 16,000 suggestions in response.[116] And the 2011 Egyptian constituent assembly used a website to solicit comments on their drafts and give the public the opportunity to vote on specific proposals. Over 68,000 individuals participated by providing over 650,000 votes and comments.[117]

If (a) and (b) are true, the numerous opportunities for rich participatory moments in the earlier stages of constitution-making provide several avenues for increasing the sociological legitimacy of a constitution if that is one's goal. Further, these other earlier procedures are more likely to be successful at doing so. For one thing, the research by Eisenstadt et al. mentioned above suggests that insofar as participation in constitution-making leads to greater levels of democracy, this effect is far more likely when the participation occurs at the beginning of the constitution-making process rather than merely at the end.[118] Moreover, the arguments connecting participation to legitimacy sketched above claim that people are more likely to deem an outcome legitimate if they feel a sense of ownership over it, identify with the results, and believe themselves to be connected to the decision-making process. In particular, Tyler's process-based approach holds that people are most likely to consider an outcome legitimate if the procedure that produced it was just, where procedural justice evaluations are affected by antecedent considerations such as having one's say, being treated as a person and taken seriously, and understanding the mechanics of a procedure and the reasons why decision-makers acted in a certain way.

All three of these antecedents can be met through elections and public consultation, the civic education campaigns that precede them, and the partially transparent constitution-making procedures that coincide with them. A person who talked with a constitution-making delegate, attended a constitutional workshop, commented on an online draft constitution, elected a delegate to a constituent assembly, watched deliberations in the assembly, or a did a combination of such things, is likely to feel that they participated and that the constitution which results is partly their creation. Moreover, the fact that constitution-drafting is ongoing during these moments of participation makes it more likely that a participant feels that they had a role to play in the constitution's development. It is unclear what the extra opportunity of ratification, in which participants only get to contribute to a veto process, would add.

To summarize this point, if a constitution-making designer dismisses the worries raised in regard to (a) and (b) and is convinced that participation leads

116 Hélène Landemore, "Inclusive Constitution-Making: The Icelandic Experiment," (2015) 23 The Journal of Political Philosophy, 174.

117 Tofigh Maboudi and Ghazal P. Nadi, "Crowdsourcing the Egyptian Constitution: Social Media, Elites, and the Populace," (2016) 69 Political Research Quarterly 716–34, 716–17.

118 Eisenstadt, LeVan, and Maboudi, *Constituents before Assembly: Participation, Deliberation, and Representation in the Crafting of New Constitutions*, 51.

to legitimacy in a constitution-making context, they are likely to enhance participation earlier in the constitution-making process. This not only comports with many current constitution-making recommendations, but also seems more like to achieve the desired effect of bringing about a sociologically legitimate constitution, for these prior participatory opportunities are far richer than merely choosing or talking to a veto player or serving as one. If this is the case, the participatory-based PSL justification for ratification rests on the assertion that adding an additional instance of low-quality participation to an already participatory process will make it even more likely that citizens will see the resultant constitution as sociologically legitimate. This is a subtler and weaker claim, one that is far more complicated to evaluate, and significantly less intuitive.

3.2.3 Manipulation

Besides skepticism of the components of the participatory PSL justification, there is another more general reason to be wary of it. Namely, that enacting ratification procedures because of a PSL justification of this type is to engage in wrongful manipulation, and thus advocating for ratification on such a basis is to encourage and commit a moral wrong. To understand this objection, I need to first sketch out a kind of manipulation and explain when and why it is wrong. Note that in doing so I avoid two issues often at the center of many philosophical discussions of manipulation. First, I do not try to give one definition of manipulation that covers all cases. This is unnecessary for my purposes and controversial. It might also be impossible, in that manipulation might be a family resemblance or cluster concept, one involving combinatory vagueness such that it admits of no single definition of necessary and sufficient conditions.[119] Second, I do not assume that manipulation is a moralized concept, in the sense that to call something manipulation is necessarily to brand it as immoral.[120] What manipulation is and whether and when it is wrong are, I believe, separate questions.

One type or set of cases of manipulation involve an agent taking an action or actions in order to lead another to believe or do something on the basis of reasons or factors that are irrelevant, bad, or distorted and known to be such by the manipulator. In this sense, the manipulation involves actions designed to trick someone into adopting a particular mental state or making a certain decision by circumventing, subverting, or adulterating their rational decision-making processes.[121] It can be distinguished from, but shares aspects of, coercion and

[119] See Felicia Ackerman, "The Concept of Manipulativeness," (1995) 9 Philosophical Perspectives 335–40, 338. The idea of family resemblance concepts comes from Ludwig Wittgenstein, *Philosophical Investigations* (4th edn, Blackwell Publishing Ltd 2009) 37e.

[120] Allen W. Wood, "Coercion, Manipulation, Exploitation," in Christian Coons and Max Weber (eds.), *Manipulation: Theory and Practice* (Oxford University Press 2014) 19–21.

[121] Claudia Mills, "Politics and Manipulation," (1995) 21 Social Theory and Practice 97–112, 100; Wood, "Coercion, Manipulation, Exploitation," 35.

persuasion. Coercion involves the threat or use of force to make someone do what you want, it forces your will on another, and works by removing options from a particular agent's choice situation such that they have no acceptable alternative.[122] Persuasion involves offering good reasons to convince another to do what you want without altering their choice situation. Manipulation, on this account, is a sort of hybrid involving the submission of your will on another by distorting their reasoning capability rather than eliminating acceptable alternatives or offering actually good reasons.[123]

Consider the following: Elif and Rachel are married and have a rule according to which both must agree to every large purchase. Elif wants to buy a bigger television but knows that Rachel is strongly against the idea because money is tight, their current television works perfectly, and it is only a year old. However, Elif also knows that after eating her favorite meal at her favorite restaurant, Rachel descends into a state of bliss in which she is likely to agree to things without thinking them through. Elif plans a trip to the restaurant, waits until Rachel finishes eating and sinks into her happy state, and asks about the television. Rachel agrees and Elif immediately places the order. This is an example of manipulation because Elif intentionally leads Rachel to make a particular decision by polluting her normal reasoning functions. That she had just eaten her favorite meal is simply irrelevant to whether Rachel should agree to buy a larger television, as Rachel herself would admit in a more lucid state. Thus, by introducing an irrelevant variable in order to sway Rachel, Elif manipulated her wife. This is distinct from a situation in which Elif threatened Rachel to secure her agreement (coercion) or offered good reasons for the new purchase (persuasion).

Intuitively, manipulation of this sort seems wrong. But what makes it so? Why exactly has someone like Elif acted wrongly? One answer is that they have intentionally subverted the autonomy of another. Manipulation involves taking an action to disrupt a person's reasoning such that they make a decision or come to a particular mental state they would not make or have if thinking clearly.[124] Like coercion, it thus involves the imposition of one's own will on the will of another.[125] It degrades a person's ability to make a free autonomous choice, and thus goes against their human capacity of setting their own life plans and making their own

[122] Raz, *The Morality of Freedom*, 378; Wood, "Coercion, Manipulation, Exploitation," 21; Robert Nozick, "Coercion," in Sidney Morgenbesser, Patrick Suppes, and Morton White (eds.), *Philosophy, Science, and Method: Essays in Honor of Ernest Nagel* (St. Martin's Press 1969).

[123] Raz, *The Morality of Freedom*, 377; Wood, "Coercion, Manipulation, Exploitation," 35.

[124] See Cave's claim that manipulation violates what he calls modest autonomy, in which an "agent need only act from concerns not thrust on her by others in ways that overwhelm her capacity over her own mental life." Eric M. Cave, "What's Wrong with Motive Manipulation," (2006) 10 Ethical Theory and Moral Practice 129–44, 138.

[125] One might see the usurpation of rational self-government not merely as an infringement of autonomy understood generally, but as a violation of our freedom of non-domination. See Wood, "Coercion, Manipulation, Exploitation," 41.

way in the world.[126] Elif knows that Rachel does not want the television and would not agree to it under normal circumstances, so she engineers a situation in which Rachel's reasoning is predictably distorted in order to assure her desired outcome. In this moment, Elif is taking self-government away from Rachel, or at the least unduly influencing or perverting it.[127] Put differently, and in a more Kantian vein, this is to wrongly treat the manipulated as a means to an end, as something that can be conformed to one's own wishes by pulling certain levels rather than by offering reasons for the free agent to consider.[128]

Some instances of manipulation are wrong for a further reason, namely that they involve explicit deception. Imagine that instead of bringing Rachel to her favorite restaurant, Elif altered the picture settings of their current television in order to make Rachel believe that it was broken. Here, Elif not only interfered with her wife's ordinary reasoning processes to get a desired outcome but did so by deliberately introducing a false belief, thereby preventing Rachel from governing herself with an accurate understanding of her circumstances.[129] This goes against, and directly interferes with, the value that rational agents place on being in touch with reality and knowing what reasons apply to them. While manipulation as an autonomy violation interferes with the value of "having the capacity to govern our own actions, the capacity to act in accordance with our own ideas of what is right and good," manipulation as deception contravenes the value of seeing "the problems and important facts that bear on them realistically and in perspective."[130]

Manipulation might be prima facie wrong, a pro tanto wrong, or some combination of the two. Regardless, in certain circumstances manipulative actions might be justified on balance.[131] Though imprecise in the case of prima facie wrongs, for

[126] A neo-Frankfurtian account of autonomy, one that better fits with compatibilism, would add a further stipulation, claiming that an autonomy violation only occurs if the affected agent objects, or would object, to the manipulation influencing the process through which they form desires, decisions, or actions. See J.S. Blumenthal-Barby, "A Framework for Assessing the Moral Status of "Manipulation," in Christian Coons and Max Weber (eds.), *Manipulation: Theory and Practice* (Oxford University Press 2014) 125–26.

[127] Scanlon describes the wrongness of manipulation as violating "the strong generic reason to want to be able to direct one's efforts and resources toward aims one has chosen and not to have one's planning co-opted," though he confines manipulation to instances in which A influences B to do X by leading B to expect that A will do Y in return for B doing X. T.M. Scanlon, *What We Owe Each Other* (Harvard University Press 1998) 298.

[128] Mills, "Politics and Manipulation," 101; Thomas E. Hill Jr., "Humanity as an End in Itself," (1980) 91 Ethics 84–99, 96.

[129] Sarah Buss, "Valuing Autonomy and Respecting Persons: Manipulation, Seduction, and the Basis of Moral Constraints," (2005) 11 Ethics 195–235, 226.

[130] Ibid., 228; Thomas E. Hill Jr., "Autonomy and Benevolent Lies," (1984) 18 Journal of Value Inquiry 251–67, 251

[131] If manipulation is a prima facie wrong it is presumptively wrong, such that in certain circumstances it is not wrong at all. If it is a pro tanto wrong, manipulation always imparts wrongness, but can be outweighed by competing sources of goodness. Alternatively, Baron articulates a convincing hybrid account in which manipulation is a prima face wrong, but when wrong, the wrongness is of the pro tanto variety Marcia Baron, "The Mens Rea and Moral Status of Manipulation," in Christian Coons and Max Weber (eds.), *Manipulation: Theory and Practice* (Oxford University Press 2014) 116–18. I am assuming that manipulation is not an absolute wrong, in that there are far too many examples

ease of explanation I will use the language of competing moral factors outweighing or overriding the wrongness of manipulation.[132] For instance, let us imagine that Elif is driven by the knowledge that replacing the current television will enhance Rachel's well-being. Perhaps Elif and Rachel love watching subtitled foreign films, and Elif knows that Rachel, though she will never admit it, is having a harder time reading the subtitles as her eyesight is worsening. A larger television will both make it easier for Rachel to watch her films and not remind her regularly of her deteriorating sight. In such an instance, it is wrong for Elif to manipulate Rachel, and it would obviously be better if she could get her desired outcome through persuasion, but nonetheless given the circumstances the manipulation might be justified or at least permissible because of the happiness it will bring Rachel and the goodness of mitigating some of her ocular anxiety.

Let us now return to ratification and attempts to justify the procedure by appealing to a PSL pathway such as the one linking legitimacy to participation. Remember, this involves justifying the implementation of ratification solely because the participation that comes from taking part in the procedure makes it more likely that a populace will see the constitution as morally legitimate. My contention is that implementing a ratification procedure for this reason is to engage in wrongful manipulation and should therefore be avoided.

For one thing, it involves trying to induce a specific belief in agents for reasons that are irrelevant to the belief itself. That a ratification procedure was used has no bearing, in itself, on whether or not a constitution is morally legitimate, and thus using this occurrence as a means of bringing about a desired legitimacy belief in the populace is to engage in widespread manipulation that wrongfully violates their autonomy. It is to trick the people, or a portion of them, into thinking that a constitution is morally legitimate for reasons unrelated to its moral legitimacy. Moreover, in some cases it also involves deception. For instance, people might come to think that a ratified constitution is morally legitimate because of their incorrect belief in some form of constituent power justification (CPJ). If this is known and encouraged by designers of the constitution-making process, then the use of ratification involves manipulation that intentionally induces false beliefs on the way to violating autonomy. The participatory PSL justification, and other possible PSL justifications, are therefore problematic and should be rejected, for in answer to the question, why should we implement ratification, they advocate for a moral wrong.

Two objections might rebut this charge. The first denies manipulation, claiming that ratification is in fact a good reason for believing a constitution is morally

of manipulation—planning a surprise party, playing poker, dressing up for date—that do not seem to involve wrongdoing.

132 If manipulation is merely a prima facie wrong, these competing factors or circumstances would not outweigh the wrong of manipulation, but would simply make clear that manipulation is not wrong in a particular instance.

legitimate. Since I have defined the kind of manipulation I am concerned with as intentionally leading an agent to decide or form a belief based on reasons that are bad and known to be bad by the manipulator, this objection would rebut my central claim. It would transform the act of implementing ratification to induce sociological legitimacy from manipulation to persuasion, which involves bringing someone to a desired mental state or action by putting forth good reasons. Ordinary cases of persuasion such as this are morally acceptable, involving the recognition rather than the rejection of a person's status as a reasoning autonomous agent, and thus a PSL justification involving persuasion would be unproblematic.

So, what would it mean for ratification to be a good and relevant reason for believing that a constitution is morally legitimate? In other words, in what ways might ratification really matter for one's assessment of whether sufficient moral reasons exist for a constitution's claim to authority? At the least, the presence of a ratification procedure, and perhaps its success, would have to increase the moral legitimacy of a constitution. How might this occur? There are two general ways that a decision-making procedure, like ratification, could have such an effect on a constitution's legitimacy. On the one hand, the occurrence of ratification might make it more likely that the content of a constitution falls within the boundaries of moral legitimacy. Thus, for example, perhaps knowledge of ratification makes framers more likely to write a constitution that is substantively morally legitimate. On the other hand, the procedure itself might serve to help legitimate the constitution, regardless of its effects on the substance of the text. For instance, perhaps a constitution is only morally legitimate if it is the explicit creation of the soon-to-be governed people, and ratification provides the best opportunity for the people to act in their creative capacity.

This should all be too familiar. In essence, this first objection to the claim that certain PSL justifications of ratification are wrongfully manipulative turns on the strength of ratification's role in substantive moral legitimation or procedural moral legitimation, in that utilizing ratification to get people to believe that a constitution is morally legitimate would only not be manipulative if it plausibly affected the actual moral legitimacy of a constitution. And, as I have discussed in the above sections, it is unlikely, and at best unclear, that ratification serves as a means of SML or PML. The first objection therefore fails.[133]

While the first objection denies the charge of manipulation, the second acknowledges it but claims that circumstances are such that manipulation is nonetheless justified. Specifically, it claims that the good of citizens seeing their constitution

[133] This is perhaps too strong. As discussed in section 2.2, ratification does procedurally legitimate a constitution according to a constitutional consent theory, so the objection will stand for those who endorse it and ratification would not be manipulative. However, as noted, this is a fringe position, not explicitly espoused by anyone, that requires one to see the moral legitimacy of a constitution as important while accepting the fact that constitutions are morally illegitimate for nearly everyone both in the past and in the future.

as sociologically legitimate negates or outweighs the wrong of manipulating the public via ratification. In the current and previous chapters, I have simply assumed that a constitution being sociologically legitimate is a good thing that produces reasons for implementing ratification. But why would that be? One can think of many reasons. Sociologically legitimate constitutions might be more likely to: stick and successfully play their role as higher law; endure and create stable legal and political conditions; or generate support and acquiescence for the governments that they structure.[134] Again, according to the second objection, good outcomes such as these, which stem from citizens believing in the existence of moral reasons in favor of the authority of their constitution, produce moral reasons that disable or override the wrongness of ratification's manipulation and thus leave the PSL justification intact.

There are two reasons why this objection is weaker than it initially appears. The first can be seen by once again returning to Elif and Rachel. Imagine that Elif is manipulating Rachel into agreeing to buy a new television at a discount website, where the type of new television one receives is unknown beforehand. They might receive a larger television, this may even be the most likely occurrence, but they also might receive a smaller television or one identical in size to their current television. In this scenario, if forced to justify why she is manipulating her wife beforehand, Elif's response regarding Rachel's eyesight and the subtitles is substantially weaker. She has no idea whether the new television will help the matter, and thus her manipulation cannot be so easily excused. The wrong of the manipulation is a given, but the competing source of goodness is not.

Something similar, I argue, is happening with this second objection. It relies on a claim of the following form: it is good, because of *x*, for a constitution to be sociologically legitimate. However, even if one assumes that such an *x* exists, regardless of what form it takes it cannot apply to all possible constitutions. That is, any reason for why a sociologically legitimate constitution is a moral good capable of outweighing the wrong of manipulation will be inapplicable to some constitutions. For instance, if *x* refers to the benefit of citizens supporting and acquiescing to the government set up by a new constitution, this will not apply to constitutions that set up autocracies or other undesirable government types. It is not a great source of good if a constitution's sociological legitimacy assists in leading citizens to blindly follow the orders of their despotic leader.

To put it differently, given a particular constitution-making setting, for every *x* one can imagine all possible constitutions divided into three sets: constitutions for which it is a good if they are seen as sociologically legitimate; constitutions for which it is a neutral thing, neither wrong nor good, if they are seen as sociologically

[134] James L. Gibson, Gregory A. Caldeira, and Lester Kenyatta Spence, "Why Do People Accept Public Policies They Oppose? Testing Legitimacy Theory with a Survey Based Experiment?," (2005) 58 Political Research Quarterly 187–201, 196.

legitimate; and constitutions for which it is a wrong if they are seen as sociologically legitimate. This means that if a constitution falls into the first category, the manipulation is justified. However, if the constitution falls into the neutral category the manipulation is still wrong overall, and if it is a part of last category, the manipulation is wrong not simply because of autonomy considerations, but also because it involves producing an outcome that is harmful. The problem is that when constructing a constitution-making process, it cannot be guaranteed which set the eventual constitution will fall into. That is, when a justification for the inclusion of ratification is needed, one cannot know whether the manipulation involved in the PSL justification is defensible or not. This undercuts the second objection considerably, in that the defense of a future act of manipulation is based on something that, for non-random or unforeseen reasons, may not happen. Those seeking to defend a PSL justification find themselves in Elif's position, trying to explain an action that will be wrong by pointing to results that might provide a good.

Second, this objection weakens once one remembers that other parts of the constitution-making process can also contribute to creating sociological legitimacy. Imagine that Elif takes other actions to help Rachel read the subtitles. She rearranges the furniture to bring the television closer to the seating area and enlarges the subtitle size on their media player. Now, whether or not the manipulation is justified turns on the added benefit, if it exists, of obtaining a larger television on the subtitle readability. The case is now much less clear-cut and intuitive, for it is uncertain if a new television is even needed. The same is true, as mentioned above, with ratification and its effects on sociological legitimacy. If participation leads to legitimacy, it is unclear why earlier moments of participation will not be sufficient. This, admittedly, is not a refutation of the second objection, but it casts further doubt on its ability to dislodge the claim that implementing ratification on the basis of a participatory PSL is to commit the moral wrong of manipulation.

4. Conclusion

The most popular and intuitive justification for ratification is the claim that the procedure should be implemented because it helps create legitimate constitutions. Ratification provides the people or their agents with the opportunity to evaluate and double-check what is meant to be their future democratic constitution. It gives them a direct, pivotal, and final role in what is usually one of the key political moments in a country's history. For those with democratic intuitions that prioritize the people's control of the political sphere, the procedure looks obviously connected to the legitimacy of the final product of the constitution-making process. However, as I argue in this and the previous chapter, the details are important. What it means for a procedure to legitimate a constitution is not straightforward, and once parsed out and analyzed the justification loses much of its initial force.

In chapter 8 I set the stage for this enquiry. Noting that legitimacy is used to mean different things across contexts, leading to much confusion, I divided ratification into three types: something is morally legitimate if its claim to authority is morally justified; sociologically legitimate if a significant portion of the population believes it to be morally legitimate and obeys or follows as a result; and legally legitimate if it is legally valid according to the legal system of which it is a part.

Moral and sociological legitimacy apply to constitutions without problem. A constitution is morally legitimate if there are good reasons for its claim to be the ultimate source of legal authority in a polity, and sociologically legitimate if people believe that such reasons exist and treat a constitution as if it were morally legitimate as a result. However, legal legitimacy does not apply in the same way. Constitutions are the source of legality within a given political and legal system, and therefore there is no legal system under which they might be legally valid. The apparent legal legitimacy of constitutions is actually based upon their sociological legitimacy, and thus legal legitimacy is irrelevant for the purposes of examining the capacity for ratification to legitimate constitutions. More generally, this means that, from a legitimacy standpoint, abiding by legally proscribed procedures of constitutional replacement is only justifiable if doing so increases the likelihood and degree to which citizens believe the new constitution is legitimate.

I next explained how ratification, like any procedure, might contribute to the actual or perceived normative status of its outcome. On the one hand, it might have a substantive effect, i.e. ratification might affect the contents of a constitution, such that it is more likely to meet some independent standard of legitimacy. On the other hand, it might have a procedural effect. When it comes to legitimacy, this means that ratification might legitimate a constitution simply because the procedure was carried out. A constitution would be legitimate not because of its content, but rather because it resulted from ratification itself.

Combined, the distinction between sociological and moral legitimacy and procedural and substantive effects produces four pathways through which ratification might legitimate a constitution: substantive moral legitimation; substantive sociological legitimation; procedural moral legitimation; and procedural sociological legitimation. The enunciation of these pathways is the major contribution of chapter 8, for it sets out a framework, lacking in the literature on constitution-making, through which the alleged legitimating effects of a whole host of constitution-making and decision-making procedures might be analyzed and tested.

In this chapter I evaluated various possible legitimacy-based justification of ratification by using my framework to examine the most popular, likely, and plausible explanations of how ratification might help produce legitimate constitutions. First, I turned toward substantive sociological and moral legitimation. Ratification might help to ensure that the contents of a constitution meet conditions of actual or perceived moral legitimacy through one of two ways: by filtering out illegitimate constitutions or preventing illegitimate constitutions from being written. The ratification-as-filter mechanism, which I developed through an analysis of Condorcet's 1789 essay, is appealing but has several weaknesses. Primarily, it assumes that ratifiers will make their decision based on legitimacy considerations and that they can identify an illegitimate constitution in the first place. Neither assumption can be made with any confidence, and ratification might therefore fail to filter much of anything. This makes the attempt to justify ratification based on its filtration capabilities unpersuasive.

Next, I scrutinized two ways through which ratification could serve as a means of content control by changing the behavior of framers. Ratification may impose a *goal constraint* by giving constitution-makers reasons to only pursue constitutions they believe ratifiers will accept, and a *justificatory constraint* by preventing framers from including provisions that cannot be justified without violating societal norms of argumentation. Both of the constraints are plausible on their face, but there are good reasons to question their effectiveness and to doubt the subsequent strength of any justification based on them. For instance, neither constraint will function if framers believe, quite plausibly, that ratifiers will not cast their votes on the basis of legitimacy or social norms violations—perhaps because of ignorance or an undesirable status quo—or that they can persuade ratifiers to accept an illegitimate constitution. Moreover, the goal constraint depends on the sort of clear and reliable pathways of communication between framers and their constituents that, as discussed in chapter 7, are absent even in well-functioning and long-standing representative democracies, and both constraints already affect the constitution-making process without ratification.

I then turned to the procedural pathways. Defending ratification by appealing to its role in procedural moral legitimation is familiar, in that constituent power justifications are examples I have already analyzed and rejected in previous chapters. I also looked at a more basic form of a PML argument, one that conceptualizes ratification as a moment of necessary direct citizen consent. Such an argument does in fact justify ratification, but at the cost of requiring one to endorse pure consent theory and its applicability to constitutions, and accept that all past, present, and future constitutions are morally illegitimate for a high supermajority of their citizens. This justification is likely to have few proponents and little chance of persuading those who are not already avowed philosophical anarchists.

Finally, I looked at whether ratification leads to procedural sociological legitimacy, i.e. whether the mere occurrence of the procedure induces people to believe in the moral authority of the constitution. I acknowledge that this effect likely occurs in places where certain norms and beliefs exist linking ratification to legitimacy, such that a constitution not submitted to ratification would be seen as illegitimate. However, one cannot assume that such norms and beliefs are widespread and common now or in the future, and thus such a PSL explanation cannot be the basis of a universal justification for ratification. A more general PSL argument requires a mechanism explaining why the procedure of ratification leads to the formation of legitimacy beliefs in the populace for content-independent reasons. The best candidate for such a mechanism is the claim that participation leads to legitimacy. The participatory PSL argument for ratification incorporates this mechanism, producing perhaps the most convincing and referenced justification for ratification examined in this book. Its claim is simple: ratification provides a means for the soon-to-be governed populace to participate in the constitution-making process, and this participation, like it allegedly does in a whole range of more common decision-making processes, leads participants to see the outcome as being supported by moral reasons.

This justification, however, suffers from problems. For one thing, it rests on an untested empirical assertion. We simply do not know if participation generally leads to legitimacy during constitution-making, let alone if participation via a ratification procedure does. Quantitative and qualitative research on the former is mixed, perhaps even tilting negative, while there is no research on the latter. Moreover, the research vindicating the participation leads to legitimacy mechanism in ordinary circumstances is also suspect, in that, among other things, legitimacy is incredibly hard to isolate in empirical studies and is usually operationalized in such a way that the underlying concept becomes distorted or lost. In addition, if participation does lead to legitimacy, it remains unclear what the weak and limited participation provided by ratification would contribute to the myriad of other aspects of a constitution-making process that can and often are made participatory. However, I should note that the possibility of other participatory procedures legitimating constitutions does not give us reason to avoid ratification. Such a determination would require weighing the pros and cons of ratification and its likely effects with other participatory components of constitution-making, and I did not perform such an analysis.

I ended the chapter reflecting on a more general reason to be wary of some arguments urging the use of ratification because of its role in procedural sociological legitimation. Namely, that enacting ratification for such a purpose would be to commit wrongful manipulation, in that it would involve attempting to lead the people to form a belief (that the constitution is morally legitimate) based on a reason that is irrelevant to said belief (that the constitution had been ratified). At the least, such manipulation violates the autonomy of the people, for it involves distorting their ability to rationally make their own judgments, and on occasion it involves deception, if the effect of ratification on sociological legitimacy comes from telling mistruths to the people.

To conclude, much of the intuitive nature of the legitimacy justification stems from ambiguity around the word legitimacy and how procedures contribute to it, our reflexive democratic tendency to see amplifying sites of participation as an unchallengeable good, and a failure to interrogate our own assumptions. This explains the numerous confident statements, by scholars and practitioners alike, linking ratification to legitimacy without a modicum of explanation. Ratification might very well be justified because its use increases the likelihood of creating a more legitimate constitution. I have presented no knock-down argument against this possibility. It remains the most natural defense of ratification, and, in my opinion, the most likely source of ratification's merits if they so exist. However, what I have tried to show is that the argument does not make itself, and that actually trying to piece together the mechanism through which the decision to use a ratification procedure produces legitimacy is incredibly difficult. I have found the likeliest such mechanisms wanting. Others surely exist. But these must be detailed, explained, examined, and defended before ratification can be justified on their basis.

10
Conclusion

Ratification is ubiquitous. In April 2020, Kyrgyzstani voters approved a new constitution using a ratification referendum. At the time of writing, the high-profile Chilean constitution-making process is scheduled to terminate with the same procedure.[1] It will likely follow on the heels of another ratification referendum in Haiti, recently rescheduled to take place in November 2021.[2] In this book I asked a simple question: should ratification procedures such as these be a standard part of constitution-making?

Answers here are important, for ratification is not only increasingly common, but has significant effects, is recommended, and is optional. However, thus far, ratification has been ignored. The procedure is rarely studied or analyzed; its worth assumed rather than explained. I argued that this is a mistake. One should not be recommending or using a procedure in a high stakes decision-making process, let alone one that distributes a veto, without good reasons for doing so.

Specifically, I sought context-independent, ex ante reasons for implementing ratification, i.e. general justifications that appeal to impartial values for including ratification within the best practices of democratic constitution-making. For many, myself once included, ratification appears to be just the sort of procedure that could be justified in this way. This project began in earnest search of a justification I believed I would find. Admittedly, this might be an American affliction, for in the United States the ratification of the federal constitution is often treated and taught as if it was an event of religious importance. But, more generally, ratification just seems intuitive—a procedure supported by so many of our basic democratic norms. How could it not have an easy and straightforward justification for its use?

However, while intuitions might be prevalent, justifications are hard to find. Few have been given by those involved in or who study constitution-making, both in the present or in the past. At least partially this might be because of the intuitive nature of the procedure; it just doesn't cry out for much of an explanation. Nonetheless, in the previous chapters, after canvassing the pre-constitutional

[1] John Bartlett, "'A New Chile': Political Elite Rejected in Vote for Constitutional Assembly" *The Guardian* (May 18, 2021) <https://www.theguardian.com/world/2021/may/18/a-new-chile-political-elite-rejected-in-vote-for-constitutional-assembly>.

[2] Andrew Paultre and Laura Gottesdiener, "Haiti Elections to Replace Slain President Postponed to Nov. 7" *Reuters* (August 11, 2021) <https://www.reuters.com/world/americas/haiti-elections-replace-slain-president-postponed-nov-7-media-2021-08-12/>. Note that Haiti's referendum, if it happens, will violate the 1987 Haitian Constitution, which explicitly prohibits referendums on constitutional reform. See Constitution of the Republic of Haiti (1987), title XIII, Art. 284-2.

Constitutional Ratification without Reason. Jeffrey A. Lenowitz, Oxford University Press. © Jeffrey A. Lenowitz 2022.
DOI: 10.1093/oso/9780198852346.003.0010

origins and extra-constitutional uses of ratification, as well as the procedure's early constitutional history, I formulated and tested what seemed to be the strongest forms of the most plausible, persuasive, and cited reasons for using ratification. All of these, as shown, came up short. This conclusion reports and reflects upon my findings and divides into three sections.

First, I summarize the results of my examination of each of the three core justifications of ratification—the constituent power justification, the representation justification, and the legitimacy justification. Second, I reflect upon my findings, discussing what we can and cannot conclude about ratification's role in the constitution-making process. I also draw out some more general lessons and observations that emerged throughout. Third, I finish this chapter by asking and sketching out answers to a new yet related question that constantly surfaced in previous discussions: what content-dependent, ex post reasons are there to use ratification? In other words, what are some general scenarios in which specific constitution-makers might rationally want to use ratification?

1. Summary of Findings

I define ratification as an optional procedure that takes place at the end of a constitution-making process. It involves an agent, independent of the drafters and plausibly claiming to act for the people, voting for or against a constitution, with approval required for enactment. There are six types of ratification, depending upon the form of the ratifying agent—a convention, an existing government body, or the people in a referendum—and whether they are acting for the people as a whole or sub-state territories. Thus, a ratification procedure can involve national conventions, sub-state conventions, a national government body, sub-state government bodies, national referendums, or sub-state referendums. Referendums are by far the most popular form of ratification.

The first core justification for this procedure links it with the theory of constituent power, the influential idea that constitutions need to be made not by governments, but by those they are to govern. Constitutions are often written to encourage this belief. The Spanish Constitution starts by announcing that "The Spanish Nation … proclaims its will," and the constitutions of South Africa, the United States, South Korea, Ghana, and many others begin with the words "We, the people … ."[3] Perhaps, then, ratification is a means of giving teeth to such expressions. On its face, this thought is quite persuasive. It fits nicely with the intuition that ratification has something to do with popular power, is the argument made by those that first invented and advocated for the procedure, and comports

[3] *The Constitution of Spain* (1978).

with what many ratifiers likely understand themselves as doing. To be precise, a constituent power justification (CPJ) holds that any authoritative constitution must be the creation of the people, and that ratification is an essential means of making this happen.

Of course, part of the persuasiveness of CPJ comes from the fact that, like many allusions to the theory of constituent power, it is blurry on the details. Specifically, we need to know the answer to the following: how is ratification involved in the people exercising their constituent power? In chapter 4, I considered and analyzed several different CPJs that varied in how they answered this question. According to a multiple moments justification, ratification is one of several instances during constitution-making in which the people exercise their constituent power. Alternatively, the reparative function justification, referencing the original reparative function of the procedure in Roman law, pitches ratification as a critical moment of constituent action used when prior attempts at manifesting the people fail. A multiple attempts justification sees ratification as one of many procedures in a constitution-making process designed to make it more likely that the constituent power acts, and an overall process justification claims that ratification is just one part of the overall constitution-making process which, taken as a whole, involves the constituent power creating its higher law.

Each of these CPJs, I argued, are inadequate. The multiple attempts justification is incoherent, for prior moments of constituent action make ratification either redundant or contradictory. The reparative function justification is at least plausible but does not produce the sort of ex ante reasons we are looking for; I will however return to it at the end of this chapter. Among other flaws, the multiple attempts justification misses the point of constituent power theory, which gains normative traction from its emphasis on the people acting, not indirectly trying to approximate or arrive at its will. The overall process justification fares worse, in that it is simply a retreat into vagueness, giving no reason for using or not using any procedure, ratification included.

The failure of all four of these CPJs pushes us toward a final way in which ratification might enable constituent power. This argument, which I call the unique site justification (USJ), claims that ratification is justified because it is the sole moment in the constitution-making process capable of allowing the people to act and make the constitution their own. I developed USJ primarily by looking at the writings of Thomas Allen and his Berkshire Constitutionalists, the group of Massachusetts revolutionaries covered in chapter 3 whose protests led to the first ratification procedure in history. Allen argued that authoritative constitutions must be created through the exercise of the people's constituent power and that this power was unalienable, for alienating it would necessarily open the people to serious harm. This means that constituent action is not only confined to the ratification process, but that it can only be deployed by the people acting directly via a referendum.

Unfortunately, despite the passionate nature of the Constitutionalists' arguments and the rich theoretical foundations of their claims, USJ falls flat. The reason is simple: constituent power logic requires that voters in a ratification referendum, tasked with creating their constitution, make a meaningful choice, i.e. a choice that reflects their understanding of the document, the likely results of its rejection, and their own beliefs, interests, and values on the subject matter. Unfortunately, through no fault of their own, voters will be too uninformed to do this. The information needed to evaluate a constitution is simply too arcane and technical, hard to obtain, and of little value in normal circumstances.

I considered and rebutted three objections to this conclusion. These suggested that framers might be too ignorant to make a meaningful choice, that information shortcuts can help ignorant ratifiers vote as if they were informed, and that targeted educational campaigns during the ratification stage can eradicate ignorance. However, these objections are unpersuasive. Meaningful choice is not meant to apply to framers. Moreover, they can become highly informed due to the intense research, deliberation, and training that they, and not citizen ratifiers, undergo. Even supporters of voting shortcuts admit that they fail in conditions like constitution-making, where elites are confused, regular cue-givers are absent or contradictory, and voters lack knowledge about who shares their values on the issues in question. Further, meaningful choice requires intentional action not inadvertent competence. Finally, education campaigns are unlikely to succeed with such a massive knowledge gap, and their effects are likely to be countered by the inevitable ratification campaigns designed to persuade confused voters by any means necessary. In the end, USJ, like all considered forms of CPJ, cannot give good reason to use ratification. Those that continue to advocate for ratification based on its role in enabling the people to act either overlook the predictable ignorance of citizen ratifiers or paper over a merely symbolic procedure with normatively charged language pretending to celebrate the demos.

The next core justification of ratification associates it with representation. Drafters of constitutions are often conceptualized as representatives of the people, and ratification seems like one way, perhaps the only way, to keep them in check. In other words, ratification seems like an excellent accountability mechanism, and if representation is something desirable in a constitution-making process, then ratification might be desirable for the same reason. However, this too falls short. While accountability mechanisms are key for the creation and maintenance of representation, ratification cannot coherently serve as one. The function of ratification, and the central task of a ratifier, is to approve or reject a proposed constitution. Accountability mechanisms are a means for principals to exert control and indicate whether they were present in their agent's action by rewarding or punishing them. These two tasks might point in opposite directions; a ratifier might wish to sanction their representative framer for failing to represent, while simultaneously approving the constitution. In such instances of evaluative divergence, ratification-as-accountability mechanism necessarily fails at one of its given tasks. Ratification, then, cannot serve as an accountability mechanism, does not play a role in a representative process, and is therefore not justified by the value of representation.

The final core justification for ratification concerns legitimacy. It claims that ratification is valuable because it helps create legitimate constitutions. This intuition is potent yet opaque, for legitimacy is a tricky concept that is used haphazardly across contexts. Much of this confusion, I argued, stems from conflating different forms of legitimacy and ignoring how procedures contribute to them. To address this, I made two distinctions that produced four legitimacy pathways. Political legitimacy divides into three types—moral, sociological, and legal—, though legal legitimacy is inapplicable for constitutions. Thus, a constitution is morally legitimate when moral reasons justify its claim to authority and sociologically legitimate when people believe it is morally legitimate. Procedures can change the normative status of an outcome by serving as normative criteria themselves (procedural effect) or altering the substance of an outcome such that it is more or less likely to meet an independent normative criterion (substantive effect). This means that ratification or any constitution-making procedure can legitimate a constitution through four pathways: substantive moral legitimation, substantive sociological legitimation, procedural moral legitimation, and procedural sociological legitimation.

I discussed what appeared to be the most likely examples of how ratification might legitimate a constitution through these pathways. I treated arguments for both substantive moral and sociological legitimation together. As an ex post procedure, ratification can only affect the content of a constitution in two ways. First, it might filter out illegitimate constitutions because ratifiers will reject such constitutions. Second, it might prevent constitutions with illegitimate content from being written in the first place by leading framers to either restrict their constitutional goals in anticipation of what ratifiers will accept or limit their provisions to those that admit to public justification. I found the ratification-as-filter argument unpersuasive because it mistakenly assumes that ratifiers will base or can be made to base their decisions solely upon legitimacy and that ratifiers will always be able to identify illegitimate constitutions. The argument that ratification will alter the content of the constitution by pushing its drafters to write something legitimate is equally flawed. It erroneously assumes that drafters have an implausible image of ratifiers as being not only able to identify partial provisions and illegitimate constitutions, but also motivated to make their decisions on that basis while being immune to persuasion.

I looked at two procedural moral legitimation arguments. The first was the constituent power justification already dismissed. The second relied on consent theory. This latter argument only applies to a ratification referendum, which it conceptualizes as involving citizens giving their necessary consent to a constitution and taking on obligations to obey as a result. Because of classic generational problems, the inability of the ignorant and coerced to give morally relevant consent, and the use of majority or supermajority thresholds in referendum, this justification implies that all past, present, and future constitutions are morally illegitimate for a supermajority of citizens. This renders the justification unpersuasive and unattractive to all those not already persuaded by the most extreme philosophical anarchist position.

Finally, I considered two arguments for how ratification could involve procedural sociological legitimation. On the one hand, the voting public might believe that ratification makes a constitution legitimate, or that a lack of ratification makes it illegitimate. This argument relies on the existence of a specific norm and/or belief that we have little reason to believe will be generally present in all or most constitution-making contexts, and thus cannot serve as the basis for ratification's general justification. On the other hand, some mechanism might exist linking the experience of ratification to the development of legitimacy beliefs. The most likely candidate is a three-part argument casting ratification as a means of participation. Specifically, such an argument claims that participation tends to lead to legitimacy beliefs, that this effect applies in constitution-making settings, and that ratification, as a participatory process, helps legitimize constitutions in this way.

This is a referenced and credible argument, yet it can be challenged. As I argued, each of its component parts have problems. For instance, the research showing that participation leads to legitimacy in other contexts is bedeviled by operationalization problems and the slippery nature of legitimacy as an object of measurement. Not only does empirical work linking ratification to legitimacy via participation not exist, but existing research on participation leading to legitimacy more generally in the constitution-making process is scant and contradictory. Moreover, there are good reasons to doubt that this mechanism would carry over to the constitution-making process. Also, the additional participation that ratification procedures provide seems minimal compared to the vast range of participatory possibilities available in earlier procedures in the constitution-making process, weakening the bite of the justification. And finally, implementing ratification based on this type of legitimacy justification is a morally problematic attempt to manipulate the populace, for it involves trying to make them take on a belief—that the constitution is morally legitimate—for reasons that we have found are irrelevant. In the end, like the previous two core justifications, the legitimacy justification does not persuade, at least in the absence of further developments.

2. Lessons and Questions

Where does this analysis leave us? Can we say that it is always a bad idea to incorporate ratification into a constitution-making process, or that there are never good reasons to do so? No. The findings and implications of this project are too modest to reach this conclusion. On the one hand, I only concentrated on the sort of general reasons that would justify including ratification in constitution-making best practices. Other types of reasons exist, and I explain some in the final section of this chapter. On the other hand, even when it comes to the kinds of reasons I was looking for, I only addressed the three core justifications of ratification. These appeared most likely to be successful—they rely on central conversations and concepts in democratic and constitutional theory, best make sense of the few positive arguments supporters of ratification make, and were persuasive on their face—but they are not comprehensive. Other justifications, yet to be forwarded and detailed, are possible.

Nonetheless, we can reach some important conclusions. Primarily, until new arguments are made, it is currently a mistake for anyone to make a blanket recommendation for ratification. The procedure has no place in the best practices of constitution-making. Attempts to link ratification to representation, constituent power and popular sovereignty, legitimacy, or similar concepts should be dismissed in the absence of extensive argumentation rebutting the above. Moreover, it is also an error for those designing constitution-making processes to reach for the procedure uncritically as a default, or even to assume that ratification has a general upside. Doing any of these things is to put faith in squishy normative intuitions that, as I have demonstrated, do not translate into good arguments.

In addition, our hunt for ratification's justification also yielded other conclusions, observations, and questions that are worth reviewing. Most generally, it is a mistake to assume that the procedural recommendations, principles, and concepts of normative democratic theory seamlessly apply to decision-making procedures such as constitution-making that fall outside the context of ordinary democratic politics. This is because, at the risk of being reductive, democratic theory tells us how best to structure the processes needed for the perpetual project of self-governance. It therefore is built upon the assumption that decisions are ongoing, that procedures are repeated, and that almost everyone involved at least has the capacity to familiarize themselves with the game. None of this is true of one-off processes such as constitution-making. If done right, constitution-making is rare within a single polity. It happens infrequently and ends soon after it starts. This means that many normative arguments built upon the routine of democracy simply do not apply.

Constitution-making occurs and will continue to do so. If we want to give countries advice about how to go about creating their founding documents, we must rely on clear concepts, well-developed normative arguments, and behavioral and psychological assumptions that take the unique context of constitution-making into consideration, not on intuitions stemming from the familiarity of certain procedures, vague connections to democratic norms, or allusions to celebrated founding myths. At the least then, this analysis should make those interested in constitution-making, or the construction of any decision-making process outside a normal democratic context, suspicious of procedures justified by hand waving toward familiar democratic norms.

Second, constituent power is not particularly helpful when it comes to procedural design. The concept is experiencing a renaissance in constitutional theory today. The idea of a unique popular power to create a morally legitimate constitution that cannot be constrained by constituted authorities is, for many, a normatively attractive one. Regardless, whatever productive uses the concept of constituent power might have—for instance to ward off attempts by constituted authorities to claim the raw power of the people or to explain the existence of unconstitutional constitutional amendments—it is unhelpful, for many reasons, when it comes to choosing procedures for a constitution-making process ex ante. Primarily, the concept and theory lack the necessary specificity. The constituent power theory assertion, for instance, that "a constitutional regime should have a democratic pedigree," meaning constitution-making should be characterized by a "degree of openness and popular participation," can perhaps help us dismiss a constitution-making process solely involving an unelected sitting government acting in complete secrecy.[4] However, it cannot help us choose which configuration of procedures, some more or less participatory and transparent, best fit together to create an optimal constitution-making process. When one tries to use constituent power theory to do so, a whole host of problems, some of which were illustrated in chapter 4, emerge.

Third, whether we can or should want to conceptualize constitution-makers as representatives, and the implications of this, needs further investigation. Both academic and journalist sources describe constitution-makers, especially those that are elected, using the language of representation. However, formal accountability mechanisms appear to be a critical part of what makes a relationship between a principal and their agent representative. While properly designed selection mechanisms might be able to impart a form of control over agents—here I am imagining something like Mansbridge's selection model of political representation—there does not seem to be a substitute procedure or means to transcend Pitkin's paradox of absent presence.[5] If this is the case, the lack of an accountability mechanism in the constitution-making process means that constitution-makers cannot be traditional representatives.[6] Is this a problem?

As I mentioned at the end of chapter 7, I do not think the answer is clear cut. On the one hand, treating constitution-makers like traditional democratic

[4] Joel Colón-Ríos, *Weak Constitutionalism: Democratic Legitimacy and the Question of Constituent Power* (Routledge 2012) 115.

[5] Jane Mansbridge, "A 'Selection Model' of Political Representation," (2009) 17 The Journal of Political Philosophy 369–98.

[6] I am excluding the possibility of creating something like the fanciful constitution-making accountability mechanisms I sketched out in chapter 7, section 4.4.

representatives makes good sense if one is trying to mimic the regime to come in the procedures used to create it. There might be good reasons to do this in some settings, for instance to familiarize citizens new to representative systems of government with its practices and norms. On the other hand, an argument can be made that we do not want those elected to write a constitution to be or think themselves to be representatives in the traditional sense. Their task, perhaps, is not to fight for their constituents, not to give them presence in the constitution-making setting, but rather to create a framework of government that will work for everyone, including both their constituents and the rest of the country in question. Perhaps moving away from the language of representation is one small way this can be made more likely to happen.

Fourth, the use of legitimacy by social scientists to promote their favored procedures and institutions remains problematic and in need of reform. On the one hand, operationalizing legitimacy and measuring it continues to throw up problems for empirical work. The concept is complex and hard to isolate and, as I argued in chapter 9, some of the most dominant attempts to do so run into thus far unavoidable obstacles. On the other hand, on the level of theory, clarity must be demanded. Saying that something promotes legitimacy is unhelpful unless the type of legitimacy is specified. This will not only bring precision to discussions of legitimacy and help inhibit the concept from being confused with something else, such as mere regime support or popularity, but also prevent projects designed to promote sociological legitimacy from quietly harnessing the built-in normativity of moral legitimacy. By this I mean that there is nothing inherently desirable about a set of people believing that something is morally legitimate. One promoting a policy initiative or procedure by showing how it creates sociological legitimacy must also explain why this is a good thing. Distinguishing legitimacy type makes this imperative more obvious. Further, the mechanism through which legitimation purportedly occurs always needs to be identified, explained, and connected to a legitimacy type. I did just that, listing four pathways through which a constitution-making procedure might assist in legitimating a constitution and using them to test ratification. This demonstrates how constitution-making procedural recommendations reliant on legitimacy should be treated, and something similar should be done to test and formulate legitimacy-based arguments in other domains.

3. Context-Dependent Reasons

In the absence of new arguments, ratification should not be treated as part of the best practices of constitution-making, for the most plausible and referenced ex ante and context-independent reasons that would justify its inclusion do not stand up to scrutiny. However, as mentioned, this does not mean there are never reasons to use ratification. Other reasons, those that depend on specific circumstances and sometimes appeal to values applicable to only certain members involved in the constitution-making process, exist. Throughout the previous chapters such reasons occasionally came to the surface, and in what follows I briefly sketch out what I tentatively take to be four persuasive ones. Thus, to end this book, I will ask and give some preliminary answers to a new question: what context-dependent reasons might justify ratification's use?

3.1 Reparative Justification

The first such reason connects constitutional ratification to its origins in ancient Rome, where it functioned in Roman law as a means of repairing and making binding defective agreements in which a promisor lacks or acts beyond the terms of their mandate, and to present-day agency law where it serves a similar purpose. In certain circumstances, when an ongoing constitution-making process appears to lack procedural legitimacy, there might be a good reason to deploy ratification in the hopes of generating some. As should be expected, this justification splits into two depending upon whether moral or sociological legitimacy is at issue.

We can understand both forms of this reparative justification by considering a hypothetical. Popular unrest prompts a sitting government to initiate a constitution-making process. They plan the following: proportional representation elections will take place in existing municipalities to fully populate the constituent convention. Once assembled, the convention will get to work drafting, airing it proceedings on national television. Delegates will meet with civil society leaders and key stakeholders and solicit public opinion on controversial issues throughout the convention. Finally, the government will enact and implement the new constitution once two-thirds of the convention approves it. Now, imagine that this process goes awry. For instance, one political party manipulates the convention election to secure a disproportionate number of seats, causing rival parties to boycott the convention entirely. Or it is revealed that the current President and her aides produced a draft constitution in secret, which is being forced through the convention in place of the participatory draft being hashed out on television.

On the one hand, a ratification procedure might serve as a means of PML, increasing the chances of a morally legitimate constitution by serving as a site of constituent power. I have in mind the reparative function justification considered in chapter 4, section 3.2. Here, the idea would be that a morally legitimate constitution must be made by the constituent power, and a distorted convention or one prevented from writing the constitution prevents this from happening during the earlier phases of the constitution-making process. Adding a properly constructed ratification procedure might in a sense repair the deficient constitution-making process, creating a space for the people to act and, if they approve the constitution, legitimate it. For those convinced by a theory of constituent power, the concept might give reason to use ratification in this instance. The problems detailed in chapter 4, and the general inability of the concept to yield specific procedural recommendations at the design stage, are less of an issue here given that most of the constitution-making process has already transpired. That is, the problems of under-specification and redundancy drop out once most stages of the constitution-making process have elapsed without any plausible room for constituent action. Of course, this argument does not apply to ratification referendums, as predictable citizen ignorance prevents them from being a reliable channel of constituent power.

As discussed in chapter 3, one way of reading some of the arguments made in Philadelphia in favor of ratification by state conventions rather than state legislatures is to see them as making this constituent power-based reparative justification. Most of the delegates were never equipped with constituent power, and thus they were acting outside the bounds of their authority by creating a constitution. By adding a form of ratification associated with popular sovereignty, the framers can be seen as trying to make up for prior deficiencies by opening up a space for the constituent power to emerge.

On the other hand, in the same scenario, the central worry might be that citizens will deem the constitution illegitimate, regardless of its content, because of the deficiencies in the process. The drafting process will be seen as corrupted, either because the constituent convention is unreflective of the country or because it is being forced to adopt a secretly made constitution not of its own making. In some contexts, a ratification procedure might be able to ameliorate some of this legitimacy deficit by serving as a means of PSL. For instance, any type of ratification procedure, assuming it avoids corruption, would introduce a new and untainted element of participation into the constitution-making process. If participation can indeed lead to legitimation in a constitution-making setting, this could be a case where ratification's relatively low degree of participation becomes meaningful because of the perceived lack of it earlier on in the process.

Of course, relying on the participation inherent in ratification to yield a sociologically legitimate constitution runs into the problem of manipulation discussed at the end of chapter 9. However, in this instance it might be possible that this wrong is negated or overridden by the good produced by the constitution in question becoming sociologically legitimate. This defense faltered when attempting to justify ratification ex ante because the nature of the uncreated constitution was unknown, for it is only a good for some constitutions to be sociologically legitimate. If the draft of a constitution is already written in the above hypothetical, it might be possible that the wrong of manipulation is countered by the constitution being of the right substantive kind.

3.2 Bargaining Advantage Justification

As discussed in chapter 2, in both treaty negotiations and collective bargaining, ratification can advantage a negotiator by favorably limiting the range of compromises they can make during the bargaining process. For instance, a union representative can exclude from further debate a make-or-break issue for her membership by pointing to the need to secure majority approval in a contract ratification referendum. Constitutional ratification can serve this function, shrinking the range of possible constitutions by eliminating those drafters deem unlikely to be ratified.[7] This gives those that stand to benefit a means to obtain a constitution more in line with their preferences, and thus a powerful reason to implement the procedure.

However, this justification has limited applicability, for ratification only confers this benefit in certain circumstances. Recall that in treaty negotiations and collective bargaining, a ratification procedure applies to just one of the parties. A country that alters its ratification requirements for certain treaties does not affect the domestic approval requirements for other countries, and a union rule requiring referendum approval does not apply to employers. The same is not true when it comes to constitutional ratification for, if present, the procedure applies to all. Thus, ratification can only impart a bargaining advantage if it takes place within a constitution-making process for a country in which discrete groups exist and these groups have predictable and opposing constitutional preferences. Practically, this means that the bargaining advantage justification will most likely apply in fractious multinational or multiethnic states. Further, ratification needs to advantage a group that is both at a disadvantage in the drafting process—for if they were not, they would have little need or incentive to rely on their veto—and is able to plausibly threaten ratification rejection by accepting the likely reversion point.

Two examples help to illustrate this bargaining advantage. The first once again pertains to the Philadelphia Convention. The initial ratification process, specified by the Congress of the Confederation and the Articles of Confederation, required unanimous agreement by state legislatures. This gave a significant bargaining advantage to the delegates in the convention interested in preserving the authority of their state or states in general. A delegate against an empowered federal government could claim that proposals designed to substantially diminish state power would be viewed negatively and rejected by their own or some other state's legislature, thereby shrinking the range of compromises and possible constitutions they could agree to.

Here we have a discrete group with an opposing preference: states and their delegates that were against a powerful federal government. This group was at a

[7] What drafters deem unlikely to be ratified is not necessarily what ratifiers dislike, but what they cannot be convinced to like. See the discussion of ratification as means of content control in chapter 9, section 1.2.

disadvantage, as they made up a minority in a convention operating in accordance with majority rule. Further, their threat was plausible, in that Rhode Island's outright refusal to send delegates and the departure of two of New York's three delegates suggested that some states found the status quo acceptable. Of course, as discussed in chapter 3, the advantage conferred by ratification was immediately recognized at the convention and is likely a major reason that the procedure was targeted so quickly for replacement by those dedicated to the federal project.

Second is the unusual ratification referendum used to ratify Iraq's 2005 constitution. Article 61 of the Transitional Administrative Law (TAL), the interim constitution at the time, specified the following: "The general referendum will be successful and the draft constitution ratified if a majority of the voters in Iraq approve and if two-thirds of the voters in three or more governorates do not reject it."[8] In other words, in addition to national majority approval, the constitution would only be ratified if no more than two of the country's eighteen provinces rejected the constitution by a threshold of two-thirds or more.

This procedure was proposed and designed to empower the Iraqi Kurds, for they controlled three provinces. This effectively gave them a veto on any constitution and amplified their power in the constitution-making body.[9] The Kurds were certainly a distinct group with competing preferences. As 20 percent of the Iraqi population, they expected to be at a disadvantage in the transitional national assembly, the constituent legislature set to be elected via proportional representation to draft the new constitution.[10] Moreover, their threat to reject the constitution was plausible, as the TAL gave the Kurds much of what they wanted out of a new constitution anyway.[11] Further, the Kurds came to the national assembly and subsequent negotiating bodies ready to exploit their veto, having "internally agreed on their nonnegotiable red-line positions, which committee members from the Kurdistan Coalition were not at liberty to modify."[12] In the end, the Kurds came out of the constitution-making process with a document favorable to their desires. Admittedly, it is difficult to say how much of this can be attributed to the ratification

[8] Law of Administration for the State of Iraq for the Transitional Period (2008), Art. 61.

[9] Michele Brandt and others, *Constitution-Making and Reform: Options for the Process* (Interpeace 2011) 299; Paul Bremer, *My Year in Iraq: The Struggle to Build a Future of Hope* (Simon & Schuster 2006) 297; Peter W. Galbraith, *The End of Iraq: How American Incompetence Created a War without End* (Simon & Schuster 2007) 144–45; Andrew Arato, *Constitution Making under Occupation: The Politics of Imposed Revolution in Iraq* (Columbia University Press 2009) 170–72, 327n129; U.S. Institute of Peace, *Iraq's Constitutional Process: Shaping a Vision for the Country's Future* (U.S. Institute of Peace 2005).

[10] In the end a large portion of Sunni Arabs boycotted the assembly elections. This allowed the Kurdistan Coalition List to pick up 75 of the 275 seats, though they were still outnumbered by the Shia United Iraqi Alliance, which won 140 seats and thus effectively controlled the assembly. Jonathan Morrow, "Deconstituting Mesopotamia: Cutting a Deal on the Regionalization of Iraq," in Laurel E. Miller (ed.), *Framing the State in Times of Transition: Case Studies in Constitution Making* (United States Institute of Peace Press 2010) 569–70; Arato, *Constitution Making under Occupation: The Politics of Imposed Revolution in Iraq*, 207.

[11] Arato, *Constitution Making under Occupation: The Politics of Imposed Revolution in Iraq*, 175–81.

[12] Morrow, "Deconstituting Mesopotamia: Cutting a Deal on the Regionalization of Iraq," 578.

advantage given the chaos that quickly engulfed the constitution-making process. Of particular note was the complete side-lining of the Sunni Arabs and the sudden replacement of the assembly's Constitutional Commission with the leadership council, a closed-door pseudo-roundtable of Shia and Kurdish leaders, as the main site of bargaining.[13]

These examples suggest two other restrictions on ratification being able to confer a bargaining advantage. First, those expected to control the drafting process must not also control the constitution-making design process, for it is unlikely that any majority group in a divided country would hand over a veto to their likely opponents. The Kurds only successfully secured their advantage because they convinced the U.S. Central Provisional Authority, who controlled the process leading to the TLA, to give it to them. The results would have almost certainly been different if Shia leaders oversaw the construction of the transitional constitution. Second, it requires that once constitution-making begins the drafting body does not follow the Philadelphia Convention's lead, deciding to change the ratification procedures to eliminate the bargaining advantage. Again, the Kurds likely only maintained their advantage because the entire process was supervised by the United States and the shift to the leadership council made Shia dominance in the assembly less exploitable.

3.3 Citizen Belief Justification

This is the simplest context-dependent justification. In chapter 9, section 3.1, I noted that in certain settings ratification could serve as a means of PSL because of citizen belief. Either a significant number of citizens expect or demand that any new constitution be submitted to the people in a ratification procedure, or conditions are such that they can predictably be convinced that the absence of ratification is a problem.[14] As discussed, we can imagine a variety of ways such a norm might arise. It might be because an operative and still authoritative constitution specifies ratification, because the country in question has a long and well-known tradition of ratifying alterations to its constitution, because something in the country's recent history made ratification look essential, or because a popular social movement involved in the constitution-making effort takes up the use of a ratification procedure as part of its cause. Whatever its origins, the result of this belief is that a constitution not subject to ratification is less likely to be accepted as legitimate. This produces a straightforward context-dependent reason to utilize a ratification procedure from the perspective of someone who believes

[13] Arato, *Constitution Making under Occupation: The Politics of Imposed Revolution in Iraq*, 216–18; Morrow, "Deconstituting Mesopotamia: Cutting a Deal on the Regionalization of Iraq," 572–74.

[14] I will focus on the former for ease of explanation.

that a sociologically legitimate constitution, regardless of its unpredictable content, is desirable. Use ratification, because if you do not the constitution will likely be deemed illegitimate.

Note, however, manipulation is still an issue here. If one found chapter 9 persuasive, such that they are convinced that being ratified has no connection to any known plausible theory of what makes a constitution morally legitimate, then implementing ratification for PSL purposes because of the beliefs of citizens is to commit a moral wrong. It fits the definition of manipulation perfectly, for it involves taking an action (implementing ratification) to lead another to believe something that you want them to believe (that the constitution is morally legitimate) for irrelevant or bad reasons (because ratification occurred).

This justification might not seem manipulative because it involves giving citizens what they want; in this instance citizens already believe that a constitution's legitimacy depends on ratification. However, this is to misunderstand what makes a reason irrelevant or bad for the purposes of determining if an act is manipulative. There is genuine debate in the literature about whether the appropriate criterion is objective, determined by the beliefs of the manipulator, or both.[15] But, it is decidedly not determined by the beliefs of the manipulated. For instance, if a co-worker erroneously believes that you are their boss and asks for assignments, and you take advantage of this by delegating your work to them, you are manipulating them. You are taking actions that lead someone else to do something you want based on reasons that you know to be bad. That they falsely believe that you are their boss is irrelevant, for you know you are not.

So, when the proper belief exists and is known to exist by those designing a constitution-making process, assuming that a sociologically legitimate constitution is wanted, there is a good reason to use ratification. However, if one accepts my arguments about ratification and manipulation, this reason's power is at least diminished because implementing the procedure on its basis involves committing morally wrong manipulation.

3.4 Deadlock Breaking Justification

A final context-dependent reason to use ratification does not pertain to ratification as we have so far understood it, but instead only applies to what I will call a *ratification trigger*. This is a rule according to which ratification only takes place if certain conditions are met. Examples of a ratification trigger can be found in the rules governing the Tunisian and South African constitution-making processes.

[15] Anne Barnhill, "What Is Manipulation?" in Christian Coons and Max Weber (eds.), *Manipulation: Theory and Practice* (Oxford University Press 2014) 65–68; Robert Noggle, "Manipulative Actions: A Conceptual and Moral Analysis," (1996) 33 American Philosophical Quarterly 43–55, 49–50.

As mentioned in chapter 1, ratification did not occur in the making of either constitution. This was as planned; constitution-making was supposed to terminate at the approval stage with enactment happening immediately after. However, both processes specified that if sufficient agreement on the draft did not occur, ratification would take place.

Specifically, according to the Constitution Act no. 6, which partially structured the Tunisian constitution-making process, the new constitution was to be adopted as follows: the national constituent assembly (NCA) was to approve each article by absolute majority and then vote on the entire draft constitution. If a two-thirds supermajority approved the draft, it would be adopted and implemented. However, if upon two attempts supermajority approval could not be obtained, the most recent draft constitution would be submitted to a national ratification referendum.[16] The interim constitution for South Africa set out a similar procedure. A draft constitution would be approved and implemented when two-thirds of the constitutional assembly voted in favor of it. However, if only majority approval was reached, the draft constitution would be sent to a panel of outside experts charged with proposing an amended version of the constitution to the assembly. If the panel of experts could not unanimously agree on an amended draft, or if two-thirds of the constitutional assembly did not approve it, whichever version of the constitution that achieved majority support would be sent to the people for a national ratifying referendum.[17]

In certain circumstances, designers of a constitution-making process have a good reason to use such a ratification trigger: it provides a means to break through possibly permanent or harmfully long deadlock in the constitution-making body. It can do this in two ways. On the one hand, if there is serious deadlock, ratification will be triggered automatically and end the constitution-making process with a definitive result. Here, the benefit of achieving a new constitution via ratification would have to be weighed against the anticipated costs of the ratification procedure.

On the other hand, provided that the procedure specified by the ratification trigger is undesirable to a significant portion of those charged with creating the draft constitution, the threat of ratification might provide an incentive to compromise. As Bulmer notes in a discussion of ordinary referendums on constitutional issues, in some contexts "the referendum is likely to extract a significant political cost, and elites may have an incentive to compromise in order to reach agreements that spare

[16] Bill Proctor and Ikbal Ben Moussa, *The Tunisian Constituent Assembly's by-Laws: A Brief Analysis* (International IDEA 2012) 27; The Carter Center, *The Constitution-Making Process in Tunisia: Final Report* (The Carter Center 2014) 30.

[17] Parliament of South Africa, Constitution [Interim] of the Republic of South Africa Act 200 (1993), chapter 5, sec. 73.

them from the unpredictability and risks of a referendum."[18] Ratification might be undesirable or costly for a variety of reasons. Drafters involved in constitution-making at the tail end of a post-conflict peacebuilding process might want to avoid the politicization and competition that often accompanies ratification, for fear that this could reignite violence. Participants in a constitution-making process that primarily involves elite negotiations might worry that the bargains struck wouldn't survive the transparency endemic to many ratification procedures. Or, members of a constituent assembly with a ratification trigger might simply want to avoid the procedure because it would serve as a public announcement of their failure.[19]

Provided that one believes encouraging compromise and ending long or permanent delays in the constitution-making process is a valuable goal, implementing a ratification trigger in situations where it is likely to have these effects is a reasonable thing to do. In some sense, this is the strongest justification for ratification that we have discussed, though admittedly it only pertains to a special kind of ratification that might not happen at all. Note, however, just how far we have come from the moral intuitions that motivated this book and the justifications examined in the previous chapters. In the end, rather than being used, ratification is being threatened. And motivating this is not some positive normative role ratification is to play—to serve as a conduit for the people, to foster representation, to help create legitimacy—but rather the predicted distaste those tasked with writing the constitution will have with it. Nonetheless, this might be an especially useful role for our old misunderstood and rarely defended constitution-making procedure. It is certainly nothing like the Berkshire Constitutionalists had in mind when they shut down the Massachusetts courts, but in the end, it might help produce healthy constitution-making processes and constitutions aimed at the common good regardless, something that Allen and his allies certainly valued.

[18] W. Elliot Bulmer, "Elite Compacts and Popular Sovereignty: The Constitutional Referendum in Comparative Context," *Annual Review of Constitution-Building Processes: 2016* (International IDEA 2017) 26.

[19] According to Thornton, this was the case in Tunisia: "For all political parties recognised that the need to hold a referendum would symbolize the failure of the NCA, Tunisia's only democratically elected institution, and consequently wanted to avoid that eventuality if at all possible." Christopher Thornton, *The Rocky Path from Elections to a New Constitution in Tunisia: Mechanisms for Consensus-Building and Inclusive Decision-Making* (Oslo Forum Background Papers 2016) 7.

Bibliography

"An Act for More Equal Representation, May 4, 1776" in Handlin O and Handlin M (eds.), *The Popular Sources of Political Authority* (Harvard University Press, 1966)

"Address from the Committee of Mechanicks" *The Constitutional Gazette* (New York, June 5, 1776) 2–3

"Address from the Committee of Mechanicks" *The New-York Gazette; and the Weekly Mercury* (New York, November 21, 1774) 3

"After Carl Becker: The Mechanics and New York City Politics, 1774–1801" (1964) 5 Labor History 215–24

"Albermarle County Instructions Concerning the Virginia Constitution, Sept–Oct, 1776" in Oberg BB and Looney JJ (eds.), *The Papers of Thomas Jefferson Digital Edition* (University of Virginia Press 2008)

Articles of Confederation (1781)

Basic Law fort he Federal Republic of Germany (1949)

"A Berkshire Convention Addresses the Superior Court, May 3, 1779" in Taylor RJ (ed.), *Massachusetts, Colony to Commonwealth: Documents on the Formation of Its Constitution, 1775–1780* (The University of North Carolina Press 1961)

"Berkshire County Remonstrance, August 26, 1778" in Handlin O and Handlin M (eds.), *The Popular Sources of Authority* (Harvard University Press 1966)

The Book of the States: 2011 (The Council of State Governments 2011)

Bürgerliches Gesetzbuch (German Civil Code)

"By Whom Shall a State Constitution Be Adopted" (1896) 9 Harvard Law Review 471–72

California Civil Code (2019)

"The Call for a Convention, June 1779" in Handlin O and Handlin M (eds.), *The Popular Sources of Political Authority* (Harvard University Press, 1966)

Civil Code of France (2016)

The Code Napoleon; or, the French Civil Code (Charles Hunter 1824)

Communications Workers of America Constitution (2019)

A Concise and Simple Narrative of the Controversy between Thomas Allen, A.M. of Pittsfield and That Part of His Church and Congregation Which Have Lately Separated from His Pastoral Care (Early American Imprints, Milo Smith & Co. 1809)

"Confederation Congress Calls the Constitutional Convention, 21 February 1787" in Jensen M (ed.), *The Documentary History of the Ratification of the Constitution: Constitutional Documents and Records, 1776–1787*, vol. 1 (The State Historical Society of Wisconsin 1976)

Constitution of Argentina (1853 (rev. 1994))

The Constitution of Spain (1978)

The Constitution of the Federative Republic of Brazil (1988 (rev. 2017))

The Constitution of Kenya (Amendment) Bill (2008)

The Constitution of the Bolivarian Republic of Venezuela (1999)

Constitution of the Federal Democratic Republic of Ethiopia (1994)

Constitution of the Federated States of Micronesia (1978)

Constitution of the National Association of Letter Carriers of the United States (2018)

Constitution of the New Zealand Nurses Organisation (2018–19)
Constitution of the Republic of Ecuador (2008)
Constitution of the Republic of Palau (1979)
Constitution of the Republic of South Africa (1996)
The Constitution of the State of Rhode Island (1986)
"Constitution Watch: Country-by-Country Updates on Constitutional Politics in Eastern Europe" (1995) 4 East European Constitutional Review 2–35
"Constitution Watch: Country-by-Country Updates on Constitutional Politics in Eastern Europe and the Ex-USSR" (1998) 7 East European Constitutional Review 2–44
The Constitution-Making Process in Tunisia: Final Report (The Carter Center 2014)
Das Bayerische Landrecht (Codex Maximilianeus Bavaricus Civilis) Von Jahre 1756 (J. Schweizer 1894)
The Decisions of the Court of Session (Bell & Bradfute 1802)
Fleckner v. U.S. Bank, 21 US 338 (1823)
"From the Proceedings of a Convention in Hampshire, March 11, 1776" in Taylor RJ (ed.), *Massachusetts, Colony to Commonwealth: Documents on the Formation of Its Constitution, 1775–1780* (The University of North Carolina Press 1961)
The Future Constitutional Treaty (European Commission 2005)
Georgia Constitution (1777)
The Governance Act (Poland) (1791)
"Iceland Election Results Announced" Iceland Review Online <http://www.icelandreview.com/icelandreview/search/news/Default.asp?ew_0_a_id=370813>
"Instructions to Pittsfield Constitutional Convention Delegate, 1779" in Handlin O and Handlin M (eds.), *The Popular Sources of Political Authority* (Harvard University Press 1966)
"Instructions to Stoughton Constitutional Convention Delegate, 1779" in Handlin O and Handlin M (eds.), *The Popular Sources of Authority: Documents on the Massachusetts Constitution of 1780* (Harvard University Press 1966)
Iraq's Constitutional Process: Shaping a Vision for the Country's Future (U.S. Institute of Peace 2005)
Journal of the Convention for Framing a Constitution of Government for the State of Massachusetts Bay, from the Commencement of Their First Session, September 1, 1779, to the Close of Their Last Session, June 16, 1780 (Dutton and Wentworth, Printers to the State 1832)
"Journal of the Convention, June 17, 1777–March 6, 1778" in Handlin O and Handlin M (eds.), *The Popular Sources of Political Authority* (Harvard University Press 1966)
Journals of the Provincial Congress, Provincial Convention, Committee of Safety and Council of Safety of the State of New York: 1775–1776–1777, vol. 1 (Thurlow Weed 1842)
The Judgment of Whole Kingdoms and Nations (Printed for T. Harrison 1713)
Kelner v. Baxter, 2 CP 174 (1866)
Louisiana Civil Code (2017)
Labor-Management Reporting and Disclosure Act of 1959
Law of Administration for the State of Iraq for the Transitional Period (2008)
"A Letter from the Chesterfield Committee of Correspondence, March 4, 1776" in Taylor RJ (ed.), *Massachusetts, Colony to Commonwealth: Documents on the Formation of Its Constitution, 1775–1780* (The University of North Carolina Press 1961)
Maharashtra State Mining Corporation v. Sunil, 5 SCC 96 (2006)
The Mavrommatis Palestine Concessions (Greece v. U.K.), PCIJ (Permanent Court of International Justice) (1924)

Civil Code of Japan (1896)
North Dakota Century Code (2019)
"New Constitution Approved by Referendum—Minimum Age for Franchise to Be Reduced to 23 Years" (1953) IX Keesing's Contemporary Archives 12950
Njoya & Others v. Attorney General & Others, KLR 4788 (High Court of Kenya) (2004)
Official Report of the National Australasian Convention Debates. Sydney, 2 March to 9 April, 1891 (George Stephen Chapman, Acting Government Printer 1891)
"Opinions of Hampshire County Towns, March 30, 1779" in Handlin O and Handlin M (eds.), *The Popular Sources of Political Authority* (Harvard University Press 1966)
The Papers of James Madison Digital Edition (University of Virginia Press 2010)
The Papers of Thomas Jefferson Digital Edition (University of Virginia Press, Rotunda 2008)
Participatory Constitution Making Process (Participatory Constitution Building in Nepal Booklet Series, 2009)
"Pittsfield Petitions, May 29, 1776" in Handlin O and Handlin M (eds.), *The Popular Sources of Political Authority* (Harvard University Press 1966)
The Political Constitution of the State of Bolivia (2009)
"Proceedings and Report of the Commissioners at Annapolis, Maryland, 11–14 September 1786" in Jensen M (ed.), *The Documentary History of the Ratification of the Constitution: Constitutional Documents and Records, 1776–1787*, vol. 1 (The State Historical Society of Wisconsin 1976)
"Proclamation of the General Court, January 23, 1776" in Handlin O and Handlin M (eds.), *The Popular Sources of Political Authority* (Harvard University Press 1966)
"Report of a Lecture by Thomas Allen on February 18, 1776" in Handlin O and Handlin M (eds.), *The Popular Sources of Political Authority* (Harvard University Press 1966)
"Resolution of the House of Representatives, September 17, 1776" in Handlin O and Handlin M (eds.), *The Popular Sources of Political Authority* (Harvard University Press 1966)
"Resolutions of an Essex County Convention, April 25, 1776" in Taylor RJ (ed.), *Massachusetts, Colony to Commonwealth: Documents on the Formation of Its Constitution, 1775–1780* (The University of North Carolina Press 1961)
"Resolve of May 5, 1777" in Handlin O and Handlin M (eds.), *The Popular Sources of Political Authority* (Harvard University Press 1966)
"Resolve on the Question of a Constitution, February 20, 1779" in Handlin O and Handlin M (eds.), *The Popular Sources of Political Authority* (Harvard University Press 1966)
"Resolves of the Stockbridge Convention, December 15, 1775" in Taylor RJ (ed.), *Massachusetts, Colony to Commonwealth: Documents on the Formation of Its Constitution, 1775–1780* (The University of North Carolina Press 1961)
The Republic of Albania: Referendum on the Constitution, 22 November 1998 (Organization for Security and Cooperation in Europe 1999)
"The Respectful Address of the Mechanicks in Union, for the City and County of New-York, Represented by Their General Committee" *The New-York Gazette; and the Weekly Mercury* (New York, June 17, 1776) 3
Restatement of the Law (Third) of Agency, vol. I (American Law Institute 2006)
"Returns of the Towns on Resolves of February 20, 1779" in Handlin O and Handlin M (eds.), *The Popular Sources of Political Authority* (Harvard University Press 1966)
"Returns of the Towns on the Constitution of 1778" in Handlin O and Handlin M (eds.), *The Popular Sources of Political Authority* (Harvard University Press 1966)
"Returns of the Towns on the Constitution of 1780" in Handlin O and Handlin M (eds.), *The Popular Sources of Political Authority* (Harvard University Press 1966)
"Returns of the Towns on the Resolution of September 17, 1776" in Handlin O and Handlin M (eds.), *The Popular Sources of Political Authority* (Harvard University Press 1966)

"Somalia: National Constituent Assembly Adopts New Constitution" Shabelle Media Network <http://allafrica.com/stories/201208020038.html>
"Sondaggio Ipr & Tecne 24 Ottobre 2016—Referendum" (2016) <http://scenaripolitici.com/2016/10/sondaggio-ipr-tecne-24-ottobre-2016-referendum.html>
"Statement of Berkshire County Representatives, November 17, 1778" in Handlin O and Handlin M (eds.), *The Popular Sources of Authority* (Harvard University Press 1966)
The Statutes at Large, from the 20th Year of the Reign of King George II to the 30th Year of the Reign of King George II, vol. 7 (Mark Basket 1764)
Support to Constitution Building: Introductory Workshops/Interaction Programmes (United Nations Development Programme, Nepal 2008)
Transitional Period Charter of Ethiopia (1991)
Unifor Constitution (2019)
Vienna Convention on the Law of Treaties vol. 1155 (Treaty Series, United Nations 1969)
"Votes of Towns in Choosing Delegates, July–October 1779" in Handlin O and Handlin M (eds.), *The Popular Sources of Political Authority* (Harvard University Press 1966)
Year Books of the Reign of King Edward the First: Year XXX–XXXI (Longman, Green, Longman, Roberts, and Green 1863)
Achen CH and Bartels LM, *Democracy for Realists: Why Elections Do Not Produce Responsive Government* (Princeton University Press 2016)
Ackerman BA, *Revolutionary Constitutions: Charismatic Leadership and the Rule of Law* (Harvard University Press 2019)
Ackerman BA, *We the People: Foundations* (Harvard University Press 1991)
Ackerman BA, *We the People: Transformations* (Belknap Press of Harvard University Press 1998)
Ackerman F, "The Concept of Manipulativeness" (1995) 9 Philosophical Perspectives 335–40
Adams J, *The Works of John Adams*, vol. 2 (Little, Brown, and Co. 1850)
Adams J, *The Works of John Adams*, vol. 3 (Little, Brown, and Co. 1851)
Adams WP, *The First American Constitutions: Republican Ideology and the Making of the State Constitutions in the Revolutionary Era* (expanded edn, Rita and Robert Kimber trs., Rowman & Littlefield 2001)
Albert R, *Constitutional Amendments: Making, Breaking, and Changing Constitutions* (Oxford University Press 2019)
Alexander L, "What Are Constitutions, and What Should (and Can) They Do?" in Paul EF, Miller FD, Jr., and Paul J (eds.), *What Should Constitutions Do?* (Cambridge University Press 2011)
Allen T, "Pittsfield Memorial, December 26, 1775" in Handlin O and Handlin M (eds.), *The Popular Sources of Political Authority* (Harvard University Press 1966)
Althusius J, *Politica: An Abridged Translation of Politics Methodically Set Forth and Illustrated with Sacred and Profane Examples* (Liberty Fund 1995)
Alvarez MR and Brehm J, *Hard Choices, Easy Answers: Values, Information, and American Public Opinion* (Princeton University Press 2002)
Amar AR, "Popular Sovereignty and Constitutional Amendment" in Levinson S (ed.), *Responding to Imperfection* (Princeton University Press 1995)
Andresassen BA and Tostensen A, "Of Oranges and Bananas: The 2005 Kenyan Referendum of the Constitution" (2006) 13 Chr Michelsen Institution Working Paper 1–8
Ankut PY, *The Role of Constitution-Building Processes in Democratization: Case Study—Rwanda* (International IDEA 2005)
Anthony DL, Heckathorn DD, and Maser S, "Rational Rhetoric in Politics: The Debate over Ratifying the U.S. Constitution" (1994) 6 Rationality and Society 489–518

Appleby J, *Liberalism and Republicanism in the Historical Imagination* (Harvard University Press 1992)
Arato A, *The Adventures of the Constituent Power* (Cambridge University Press 2017)
Arato A, "Carl Schmitt and the Revival of the Constituent Power in the United States" (1999–2000) 21 Cardozo Law Review 1739–47
Arato A, *Civil Society, Constitution, and Legitimacy* (Rowman & Littlefield Publishers 2000)
Arato A, *Constitution Making under Occupation: The Politics of Imposed Revolution in Iraq* (Columbia University Press 2009)
Arato A, *Post Sovereign Constitution Making* (Oxford University Press 2016)
Arato A and Miklosi Z, "Constitution Making and Transitional Politics in Hungary" in Miller LE (ed.), *Framing the State in Times of Transition: Case Studies in Constitution Making* (United States Institute of Peace Press 2010)
Archard D, "Informed Consent: Autonomy and Self-Ownership" (2008) 25 Journal of Applied Philosophy 19–34
Aristotle, *Politics* (Hackett Publishing Company 1998)
Ashcraft R, *Locke's Two Treatises of Government* (Allen & Unwin 1987)
Ashcraft R, *Revolutionary Politics & Locke's Two Treatises of Government* (Princeton University Press 1986)
Ashcraft R and Goldsmith MM, "Locke, Revolution Principles, and the Formation of Whig Ideology" (1983) 26 The Historical Journal 773–800
Augustin E, "Cuba Overwhelmingly Approves New Constitution Affirming 'Irrevocable' Socialism" *The Guardian* (25 February 2019) <https://www.theguardian.com/world/2019/feb/25/cuba-approves-new-socialist-constitution>
Aust A, *Modern Treaty Law and Practice* (3rd edn, Cambridge University Press 2013)
Austin J, *The Province of Jurisprudence Determined* (Cambridge University Press 1995)
Bacon GC, "The State Constitution (1777–1780)" in Hart AB (ed.), *Commonwealth History of Massachusetts*, vol. 3 (Russell & Russell 1966)
Baczko B, "The Social Contract of the French: Sieyes and Rousseau" (1988) 60: Supplement The Journal of Modern History S98–S125
Bailyn B, *The Ideological Origins of the American Revolution* (Harvard University Press 1992)
Baker KM, *Condorcet, from Natural Philosophy to Social Mathematics* (University of Chicago Press 1975)
Banks AM, "Expanding Participation in Constitution Making: Challenges and Opportunities" (2008) 49 William and Mary Law Review 1043–69
Banks AS and Wilson KA, *Cross-National Time-Series Data Archive* (Databanks International 2019)
Banks WC and Alvarez E, "The New Colombian Constitution: Democratic Victory or Popular Surrender" (1991) 23 Inter-American Law Review 39–92
Bannon AL, "Note: Designing a Constitution-Drafting Process: Lessons from Kenya" (2007) 116 Yale Law Journal 1830–72
Barber B, *Strong Democracy: Participatory Politics for New Age* (University of California Press 1984)
Barnave A, "On National Conventions and Constituent Power" in Goldstein MA (ed.), *Social and Political Thought of the French Revolution, 1788–1797: An Anthology of Original Texts* (Peter Lang 1997)
Barnhill A, "What Is Manipulation?" in Coons C and Weber M (eds.), *Manipulation: Theory and Practice* (Oxford University Press 2014)
Baron M, "The Mens Rea and Moral Status of Manipulation" in Coons C and Weber M (eds.), *Manipulation: Theory and Practice* (Oxford University Press 2014)

Bartels LM, "Uninformed Votes: Information Effects in Presidential Elections" (1996) 40 American Journal of Political Science 194–230

Bartels LM and Achen CH, *Democracy for Realists: Why Elections Do Not Produce Responsive Government* (Princeton University Press 2016)

Bartlett J, "A New Chile": Political Elite Rejected in Vote for Constitutional Assembly" *The Guardian* (May 18, 2021) <https://www.theguardian.com/world/2021/may/18/a-new-chile-political-elite-rejected-in-vote-for-constitutional-assembly>

Basu DD, *Introduction to the Constitution of India* (20th edn, LexisNexis Butterworths Wadhwa Nagpur 2011)

Becker C, *The History of Political Parties in the Province of New York, 1760–1776* (University of Wisconsin 1909)

Beckman L, "Democratic Legitimacy Does Not Require Referendum. On the 'Constitution' in Theories of Constituent Power" (2018) 14 European Constitutional Law Review 567–83

Beetham D, *The Legitimation of Power* (MacMillan 1991)

Bendersky CH, Heiss C, Eigueta E, Contesse J, and Sanhueza C, *An Assessment of the Chilean Constituent Process* (Observatory of the Chilean Constituent Process 2018)

Benjamin G, "The Mandatory Constitutional Convention Question Referendum: The New York Experience in National Context" (2002) 65 Albany Law Review 1017–50

Benomar J, "Constitution-Making after Conflict: Lessons for Iraq" (2004) 15 Journal of Democracy 81–95

Benomar J, *Constitution-Making and Peace Building: Lessons Learned from the Constitution-Making Processes of Post-Conflict Countries* (United Nations Development Programme 2003)

Beran H, *The Consent Theory of Political Obligation* (Croom Helm 1987)

Berelson BR, Lazarsfeld PF, and McPhee WN, *Voting: A Study of Opinion Formation in a Presidential Campaign* (University of Chicago 1954)

Berhanu K, "Ethiopia Elects a Constituent Assembly" (1995) 22 Review of African Political Economy 129–35

Bernal AM, *Beyond Origins: Rethinking Founding in a Time of Constitutional Democracy* (Oxford University Press 2017)

Bernal C, "Constitution-Making (without Constituent) Power: On the Conceptual Limits of the Power to Replace and Revise the Constitution" in Albert R, Bernal C, and Benvindo JZ (eds.), *Constitutional Change and Transformation in Latin America* (Hart Publishing 2019)

Bernal C, "How Constitutional Crowdsourcing Can Enhance Legitimacy in Constitution Making" in Landau D and Lerner H (eds.), *Comparative Constitution Making* (Edward Elgar 2019)

Berry CR and Howell WG, "Accountability and Local Elections: Rethinking Retrospective Voting" (2007) 69 The Journal Of Politics 844–58

Bickerton C and Tuck R, "Popular Sovereignty and 'Taking Back Control': What It Means and Why It Matters" The Full Brexit <https://www.thefullbrexit.com/popular-sovereignty>

Birdsall RD, "The Reverend Thomas Allen: Jeffersonian Calvinist" (1957) 30 The New England Quarterly 147–65

Birks P, *The Roman Law of Obligations* (Oxford University Press 2014)

Blackstone W, *Commentaries of the Laws of England in Four Books*, vol. 1 (J. B. Lippincott Company 1893)

Blix H, "The Requirement of Ratification" (1953) 30 British Year Book of International Law 352–80

Blount J, "Participation in Constitutional Design" in Ginsburg T and Dixon R (eds.), *Comparative Constitutional Law* (Edward Elgar 2011)

Blount J, Elkins Z, and Ginsburg T, "Does the Process of Constitution-Making Matter?" in Ginsburg T (ed.), *Comparative Constitutional Design* (Cambridge University Press 2012)

Blumenthal-Barby JS, "A Framework for Assessing the Moral Status of 'Manipulation'" in Coons C and Weber M (eds.), *Manipulation: Theory and Practice* (Oxford University Press 2014)

Bockenforde M, Hedlin N, and Wahiu W, *A Practical Guide to Constitution Building* (International Institute for Democracy and Electoral Assistance 2011)

Boland PJ, "Majority Systems and the Condorcet Jury Theorem" (1989) 38 Journal of the Royal Statistical Society Series D (The Statistician) 181–89

Bonime-Blanc A, "Constitution Making and Democratization: The Spanish Paradigm" in Miller LE (ed.), *Framing the State in Times of Transition: Case Studies in Constitution Making* (United States Institute of Peace 2010)

Bonnefoy P, "Chile's President Says He Will Support a New Constitution" *New York Times* (November 12, 2019) A12

Bonnefoy P, "'An End to the Chapter of Dictatorship': Chileans Vote to Draft a New Constitution" *New York Times* (October 26, 2020) A11

Bottoms A and Tankebe J, "Beyond Procedural Justice: A Dialogic Approach to Legitimacy in Criminal Justice" (2012) 102 The Journal of Criminal Law & Criminology 119–17

Bourne HE, "Municipal Politics in Paris in 1789" (1906) 11 The American Historical Review 263–86

Bowen RL, Jr., "New York Porter Mugs and Porterhouses" (1977) 7 The Pewter Collectors Club of America Bulletin 186–91

Bowler S and Donovan T, *Demanding Choices: Opinion, Voting, and Direct Democracy* (University of Michigan Press 1998)

Bowler S, Donovan T, and Karp JA, "Enraged or Engaged? Preferences for Direct Citizen Participation in Affluent Democracies" (2007) 60 Political Research Quarterly 351–62

Bracton HD, *On the Laws and Customs of England*, vol. 3 (Samuel Thorne and George Woodbine eds, Belknap Press 1977)

Brady HE and Sniderman PM, "Attitude Attribution: A Group Basis for Political Reasoning" (1985) 79 American Political Science Review 1061–78

Brady P, "Social, Political and Philosophical Foundations of the Irish Constitutional Order" in Galligan DJ and Versteeg M (eds.), *Social and Political Foundations of Constitutions* (Cambridge University Press 2013)

Braley AL, "Provisional Government of Massachusetts" in Hart AB (ed.), *Commonwealth History of Massachusetts*, vol. 3 (Russell & Russell 1966)

Brandt M and others, *Constitution-Making and Reform: Options for the Process* (Interpeace 2011)

Bremer P, *My Year in Iraq: The Struggle to Build a Future of Hope* (Simon & Schuster 2006)

Brennan G and Hamlin A, "On Political Representation" (1999) 29 British Journal of Political Science 109–27

Brennan J, *Against Democracy* (Princeton University Press 2016)

Brewer-Carias AR, "The 1999 Venezuelan Constitution-Making Process as an Instrument for Framing the Development of an Authoritarian Political Regime" in Miller LE (ed.), *Framing the State in Times of Transition: Case Studies in Constitution Making* (United States Institute of Peace Press 2010)

Brockner J and others, "The Moderating Effect of Self-Esteem in Reaction to Voice: Converging Evidence from Five Studies" (1998) 75 Journal of Personality and Social Psychology 394–407

Brooke JL, "To the Quiet of the People: Revolutionary Settlements and Civil Unrest in Western Massachusetts, 1774–1789" (1989) 46 The William and Mary Quarterly 425–62

Brookshire ML, "Centralized Bargaining Structures and Referendums" (1976) 2 Southern Business Review 12–27

Brutus SJ, *Vindiciae, Contra Tyrannos* (George Garnett tr., Cambridge University Press 1994)

Buchanan A, "Political Legitimacy and Democracy" (2002) 112 Ethics 689–719

Buchanan JM and Tullock G, *The Calculus of Consent: Logical Foundations of Constitutional Democracy*, vol. 3 (The Collected Works of James M Buchanan, Liberty Fund 1999)

Budge I, *The New Challenge of Direct Democracy* (Polity Press 1996)

Bulmer WE, "Elite Compacts and Popular Sovereignty: The Constitutional Referendum in Comparative Context", *Annual Review of Constitution-Building Processes: 2016* (International IDEA 2017)

Burgh J, *Political Disquisitions*, vol. 1 (Edward and Charles Dilly 1774)

Burlamaqui J-J, *The Principles of Natural and Politic Law* (Thomas Nugent tr., Petter Korkman ed., Liberty Fund 2006)

Busch D, "Unauthorised Agency in Dutch Law" in Busch D and Macgregor L (eds.), *The Unauthorised Agent: Perspectives from European and Comparative Law* (Cambridge University Press 2009)

Busch D and Macgregor L, "Comparative Law Evaluation" in Busch D and Macgregor L (eds.), *The Unauthorised Agent: Perspectives from European and Comparative Law* (Cambridge University Press 2009)

Busch D and Macgregor L (eds.), *The Unauthorised Agent: Perspectives from European and Comparative Law* (Cambridge University Press 2009)

Buss S, "Valuing Autonomy and Respecting Persons: Manipulation, Seduction, and the Basis of Moral Constraints" (2005) 11 Ethics 195–235

Cairns JW and Plessis Pd (eds.), *The Creation of the Ius Commune* (Edinburgh University Press 2010)

Cambell A and others, *The American Voter* (The University of Chicago Press 1960)

Caplan B, *The Myth of the Rational Voter: Why Democracies Choose Bad Policies* (Princeton University Press 2007)

Cappelli P and Sterling WP, "Union Bargaining Decisions and Contract Ratifications: The 1982 and 1984 Auto Agreements" (1988) 41 Industrial & Labor Relations Review 195–209

Cardona D and Ponsatí C, "Representing a Democratic Constituency in Negotiations: Delegation Versus Ratification" (2015) 45 Social Choice and Welfare 399–414

Carey JM, "Does It Matter How a Constitution Is Created?" in Barany Z and Moser RG (eds.), *Is Democracy Exportable?* (Cambridge University Press 2009)

Carey JM, "Parchment, Equilibria, and Institutions" (2000) 33 Comparative Political Studies 735–61

Carlson SN, "The Drafting Process for the 1998 Albanian Constitution" in Miller LE (ed.), *Framing the State in Times of Transition: Case Studies in Constitution Making* (United States Institute of Peace Press 2010)

Castiglione D, "The Political Theory of the Constitution" (1996) XLIV Political Studies 417–35

Cave EM, "What's Wrong with Motive Manipulation" (2006) 10 Ethical Theory and Moral Practice 129–44

Cella AJ, "The People of Massachusetts, a New Republic, and the Constitution of 1780: The Evolution of Principles of Popular Control of Political Authority, 1774–1780" (1980) 14 Suffolk University Law Review 975–1006

Chambers S, "Contract or Conversation? Theoretical Lessons from the Canadian Constitutional Crisis" (1998) 26 Politics and Society 143–72

Chambers S, "Democracy, Popular Sovereignty and Constitutional Legitimacy" (2004) 11 Constellations 153–73

Champagne RJ, "Liberty Boys and Mechanics of New York City, 1764–1774" (1967) 8 Labor History 115–35

Chastellux MD, *Travels in North America in the Years 1780, 1781, 1782* (New York 1828)

Chicago Tribune Wire, "Moroccan Voters Pass Constitutional Reforms" *Chicago Tribune* (Pre-1997 Full text) <http://resources.library.brandeis.edu/login?url=https://search-proquest-com.resources.library.brandeis.edu/docview/283393795?accountid=9703.>

Chong D and Druckman JN, "A Theory of Framing and Opinion Formation in Competitive Elite Environments" (2007) 57 Journal of Communication 99–118

Christin T, Hug S, and Sciarini P, "Interests and Information in Referendum Voting: An Analysis of Swiss Voters" (2002) 41 European Journal of Political Research 759–76

Clark I, "Legitimacy in a Global Order" (2003) 29 Review of International Studies 75–95

Clarke HD and Kornberg A, "The Politics and Economics of Constitutional Choice: Voting in Canada's 1992 National Referendum" (1994) 56 The Journal of Politics 940–62

Clarke HD, Kornberg A, and Stewart MC, "Referendum Voting as Political Choice: The Case of Quebec" (2004) 24 British Journal of Political Science 345–55

Cohen J, "Deliberation and Democratic Legitimacy" in Hamlin A and Pettit P (eds.), *The Good Polity: Normative Analysis of the State* (Blackwell 1989)

Coke E, *The Fourth Part of the Institute of the Laws of England* (W. Clarke and Sons 1809)

Coleman JL, *The Practice of Principle* (Clarendon Press 2001)

Coleman K, *The American Revolution in Georgia: 1763–1789* (University of Georgia Press 1958)

Colón-Ríos J, "The Legitimacy of the Juridical: Constituent Power, Democracy, and the Limits of Constitutional Reform" (2010) 48 Osgood Hall Law Journal 199–245

Colón-Ríos J, "Rousseau, Theorist of Constituent Power" (2016) 36 Oxford Journal of Legal Studies 885–908

Colón-Ríos J, *Weak Constitutionalism: Democratic Legitimacy and the Question of Constituent Power* (Routledge 2012)

Commission AE, *Costs of Elections and Referendums* (2019)

Conceição-Heldt E and Mello PA, "Two-Level Games in Foreign Policy Analysis" Oxford Research Encylopedias—Politics <https://oxfordre.com/politics/view/10.1093/acrefore/9780190228637.001.0001/acrefore-9780190228637-e-496>

Condorcet M, "Essay on the Application of Mathematics to the Theory of Decision-Making" in Baker KM (ed.), *Condorcet: Selected Writings* (Bobbs-Merrill 1976)

Condorcet M, "Declaration of Rights" in McLean I and Hewitt F (eds.), *Condorcet: Foundations of Social Choice and Political Theory* (Edward Elgar 1994)

Condorcet M, "On the Need for the Citizens to Ratify the Constitution" in McLean I and Hewitt F (eds.), *Condorcet: Foundations of Social Choice and Political Theory* (Edward Elgar 1994)

Condorcet M, "A Survey of the Principles Underlying the Draft Constitution" in McLean I and Hewitt F (eds.), *Condorcet: Foundations of Social Choice and Political Theory* (Edward Elgar 1994)

Condorcet M, "The Principle of, the Justifications for, the New Constitution" in Goldstein MA (ed.), *Social and Political Thought of the French Revolution, 1788–1797: An Anthology of Original Texts* (Peter Lang 1997)

Condorcet M, "Ideas on Despotism: For the Benefit of Those Who Pronounce This Word without Understanding It" in Ansart G (ed.), *Condorcet: Writings on the United States* (The Pennsylvania State University Press 2012)
Conley PT, *The Rhode Island State Constitution: A Reference Guide* (Praeger 2007)
Coons C and Weber M (eds.), *Manipulation: Theory and Practice* (Oxford University Press 2014)
Cornwell EE, Goodman JS, and Swanson WR, *State Constitutional Conventions: The Politics of the Revision Process in Seven States* (Praeger 1975)
Council of Europe, *Treaty Making: Expression of Consent by States to Be Bound by a Treaty* (Kluwer Law International 2001)
Countryman E, *A People in Revolution: The American Revolution and Political Society in New York, 1760–1790* (John Hopkins University Press 1981)
Crennan S, "Federation" in Saunders C and Stone A (eds.), *The Oxford Handbook of the Australian Constitution* (Oxford University Press 2018)
Crisp BF and others, "Elections as Instruments for Punishing Bad Representatives and Selecting Good Ones" (2014) 32 Electoral Studies 658–69
Croissant A, "Ways of Constitution-Making in Southeast Asia: Actors, Interests, Dynamics" in Bünte M and Dressel B (eds.), *Politics and Constitutions in Southeast Asia* (Routledge 2017)
Cronin TE, *Direct Democracy: The Politics of Referendum, Initiative, and Recall* (Harvard University Press 1989)
Cushing HA, *History of the Transition from Provincial to Commonwealth Government in Massachusetts* (Columbia University 1896)
Cushing HA, "Political Activity of Massachusetts Towns During the Revolution", *Annual Report of the American Historical Association for the Year 1895* (Government Printing Office 1896)
Dahl RA, *On Democracy* (Yale University Press 2000)
Dann P and Al-ali Z, "The Internationalized *Pouvoir Constituant*—Constitution-Making under External Influence in Iraq, Sudan and East Timor" (2006) 10 Max Plank Yearbook of United Nations Law 423–63
Dann P and others, *Lessons Learned from Constitution-Making: Processes with Broad Based Public Participation* (Democracy Reporting International 2011)
Dardanelli P, "The Emergence and Evolution of Democracy in Switzerland" in Malone M (ed.), *Achieving Democracy: Democratization in Theory and Practice* (Continuum 2011)
de Covarrubias y Lieva D, *Relectio Cap. Quamuis Pactum, De Pactis, Regul* (1558)
de Raadt J, "Contested Constitutions: Legitimacy of Constitution-Making and Constitutional Conflict in Central Europe" (2009) 23 East European Politics and Societies 315–38
de Vreese CH, "Context, Elites, Media and Public Opinion in Referendums: When Campaigns Really Matter" in de Vreese CH (ed.), *The Dynamics of Referendum Campaigns: An International Perspective* (Palgrave Macmillan 2007)
Delli Carpini MX and Keeter S, *What Americans Know About Politics and Why It Matters* (Yale University Press 1996)
DeMott DA, "Ratification: Useful but Uneven" (2009) 17 European Review of Private Law 987–1002
Denver DT and Hands G, *Modern Constituency Electioneering: Local Campaigning in the 1992 General Election* (Frank Cass 1997)
DeSorbo FA, "Reverend Thomas Allen and Revolutionary Politics in Western Massachusetts" (Dissertation, New York University 1995)

Devereux A, *Timor-Leste's Bill of Rights: A Preliminary History* (Australian National University Press 2015)

Diagne SB, "The Constitution of a 'Laïc' African and Muslim Country: Senegal" in Bâli AÜ and Lerner H (eds.), *Constitution Writing, Religion and Democracy* (Cambridge University Press 2017)

Diehl K and others, *Structures and Principles of a Constitution* (Max Planck Manuals on Constitution Building 2009)

Dinan JJ, "'The Earth Belongs Always to the Living Generation': The Development of State Constitutional Amendment and Revision Procedures" (2000) 62 Review of Politics 645–74

Dinan JJ, *The Virginia State Constitution* (Oxford University Press 2011)

Dixon M, Franklin D, Holmes S, Maric V, and Semler D, "Constitution Watch" (1992) 1 East European Constitutional Review 2–8

Disch L, "Toward a Mobilization Conception of Democratic Representation" (2011) 105 American Political Science Review 100–114

Djordjevic J, "The Creation of the 1974 Constitution of the Socialist Federal Republic of Yugoslavia" in Goldwin RA and Kaufman A (eds.), *Constitution-Makers on Constitution Making: The Experience of Eight Nations* (American Enterprise Institute 1988)

Dodd WF, *Revision and Amendment of State Constitutions* (The John Hopkins Press 1910)

Dornbach A, "Special Reports: Retroactivity Law Overturned in Hungary" (1992) 7 East European Constitutional Review 7–8

Dovi S, *The Good Representative* (Blackwell Publishing 2007)

Downs A, *An Economic Theory of Democracy* (Harper and Row 1957)

Doyle O, "Populist Constitutionalism and Constituent Power" (2018) 20 German Law Journal 161–80

Dressel B, "Thailand's Elusive Quest for a Workable Constitution, 1997–2007" (2009) 31 Contemporary Southeast Asia 296–325

Dullea HN, *Charter Revision in the Empire State: The Politics of New York's 1967 Constitutional Convention* (Rockefeller Institute Press 1997)

Dunning T and others, "Voter Information Campaigns and Political Accountability: Cumulative Findings from a Preregistered Meta-Analysis of Coordinated Trials" (2019) 5 Science Advances 1–10

Dworkin R, *Law's Empire* (Harvard University Press 1986)

Dyzenhaus D, "The Politics of the Question of Constituent Power" in Loughlin M and Walker N (eds.), *The Paradox of Constitutionalism: Constituent Power and Constitutional Form* (Cambridge University Press 2007)

Dyzenhaus D, "Constitutionalism in an Old Key: Legality and Constituent Power" (2012) 1 Global Constitutionalism 229–60

Ebrahim H, Fayemi K, and Loomis S, *Promoting a Culture of Constitutionalism and Democracy in Commonwealth Africa: Recommendations to Commonwealth Heads of Government* (Commonwealth Human Rights Initiative 1999)

Ebrahim H and Miller LE, "Creating the Birth Certificate of a New South Africa: Constitution Making after Apartheid" in Miller LE (ed.), *Framing the State in Times of Transition: Case Studies in Constitution Making* (United States Institute of Peace 2010)

Eisenstadt TA, LeVan AC, and Maboudi T, *Constituents before Assembly: Participation, Deliberation, and Representation in the Crafting of New Constitutions* (Cambridge University Press 2017)

Eisenstadt TA, LeVan AC, and Maboudi T, *Constitutionalism and Democracy Dataset, Version 1.0* (American University's Digital Research Archive 2017)

Eisenstadt TA and Maboudi T, "Being There Is Half the Battle: Group Inclusion, Constitution-Writing, and Democracy" (2019) 52 Comparative Political Studies 2135–70

Elkins Z, Ginsburg T, and Blount J, "The Citizen as Founder: Public Participation in Constitutional Approval" (2008) 81 Temple Law Review 361–82

Elkins Z, Ginsburg T, and Melton J, "The Lifespan of Written Constitutions" (World Justice Forum 2008)

Elkins Z and Hudson A, "The Constitutional Referendum in Historical Perspective" in Landau D and Lerner H (eds.), *Comparative Constitution Making* (Edward Elgar 2019)

Elkins Z, Melton J, and Ginsburg T, *The Endurance of National Constitutions* (Cambridge University Press 2009)

Elster J, "Constitution-Making in Eastern Europe: Rebuilding the Boat in the Open Sea" (1993) 71 Public Administration 169–217

Elster J, "Constitutional Bootstrapping in Philadelphia and Paris" in Rosenfeld M (ed.), *Constitutionalism, Identity, Difference, and Legitimacy: Theoretical Perspectives* (Duke University Press 1994)

Elster J, "Forces and Mechanisms in the Constitution-Making Process" (1995) 45 Duke Law Review 364–96

Elster J, "The Role of Institutional Interest in East European Constitution-Making" (1996) 5 East European Constitutional Review 169–217

Elster J, *Alchemies of the Mind: Rationality and the Emotions* (Cambridge University Press 1998)

Elster J, "Deliberation and Constitution Making" in Elster J (ed.), *Deliberative Democracy* (Cambridge University Press 1998)

Elster J, "Accountability in Athenian Politics" in Przeworski A, Manin B, and Stokes SC (eds.), *Democracy, Accountability, and Representation* (Cambridge University Press 1999)

Elster J, "Arguing and Bargaining in Two Constituent Assemblies" (1999–2000) 354 University of Pennsylvania Journal of Constitutional Law 345–421

Elster J, *Ulysses Unbound* (Cambridge University Press 2000)

Elster J, "Legislatures as Constituent Assemblies" in Bauman RW and Kahana T (eds.), *The Least Examined Branch: The Role of Legislatures in the Constitutional State* (Cambridge University Press 2006)

Elster J, *Explaining Social Behavior: More Nuts and Bolts for the Social Sciences* (Cambridge University Press 2007)

Elster J, "Clearing and Strengthening the Channels of Constitution Making" in Ginsburg T (ed.), *Comparative Constitutional Design* (Cambridge University Press 2012)

Elster J, "The Optimal Design of a Constituent Assembly" in Landemore H and Elster J (eds.), *Collective Wisdom: Principles and Mechanisms* (Cambridge University Press 2012)

Elster J, *Securities against Misrule: Juries, Assemblies, Elections* (Cambridge University Press 2013)

Elster J and others, "Introduction" in Elster J and others (eds.), *Constituent Assemblies* (Cambridge University Press 2018)

Esaiasson P, Gilljam M, and Persson M, "Which Decision-Making Arrangements Generate the Strongest Legitimacy Beliefs? Evidence from a Randomised Field Experiment" (2012) 51 European Journal of Political Research 785–808

Espejo PO, *The Time of Popular Sovereignty: Process and the Democratic State* (The Pennsylvania State University Press 2011)

Eule JN, "Judicial Review of Direct Democracy" (1990) 99 Yale Law Journal 1503–90

European Commission for Democracy Through Law, *Opinion on the Fourth Amendment to the Fundamental Law of Hungary* (Council of Europe 2013)

Fallon RH, Jr., "Legitimacy and the Constitution" (2005) 118 Harvard Law Review 1787–1853

Farrand M (ed.), *The Records of the Federal Convention of 1787*, vol. 1 (Yale University Press 1914)

Farrand M (ed.), *The Records of the Federal Convention of 1787*, vol. 2 (Yale University Press 1914)

Farrand M (ed.), *The Records of the Federal Convention of 1787*, vol. 3 (Yale University Press 1914)

Farrell DM and Schmitt-Beck R, *Do Political Campaigns Matter? Campaign Effects in Elections and Referendums* (Routledge 2002)

Fearon JD, "Deliberation as Discussion" in Elster J (ed.), *Deliberative Democracy* (Cambridge University Press 1998)

Fearon JD, "Electoral Accountability and the Control of Politicians: Selecting Good Types Versus Sanctioning Poor Performance" in Przeworski A, Manin B, and Stokes SC (eds.), *Democracy, Accountability, and Representation* (Cambridge University Press 1999)

Ferejohn J, *Why the People: A Reflection on Democratic Constitutionalism* (Stanford University 2004)

Ferejohn J and Rosenbluth F, "Electoral Representation and the Aristocratic Thesis" in Shapiro I and others (eds.), *Political Representation* (Cambridge University Press 2009)

Fink EC and Riker WH, "The Strategy of Ratification" in Grofman B and Wittman D (eds.), *The Federalist Papers and the New Institutionalism* (Agathon Press 1989)

Fiorina MP, *Retrospective Voting in American National Elections* (Yale University Press 1980)

Fiske ST and Taylor SE, *Social Cognition* (2nd edn, McGraw-Hill 1992)

Fleming C, "'Biggest Strike NZ Has Ever Seen' on the Way as Teachers Turn Out" *Bay of Plenty Times* (Tauranga, New Zealand, May 28, 2019) A:2

Flynt W, "Alabama's Shame: The Historical Origins of the 1901 Constitution" (2002) 53 Alabama Law Review 67–76

Ford WC and others (eds.), *Journals of the Continental Congress, 1774–1789*, vol. 1 (U.S. Government Printing Office 1904)

Ford WC and others (eds.), *Journals of the Continental Congress, 1774–1789*, vol. 2 (U.S. Government Printing Office 1904–1937)

Ford WC and others (eds.), *Journals of the Continental Congress, 1774–1789*, vol. 4 (U.S. Government Printing Office 1906)

Forsyth MG, *Reason and Revolution: The Political Thought of the Abbè Sieyès* (Leicester University Press 1987)

Forsyth MG, "Hobbes's Contractarianism: A Comparative Analysis" in Boucher D and Kelly P (eds.), *The Social Contract from Hobbes to Rawls* (Routledge Press 1994)

Forsyth MG, "Thomas Hobbes and the Constituent Power of the People" (2006) XXIX Political Studies 191–203

Fox DT, Gallon-Giraldo G, and Stetson A, "Lessons of the Colombian Constitutional Reform of 1991: Toward the Securing of Peace and Reconciliation?" in Miller LE (ed.), *Framing the State in Times of Transition: Case Studies in Constitution Making* (United States Institute of Peace Press 2010)

Franck TM and Thiruvengadam AK, "Norms of International Law Relating to the Constitution-Making Process" in Miller LE (ed.), *Framing the State in Times of Transition: Case Studies in Constitution Making* (United States Institute of Peace Press 2010)

Franklin JH, *John Locke and the Theory of Sovereignty: Mixed Monarchy and the Rights of Resistance in the Political Thought of the English Revolution* (Cambridge University Press 1978)

Franklin MN, Eijk CVD, and Marsh M, "Referendum Outcomes and Trust in Government: Public Support for Europe in the Wake of Maastricht" (1995) 18 West European Politics 101–17

Friedman RS and Stokes S, "The Role of Constitution-Maker as Representative" (1965) 9 Midwest Journal of Political Science 148–66

Friedrich C, *Man and His Government* (McGraw-Hill 1963)

Frohlich N and Oppenheimer JA, *Choosing Justice: An Experimental Approach to Ethical Theory* (University of California Press 1993)

Fung A, "Varieties of Participation in Complex Governance" (2006) 66 Public Administration Review 66–75

Fung A, "Democratic Theory and Political Science: A Pragmatic Model of Constructive Engagement" (2007) 101 American Political Science Review 443–58

Fung A, "Putting the Public Back into Governance: The Challenges of Citizen Participation and Its Future" (2015) 75 Public Administrative Review 513–22

Furneaux P, *Letters to the Honourable Mr. Justice Blackstone* (T. Cadell 1770)

Gage T, "By the Governour—A Proclamation, September 18, 1774" in Force P (ed.), *American Archives: Fourth Series* (Northern Illinois University Libraries 1837)

Galbraith PW, *The End of Iraq: How American Incompetence Created a War without End* (Simon & Schuster 2007)

Galie PJ, *The New York State Constitution: A Reference Guide* (Greenwood Press 1991)

Gamnson WA and Modigliani A, "Media Discourse and Public Opinion on Nuclear Power: A Constructionist Approach" (1989) 95 American Journal of Sociology 1–37

Garlicki L and Garlicka ZA, "Constitution Making, Peace Building, and National Reconciliation: The Experience of Poland" in Miller LE (ed.), *Framing the State in Times of Transition: Case Studies in Constitution Making* (United States Institute of Peace Press 2010)

Gasamagera W, "The Constitution Making Process in Rwanda: Lessons to Be Learned" (7th Global Forum for Reinventing Government)

Gathii JT, "Popular Authorship and Constitution Making: Comparing and Contrasting the DRC and Kenya" (2008) 49 William and Mary Law Review 1109–38

General Assembly of Georgia, "Acts of the General Assembly of the State of Georgia Commencing the 1st of January, 1788" in *Early American Imprints: Series I Evans* (Readex 1984) microfilm 21107

Ghai Y, *The Role of Constituent Assemblies in Constitution Making* (Institute for Democracy and Electoral Assistance 2007)

Ghai Y and Cottrell J (eds.), *Creating the New Constitution: A Guide for Nepali Citizens* (International IDEA 2008)

Ghai Y and Galli G, *Constitution Building Processes and Democratization* (International IDEA 2006)

Gibson JL, Caldeira GA, and Spence LK, "Why Do People Accept Public Policies They Oppose? Testing Legitimacy Theory with a Survey Based Experiment?" (2005) 58 Political Research Quarterly 187–201

Gilley B, *The Right to Rule: How States Win and Lose Legitimacy* (Columbia University Press 2009)

Ginsburg T and Dixon R, "Introduction" in Ginsburg T and Dixon R (eds.), *Comparative Constitutional Law* (Edward Elgar 2011)

Ginsburg T, Elkins Z, and Blount J, "Does the Process of Constitution-Making Matter?" (2009) 5 Annual Review of Law and Social Science 201–23

Ginsburg T and Ganzorig G, "Constitutional Reform and Human Rights" in Brunn O and Odgaard O (eds.), *Mongolia in Transition: Old Patterns, New Challenges* (Routledge 1996)

Glencross A and Trechsel A, "First or Second Order Referendum? Understanding the Votes on the Eu Constitutional Treaty in Four Eu Member States" (2011) 34 West European Politics 755–72

Gloppen S, *South Africa: The Battle over the Constitution* (Ashgate 1997)

Goddard EC, "Ratification by an Undisclosed Principal" (1903) 2 Michigan Law Review 25–45

Goldey DB, "The French Referendum and Election of 1962" (1963) 11 Political Studies 287–307

Goldman AL and Corrada RL, *Labour Law in the USA* (Kluwer Law International 2014)

Goneng L, *Prospects for Constitutionalism in Post-Communist Countries*, vol. 50 (Law in Eastern Europe, Martinus Nijhoff Publishers 2002)

Gonzalez CE, "Representational Structure through Which We the People Ratify Constitutions: The Troubling Original Understanding of the Constitution's Ratification Clauses" (2005) 38 UC Davis Law Review 1373–1504

Gooch RK, "Recent Constitution-Making in France" (June 1947) 41 The American Political Science Review 429–32

Goodin RE, *Innovating Democracy: Democratic Theory and Practice after the Deliberative Turn* (Oxford University Press 2008)

Goodin RE and Niemeyer SJ, "When Does Deliberation Begin? Internal Reflection Versus Public Discussion in Deliberative Democracy" (2003) 51 Political Studies 627–49

Goodin RE and Spiekermann K, *An Epistemic Theory of Democracy* (Oxford University Press 2018)

Gordon SC and Huber GA, "The Empirical Study of Legitimate Authority: Normative Guidance for Positive Analysis" in Knight J and Schwartzberg M (eds.), *Political Legitimacy: NOMOS LXI* (New York University Press 2019)

Gönenç L, *Prospects for Constitutionalism in Post-Communist Countries* (Martinus Nijhoff Publishers 2002)

Goss KC, *The Arkansas State Constitution: A Reference Guide* (Greenwood Press 1993)

Grafstein R, "The Failure of Weber's Conception of Legitimacy: Its Causes and Implications" (1981) 43 The Journal of Politics 45–472

Grant R, *John Locke's Liberalism* (Chicago University Press 1987)

Grant RW and Keohane RO, "Accountability and Abuses of Power in World Politics" (2005) 99 American Political Science Review 29–43

Green L, "Law, Legitimacy, and Consent" (1989) Southern California Law Review 795–825

Greenawalt K, *Conflicts of Law and Morality* (Clarendon Press 1987)

Grewal DS and Purdy J, "The Original Theory of Constitutionalism" (2018) 127 The Yale Law Journal 2–42

Grey TC, "Constitutionalism: An Analytic Framework" in Pennock RJ and Chapman JW (eds.), *Constitutionalism: NOMOS XX* (New York University Press 1979)

Griffin J, "Incommensurability: What's the Problem?" in Chang R (ed.), *Incommensurability, Incomparability, and Practical Reason* (Harvard University Press 1997)

Grigsby HB, *The Virginia Convention of 1776* (Da Capo Press 1969)

Grimm D, *Constitutionalism: Past, Present, and Future* (Oxford University Press 2016)

Groseclose T and McCarty N, "The Politics of Blame: Bargaining before an Audience" (2001) 45 American Journal of Political Science 100–119

Grossman G and Baldassarri D, "The Impact of Elections on Cooperation: Evidence from a Lab-in-the-Field Experiment in Uganda" (2012) 56 American Journal of Political Science 964–85

Grotius H, *The Rights of War and Peace*, vol. II (Liberty Fund 2005)

Gunderson M, "Justifying a Principle of Informed Consent: A Case Study in Autonomy-Based Ethics" (1990) 4 Public Affairs Quarterly 249–65

Gutmann A and Thompson DF, *Democracy and Disagreement* (Harvard University Press 1996)

Habermas J, *Between Facts and Norms: Contributions to a Discourse Theory of Law and Democracy* (The MIT Press 1996)

Habermas J, "Constitutional Democracy: A Paradoxical Union of Contradictory Principles" (2001) 29 Political Theory 766–81

Habermas J, *The Inclusion of the Other: Studies in Political Theory* (The MIT Press 1996)

Hall WE, *A Treatise on International Law* (4th edn, Clarendon Press 1895)

Haller H and Holden S, "Ratification Requirement and Bargaining Power" (1997) 38 International Economic Review 825–51

Hamburger PA, "Natural Rights, Natural Law, and American Constitutions" (1993) 102 The Yale Law Journal 907–60

Hammett TM, *The Revolutionary Ideology in Its Social Context: Berkshire County, Massachusetts 1725–1785* (Dissertation, Brandeis University 1976)

Hammett TM, "Revolutionary Ideology in Massachusetts: Thomas Allen's "Vindication" of the Berkshire Constitutionalists, 1778" (1976) 33 The William and Mary Quarterly 514–27

Handlin O and Handlin M, "Introduction" in Handlin O and Handlin M (eds.), *The Popular Sources of Political Authority* (Harvard University Press 1966)

Hansen MH, *The Athenian Democracy in the Age of Demosthenes: Structure, Principle, and Ideology* (Oxford University Press 1991)

Hardin R, *Liberalism, Constitutionalism, and Democracy* (Oxford University Press 1999)

Hart HLA, *Essays in Jurisprudence and Philosophy* (Clarendon Press 1983)

Hart HLA, *The Concept of Law* (2nd edn, Oxford University Press 1994)

Hart V, *Democratic Constitution Making*, Special Report 107 (United States Institute of Peace 2003)

Hart V, "Constitution Making and the Right to Take Part in a Public Affair" in Miller LE (ed.), *Framing the State in Times of Transition: Case Studies in Constitution Making* (United States Institute of Peace Press 2010)

Hartwell EM, "Referenda in Massachusetts and Boston" (1910) 12 Publications of the American Statistical Association 230–73

Hatchard J, "Re-Establishing a Multi-Party State: Some Constitutional Lessons from the Seychelles" (1993) 31 Journal of Modern African Studies 601–12

Hatchard J, "Some Lessons on Constitution-Making from Zimbabwe" (2001) 54 Journal of African Law 210–16

Hayward CR, "Making Interest: On Representation and Democratic Legitimacy" in Shapiro I and others (eds.), *Political Representation* (Cambridge University Press 2009)

Hazel R, "You Want a Constitutional Convention? This Is What You Need to Think through First" *The Constitution Unit, UCL* (8 October 2014) <https://constitution-unit.com/2014/10/08/you-want-a-constitutional-convention-this-is-what-you-need-to-think-through-first/>

Heinhard S, "Peace Treaties from Paris to Versailles" in Lesaffer R (ed.), *Peace Treaties and International Law in European History* (Cambridge University Press 2004)

Higley J and McAllister I, "Elite Division and Voter Confusion: Australia's Republic Referendum in 1999" (2002) 41 European Journal of Political Research 845–61

Hill TE Jr., "Humanity as an End in Itself" (1980) 91 Ethics 84–99

Hill TE Jr., "Autonomy and Benevolent Lies" (1984) 18 Journal of Value Inquiry 251–67

Hinsch W, "Justice, Legitimacy, and Constitutional Rights" (2010) 13 Critical Review of International Social and Political Philosophy 39–51

Hoar RS, *Constitutional Conventions, Their Nature, Powers, and Limitations* (Little, Brown and Company1917)
Hobbes T, *Leviathan* (Cambridge University Press 1996)
Hobolt SB, "Taking Cues on Europe? Voter Competence and Party Endorsements in Referendums on European Integration" (2007) 46 European Journal of Political Research 151–82
Hodson D and Maher I, "British Brinkmanship and Gaelic Games: EU Treaty Ratification in the UK and Ireland from a Two Level Game Perspective" (2014) 16 The British Journal of Politics and International Relations 645–61
Holmes S, *Passions and Constraint: On the Theory of Liberal Democracy* (University of Chicago Press 1995)
Holmes S and Elster J, "New Constitutions Adopted in Bulgaria and Romania" (1992) 1 East European Constitutional Review 11–12
Horne C, "A Social Norms Approach to Legitimacy" (2009) 53 American Behavioral Scientist 400–415
Horowitz DL, "Conciliatory Institutions and Constitutional Processes in Post-Conflict States" (2008) 49 William and Mary Law Review 1213–48
Horowitz DL, "Constitution-Making: A Process Filled with Constraint" (2006) 12 Review of Constitutional Studies 1–17
Hough FB, *New York Convention Manual* (Weed, Parsons & Company 1867)
Hudson A, "Political Parties and Public Participation in Constitution Making: Legitimation, Distraction, or Real Impact" (Forthcoming) Comparative Politics 1–21
Huffcut EW, *The Law of Agency: Including the Law of Principal and Agent and the Law of Master and Servant* (2nd edn, Little, Brown, and Company 1901)
Hug S, "Some Thoughts About Referendums, Representative Democracy, and Separation of Powers" (2009) 20 Constitutional Political Economy 251–66
Hug S and Tsebelis G, "Veto Players and Referendums around the World" (2002) 14 Journal of Theoretical Politics 465–515
Hume D, *Essays: Moral, Political, and Literary* (Liberty Fund 1985)
Hussein A, "Somalia Faces Tough Road in Its Transition to Federal Rule" Sabahi <http://sabahionline.com/en_GB/articles/hoa/articles/features/2012/05/21/feature-01>
Hutcheson F, *An Inquiry into the Original of Our Ideas of Beauty and Virtue in Two Treatises* (Liberty Fund 2004)
Ipsos MORI and the Policy Institute at King's College London, "Brexit Misperceptions" <https://www.kcl.ac.uk/policy-institute/assets/brexit-misperceptions.pdf>
Ipsos MORI and UK in a Changing Europe, "The Perils of Perception and the EU" <https://www.ipsos.com/ipsos-mori/en-uk/perils-perception-and-eu>
Jackson VC, "What's in a Name? Reflections on Timing, Naming, and Constitution-Making" (2008) 49 William and Mary Law Review 1249–1305
Jameson JA, *The Constitutional Convention; Its History, Powers, and Modes of Proceeding* (Charles Scribner and Company 1867)
Jameson JA, "Conventions, the Constitutional" in Lalor JJ (ed.), *Cyclopedia of Political Science, Political Economy, and of the Political History of the United States*, vol. 1 (Rand, McNally & Company 1882)
Jaume L, "Constituent Power in France: The Revolution and Its Consequences" in Loughlin M and Walker N (eds.), *The Paradox of Constitutionalism: Constituent Power and Constitutional Form* (Cambridge University Press 2007)
Jefferson T, *Thomas Jefferson: Writings* (Library of America 1984)
Jensen M (ed.), *The Documentary History of the Ratification of the Constitution: Constitutional Documents and Records, 1776–1787* (The State Historical Society of Wisconsin 1976)

Jewell ME, "Legislator-Constituency Relations and the Representative Process" (1983) 8 Legislative Studies Quarterly 303–37
Johnson C, "Local Civic Participation and Democratic Legitimacy: Evidence from England and Wales" (2014) 63 Political Studies 765–92
Johnson S, *A Dictionary of the English Language* (3rd edn, W.G. Jones 1768)
Jones DR, "Air Talks Reach 'Serious Impasse'" *New York Times* (New York, July 15, 1966)
Jones JM, *Full Powers and Ratification: A Study in the Development of Treaty-Making Procedure* (University of Cambridge Press 1946)
Junius, "To the Printer of the Public Advertiser", *The Letters of Junius* (Leavitt, Trow & Co 1848)
Kahneman D, Knetsch JL, and Thaler RH, "Anomalies: The Endowment Effect, Loss Aversion, and Status Quo Bias" (1991) 5 The Journal of Economic Perspectives 193–206
Kalt JP and Zupan MA, "The Apparent Ideological Behavior of Legislators: Testing for Principal-Agent Slack in Political Institutions" (1990) 33 Journal of Law and Economics 103–32
Kalyvas A, "Sovereignty, Democracy, and the Constituent Power" (2005) 12 Constellations 223–44
Kalyvas A, *Democracy and the Politics of the Extraordinary* (Cambridge University Press 2008)
Kampo VM, "Dissenting Opinion of Justice of the Constitutional Court of Ukraine V.M. Campo Pertaining to Decision No.6-Rp/2008 of April 16, 2008" (2009) 44 Statutes and Decisions 93–96
Karim QA and others, "Informed Consent for HIV Testing in a South Africa Hospital: Is It Truly Informed and Truly Voluntary" (1998) 88 American Journal of Public Health 637–40
Kau JB and Rubin PH, "Ideology, Voting, and Shirking" (1993) 76 Public Choice 151–72
Kay RS, "The Illegality of the Constitution" (1987) 4 Constitutional Commentary 57–80
Kay RS, "Constituent Authority" (2011) 59 American Journal of Comparative Law 715–61
Kelsen H, *General Theory of Law and State* (Transaction Publishers 2006)
Kenyon JP, *Revolution Principles: The Politics of Party, 1689–1720* (Cambridge University Press 1977)
Key VO, *The Responsible Electorate* (Vintage 1966)
Khalil A, *The Enactment of Constituent Power in the Arab World: The Palestinian Case* (Dissertation, University of Fribourg 2006)
Kildea P and Smith R, "The Challenge of Informed Voting at Constitutional Referendums" (2016) 39 UNSW Law Journal 368–400
King P, "Neo-Bolivarian Constitutional Design" in Galligan DJ and Versteeg M (eds.), *Social and Political Foundations of Constitutions* (Cambridge University Press 2013)
Klarman MJ, *The Framers' Coup: The Making of the United States Constitution* (Oxford University Press 2016)
Klein C, "A Propos Constituent Power: Some General Views in a Modern Context" in Jyranki A (ed.), *National Constitutions in the Era of Integration* (Kluwer Law International 1999)
Klein C and Sajó A, "Constitution-Making: Process and Substance" in Rosenfeld M and Sajó A (eds.), *The Oxford Handbook of Comparative Constitutional Law* (Oxford University Press 2012)
Klein MM, "Democracy and Politics in Colonial New York" (1959) 40 New York History 221–46
Klosko G, *Political Obligation* (Oxford University Press 2005)

Koch HW, *A Constitutional History of Germany in the Nineteenth and Twentieth Centuries* (Longman 1984)

Konold D, "Farm Interests as Bargaining Chips: France in the Eu-Mercosur Free Trade Negotiations" (2010) 30 Journal of Public Policy 321–43

Kriesi H, "The Participation in Swiss Direct-Democratic Votes" in de Vreese CH (ed.), *The Dynamics of Referendum Campaigns: An International Perspective* (Palgrave Macmillan 2007)

Kruman MW, *Between Authority and Liberty: State Constitution Making in Revolutionary America* (University of North Carolina Press 1997)

Kuehne DS, *Massachusetts Congregationalist Political Thought, 1760–1790: The Design of Heaven* (University of Missouri Press 1996)

Kuklinski JH and Quirk PJ, "Reconsidering the Rational Public: Cognition, Heuristics, and Mass Opinion" in Lupia A, McCubbins M, and Popkin S (eds.), *Elements of Reason: Cognition, Choice, and the Bounds of Rationality* (Cambridge University Press 2000)

Kuklinski JH and Quirk PJ, "Conceptual Foundations of Citizen Competence" (2001) 23 Political Behavior 285–311

Kyvig DE, *Explicit & Authentic Acts: Amending the U.S. Constitution, 1776–2015* (University Press of Kansas 2016)

Lahne HJ, "Union Contract Ratification Procedures" (1968) 91 Monthly Labor Review 7–10

Lal BV, "Constitutional Engineering in Post-Coup Fiji" in Reynolds A (ed.), *The Architecture of Democracy: Constitutional Design, Conflict Management, and Democracy* (Oxford University Press 2002)

Landau D, "Constitution-Making Gone Wrong" (2013) 64 Alabama Law Review 923–80

Landemore H, "Inclusive Constitution-Making: The Icelandic Experiment" (2015) 23 The Journal of Political Philosophy 166–91

Lantis JS, *The Life and Death of International Treaties: Doubled-Edged Diplomacy and the Politics of Ratification in Comparative Perspective* (Oxford University Press 2008)

Laslett P, "Introduction" in Laslett P (ed.), *Two Treatises of Government* (Cambridge University Press 2002)

Lau RR and Redlawsk DP, "Voting Correctly" (1997) 91 American Political Science Review 585–98

Lau RR and Redlawsk DP, "An Experimental Study of Information Search, Memory, and Decision Making During a Political Campaign" in Kuklinski J (ed.), *Citizens and Politics, Perspectives from Political Psychology* (Cambridge University Press 2001)

Law DS and Versteeg M, "Sham Constitutions" (2013) 101 California Law Review 863–952

Lawson G, *An Examination of the Political Part of Mr. Hobbs His Leviathan* (London 1657)

Lawson G, *Politica Sacra Er Civilis* (Cambridge University Press 1992)

Le Roy K, *Public Participation in Constitution-Making: The Pacific Islands* (Interpeace 2011)

Leary P, "Harley-Davidson Workers Reportedly Reject Contract Offer" *Milwaukee Business Journal* <https://www.bizjournals.com/milwaukee/news/2019/04/01/harley-davidson-workers-reportedly-reject-contract.html?iana=hpmvp_mil_news_headline>

LeDuc L, *The Politics of Direct Democracy: Referendums in a Global Perspective* (Broadview Press 2003)

LeDuc L, "Referendums and Elections: How Do Campaigns Differ?" in Farrell DM and Schmitt-Beck R (eds.), *Do Political Campaigns Matter? Campaign Effects in Elections and Referendums* (Routledge 2002)

LeDuc L, "Opinion Formation and Change in Referendum Campaigns" in de Vreese CH (ed.), *The Dynamics of Referendum Campaigns: An International Perspective* (Palgrave Macmillan 2007)

Lee D, "Private Law Models for Public Law Concepts: The Roman Law Theory of Dominium in the Monarchomach Doctrine of Popular Sovereignty" (2008) 70 The Review of Politics 370–99
Lee D, *Popular Sovereignty in Early Modern Constitutional Thought* (Oxford University Press 2016)
Lenowitz J and Schwartzberg M, "Insomnia and Other Constitutional Pathologies" (2019) 16 Modern Intellectual History 295–308
Lenowitz JA, "On the Empirical Measurement of Legitimacy" in Schwartzberg M and Knight J (eds.), *Political Legitimacy: NOMOS LXI* (New York University Press 2019)
Lerner H, *Making Constitutions in Deeply Divided Societies* (Cambridge University Press 2011)
Lerner H, "Constituent Assemblies and Political Continuity in Divided Societies" in Elster J and others (eds.), *Constituent Assemblies* (Cambridge University Press 2018)
Lesaffer R, "Peace Treaties from Lodi to Westphalia" in Lesaffer R (ed.), *Peace Treaties and International Law in European History* (Cambridge University Press 2004)
Levinthal IH, "The Jewish Law of Agency" (1922) 13 The Jewish Quarterly Review 117–91
Levy PA, "Membership Rights in Union Referenda to Ratify Collective Bargaining Agreements" (1987) 4 Hofstra Labor and Employment Law Journal 225–67
Lincoln CZ, *The Constitutional History of New York*, vol. 1 (The Lawyers Co-operative Publishing Company 1906)
Lincoln W (ed.), *The Journals of Each Provincial Congress of Massachusetts in 1774 and 1775* (Dutton and Wentworth 1838)
Lindahl H, "The Paradox of Constituent Power: The Ambiguous Self-Constitution of the European Union" (2007) 20 Ratio Juris 485–505
Lindahl H, "Possibility, Actuality, Rupture: Constituent Power and the Ontology of Change" (2015) 22 163–74
Linington G, *Constitutional Law of Zimbabwe* (Legal Resources Foundation 2001)
Lintott A, *Imperium Romanum: Politics and Administration* (Routledge 1993)
Lo B, "Assessing Decision-Making Capacity" (1990) 18 Law, Medicine, & Health Care 193–201
Lobingier CS, *The People's Law or Popular Participation in Law-Making: From Ancient Folk-Moot to Modern Referendum* (The Macmillan Company 1909)
Locke J, "A Letter Concerning Toleration", *The Works of John Locke*, vol. 5 (12th edn, Rivington 1824)
Locke J, *Two Treatises of Government* (1698, Cambridge University Press 2002)
Loughlin M, "On Constituent Power" in Dowdle MW and Wilkinson MA (eds.), *Constitutionalism Beyond Liberalism* (Cambridge University Press 2017)
Loughlin M and Walker N, "Introduction" in Loughlin M and Walker N (eds.), *The Paradox of Constitutionalism: Constituent Power and Constitutional Form* (Cambridge University Press 2007)
Loughran CS, *Negotiating a Labor Contract: A Management Handbook* (The Bureau of National Affairs, Inc. 1984)
Ludwikowski RR, "Constitution Making in the Countries of Former Soviet Dominance: Current Development" (1993) 33 Georgia Journal of International and Comparative Law 155–267
Lupia A, "Shortcuts Versus Encyclopedia: Information and Voting Behavior in California Insurance Reform Elections" (1994) 88 The American Political Science Review 63–76
Lupia A, "How Elitism Undermines the Study of Voter Competence" (2006) 18 Critical Review 217–32

Lupia A and Matsusaka JG, "Direct Democracy: New Approaches to Old Questions" (2004) 7 Annual Review of Political Science 463–82

Lupia A and McCubbins M, *The Democratic Dilemma: Can Citizens Learn What They Need to Know* (Cambridge University Press 1998)

Luskin RC and others, *Deliberation and Referendum Voting* (The Center for Deliberative Democracy 2005)

Lusztig M, "Constitutional Paralysis: Why Canadian Initiatives Are Doomed to Fail" (1994) 27 Canadian Journal of Political Science 747–71

Lutz DS, "The Theory of Consent in the Early State Constitutions" (1979) 9 Publius 11–42

Lutz DS, "From Covenant to Constitution in American Political Thought" (1980) 10 Publius 101–33

Lutz DS, *The Origins of American Constitutionalism* (Louisiana State University Press 1988)

Lutz DS (ed.), *Colonial Origins of the American Constitution: A Documentary History* (Liberty Fund 1998)

Lutz DS, *Principles of Constitutional Design* (Cambridge University Press 2006)

Lynd S, "The Mechanics in New York Politics, 1774–1788" (1964) 5 Labor History 225–46

Maboudi T and Nadi GP, "Crowdsourcing the Egyptian Constitution: Social Media, Elites, and the Populace" (2016) 69 Political Research Quarterly 716–34

Macdonald T, *Global Stakeholder Democracy: Power and Representation Beyond Liberal States* (Oxford University Press 2008)

Macdonald T and Macdonald K, "Non-Electoral Accountability in Global Politics: Strengthening Democratic Control within the Global Garment Industry" (2006) 17 The European Journal of International Law 89–119

MacDonald W (ed.), *Select Charters and Other Documents Illustrative of American History: 1606–1775* (The MacMillan Company 1899)

Madison J, *The Writings of James Madison: 1787–1790*, vol. 4 (G.P. Putnam's Sons 1903)

Madison J, *The Papers of James Madison*, vol. 8 (The University of Chicago Press 1973)

Madison J, *The Papers of James Madison*, vol. 9 (The University of Chicago Press 1975)

Madison J, Hamilton A, and Jay J, *The Federalist Papers* (Penguin Books 1987)

Magleby D, *Direct Legislation: Voting on Ballot Propositions in the United States* (The John Hopkins University Press 2001)

Maier P, *Ratification: The People Debate the Constitution, 1787–1788* (Simon & Schuster 2010)

Maimonides, *Book 12: The Book of Acquisition* (The Code of Maimonides, Yale University Press 1951)

Maistre JM, "On the Sovereignty of the People" in Lebrun R (ed.), *Against Rousseau: "On the State of Nature" and "on the Sovereignty of the People"* (McGill-Queen's Press 1995)

Maloy JS, *The Colonial American Origins of Modern Democratic Thought* (Cambridge University Press 2008)

Manin B, *The Principles of Representative Democracy* (Cambridge University Press 1997)

Manin B, Przeworski A, and Stokes S, "Elections and Representation" in Manin B, Przeworski A, and Stokes SC (eds.), *Democracy, Accountability, and Representation* (Cambridge University Press 1999)

Manin B, Przeworski A, and Stokes S, "Introduction" in Przeworski A, Manin B, and Stokes SC (eds.), *Democracy, Accountability, and Representation* (Cambridge University Press 1999)

Mansbridge J, "Rethinking Representation" (2003) 97 American Political Science Review 515–28

Mansbridge J, "A 'Selection Model' of Political Representation" (2009) 17 The Journal of Political Philosophy 369–98

Manson NC and O'Neil O, *Rethinking Informed Consent in Bioethics* (Cambridge University Press 2007)

Maravall JM, "Accountability and Manipulation" in Manin B, Przeworski A, and Stokes SC (eds.), *Democracy, Accountability, and Representation* (Cambridge University Press 1999)

Marks SP, "The Process of Creating a New Constitution in Cambodia" in Miller LE (ed.), *Framing the State in Times of Transition: Case Studies in Constitution Making* (United States Institute of Peace Press 2010)

Marshall D, Denny A, and Marshall S, *Communication of the Sante' Mawi' omi Wjit Mikmaq under the Optional Protocol to the International Covenant on Civil and Political Rights* (Santeioi Maoaiomi Mikmaoei 1986)

Martin JE and Berthiaume RD, "Predicting the Outcome of a Contract Ratification Vote" (1995) 38 The Academy of Management Journal 916–28

Maslan S, "Resisting Representation: Theater and Democracy in Revolutionary France" (1995) Representations 27–51

Massachusetts House of Representatives, "A Letter to Dennis Deberdt, Esq; Agent for the House of Representatives" *The Boston Chronicle* (April 11, 1768) 145–48, available in *America's Historical Newspapers* (Readex 2021)

McAllister I, "Civic Education and Political Knowledge in Australia" (1998) 33 Australian Journal of Political Science 7–23

McConnell T, "The Nature and Basis of Inalienable Rights" (1984) 3 Law and Philosophy 25–59

McCoy JL, "Venezuela's Controversial New Constituent Assembly, Explained" (*The Washington Post*, August 1, 2017) <https://www.bbc.com/news/world-latin-america-41094889>

McDonald F, *Novus Ordo Seclorum: The Intellectual Origins of the Constitution* (University of Kansas Press 1985)

McGuire RA and Ohsfeldt RL, "Self-Interest, Agency Theory, and Political Voting Behavior: The Ratification of the United States Constitution" (1989) 79 The American Economic Review 219–34

McKelvey RD and Ordeshook PC, "Information, Electoral Equilibria, and the Democratic Ideal" (1985) 48 Journal of Politics 909–37

McLaughlin AC, "American History and American Democracy" (1915) 20 The American Historical Review 255–76

McLean I and Hewitt F (eds.), *Condorcet: Foundations of Social Choice and Political Theory* (Edward Elgar 1994)

McLean I and Urken AB, "Did Jefferson or Madison Understand Condorcet's Theory of Social Choice?" (1992) 73 Public Choice 445–57

McMahon C, *Collective Rationality and Collective Reasoning* (Cambridge University Press 2001)

McWhinney E, *Constitution-Making: Principles, Process, Practice* (University of Toronto Press 1981)

Mechanics of Boston, "To the Printer" *The New-York Journal; or, The General Advertiser* (New York, September 29, 1774)

Mechem FR, *A Treatise on the Law of Agency* (Callaghan and Company 1914)

Mechem P, "The Rationale of Ratification" (1952) 100 University of Pennsylvania Law Review 649–78

Medhanie T, *Constitution-Making, Legitimacy and Regional Integration: An Approach to Eritrea's Predicament and Relations with Ethiopia* (DIIPER Research Series, 2008)

Meinecke F, *Cosmopolitanism and the National State* (Princeton University Press 1970)

Mendez F and Wheatley J, "Patterns of Constitution-Making over Time and Space" in Wheatley J and Mendez F (eds.), *Patterns of Constitutional Design: The Role of Citizens and Elites in Constitution-Making* (Routledge 2016)

Merkl P, *The Origins of the West German Republic* (Oxford University Press 1963)

Meron T, "The Authority to Make Treaties in the Late Middle Ages" (1995) 89 The American Journal of International Law 1–20

Michelman FI, "Ida's Way: Constructing the Respect-Worthy Governmental System" (2004) 72 Fordham Law Review 345–65

Michelman FI, "Is the Constitution a Contract for Legitimacy?" (2003) 8 Review of Constitutional Studies 101–28

Miller D, "Democracy's Domain" (2009) 37 Philosophy & Public Affairs 201–28

Miller LE, "Designing Constitution-Making Processes: Lessons from the Past, Questions for the Future" in Miller LE (ed.), *Framing the State in Times of Transition: Case Studies in Constitution Making* (United States Institute of Peace Press 2010)

Mills C, "Politics and Manipulation" (1995) 21 Social Theory and Practice 97–112

Mo J, "Domestic Institutions and International Bargaining: The Role of Agent Veto in Two-Level Games" (1995) 89 American Political Science Review 914–24

Moehler DC, "Public Participation and Support for the Constitution in Uganda" (2006) 44 The Journal of Modern African Studies 275–308

Moehler DC, *Distrusting Democrats: Outcomes of Participatory Constitution Making* (University of Michigan Press 2008)

Molina O, "Social Pacts, Collective Bargaining and Trade Union Articulation Strategies" (2008) 14 Transfer: European Review of Labour and Research 399–418

Mondak JJ, "Public Opinion and Heuristic Processing of Source Cues" (1993) 15 Political Behavior 167–92

Moravcsik A, "Integrating International and Domestic Theories of International Bargaining" in Evans PB, Putnam RD, and Jacobson HK (eds.), *Double-Edged Diplomacy: International Bargaining and Domestic Politics* (University of California Press 1993)

Morgan ES, *Inventing the People: The Rise of Popular Sovereignty in England and America* (W.W. Norton & Company, Inc. 1988)

Morison SE, *A History of the Constitution of Massachusetts* (Wright & Potter Printing Co. 1917)

Morison SE, "The Struggle over the Adoption of the Constitution of Massachusetts, 1780", *Massachusetts Historical Society Proceedings*, vol. L (Massachusetts Historical Society 1917)

Morrow J, "Deconstituting Mesopotamia: Cutting a Deal on the Regionalization of Iraq" in Miller LE (ed.), *Framing the State in Times of Transition: Case Studies in Constitution Making* (United States Institute of Peace Press 2010)

Mosoku G, "We Are Ready to Conduct the Referendum, Which Will Cost Sh12b: Iebc" *The Standard* (Nairobi, October 8, 2018) <https://www.standardmedia.co.ke/politics/article/2001298246/we-are-ready-for-referendum-but-it-will-cost-you-billions-iebc>

Mueller DC, *Constitutional Democracy* (Oxford University Press 1996)

Mulgan R, "'Accountability': An Ever-Expanding Concept" (2000) 78 Public Administration 555–73

Murphy W, *Constitutional Democracy: Creating and Maintaining a Just Political Order* (John Hopkins University Press 2007)

Murray C, "Negotiating Beyond Deadlock: From the Constitutional Assembly to the Court" (2004) 32 International Journal of Legal Information 322–50

National Assembly of Tanzania, *The Constitutional Review Commission Act* (2011)

Ndulo M, "Constitution-Making in Africa: Assessing Both the Process and Content" (2001) 21 Public Administration and Development 101–17

Ndulo M, "Zimbabwe's Unfulfilled Struggle for a Legitimate Constitutional Order" in Miller LE (ed.), *Framing the State in Times of Transition: Case Studies in Constitution Making* (United States Institute of Peace Press 2010)

Negretto GL, "Replacing and Amending Constitutions: The Logic of Constitutional Change in Latin America" (2012) 46 Law & Society Review 749–79

Negretto GL, "Constitution Making in Democratic Constitutional Orders: The Challenge of Citizen Participation" in Ruth S, Welp Y, and Whitehead L (eds.), *Let the People Rule? Direct Democracy in the Twenty-First Century* (ECPR Press 2017)

Negretto GL, *Constitution-Building Processes in Latin America: International Idea Discussion Paper 3/2018* (2018)

Negretto GL, "Democratic Constitution-Making Bodies: The Perils of a Partisan Convention" (2018) 16 International Journal of Constitutional Law 254–79

Negretto GL, "Constitution-Making and Liberal Democracy: The Role of Citizens and Representative Elites" (2020) 18 International Journal of Constitutional Law 206–32

Negretto GL, "Constitution-Making in Comparative Perspective" Oxford Research Encyclopedia of Politics <https://oxfordre.com/politics/view/10.1093/acrefore/9780190228637.001.0001/acrefore-9780190228637-e-66.>

Negretto GL and Talanquer MS, "Constitutional Origins and Liberal Democracy in Comparative Perspective" (ICON*S Conference: Public Law in Times of Change 2019)

Negri A, *Insurgencies: Constituent Power and the Modern State* (The University of Minnesota Press 2009)

Neuman WR, *The Paradox of Mass Politics: Knowledge and Opinion in the American Electorate* (Harvard University Press 1986)

Niemi RG and Weisberg HF, *Controversies in Voting Behavior* (4th edn, CQ Press 2001)

Noggle R, "Manipulative Actions: A Conceptual and Moral Analysis" (1996) 33 American Philosophical Quarterly 43–55

Nozick R, "Coercion" in Morgenbesser S, Suppes P, and White M (eds.), *Philosophy, Science, and Method: Essays in Honor of Ernest Nagel* (St. Martin's Press 1969)

O'Connell DP, *International Law*, vol. 1 (Stevens & Son Limited 1965)

Odewahn CA and Krislov J, "Contract Rejections: Testing the Explanatory Hypotheses" (1973) 12 Industrial Relations 289–96

Olken BA, "Direct Democracy and Local Public Goods: Evidence from a Field Experiment in Indonesia" (2010) 104 American Political Science Review 243–67

Oppenheim L, *International Law: A Treatise*, vol. 1 (8th edn, David McKay Company Inc 1955)

Oscarsson H, "The Ideological Response: Saying No to the Euro" in de Vreese CH (ed.), *The Dynamics of Referendum Campaigns: An International Perspective* (Palgrave Macmillan 2007)

Ottaway M and Brown NJ, "Egypt's Transition in Crisis: Falling into the Wrong Turkish Model?" (*Carnegie Endowment for the International Peace*, 2012) <https://carnegieendowment.org/2012/03/30/egypt-s-transition-in-crisis-falling-into-wrong-turkish-model-pub-47696>

Page BI and Shapiro RY, *The Rational Public: Fifty Years of Trends in Americans' Policy Preferences* (University of Chicago Press 1992)

Paine T, *Collected Writings* (The Library of America 1995)

Paine T, *Rights of Man, Common Sense, and Other Political Writings* (Oxford University Press 1998)

Parau CE, "Romania's Transnational Constitution: A Tradition of Elite Learning and Self-Empowerment" in Galligan DJ and Versteeg M (eds.), *Social and Political Foundations of Constitutions* (Cambridge University Press 2013)

Parliament of New Zealand, Employment Relations Act (2000)

Parliament of South Africa, Constitution [Interim] of the Republic of South Africa Act 200 (1993)

Parsons T, "The Essex Result, 1778" in Handlin O and Handlin M (eds.), *The Popular Sources of Political Authority* (Harvard University Press 1966)

Pateman C, *Participation and Democratic Theory* (Cambridge University Press 1970)

Patterson SE, *Political Parties in Revolutionary Massachusetts* (University of Wisconsin Press 1973)

Paultre A and Gottesdiener L, "Haiti Elections to Replace Slain President Postponed to Nov. 7" *Reuters* (August 11, 2021) <https://www.reuters.com/world/americas/haiti-elections-replace-slain-president-postponed-nov-7-media-2021-08-12/>

Persson M, Esaiasson P, and Gilljam M, "The Effects of Direct Voting and Deliberation on Legitimacy Beliefs: An Experimental Study of Small Group Decision-Making" (2006) European Political Science Review 1–19

Peters RM, *The Massachusetts Constitution of 1780: A Social Compact* (The University of Massachusetts Press 1978)

Pettit P, "Varieties of Public Representation" in Shapiro I and others (eds.), *Political Representation* (Cambridge University Press 2009)

Phillips A, *The Politics of Presence* (Oxford University Press 1995)

Philp M, "Review of Richard Tuck's 'The Sleeping Sovereign: The Invention of Modern Democracy'" (2019) CXXXIV The English Historical Review 469–72

Pickard D, "Prospects for Implementing Democracy in Tunisia" (2014) 19 Mediterranean Politics 259–64

Pitkin HF, *The Concept of Representation* (University of California Press 1967)

Pitkin HF, "Commentary: The Paradox of Representation" in Pennock RJ and Chapman JW (eds.), *Representation* (Atherton 1968)

Pitkin HF, "Representation and Democracy: Uneasy Alliance" (2004) 27 Scandinavian Political Studies 335–42

Plessis PD and Borkowski A, *Borkowski's Textbook on Roman Law* (5th edn, Blackstone Press Limited 2015)

Pocock JGA, *The Machiavellian Moment: Florentine Political Thought and the Atlantic Republican Tradition* (Princeton University Press 1975)

Pole JR, *Political Representation in England and the Origins of the American Republic* (MacMillan 1966)

Polybius, *The Rise of the Roman Empire* (Penguin Classics 1980)

Poore BP (ed.), *Federal and State Constitutions, Colonial Charters, and Other Organic Laws of the United States*, vol. 1 (Government Printing Office 1877)

Popkin S, *The Reasoning Voter: Communication and Persuasion in Presidential Campaigns* (University of Chicago Press 1991)

Pressman A, "AT&T Sees Its First Labor Problem in Years with Rejected Contract Proposal" *Fortune Magazine* <http://fortune.com/2016/07/18/att-labor-problems/>

Pressman A, "AT&T Wireless Workers Approve New Benefits Contract" *Fortune Magazine* <http://fortune.com/2016/08/31/att-wireless-workers-approve-contract/>

Preuss UK, "Constitutional Powermaking for the New Polity: Some Deliberations on the Relations between Constituent Power and the Constitution" in Rosenfeld M (ed.), *Constitutionalism, Identity, Difference, and Legitimacy: Theoretical Perspectives* (Duke University Press 1994)

Preuss UK, "Perspectives on Post-Conflict Constitutionalism: Reflections on Regime Change through External Constitutionalization" (2006) 51 New York Law School Law Review 467–94

Price R, "Two Tracts on Civil Liberty, the War with America, and the Debts and Finances of the Kingdom" in Thomas DO (ed.), *Richard Price: Political Writings* (Cambridge University Press 1991)

Procaccia G, "On the History of Agency" (1976) 2 Tel Aviv University Studies in Law 56–87

Procaccia G, "On the Theory and History of Ratification in the Law of Agency" (1978–1979) 4 Tel Aviv University Studies in Law 9–32

Proctor B and Ben Moussa I, *The Tunisian Constituent Assembly's by-Laws: A Brief Analysis* (International IDEA 2012)

Przeworski A, "Minimalist Conception of Democracy: A Defense" in Shapiro I and Hacker-Cordsn C (eds.), *Democracy's Value* (Cambridge University Press 1999)

Pufendorf S, *De Jure Naturae Et Gentium Libri Octo*, vol. 2 (Clarendon Press 1934)

Pufendorf S, *The Whole Duty of Man According to the Law of Nature* (Liberty Fund 2003)

Pufendorf S, *Two Books of the Elements of Universal Jurisprudence* (Liberty Fund 2009)

Putnam RD, "Diplomacy and Domestic Politics: The Logic of Two-Level Games" (1988) 42 International Organization 427–60

Qvorthup M, "A Comparative Study of Referendums: Government by the People" (Manchester University Press 2002)

Rakove JN, *Original Meanings: Politics and Ideas in the Making of the Constitution* (A.A. Knopf 1996)

Rawls J, *A Theory of Justice* (revised edn, Harvard University Press 1999)

Raz J, "On Lawful Governments" (1970) 80 Ethics 296–305

Raz J, *The Morality of Freedom* (Oxford University Press 1986)

Raz J, *On the Authority and Interpretation of Constitutions: Some Preliminaries* (Cambridge University Press 1998)

Raz J, "The Problem of Authority: Revisiting the Service Conception" (2006) 90 Minnesota Law Review 1003–44

Raz J, *The Authority of Law* (2nd edn, Oxford University Press 2009)

Raz J, *Between Authority and Interpretation: On the Theory of Law and Practical Reason* (Oxford University Press 2009)

Raz J, *From Normativity to Responsibility* (Oxford University Press 2011)

Regan D, "Value, Comparability, and Choice" in Chang R (ed.), *Incommensurability, Incomparability, and Practical Reason* (Harvard University Press 1997)

Regassa T, "The Making and Legitimacy of the Ethiopian Constitution: Towards Bridging the Gap between Constitutional Design and Constitutional Practice" (2010) 23 Afrika Focus 85–118

Rehfeld A, *The Concept of Constituency: Political Representation, Democratic Legitimacy, and Institutional Design* (Cambridge University Press 2005)

Rehfeld A, "Towards a General Theory of Political Representation" (2006) 68 The Journal of Politics 1–21

Rehfeld A, "Representation Rethought: On Trustees, Delegates, and Gyroscopes in the Study of Political Representation and Democracy" (2009) 103 American Political Science Review 214–30

Rehfeld A, "The Concepts of Representation" (2011) 103 American Political Science Review 631–41

Rehfeld A, "What Is Representation? On Being and Becoming a Representative" in Viera MB (ed.), *Reclaiming Representation: Contemporary Advances in the Theory of Political Representation* (Routledge 2017)

Reuters Staff, "Chad Parliament Approves New Constitution Expanding President's Powers" *Reuters* (May 4, 2018) <https://www.reuters.com/article/us-chad-politics/chad-parliament-approves-new-constitution-expanding-presidents-powers-idUSKBN1I11RC>

Reyntjens F, "Constitution-Making in Situations of Extreme Crisis: The Case of Rwanda and Burundi" (1996) 40 Journal of African Law 234–42

Richards LL, *Shay's Rebellion: The American Revolution's Final Battle* (University of Pennsylvania Press 2002)

Robert F, "Republicanism Adapted to France" in Goldstein MA (ed.), *Social and Political Thought of the French Revolution, 1788–1797: An Anthology of Original Texts* (Peter Lang 1997)

Roby HJ, *Roman Private Law: In the Times of Cicero and of the Antonines* (reprint edn, Gaunt Inc. 1998)

Rogowski R, *Rational Legitimacy: A Theory of Political Support* (Princeton University Press 1974)

Rosenn KS, "Brazil's New Constitution: An Exercise in Transient Constitutionalism for a Transitional Society" (1990) 38 The American Journal of Comparative Law 773–802

Rosenn KS, "Conflict Resolution and Constitutionalism: The Making of the Brazilian Constitution of 1988" in Miller LE (ed.), *Framing the State in Times of Transition: Case Studies in Constitution Making* (United States Institute of Peace Press 2010)

Rothenberg LS and Sanders MS, "Lame-Duck Politics: Impending Departure and the Votes on Impeachment" (2000) 3 Political Research Quarterly 523–36

Rousseau JJ, *The Government of Poland* (Hackett Publishing Company, Inc. 1985)

Rousseau JJ, "Of the Social Contract" in Gourevitch V (ed.), *Rousseau: The Social Contract and Other Later Political Writings* (Cambridge University Press 1997)

Roznai Y, *Unconstitutional Constitutional Amendments* (Oxford University Press 2017)

Rubenfeld J, *Legitimacy and Interpretation* (Cambridge University Press 1998)

Rubinelli L, *Constituent Power: A History* (Cambridge University Press 2020)

Rudolph L and Däubler T, "Holding Individual Representatives Accountable: The Role of Electoral Systems" (2016) 78 Journal of Politics 746–62

Runciman D, "The Paradox of Political Representation" (2007) 15 The Journal of Political Philosophy 93–114

Runciman D and Vieira MB, *Representation* (Polity Press 2008)

Saati A, *The Participation Myth: Outcomes of Participatory Constitution Building Processes on Democracy* (Umeå University, Department of Politics 2015)

Samoy I, "Unauthorised Agency in Belgian Law" in Busch D and Macgregor L (eds.), *The Unauthorised Agent: Perspectives from European and Comparative Law* (Cambridge University Press 2009)

Samuels K, *Constitution Building Processes and Democratization: A Discussion of Twelve Case Studies* (International IDEA 2006)

Samuels K and Wyeth VH, *State-Building and Constitutional Design after Conflict* (International Peace Academy 2006)

Sartorius R, "Political Authority and Political Obligation" (1981) 67 Virginia Law Review 3–17

Saward M, "Authorisation and Authenticity: Representation and the Unelected" (2009) 17 The Journal of Political Philosophy 1–22

Saye AB, *A Constitutional History of Georgia: 1732–1945* (The University of Georgia Press 1948)

Scanlon TM, *What We Owe Each Other* (Harvard University Press 1998)

Schauer F, "Amending the Presuppositions of a Constitution" in Levinson S (ed.), *Responding to Imperfection: The Theory of Practice of Constitutional Amendment* (Princeton University Press 1995)

Schelling T, *The Strategy of Conflict* (Harvard University Press 1980)

Schmidt-Kessel M and Baide A, "Unauthorised Agency in German Law" in Busch D and Macgregor L (eds.), *The Unauthorised Agent: Perspectives from European and Comparative Law* (Cambridge University Press 2009)

Schmitt C, *Constitutional Theory* (Duke University Press 2008)

Schuck ART and De Vreese CH, "Public Support for Referendums: The Role of the Media" (2011) 34 West European Politics 181–207

Schumpeter JA, *Capitalism, Socialism, and Democracy* (3rd edn, Harper & Row 1950)

Schwartzberg M, "The Arbitrariness of Supermajority Rules" (2010) 49 Social Science Information 61–82

Selassie BH, "Constitution Making in Eritrea: A Process-Driven Approach" in Miller LE (ed.), *Framing the State in Times of Transition: Case Studies in Constitution Making* (United States Institute of Peace Press 2010)

Selejan-Gutan B, *The Constitution of Romania: A Contextual Analysis* (Constitutional Systems of the World, Hart Publishing 2013)

Setälä M, "On the Problems of Responsibility and Accountability in Referendums" (2006) 45 European Journal of Political Research 699–721

Shaeffer JN, "Georgia's 1789 Constitution: Was It Adopted in Defiance of the Constitutional Amending Process?" (1977) 61 The Georgia Historical Quarterly 329–41

Shair DI, "The Mythology of Labor Contract Rejections" (1970) 21 Labor Law Journal 88–94

Shapiro S, "Authority" in Coleman JL and Shapiro S (eds.), *The Oxford Handbook of Jurisprudence and Philosophy of Law* (Oxford University Press 2002)

Sharp G, *A Declaration of the People's Natural Right to a Share in the Legislature* (Applewood Books 2009)

Shaw MN, *International Law* (6th edn, Cambridge University Press 2008)

Sheafer T, "Detecting Campaign Effects in Imbalanced Campaigns: The Likud's Interparty Refererndum over Sharon's Disengagement Plan" (2005) 10 The Harvard International Journal of Press/Politics 85–93

Sheehan CA and McDowell GL (eds.), *Friends of the Constitution: Writings of the "Other" Federalists, 1787–1788* (Liberty Fund 1998)

Shepsle KA, "The Positive Theory of Legislative Institutions: An Enrichment of Social Choice and Spatial Models" (1986) 50 Public Choice 135–78

Sidney A, *Discourses Concerning Government* (Liberty Fund 1996)

Sieyès EJ, "Reasoned Exposition of the Rights of Man and Citizen" in Goldstein MA (ed.), *Social and Political Thought of the French Revolution, 1788–1797* (Peter Lang Publishers 1997)

Sieyès EJ, "Views of the Executive Means" in Sonenscher M (ed.), *Political Writings: Including the Debate between Sieyès and Tom Paine in 1791* (Hackett Publishing Company 2003)

Sieyès EJ, "What Is the Third Estate?" in Sonenscher M (ed.), *Political Writings: Including the Debate between Sieyès and Tom Paine in 1791* (Hackett Publishing Company 2003)

Silva JF, *The California Initiative Process: Background and Perspective* (Resource Material for the Speaker's Commission on the California Initiative Process, 2000)

Simkin WE, "Refusals to Ratify Contracts" (1968) 21 Industrial and Labor Relations Review 518–40

Simmons AJ, *Justification and Legitimacy: Essays on Rights and Obligations* (Cambridge University Press 2001)

Simmons AJ, *Moral Principles and Political Obligations* (Princeton University Press 1979)
Simmons AJ, *On the Edge of Anarchy: Locke, Consent, and the Limits of Society* (Princeton University Press 1993)
Skinner Q, *The Foundations of Modern Political Thought: The Age of Reformation*, vol. 2 (Cambridge University Press 1978)
Skjelton S, *A People's Constitution: Public Participation in the South-African Constitution-Making Process* (Institute for Global Dialogue 2006)
Smith FE, *International Law* (6th edn, J.M Dent & Sons 1927)
Smith JEA, "Chapter XIX: Town of Pittsfield (Continued)" in Cushing T (ed.), *History of Berkshire County, Massachusetts, with Biographical Sketches of Its Prominent Men*, vol. 2 (J.B. Beers & Co. 1885)
Smith JEA, *The History of Pittsfield (Berkshire Country), Massachusetts* (Lee and Shepard 1869)
Smith MBE, "Is There a Prima Facie Obligation to Obey the Law?" (1973) 82 Yale Law Journal 950–76
Sniderman PM, Brody RA, and Tetlock PE, *Reasoning and Choice: Explorations in Political Psychology* (Cambridge University Press 1991)
Sniderman PM and Theriault SM, "The Structure of Political Argument and the Logic of Issue Framing" in Saris WE and Sniderman PM (eds.), *Studies in Public Opinion: Gauging Attitudes, Nonattitudes, Measurement Error and Change* (Princeton University Press 2004)
Soboul A, *The French Revolution 1787–1799: From the Storming of the Bastille to Napoleon* (NLB 1974)
Somek A, "The Owl of Minerva: Constitutional Discourse before Its Conclusion" (2008) 71 The Modern Law Review 473–89
Somin I, *Democracy and Political Ignorance: Why Smaller Government Is Smarter* (Stanford Law Books 2013)
Somos M, *American State of Nature: The Origins of Independence, 1761–1775* (Oxford University Press 2019)
Stagner R and Rosen H, *Psychology of Union-Management Relations* (Wadsworth Publishers, Inc. 1965)
Stein P, *Regulae Iuris: From Juristic Rules to Legal Maxims* (Edinburgh University Press 1966)
Stein P, *Roman Law in European History* (Cambridge University Press 2004)
Steytler N, "South Africa" in Kincaid J and Tarr GA (eds.), *Constitutional Origins, Structure, and Change in Federal Countries* (McGill-Queen's University Press 2005)
Stokes SC, "What Do Policy Switches Tell Us About Democracy" in Manin B, Przeworski A, and Stokes SC (eds.), *Democracy, Accountability, and Representation* (Cambridge University Press 1999)
Story J, *Commentaries on the Law of Agency as a Branch of Commercial and Maritime Jurisprudence* (Little, Brown and Company 1863)
Sturm AL, "The Development of American State Constitutions" (1982) 12 Publius 57–98
Sturm AL, *Thirty Years of State Constitution-Making, 1938–1968; with an Epilogue: Developments During 1969* (National Municipal League 1970)
Sturm AL, *Trends in State Constitution-Making, 1966–1972* (Council of State Governments 1973)
Suksi M, *Bringing in the People: A Comparison of Constitutional Forms and Practices of the Referendum* (Martinus Nijhoff Publishers 1993)
Summers CW, "Ratification of Agreements" in Dunlop JT and Chamberlain NW (eds.), *Frontiers of Collective Bargaining* (Harper & Row 1967)

Suteu S and Tierney S, "Squaring the Circle? Bringing Deliberation and Participation Together in Processes of Constitution-Making" in Levy R and others (eds.), *The Cambridge Handbook of Deliberative Constitutionalism* (Cambridge University Press 2018)

Sutter M, Haigner S, and Kocher MG, "Choosing the Carrot or the Stick? Endogenous Institutional Choice in Social Dilemma Situations" (2010) 77 Review of Economic Studies 1540–66

Swinburne H, *A Treatise of Spousals, or Matrimonial Contracts* (2nd edn, London 1711)

Tamanaha BZ, "Battle between Law and Society in Micronesia" in Galligan DJ and Versteeg M (eds.), *Social and Political Foundations of Constitutions* (Cambridge University Press 2013)

Tamaru N and O'Reilly N, *A Women's Guide to Constitution Making* (Inclusive Security 2018)

Tarr GA, *Understanding State Constitutions* (Princeton University Press 1998)

Tate TW, "The Social Contract in America, 1774–1787: Revolutionary Theory as a Conservative Instrument" (1965) 22 The William and Mary Quarterly 375–91

Taylor RJ, "Introduction and Notes" in Taylor RJ (ed.), *Massachusetts, Colony to Commonwealth: Documents on the Formation of Its Constitution, 1775–1780* (University of North Carolina Press 1961)

Taylor RJ, *Western Massachusetts in the Revolution* (Brown University Press 1954)

Tekin S, *Founding Acts: Constitutional Origins in a Democratic Age* (University of Pennsylvania Press 2016)

Thompson MP, "Significant Silences in Locke's Two Treatises of Government: Constitutional History, Contract and Law" (1988) 31 The Historical Journal 275–94

Thornhill C, *A Sociology of Constitutions: Constitutions and State Legitimacy in Historical-Sociological Perspective* (Cambridge University Press 2011)

Thornton C, *The Rocky Path from Elections to a New Constitution in Tunisia: Mechanisms for Consensus-Building and Inclusive Decision-Making* (Oslo Forum Background Papers, 2016)

Tierney S, "Constitutional Referendums: A Theoretical Enquiry" (2009) 72 The Modern Law Review 360–83

Tierney S, *Constitutional Referendums: The Theory and Practice of Republican Deliberation* (Oxford University Press 2012)

Tiitinen S, "Constitutional Reform in Finland", *Constitutional & Parliamentary Information* (Association of Secretaries General of Parliaments 1999)

Trenchard J and Gordon T, *Cato's Letters, or Essays on Liberty, Civil and Religious, and Other Important Subjects*, vol. 1 (W. Wilkins, T. Woodward, J. Walthoe, and J. Peele 1737)

Tridimas G and Tridimas T, "Electorates V. Politicians: The 2005 French and Dutch Referendums on the Eu Constitutional Treaty" in Albi A and Ziller J (eds.), *The European Constitution and National Constitutions: Ratification and Beyond* (Kluwer Law International 2006)

Tripp AM, "The Politics of Constitution Making in Uganda" in Miller LE (ed.), *Framing the State in Times of Transition: Case Studies in Constitution Making* (United States Institute of Peace Press 2010)

Tsebelis G, "Veto Players and Institutional Analysis" (2000) 13 Governance: An International Journal of Policy, Administration, and Institutions 441–74

Tsebelis G, *Veto Players: How Political Institutions Work* (Princeton University Press 2002)

Tsebelis G and Nardi DJ, "A Long Constitution Is a (Positively) Bad Constitution: Evidence from OECD Countries" (2016) 46 457–78

Tuck R, "Brexit: A Prize in Reach for the Left" Policy Exchange <https://policyexchange.org.uk/pxevents/brexit-a-prize-in-reach-for-the-left/>

Tuck R, *Natural Rights Theories: Their Origin and Development* (Cambridge University Press 1979)

Tuck R, *The Sleeping Sovereign: The Invention of Modern Democracy* (Cambridge University Press 2016)

Tushnet M, "Constitution-Making: An Introduction" (2012) 91 Texas Law Review 1983–2013

Tversky A and Kahneman D, "Judgment under Uncertainty: Heuristics and Biases" (1974) 185 Science 1124–31

Tyler TR, "Enhancing Police Legitimacy" (2004) 593 The Annals of the American Academy of Political and Social Sciences 84–99

Tyler TR, "Evaluating Consensual Models of Governance: Legitimacy Based Law" in Knight J and Schwartzberg M (eds.), *Political Legitimacy: NOMOS LXI* (New York University Press 2019)

Tyler TR, "Procedural Justice and Policing" in Lind EA (ed.), *Social Psychology and Justice* (Routledge 2019)

Tyler TR, "Procedural Justice, Legitimacy, and the Effective Rule of Law" (2003) 30 Crime and Justice 283–357

Tyler TR, *Why People Obey the Law* (Yale University Press 1990)

Tyler TR and Blader S, "Can Businesses Effectively Regulate Employee Conduct? The Antecendets of Rule Following in Work Settings" (2005) 48 The Academy of Management Journal 1143–58

Tyler TR, Callahan PE, and Frost J, "Armed, and Dangerous(?): Motivating Group Adherence among Agents of Social Control" (2007) 41 Law & Society Review 457–92

Tyler TR, Casper JD, and Fisher B, "Maintaining Allegiance Towards Political Authorities" (1989) 33 American Journal of Political Science 629–52

Tyler TR and Huo YJ, *Trust in the Law: Encouraging Public Cooperation with the Police and Courts* (Russell-Sage Foundation 2002)

Tyler TR and Jackson J, "Future Challenges in the Study of Legitimacy and Criminal Justice" in Tankebe J and Liebling A (eds.), *Legitimacy and Criminal Justice: An International Exploration* (Oxford University Press 2013)

Tyler TR and Jackson J, "Popular Legitimacy and the Exercise of Legal Authority: Motivating Compliance, Cooperation and Engagement" (2014) 20 Psychology, Public Policy, and the Law 78–95

Uibopuu H-J, "The Constitutional Development of the Estonian Republic" (1973) 4 Journal of Baltic Studies 11–35

Uleri P, "Introduction" in Gallagher M and Uleri P (eds.), *The Referendum Experience in Europe* (Macmillan Press 1996)

Ullmann W, *Law and Politics in the Middle Ages* (Cambridge University Press 1975)

Unger D, "Transit Workers Reject Latest Offer; but Willing to Take Smaller Wage Hike in Exchange for Safer Working Conditions" *The Winnipeg Sun* (Winnipeg, August 17, 2019) A.3

UNSG, *Guidance Note of the Secretary-General: United Nations Assistance to Constitution-Making Processes* (United Nations 2009)

Urbinati N, "Representation as Advocacy" (2000) 28 Political Theory 758–86

Urbinati N, *Representative Democracy: Principles and Genealogy* (University of Chicago Press 2008)

Urbinati N and Warren M, "The Concept of Representation in Contemporary Democratic Theory" (2008) 11 Annual Review of Political Science 387–412

Van Giffen H, *Tractatus De Diversis Regulis Juris Antiqui Utilissimus* (Strasbourg 1607)

Varadkar L, *Written Answers: Tuesday, 26 March 2019* (Dáil Éireann 2019) <https://www.oireachtas.ie/en/debates/question/2019-03-26/123/#pq_123>

Vattel E, *The Law of Nations* (Liberty Fund 2008)

Venter F, "Constitution Making and the Legitimacy of the Constitution" in Jyranki A (ed.), *National Constitutions in the Era of Integration* (Kluwer Law International 1999)

Vermeule A, *The System of the Constitution* (Oxford University Press 2011)

Verol OO, "Temporary Constitutions" (2014) 102 California Law Review 409–64

Viera MB, "Introduction" in Viera MB (ed.), *Reclaiming Representation: Contemporary Advances in the Theory of Political Representation* (Routledge 2017)

Voigt S, "The Consequences of Popular Participation in Constitutional Choice: Towards a Comparative Analysis" in Aaken AV, List C, and Luetge C (eds.), *Deliberation and Decision: Economics, Constitutional Theory, and Deliberative Democracy* (Ashgate Publishing, Ltd. 2004)

Von Dornum DD, "The Straight and the Crooked: Legal Accountability in Ancient Greece" (1997) 97 Columbia Law Review 1483–1518

Von Martens GF, *A Compendium of the Law of Nations* (Cobbett and Morgan 1802)

Waliggo J, "The Main-Actors in the Constitution-Making Process in Uganda" in Hyden G and Venter D (eds.), *Constitution-Making and Democratisation in Africa* (Africa Institute of South Africa 2001)

Wallis J, *Constitution Making During State Building* (Cambridge University Press 2014)

Walzer M, *Obligations: Essays on Disobedience, War, and Citizenship* (Harvard University Press 1970)

Wambaugh E, "A Problem as to Ratification" (1895) 9 Harvard Law Review 60–71

Wandan S, "Nothing out of the Ordinary: Constitution Making as Representative Politics" (2015) 22 Constellations 44–58

Wapakhabulo J, "Managing the Constitution-Making Process in Uganda" in Hyden G and Venter D (eds.), *Constitution-Making and Democratisation in Africa* (Africa Institute of South Africa 2001)

Ward L, *The Politics of Liberty in England and Revolutionary America* (Cambridge University Press 2004)

Warren ME, "Deliberative Democracy and Authority" (1996) 90 The American Political Science Review 46–60

Watson A, *The Spirit of Roman Law* (The University of Georgia Press 1995)

Watson A, Mommsen T, and Krueger P (eds.), *The Digest of Justinian*, vol. I (revised edn, University of Pennsylvania Press 1985)

Watson A, Mommsen T, and Krueger P (eds.), *The Digest of Justinian*, vol. IV (University of Pennsylvania Press 1985)

Weber M, *Economy and Society: An Outline of Interpretive Sociology*, vol. 1 (University of California Press 1978)

Weston CC, "England: Ancient Constitution and Common Law" in Burns JH and Goldie M (eds.), *The Cambridge History of Political Thought, 1450–1700*, vol. III (Cambridge University Press 1991)

Wheatley J and Germann M, "Outcomes of Constitution-Making: Democratization and Conflict Resolution" in Wheatley J and Mendez F (eds.), *Patterns of Constitutional Design: The Role of Citizens and Elites in Constitution-Making* (Routledge 2016)

Wheatley J and Mendez F, "The Constitution-Making Process: An Analytical Framework" in Wheatley J and Mendez F (eds.), *Patterns of Constitutional Design: The Role of Citizens and Elites in Constitution-Making* (Routledge 2016)
Wheatley J and Mendez F (eds.), *Patterns of Constitutional Design: The Role of Citizens and Elites in Constitution-Making* (Routledge 2016)
Wheaton H, *Elements of International Law* (2nd edn, Stevens & Sons 1880)
Whitaker BE and Giersch J, "Voting on a Constitution: Implications for Democracy in Kenya" (2009) 27 Journal of Contemporary African Studies 1–20
White M, *The Philosophy of the American Revolution* (Oxford University Press 1978)
Whiting W, "An Address to the Inhabitants of Berkshire County, Mass. (1778)" in Hyneman CS and Lutz DS (eds.), *American Political Writing During the Founding Era, 1760–1805*, vol. I (Liberty Press 1983)
Wicclair MR, "Patient Decision-Making Capacity and Risk" (1991) 5 Bioethics 91–101
Wicquefort Ad, *The Embassador and His Functions* (Bernard Lintott 1716)
Widner J, "Constitution Writing and Conflict Resolution," (2005) 9 The Commonwealth Journal of International Affairs 503–18
Widner J, "Constitution Writing and Conflict Resolution Project" <http://www.princeton.edu/~pcwcr/>
Widner J, "Constitution Writing in Post-Conflict Settings: An Overview" (2008) 49 William and Mary Law Review 1513–42
Wieacker F, *A History of Private Law in Europe* (Clarendon Press 1996)
Wiechers M, "Namibia's Long Walk to Freedom: The Role of Constitution-Making and the Right to Take Part in a Public Affair" in Miller LE (ed.), *Framing the State in Times of Transition: Case Studies in Constitution Making* (United States Institute of Peace Press 2010)
Wiggins D, "Incommensurability: Four Proposals" in Chang R (ed.), *Incommensurability, Incomparability, and Practical Reason* (Harvard University Press 1997)
Williams A, "An Election Sermon: Boston, 1762" in Hyneman CS and Lutz DS (eds.), *American Political Writing During the Founding Era: 1760–1805*, vol. 1 (Liberty Fund 1983)
Williams K, "School Mega-Strike Still under Consideration" *Manawatu Standard* (Palmerston North, New Zealand, April 9, 2019) 7
Williams MS, *Voice, Trust, and Memory: Marginalized Groups and the Failings of Liberal Representation* (Princeton University Press 1998)
Wilson J, *Collected Works of James Wilson* (Liberty Fund 2007)
Wing SD, *Constructing Democracy in Transitioning Societies of Africa: Constitutionalism and Deliberation in Mali* (Palgrave Macmillan 2008)
Wittgenstein L, *Philosophical Investigations* (4th edn, Blackwell Publishing Ltd 2009)
Wolfers EP, "'Joint Creation': The Bougainville Peace Agreement and Beyond" (2010) 12 Accord 44–50
Wolff C, *Jus Gentium Methodo Scientifica Pertractatum*, vol. 2 (1764, Clarendon Press 1934)
Wood AW, "Coercion, Manipulation, Exploitation" in Coons C and Weber M (eds.), *Manipulation: Theory and Practice* (Oxford University Press 2014)
Wood GS, *The Creation of the American Republic, 1776–1787* (The University of North Carolina Press 1998)
Wood GS, "Foreword: State Constitution-Making in the American Revolution" (1992–93) 24 Rutgers Law Journal 911–26
Young IM, *Inclusion and Democracy* (Oxford University Press 2000)

Young T, "Thomas Young to the People of the Grants" in Morgan C (ed.), *The Documentary History of the State of New York* (Charles Van Benthuysen 1851)
Zelditch M, "Processes of Legitimation: Recent Developments and New Directions" (2001) 64 Social Psychology Quarterly 4–17
Zimmermann R, *The Law of Obligations: Roman Foundations of the Civilian Tradition* (Oxford University Press 1996)
Zimmerman JF, *The Referendum: The People Decide Public Policy* (Praeger Publishing 2001)
Zook MS, *Radical Whigs and Conspiratorial Politics in Late Stuart England* (The Pennsylvania State University Press 1999)

Name Index

For the benefit of digital users, indexed terms that span two pages (e.g., 52–53) may, on occasion, appear on only one of those pages.

Subject Index

For the benefit of digital users, indexed terms that span two pages (e.g., 52–53) may, on occasion, appear on only one of those pages.